14th International Conference on Theoretical and Computational Acoustics (ICTCA 2019)

Beijing, China
28 July – 1 August 2019

Editors:

Juan Zeng
Xiuming Wang

ISBN: 978-1-5108-9729-8

Printed from e-media with permission by:

Curran Associates, Inc.
57 Morehouse Lane
Red Hook, NY 12571

Some format issues inherent in the e-media version may also appear in this print version.

Printed with permission by Curran Associates, Inc. (2020)

For permission requests, please contact Institute of Acoustics, Chinese Academy of Sciences at the address below.

Institute of Acoustics, Chinese Academy of Sciences
No. 21 North 4th Ring Road,
Haidian District, 100190
Beijing, China

http://english.ioa.cas.cn/

Additional copies of this publication are available from:

Curran Associates, Inc.
57 Morehouse Lane
Red Hook, NY 12571 USA
Phone: 845-758-0400
Fax: 845-758-2634
Email: curran@proceedings.com
Web: www.proceedings.com

CONTENT

Underwater Acoustics

Institute of Acoustics, Chinese Academy of Sciences

14th International Conference on Theoretical and Computational Acoustics

28 July- 1 August 2019, Beijing, China

ICTCA2019

Beijing

Proceedings of the 14th International Conference on Theoretical and Computational Acoustics

Edited by

Juan Zeng

and

Xiuming Wang

Proceedings of the 14th International Conference on Theoretical and Computational Acoustics

Beijing, China
July 28-August 1, 2019

Edited by

Juan Zeng

and

Xiuming Wang

Chinese Academy of Sciences, China

PREFACE

With more than 200 participants working at universities, Institutes, and industrial laboratories in 13 different countries, the 14th International Conference on Theoretical and Computational Acoustics (ICTCA2019) held at the Beijing International Convention Center in Beijing, China July 28-August 1, 2019 is a technic forum for active scientists in various fields of acoustics to share with state-of-the art research results in their work, to exchange ideas, as well as to stimulate future research in the jointed acoustic fields. It is also a "young" ICTCA with about 1/4 talks presented by graduate students.

We would like to give the great thanks to the plenary speakers, the structured session organizers, and all of the people who enthusiastically participate in the conference. Without their efforts and hard work, ICTCA2019 would never happens. Just like an old Chinese saying, a great cooker could do nothing without the food supplies. We would like to extend our thanks to the office of Naval Research Global (ONRG) for its supports and contributions of the conference. We also would like to acknowledge the supports of the Acoustical Society of China (ASC) and the Institute of Acoustics in Chinese Academy of Sciences (IACAS).

We originally called for papers in 20 different structured sessions. For the present proceedings we decided to simply re-categorize the papers into two parts, underwater acoustics and ultrasonics. We would like to thank the contributors for their efforts and especially for their promptness in providing the editors with their full-length manuscripts.

Juan Zeng

Xiuming Wang

Beijing, China

November 2019

A practical bottom rough surface reverberation model in shallow water

Jinrong Wu[1,2], Peng Li[1,2,3], Erchang Shang[1,2], Zhendong Zhao[1,2]
[1]Key Laboratory of Underwater Acoustic Environment, CAS, Beijing, China
[2]Institute of Acoustics, CAS, Beijing, China
[3]University of Chinese Academy of Sciences, Beijing, China
No.21, BeiSiHuan XiLu, Haidian District, Beijing, China, 100190
wujinrong@mail.ioa.ac.cn

Bottom rough surface scattering is the dominating source of low to mid frequency reverberation in shallow water. It is difficult to test the traditional full wave reverberation model using experiment data because many environmental parameters in the model are not easy to get. A three parameters model of shallow water waveguide reverberation based on full wave reverberation model was proposed. The three unknown environmental parameters in the new model include: bottom reflection attenuation parameter P, bottom reflection phase parameter Q, and bottom backscattering parameter μ. These parameters can be measured or inversed easily, and have clear physical pictures. This new practical shallow water reverberation model was compared with the Yellow Sea low frequency reverberation experiment data. The results show that the new proposed model can explain low frequency shallow water reverberation well.

1. Introduction

Reverberation is the main interference to active detection, and for this reason reverberation has been of interest for a long time, especially in the case of shallow water waveguides. There are many factors can cause low frequency reverberation in the shallow water. In many cases, sea floor rough surface is the dominant factor contributing to reverberation in shallow water, especially for a negative sound speed profile in the water. There have appeared many sea floor rough surface shallow water reverberation models, such as normal mode model[1-5], energy-flux model[6,7], spectral representation model[8], PE model[9] and so on. But most of the reverberation models have not been tested by shallow water reverberation data because some environmental parameters in the model are difficult to obtain. J.R.[10] has developed a new energy-flux reverberation model based on Perturbation theory. This model just contained three unknow parameters, bottom reflection coefficient parameters P and Q, and rough surface backscattering parameter μ. It is a practical reverberation model, however, the model only considers average reverberation intensity, and has neglected many factors such as source depth, receiver depth, and so on.

In this paper, a extended practical model of waveguide reverberation based on full wave reverberation model was presented. The new model also has three unknown environmental parameters, which can be measured or inversed easily. This paper is organized as follows: the modal reverberation model based on the Perturbation theory is introduced in Section 2. In Section 3, the practical shallow water reverberation model based on P and Q is presented.

Numerical simulation cases and theory- experiment data comparsion are presented in section 4. The summary and conclusions are addressed in section 5.

2. Full wave reverberation model in shallow water waveguide

The typical shallow-water bottom rough interface reverberation problem is depicted in Fig.1. We have a stratified water column with a sound speed profile c0(z), constant density ρ0 and a constant water depth H. The water-sediment rough interface has a fluctuated height η, with <η> = 0. In the sediment, the sound speed and density have a constant mean values of cb and ρb. In water column, R0 represents the source point, R represents the reverberation field point and R1 represents the scattering point.

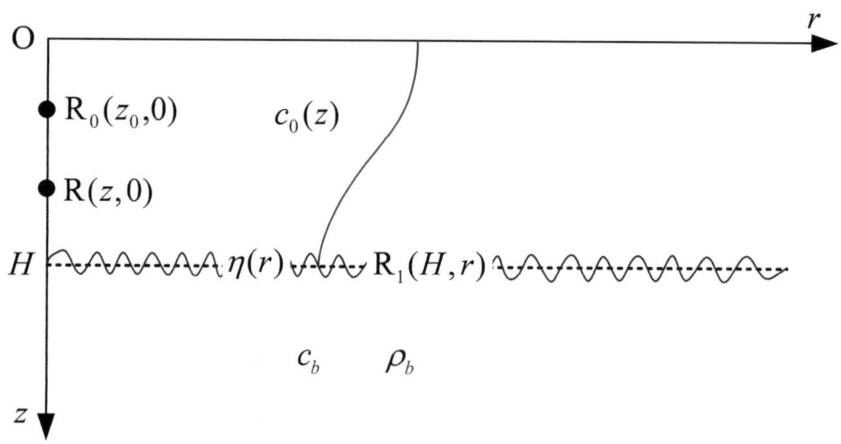

Fig.1 Shallow-water reverberation scenario

By using the Bass perturbation theory, the continuities of the field at the rough surface can be replaced by the inhomogeneous boundary conditions at the smooth interface z = H, as follows [11,12,13]

$$\frac{\partial u_1(\mathrm{R},\mathrm{R}_1)}{\partial z}-\frac{\partial u_2(\mathrm{R},\mathrm{R}_1)}{\partial z}=V(\mathrm{R}_1)G^i(\mathrm{R}_1,\mathrm{R}_0) \tag{1}$$

$$\rho_0 u_1(\mathrm{R},\mathrm{R}_1)-\rho_b u_2(\mathrm{R},\mathrm{R}_1)=p(\mathrm{R}_1)G^i(\mathrm{R}_1,\mathrm{R}_0) \tag{2}$$

where

$$V(\mathrm{R}_1)=(k_0^2-k_b^2/\alpha)\eta(\mathrm{R}_1)+(1-1/\alpha)\nabla_\perp\bullet(\eta\nabla_\perp) \tag{3}$$

$$p(\mathrm{R}_1)=(\rho_b-\rho_0)\eta(\mathrm{R}_1)\frac{\partial}{\partial z} \tag{4}$$

here k = ω/c0(H), kb = ω/cb, α = ρb/ρ0 , and u2 , u1 are the reverberation field under and above the interface respectively. The initial incident field Gi (R1,R0) (with η = 0) of a unit point source at R0 can be written as a summation of proper modes :

$$G^i(\mathrm{R}_0,\mathrm{R}_1)=i\pi\sum_m^M\phi_m(z_0)\phi_m(H)H_0^{(1)}(K_m r) \tag{5}$$

where $H_0^{(1)}$ is the first kind zero order Hankel function, $\phi_m(z)$ is the normalized mode function, K_m is the complex modal wave number : $K_m = k_m + i\beta_m$, and r is the center range of the scattering area. M is the number of effective normal mode in the waveguide.

According to the Green's theorem, under Born approximation, the scattered field of a point source in the water is given by :

$$u_1(\mathrm{R}_0,\mathrm{R}) = \int d\mathrm{R}_1 \{G(\mathrm{R},\mathrm{R}_1)V(\mathrm{R}_1)G^i(\mathrm{R}_1,\mathrm{R}_0) - \frac{1}{\rho_w}\frac{\partial G(\mathrm{R},\mathrm{R}_1)}{\partial z}p(\mathrm{R}_1)G^i(\mathrm{R}_1,\mathrm{R}_0)\} \tag{6}$$

Substituting eq.(3), eq.(4) and eq.(5) into eq.(6), we get

$$u_1(\mathrm{R}_0,\mathrm{R}) \cong \frac{2\pi i}{k_0 r_c}\sum_m^M\sum_n^M \phi_m(z_0)\phi_n(z)\exp[-(\beta_m+\beta_n)r]S_{mn}^R K^R(k_m,k_n) \tag{7}$$

where

$$S_{mn}^R \equiv \phi_m(H)C_{mn}^R\phi_n(H) \tag{8}$$

$$C_{mn}^R = [k_0^2 - k_b^2/\alpha + (1+\alpha)k_m k_n + (1-\alpha)(\alpha^{-2})\gamma_m\gamma_n] \tag{9}$$

$$\gamma_m = (k_m^2 - k_b^2)^{1/2} \quad , \qquad k_m = k_0\cos\theta_m \tag{10}$$

$$K^R(k_m,k_n) \equiv \int dr\eta(r)\exp[i(k_m+k_n)r] \tag{11}$$

Take the statistical average of the incoherent summation of $<|u_1(R_0, R)|^2_{inc}>$ as the intensity of the reverberation - $I_R(R_0, R)$, and consider the insonified area is a ring with area: $A = 2\pi r_c\Delta r$, and $\Delta r \cong c_0\tau_0/2$, where τ_0 is the duration of the signal s(t), we get

$$I_R(\mathrm{R}_0,\mathrm{R}) = (\frac{2\pi}{k_0 r_c})^2(2\pi r_c)\sum_m^M\sum_n^M \phi_m^2(z_0)\phi_n^2(z)\exp[-2(\beta_m+\beta_n)r_c][S_{mn}^R]^2\Gamma(k_m,k_n) \tag{12}$$

Assume Δr is much larger than the bottom rough surface correlation scale L, we get

$$\Gamma(k_m,k_n) \cong (\Delta r)\sigma_\eta^2\int_0^\infty dxR^\eta(x)\exp(i2k_0x) = \frac{c_0\tau_0}{2}\sigma_\eta^2 P^\eta(2k_0) \tag{13}$$

where $R_\eta(x)$ and σ_η^2 are the correlation function and mean square (MS) value of the fluctuation η respectively. P_η is the power spectrum of the fluctuation η.

Substituting eq.(13) into eq.(12), we get

$$I_R(\mathrm{R}_0,\mathrm{R}) = E_0(\frac{2\pi}{k_0 r_c})^2(\pi r_c c_0)\sum_m^M\sum_n^M \phi_m^2(z_0)\phi_n^2(z)\exp[-2(\beta_m+\beta_n)r_c]\Theta_{mn}^R \quad (14)$$

where E0 is the energy of the initial pulse signal, and the MBSM is given by

$$\Theta_{mn}^R = \sigma_\eta^2 P^\eta(2k_0)[S_{mn}^R]^2 \quad (15)$$

We consider a widely accepted spectrum of the interface roughness – the Goff-Jordan spectrum[14] :

$$P^\eta(2k_0) = \pi L[1+(2k_0 L)^2]^{-3/2} \quad (16)$$

Take eq.(15) and eq.(16) into eq.(14), we can get

$$I_R(\mathrm{R}_0,\mathrm{R}) = E_0(\frac{2\pi}{k_0 r_c})^2(\pi r_c c_0)\sum_m^M\sum_n^M \phi_m^2(z_0)\phi_m^2(H)\phi_n^2(z)\phi_n^2(H)\exp[-2(\beta_m+\beta_n)r_c]\mu_{mn}^R \quad (17)$$

where the μ_{mn}^R is given by

$$\mu_{mn}^R = \sigma_\eta^2 P^\eta(2k_0)[C_{mn}^R]^2 \quad (18)$$

Eq.(17) and eq.(18) are the analytic expressions for sea floor rough surface reverberation in shallow water waveguide.

3. Three parameters reverberation model

In traditional full wave reverberation theory, eq.(17), there are many unknow environmental parameters, such as sea floor geo-acoustic parameters: bottom sound speed cb, bottom density ρb, and bottom attenuation α, and rough surface parameters: rough surface correlation length L and root of mean square (MS) value of the rough surface fluctuation σ . It is not easy to measure these unknown parameters directly. In this section, we use the other set of sea floor parameters to describe full wave reverberation theory.

Firstly, we consider the backscattering term μ_{mn}^R . Taking eq.(9) and eq.(16) into eq.(18), we can get

$$\mu_{mn}^R \approx k_0\sigma_\eta^2\frac{\pi}{8L^2}[c_{mn}^R]^2 \quad (19)$$

here

$$c_{mn}^R = \{1-(c_0/c_b)^2/\alpha+(1-\alpha^{-1})\cos\theta_m\cos\theta_n+(1-\alpha)(\alpha^{-2}) \times[\cos^2\theta_m-(c_0/c_b)^2]^{1/2}[\cos^2\theta_n-(c_0/c_b)^2]^{1/2}\} \quad (20)$$

Numerical calculations show that the mode coupling kernel μ_{mn}^{R} can be approximated as a constant in small grazing angle area from $\theta_m = 0$ to critical angle $\theta^{*} = \cos^{-1}(c_0 / c_b)$ for the case of single frequency. Table 1 illustrates the values of μ_{mn}^{R} for sediment type 1 as classified by Hamilton[15], the bottom parameters are listed as following: cb = 1836 m/s, ρb = 2.03, P = 7.04, σ = 0.1 m, L = 10 m .

Table 1. The values of μ_{mn}^{R} for sediment type 1

θ_m (degree)	f = 150 Hz	f = 300Hz
0	0.2961×10^{-6}	0.5922×10^{-6}
5	0.2950×10^{-6}	0.5901×10^{-6}
10	0.2919×10^{-6}	0.5838×10^{-6}
15	0.2868×10^{-6}	0.5737×10^{-6}
20	0.2801×10^{-6}	0.5601×10^{-6}
25	0.2718×10^{-6}	0.5435×10^{-6}
30	0.2623×10^{-6}	0.5247×10^{-6}
35	0.2521×10^{-6}	0.5042×10^{-6}

As we can see from table 1 and eq.(19), the μ_{mn}^{R} has a very weak dependengt on grazing angle, and is proportional to frequency. So μ_{mn}^{R} can be approximated as a constant μ for the case of single frequency. And the eq.(17) can be written as

$$I_R(R_0, R) = E_0 \left(\frac{2\pi}{k_0 r_c}\right)^2 \pi r_c c_0 \mu \sum_{m}^{M}\sum_{n}^{M} \phi_m^2(z_0)\, \phi_m^2(H)\, \phi_n^2(z)\, \phi_n^2(H) \exp[-(\beta_m + \beta_n)\, 2 r_c] \quad (21)$$

In the full wave reverberation model, eq.(21), bottom backscattering is extracted as one parameter, it is frequency dependent, and is range and angle free.

The double sum part of the eq.(21) is two-way propagation term. For normal mode theory, there are three key terms need to calculate. Normal mode eigenfunction ϕ_m and real part of normal mode eigenvalue k_m and image part of normal mode eigenvalue β_m.

Traditionally, A series of fast numerical codes can be used to calculate the normal mode eigenfunction and eigenvalue for any SSP in the water column and any layered sediment bottom, such as KRAKEN, ORCA, MOATAL and so on. But in practical, the bottom GA parameters, include the layer structure of the bottom and the sound speed, density and attenuation in each layer, are difficult to measure directly.

Alternatively, the boundary effect of the bottom on the underwater sound field can be concentrated in one physical measurement – the bottom reflection coefficient V(θ) and the corresponding derivation of Green's function has been discussed[16]. Furthermore, the bottom reflection coefficient can be approximated by two parameters (P, Q) for small grazing angle where linear approximation can be made[15]. In the far field only the reflection character for angles less than the bottom critical angle makes sense, therefore in most practical applications only the reflection parameter (P, Q) and the bottom reflection characters in small grazing angle are as in the following.

$$\ln|V(\theta)| \approx -Q\theta \tag{22}$$

$$\arg V(\theta) \approx -\pi + P\theta \tag{23}$$

The grazing angle satisfied $0<\theta<\theta cr$, where θcr refers to the critical angle of the given waveguide.

By using the WKB approximation, the real part km and imaginary part βm of the modal horizontal wavenumber describes the phase and attenuation of modes and respectively has the following relationship with parameters P and Q.

$$2\int_0^H \sqrt{k_0^2(z)-k_m^2}\,dz + P\theta_m = 2m\pi \tag{24}$$

$$\beta_m = \frac{Q\theta_m}{S_m+\delta_m} \tag{25}$$

where θm is the modal grazing angle, and Sm+δm indicates the modal cycle distance given by

$$S_m = 2\int_0^H \left(k_m / \sqrt{k_0^2(z)-k_m^2}\right) dz \tag{26}$$

$$\delta_m \approx P/(k_0\theta_m) \tag{27}$$

We can use the depth-separated wave equation to propagate (or shoot) a mode depth function ϕm(z) from initial values at the surface to the bottom.

$$\frac{d\phi^2}{dz^2} + \left(\frac{\omega^2}{c^2(z)} - k_{rm}^2\right)\phi_m(z) = 0 \tag{28}$$

Through the finite difference representation of eq.(28), we can get eigenfunction of the normal mode theory.

So the eigenfunction and the eigenvalue of the normal modes can be calculated by P and Q with any SSP. Furthermore, the full wave reverberation model can be approximated as three unknow parameters model. It turns out that the angular pattern of the sea floor rough surface scattering is mainly determined by the angular dependency of $\varphi_m(H)\varphi_n(H)$.

4. Case study

4.1. Numerical simulation on a Pekeris waveguide

In the numerical simulation, the environmental parameters were listed in figure 2: a Pekeris waveguide with water depth H = 50 m, sound speed in water c0 = 1500 m/s, sound speed in sediment cb = 1600m/s, the density in sediment ρb = 1.77 g/cm3, and the attenuation in sediment αb = 0.673 dB/kHz-m. For rough interface, consider RMS value of roughness σ = 0.1m, the space correlation scale L = 10 m.

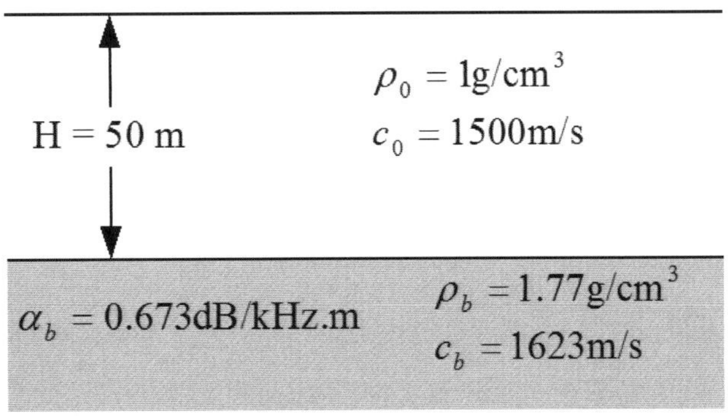

Fig.2 Pekeris waveguide

Acorrding to the PQ definition in reference [15], P = 9.27 and Q = 0.88 for the Pekeris waveguide shown in figure 2. The reverberation data was calculated based on the theories listed in section 2 and section 3. Figure 3 and figure 4 are the comparison between modal reverberation model and energy-flux reverberation model corresponding to fc = 300 Hz and fc = 900 Hz respectively. In the comparison, sounce depth and the receiver depth are both 25 m. The two theories agree well. But they don't agree well near the boundary, for example, source depth and receiver depth are both 5 m, see figure 5. However, the two theories agree well in most part of the water column.

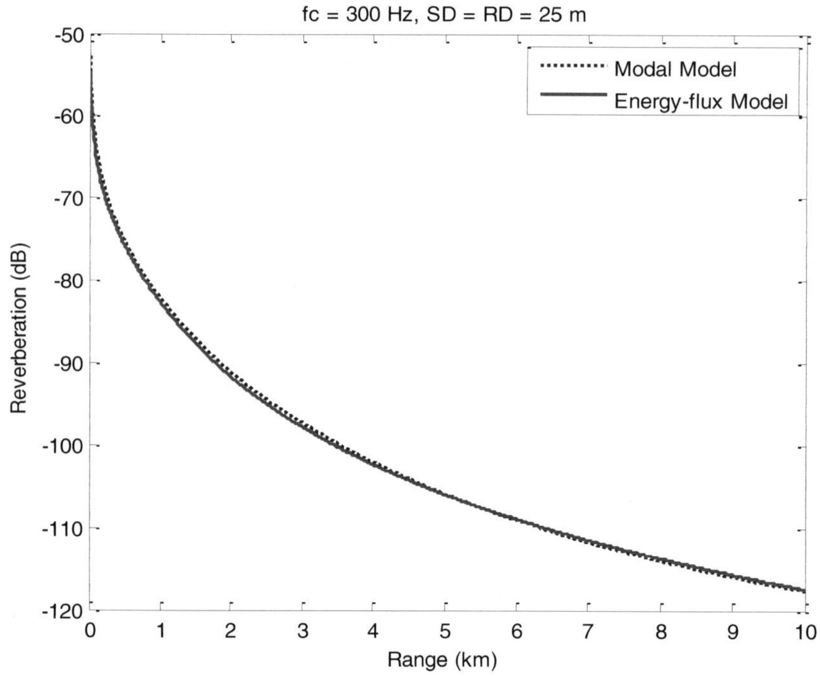

Fig.3 Comparison between modal model and energy-flux model(fc = 300 Hz)

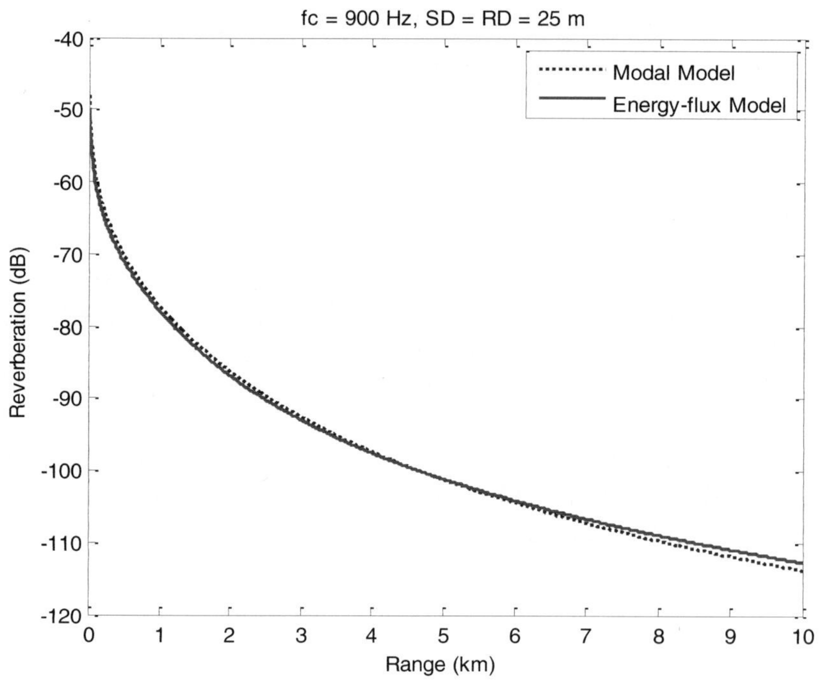

Fig.4 Comparison between modal model and energy-flux model(fc = 900 Hz)

4.2. Model-data comparison for a Pekeris waveguide (Qingdao)

The experiment was carried out at Yellow Sea (China) in November 2005. It can be approximated as an iso-velocity profile from the sound speed profile (figure 6) measured at the experiment, and the sound speed in the water c_0 = 1513 m/s. The water depth in the experiment area is 32 m. And we have got P = 9 and Q(f = 300 Hz) = 0.24, Q(f = 600 Hz) = 0.29, Q(f = 900 Hz) = 0.35 in this area through geoacoustic inversion using sound propagation data. The explosive source (70g) was used in the experiment. From the reverberation data, we can inverse μ (f = 300 Hz) = -39 dB, μ (f = 600 Hz) = -39 dB and μ (f = 900 Hz) = -40 dB with the new reverberation model.

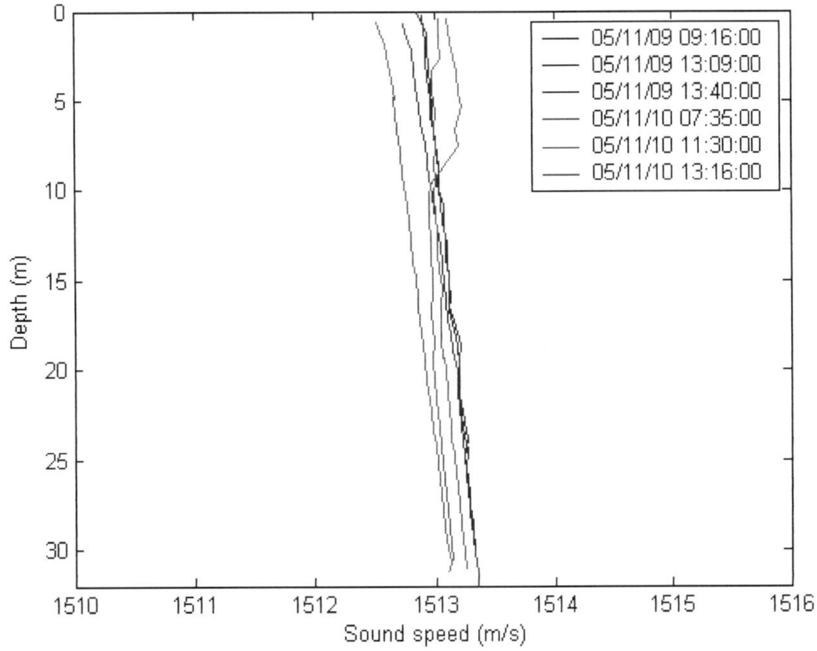

Fig.5 Sound speed profile during 2005 Yellow Sea experiment

Using the new energy-flux model of waveguide reverberation based on Perturbation theory and the environmental parameters (μ, P and Q) for each frequency, the reverberation data in the experiment area can be predicted. The source strength for f = 300,600 and 900 Hz was 184, 183, and 181 dB, and the sensitivity of hydrophone is -171 dB. With these data, the reverberation data filtered in 1/3 octave band was calibrated. Model-data comparison with f = 300, 600 and 900 Hz was shown in the figure 6,7 and 8 respectively.

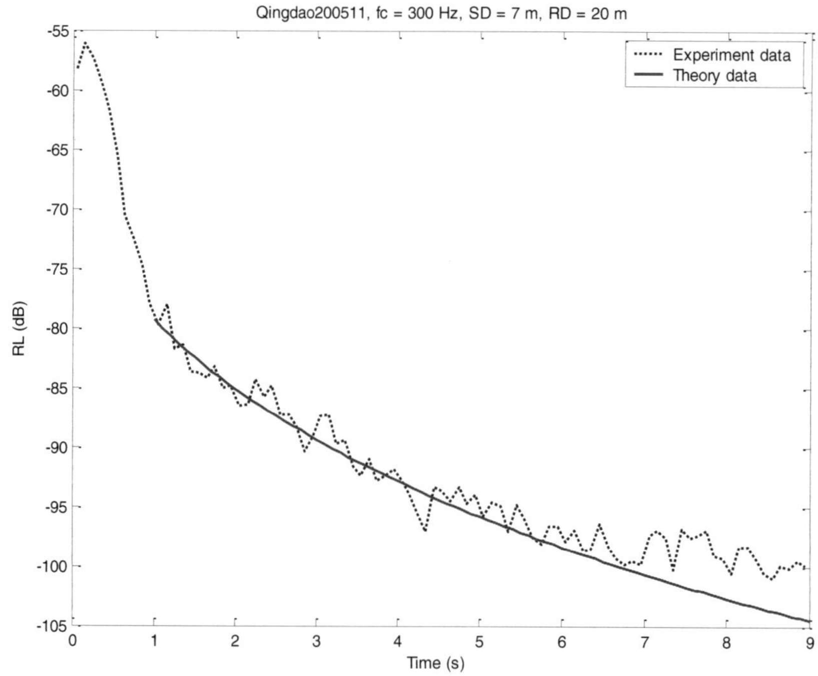

Fig.6 Model-data comparison (f = 300 Hz)

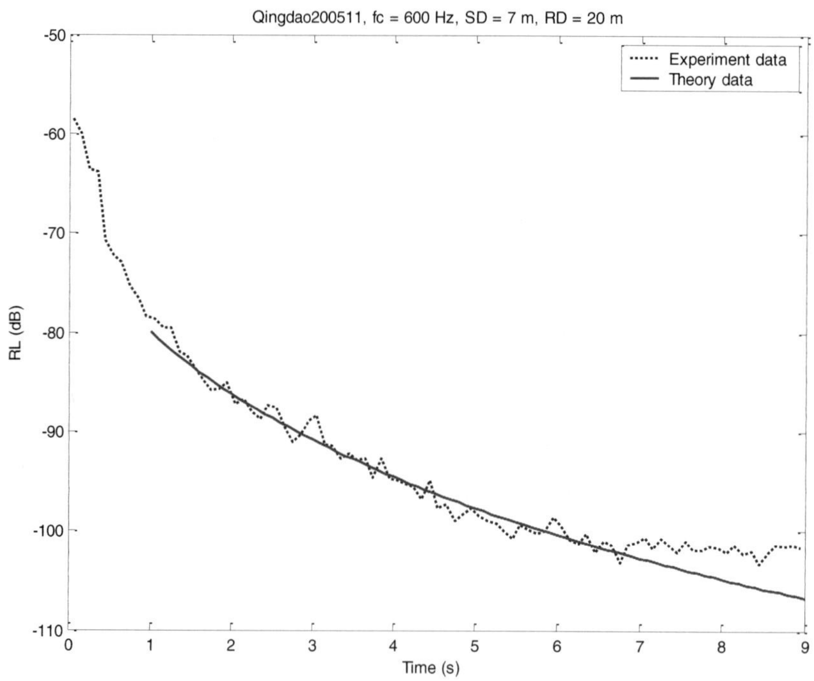

Fig.7 Model-data comparison (f = 600 Hz)

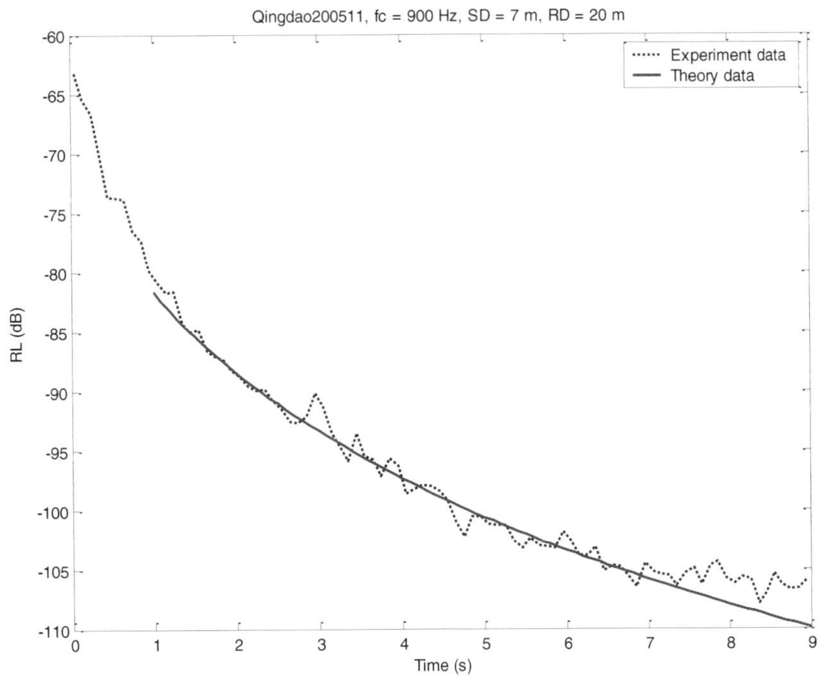

Fig.8 Model-data comparison (f = 900 Hz)

In figure 6,7,8, the dotted line is experiment data, and the solid line is theory data. Model and data comparison shows the new energy-flux reverberation theory can explain the experiment data well.

5. Conclusion

A practical shallow water reverberation model based on bottom reflection parameters was given in this paper. The new model has only three environmental parameters (P, Q and μ). P illustrates the angular dependency of backscattering; Q controls the reverberation intensity decaying; and μ shows the backscattering strength in the model. The three parameters can be inverted easily. It can calculate average reverberation intensity, and has considered many factors such as source depth, receiver depth, and so on. Theory – experiment data comparison shows that the new model can explain the low frequency reverberation data well.

Acknowledgments

This work was supported by the National Natural Science Foundation of China under No. 11774375 and No. 11974375.

Reference

[1] H.P. Bucker and H.E. Morris, "Normal-mode reverberation in channels or ducts," J. Acoust. Soc. Am. 44, pp.827-828, 1968.

[2] R.H. Zhang and G.L. Jin, " Normal mode theory of average reverberation intensity in shallow-water," J. Sound and Vib, 119, pp.215-223, 1987.

[3] D.D.Ellis,"A shallow-water normal mode reverberation model," J. Acoust. Soc. Am.,97, pp.2804-2814, 1995.

[4] K. LePage, "Bottom reverberation in shallow-water: coherent properties as a function of bandwidth, waveguide characteristics and scatterer distribution," J. Acoust. Soc. Am., 106, pp.3240-3254, 1999.

[5] J.X. Zhou, D. Guan , E.C. Shang and E. Luo, "Long-range reverberation and bottom scattering in shallow-water, Chinese J. Acoustics, 1, pp. 54-63, 1982.

[6] C.H. Harrison, "Closed-form solutions for reverberation and signal excess with mode-stripping and Lambert's law," J. Acoust.Soc,Am., 114, pp.2744-2756, 2003.

[7] B.H. Tracy and H. Schmidt, "Seismo-Acoustic field statistics in shallow water," IEEE,JOE, 22, pp.317-331, 1997.

[8] G.Bouchage, K.D.LePage, "A shallow-water reverberation PE model," Proceedings of the Sixth European Conference on Underwater Acoustics, ECUA'2002, pp.125-130, 2002.

[9] J.R.Wu, E.C.Shang, and T.F.Gao, "A new energy-flux model of waveguide reverberation based on perturbation theory," Journal of Computational Acoustics, Vol.18(3), pp209-225, 2010.

[10] T.F. Gao, "Relation between waveguide and non-waveguide scattering from a rough interface," Acta Acust. 14, pp.126-132, 1989.

[11] D.J. Tang, "Shallow-water reverberation due to sediment volume inhomogeneities," in *Shallow-water Acoustics,* Ed. by R.H. Zhang and J.X. Zhou, pp.323-328, 1997.

[12] E.C.Shang, T.F.Gao and J.R.Wu, "A shallow-water reverberation model based on Perturbation theory," IEEE, Journal of Oceanic Engineering, Vol.33(4), pp.451- 461, 2008.

[13] J.A. Goff and T. Jordan, "Stochastic modeling of seafloor morphology : Inversion of sea beam data for second order statistics,"JGR, 93, pp. 13589-13608, 1993.

[14] T.C. Wang and E.C. Shang, *Underwater Acoustics* ,(in Chinese), Scientific Publisher, Beijing China, 1981.

[15] L.M.Brekhovskikh, *Waves in Layered Media*, 2nd ed, Academic, New York, 1980.

Effects of rough sea-ice on the sound propagation in the Arctic ocean

Qianqian Li[1, 2, 3*], Juan Shi[2], Zhenglin Li[3]

1 College of Underwater Acoustic Engineering, Harbin Engineering University, Harbin 150001, China

2 College of Geomrtics, Shandong University of Science and Technology, Qingdao 26690, China;

3 State Key Laboratory of Acoustics, Institute of Acoustics, Chinese Academy of Sciences, Beijing 100190, China;

* Correspondence: lqq@mail.ioa.ac.cn; Tel.: +86-1586-300-1888

Aiming at the complex and variable environment of Arctic ice, a stochastic physical model of sea ice is proposed to better represent the roughness of sea ice and study the acoustic characteristics of typical Arctic ice. The sea-ice is regarded as the uniform elastomer with rough interface, and the randomly distributed protuberance on the lower layer of the sea-ice are ice ridges. Referring to the BT scattering model, the sea-ice thickness data measured by the up-looking sonar, which released from the National Snow and Ice Data Center. and the randomly distributed ice ridge is regarded as a randomly distributed isosceles triangle to establish a random sea ice physical model, combined with plane elasticity. The ice layer reflection model is used to obtain the ice layer reflection coefficient; The last year's data is used as the test group, and the rest as the training group, the ray theory model is used to calculate the propagation loss under the ice covered and compare them. The results show that there is scattering phenomenon when sound waves propagate under the rough ice interface. It is difficult to observe the sound shadow region under rough ice. Comparing the sound field under sea-ice between the training group and the test group, it is found that the sound transmission loss of the two groups is consistent on the whole. It indicates that the rough sea ice model proposed can better characterize the roughness of the interface under the real ice layer.

Keyword: rough sea-ice; acoustic reflecting; Arctic sea

1. Introduction

The complex and variable environment of the Arctic ice layer adds to the difficulty of modeling the Arctic acoustic field. In recent years, as global warming accelerates the melting of Arctic sea ice, the related technologies for the development of polar resources continue to advance, making the Arctic increasingly the focus of attention of surrounding countries, and injecting great vitality into Arctic underwater sound research [1]. Sound waves are the only form of energy that can transmit long distances underwater [2]. Moreover, sound waves propagate in the ice-covered polar regions, which is different from in shallow seas and deep seas. To make good use of the resources in the arctic, it is necessary to first understand the characteristics of acoustic propagation in the arctic environment [3]. Polar waters are

completely different from acoustic fields in ice-free waters, taking into account the effects of reflection and scattering of sea ice during the propagation of sound waves [4].Burke and Twersky regarded the ice ridges as the semielliptic protuberances on rigid base planes and established a Burke-Twersky (BT) model for calculating the acoustic field under sea-ice [5]. Afterwards, Diachok [6] regarded the ice ridge as elliptical half-cylinders on rigid to establish a sea-ice model, and studied the acoustic reflection coefficient of sea-ice. Yew C H [7] takes sea-ice as fluid-saturated porous elastic medium to study its reflection and scattering effects on sound waves. Chen Wenjian, Yin Jingwei et al. [8] simplified the rough sea-ice into a plane ice layer, and using the reflection model proposed by Mccammon [9], the plane single-layer ice reflection model is derived to calculate the reflection coefficient. The coefficient as the input data of the ray acoustic model Bellhop, the characteristics of the acoustic propagation loss under the plane sea ice are analyzed, and the frequency selective conclusion of the acoustic propagation under the sea ice cover is obtained.
This paper we use the sea-ice thickness data measured by the up-looking sonar, which released from the NSIDC, and refer to the BT scattering model to determine the mean value of sea ice thickness, the average number of ice ridges per kilometer and its distribution law, and consider the ice ridge as a randomly distributed isosceles triangle, establish a random sea-ice physical model, and obtain the value of sea-ice thickness varying with distance. On the basis of the literature [8], combined with the plane elastic ice reflection model, the ice reflection coefficient is obtained. Additionally, the last year data in the history data is used as the test group, and the rest as the training group, The propagation losses under ice cover were calculated and compared by using the ray theory model.

2. Theory and model

2.1. Acoustic reflection characteristics of elastic ice

Chen Wenjian and Yin Jingwei et al. conducted theoretical research on the underwater acoustic environment characteristics of the polar ice region. The reflection coefficient model of air-ice-water structure was initially establish based on the multilayer elastic sea-ice reflection model [8]. Fig. 1 shows the schematic diagram of ice layer.

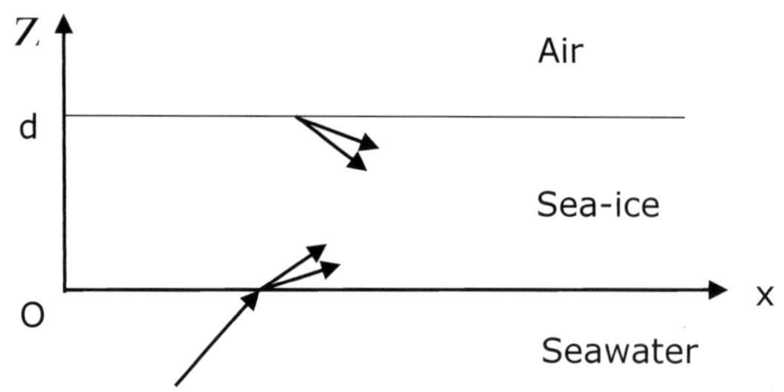

Fig.1 Schematic diagram of ice layer

According to the boundary conditions of the sound wave propagation to the water-ice interface and the ice-air interface, the reflection coefficient R of the plane sound wave under the sea-ice model can be obtained. See Ref.8 for other specific formula:

$$R = \frac{Z_{ice\_air} - Z_{water}}{Z_{ice\_air} + Z_{water}} \quad (1)$$

Where

$$Z_{ice\_air} = \frac{i\omega Z_{air} M_{33} - M_{32}}{i\omega M_{22} + \omega^2 Z_{air} M_{32}} \quad (2)$$

$$Z_{water} = \frac{\rho_{water} c_{water}}{cos\theta_{water}} \quad (3)$$

$$Z_{air} = \frac{\rho_{air} c_{air}}{cos\theta_{air}} \quad (4)$$

$$M_{ik} = a_{ik} - \frac{a_{i1} a_{4k}}{a_{41}}, i, k = 2,3,4 \quad (5)$$

Among the a_{ik} satisfies the following relationship:

$$a_{21} = i[2cot\theta_p sin^2\theta_s \sin(\alpha d) - tan\theta_s cos2\theta_s \sin(\beta d)] \quad (6)$$

$$a_{22} = cos2\theta_s \cos(\alpha d) + 2sin^2\theta_s cos(\beta d) \quad (7)$$

$$a_{23} = [cos\theta_p \sin(\alpha d) + tan\theta_s sin\theta_p \sin(\beta d)]/\omega\rho_{ice} c_p \quad (8)$$

$$a_{31} = -2i\omega\rho_{ice} s_s sin\theta_s \cos2\theta_s [\cos(\beta d) - \cos(\alpha d)] \quad (9)$$

$$a_{32} = -\omega\rho_{ice}\left[\frac{c_p cos^2 2\theta_s}{cos\theta_p \sin(\alpha d)} + 4s_s cos\theta_s sin^2\theta_s sin(\beta d)\right] \quad (10)$$

$$a_{33} = cos2\theta_s \cos(\alpha d) + 2sin^2\theta_s cos(\beta d)) \quad (11)$$

$$a_{41} = -\omega\rho_{ice} s_s^{\,2}[4/c_p cos\theta_p sin^2\theta_s \sin(\alpha d) + cos^2 2\theta_s / s_s cos\theta_s sin(\beta d)] \quad (12)$$

$$a_{42} = -2i\omega\rho_{ice} s^2{}_s sin\theta_p \cos2\theta_s [\cos(\beta d) - \cos(\alpha d)]/c_p \quad (13)$$

$$a_{43} = is^2{}_s\left[\frac{sin2\theta_p}{c^2{}_p \sin(\alpha d)} - cos2\theta_s / s_s^{\,2} tan\theta_s \sin(\beta d)\right] \quad (14)$$

When sound waves propagate in sea-ice, energy is absorbed by sea-ice[10]. In formula (6-14), d represents the thickness of the ice layer, α、β represent the absorption coefficients of the longitudinal and transverse waves, respectively. Reference [8] can be used to find the approximate formula of acoustic absorption coefficient of longitudinal and transverse waves:

$$\alpha = 0.06f\ dB/m \quad (15)$$

$$\beta = 6\alpha\ dB/m \quad (16)$$

If the density of water ρ_{water}, the propagation velocity of sound waves in water c_{water}, the density of sea-ice ρ_{ice}, the velocity c_p of the longitudinal wave in sea-ice, the velocity s_s of the transverse wave in sea-ice, the density of air ρ_{air}, and the propagation of sound waves in the air c_{air} are known, then the reflection coefficient corresponding to sea-ice thickness d can be obtained.

2.2. Model of sea-ice ridges

The rough surface is described by a random function of coordinates, so the acoustic diffraction of the surface in sea-ice can be regarded as a statistical problem [11]. Different distributions have corresponding skewness and kurtosis, where kurtosis represents the flatness of the data distribution, and skewness represents the symmetry of the distribution. As can be seen from Figure 2, the typical normal distribution has the skewness of 0 and the kurtosis of 3.

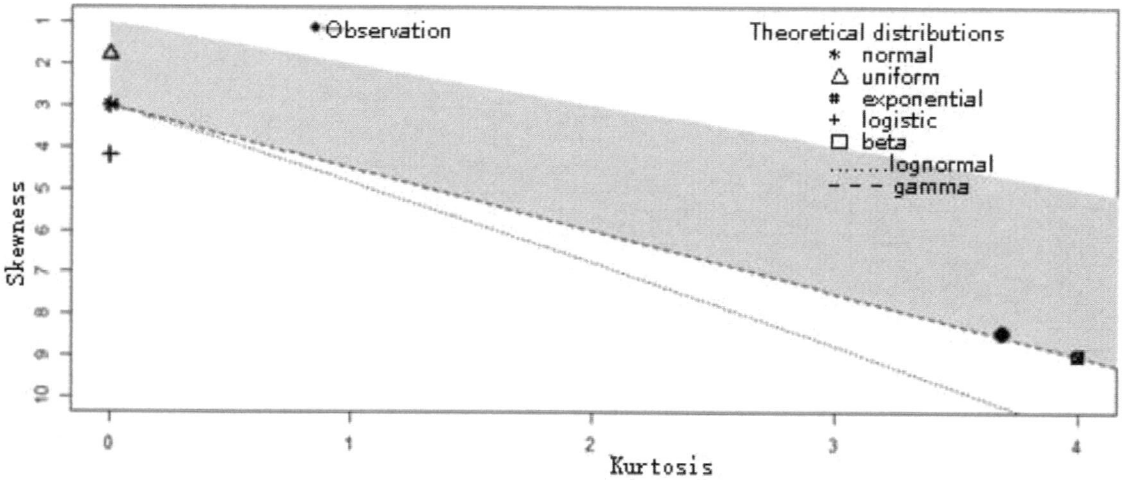

Fig. 2 Skewness and kurtosis

With reference to the BT model, this paper establishes a random thickness model of sea-ice, which is described as follows: Firstly, the skewness and kurtosis of a measured sea-ice thickness data can be gained by calculating and analyzing, and estimating which type of distribution the thickness probability function belongs to. Secondly, determining the probability distribution function of measured sea-ice thickness $f(h)$. Thirdly, counting the number of ice ridges per kilometer and the average thickness by the measured sea-ice data, and used it as thickness of the plane ice layer. Finally, by observing the measured contours shapes, as illustrated in Fig.2., the sea-ice may be described as a plurality of isosceles triangles randomly distributed under the plane ice layer, and the bottom edge height h is randomly given by the measured sea-ice thickness probability distribution function, at the same time, the length of the bottom side is twice the height. As shown in Figure 3.

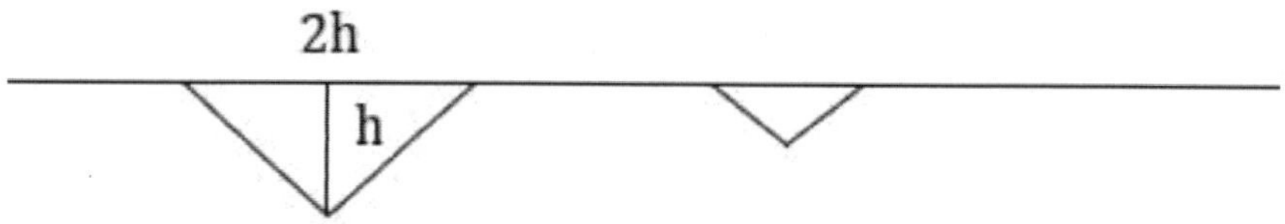

Fig.3 Schematic diagram of model ice

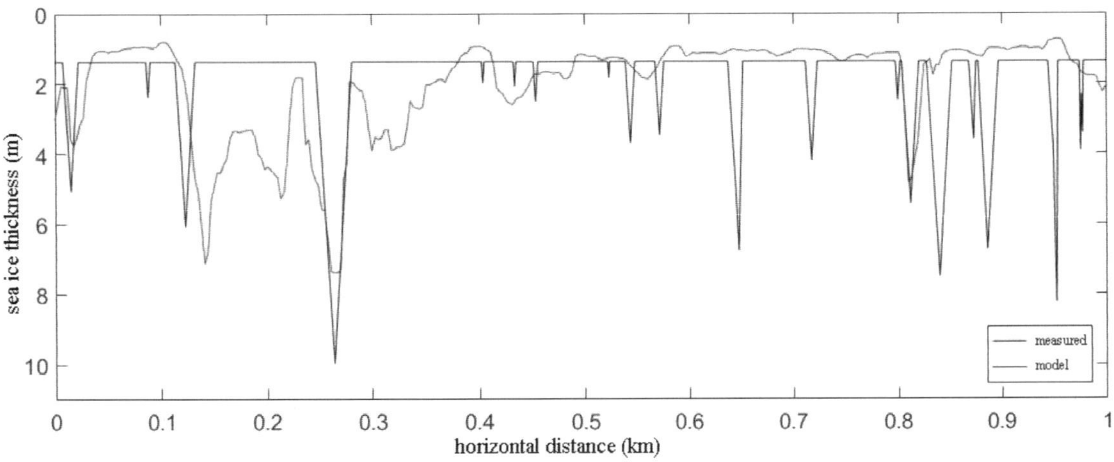

Fig.4 Measured ice and model ice

In the sea-ice model, the random ice thickness data can be generated from the measured sea-ice thickness data. Figure 4 shows the thickness comparison of measured ice and model ice for a certain kilometer. The thickness of sea-ice is rough, but the Bellhop model can only deal with the constant thickness of sea-ice, in other words, it cannot handle the case that sea-ice thickness varies with distance. During the propagation of sound waves, the sound rays will reflect with sea-ice of varying thickness[12]. As shown in Figure 5(a), the sea-ice thickness corresponding to reflection point A and B are not equal.

The Bellhop model can only deal with the situation shown in Figure 5(b). When calculating the energy change of the sound rays at the reflection point A and the B, particularly, the effect of ice thickness change on the energy loss of acoustic wave propagation cannot be considered.

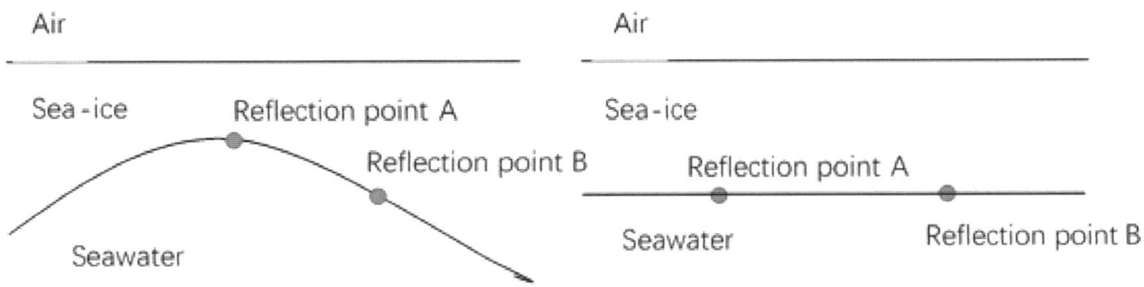

(a) Schematic diagram of rough ice (b) Schematic diagram of plane ice

Fig.5 Schematic diagram of reflection point

In response to the above defects, the Bellhop model was improved, and the previous single-layer elastic sea-ice acoustic reflection model was embedded in the Bellhop model. The improved model can update the reflection coefficient in real time according to the thickness of the sea-ice corresponding to the sound reflection point.

3. Sound transmission loss under rough ice-covered

Since 1960, the National Snow and Ice Data Center has collected and published data about polar sea-ice thickness which is measured by up-looking sonar. There are 2,270 valid data files, among which the length of the accumulative route is 65,900 km, and a total of 41.455 million sea-ice thicknesses are sampled. The track summary of up-looking sonar is shown in Figure 6.

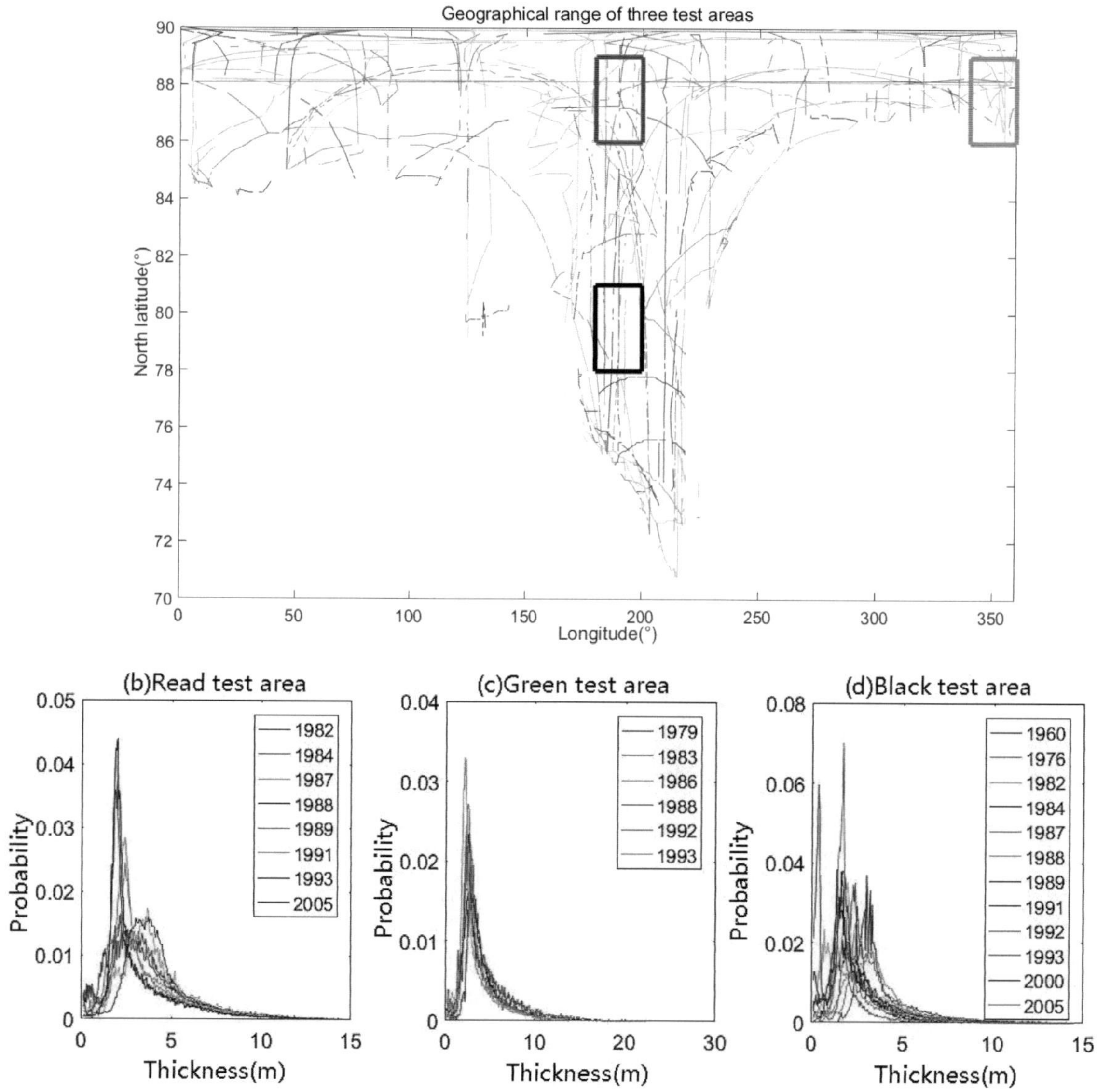

Fig.6 Track summary of up-looking sonar and test area

Sound velocity profile is one of the important underwater acoustic environment parameters of sound wave propagation, which can directly affect the results of simulation experiments. The Arctic Ocean environment is relatively stable. Therefore, this paper uses the sound velocity profile of the positive sound velocity gradient to simulate the experiment, as shown in Figure 7. [12]

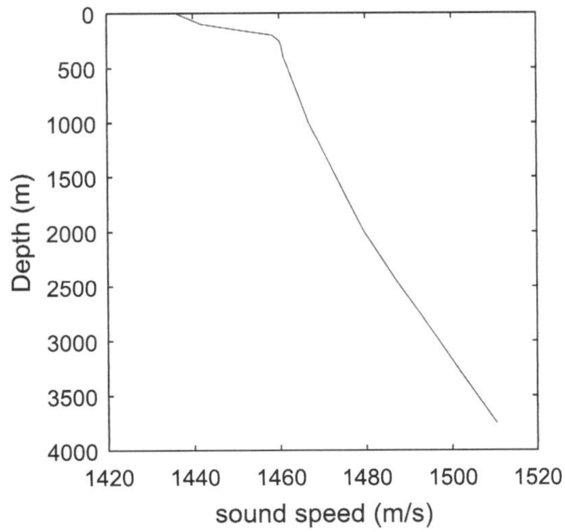

Fig.7 Typical subsea sound velocity profiles in the Arctic sea-ice

This paper calculates the acoustic field of the measured ice and model ice, then, selects three areas, which are represented by red box, green box and black box respectively. Each area contains historical sea-ice thickness data for several years. The probability distribution of sea-ice thickness over the years in the test area corresponds to Figures 6(b), 6(c), and 6(d), respectively.

This paper hypothesizes that sea-ice thickness has temporal-spatial correlation, then takes the probability distribution of sea-ice thickness in previous years as the distribution of sea-ice thickness density in the last year, and uses the data of previous years to predict the number of ice ridges in the last year, generates the data of random ice. Finally, uses the typical Arctic sound velocity profile to calculate the transmission loss of measured ice and model ice at 20, 100, and 500 m in each test area.

1. Red test area: The measured ice is taken from the data of 2005. The data of model ice is randomly generated from the random model of sea-ice thickness based on the measured data of the remaining years.

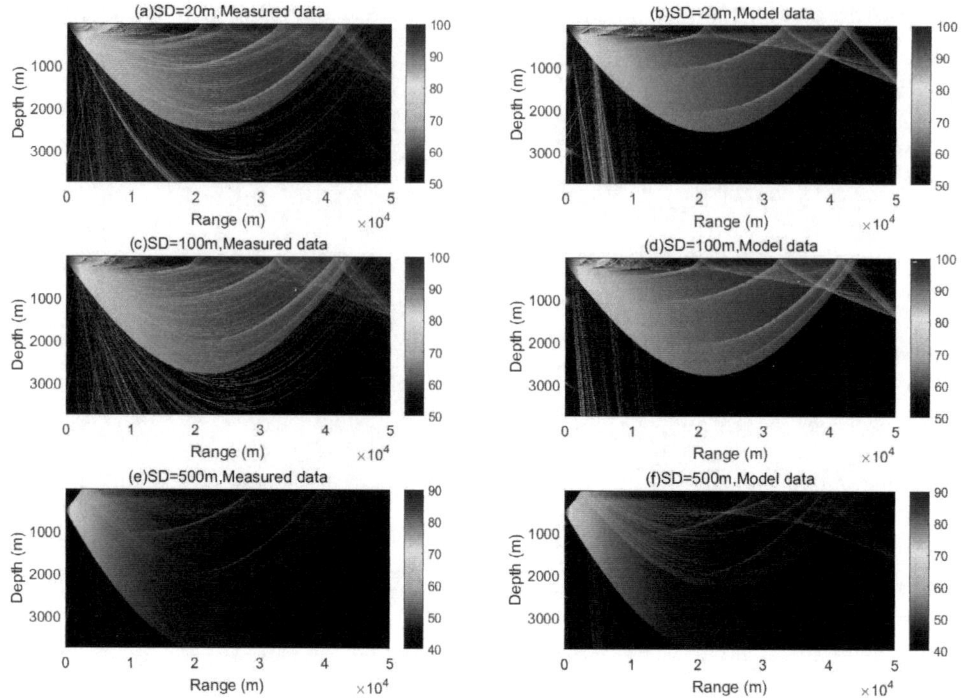

Fig.8 Transmission loss of red test area

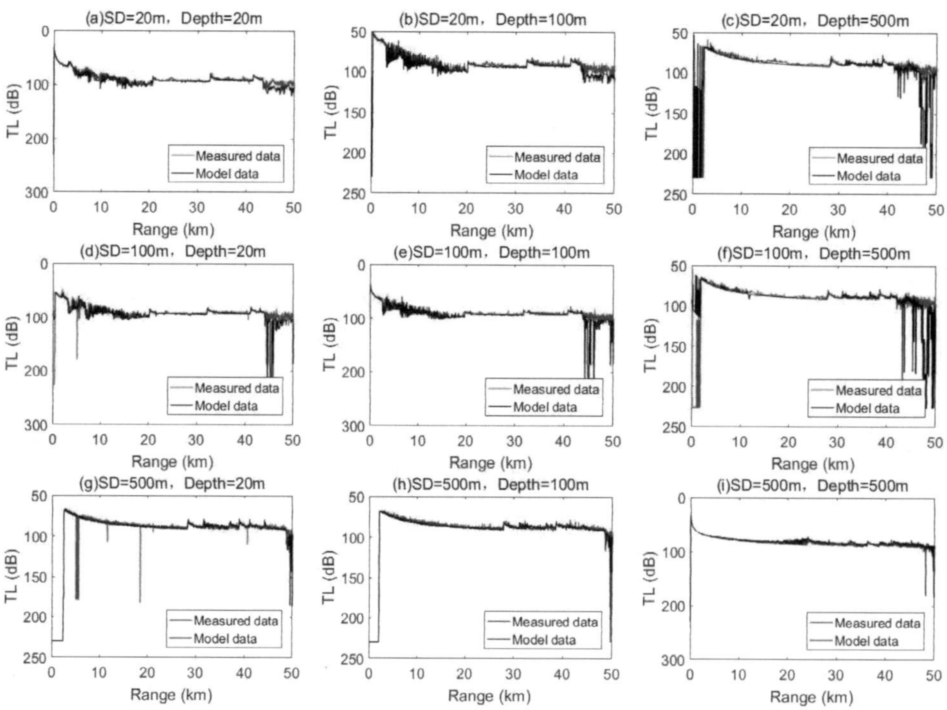

Fig.9 Transmission loss of red test area

2. Green test area: The measured ice is taken from the data of 1993. The data of model ice is randomly generated from the random model of sea-ice thickness based on the measured data of the remaining years.

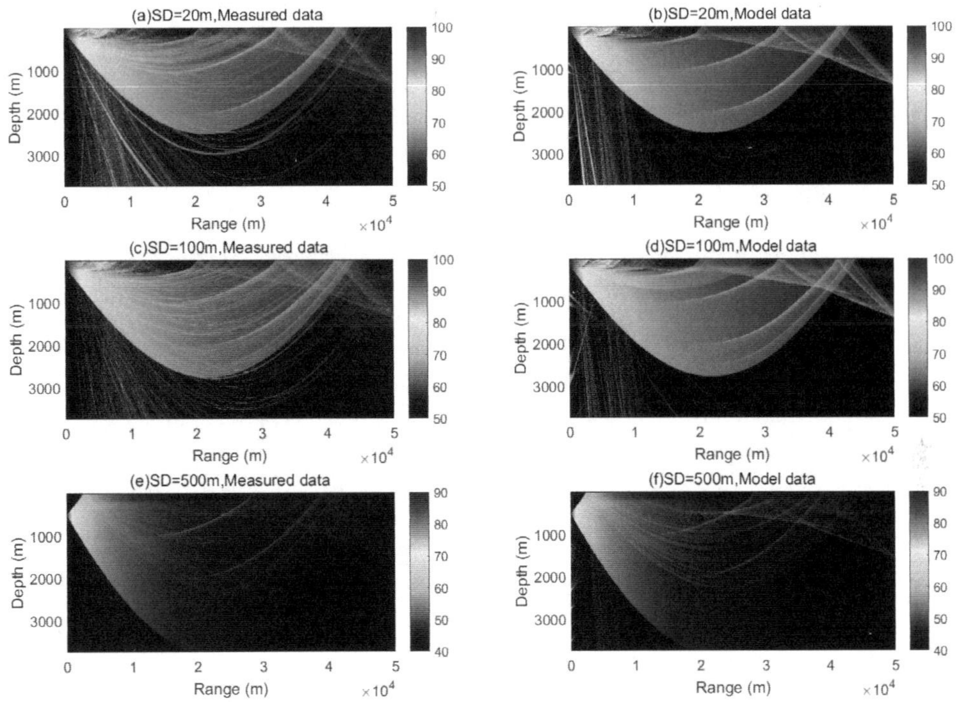

Fig.10 Transmission loss of green test area

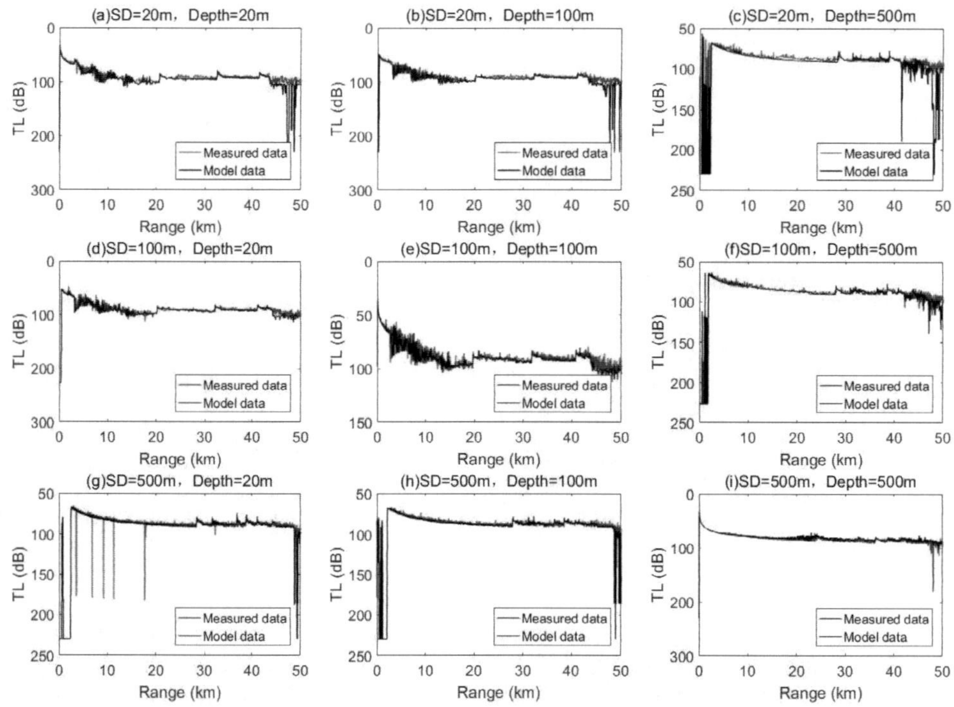

Fig.11 Transmission loss of red test area

3. Black test area: The measured ice is taken from the data of 2005. The data of model ice is randomly generated from the random model of sea-ice thickness based on the measured data of the remaining years.

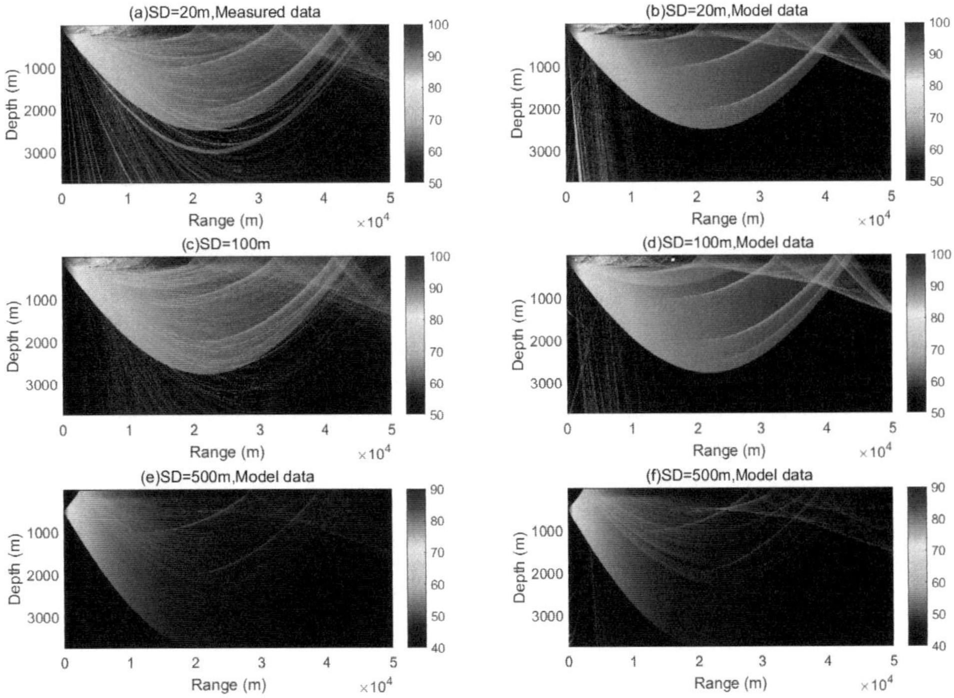

Fig.12 Transmission loss of black test area

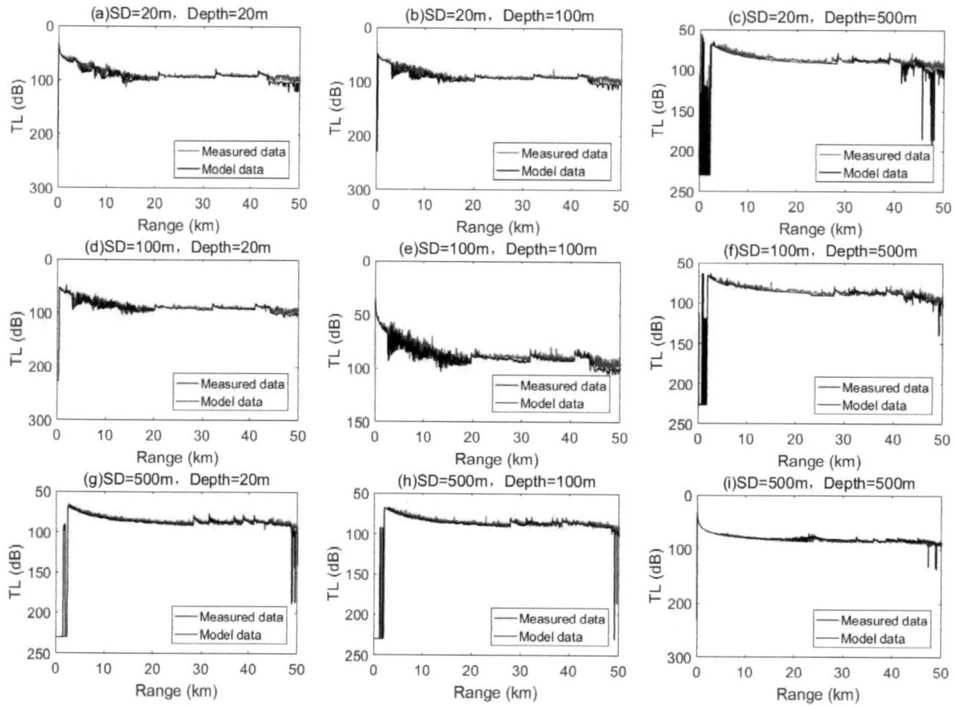

Fig.13 Transmission loss of red test area

Although the measured ice is rough and the thickness distribution is random, the acoustic field under the ice can be predicted to some extent by means of probability statistics and modeling.

4. Conclusions

The propagation loss under the ice surface is different from other surfaces, and the roughness of the sea ice is different. Therefore, in this paper, the ice ridges in the typical positive sound velocity gradient environment of the Arctic Ocean are modeled, and the acoustic field modeling is studied. According to the historical data of sea ice thickness, the BT model is used to establish a random sea-ice physical model for the uniform elastic layer under the rough interface. The sound field under the test group and the sample group is calculated, and found that there is scattering under the rough sea ice, the sound energy is scattered to all directions, so it is difficult to observe the sound shadow region under rough ice; The sound transmission loss under the two interfaces is consistent with the overall trend, and the absolute difference between the two is less than 3 db. This indicates that the rough sea-ice model proposed in this paper can better characterize the roughness of the real ice interface.

In addition, since the number of points in the random ice thickness model is far less than the measured sea-ice, the time required to calculate the acoustic field is less, the calculation efficiency of the acoustic field under the model ice is higher, which provides a way to improve the calculation efficiency of the sea-ice acoustic field.

The polar ice layer has a complex structure. This paper only makes a preliminary exploration of the polar sea ice model, which is of certain significance for understanding the acoustic field characteristics under polar ice and improve environmental adaptability of sonar equipment. In reality, the structure of the ice layer is complex, and various factors will affect the acoustic reflection coefficient. Therefore, in the subsequent work, the acoustic field model still needs to be improved. So a more complex ice reflection or scattering model is established to further study the acoustic characteristics of rough sea-ice, so as to acoustic characteristics closer to the actual sea-ice condition.

Acknowledgments

The National Natural Science Foundation of China under contract No. 11704225; State Key Laboratory of Acoustics, Chinese Academy of Sciences under contract No. SKLA201902; National Key R&D Program of China under contract No. 2018YFC1405900; SDUST Research Fund under contract No. 2019TDJH103.

Reference

[1] Qihu L I , Ning W , Jinping Z , et al. Arctic underwater acoustics: an attractive new topic in ocean acoustics[J]. Journal of Applied Acoustics, 2014.

[2] Chun-Xia M , Gui-Juan L I , Xiu-Wei L I . The research on methods of seafloor parameters inversion[J]. Ship Science and Technology, 2007.

[3] Chonglei L ,Tao L ,Li Y ,Haining H ,Acoustic propagation properties of two-axes channel under sea ice in the Arctic [J]. Applied acoustic,2016,35(04):309-315.

[4] Jin G , Lynch J F , Pawlowicz R , et al. Acoustic scattering losses in the Greenland Sea marginal ice zone during the 1988-89 tomography experiment[J]. The Journal of the Acoustical Society of America, 1994, 96(5):3045-3053.

[5] Burke, J. E . Scattering and Reflection by Elliptically Striated Surfaces[J]. The Journal of the Acoustical Society of America, 1966, 40(4):883.

[6] Diachok, O. I . Effects of sea-ice ridges on sound propagation in the Arctic Ocean[J]. The Journal of the Acoustical Society of America, 1976, 59(5):1110.

[7] Yew C H , Weng X . A study of reflection and refraction of waves at the interface of water and sea ice[J]. Journal of the Acoustical Society of America, 1987, 82(1):342-353.

[8] Wenjian C, Jingwei Y, Huanling Z, Guangping Z, Hui S. Characteristic analysis of acoustic transmission loss in water under plane ice cover [J].Chinese Journal of Polar Research, 2017, 29(02):194-203.

[9] Mccammon D F , Mcdaniel S T . The influence of the physical properties of ice on reflectivity[J]. The Journal of the Acoustical Society of America, 1998, 77(2):499-507.

[10] Squire V A, Williams T D. Wave propagation across sea-ice thickness changes[J]. Ocean Modelling, 2008, 21(1):1-11.

[11] Fuks, I. M . Wave scattering from statistically rough surfaces[M].

[12] Bukatov A E , D. D. Zav' yalov. Incidence of flexural gravitational waves on the line of contact of two floating ice plates of different thickness[J]. Physical Oceanography, 1999, 10(1):11-20.

[13] Fox C, Squire V A. Reflection and transmission characteristics at the edge of shore fast sea ice[J]. Journal of Geophysical Research Oceans, 1990, 95(C7):11629-11639.

Extracting Bottom Roughness Parameters Using Broadband Reverberation Data in Shallow Water

HOU QIANNAN, SHANG ERCHANG, WU JINRONG

Key Laboratory of Underwater Acoustic Environment, Institute of Acoustics, Chinese Academy of Sciences, Beijing, 100190, China
Houqiannan13@mails.ucas.ac.cn

Though reverberation is an exceptive interfering signal for sonar, it contains lots of information of bottom in shallow water, especially rough interface. The full-wave reverberation theory, based on Bass perturbation theory, proposes that bottom roughness is considered as "sub-source" in wave function, Sound scattering field and reverberation field can be obtained through solving such function. In this model, the bottom roughness is narrated as spectrum and characterizes backscattering strength, which provides the theory physical basis for extracting of bottom roughness. Goff-Jordan spectrum corrected Gaussian spectrum based on measured data and give a clear expression with variance, correlate scale and exponent term of frequency. These three parameters are what we want to extract from broadband reverberation data based on Goff-Jordan spectrum one by one. Numerical simulation and experiment at sea will both give the proofs of the rationality of such method and the accuracy of the result.

Keywords: broadband reverberation ; bottom roughness parameters;

1. General Appearance

Multi-beam Sound System is applied to measure the bottom bathymetry. But the accuracy of bottom roughness cannot be satisfied for perturbed scattering theory in generally. In recent years, the high-frequency multi-beam sonar is applied to provide the accuracy, while the problems of high-cost and time-consuming still exist. So, a method of extracting bottom roughness parameters is proposed.

The bottom perturbed fluctuation is considered as a statistics variable and applies roughness spectrum to describe it. There are several spectrum functions, such as Gaussian spectrum, Exponential spectrum, are frequently used, but they are not matched with the actual data. Thereby, a new spectrum function, here call it Goff-Jordan spectrum[1], is proposed through correcting the Gaussian spectrum based on the bottom roughness. This spectrum has also been applied by several researchers to model scattering due to bottom roughness[2-3].

In this paper, the full-wave reverberation theory described bottom roughness as a spectrum function and give a clear expression between reverberation average intensity and spectrum, which gives a fundamental of extracting roughness parameters using reverberation data. The reverberation due to bottom roughness was proposed by Gao Tianfu in 1979 primarily[4]. He said that bottom scattering field due to rough interface was considered as a "sub-source" to radiate sound intensity into waveguide and the "sub-source" was obtained through Bass perturbation theory. Then, the reverberation due to sediment volume inhomogeneous was proposed by Tang Dajun in 1980[5]. Shang E C combined the above two as an unified model and gave an explicitanalytic expression of modal backscattering matrix (abbreviated as MBSM in this paper) using bottom roughness spectrum[6].

This method is divided into two steps. In the first, bottom roughness spectrum is obtained using broadband reverberation data; In the second, extract bottom roughness parameters one by one according to Goff-Jordan spectrum.

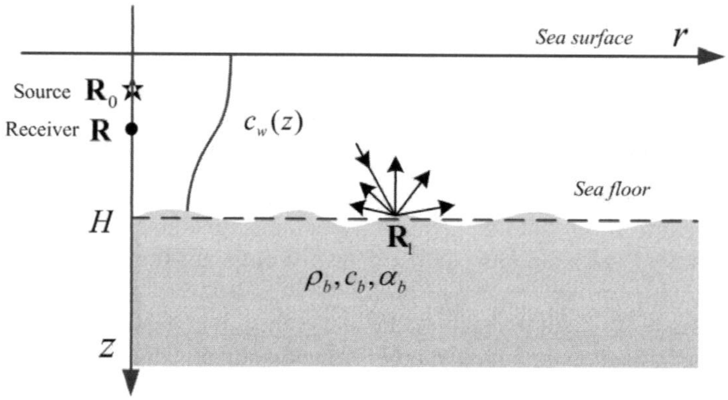

Fig.1. Geometry of shallow water.

2. Bottom Rough Water-sediment Interface

Here we assume that the bottom backscattering come from rough water-sediment interface only because of that backscattering due to the internal layer interfaces is too weak and can be ignored. The fluctuation of such rough interface is very small and distribute randomly, so that it can be described as a spectrum function in statistics. The bottom rough interface $\eta(r)$, as shown in Fig.1, is regarded as a perturbation to the average bottom depth H_0, and the statistics average value equals zero. In statistics, the spectrum function is the Fourier transformation of the auto-correlation function,

$$K(k) = \int_{r_1}^{r_2}\int_{r_1}^{r_2} < \eta(r')\eta(r'') > e^{ik(r'-r'')} dr' dr'' \quad (2.1)$$

where, $k = 2\pi f / c_h$ is the wavenumber at sea bottom.

In general, the Gaussian spectrum is the first choice, and the exponential spectrum is also applied. There are two parameters to describe such spectrum, because the average of such fluctuation equal to zero. Then, the first parameter is variance, which is to judge the relative height to the average value. The second is correlate scale, which describe the correlation range of bottom rough interface. While, both of these two spectrums cannot match the actual data well. So, Goff-Jordan spectrum is made by John A. Goff and Thomas H. Jordan in 1988. They corrected Gaussian spectrum according to the measured data and analyzed its statistics characteristic, then gave an explicit expression[1]

$$K^{\eta}_{G-J}(k) = \sigma^2 \pi L[1 + (2kL)^2]^{-(1+\nu)} \quad (2.2).$$

This spectrum introduced a particular parameter, exponent term v of frequency, to describe frequency dependency of spectrum, which presents the smooth degree of such interface and varies from 0 to 1 with the interface getting less smooth shown as in Fig.2. The larger v, the smoother interface. So, there are three important parameters to describe such roughness: variance σ^2, correlate scale L, and exponent term of frequency v. In this paper, we illustrate a method of extracting these three parameters according to Goff-Jordan spectrum.

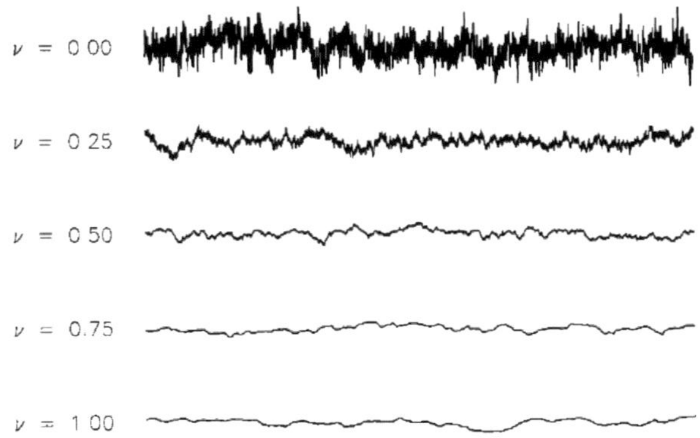

Fig.2. Profile of bottom water-sediment interface with different v (quote in Ref.1)

The full wave reverberation modal has already given an explicit expression of reverberation average intensity using bottom roughness spectrum. This proposes that it is available to extract bottom roughness parameters using reverberation data.

3. Full-Wave Reverberation Theory

For monostatic reverberation, receiver and source at the same location. The sound propagates from source to bottom; then scattering by bottom rough interface mainly; finally, all these scattering echoes are received by receiver at one time. The first and third processes both are propagation, and propagation modal have also matured which is superposition of normal modes in shallow water. The explicit physical modal of backscattering using bottom roughness spectrum has been expressed in the full wave reverberation theory. Here, a short introduction for it is done.

In Fig.1, bottom water-sediment interface is described as a perturbation variable $\eta(r)$ compared with average depth of bottom H_0. The average value of such perturbation variable is zero and the variance is σ^2. Bottom sediment is an infinite half-space medium with geoacoustic parameters (such as sound speed, density and attenuation coefficient) are c_b, ρ_b and α_b. In reverberation modal, the distribution of scatterers is isotropy, which means it has a similar distribution in all azimuth angle. In shallow water waveguide, reverberation averaged intensity can be described by the superposition of normal modes[6]

$$I_\eta(r,f) = E_0(\frac{2\pi}{r})^2 \pi r c_w(H_0)\sum_n^M\sum_m^M \varphi_m^2(z)\varphi_m^2(H_0)M_{mn}\varphi_n^2(H_0)\varphi_n^2(z_s)\frac{e^{-2(\beta_m+\beta_n)r}}{k_m k_n} \tag{3.1}$$

$$M_{mn} = C_{mn} K(k_m + k_n) \tag{3.2}$$

$$K(k_m + k_n) = \int_{r_1}^{r_2} \int_{r_1}^{r_2} < \eta(r')\eta(r'') > e^{i(k_m+k_n)(r'-r'')} dr' dr'' \tag{3.3}$$

$$C_{mn} = [1 - \frac{k_b^2}{\rho_b k_h^2} + (1 - \frac{1}{\rho_b}) \frac{k_m k_n}{k_h^2} + (\frac{1-\rho_b}{\rho_b^2}) \frac{\gamma_m \gamma_n}{k_h^2}]^2 \cdot k_h^4 \tag{3.4}$$

$$\gamma_{m,n} = \sqrt{k_{m,n}^2 - k_b^2} \tag{3.5}$$

where, E_0 is initial source signal intensity, and for short pulse $s(t)$ with pulse length τ, $E_0 \approx s^2(t) \cdot \tau$. $\varphi_m(z)$ represent eigenfunction, k_m and β_m is the real part and image part of eigenvalue. The ratio of density in sediment and water is κ. The grazing angle $\theta_m(z)$ satisfies Snell Law $k_w(z_1)\cos(\theta_m(z_1)) = k_w(z_2)\cos(\theta_m(z_2))$ and $k_{w,b}(z) = 2\pi f / c_{w,b}(z)$ is the wavenumber with subscript w in water and b in bottom sediment. M_{mn}, shown in Eq.(3.2), is the bottom backscattering coefficient due to bottom rough water-sediment interface, which depends on bottom roughness spectrum and coherence coefficient of normal modes. C_{mn} is a coherent coefficient of incident and scattering mode to describe the effect of bottom on sound scattering. $K(k_m + k_n)$ is bottom rough interface spectrum.

Analysis Eq.(3.1), the MBSM due to bottom rough interface is

$$\Theta_{mn} = \varphi_m^2(H_0) M_{mn} \varphi_n^2(H_0) \tag{3.6}$$

where, $\varphi_m(H_0)$, which is restricted by Green function of shallow water waveguide, is the incident mode average bottom depth. And $\varphi_n(H_0)$ is the scattering mode at average bottom depth. The bottom roughness spectrum can decide backscattering intensity directly according to Eq.(3.2).

Some simplification for the bottom roughness spectrum been done to isolate from normal mode. For long range condition in shallow water, there are only a fewer lower order normal modes persist. Here an assumption, $k_m \approx k_n \approx k_h = 2\pi f / c_w(H_0)$, is typical for many normal mode approximate modalities. $K(k_m + k_n)$ can also be simplified as

$$K(2k_h) = \int_{r_1}^{r_2} \int_{r_1}^{r_2} < \eta(r')\eta(r'') > e^{i2k_h(r'-r'')} dr' dr'' \tag{3.7}$$

As a result, the bottom roughness spectrum is independent on the normal modes and can be alone with the superposition. The Eq.(3.1) is deformed

$$I_\eta(r, f) = E_0 \frac{4\pi^3 c_w(H_0)}{k_h^2 r} \cdot K(2k_h) \cdot \sum_m^M \sum_n^M \varphi_m^2(z) \varphi_m^2(H_0) C_{mn} \varphi_m^2(H_0) \varphi_m^2(z_s) e^{-2(\beta_m + \beta_n) r} \tag{3.8}$$

This simplification can be accepted exactly as shown in Fig.3, where simulation environment is a 100m water layer with 1500m/s iso-velocity laying on a flat bottom with the sixth type sediment given by Hamilton[7] and the geoacoustic parameters are that sound speed 1623m/s, density 1.77g/cm^3, attenuation 0.3 dB/λ. The variance, correlate scale and exponent term of frequency for Goff-Jordan spectrum is 0.01m^2, 10m and 0.5, respectively. The depth of source and receiver both are 25m. As a result, such deformation makes full wave reverberation model an attractive modality to show potential in extracting bottom rough spectrum parameters using reverberation data.

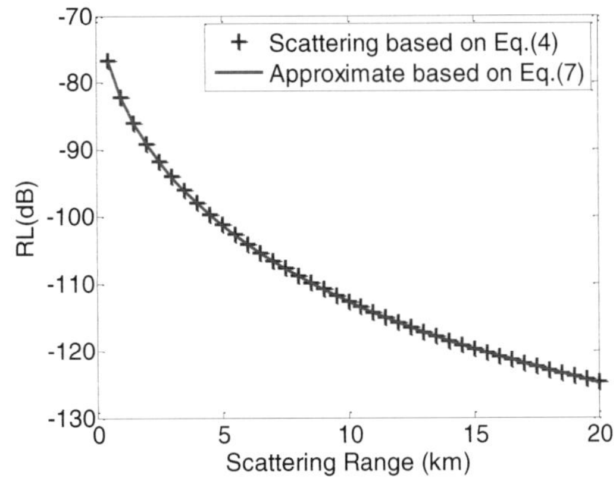

Fig.3. Compare RL before and after the long-range approximation

4. Extracting Spectrum Parameters

Defined a function $g(r)$

$$g(r,f) = \frac{4\pi^3 c_w(H_0)}{k_h^2 r} \cdot \sum_m^M \sum_n^M \varphi_m^2(z)\varphi_m^2(H_0) C_{mn} \varphi_m^2(H_0)\varphi_m^2(z_s) e^{-2(\beta_m+\beta_n)r} \tag{4.1}$$

Which is dependent on the geometry of shallow water waveguide and its environment parameters, except for the bottom water-sediment interface roughness characteristics. On the other words, $g(r,f)$ can be simulated according to the environment parameters has already been known. As a consequence, the Eq.(3.8) formulates three parts and isolates the roughness spectrum from reverberation average intensity as follow

$$K(2k_h) = \frac{I_\eta(r,f)}{E_0(f)\cdot g(r,f)} \tag{4.2}$$

or the formulation in decibel as

$$SP(2k_h) = RL(r,f) - SL(f) - G(r,f) \tag{4.3}$$

where, $I_\eta(r,f)$ (or $RL(r,f) = 10\lg(I_\eta(r,f))$) is the measured broadband data of reverberation average intensity; $E_0(f)$ (or $SL(f) = 10\lg(E_0(f))$) is source signal intensity for corresponding frequency and also can be measured through monitoring hydrophone or another method; and $g(r,f)$ (or $G(r,f) = 10\lg(g(r,f))$) can be simulated according to Eq.(4.1).

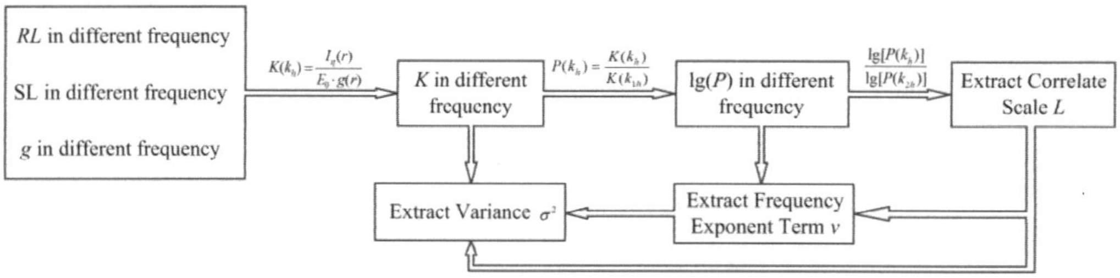

Fig.4. Method of extracting bottom roughness parameter.

Now, the bottom water-sediment interface roughness spectrum is obtained based on the broadband reverberation average intensity, and the expression of bottom roughness spectrum has been determined clearly. So, the parameters of bottom roughness can be inversed from reverberation intensity directly. Here, some procession has been done for it. Choosing a referent frequency, a ratio of spectrum at different frequency to the referent frequency has been done, so that the variance can be relieved according with Eq.(2.2)

$$P_{G-J}(k_h) = \frac{K_{G-J}(2k_h)}{K_{G-J}(2k_{1h})} = \left[\frac{1+(2k_h L)^2}{1+(2k_{1h}L)^2}\right]^{-(1+\nu)} \tag{4.4}$$

where, k_{1h} is the reference wavenumber. The ratio is function of correlate scale L and frequency exponent term ν . in order to clear up the effect of frequency exponent term ν , we take logarithm to $P_{G-J}(k_h)$

$$\Delta SP(k_h) = \lg[P(k_h)] = -(1+\nu)\{\lg[1+(2k_h L)^2] - \lg[1+(2k_{1h}L)^2]\} \tag{4.5}$$

Then, choose another reference wave number k_{2h}, process to Eq.(4.5) as follow

$$\Lambda(k_k) = \frac{\Delta SP(k_h)}{\Delta SP(k_{2h})} = \frac{\lg[1+(2k_h L)^2] - \lg[1+(2k_{1h}L)^2]}{\lg[1+(2k_{2h}L)^2] - \lg[1+(2k_{1h}L)^2]} \tag{4.6}$$

where, $\Lambda(k_h)-f$ curve is only relay on the correlate scale L . So extracting L in according with this curve is both accurate and efficient. Then, match ν based on $\Delta SP(k_h)-f$ curve by Eq.(4.5) after L has been obtained. Finally, evaluate variance according to $K(2k_h)-f$ curve. The basic extracting method shown as Fig.4, which gains the bottom roughness parameters in proper sequence accurately one by one.

Here numerical experiment gives a proof for the method of extracting bottom roughness parameters. The range independent shallow water waveguide and environment parameters as shown in Fig.1 is applied. Here we assume that source level is 0dB and simulate a reverberation average intensity for frequency from 100Hz to 1000Hz as measure data. At the same time, 1dB random fluctuation has been considered for the reverberation average intensity at 4s as displaying in Fig.5-a. The decaying term is simulated based on environment parameters as shown in Fig.5-b. Then the frequency dependency of the bottom roughness spectrum is obtained according to Eq.(4.2) or Eq.(4.3). Firstly, the correlate scale and exponent term of frequency is 10.17m and 0.478 obtained according to the frequency dependency of spectrum based on Eq.(4.6) and Eq.(4.5) one by one, shown as the red circle curve in Fig.6-a, which matches experiment data (the blue '+' curve) and real data (the black line) very well. The error is available compared with actual data is 10m and 0.5. Secondly, the variance of bottom roughness is $0.0083m^2$ as shown in Fig.6-b compared with actual data $0{,}01m^2$.

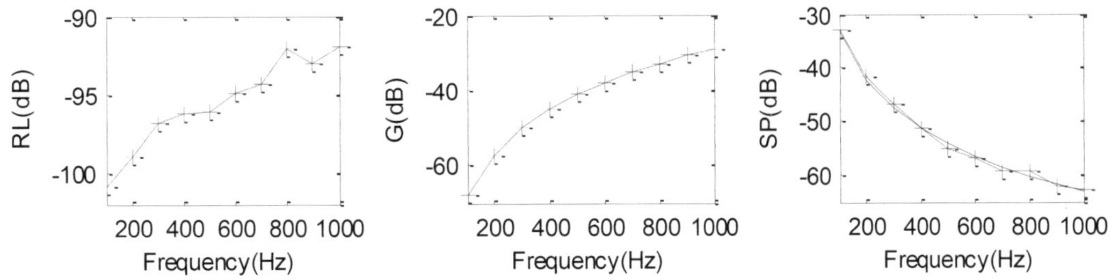

Fig.5. Extracted bottom roughness spectrum varies from 100Hz to 1000Hz at 4s. (a)reverberation level, (b)the decaying term, (c)the bottom roughness spectrum

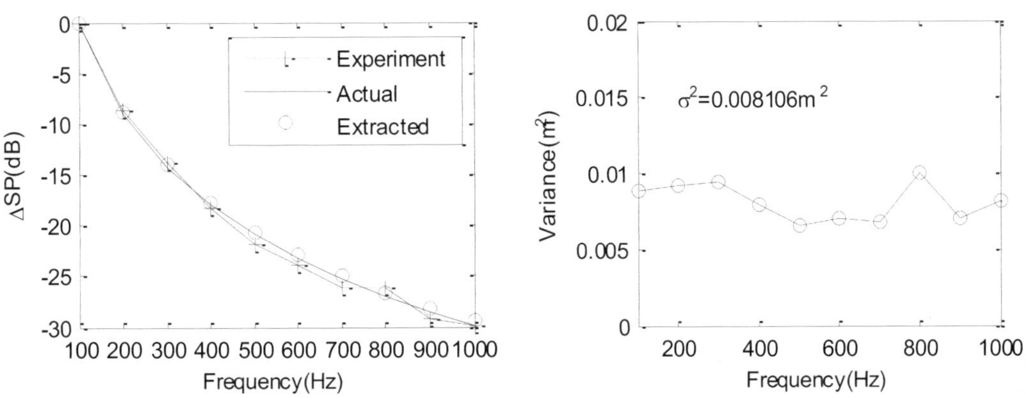

Fig.6. Extracted bottom roughness parameters. (a) the correlation scale and the exponent term of frequency, (b)the variance

5. At-Sea Experimentation

An experiment at sea has been conducted for testing this method is effect. The geometry of experiment environment is shown in Fig.7, where the Sound Speed Profile (short SSP) is considered as iso-velocity with 1487m/s. The half-space sediment geoacoustic parameters are: velocity 1520m/s, density $0.9g/cm^3$, attenuation coefficient $0.1dB/\lambda$. Standard explosive sound signals, containing the equivalent of 1kg TNT, detonate at depth of 25m and about 100m horizontally from the research vessel. A vertical line array of 37 homogeneous hydrophones with an over-all length of 29.6m is suspended from an anchored research vessel and the deepest hydrophone is located at depth of 31.6m. During this experiment the sea surface is very smooth, so reverberation come from bottom scattering mainly.

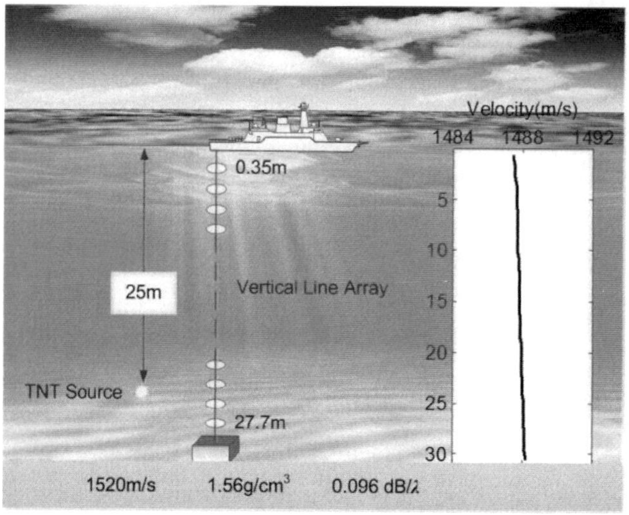

Fig.7. Geometry of reverberation experiment.

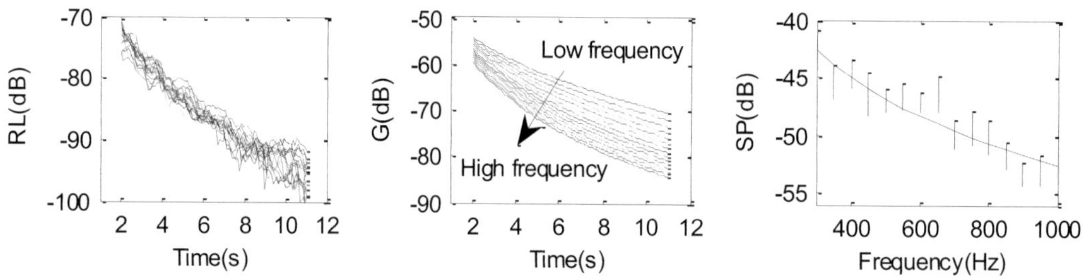

Fig.8. Data processing for frequency from 300Hz to 1000Hz. (a)reverberation level from experiment data, (b)the decaying term simulated according to environment, (c)the bottom roughness spectrum extracted through (a) minus (b).

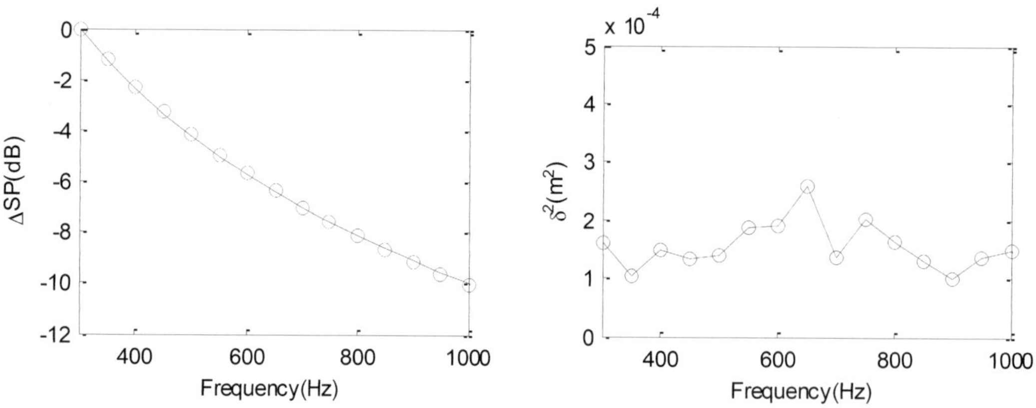

Fig.9. The extracted parameters of bottom roughness spectrum. (a) the correlation scale and the exponent term of frequency, (b)the variance

Experiment data varies from 300Hz to 1000Hz is processed to extract bottom roughness parameters. The reverberation average intensity decay from 2s to 11s with the source level is 0dB as shown in Fig. 8-a, and different curve represent different frequency. Then simulate the decaying term according to the measured environment parameters as shown in Fig.8-b. Reverberation average intensity minus the decaying term according Eq.(4.3) in decibel, we obtain the frequency dependency of bottom roughness spectrum as black point in Fig.8-c. The blue line is 1 order logarithm asymptotic expression of such spectrum data, which is considered as the standard data to extract bottom roughness parameters. Then the extracted result of correlate scale is 15m and exponent term of frequency is 0.5 as shown in Fig.9-a and the variance of bottom roughness is 1m as shown in Fig.9-b. In this paper, reverberation average intensity has been predicted for another frequency according to the above extracted bottom roughness parameters.

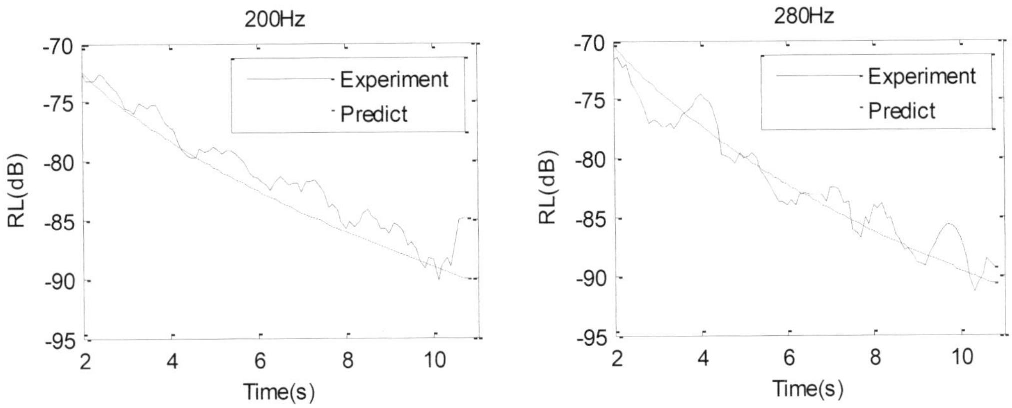

Fig.10. The extracted data of bottom roughness spectrum.

6. Summarys

In this paper, the authors propose a method of extracting bottom roughness parameters using broadband reverberation average intensity data according to Goff-Jordan spectrum. There are three parameters of Goff-Jordan spectrum to be extracted, variance, correlate scale and exponent term of frequency. These three parameters can be isolated through some processing to bottom roughness spectrum, so that extracting them one by one to make the result much more accurate. In order to obtain these parameters, there are several variables to input: the first is broadband reverberation average level, the second is source intensity of corresponding frequency, the third is decaying term of corresponding frequency. the former two are measured and the last is simulated according to the measured environment parameters, such as sediment geoacoustic parameters, sea depth, sound speed profile and source depth. Numerical simulation illustrates this method is available, and experiment at sea states the extracted result is accurate and this extracting method is effective.

Acknowledgments

This work is supported by the National Natural Science Foundation of China under No. 11904383.

References

[1] J. A. Goff, T. H. Jordan, Stochastic Modeling of Seafloor Morphology Inversion of Sea Beam Data for Second-Order Statistics, *J. Geophys. Res.*, 93(B11) (1988), pp. 13589-13608

[2] S. E. Hough, On the use of spectral methods for the determination of fractal dimension, *Geophysical Research Letters,* 16(7) (1989,pp. 673-676

[3] R Lim, K. L. Williams, E. I. Thorsos, Acoustic scattering by a three-dimensional elastic object near a rough surface,*J. Acoust. Soc. Am.,*107(3) (2000),pp. 1246-1262

[4] T. F. Gao, Relation between waveguide and non-waveguide scattering from a rough interface, *Acta Acoust.*, 14(2) (1989), pp. 126-132

[5] D.J. Tang, Sediment volume inhomogeneity and shallow water reverberation, *International Conference on shallow water Acoustics*, Beijing, China, 21-25 April, 1997

[6] E.C. Shang, T. F. Gao, J.R. Wu, A shallow-water reverberation model based on perturbation theory, *IEEE. J. Ocean Eng.,* 33(4) (2008), pp. 451-461.

[7] D. Z. Wang, E. C. Shang,Underwater Acoustics (2nd Edition) (in Chinese),Beijing: Science Press,2013, pp.69

Acoustic Intensity Fluctuation Due to Internal Tide in the Yellow Sea

Li Fan[1], Hu Tao[1], Guo shengming[1]

1, Key Laboratory of Underwater Acoustics Environment, Institute of Acoustics, Chinese Academy of Science,No.21 North 4thRing Road, Haidian District, Beijing, 100190, China

lifan@mail.ioa.ac.cn

In the paper, the least square harmonic analysis method is used to analyze the primary characteristic of internal tide in the Yellow Sea and the simplified internal tide propagation model is set up. Using the simplified internal tide propagation model, we simulate the horizontal non-uniform distribution and temporal variation along the acoustic propagation path. The fluctuation in acoustic propagation energy over time is predicted for 500 consecutive minutes and compared with the experimental measurement data. The comparison shows that the prediction results of depth integral for the fluctuation of acoustic field energy with time agree with experimental results. The prediction results show that the internal tide in the Yellow Sea is the primary cause of the fluctuation of acoustic field. The dynamic prediction of acoustic field in the Yellow Sea is realized

Keywords: Yellow Sea; internal tide; acoustic field prediction; energy fluctuation.

1. Introduction

In shallow water, the influence of sea water and sea bottom on acoustic channel results in acoustic fluctuation. Water mass, mesoscale eddy, internal wave cause the temporal and spatial variation of ocean waveguide environment and the fluctuation of acoustic propagation is caused. The internal wave in shallow water include internal tide, soliton wave and linear wave, etc. The internal tide is the internal wave with diurnal or semi-diurnal tidal frequency produced by astronomical tide forced topographic force in the density stratification seawater. According to the observation results, internal tide usually occurs at the sloping seafloors such as seamount, submarine trench and the fringes of the continental shelf [1]. LOUIS ST. LAURENT *et al* [2] discussed that the formation and propagation of internal waves on the knife-like ridge boundary, the steps border, finite width boundary and slope border. The internal wave activity in shallow sea is the main factor that causes the fluctuation of acoustic field and seriously affects the reliability of acoustic field prediction. In recent years, the interaction between internal wave and acoustic field has become one of the research hot issues in underwater acoustics. But most of them focus on the influence of nonlinear soliton on acoustic propagation. The researches shows that nonlinear soliton internal waves can lead to the mode coupling between normal modes, horizon refraction, signal intensity and arrival time fluctuation [3-7]. Internal tides are relatively easier to form than soliton. In summer, internal tides exist in almost all shallow water and the spatial continuous distribution characteristics of the internal tides will give rise to the horizontal non-uniform variation of sound speed profile over the whole propagation distance. As a result, the research on the influence of internal tide on sound propagation is more universal. In the paper, the observation data of internal tide in the Yellow Sea in summer are analyzed and the characteristics of the internal tides in the Yellow Sea are obtained. According to the characteristics and internal tide model, the horizontal non-uniform distribution of sound speed profile in the presence of internal tide are gotten. Using predicted sound speed profile, we predict the acoustic intensity fluctuation with time and compare the predicted result with experimental result. The comparison result shows that predicted results have good agreement with the experimental results of acoustic field energy fluctuation with depth integral within 500 minutes.

2. Internal tide model of the Yellow Sea

2.1. Internal tidal experiment in the Yellow Sea

The combined acoustics/physical oceanography experiment was conducted in the yellow sea in summer 2009. The source of 260Hz. Hydrophones were used to receive signals and the spacing of adjacent elements was 1.5m.The range between the source and receiving array was 10.8km during the propagation experiments. The water depth of experiments site is almost 35m and relatively flat bottom. The thermistor-chains was employed to record the 40 hours temperature variation induced by internal tide. The pressure sensor of the temperature chain was employed to correct the array shape. Figure 1 showed the temperature profile. The temperature profile of the Yellow Sea has typical negative thermocline structure as shown in the figure1.The upper and lower layers was isothermal layers and the isothermal layer thickness was respectively 14m and 16m.The intermediate layer varied with linearly was negative thermocline and the thickness was 5m.The temperature fully conforms to the typical three layer ocean medium structure model. Figure 2 is 60 hours experimental measurement data of the temperature-time fluctuation pseudo-color image. From the figure, the semi-diurnal and full-diurnal tides can be observed and semi-diurnal tide (M2) have dominant contribution.

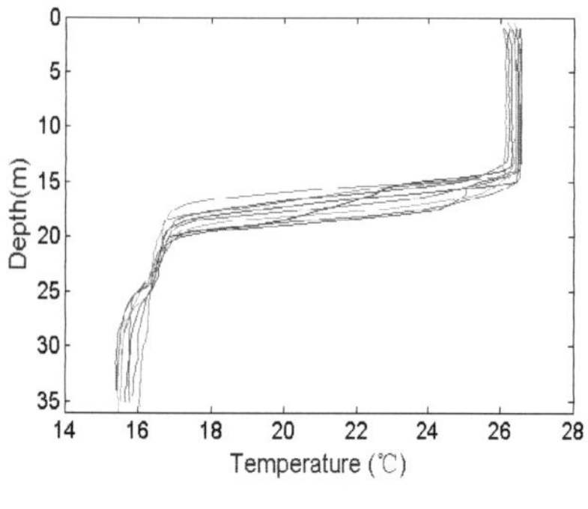

Fig.1. Temperature profile during the experiment

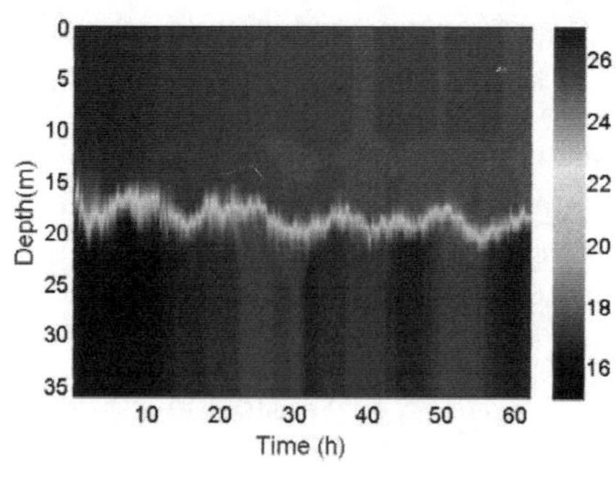

Fig.2. Experimental temperature fluctuation

2.2. Internal tide model of the Yellow Sea

2.2.1. The harmonic analysis of internal tide in the Yellow Sea

The least square harmonic analysis method [8] is used to analyze isotherm fluctuation data and obtain the amplitude and characteristic parameters of each component of internal tide. Let's assume that $\eta(t)$ is the experiment fluctuation data during $[T_b, T_e]$, T_b, T_e are the start and end time of the data respectively. $\eta_n(t)$ represents the fitting fluctuation data during $[T_b, T_e]$ by harmonic analysis of n tidal components.

$$\eta_n(t) = x_1 + \sum_{i=1}^{n} x_{i+1} \cos \omega_i t + \sum_{i=1}^{n} x_{i+n+1} \sin \omega_i t = \zeta X \qquad t \in [-\Delta, \Delta] \tag{2.1}$$

Where $\Delta = (T_e - T_b)/2$, $\zeta = \{\zeta_i(t)\}_{1\times(2n+1)}$

$$\zeta_i(t) = \begin{cases} 1, & i = 1; \\ \cos(\omega_{i-1} t), & i = 2, \cdots, n+1; \\ \sin(\omega_{i-n-1} t), & i = n+2, \cdots, 2n+1. \end{cases} \tag{2.2}$$

$$X = \{x_i\}_{(2n+1)\times 1} \tag{2.3}$$

Notice that the zero of time has shifted. The target function is set up:

$$\varphi(X) = \int_{-\Delta}^{\Delta} [\eta(t) - \eta_n(t)]^2 dt \tag{2.4}$$

In order to minimize the target function φ:

$$\frac{\partial \phi}{\partial x_i} = 0, i = 1, 2, \cdots, 2n+1 \tag{2.5}$$

The linear equation of coefficient x_i is gotten where the coefficient matrix A is a symmetric matrix:

$$AX = H \tag{2.6}$$

$$A = \{a_{ij}\}_{(2n+1)\times(2n+1)}, a_{ij} = a_{ji} = \int_{-\Delta}^{\Delta} \zeta_i(t)\zeta_j(t) dt \tag{2.7}$$

The right-hand-side vector H is:

$$H = \{h_i\}_{(2n+1)\times 1}, h_i = \int_{-\Delta}^{\Delta} \eta(t)\zeta_i(t) dt \tag{2.8}$$

The equation (2.6) is solved to get the coefficient vector **X** which correspond to parameters of each tidal component. Figure 3 shows the comparison isothermal line with results of harmonic analysis. The temperatures of the isothermal line are 18 C°、 19 C° and 20 C° respectively. The red line is the result of harmonic analysis and the blue line is the experimental data. The two lines fit well that indicate the isotherm fluctuation is induced by internal tides and remarkably periodic. Table 1 shows amplitude of different tidal components from harmonic analysis method. The dominant contribution to the isothermal fluctuation is at the M2 tidal frequency. According to the comparison depth distribution with the mode of tidal fluctuation, the distribution of tidal amplitude at six depths are basically consistent with the first order mode as shown in the figure 4. As a results the first order mode controls the internal tides.

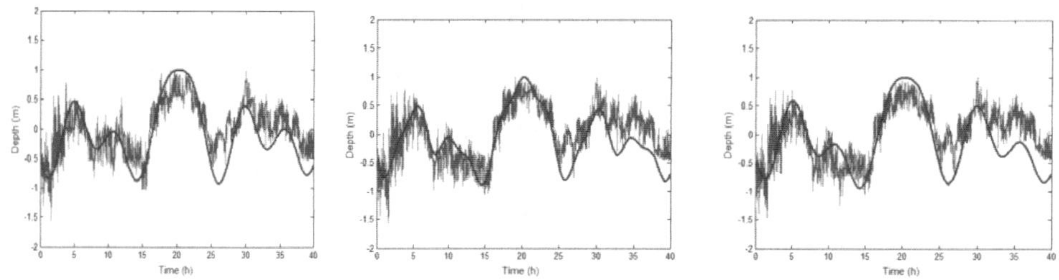

(a) 18C° (b) 19C° (c) 20C°

Fig.3. Comparing isothermal line with results of harmonic analysis

(a) 18C° isothermal line (b) 19C° isothermal line (c) 20C° isothermal line

Table 1. The amplitude of different tidal components of harmonic analysis of isothermal line

Isothermal line(C°)	24h K1	12h M2	8h M3	6h M4
23	0.45	0.70	0.36	0.35
22	0.45	0.69	0.35	0.33
21	0.46	0.69	0.32	0.31
20	0.45	0.70	0.308	0.29
19	0.45	0.72	0.31	0.27
18	0.43	0.71	0.32	0.29

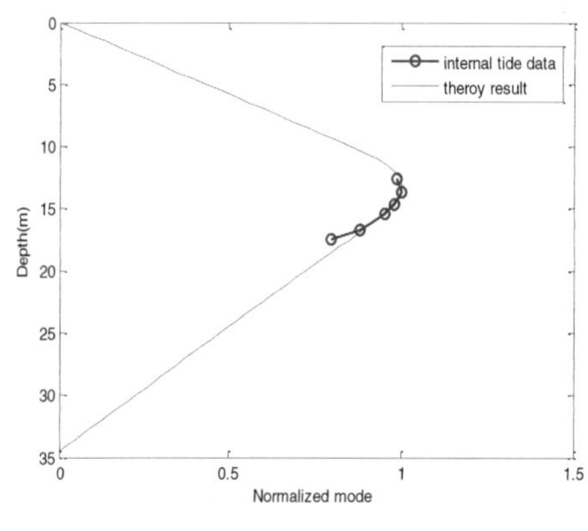

Fig.4. Comparison depth distribution with the mode of tidal fluctuation

2.2.2.The modeling of internal tide in the Yellow Sea

According to the Fig.1, the temperature profile of the experiment accords with the typical three-layer medium thermocline structure that is the upper and lower layers of the temperature profile are isodensity and the intermediate layer is the transition layer. In the case, the vertical mode equation of the internal wave can be expressed as [9]:

$$\begin{cases} \dfrac{\partial^2 W}{\partial z^2} - k^2 W = 0 & -H_1 < z < 0, and, -H < z < -(H_1 + d) \\ \dfrac{\partial^2 W}{\partial z^2} + k_z{}^2 W = 0 & k_z = k\sqrt{N_0^2 / \omega^2 - 1}, -(H_1 + d) < z < -H_1 \end{cases} \tag{2.9}$$

Where $k = \omega / c$ is wavenumber of internal tide, ρ_1 and ρ_2 are density of the upper layer and lower layer respectively. H is sea depth, H_1、d、H_3 are the thickness of the upper layer, middle layer and lower layer respectively. The internal wave solutions in the three layer are respectively:

$$W_1 = A\sinh(kz) \tag{2.10a}$$

$$W_2 = B\cos\left[k_z(z + H_1)\right] + C\sin\left[k_z(z + H_1)\right] \tag{2.10b}$$

$$W_3 = D\sinh\left[k(z + H)\right] \tag{2.10c}$$

The boundary conditions of seabed and sea surface and the continuity conditions of interface are used to derive the dispersion equation as follow:

$$k_z^2 = k_z k\cot(k_z d)\left[\coth(kH_1) + \coth(kH_3)\right] + k^2\coth(kH_1)\coth(kH_3) \tag{2.11}$$

$$\cot(k_z d) = \frac{k_z / k - (k / k_z)\coth(kH_1)\coth(kH_3)}{\coth(kH_1) + \coth(kH_3)} \tag{2.12}$$

The cotangent function in the dispersion equation (2.12) is a multi-value function that is $\cot(k_2 d + n\pi) = \cot(k_2 d)$. As a result, the dispersion equation has multiple solutions and each solution corresponds to a mode that is normal mode. In general, the dispersion equation has no analytic solution. When $\omega_0{}^2 << \omega^2 << N_0^2$, $k_z^2 H_1 H_3 >> 1$ is always true [10]. So the equation (2.12) can be approximated to:

$$\cot(k_z d) = \frac{k_z / k}{\coth(kH_1) + \coth(kH_3)} \tag{2.13}$$

The solution to the dispersion equation (2.13) can be expressed as:

$$k_{zn} d = (n-1)\pi + \arctan\left\{(k / k_{zn})\left[\coth(kH_1) + \coth(kH_3)\right]\right\} \tag{2.14}$$

The group velocity and phase velocity are discussed for the first order mode because internal tide of the experimental area is mainly controlled by the first order mode. For the first order normal mode ($n = 1$), the equation (2.14) in the short wavelength approximation ($kH_1 >> 1, kH_3 >> 1$) can be transformed as:

$$k_{z1}^2 = 2k \tag{2.15}$$

As a result, the phase velocity is:

$$c_1 = \frac{N_0^2 d}{2\omega} = N_0\sqrt{\frac{d}{2k}} \tag{2.16}$$

The group velocity is:

$$c_g^{(1)} = \frac{\partial\omega}{\partial k} = c_1 / 2 \tag{2.17}$$

The equation (2.14) in the long wavelength approximation $kH_1 << 1$, $kH_3 << 1$, $k_z \approx (N_0 / \omega)k$ can be transformed as:

$$k_{z1}^2 d = (1/H_1 + 1/H_3) \tag{2.18}$$

In this case, the group velocity is equal to the phase velocity, that is:

$$c_g^{(1)} = c_1 = N_0 \sqrt{\frac{dH_1 H_3}{H}} \tag{2.19}$$

The above analysis show that when the short wavelength approximation is true, internal wave of different wavelength have different group velocity for the first order normal mode under the three-layer model. This is because high frequency component of internal wave has obvious waveform distortion during propagation; On the contrary, the group velocity is the same as the phase velocity when the long wavelength approximation is true. Only when submarine topography and thermocline variation change, high frequency component of internal wave has obvious waveform distortion during propagation. The internal tide discussed in this paper is low frequency internal wave and satisfies the long wave approximation condition. For the experiment environment, the group velocity and phase velocity are calculated by the equation (2.19):

$$c_g^{(1)} = c_1 = 0.34m/s \tag{2.20}$$

3. Prediction of acoustic intensity fluctuation due to internal tides in Yellow Sea

3.1. Prediction of sound speed profile in the internal tides

Sound speed field can be usually expressed as the sum of the average sound speed and random disturbances using the equation (2.21). For the sound speed profile in the internal tides, the harmonic analysis method is used to analyze isotherm fluctuations and obtain the amplitude and characteristic parameters of each component of internal tide. The internal tide linear equation [11] is obtained by equation (2.23) on the flat bottom. The distribution of sound speed profiles in the internal tides in Yellow Sea is obtained by substituting equation (2.23) into equation (2.21) and (2.22).

$$c = c_0 + \delta c \tag{2.21}$$

$$\delta c = \left(\frac{dc}{dz}\right)_p \xi \tag{2.22}$$

$$\xi(x,z,t) = \sum_{n=1}^{N} \sum_{i=1}^{\infty} A(\omega_i) W_n(z,\omega_i) \cos(k_{n,i} x + \omega_i t + e_{n,i}) \tag{2.23}$$

Where $(dc/dz)_p$ is sound speed gradient, ξ is isothermal displacement, $W_{n,i}(z,\omega_i)$ is the solution of internal wave vertical mode equation, $k_{n,i}$ is the horizontal wave number of internal wave and can be obtained by equation (2.14), ω_i is different frequency component of internal tides, $e_{n,i}$ is initial phase, N is the number of normal modes, $A(\omega_i)$ is the amplitude of different frequency components and can be obtained by equation (2.6). Using above equation, sound speed profiles are predicted from experiment data of internal tide.

3.2. Prediction of acoustic intensity fluctuation in Yellow sea

The combined acoustics/physical oceanography experiment was conducted in the yellow sea in summer 2009. The frequency of source was 260Hz. The experiment was conducted by fixed-point transmission and record. The distance between source and receiver is 10.8km. Hydrophones were used to receive signals and the spacing of adjacent elements was 1.5m. The water depth of experiments site is almost 35m and relatively flat bottom. The thermistor-chains was employed to record the temperature variation during the experiments. The energy fluctuation acoustic field measured in the experiments with time is shown in figure 5.

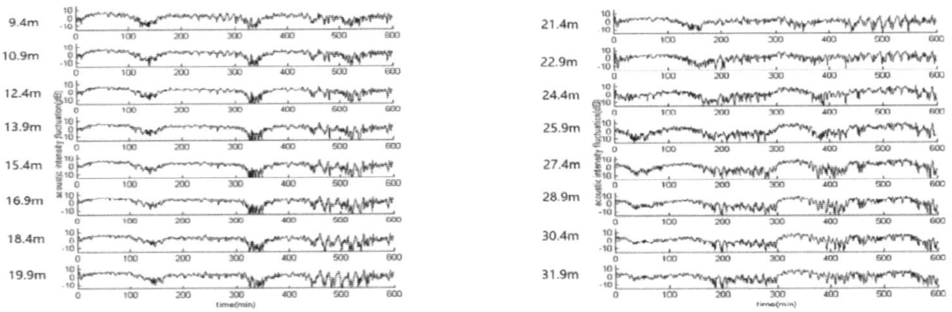

Fig.5. Energy fluctuation acoustic field measured in the experiments with time

Using temperature chain data measured, the horizontal non-uniform distribution of sound speed profiles was predicted according to internal tides model and equations. The energy fluctuation of acoustic field was simulated according to predicted sound speed profile. Acoustic field was simulated by range-dependent acoustic model (RAM) [12]. The source is 260Hz and sea depth 35m. The model of the shallow-water waveguide is the same as the experiment environment. The intensity fluctuations of acoustic field with different depth obtained by simulation were compared with experiment results during 10 hours. The range from source to receiver was 10.8km and internal tidal velocity was 0.34m/s. The figure 6 show the comparison curves at 8 receiver depth and depth intervals was 3m. Red line is simulation result and blue one is experiment result. Figure 7 shows the comparison experiment data with simulation data of the acoustic field energy fluctuation with depth integral of 16 array. The simulation result are shown have good agreement with the experimental data. The differences between prediction data and experimental data at single receive depth were maybe caused by the waveform changed during the propagation of internal tides. The acoustic field energy fluctuation with depth integral of 16 array can offset the effect.

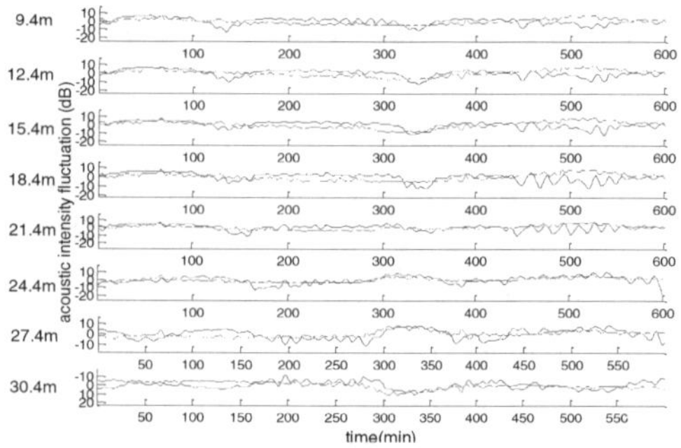

Fig.6. Comparison acoustic intensity at 8 depths
red: experiment blue: theory result

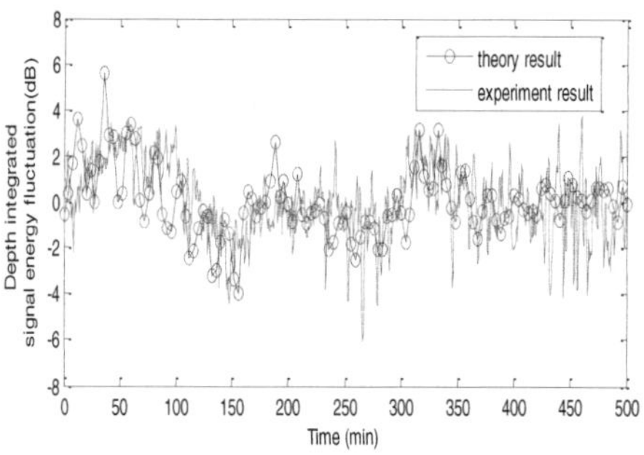

Fig.7. Comparison energy fluctuation with depth integral of 16 array

4. Conclusion

We set up the "idealized" internal tide model in Yellow Sea and predict the horizontal non-uniform distribution and temporal variation of SSP in the Yellow Sea by the harmonic analysis method and temperature data measured from experiments. On this basis, Ocean dynamics model and acoustic field model are combined to realize the true dynamic forecast of acoustic field in the internal tide. Acoustical intensity fluctuations with depth integral of 16 arrays have good agreement with the experimental data. It is verified that the internal tide in the Yellow Sea is the main cause of energy fluctuation of acoustic field. The prediction data at the single receive depth is consistent with experimental data and there is some error at some point. The differences between them are maybe caused by the waveform changed during the propagation of internal tides and we will model the environment more precisely.

Acknowledgments

This work was supported by the National Natural Science Foundation of China (No.11274338 and No.11204344)

References

[1] BAINES P G. "On internal generation models," Deep-sea Research, 1982, 29(3A): 307-338.

[2] LOUIS S T. Laurent, Steven Stringer, "The generation of internal tide at abrupt topography," Deep-sea Research, 2003, 50: 987-1003.

[3] APEL J R, BADIEY M, CHIU C S, FINETTE S, et al. "An overview of the 1995 SWARM shallow water internal wave acoustic scattering experiment," IEEE, Journal of Oceanic Engineering, 1997, 22(3): 465-500.

[4] FINETTE S. "Acoustic Field Variability Induced by Time-Evolving Internal Wave Fields," Journal Acoustical Society of America, 1999, 108: 975-972. 999FINETTE S. "Acoustic field variability induced by time evolving internal wave fields," Journal Acoustical Society of America, 2000, 108(3): 957-972.

[5] BADIEY M. "Temporal and Azimuthal Dependence of Sound Propagation in Shallow Water with Internal Waves," IEEE Journal of Oceanic Engineering, 2002, 27: 117-129.

[6] JAMES C P. DUDA T F. "Coupled acoustic mode propagation through continental-shelf internal solitary waves," IEEE J. of Oceanic engineering, 1997 22(2): 256-269.
[7] ROUSEFF D. "Coherence of acoustic modes propagating through shallow water internal waves," Journal Acoustical Society of America, 2002, 111(4): 1655-1665.
[8] Pawlowicz R. Beardsley R. "Classical tidal harmonic analysis including error estimates in MATLAB using T-TIDE," Computers &Geosciences, 2002, 28:929.
[9] LEE O S. "Fixed path acoustic transmission in the presence of internal wave," Journal Acoustical Society of America, 1960, 32: 1514.
[10] HU Tao. "Shallow Water Internal Waves and Their Effect on Acoustic Propagation [D]," Beijing, Institute of acoustics CAS, 2007: 18-24.
[11] BAINES P G. "On internal generation models," Deep sea Research, 1982, 29(3A): 307-338.
[12] MICHAEL D C. "Generalization of the split-step pade solution," Journal Acoustical Society of America, 1994, 96(1): 382-385.

Numerical Modeling of the Sound Propagation Under Rough Sea Surface of the PM Spectrum

MEIJUAN YAO, LICHENG LU, Li MA, SHENGMING GUO

Key Laboratory of Underwater Acoustic Environment,
Institute of Acoustics, CAS, Beijing, 100190, China
yaomeijuan88@mail.ioa.ac.cn
lulicheng@mail.ioa.ac.cn
guoshengming@mail.ioa.ac.cn
mali@mail.ioa.ac.cn

Sea surface, acting as the top boundary of the waveguide, can significantly affect underwater acoustic propagation. The rough sea surface has, not only reflection effect, but also scattering effect on acoustic wave, which leads to reflection loss. Based on Kirchhoff Approximation scattering theory and Small Slope Approximation scattering theory, Krakenc-KA(Kirchhoff Approximation, KA) and Krakenc-SSA (Small Slope Approximation, SSA) sound propagation models are put forward. The numerical simulation result shows that the horizontal locations of the interference peak and trough of acoustic field are changed when Krakenc-SSA model is used as the reflection coefficient calculated using SSA theory can change the phase of the field, while it is not like that when Krakenc-KA model is used. Moreover, using monte-carlo method to generate one-dimensional rough sea surface, Ramsurf sound propagation models are compared with Krakenc-KA model and Krakenc-SSA model under rough sea surface of PM spectrum.

Keywords: Rough sea surface; Sound propagation; Reflection coefficient.

1. Introduction

Sea surface, acting as the upper boundary of the waveguide, is of great significance for acoustic propagation, especially when there is a surface duct. The characteristics of the surface boundary is actually a significant environmental parameter. The sea surface is usually considered to be an absolute soft boundary when there is no wind or the wind speed is almost zero. The smooth surface has perfect reflection effect and there is almost no reflection loss. However, sea surface is always rough due to the wind and there is scattering besides reflection. JiXun Zhou[1] said small changes in loss-per-bounce values could have cumulative effects on long-range reverberation and propagation.

There has been some research on the reflection coefficients of the rough sea surface in the past few years. William[2] compared the coefficients calculated using KA (Kirchhoff Approximation, KA) method and SSA (small slope approximation, SSA) method in 2004. Jones[3] did research on the existing surface reflection loss model in 2010～2016. While most

of the researchers focus on the reflection coefficients and the reflection loss of the rough sea surface, this article directly aims at propagation models under rough sea surface.
Firstly, the PM spectral is introduced. Secondly, based on KA scattering theory and SSA scattering theory, Krakenc-KA and Krakenc-SSA sound propagation models are put forward. Then, using monte-carlo method to generate one-dimensional rough sea surface, Ramsurf sound propagation models are compared with Krakenc-KA and Krakenc-SSA models under rough sea surface of Pierson-Moskowitz (PM) spectrum[4].

2. The Theory

2.1. Surface-wave spectrum

There are many kinds of surface wave spectrum for a fully developed sea. Here, Pierson-Moskowitz (PM) wave spectrum, which is widely used internationally, is of interest. The frequency spectrum and the rms roughness of PM are:

$$S(\Omega)=\frac{a_0 g^2}{\Omega^5}\exp\left[-\beta g^4/(\Omega v_{19.5})^4\right] \tag{2.1}$$

$$h_\sigma \approx 5.3\times10^{-3} {v_{19.5}}^2 \tag{2.2}$$

Here, $a_0 = 8.1\times10^{-3}$, $\beta = 0.74$. g is the acceleration of gravity. $v_{19.5}$ is the wind speed with the measurement height being 19.5m.

2.2. Sound propagation models under rough sea surface: Krakenc-KA and Krakenc-SSA

One can use different scattering theories to get the mean reflection coefficients such as the KA theory and the SSA theory[5][6]. According to the scattering theory we use, we can call the sound propagation models under rough sea surface to be Krakenc-KA model and Krakenc-SSA model respectively. In the following, we will give the equations to calculate the mean reflection coefficients using KA theory and SSA theory.
One can denote the rough sea surface by: $z = f(x)$. And the incident field is a scalar plane wave which is denoted as $\exp(i\mathbf{k}_i\Box\mathbf{r})$.Here, $\mathbf{r}=(x,z)$, $\mathbf{k}_i=(k_{ix},k_{iz})=(k_{ix},-\kappa_{iz})$.Also we have : $-\kappa_{iz}=\left[k^2-k_{ix}^2\right]^{1/2}>0$. Here , $k=\omega/c$ is the wavenumber. One can define: $\boldsymbol{v}=\boldsymbol{k}_i-\boldsymbol{k}_s=(v_x,-v_z)$, $v_x=k_{ix}-k_{sx}$, $v_z=\kappa_{iz}+k_{sz}$, and $k\beta_{i+1}=\left[k^2-(K_1+k_{ix})^2\right]^{1/2}$, $k\beta_{s-1}=\left[k^2-(k_{sx}-K_1)^2\right]^{1/2}$. Here k_{ix} is the horizontal component of the wave number : $k_{ix}\equiv k_{sx}=k\sin\theta_i$. κ_{iz} is the vertical component of the wave number: $\kappa_{iz}\equiv|k_{sz}|=k\cos\theta_i$. $g(K_1)=k\beta_{i+1}+k\beta_{s-1}-v_z$.
$W(K_1)$ is the roughness spectrum of the sea surface. One can finally get the reflection coefficient by SSA theory:

$$R_A(k_{ix})\approx\exp\left[-\frac{v_z^2h^2}{2}\right]\left[-1+\kappa_{iz}\int dK_1 W(K_1)g(K_1)\right] \tag{2.3}$$

What's more, the first part in the right side of the equation is the reflection coefficient calculated by KA method.

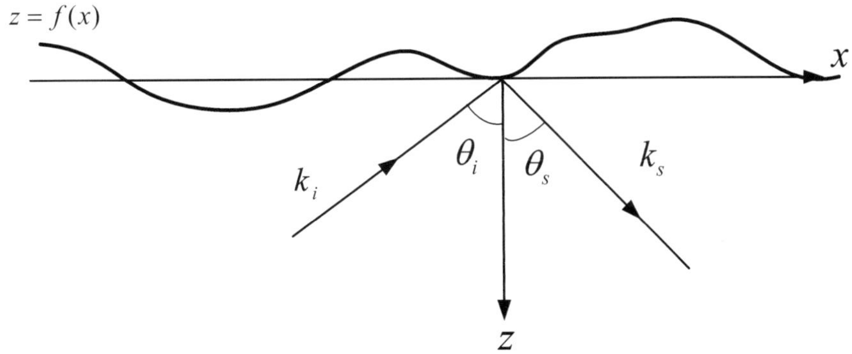

Fig. 1 Scattering sketch map for one-dimensional rough sea surface

2.3. Sound propagation models under rough sea surface: Ramsurf

The sound propagation model under the rough sea surface—Ramsurf sound propagation model is a modified PE sound model. One can, based on different wave spectrum, use monte-carlo method to generate one-dimensional rough sea surface and take it as the parameters of the top boundary of the Ramsurf model. Here, the Ramsurf model only considers the forward scattering of the field and is not fit for the backward scattering problem caused by strongly rough sea surface.
In the following, the monte-carlo method of modelling one-dimensional rough sea surface is introduced:
One can use the following equation to generate the one-dimensional rough sea surface with the length L :

$$f(x_n) = \frac{1}{L} \sum_{j=-N/2+1}^{N/2} F(k_j) e^{ik_j x_n} \tag{2.4}$$

3. Simulation modeling

3.1. Krakenc-KA propagation model under rough sea surface

There are two ways to write the parameters of rough sea surface into the Krakenc model. One way is to set up the value of sigma (rms roughness) in the ENV file and the other way is to put the reflection coefficient in the TRC file. For the Krakenc-KA model, the two methods are equivalent to each other.
The water depth of the underwater environment is 30 meters. The sound speed is 1500m/s and the frequency is 1000Hz. The source depth is 7m and the receiver depth is 7m. What is shown in fig.2 is the comparison of the Transmission Loss (TL) curves. The red line is the TL curve with a smooth surface while the other two lines are those with the wind speed being 12m/s. The green line is that using the first way to write the parameters of rough sea surface

into the Krakenc model while the black line is that using the seconway. One can see that the green line and the black line coincide well with each other.

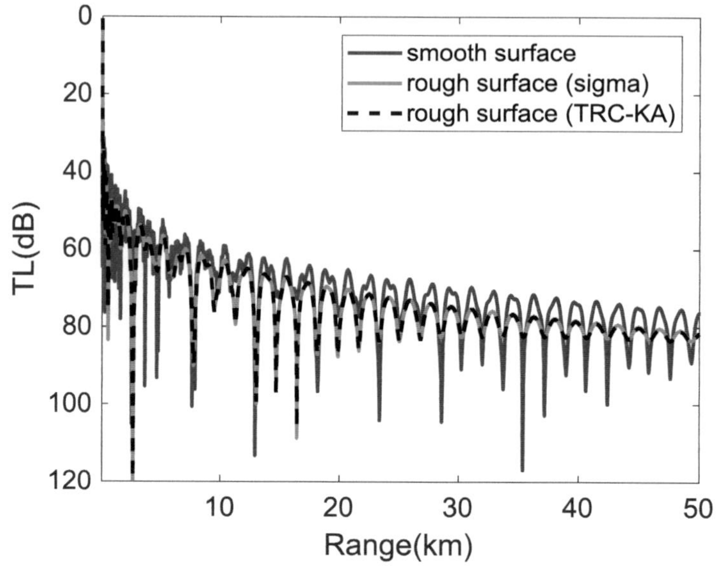

Fig.2 Comparison of the two realization ways for Krakenc-KA propagation model with rough sea surface

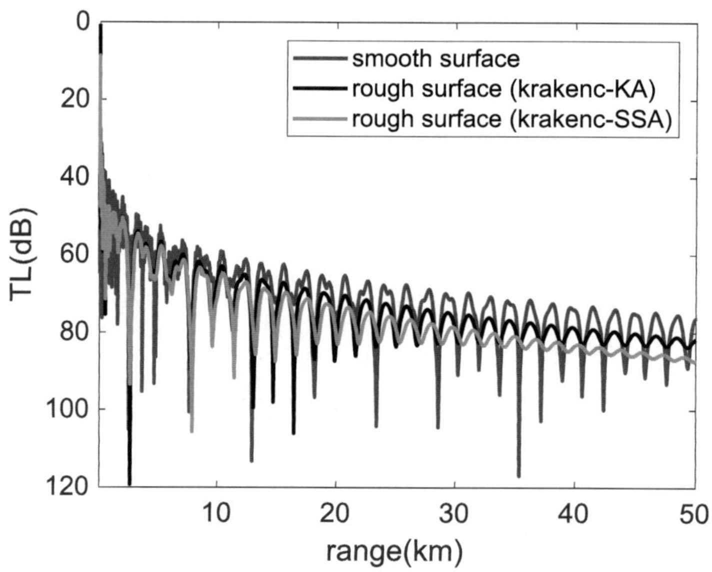

Fig.3 Comparison of TL curves by different scattering method to calculate mean reflection coefficient

3.2. Krakenc-KA propagation model under rough sea surface

The Krakenc-SSA propagation model uses the SSA scattering theory to calculate the mean reflection coefficients. The underwater environment, the source depth and the receiver depth are the same as those in section 3.1. One can get the simulation results, using Krakenc-KA model and Krakenc-SSA model, shown as fig.3. The red line is the TL curve with a smooth surface while the other two lines are those with the wind speed being 12m/s. The black line is the TL loss curve calculated by Krakenc-KA model while the green line is that calculated by Krakenc-SSA model. One can see that the curves are close to each other at short range but there is a obvious difference at long range because of the cumulative effects of the rough sea surface. And also, one can see that the horizontal range of the interference peak and valley of the sound field calculated by Krakenc-SSA model are changed while those by Krakenc-KA model are not changed.The reason is that sea surface mean reflection coefficients calculated by SSA can change the phase of the sound field while that by KA theory don't change the phase of the sound field.

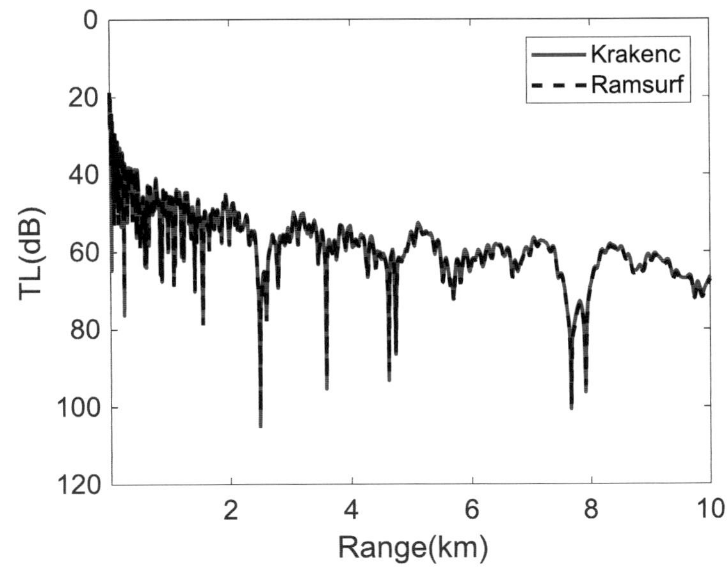

Fig.4 Comparison of TL curves by Ramsurf and Krakenc with a rough sea surface

3.3. Ramsurf propagation model under rough sea surface

3.3.1. Comparison between Krakenc model and Ramsurf model under smooth sea surface

The underwater environment, the source depth and the receiver depth are the same as those in section 3.2. What is shown in fig.4 is the comparison between the Krakenc model and the Ramsurf model under smooth sea surface. One can see that the two curves coincide well with each other.

3.3.2. Comparison between Krakenc model and Ramsurf model under rough sea surface

Ramsurf propagation model is based on monte-carlo method to generate one-dimensional rough sea surface. And also, Ramsurf model can deal with the range-dependent submarine topography. What is shown in fig.5 is the comparison of TL curves by Krakenc-KA model, Krakenc-SSA model and Ramsurf model with rough sea surface of the same roughness caused by a wind speed of 12m/s. Here, the simulation result of Ramsurf model is the average of 100 monte-carlo realizations .

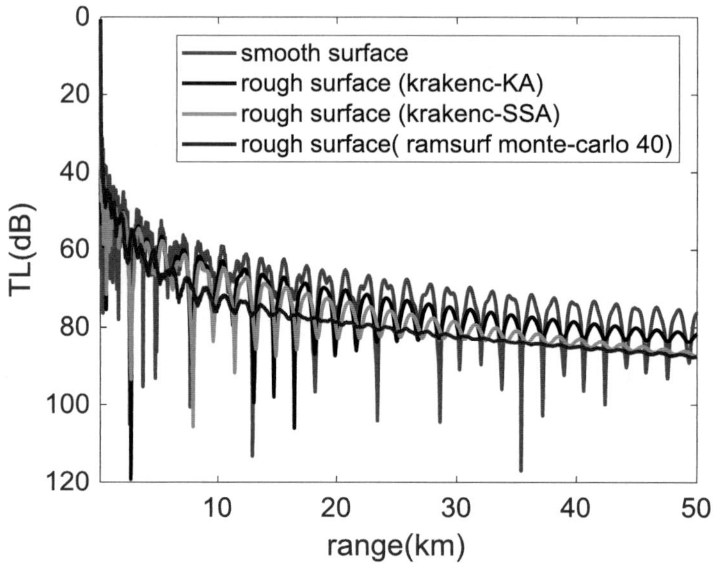

Fig.5 Comparison of TL curves by different propagation models

4. Summary

In this article, based on KA scattering theory and SSA scattering theory, the sound propagation under rough sea surface —Krakenc-KA model and Krakenc-SSA model are put forward. And Ramsurf model is compared with Krakenc-KA model and Krakenc-SSA model by numerical simulation. Here are the conclusions:

First, sea surface mean reflection coefficients calculated by SSA theory can change the phase of the sound field while that by KA theory don't change the phase of the sound field. The horizontal range of the interference peak and valley of the sound field calculated by Krakenc-SSA model are changed while those by Krakenc-KA model are not changed.

Second, Krakenc sound propagation model is based on kinds of scattering theories to calculate the mean reflection coefficients. Ramsurf model is based on monte-carlo method to generate one-dimensional sea surface. One needs to take the average value of more than 40 relizations. Therefore, the computational efficiency of Krakenc model is higher. But , one can get the fluctuation characteristics of the sound field using Ramsurf model.

Third, Ramsurf model is more suitable for the environment with varied topography.

References

[1] Ji-Xun Zhou and Xue-Zhen Zhang, Zhaohui Peng, James S. Martin, "Sea surface effect on shallow-water reverberation, " *J. Acoust. Soc. Am.* 121(1) (2007), 98-107
[2] K.L. Williams, E.I. Thorsos, and W.T. Elam, "Examination of coherent surface reflection coefficient (CSRC) approximations in shallow water propagation," *J. Acoust. Soc. Am* 116 (4)(2004), 1975 –1984.
[3] A.D. Jones, A.J. Duncan, A.Maggi, "A detailed comparison between a small- slope model of acoustical scattering from a rough sea surface and stochastic modeling of the coherent surface Loss". *IEEE JOURNAL OF OCEANIC ENGINEERING*, 41(3) (2016), 689-708
[4] E.I.Thorsos, "Acoustic scattering from a Pierson-Moskowita Sea surface". *J.Acoust.Soc.Am.* 88(1)(1990), 3335-349
[5] E. I. Thorsos and S. L. Broschat, "An investigation of the small slope approximation for scattering from rough surfaces. Part I. Theory, "J.Acoust. Soc. Am. 97(4)(1995), 2082–2093
[6] S. L. Broschat and E. I. Thorsos, "An investigation of the small slope approximation for scattering from rough surfaces. Part II. Numerical studies," *J. Acoust. Soc. Am.* 101(5)(1997), 2615–2625 .

Matched-field geoacoustic inversion using propagation invariant in the presence of nonlinear internal waves

Wenhua Song[1], PengYu Wang[2]

1, Department of Physics, Ocean University of China, 238 Songling Road, Qingdao, 266100, China
songwenhua@ouc.edu.cn
2, Department of electronic engineering, Ocean University of China, 238 Songling Road,
Qingdao, 266100, China
swangpengyu@ouc.edu.cn

Matched-field processing (MFP) has been applied successfully in geoacoustic inversion for the seabed parameters. However, the prediction capability of the matched-field processor can be destroyed by variabilities in the environment, such as changes in bathymetry, internal waves in the water column, or abrupt changes in the seabed properties. It is impossible to include all these variabilities in the numerical modeling required for the MFP inversion. In this paper a field transformation of acoustic data is proposed, referred to as propagation invariant (PI). PI is purely data-driven and most importantly can eliminate the effect of the intermediate propagation process, which means that the received acoustic data is same as that propagated through a range independent waveguide. Therefore, propagation invariant can provide the matched-field processor with ideal forward propagation model. A towed sound source is used with a moored VLA in the simulation, and results show good performance of MFP geoacoustic inversion even in a highly range-dependent waveguide.

Keywords: Matched field inversion; sea bottom sediment; range dependency; propagation invariant.

1. Introduction

Matched field inversion (MFI) had been reported to work well using an acoustic source and a vertical line array (VLA) of hydrophones spanning a large portion of the water column [1,2,3]. Since then other configurations with towed [4,5,6] and bottom-moored [7-9] horizontal line arrays (HLAs) have been fully studied. As a model-based inversion method, MFI can successfully estimate geoacoustic parameters of marine sediments using the accurate forward propagation models that can produce reasonable match with the measurement of acoustic fields. Global optimization methods, such as genetic algorithm or simulated annealing may be utilized to infer the bottom sediment properties [10,11].

For the dynamic ocean, the bathymetry and the acoustic properties of seabed could be quite range dependent and the sound speed profiles (SSP) of the water column can be variant in space and time. These variances can highly degrade the performance of MFI. Firstly, evidence shows that in a range dependent waveguide the uncertainties of the inversion result is increasing for longer separation between source and VLA [10, 11], and it is recommended that the separation should be less than 2 km [11]. Secondly, MFI can only give sea bottom properties which are averaged along the sound path. However, this is not the result one needs especially when the bottom types are distinct along the sound path; in fact, one needs the "local" information of sea bottom. In this paper, "local" means`estimating the bottom sediment properties at a specific location, and is on the contrary to range-averaged. Third, the time variance in the data, which is caused by the fluctuations of the water column, can introduce time-changing characteristics in the inversion result although the bottom is actually not time-changing.

In order to solve these problems, the forward model must be able to corporate with these range dependencies. However, instead of trying to describe this propagation process with complicated models, such as mode coupling theory, we intend to find a way to eliminate the influence of the inhomogeneity in the intermediate zone, that is propagation invariant (PI) [12]. In this paper, propagation invariant is used for geoacoustic inversion with the configuration of a moving source and a fixed VLA that spans the whole water column. In sec. II, the basic theory of PI and the relevant process of MFI will be introduced. In sec. III, simulations are used to illustrate the feasibility of this method. Summary and conclusions are given in sec. IV.

2. Basic theory for propagation invariant

2.1. The concept of Propagation Invariant in ocean waveguide

In this subsection, a concrete realization of the idea of propagation invariant is presented in a two-dimensional ocean waveguide. To verify the notion, a typical experiment setup is used, which consists of a fixed vertical line array (VLA) of N_Z hydrophones and a source that moves outward (or inward) in range, as in Fig. 1. The acoustic field is continually recorded by the hydrophones over a period of time (denoted as T) during which the source-receiver ranges are $r_1, r_2, r_3, \ldots, r_{NS}$ respectively. The hydrophones are located at the depths of $z_1, z_2, \ldots, z_{NZ}$ while the sources are at the fixed depth of z_s. For simplicity we use the range independent case to show the concept of PI, and the deduction can be directly extended to the range dependent case.

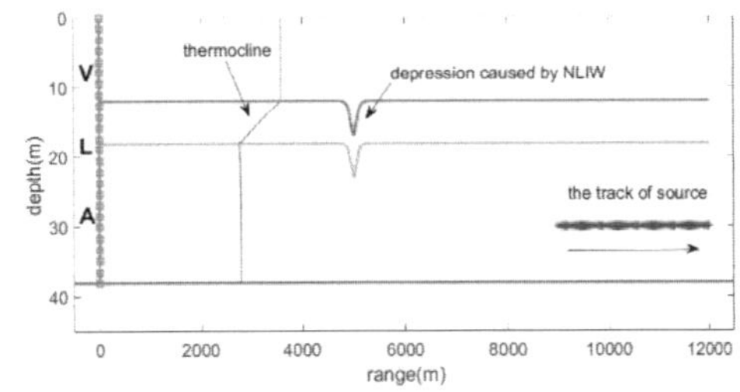

Fig. 1 The geometry used for demonstrating the concept of propagation invariant. The vertical linear array of hydrophones is fixed while the acoustic source ship moves outward in the range.

As the source ship travels during a period of time T, we can get a $N_z \times N_s$ complex matrix $\boldsymbol{P}_r$ at the frequency f_0,

$$\begin{bmatrix} p(z_1,r_1) & p(z_1,r_2) & \cdots & p(z_1,r_{NS}) \\ p(z_2,r_1) & \ddots & \cdots & \cdots \\ \vdots & & & \vdots \\ p(z_{Nz},r_1) & p(z_{Nz},r_2) & & p(z_{Nz},r_{NS}) \end{bmatrix} \quad (1)$$

Based on the normal mode theory, the elements of the matrix may be written as follows,

$$p_{ql}(z_q,r_l;z_s) = \frac{\sqrt{2\pi}e^{i\pi/4}}{\rho(z_s)} \sum_{m=1,n=1}^{M_e} \phi_m(z_q) \left[\frac{e^{ik_m r_1}}{\sqrt{k_m r_1}} \delta_{mn}\right] \left[\phi_n(z_s) \frac{e^{ik_n(r_l-r_1)}}{\sqrt{(r_l-r_1)/r_1}}\right] \quad (2)$$

where $q = 1,2,\cdots N_z, l = 1,2,\cdots N_s$ and M_e denotes the effective number of trapped modes, $k_m = k_{rm} + i\alpha_m$ denotes the complex horizontal wavenumber of the mth mode, and ϕ_m denotes the corresponding orthogonal modal depth function.

In the following part of this subsection, we assume $N_S = N_Z = M_e = N$ and $\rho(z) = 1.0$ for simplicity. Thus, ali matrices defined below are square. Now we rewrite Eq.(1) in a matrix form,

$$\boldsymbol{P}_r = \frac{\sqrt{2\pi}e^{i\pi/4}}{\rho(z_s)} \boldsymbol{\Phi\Lambda V}_r, \quad (3)$$

where

$$\boldsymbol{\Phi} = \begin{bmatrix} \phi_1(z_1) & \phi_2(z_1) & \cdots & \phi_N(z_1) \\ \phi_1(z_2) & \ddots & & \vdots \\ \vdots & & & \\ \phi_1(z_N) & \phi_2(z_N) & & \phi_N(z_N) \end{bmatrix}, \boldsymbol{V}_r = \begin{bmatrix} \phi_1(z_s) & \phi_1(z_s)e^{ik_1(r_2-r_1)} & \cdots & \phi_1(z_s)e^{ik_1(r_N-r_1)} \\ \phi_2(z_s) & \ddots & & \vdots \\ \vdots & & & \\ \phi_N(z_s) & \phi_N(z_s)e^{ik_N(r_2-r_1)} & & \phi_N(z_s)e^{ik_N(r_N-r_1)} \end{bmatrix}, \quad (4)$$

$$\boldsymbol{\Lambda} = \begin{bmatrix} \frac{e^{ik_1 r_1}}{\sqrt{k_1 r_1}} & 0 & 0 & 0 \\ 0 & \frac{e^{ik_2 r_1}}{\sqrt{k_2 r_1}} & 0 & 0 \\ \vdots & 0 & \ddots & 0 \\ 0 & 0 & \cdots & \frac{e^{ik_N r_1}}{\sqrt{k_N r_1}} \end{bmatrix}, \quad (5)$$

where we have used the approximation: $(r_l - r_1)/r_1 << 1, l = 1,2,\ldots,N$. The matrices in Eq.(3) have the following physical interpretation: the matrix $\boldsymbol{\Phi}$ denotes the receiver weight matrix, $\boldsymbol{\Lambda}$ denotes the propagating matrix, and $\boldsymbol{V}_r$ denotes the source weight matrix, respectively.

To define propagation invariant, we introduce an additional received acoustic signal $p_1(z_q, r_{N+1})$ by the VLA, which is generated by the source at a different range r_{N+1} and same source depth z_s. Similarly, the acoustic signal p_1 can be written in matrix form as,

$$\vec{P}_1 = \frac{\sqrt{2\pi}e^{i\pi/4}}{\rho(z_s)}\boldsymbol{\Phi}\boldsymbol{\Lambda}\vec{V_1}, \quad \textbf{(6)}$$

where

$$\vec{V_1} = [\phi_1(z_s)e^{ik_1(r_{N+1}-r_1)}, \phi_2(z_s)e^{ik_2(r_{N+1}-r_1)}, \cdots \phi_N(z_s)e^{ik_N(r_{N+1}-r_1)}]^T \quad \textbf{(7)}$$

Thus, it can be seen that the difference between $\boldsymbol{P}_r$ and $\vec{P}_1$ only comes from the variance of acoustic source, as the propagating matrix $\boldsymbol{\Lambda}$ is common for all the received signals. Propagation invariant can be achieved by the transformation $\boldsymbol{P}_r^{-1}\vec{P}_1$, and with the above equations, one can get

$$\boldsymbol{P}_r^{-1}\vec{P}_1 = \boldsymbol{V}_r^{-1}\vec{V_1} \cong \begin{bmatrix} 1 & e^{ik_1(r_2-r_1)} & \dots & e^{ik_1(r_N-r_1)} \\ 1 & & & \\ \vdots & & & \\ 1 & e^{ik_N(r_2-r_1)} & \dots & e^{ik_N(r_N-r_1)} \end{bmatrix}^{-1} \begin{bmatrix} e^{ik_1(r_{N+1}-r_1)} \\ e^{ik_2(r_{N+1}-r_1)} \\ \vdots \\ e^{ik_N(r_{N+1}-r_1)} \end{bmatrix}. \quad \textbf{(8)}$$

To get Eq.(8), the water column must be sampled enough to ensure the orthogonality of the acoustic modes, i.e. N_z must be large enough. From Eq.(8) it can be seen that the vector $\boldsymbol{P}_r^{-1}\vec{P}_1$ is equal to the vector $(\boldsymbol{V}_r^{-1}\vec{V_1})$ which is determined by the relative ranges of the acoustic sources' movement and the acoustic mode wavenumbers (of the local area around the source). Moreover, one can notice that the propagating matrix plays no role in this relationship. In this sense, the vectors determined by the above equation is independent of the intermediate propagating process, thus named Propagation Invariant (PI) [12].

In the above deduction, we have assumed the matrices involved being square and invertible, however, this is not a necessary condition; we did this only to make the deduction intuitive and clear. When the number of hydrophones, the number of acoustic modes, and the number of signals is not equal, the inverse matrix in Eq.(8) can be replaced by the generalized inverse matrix.

It must be stressed that in the above deduction we have assumed the waveguide is range independent and the conclusion holds for the general situations where there are inhomogeneities in-between. For example, when there are nonlinear internal waves (NLIWs), it can introduce mode coupling among acoustic modes, which can be described by mode coupling matrix [13,14], and in such cases the expressions in Eq.(4), (5) and (7) are exactly the same and the only difference lies in the propagation matrix $\boldsymbol{\Lambda}$ which now is non-diagonal. However, by taking the generalized inverse operation, $\boldsymbol{\Lambda}$ is also cancelled out by the definition of PI.

2.2. PI-based MFI in a range dependent waveguide.

In this subsection, we will show how PI can be used in matched field inversion. Because PI eliminates the influence of the intermediate inhomogeneities in the waveguide, it can extremely decrease the complexity of the forward propagation model. More importantly, PI provides the "local sound field" which can be used to infer the "local" bottom sediment properties. The PI-based matched field inversion can be summarized as follows.

- The frequency components of the time series are obtained by performing a fast Fourier transform (FFT), and $\boldsymbol{P}_r$ and $\vec{P}_1$ are then obtained. The PI vector $\boldsymbol{P}_r^{-1}\vec{P}_1$ is denoted as $\boldsymbol{X}$.
- The forward model is taken to be range independent. For each trial value of bottom property, *kraken* is used to calculate the acoustic modal wavenumber, then combined with the source's position, the replica PI vector is calculated $\boldsymbol{Y} = \boldsymbol{V}_r^{+}\vec{V}_1$.
- The two PI vectors are matched by the cost function Q, which is defined as $Q = \frac{|\sum_i X_i Y_i^*|}{\sqrt{\sum_i Y_i Y_i^*}\sqrt{\sum_i X_i X_i^*}}$.

As comparison, the conventional MFI is also performed. The conventional MFI matches the signals with replica signals directly while the PI-base MFI matches the PI vectors, i.e. ***X*** and ***Y*** as mentioned above.

3. Simulations

In the simulation, the geometry shown in Fig. 1 is used. A typical sound speed profile (SSP) with thermocline is used which is obtained from Yellow Sea of China, as shown in Fig. 2 (a). There is also NLIW in the waveguide, which causes the thermocline depressed by a vertical displacement η,

$$\eta = \eta_0 \mathrm{sech}^2\left(\frac{r-r_0}{\Delta}\right), \tag{9}$$

where η_0, Δ and r_0 is the amplitude, half width and central position of NLIW. In the simulation, they take the value of 5 m, 75 m and 5000 m respectively. The bottom sediment is set to be half space medium with the sound speed $c_b = 1584$ m/s, $\rho_b = 1.6$ g/cm3, $\alpha_b = 0.1052$ dB/λ.

In the simulation, VLA is fixed at the origins. While, the source is initially at the position of 12500 m and moves away from VLA at the speed of 10 knots. The source emits a CW signal of 700 Hz every second as it moves. It is stressed that the source moves at a speed of c_s=5 m/s while the NLIW moves at a speed of c_x=0.5 m/s.

To calculate the sound pressure, the coupling matrix $\boldsymbol{C}(r_{x2}, r_{x1})$ is computed with Dyson series[14]. The received sound pressure at 700Hz in 200 s is shown in Fig. 2 (b).

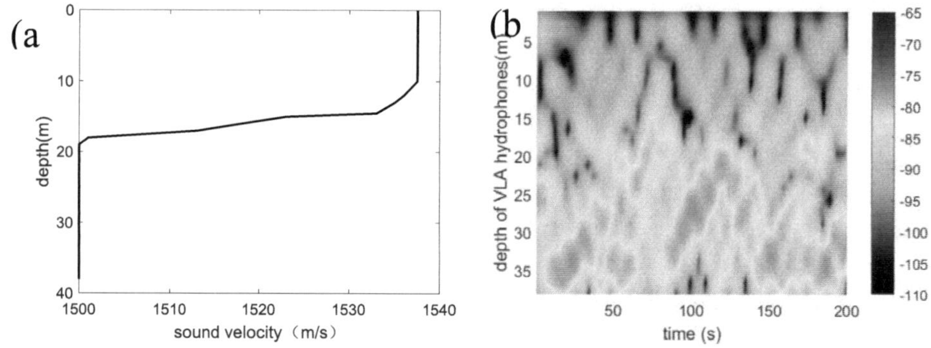

Fig. 2 (a)The background sound speed profile of the water column used in the simulation;(b)the received VLA data.

In the following, the PI vector $\boldsymbol{X} = \boldsymbol{P}_r^{-1}\vec{P}_1$ is calculated using VLA data while the PI vector $\boldsymbol{Y} = \boldsymbol{V}_r^{-1}\vec{V}_1$ is calculated by the forward model as mentioned in sec. 2.2. When NLIW does not move, $\boldsymbol{X}$ and $\boldsymbol{Y}$ (when calculating $\boldsymbol{Y}$, seabed sediment properties are exactly known) are given in Fig. 3 (a). One can find that $\boldsymbol{X}$ agrees very well with $\boldsymbol{Y}$, the cost function Q=0.997. However, one can observe that $\boldsymbol{X}$ and $\boldsymbol{Y}$ are quite different when NLIW moves, as in Fig. 3 (b).

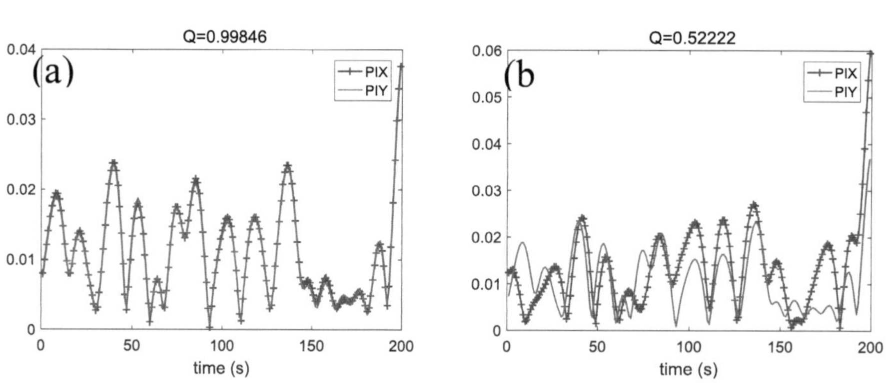

Fig. 3 The comparison of $\boldsymbol{X}$ and $\boldsymbol{Y}$. (a) when there is NLIW but it is fixed in position. (b) when there is NLIW moving at a speed of 1 knot. T=200s.

Before going forward to MFI, we want to see how the cost function Q varies as the time length T increases. The results are given in Fig. 4. One can find that the concept of PI holds for T less than 60 s, but is no longer suitable when T is larger.

This can be qualitatively explained by the acoustic modal interference distance. From mode coupling theory[13,14], the non-diagonal elements of the propagating matrix $\boldsymbol{\Lambda}$ contains an exponential term $e^{-ik_{mn}r_x}$, where k_{mn} is the wavenumber difference of acoustic modes and r_x is the position of NLIW. At this situation, if the acoustic data is acquired in such a short time (T) that NLIW moves a relatively shorter distance compared modal interference distance, i.e.

$$k_{mn}c_xT \ll 1 \rightarrow c_xT \ll D_{mn}, \tag{10}$$

the propagating matrix $\boldsymbol{\Lambda}$ can be regarded as unchanged. The modal interference distance is defined as $D_{mn} = 2\pi/k_{mn}$.

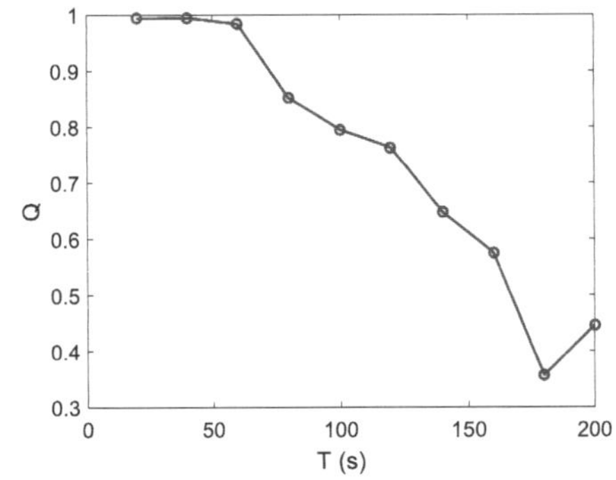

Fig. 4 The value of cost function Q as *T* (the length of time to receive data) increases. the NLIW moves at the speed of cx=0.5m/s while the source moves at the speed of cs=5 m/s.

The modal interference distance D_{mn} for the waveguide at 700 Hz is given in table 1 (only the first 5 modes are given). It is the values of $\mathrm{D_{mn}}$ for the adjacent modes ($m - n = 1$) that should be paid more attention, because the coupling caused by NLIW among adjacent modes dominated over non-adjacent modes [[13]]. The minimum D_{mn} is about 300m and the NLIW moves about 30 m in *T*=60 s. Thus, combing the data in table 1 with Fig. 4, it can be concluded that the distance of NLIW's movement should be less than 10% of the minimum of $\mathrm{D_{mn}}$ of the adjacent modes to ensure the concept of PI. This can be fulfilled by acquiring acoustic data during a relatively short time; in this simulation it is 60 seconds for 700Hz signals. This is not a tough condition considering that NLIW usually moves at a low speed compared to ships.

Table 1. The interference distance of acoustic modes in the waveguide at 700 Hz. (Units: m)

mode number	n=2	n=3	n=4	n=5
m=1	745.1	282.0	153.7	101.5
m=2		453.7	193.6	117.6
m=3			337.6	158.7
m=4				299.4

Now one can perform PI-based MFP geoacoustic inversion. As discussed above, we select received signals that the acoustic source transmitted in 40 seconds, PI can still eliminate the effect of mode coupling caused by NLIW, and the forward model for MFI can use range independent model, which significantly reduces the complexity of inversion problem.
Following the steps in sec. 2.2, the bottom sound velocity c_b is inversed, and the result is given in Fig. 5 (a). As a comparison, the "conventional" MFI inversion results are also given in Fig. 5 (b). From Fig. 5 one can see PI-based geoacoustic inversion can give accurate estimate value of bottom parameters, while the "conventional" MFI fails to do so. The reason for the failure of the conventional MFI may be explained by the time variance in the data, i.e. the data can give different estimations as time passes, resulting multiple peaks as in Fig. 5 (b).

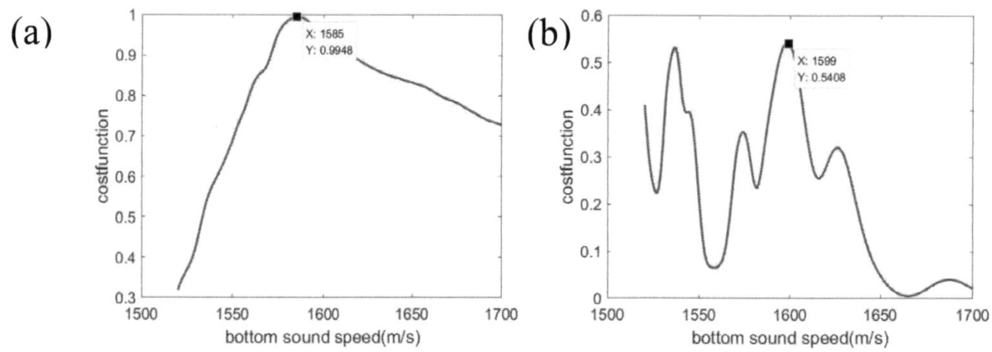

Fig. 5 (a) inversion results of sediment sound velocity c_b. (b) inversion results of sediment sound velocity using the conventional MFP inversion. The true values for the three parameters are $c_b = 1584\ \mathrm{m/s}$.

4. Summary and Conclusions

In this paper, the method for matched field geoacoustic inversion in a range dependent waveguide is presented. This method utilizes the concept of propagation invariant (PI). PI can benefit MFI as it can eliminate the effect of range dependency in the waveguide and provide the "local sound field". The inversion scheme is verified by simulations when there is a moving NLIW in the waveguide. The movement of NLIW is also considered and the result is that the concept of PI is valid as long as NLIW moves a rather shorter distance compared with modal interference distance.

The concept of PI provides a quite efficient method for geoacoustic inversion, and we believe it can also benefit source location and underwater communication in a complex environment.

Acknowledgments

This research was supported by the National Natural Science Foundation of China (Grant No.11674294) and the Fundamental Research Funds for the Central Universities (Grant No.201713056).

References

[1] D. F. Gingras and P. Gerstoft, ''Inversion for geometric and geoacoustic parameters in shallow water: Experimental results,'' *J. Acoust. Soc. Am.* **97** (1995)3589–3598.

[2] J. P. Hermand and P. Gerstoft, ''Inversion of broadband multi-tone acoustic data from the Yellow Shark summer experiments,'' *IEEE J. Ocean.Eng.* **21**(4) (1996) 324–346.

[3] N. R. Chapman and A. Tolstoy, ''Special issue: Benchmarking geoacoustic inversion methods,'' *J. Comput. Acoust.* **6**(1&2) (1998) ,1–289.

[4] M. Siderius, P. L. Nielsen, and P. Gerstoft, "Range-dependent seabed characterization by inversion of acoustic data from a towed receiver array," *J.Acoust. Soc. Am.* **112** (2002),1523–1535

[5] D. J. Battle, P. Gerstoft, W. S. Hodgkiss, W. A. Kuperman, and P. L.Nielsen, "Bayesian model selection applied to geoacoustic inversion," *J.Acoust. Soc. Am.* **116** (2004), 2043–2056

[6] L. T. Fialkowski, T. C. Yang, K. Yoo, E. Kim, and D. C. Dacol, "Consistency and reliability of geoacoustic inversions with a horizontal line array," *J. Acoust. Soc. Am.* **120** (2006), 231–246.

[7] D. P. Knobles, R. A. Koch, L. A. Thompson, K. C. Focke, and P. E.Eisman, "Broadband sound propagation in shallow water and geoacoustic inversion," *J. Acoust. Soc. Am.* **113** (2003), 205–222

[8] R. A. Koch and D. P. Knobles, "Geoacoustic inversion with ships as sources," *J. Acoust. Soc. Am.* **117** (2005), 626–637.

[9] D. Tollefsen, S. E. Dosso, and M. J. Wilmut, "Matched-field geoacoustic inversion with a horizontal array and low-level source," *J. Acoust. Soc.Am.* **120** (2006), 221–230.

[10] Tollefsen D , Dosso S E , "Bayesian geoacoustic inversion of ship - noise data from a bottom - moored horizontal line array". *J. Acoust. Soc. Am.* **122**(122) (2007), 2941-2941

[11] M. Siderius, P. Nielsen, J. Sellschopp, M. Snellen, and D. Simons, ''Experimental study of geoacoustic inversion uncertainty due to ocean sound speed fluctuations,'' *J. Acoust. Soc. Am.* **110** (2001), 769–781.

[12] Pengyu Wang, (2019) "Linear signal systems and signals invariants: Photometric transformation differential and acoustic propagation invariant", (Doctoral dissertation, Ocean university of China) (in Chinese)

[13] Song Wenhua , Wang Ning , Gao Dazhi , "The influence of mode coupling on waveguide invariant". *J. Acoust. Soc. Am.,* **142** (4) (2017), 1848-1857.

[14] T. C. Yang, "Acoustic mode coupling induced by nonlinear internal waves: Evaluation of the mode coupling matrices and applications," *J. Acoust. Soc. Am.* **135** (2014), 610–625.

An Underwater Acoustic Network Positioning Algorithm Combined with its Protocol

YI-XUAN FENG[1 2] DONG XIAO[1*] YAN CHEN[1] LI-PING WEI[1] MIN ZHAO[3] LI MA[1]

1, Institute of Acoustics, CAS, No.21, North 4th Ring Road, Haidian, Beijing, China
2, University of CAS, No.19, Yuquan Road, Shijingshan, Beijing, China
3,Economic Research Institute, State Grid Jibei Electric Power Company Limited
No.21, Yangfangdian East Road, Haidian, Beijing, China
* xiaodong@mail.ioa.ac.cn

Global positioning system (GPS) cannot be used in underwater acoustic sensor network (UASN), because radio waves suffer severe absorption in water. And, water flow always washes the node away during its deployment. The node needs to be positioned after deployment. An underwater network node positioning algorithm combined with the network protocol is proposed in this paper. Before each node is deployed into water, it is initiated with a GPS value. Then, the nodes are deployed according to certain rules, which are each node must have two other nodes in its communication range and the two other nodes can also communication with each other. Combined with our network self-organization protocol, the distances between two nodes are ranged by time of arrival algorithm. The initial GPS values are correcting according to the distances. Simulations show that the offset can be reduced to 50% or less averagely if the directions of all the offset are random, and the energy consumption is lower than the traditional method. This algorithm makes an attempt in underwater network node positioning combined with protocol, simplifies the positioning process and saves the energy. It may promote underwater network development and accelerate ocean exploitation and utilization.

Keywords: Underwater Acoustics Network; Relative Positioning; Self-Organization.

1. Introduction

Underwater acoustic networks consist of network nodes that are distributed underwater. Owing to the great propagation loss of radio waves in water, the global positioning system (GPS), which is often used in daily life, cannot be effectively used underwater [1–3]. Even if the initial value of the GPS is measured before the node is deployed, it will deviate from the initial position owing to the influence of ocean current during the deployment process [4]; further, the deviation is difficult to calculate. The location information of network nodes is usually the basic information of underwater acoustic networks. Therefore, in recent years, increased attention has been given to the positioning of underwater acoustic network nodes both domestically and internationally.

Range-based positioning methods generally obtain the distance between nodes through algorithms such as received signal strength indicator (RSSI) [5], time of arrival (TOA), time difference of arrival (TDOA), and angle of arrival (AOA) [6–9] and others [10-11]. Because the accuracy of the positioning algorithm based on non-ranging [12-17] is relatively low, ranging-based positioning method is used in our study.

Traditional calibration methods need to communicate with each node and synchronize as accurately as possible (the least synchronization error should be less than 1 ms), which not only requires a long positioning time, but also wastes the energy of the nodes. To solve the above issues, our study proposed a node self-localization method based on underwater acoustic network self-organization protocol in the absence of precise synchronization clocks between nodes.

2. Core Algorithm

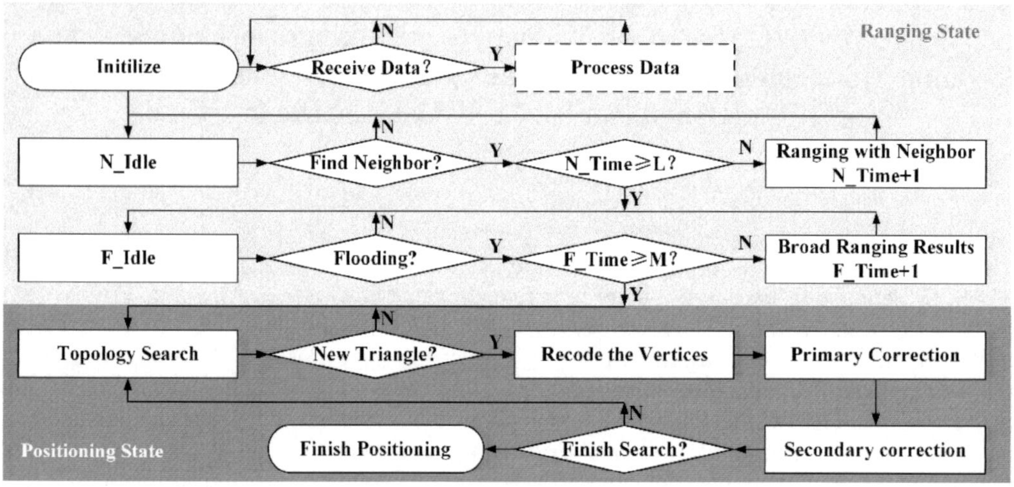

Fig.1: Overall flow chart

The overall flow of the algorithm is shown in Fig.1, which mainly includes two parts of ranging state and positioning state.

2.1. Ranging Combined with Self-Organization Network Protocol

Before the deployment of nodes, the initial GPS values and time of the communicable nodes within one hop were obtained. The rules for node deployment are as follows: There should be a minimum of two other nodes that can communicate with each other within the communication range of any one node, making this node form a triangle with a minimum of two other nodes. After deployment of the nodes, the clock synchronization between nodes is no longer performed during the entire period of ranging and positioning. The number of nodes is set as T.

In ranging state, when the nodes start to broadcast information, including their own initial GPS values. Taking two nodes A and B that can communicate in one hop as an example, node A broadcasts its own initial GPS value at t1. Upon receiving this information, node B records the initial GPS value of node A, and sends a reply packet after a fixed delay time τb. The reply packet includes the initial GPS value of node b and the delay time τb (the fixed delay time of all nodes is unequal, and its length is longer than the reply packet to avoid conflicts). After receiving the reply packet at t2, node A records the initial GPS value of node B and calculates the distance dab between node A and B according to the following equation:

$$d_{ab} = \left(\left(t_2 - t_1 - \tau_b\right)/2 - t_f\right) \times c \tag{2.1}$$

where c is the velocity of sound in seawater, tf is the time length of frame transmission.
The calculated distances are recorded in row B and column A of the distance matrix (T*T). After node A receives the reply packets from all communicable nodes within one hop, the column A of the distance matrix is completed. In the ranging stage, the nodes are broadcast in a sequence and are cycled three times to ensure that no node misses the ranging process owing to bit errors.
In the flooding stage, each node broadcasts its own column of the distance matrix. Once the other nodes received these columns, the corresponding columns of their distance matrix will be filled. Subsequently, the ranging average is calculated according to the diagonal line.

2.2. Relative Positioning

After ranging is completed using the network protocol, the node decides with which other nodes it can form a triangle that has known trilateral lengths according to the topology. Further, it records the serial number of the selected nodes. Considering that the initial value of GPS and the ranging results both have errors, a two-time correction method is proposed to locate the nodes relative to each other according to the stability of the triangle.

2.2.1. Primary correction

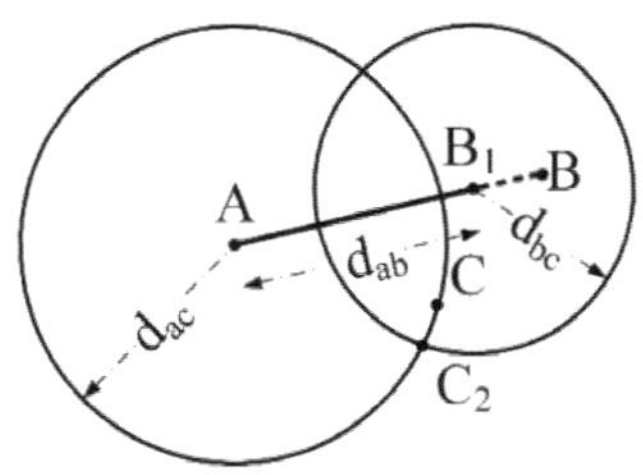

Fig.2: Primary correction:A as the origin of the coordinate

There are three known items for each node at present: The node value that can form triangles with all three known side lengths, initial GPS value of the node, and received initial GPS values of the communicable nodes in one hop. Based on these, the GPS of the three nodes in each triangle is corrected. The following is an example of a triangle composed of nodes A B C, where A, B, C $\in$ [0, T] and the values of A, B, C are not equal.
Fig.2 shows a primary correction process. First, vertex A was set as the origin of the coordinate. The corrected coordinate B_1 of point B was calculated using the GPS slope of A B and the ranging result d_{ab} of A B. Next, the corrected coordinate C_2 of point C was calculated by taking the point at which the circle with A as the center and d_{ac} as the radius and circle with B_1 as the center and d_{bc} as the radius intersect. Similarly, we can get B_2 and C_1. Next, B and C were set as the coordinate origins, and correction of A, C and A, B, were performed, respectively. After the correction, each of the three vertices in the triangle had four pairs of correction values. Last, the average values of all corrections and the initial values of the nodes were counted as the result of one correction.

2.2.2. Secondary correction

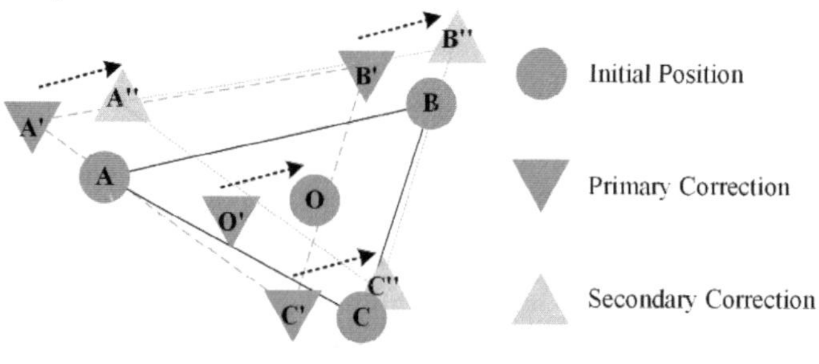

Fig.3: Seconday correction

The centroid of the initial triangle ABC consisting of the initial GPS value was set as O. The vertex of the triangle after primary correction is A', B', C', with the centroid as O'. As shown in Fig.3, move O' to O and record the offset, then move A', B', C' by the same offset. And we get A", B", C" as the result of secondary correction. Each triangle is corrected according to the above steps. The relative positioning is completed.

3. Opnet Simulations

A semi-duplex underwater acoustic communication method was designed. And the underwater acoustic communication parameters were set as: binary phase shift keying (BPSK) modulation, semi-duplex mode, 6 kHz of center frequency, 4 kHz of bandwidth, 1 kbps of communication rate, and approximately 5 km of effective distance between nodes, transmission power 10W, and standby power 0.05W.

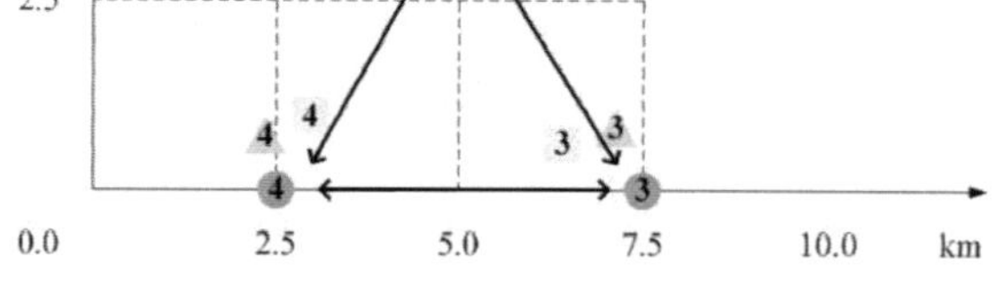

Fig.4: Simulation topology 1: 5-nodes_1

Considering the above rules, a five-node star topological structure was selected for the software simulation, as shown in Fig.4, in which "Real Position" is the real position of the node after deployment, "Initial Position" is the initial GPS value set to the node before deployment, "Corrected Position" is the position of the node after relative positioning.

3.1. Energy consumption analysis of ranging

In the traditional TOA ranging method, if a node wants to acquire the distance of all communicable nodes in one hop, it must send the ranging signal to each node successively in a question-and-answer mode. Our study combined the network protocol based on a ranging method similar to TOA for the completion of ranging between nodes; a one-question and multi-answer mode was achieved. Therefore, the combination of network protocols used in our study reduced the number of signals sent by the nodes, and thus, reduced the energy consumed.

Table 1. Energy consumption of two ranging methods at different time points

Energy Consumption (J)	Time 1	Time 2	Time 3	Time 4
Proposed	18.47	68.57	276.72	346.86
Traditional	51.60	256.80	495.75	840.26

After the ranging is completed, the distance matrix of all nodes is formed, which are the same. Table 1 lists the energy consumed by two ranging methods at specific time points. The table also presents that the ranging method similar to TOA reduced the energy consumed by a minimum of 50% compared with the traditional TOA ranging method.

3.2. Ranging analysis

Table 2: Ranging Results for the topology in Fig.4

Node/ Node	0	1	2	3
0	0	4985.56	4992.17	4999.27
1	4985.56	0	4990.00	-
2	4992.17	4990.00	0	-
3	4999.27	-	-	0
4	5010.41	-	-	5050.96

For the topology in Fig.4, distances between each two nodes which can communication within one hop are all about 5km. The ranging results are shown in Table 2. We have compared the ranging results with the real distances. The differences are no more than 5m.

3.3. Positioning analysis

Table 3: GPS value error before and after relative positioning

Longitude / Latitude (×10-4 °)	before correction	after primary correction	after secondary correction
Node 0	-1.20/-1.30	-1.66/-0.92	-0.71/-1.22
Node 1	2.10/1.53	0.25/0.61	1.26/0.99
Node 2	-2.10/1.68	-1.14/0.99	-1.72/1.45
Node 3	1.58/1.60	0.15/1.91	0.86/0.31
Node 4	-1.79/1.91	-0.31/2.44	-1.03/0.15

The GPS value errors before and after relative positioning are listed in Table 3. In each cell of the table, the number on the left of "/" is longitude value error, and the number on the right of "/" is latitude value error. It can be told from this table that, both longitude and latitude values get more accurate after secondary correction.

3.4. Ranging error analysis

As we know, there are four aspects which affect the ranging results: sound curve during propagation, measurement error of sound velocity, multipath structure in ranging communication, hardware clock precision. After Bellhop ray trace simulation, hardware clock precision and measurement error confirmation, it is found that the ranging error will not be more than tens of meters in our situation. Reduction rate is define as following:

$$Reduction\ Rate = \frac{|Secondary\ Correction\ GPS - Real\ GPS| - |Initial\ GPS - Real\ GPS|}{|Initial\ GPS - Real\ GPS|} \times 100\% \tag{3.1}$$

Some ranging errors are add into our ranging results manually, the position error reduction rates are listed in Table 4. The performance of proposed algorithm depends on ranging error.

Table 4. Position error reduction rates with different ranging errors added manually

Ranging error	0m	0~10m	11~20m	21~30m
Positioning error reduction rates	-42.4%	-40.4%	-27.5%	-4.1%

4. Conclusion

In this study, a node positioning method based on underwater acoustic network protocol is proposed. In combination with the network protocol, our method uses a ranging method similar to TOA to complete the node-to-node ranging in the self-organization process, and then performs a correction based on the recorded initial GPS value when the nodes are deployed. This ranging-based positioning method reduces the number of communications between nodes during ranging and is relatively simple. It can acquire a more accurate GPS value when energy consumed is less, which effectively improves the positioning accuracy. Further, it achieves high node positioning accuracy while consuming less energy.

But, it is only suitable for relative positioning, the topology must be based on triangle structures, and the performance depends on ranging error.

Acknowledgements

This work was supported by the National Natural Science Foundation of China (Grant No.61302109) and IACAS Young Elite Researcher Project (Grant No. QNYC201702).

References

[1] D.H.Chen, X.M.Zhang, and K.He, "Research on Node Localization in Underwater Acoustic Sensor Networks", Elementary Electroacoustics, 33(2) (2009), pp.45-51.

[2] Y.Liang, Z.Liu, and Q.T.Xia, "The Researches on Node Localization Algorithm and Self-Organization Process in UASNs", Chinese Journal of Sensors and Actuators, 24(3) (2011), pp.402-406.

[3] Y.Liu, J.Chen, and Z.Xu, "Improved DV-Hop Localization Algorithm Based on Bat Algorithm in Wireless Sensor Networks". Ksii Transactions on Internet &Information Systems, 11(1) (2017), pp.215-236.

[4] Z.Y.Jin, W.J.Lv, and L.P.Liu, "Real-time Localization Algorithm Based on Current Model for Underwater Sensor Networks", Transducer and Microsystem Technologies, 36(12) (2017), pp.149-152.

[5] Z.Lv, P.L.Tan, "Triangle Centroid Location Algorithm Based on RSSI Correction", Transducer and Microsystem Technologies, 29(5) (2010), pp.122-124.

[6] F.Gao, "Research on Localization Algorithms and Routing Technology for Underwater Sensor Network", Beijing Jiaotong University Master Dissertation, 2018.

[7] Z.P.Li, S.B.Cai, J.Zhang, Z.G. Gao, and J. Zhao, "Survey on Node Localization Technology of Underwater Acoustic Sensor Networks", Journal of Chinese Computer Systems, 33(3) (2012), pp.442-447.

[8] H.Ruan, "The Design and Implementation of Node Localization Algorithm in Underwater Wireless Sensor Netowrk", Nanjing University Master Dissertation, 2013.

[9] Z.Wang, X.N.Feng, G.J.Han, et al., "EODL: Energy Optimized Distributed Localization Method in Three-Dimensional Underwater Acoustic Sensors Networks", Computer Networks, 141 (2018), pp.179-188.

[10] Y.F.Han, C.E.Zheng, and D.J.Sun, "A High Precision Calibration Method for Long Baseline Acoustic Positioning Systems", ACTA ACUSTICA, 41(4) (2016), pp.456-464.

[11] P.Wang, S.J.Zheng, Y.Huang, and J.Y.Liu., "Range Estimation Based on Waveguide Invariant Using Beam Intensity Striations for Moving Target in Shallow Water", ACTA ACUSTICA, 40(6) (2015), pp.789-798.

[12] W.Fang, "Design and Implementation of Underwater Acoustic Communication Networks System and Localization", Northwestern Polytechnical University Master Dissertation, 2015.

[13] Q.Q.Shi, "Researcyh on Node Localization System and Algorithm for Wireless Sensor Networks", Shanghai Jiaotong University Doctor Dissertation, 2009.

[14] J.L. Liu, Z.Wang, M.W.Yao, and Z.L. Q, "VN-APIT: Virtual Nodes-based Range-Rree APIT Localization Scheme for WSN". Wireless Networks, 22(3) (2016), pp.867-878.

[15] X.P.Wu, Z.H.Gu, H.B.Shu, and H.L. Feng., "An Accurate Localization Approach of Acoustic Source Target with Linear Least Square Method", ACTA ACUSTICA, 41(1) (2016), pp.87-93.

[16] Y.C.Kang, Q.Y.Li, X.H.Zhang, and J.Li., "Direction of Arrival Estimation and Signal Recovery Based on Single Snapshot Compressed Sensing in Frequency Domain", ACTA ACUSTICA, 41(2) (2016), pp.174-180.

[17] B.Wang, Z.H.Zhu, and Y.W.Dai, "A Fast Underwater Acoustic Target Direction of Arrival Estimation Method Based on Sparse Bayesian Learning", ACTA ACUSTICA, 41(1) (2016), pp.81-85.

Analysis on the Sound Propagation Caused by Very Low Frequency Sound Source near the Sloped Seabed

XU Liang[1] ZHANG Haigang[2]
1, College of Underwater Acoustic Engineering, Harbin Engineering University, Harbin, 150001, China
2013053118@hrbeu.edu.cn
2, Acoustic Science and Technology Laboratory, Harbin Engineering University, Harbin,
Harbin, 150001, China
3, Key Laboratory of Marine Information Acquisition and Security, Ministry of Industry and Information Technology, Harbin, 150001, China
zhanghaigang@hrbeu.edu.cn

Simulating the sound field near the very low frequency seabed is a challenging task. Experience and extensive knowledge are needed to select parameters that conform to physical laws and appropriate grids to ensure robustness and reliability. A grid of one-sixth wavelength is usually used empirically, but simulations have shown that it is not sufficient to use a one-sixth wavelength for fluid and elastomer coupling fields. The purpose of this paper is to demonstrate the superiority of parabolic equations in the computation of this problem and to verify some of the seismic acoustics conclusions using a non-uniform grid approach. Finally, the effects of different depth grids on the calculation results are shown.
Keywords: Parabolic Equation; Non-uniform depth grid; Sound Propagation.

1. Introduction

The acoustic energy flow of the very low frequency source is transmitted to the sea floor and is reflected back into the water column after multiple reflections. Therefore, the composition of the sound field near the seabed is more complicated, especially the sound field near the seabed. According to the results in other literatures, the inclined seabed is conducive to the coupling of the submarine elastic wave and the general mode, and there will be a strong interference structure near the inclined seabed. In order to solve the above problems, this paper demonstrates the work experience in simulation and the verification of relevant conclusions.

Currently, the models available for this problem are the Finite element method, Normal Mode Method, Parabolic Equation Method, Matric Method. et al. The principle of judging is that there is a high frequency approximation for the model, and whether the seabed is processed only retains some of the properties so that the calculated sound field components are missing. Under the above principles, the finite element method can theoretically be used for calculation, but the development of FEM is still a hot issue, so we do not consider this method for the time being; the simplified wave method has a mature calculation program KRAKENC, which can be effective. The horizontal wave number is calculated, but the sound field calculated by the N-order normal wave superposition method cannot describe the sound field excited by the sea bottom reflection; the parabolic equation model is used for step calculation of the operator, and the step size is related to the frequency, which is suitable for the simulation of the very low frequency sound field..

2. Theory

2.1. Parabolic Equation

The elastic parabolic equation calculation program RAMs, written by M. D. Collins, calculates the displacement field of the elastic body and the sound field in the water, and can calculate the distance-related problem. The equation of elasticity can be written as:

$$\begin{cases} \rho w^2 u+(\lambda+2\mu)\dfrac{\partial^2 u}{\partial r^2}+\mu\dfrac{\partial^2 u}{\partial z^2}+(\lambda+\mu)\dfrac{\partial^2 w}{\partial r\partial z}+\dfrac{\partial\mu}{\partial z}\dfrac{\partial u}{\partial z}+\dfrac{\partial\mu}{\partial z}\dfrac{\partial w}{\partial r}=0 \\ \rho w^2 w+(\lambda+2\mu)\dfrac{\partial^2 w}{\partial z^2}+\mu\dfrac{\partial^2 w}{\partial r^2}+(\lambda+\mu)\dfrac{\partial^2 u}{\partial r\partial z}+\dfrac{\partial\lambda}{\partial z}\dfrac{\partial u}{\partial r}+(\dfrac{\partial\lambda}{\partial z}+2\dfrac{\partial u}{\partial z})\dfrac{\partial w}{\partial z}=0 \end{cases} \tag{2.1}$$

Where and are the Lame coefficient setting operators, where L, M is the media parameter operator matrix of depth. Write the equation Eq (2.1) as a parabolic equation:

$$\frac{\partial^2}{\partial r^2}\begin{pmatrix}\Delta\\ w\end{pmatrix}+L^{-1}M\begin{pmatrix}\Delta\\ w\end{pmatrix}=0. \tag{2.2}$$

where $\Delta=\partial u/\partial r+\partial w/\partial z$, the decomposition of Eq. (2.2) and the padé approximation of the operator can get the recursive equation:

$$\begin{pmatrix}\Delta\\ w\end{pmatrix}_{r+\Delta r}=e^{ik_0\Delta r}\prod_{j=1}^{n}\frac{1+\alpha_{j,n}X}{1+\beta_{j,n}X}\begin{pmatrix}\Delta\\ w\end{pmatrix}_r. \tag{2.3}$$

Eq. (2.3) is used to implement the governing equations computed on the computer. Because the step operator is related to displacement, it is possible to calculate two physics coupling problems. The horizontal step is used in the calculation. The horizontal grid step size is related to the horizontal environment change speed. The depth grid length affects the calculation accuracy in each step operator. In order to calculate the sound field near the seabed more accurately, non-uniform depth grids could be useful.

3. Experiments

In order to study the sound field of the very low frequency sound source excited near the sound field of the seabed, an explosion sound test was carried out. In this article, only an acoustic signal excited at a depth of 1180 m and received at a depth of 1640 m is shown, taking into account the time domain arrival and time-frequency characteristics of the received signal.

3.1. Environment

The test sea area is a wedge-shaped sea area, and the sound velocity gradient in water is measured by XBT. Sound Speed Profile in the test area, see Fig. 1. The test sea area is a non-complete channel, and the channel axis is at a depth of about 1000 m. The sound level of the explosion sound is greater than 222dB and only explodes when it falls to the bottom of the sea. The receiving system consists of a bottom vector mark and a submarine pick-up, which can be time-aligned to form a joint receiving system.

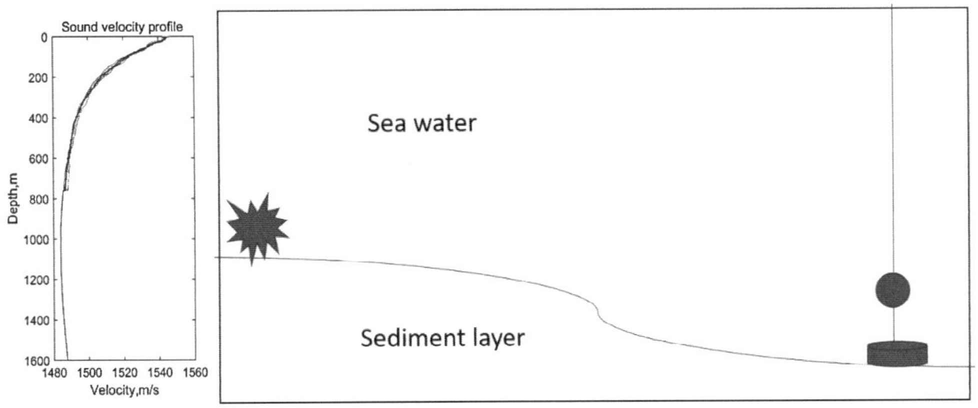

Figure. 1. Schematic of sound velocity profile and deployment of the test

In the receiving system, only the vector channel of the subsea shock absorber receives the vibration velocity in the seabed, and the other channels receive the vibration velocity and sound pressure in the seawater.

3.2. Result

The time domain waveform of the received signal, see Fig. 2. The signal received around 1.5s is the direct sound of the explosion sound, and then arrives at the signal that arrives in multiple ways, and the signal that is reflected by the submarine route is reached before.

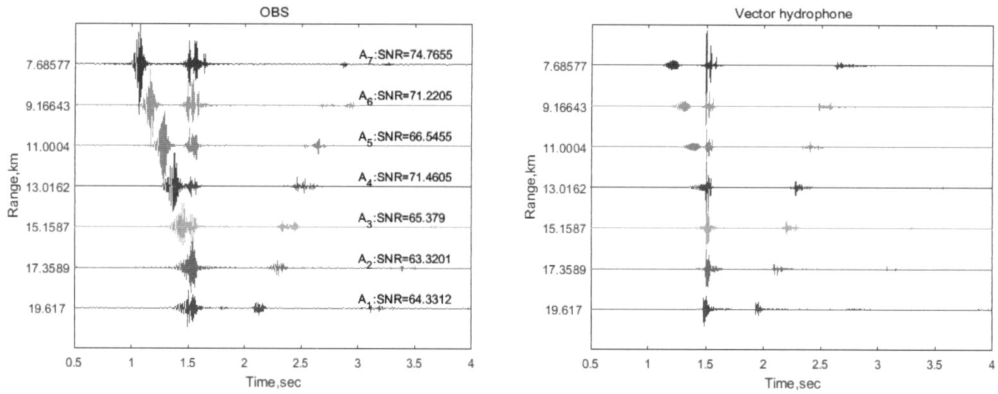

Figure. 2. The time series result of test

Further seek the pseudo-Wigner vile distribution of the three-path signal, see Fig. 3. It can be seen that the signals of the three channels are in the very low frequency band. From the test results, we can analyze that the signal reflected by the seabed route in the VLF sound field near the inclined seabed cannot be ignored. In the calculation of the sound field, it is necessary to comprehensively consider the components of various ways.

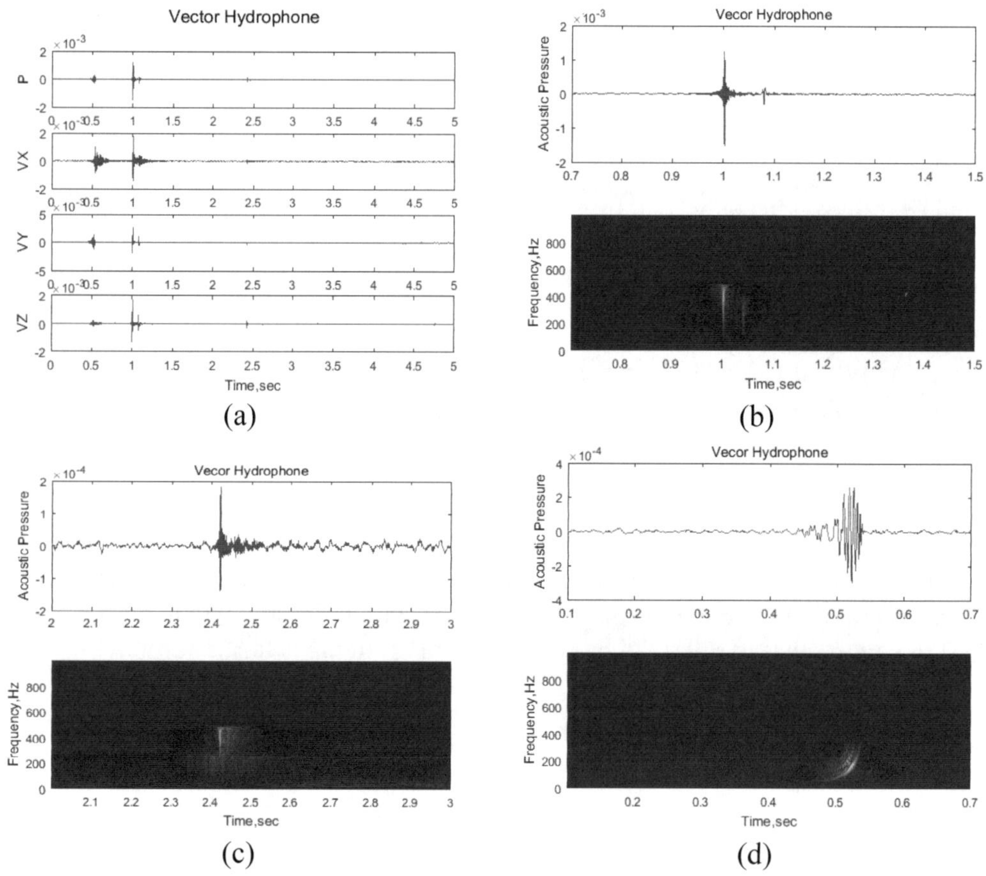

Figure. 3. receive signal of vector hydrophone: (a)The time series of the test. (b)Pseudo Wigner-Ville distribution (PWVD) of direct arrival signal. (c) PWVD of signal from multipath arrival (d) PWVD of signal from seabed arrival

4. Simulation

In this paper, two examples are calculated. The first example can prove that the results of the non-uniform depth mesh and the uniform mesh in the non-deposited layer model can be consistent under the grid scheme. The second example is to illustrate The results of non-uniform mesh and uniform mesh in the model with sedimentary layer are different. The grid method with one-sixth wavelength will lead to large errors in the calculation results, especially the simulation results of the very low-frequency sound field near the inclined seabed are larger.

4.1. Example 1: Method Verification

In Example 1, the parameters shown in Table 1 are used, and the same meshing method is used for calculation under the parameters in the table 1.
space should be left above and below the table.

Table 1. Value of simulation environment parameters

Layered Media	Density(g/cm^3)	Compression wave speed(m/s)	Shear wave speed(m/s))	Depth grid(m)
Fluid Layer	1.0	1500	\	1.0
Sediment Layer	1.2	1680	800	0.1
Half-Space	1.5	2400	1200	10.0

Fig. 4 shows the propagation loss at the seabed interface in both the horizontal layered model and the wedge layered model. The results show that the program of the non-uniform depth grid differs greatly from the program results of the uniform depth grid when the same grid is used.

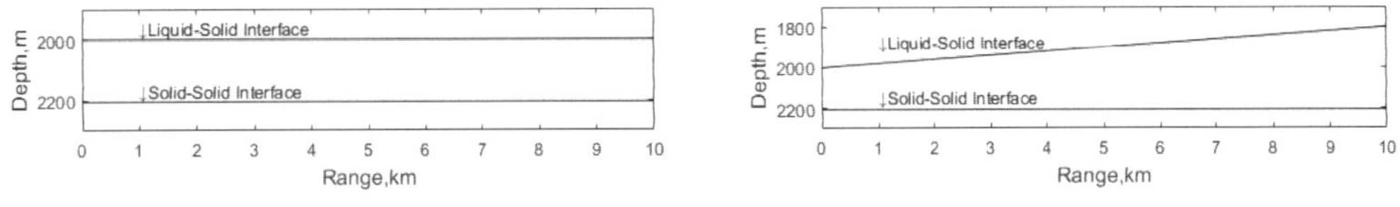

Figure. 4. The curse of Transmission Loss at 100m

4.2. Example 2: Sloped Seabed

Example 1 verifies the effectiveness of the method, and then we further study the grid selection problem of the inclined seabed. The simulation parameters are shown in Table 2. In the simulation of this example, the model in the literature was used and the simulation was performed according to the parameters shown in Table 2.

Table 2. Value of simulation environment parameters

Layer Property	Density(g/cm^3)	Compression wave speed(m/s)	Shear wave speed(m/s))	Depth grid(m
Fluid Layer	1.0	1500	\	1.0
Sediment Layer	1.2	1680	340	0.1
Half-Space	1.5	2000	1000	10.0

The result see fig. 5.

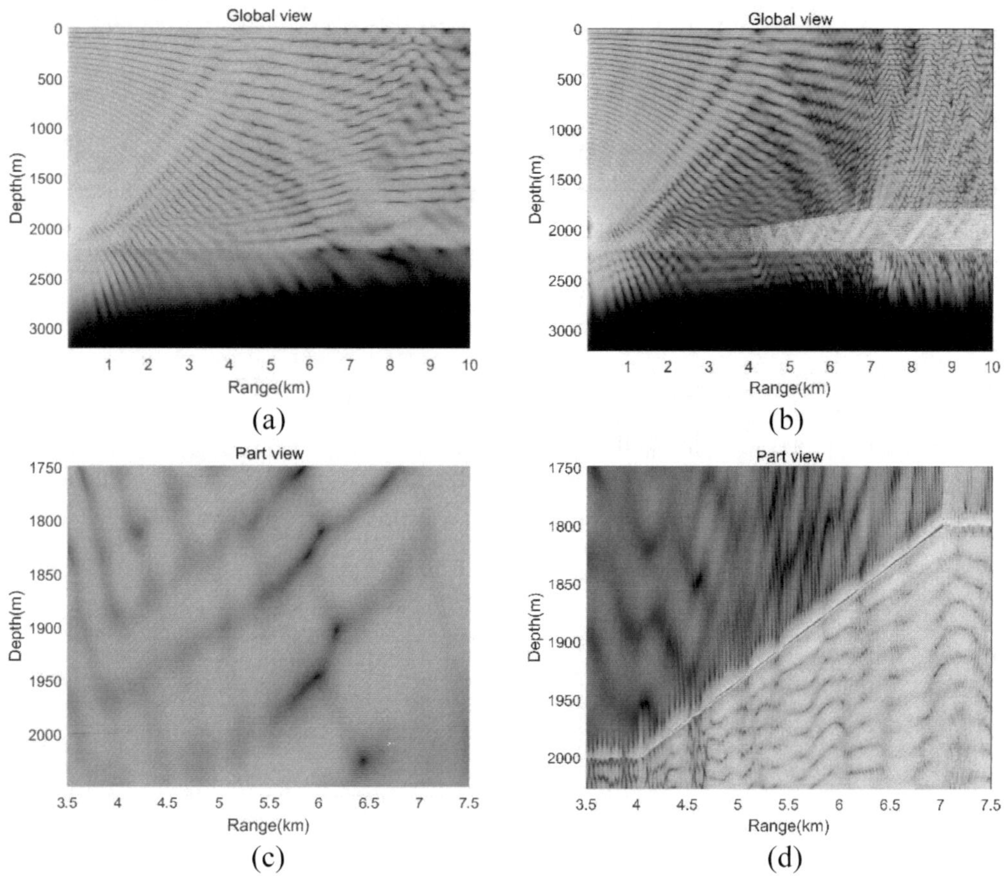

Figure. 5 The pseudo color map of transmission loss: (a)The global view of untreated RAMs. (b)The global view of treated RAMs. (c)Part view of fig.5(a). (d)Part view of fig.5(b)

The results shown in fig. 5 are calculated using different depth grids. Using a non-uniform mesh can calculate the sound field in a coarse-to-fine mesh combination, while a uniform mesh using a consistent coarse mesh will result in inaccurate results, and a uniform fine mesh will diverge. As shown in Fig. 6, there may be a difference of more than 30 dB in the sloped seafloor portion, which indicates that a depth grid using a one-sixth wavelength is not always effective. Because the result convergence is related to the padé approximation coefficient, depth grid, and distance grid, it is difficult to determine whether the obtained result is valid or not by simulation test, which needs to further solve the benchmark problem.

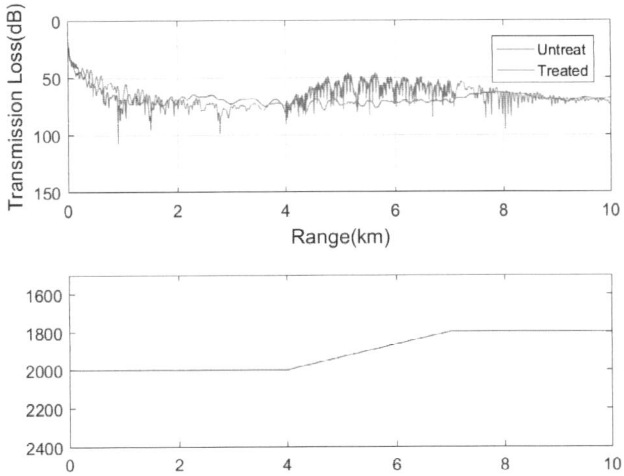

Figure. 6 The curves of transmission loss at the interface

Acknowledgments

Thanks to the National Natural Science Foundation For funding. Thanks for funding from the National Key R&D Program.

References

[1] Sanders, William M., and Michael D. Collins. "Nonuniform depth grids in parabolic equation solutions." *The Journal of the Acoustical Society of America* 133.4 (2013): 1953-1958.

[2] Collins, Michael D., Henrik Schmidt, and William L. Siegmann. "An energy-conserving spectral solution." *The Journal of the Acoustical Society of America* 107.4 (2000): 1964-1966.

[3] Zheng, Yingcai, et al. "Scholte waves generated by seafloor topography." *arXiv preprint arXiv:1306.4383* (2013).

[4] Jensen, Finn B., et al. *Computational ocean acoustics*. Springer Science & Business Media, 2011.

At-sea Observation and Theoretical Simulation on Very-low-frequency Sound Propagation in Shallow Water

Jingpu Cao[1, 2], Shuyuan Du[1], Shihong Zhou[1], Yubo Qi[1]

1, State Key Laboratory of Acoustics, Institute of Acoustics, Chinese Academy of Sciences, Beijing, China
caojingpu@mail.ioa.ac.cn
2, University of Chinese Academy of Sciences, Beijing, China

A very-low-frequency (VLF) sound propagation experiment with a reflective and refractive wide-angle Ocean Bottom Seismometer (OBS) and a large volume air-gun was conducted across the northeastern continental margin of the South China Sea (SCS). With air-gun shot spacing of approximately 190 m, high-quality Scholte wave data was recorded by the horizontal and vertical geophones of OBS within 0.4-6 km offset. At least four modal phase-velocity dispersion curves of Scholte waves in the frequency band of 1.2-3 Hz were extracted from common receiver gathers (CRGs) using phase-shift method. We retrieved the first three higher modes from the horizontal component, and the fundamental and the first higher mode can be extracted from the vertical component, but no Scholte wave was found on the hydrophone. The dispersion results show that the phase velocity of the fundamental Scholte wave varies from 240 m/s to 400 m/s, and the phase velocity of the higher order of Scholte waves vary from 400 m/s to 1000 m/s.

Keywords: Scholte wave; Dispersion curve; Phase shift method; Shallow water.

1. Introduction

The VLF sound has significant potential for developing underwater long-range target detection and seafloor inversion. In marine geological surveys, receivers such as OBSs located on the shallow water seabed can often record Scholte waves, characterized by very low frequency and large amplitude.[86] The dispersion phenomenon will occur when surface waves propagate in the layered medium, and its characteristics are closely related to the underlying medium parameters.[8] So, as a kind of surface wave, Scholte wave always carry abundant sediment information during propagation. Therefore, studying the propagation of Scholte waves in shallow water, extracting and analyzing the Scholte wave dispersion curves have important theoretical significance and application value for underwater acoustic engineering and seafloor inversion.

Two methods are usually utilized to extract surface wave dispersion curves from seismic recordings. The spectral analysis of surface waves (SASW) method[7] can only retrieve the fundamental mode of the dispersion curve by using two receivers at various distances, and its quality control and phase unwrapping uncertainty problems are difficult to solve. For this reason, the multichannel analysis of surface waves (MASW) approach which uses many channels of surface wave data to construct the fundamental and overtone dispersion curves has gradually replaced SASW method.[5] After obtaining common receiver gathers, we can calculate the energy spectrum at different frequencies, then the energy maximum value points can be picked to get the dispersion curve. To calculate the energy spectrum, three different types of techniques are often used: frequency-wavenumber (f-k)[2], slant-stack (τ-p)[3] and phase shift method[4]. Some detailed and comparative description of each method has been presented and it claims that the phase shift method results in the most accurate extraction of multimodal dispersion curves under a wide range of realistic situations. [1]

In this paper, a sound propagation experiment conducted in SCS in May 2018 is introduced. Seismic data from a 4C OBS and a large volume air-gun were used to study the VLF sound propagation in shallow water. Benefiting from the relative lower frequency band of the OBS and large volume air-gun, high signal-to-noise-ratio (S/N) surface wave within offset 0.4-6 km were clearly recorded, enabling the extraction of high-resolution phase velocity dispersion curves. The fundamental and first three higher modal dispersion curves of surface wave in the frequency band of 1.2-3.0 Hz were extracted by the phase shift method and its phase velocity vary from 240 m/s to 1000 m/s, which provide important information for seafloor parameters inversion.

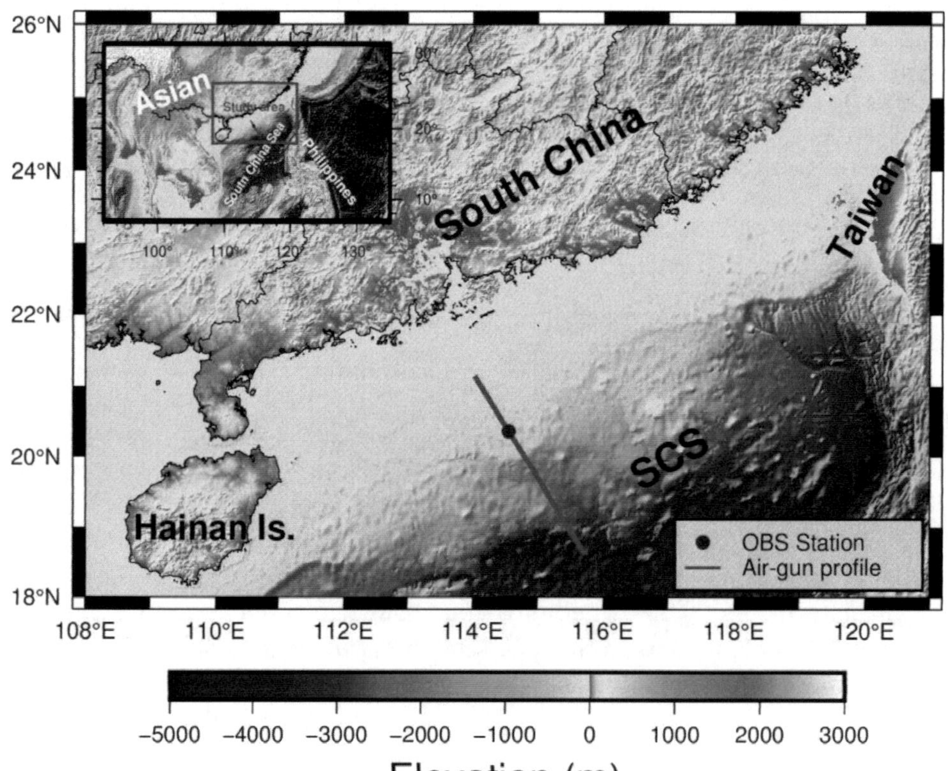

Fig.1. ocation of the study area and the survey profile. The shot positions are denoted by red dots and the blue dot indicates the OBS station position.

2. Experiment Setup

A northwest-southeast-oriented OBS survey profile with a total length of approximately 330 km was conducted in the South China Sea (SCS) in May 2018 (Fig. 1). The water depth along the survey profile varies from 73 m to 3780 m and the OBS was located at a depth of 126 m. The OBS contains a three-axis geophone which measures the inline horizontal, the cross line horizontal and the vertical component of particle velocity just below the sediment-water interface and a hydrophone which is mounted just above the interface and thus measures the acoustic pressure in the water column. An active large volume air-gun was shot at a depth of 10 m below sea level with an average distance of 190 m to each shot. The OBS data are of good quality at a sample rate of 0.004 s, recording abundant seismo-acoustic signals from the water to the sediment interface.

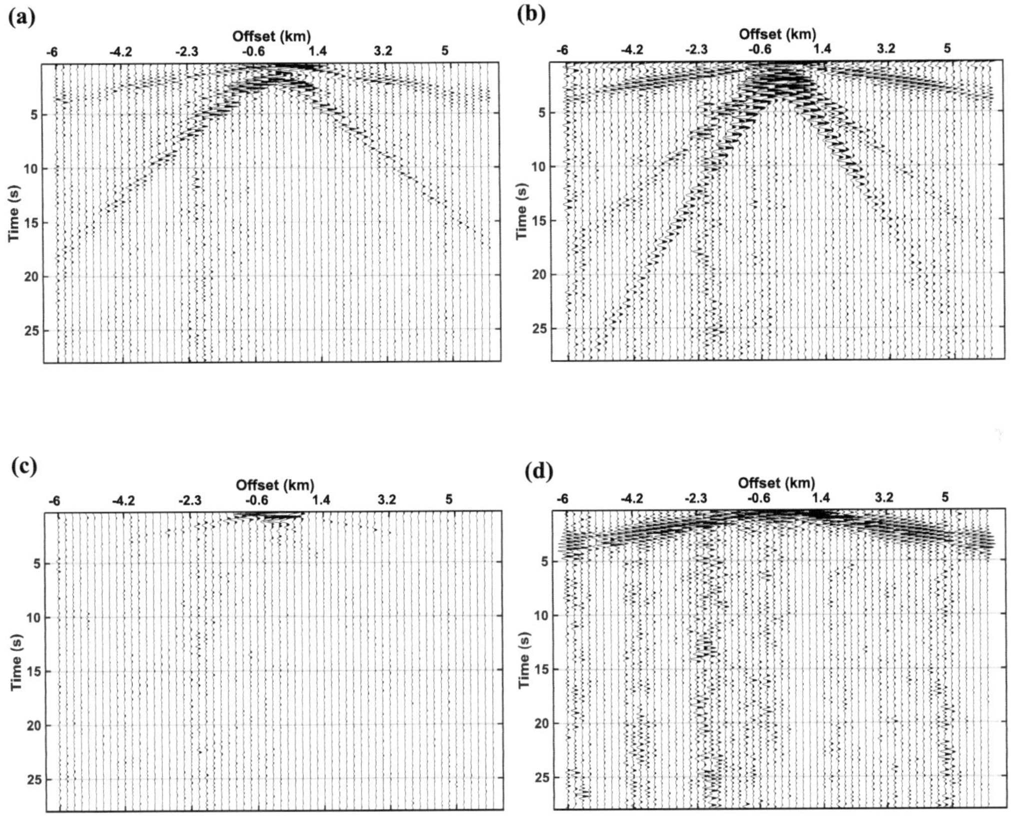

Fig.2.The CRG of (a) **radial** component, (b) **vertical** component, (c) **tangential** component and (d) **pressure** component recorded by OBS. The radial and tangential components were rotated from the inline horizontal and the cross line horizontal components. After a 1.2-3 Hz band-pass filter, it shows that obvious Scholte waves were observed on the CRG seismogram of radial and vertical component, but there is no response or weak

After the clock drift correction, the CRGs data group including pressure and velocity field was obtained from the raw 4C broadband OBS data. It is necessary to rotate the inline horizontal and the cross line horizontal component to radial (shot to receiver direction) and tangential (perpendicular to the radial direction) component. The Scholte wave propagates on the plane defined by the radial and vertical axis while the Love wave propagates on the plane defined by the tangential and vertical axis. There is little energy on tangential component when the medium is isotropic.

To guarantee the high S/N of the surface wave data, the maximum source-receiver offset was set to approximately 6000 m. Not only this, a band-pass filter of 1.2-3 Hz were implemented for each trace to improve the S/N of the Scholte wave. After the data preprocessing, obvious Scholte waves were observed on the CRG seismograms of radial and vertical component, but there is no response or weak Scholte wave on the pressure and tangential seismogram, which are presented in Fig. 2. Next, the recorded CRG seismograms were analyzed using the multichannel dispersion analysis described in the next section.

3. Dispersion Analysis

3.1. Phase shift method

In this study, the MASW method which allows direct construction of a high-resolution image of multimodal dispersion curves from multi-channel records with a relatively small number of traces is used. To obtain the dispersion energy image, the phase-shift method is applied to the Fourier transform of the shot gathers after normalization. The extensive application of phase shift method in extracting the dispersion curve is based on the analysis of the dispersion properties of surface waves, *i.e.* the dependence of propagation velocity of different spectral components of the waves upon their frequency. The extraction of dispersion curve can be defined as an procedure which includes the following steps:

- Transform the CRG from the original *x-t* (offset-time) domain into *x-f* (offset-frequency) domain using the 2-D Fourier transform;
- Normalize the CRG spectrum generated in the previous step with respect to offset compensating for the effects of geometrical spreading, attenuation or source strength variation;
- Perform the summation over the offset in the frequency domain after applying an offset-dependent phase shift.

Thus, a *f-v* (frequency-velocity) spectrum can be generated, where the dispersion curves of all excited modes become apparent through the amplitude maxima.

3.2. Dispersion curve extraction and analysis

Two Scholte wave dispersion energy images were generated from the left and the right sides of the CRG of each component by the phase shift method, which are shown in the frequency-velocity domain in Fig. 3. As shown in Fig. 3, at least total four modes of dispersion curves can be clearly found in the dispersion energy images of radial and vertical components. We retrieved the fundamental and the first higher dispersion curves from the vertical component and the first three higher modes from the radial component. The fundamental mode is shown between 1.2 and 2.0 Hz with strong amplitudes and good continuity. Except that, the first higher modal dispersion curve can also be identified between 1.4 and 2.5 Hz with a high resolution, and the other higher mode dispersion curves observed between 1.5 and 3.0 Hz have lower energy amplitude and resolution. We tested the left offset and the right offset data to construct dispersion images. Both dispersion energy images for the left and the right sides of seismogram are characterized by similar dispersion curves. The phase velocity of the fundamental Scholte wave varies from 240 m/s to 400 m/s, while the phase velocity of the higher order Scholte wave varies from 400 m/s to 1000 m/s.

In addition to the above results, the surface wave dispersion curve on T component is hard to extract and there is no surface wave response in pressure component. The phenomenon suggests that the geophone captured more abundant VLF signals than the hydrophone and the lower mode of Scholte wave dominants in the vertical component of geophone while the higher mode is obvious in the horizontal component.

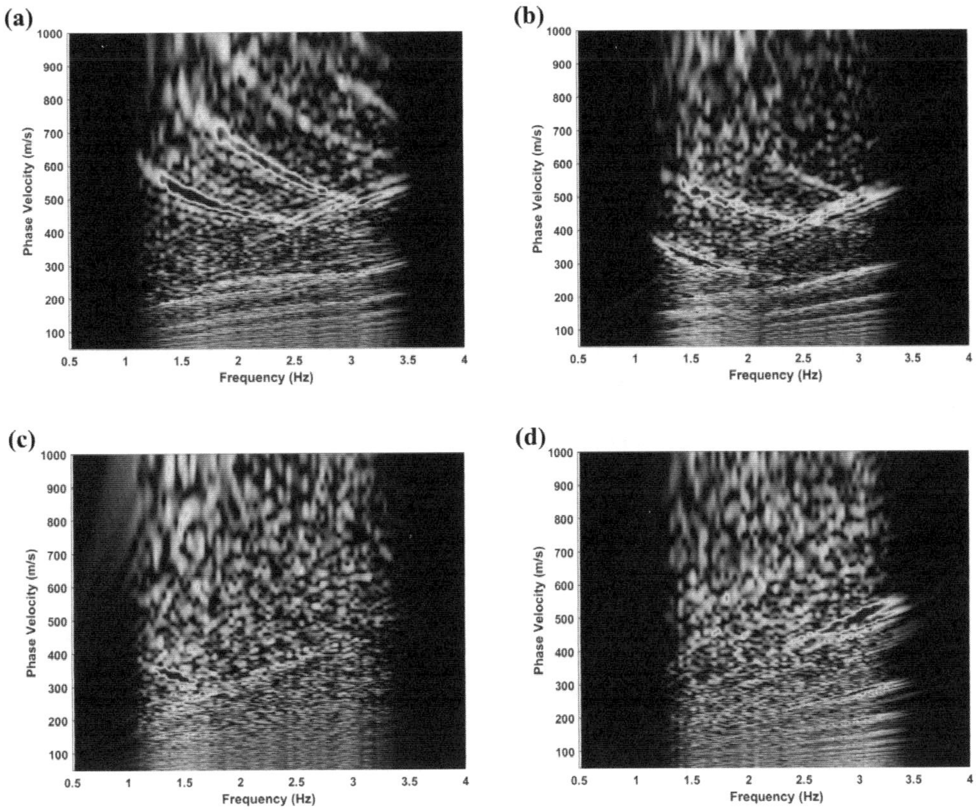

Fig.3.The dispersion energy images in the *f-v* domain generated by the phase shift method. The dispersion energy images shown in (a-d) correspond to the left (negative offset value) branches of the CRGs shown in

4. Conclusions

Obvious Scholte waves excited by a large volume air-gun were recorded by vertical and horizontal geophones of a 4C OBS within the offset 0.4-6 km. Dispersion energy images were generated on the CRGs directly by the phase shift method for studying the dispersion characteristics of surface waves. From these dispersion energy images in the *f-v* domain, It was found that at least four modes of dispersion curves in the frequency band of 1.2-3 Hz were clearly identified in horizontal and vertical velocity wave field, and the vertical component has even lower velocity and lower-frequency surface wave signals than the horizontal component while pressure field has very few Scholte wave signals. In addition, these dispersion energy images also show that the phase velocity of the fundamental Scholte wave travels 400 m/s at 1.2 Hz to 240 m/s at high frequencies of 2 Hz, and the higher modes have phase velocities between 600 m/s and 1000 m/s at 1.5 Hz which slow down to 400 m/s at frequencies of 3 Hz. Dispersion of surface waves is closely related to the structure and properties of the subsurface material and, in particular, to shear wave velocity. Therefore, the above results would provide important information for seafloor parameters inversion in the South China Sea area.

Acknowledgments

We are grateful to the investigators and the crew members on the *Bochuang*, all of whom took part in the survey work at sea. This work is supported by funding from the National Natural Science Foundation (11804362, 11804364) and the Frontier Science Research Project of Chinese Academy of Sciences (Grant No. QYZDY-SSW-SLH005).

References

[1] Dal Moro G, Pipan M, Forte E, et al. Determination of Rayleigh Wave Dispersion Curves For Near Surface Applications In Unconsolidated Sediments[J]. *Seg Technical Program Expanded Abstracts*, 2003, 22(1):1247.

[2] Gabriels P, Snieder R, Nolet G. IN SITU MEASUREMENTS OF SHEAR-WAVE VELOCITY IN SEDIMENTS WITH HIGHER-MODE RAYLEIGH WAVES[J]. *Geophysical Prospecting*, 1987, 35(2):187-196.

[3] Mcmechan G. A., Yedlin M. J., Analysis of dispersive waves by wave field transformation[J]. *GEOPHYSICS*, 1981, 46(6):869-874.

[4] Park C. B., Miller R. D. and Xia J. H., Imaging dispersion curves of surface waves on multichannel records, *SEG Expanded Abstracts*, 17(1998), 1377-1380.

[5] Park C B, Miller R D, Xia J . Multichannel analysis of surface waves[J]. *GEOPHYSICS*, 1999, 64(3):800-808.

[6] Schirmer F. Experimental Determination of Properties of the Scholte Wave in the Bottom of the North Sea. In: Kuperman W.A., Jensen F.B. (eds) *Bottom-Interacting Ocean Acoustics. NATO Conference Series (Marine Sciences)*, vol 5. Springer, Boston, MA, 1980

[7] Sheu, J. C, et al. "Applications and limitations of the spectral-analysis-of-surface-waves method." *Texas Univ Austin Report* (1986).

[8] Xia J, Miller R. D., Park C. B., Estimation of near-surface shear-wave velocity by inversion of Rayleigh waves[J]. *GEOPHYSICS*, 1999, 64(3):691-700.

Simulations of VLF Underwater- and Seismo-acoustic Propagation Fields in the Wedge Coast and the Borehole Onshore

ShuyuanDu[1] ShihongZhou[1] YuboQi[1]
1, Key Laboratory of Acoustics,Institute of Acoustics, Chinese Academy of Sciences, Beijing, China
dushuyuan@mail.ioa.ac.cn

The coastal continental shelf area is a wedge-shaped shallow-water waveguide consisting of water column and layered elastic bottom. In this kind of environment, it is necessary to learn the propagation physics of the very-low-frequency (VLF) underwater-acoustic or seismo-acoustic field, which is radiated from the underwater source, propagates through the water media, propagates over sloping layered elastic bottom and is received in the wedge coast and the borehole onshore. Considering the effects of elastic sea-bottom, the full wave fields including underwater-acoustics and seismo-acoustics below 20 Hz both in water and in borehole onshore are calculated using the 2-D Spectral Element Method (SPECFEM-2D) and the mesh tool CUBIT. Waveforms and spatial energy distribution at different frequencies are predicted. The results show that the very low frequency acoustic field can be coupled to seabed in form of Scholte wave propagating through the upper interface of the rock layer and it is better to capture it in the borehole onshore at the boundary depth of rock layer than on the seafloor in the duct.

Keywords: Scholte wave, spectral element method, low frequency seismo-acoustic.

1. Introduction

There is always Scholte wave developed on seismic data from shallow water area. The dispersion curve of Scholte wave is strongly correlated with the velocity structure, especially the shear wave velocity structure of sea bottom, therefore it is usually applied to inversion of shear wave velocity which is an important parameter for multi-component exploration in static correction, and also used in ocean project construction as an indirect tool for measuring the anti-deformation ability of marine sediment. Recently with the development of ocean acoustics towards very low frequency even ultra-low frequency, it is important to consider the full-wave field accurately including underwater-acoustics and low-frequency seismo-acoustics due to effect of elastic bottom.

There is analytical solution of wave field in horizontal layered medium while the solution for seabed undulation situation can be obtained by numerical simulation. The weak form of the wave equation with the boundary condition implicitly satisfied in the wave equation itself is suitable for the exact simulation of interface wave in complex topography model.

There is always a wedge-shaped shallow water waveguide with gradual change of water depth in coastal continental shelf area. In this kind of environment, there will be mode cutoff for low-frequency sound propagation in the wedge-shaped duct caused by energy coupling and leakage from water into the sea bottom, and part of them propagating as Scholte wave on the interface of layered elastic bottom. As a kind of interface wave, Scholte wave might be weak due to the thick and soft sediment in the coast but maybe strongly propagate on the upper surface of the basement and can be received in certain depth of the borehole onshore. In this article a simulation of wedge-shaped shallow water model is given, with the whole progress including geometry building and mesh grid building shown, followed by the waveform and spatial energy distribution and relative transmission loss analysis. It is hoped for clarifying the propagation mechanism of low-frequency seismo-acoustics and providing a basis for the application of sea-bottom parameter inversion, underwater detection or communications.

2. Simulation Example

There is always wedge bottom and shallow water in the continental shelf area. In this model the water depth vary from 200m to 0m in 20km range, with fluid sediment of 100m (yellow area) overlaying the semi-infinite basement(brown area) shown in Fig.1.

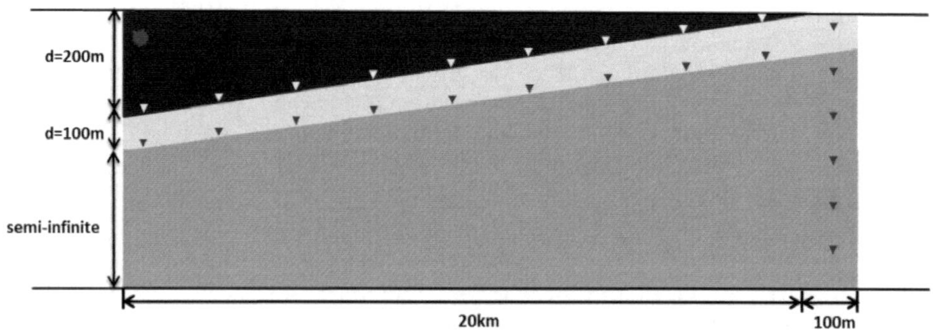

Figure 4 Simulation model.

There are three kinds of material, water, fluid sediment and rock basement with properties of each layer shown in table 1. The shot is at 0m underwater 180m, indicated by red point in Fig. 1, using Ricker wavelet with frequency bandwidth of 0-20 Hz. There are three groups of receivers: first ones lay on the bottom of the fluid sediment indicated by white triangle, second ones locate on the interface of sediment and basement indicated by horizontal black triangle and the last ones are in the borehole onshore indicated by vertical black triangle.

Table 1 The material parameters of each layer of the simulation model

Medium	Vp(m/s)	Vs(m/s)	Density(kg/m^3)	Thickness (m)
Water	1500	0	1000	200~0
Sediment	1600	0	1800	100
Basement	2400	1200	2000	semi-infinite

Spectral element method is a generalized spectral method, based on the variational or weak form theory of wave equation (AndreasFichtner, 2011). There is an obvious advantage that the boundary conditions is implicitly satisfied, so the weak form is convenient for dealing with complicated geometric structures and boundary conditions, suitable for exact simulation for interface wave.

Here we use SPECFEM-2D software for the simulation. The SPECFEM package is released open-source and can be downloaded on website https://github.com/geodynamics. It was first developed by Dimitri Komatitsch etc. in Paris, France. It can be used for 2D, 3D and even global seismic wave propagation in acoustic, elastic, viscoelastic, and poroelastic medium(Komatitsch D etc., 2002a; 2002b). In the past few years, there is a lot of progress of SEM (spectral element method) in geophysics and it has been introduced into ocean acoustic in recent years (Dong Yang, 2016).

Numerical simulation is implemented in finite area, therefore boundary treatment is necessary. PML (perfectly matched layer) is an effective boundary absorption technology and widely used in elastic wave simulation.

Before the simulation, mesh building of the calculation area is needed. Here we use Trelis software (or CUBIT) to generate mesh grid.

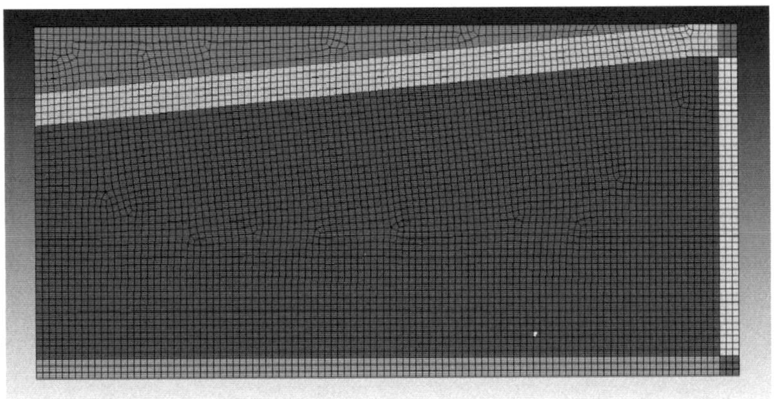

Figure 5 The mesh grid of the calculation area (for display, not the real size of the model). The green, yellow and purple area are model area, the other area are PML boundary area.

The waveforms of horizontal and vertical velocity field received on the sea bottom, upper surface of the basement and in the borehole are shown respectively.

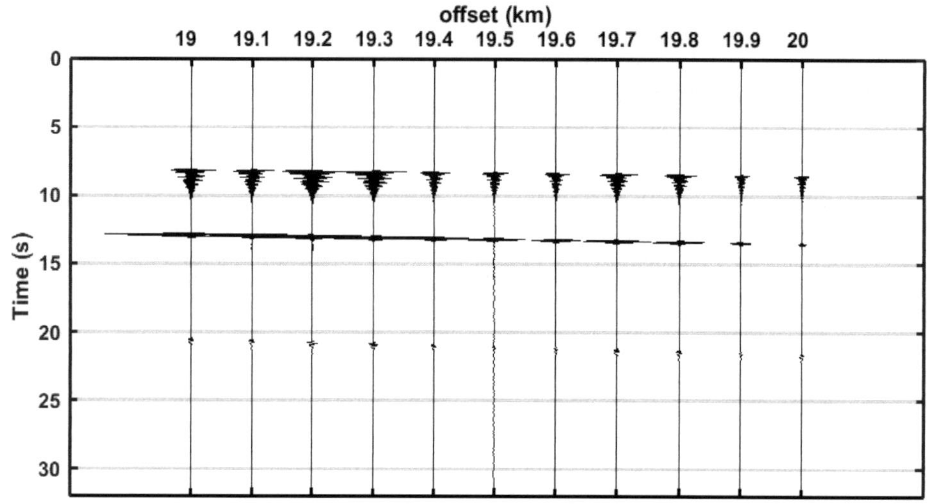

Figure 6 The velocity x component on the mud.

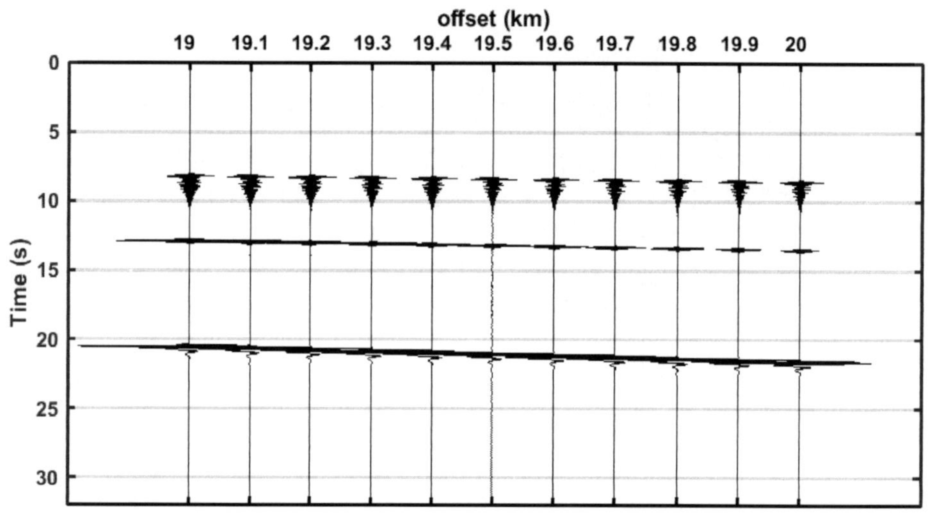

Figure 7 The velocity x component on the surface of basement.

The horizontal velocity field received by the first receiver group is shown in Figure 6, the x axis is offset, from 19 km to 20 km with interval 0.1 km; y axis is time from 0 to 30 seconds. There is obvious P-arrived between 5 s to 10 s which propagates in the basement with velocity of 2400 m/s. The acoustic wave propagating in water arrives around 13 s. The slowest Scholte wave arrives after 20 s and it is weak on the surface of fluid sediment. On the upper interface of the basement shown in Fig. 4, the Scholte wave is much stronger at the same offset.

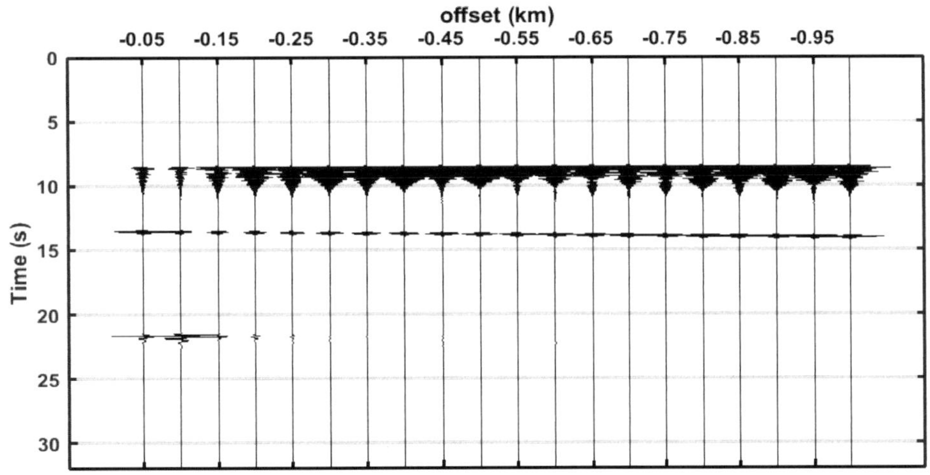

Figure 8 The velocity x component in the borehole onshore..

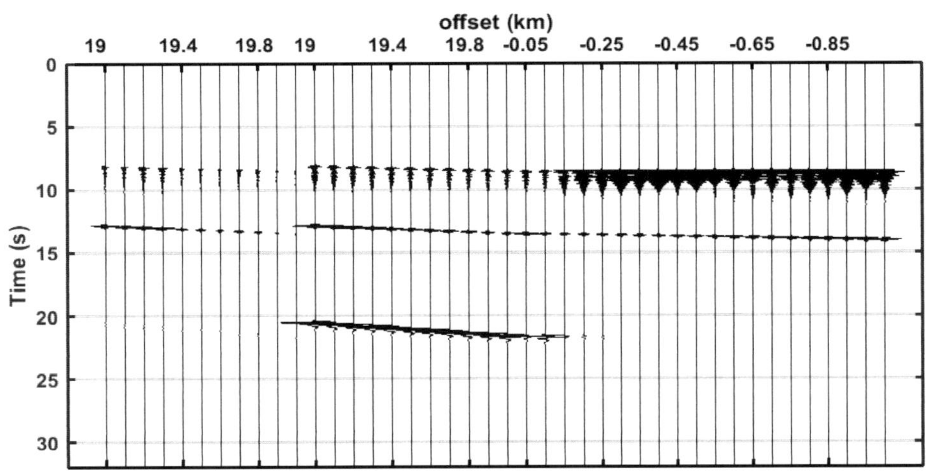

Figure 9 The velocity x component from three groups of receivers.

The horizontal velocity fields received by the third group of receivers are shown in Fig.5. x axis is depth from 50 m to 1000 m with interval 50 m; y axis is time from 0 to 30 seconds. There is strong P-arrived between 5 s to 10 s propagating in the basement with velocity of 2400 m/s. The acoustic wave propagating in water arrived around 13 s. There is Scholte wave received at depth 50 m to 200 m with maxima at depth 100 m. The waveforms received at three different locations are compared in Fig. 6. The x axis, from left to right, are the left 11 traces from the first group of receivers locating on sea bottom with offset range of 19 km to 20 km, the middle 11 traces from the upper interface of basement with offset range of 19km to 20km, and the right 20 traces from the borehole with depth of 50 m to 1000 m. Y axis is time from 0 to 30 seconds. It is shown that the Scholte wave is the strongest on the second group of receivers and certain depths of the third group of receivers.

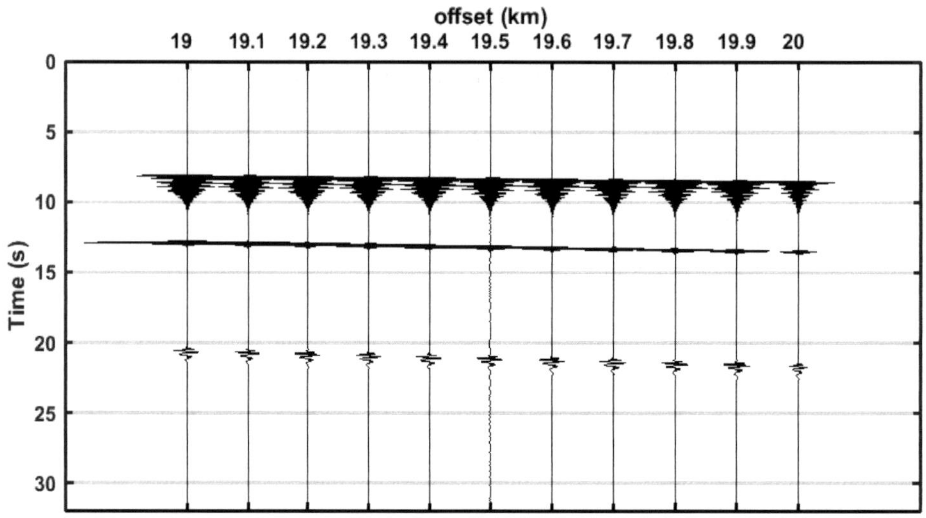

Figure 10 The velocity z component on the mud.

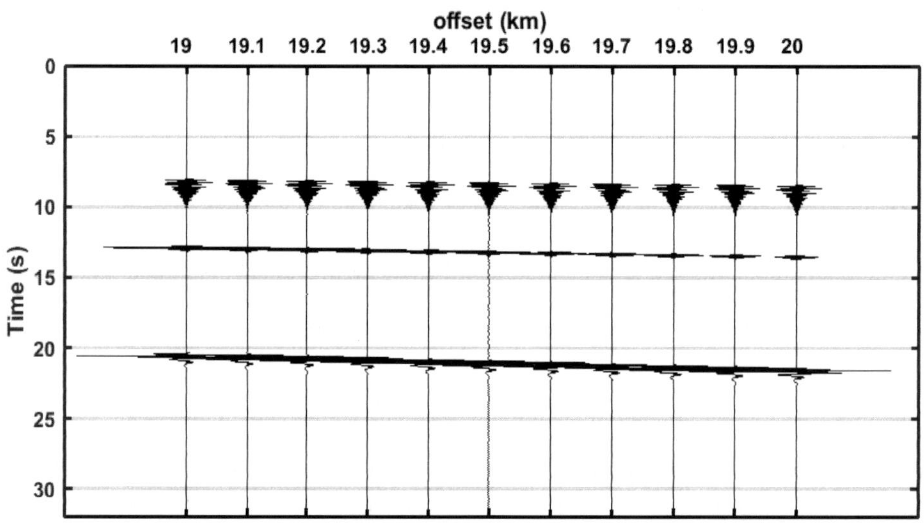

Figure 11 The velocity z component on the interface of basement.

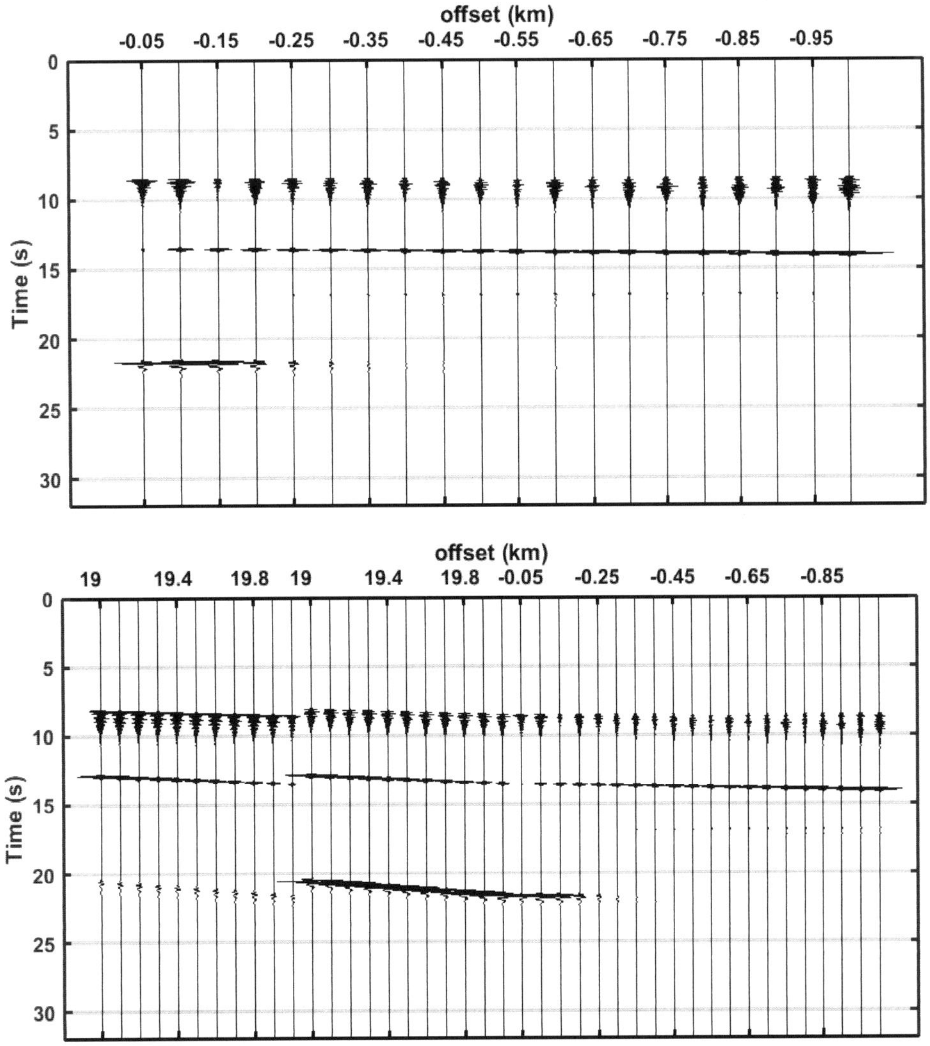

Figure 10 The velocity z component from three groups of receivers.

The vertical velocity fields received by the three groups of receivers are shown in Fig. 8-Fig.10. The conclusion is similar to the horizontal component. From the previous analysis of horizontal and vertical components and contrast of the waveforms from three different locations, it is shown that Scholte wave is weak on the surface of sea bottom due to the thick fluid sediment while there is obvious signal received on the interface of elastic basement and certain depths in borehole.

The energy distribution of the simulation area at frequency 4 Hz, 6 Hz, 8 Hz and 10 Hz are shown in Fig. 11-Fig.12 for velocity x component and Fig. 13-Fig.14 for vertical velocity component. X axis is distance (unit km) and y axis is depth (unit meter). The interfaces of different layers are indicated by the dashed line. The red color means strong energy and the blue color means weak energy. It is shown that there is energy propagating on the interface of elastic basement at far distance.

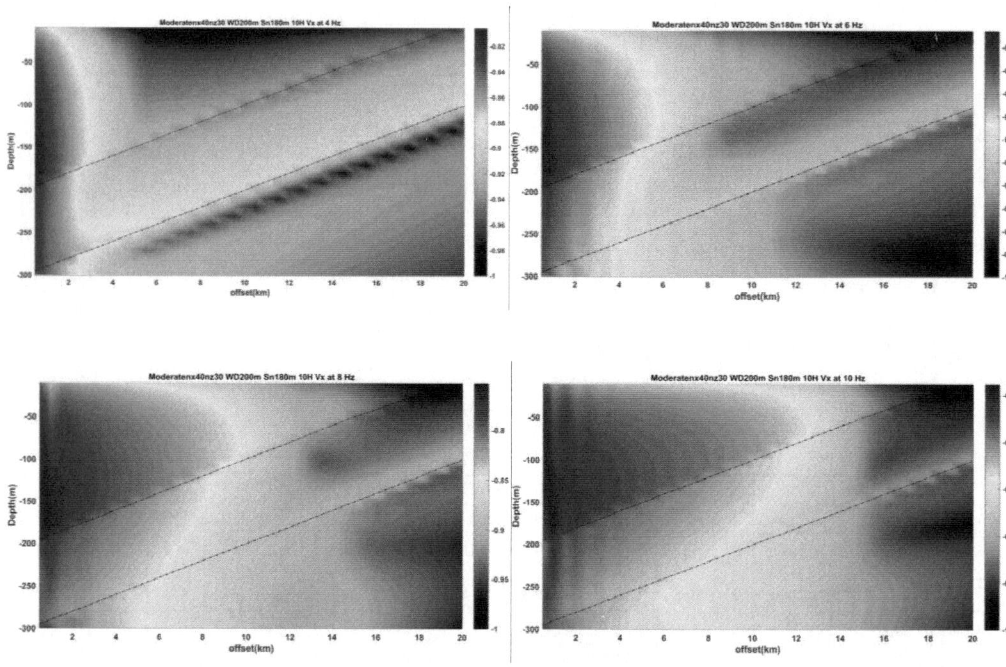

Figure 12 Energy distribution map of velocity x of the simulation area at 8 Hz(left) and 10 Hz(right).

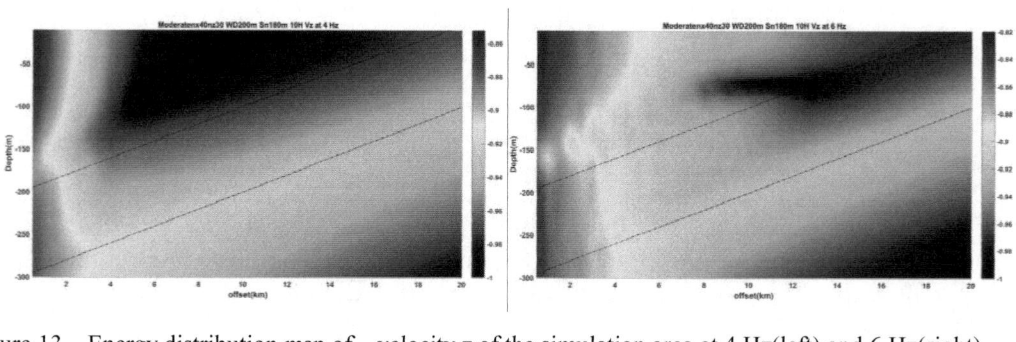

Figure 13 Energy distribution map of velocity z of the simulation area at 4 Hz(left) and 6 Hz(right).

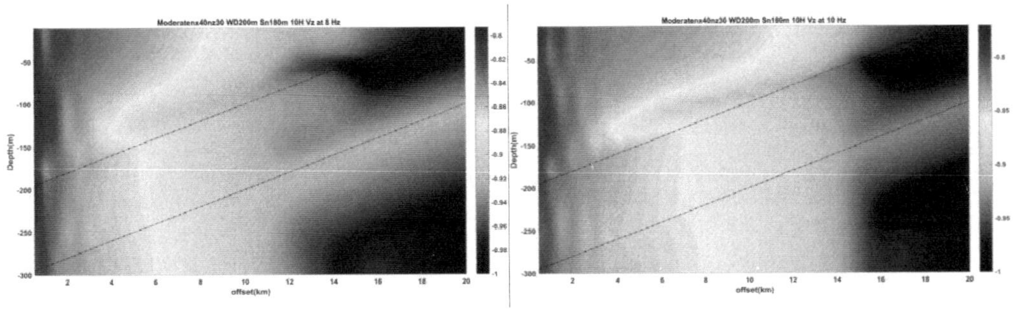

Figure 14 Energy distribution of velocity z of the simulation area at 8 Hz(left) and 10 Hz(right).

The relative energy loss (not the absolute value) of horizontal component and vertical component at 4 Hz, 6 Hz, 8 Hz and 10 Hz are shown in Fig.15-Fig.18. The red line indicates the relative energy loss received on the interface of the elastic basement and the blue line is received on the surface of sea bottom. With the frequency becomes lower, there is more energy propagating on upper interface of the elastic basement than in the water column. For very low frequency Scholte wave it is better to catch the wave field on the interface of the elastic basement than at the sea bottom.

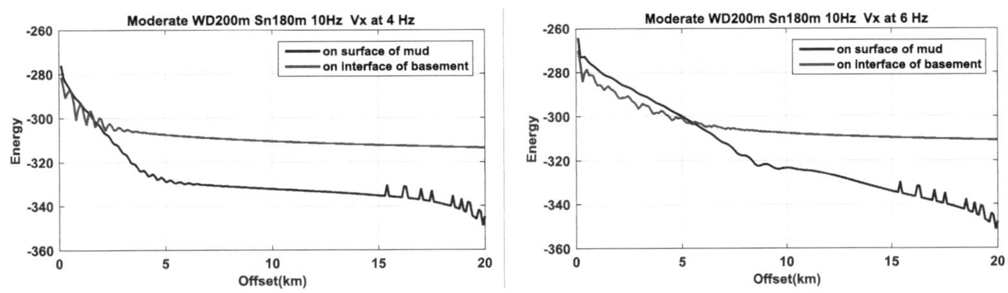

Figure 15 The curve of energy of velocity x as function of distance at 4 Hz(left) and 6 Hz(right) received at the sea bottom(blue line) and at the interface of the basement(red line) respectively.

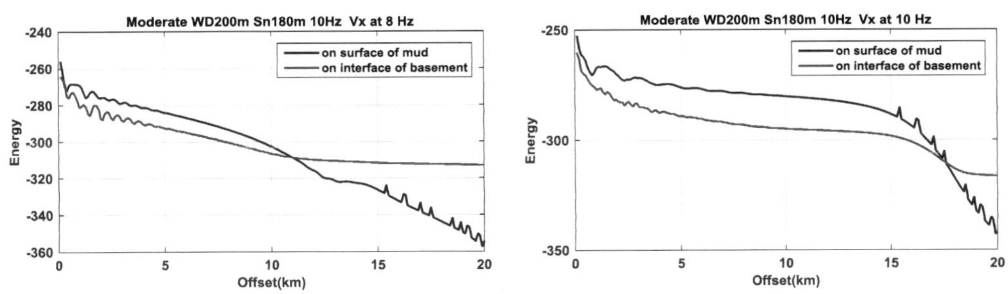

Figure 16 The curve of energy of velocity x as function of distance at 8 Hz(left) and 10 Hz(right) received at the sea bottom(blue line) and at the interface of the basement(red line) respectively.

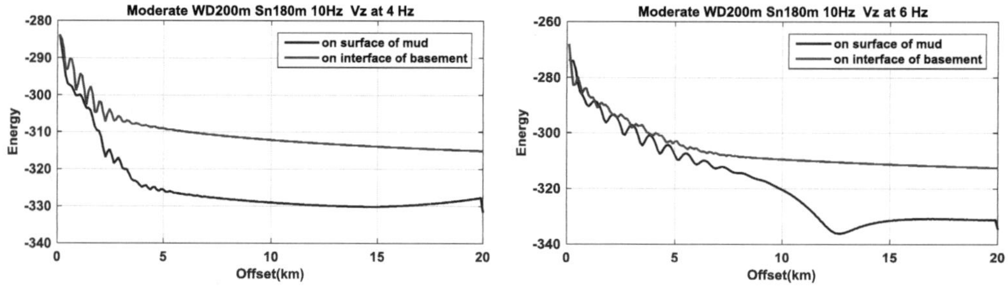

Figure 17 The curve of energy of velocity z as function of distance at 4 Hz(left) and 6 Hz(right) received at the sea bottom(blue line) and at the interface of the basement(red line) respectively.

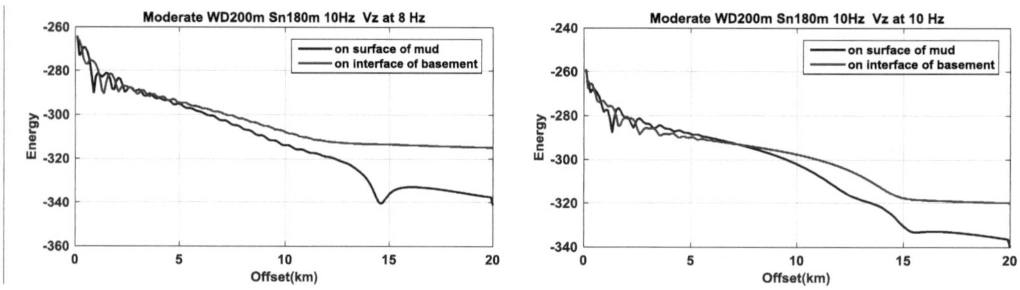

Figure 18 The curve of energy of velocity z as function of distance at 8 Hz(left) and 10 Hz(right) received at the sea bottom(blue line) and at the interface of the basement(red line) respectively.

3. Discussion and summary

From comparison of waveforms received on the surface of sea bottom, on the interface of the elastic basement and in the borehole respectively, it is shown that there is obvious Scholte wave propagating on the interface of the mud and the basement while little Scholte wave received on the surface of sea bottom due to the thick soft mud layer. This Scholte wave can also be received in the borehole at the depth of upper interface of basement.

From the spatial energy distribution map, it can be seen that low frequency energy spreads far away (here below 10 Hz at distance of 16 km) by the upper interface of basement as interface wave rather than through the water column, what is the mode cut-off phenomenon in shallow water wave guide.

The curve of relative energy loss indicates visually that for low frequency (here below 10 Hz at distance of 16 km) it is better to receive the wave field on the upper interface of basement than on surface of the sea bottom especially at far distance in shallow water area.

Of course it is difficult to locate the receiver on the upper interface of basement in field experiment, but it is more possible to receive such low frequency interface wave at the corresponding depth in the borehole onshore.

Here is just a pure simulation with ideal wedge-shaped topography and assumed properties of the elastic basement layers. In real ocean environment it may be difficult to excite interface wave due to very low shear wave velocity or thickness of fluid sediment layer or it would be hard to detect Scholte wave at far distance attributed to the strong scattering caused by the fluctuation and heterogeneity of the sea bottom. Work considering these complex factors in modeling is needed in future.

Acknowledgments

This research is supported by the Frontier Science Research Project of Chinese Academy of Sciences (Grant No. QYZDY-SSW-SLH005) and the National Natural Science Foundation of China (Grant No.11804364, 1180462).

References

[1] AndreasFichtner. Full Seismic Waveform Modelling and Inversion[M]. Springer Berlin Heidelberg, 2011.
[2] Komatitsch D , Tromp J . Spectral-element simulations of global seismic wave propagationa- I. Validation[J]. Geophysical Journal International, 2002a, 149(2):390-412.
[3] Komatitsch D , Tromp J . Spectral-element simulations of global seismic wave propagationa-II. Three-dimensional models, oceans, rotation and self-gravitation[J]. Geophysical Journal International, 2002b, 150(1):303-318.
[4] DongYang. The Spectral Element Method Applied to Ocean Acoustic [D]. 2016.

The Analysis of Multi-layered Effect for Sea Bottom at Low-frequency Acoustic Propagation

Ya-Xiao Mo[1,2†] Chao-Jin Zhang[1,2,3] Li-Cheng Lu[1,2] Bing-Wen Sun[1,2] Sheng-Ming Guo[1,2]

1, Institute of Acoustics, Chinese Academy of Sciences,
No. 21 North 4th Ring Road, Haidian District, Beijing 100190, P. R. China
† moyaxiao@mail.ioa.ac.cn
2, Key Laboratory of Underwater Acoustic Environment, Chinese Academy of Sciences,
No. 21 North 4th Ring Road, Haidian District, Beijing 100190, P. R. China
3, University of Chinese Academy of Sciences,
No. 19(A) Yuquan Road, Shijingshan District, Beijing 100149, P. R. China

As development of the noise reduction technology, the low/very-low frequency radiation noise turn into a primary way in underwater detection. However, with the reducing of the frequency, the sea bottom affects are more prominent in acoustic propagation. The change of submarine topography may seriously cause energy leakage and the variation of the acoustic interference structure. Meanwhile the layered structure of the bottom and the shear wave inside would modulate the energy transmission. Compared with the effect caused by the bottom shear wave and the submarine topography, how the layered structure affects the propagation is not as explicit. For the effect of multi-layered sea bottom, an acoustic propagation model is developed based on mapping approach in parabolic equation method. And with this model, the influence of frequency and sediment thickness is analysis on low frequency acoustic propagation. Simulated results indicate that acoustic signal is transmitted more efficiently in the wave guide made up of multi-layered bottom. And it is noticeable that the efficiency is determined by the wavelength. Especially in the beach or reefs environment, due to the effect of multi-layered sea bottom, the acoustic signal can be received on the shore or after reefs.

Keywords: acoustic propagation; multi-layered elastic sea bottom; low-frequency.

1. Introduction

Due to the result of application of silencing technology, the low frequency (LF) or very low frequency noise (VLF) radiation is a primary approach for underwater sound detection. Meanwhile, energy penetrates more to the bottom, and the bottom interface modulate the signal form and limit the sound field transmitted capability more seriously.

To analyze the bottom effect on LF acoustic propagation, many models were built, such as the coupled normal mode model [1-2] and the parabolic equation (PE) model [3-4]. By these model, the bathymetric effects are explained. However, not only the bathymetric affects the propagation, but the shear wave and the submarine stratification are non-negligible factors at LF acoustic propagation [5]. When the elastic property is considered in sea bottom, there will appear interfacial wave along the boundary [6]. And in shallow waveguide, the LF acoustic energy may be transmitted mainly as the interfacial wave [7]. For the submarine stratification, the PE models are built based on energy convergence, rotating coordinates or single-scattering method to solve the parameter discontinuity on the elastic boundary [8-9]. Compared with the shear wave and multi-layered model, the effect on propagation caused by multi-layered bottom is lack analysis systematically.

For this reason, a robust computational model that based on PE is introduced. In this model, the air-fluid-elastic boundary condition is carefully considered by the coordinate mapping and the reasonable physical quantities. Then, on the basis of model analysis, the common influence of frequency and sediment thickness on LF acoustic propagation is researched. Especially in the waveguides onshore or with reefs and seamount, the influence rule of multi-layered bottom has been shown. Finally, summarize the results and conclusions from the work.

2. Acoustic propagation model

The PE method is a powerful approach for solving range-dependent wave propagation problems. The equations of motion for fluid and elastic media with a cylindrical coordinate system are

$$-\rho\omega^2\Delta=\frac{\lambda}{r}\frac{\partial}{\partial r}(r\frac{\partial\Delta}{\partial r})+\frac{\partial}{\partial z}(\lambda\frac{\partial\Delta}{\partial z})+\frac{\partial}{\partial z}(\frac{\partial\lambda}{\partial z}\Delta)\cdot \tag{2.1a}$$

$$-\rho\omega^2u_r=(\lambda+2\mu)\frac{\partial^2}{\partial r^2}[\frac{1}{r}\frac{\partial}{\partial r}(ru)]+\frac{\partial^2}{\partial r\partial z}(\mu\frac{\partial u}{\partial z})+\frac{\partial\mu}{\partial z}\frac{\partial^2 w}{\partial r^2}+(\lambda+\mu)\frac{\partial^3 w}{\partial r^2\partial z}. \tag{2.1b}$$

$$-\rho\omega^2 w=\frac{\mu}{r}\frac{\partial}{\partial r}(r\frac{\partial u}{\partial z})+\frac{\partial}{\partial z}[\lambda\frac{1}{r}\frac{\partial}{\partial r}(ru)]+\frac{\mu}{r}\frac{\partial}{\partial r}(r\frac{\partial w}{\partial r})+\frac{\partial}{\partial z}[(\lambda+2\mu)\frac{\partial w}{\partial z}]. \tag{2.1c}$$

where compression amount $\Delta=\nabla\cdot\vec{u}$ and vertical displacement w are used in the fluid equation. Meanwhile, due to the continuous between elastic layers, the derivative of the horizontal displacement $u_r=\partial u/\partial r$ and the vertical displacement w are used in the elastic equation.

In far field, replace the physical quantities with factor $1/\sqrt{r}$, and introduce the operator theory, Eqs (2.1a), (2.1b) and (2.1c) can be described as:

$$L_{11}^{l}\frac{\partial^2\Delta}{\partial r^2}+M^{l}\Delta=0. \tag{2.2a}$$

$$\boldsymbol{L}^{s}\frac{\partial^2}{\partial r^2}\begin{bmatrix}u_r\\ w\end{bmatrix}+\boldsymbol{M}^{s}\begin{bmatrix}u_r\\ w\end{bmatrix}=0. \tag{2.2b}$$

Assuming that outgoing energy dominates, and extracting the phase factor, the fluid parabolic differential equation and elastic differential parabolic equation can be obtained,

$$\frac{\partial\Delta}{\partial r}=ik_0(-1+\sqrt{1+X_l})\Delta. \tag{2.3a}$$

$$\frac{\partial}{\partial r}\begin{bmatrix}u_r\\ w\end{bmatrix}=ik_0(-\boldsymbol{I}+\sqrt{\boldsymbol{I}+\boldsymbol{X}_s})\begin{bmatrix}u_r\\ w\end{bmatrix}. \tag{2.3b}$$

where fluid operator and elastic operator matrix are respectively

$$k_0^2 X_l = L_{11}^{l\ -1} M^l - k_0^2,\ \ k_0^2 \boldsymbol{X}_s = \boldsymbol{L}^{s^{-1}} \boldsymbol{M}^s - k_0^2 \boldsymbol{I}.$$

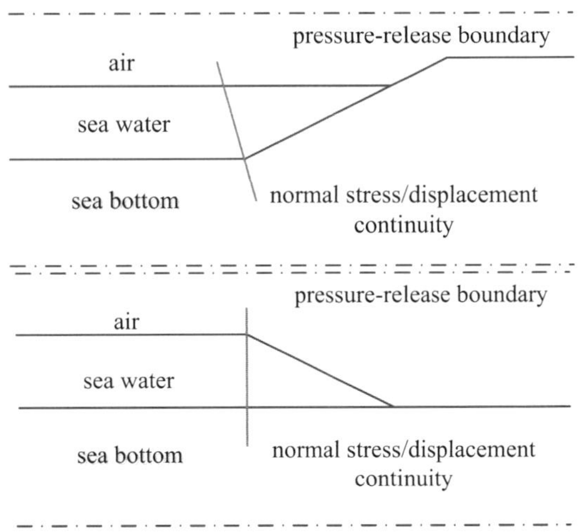

(a) Waveguide before mapping ++ (b) Waveguide after mapping

Fig. 1. The range-dependent waveguide before and after the mapping.

The physical quantities are continuous in fluid or elastic media, so the differential parabolic equation can be computed directly using a discrete algorithm. At the interface of fluid to elastic, only the continuum conditions cannot express the boundary conditions properly. Then, some corrections based on energy-conserving, single-scattering under steps approximation [3,8-9] have been developed. These approaches provide improved accuracy, but the problem has not been fully resolved. For this reason, a coordinate mapping approach is considered in the paper. The approach can map the range-dependent fluid-elastic interface to range-dependent surface boundary, as shown in Fig. (1). Assuming $H(r)$ is the ocean depth and H_0 is the constant depth, make the coordinate mapping as:

$$\begin{bmatrix} \widetilde{r} \\ \widetilde{z} \end{bmatrix} = \begin{bmatrix} r \\ z - H(r) + H_0 \end{bmatrix}. \tag{2.4}$$

By the coordinate mapping approach and the high-order Padé theory, the outgoing recursion equation can be written as:

$$\Delta(\widetilde{r} + \Delta\widetilde{r}, \widetilde{z}) = \prod_{j_p=1}^{N_p} [1 + \beta_{j_p}^{N_p} \widetilde{X}_l]^{-1} [1 + \alpha_{j_p}^{N_p} \widetilde{X}_l] \Delta(\widetilde{r}, \widetilde{z}). \tag{2.5a}$$

$$\begin{bmatrix} u_r(\widetilde{r} + \Delta\widetilde{r}, \widetilde{z}) \\ w(\widetilde{r} + \Delta\widetilde{r}, \widetilde{z}) \end{bmatrix} = \prod_{j_p=1}^{N_p} [\boldsymbol{I} + \beta_{j_p}^{N_p} \widetilde{\boldsymbol{X}}_s]^{-1} [\boldsymbol{I} + \alpha_{j_p}^{N_p} \widetilde{\boldsymbol{X}}_s] \begin{bmatrix} u_r(\widetilde{r}, \widetilde{z}) \\ w(\widetilde{r}, \widetilde{z}) \end{bmatrix}. \tag{2.5b}$$

where $\Delta\widetilde{r}$ is the range step, $\alpha_{j_p}^{N_p}$ and $\beta_{j_p}^{N_p}$ are the parameters of the Padé approximation of order N_p. In these equations, high order term $H'(r)\partial/\partial z$ is neglect when assume the slope of the interface is small. Though the Eqs (2.5) are the same form with (2.3), in Eqs (2.5) there's no need to use steps approximation and there wouldn't be sudden change for parameters at fluid to elastic vertical steps interface.

Since the mapping is not conformal, terms that depend on slope are introduced into the equation. The sound field in the mapping coordinate isn't corresponding to the sound field in the original coordinate and it is not continuous. According to the Eq (2.4), the Δ, w and u_r can be corrected as Eqs (2.6) based on the geometry and rotating coordinate.

$$\begin{bmatrix}\Delta(\tilde{r},\tilde{z})\\ w(\tilde{r},\tilde{z})\end{bmatrix}\Bigg|_r = \exp[-ik_0(\tilde{z}-H_0)\sin\delta]\begin{bmatrix}\Delta(\tilde{r},\tilde{z})\\ w(\tilde{r},\tilde{z})\end{bmatrix}\Bigg|_l . \tag{2.6a}$$

$$\begin{bmatrix}u_r(\tilde{r},\tilde{z})\\ w(\tilde{r},\tilde{z})\end{bmatrix}\Bigg|_r = \exp[-ik_0(\tilde{z}-H_0)\sin\delta]\begin{bmatrix}u_r(\tilde{r},\tilde{z})\\ w(\tilde{r},\tilde{z})\end{bmatrix}\Bigg|_l . \tag{2.6b}$$

In the Eqs (2.6), δ is the change in slop between two regions, the exponential term is the leading-order correction.

3. The model analysis

To indicate the advantage of the coordinate mapping method for the waveguide with fluid-elastic interface, a sloping waveguide with parameters as shown in Fig. (2) is considered, and the sound fields are computed by the energy-conservation method and the coordinate mapping method. The transmission losses (TLs) are compared in Fig. (3).

The results illustrate that the TL become different from the beginning of the upslope, and the difference increases cumulatively with the range increasing. For this difference, the cause is that the energy-conservation term only affects the amplitude of the physical field and it only correct the expansion quantity in the paraxial. Meanwhile, an obvious fluctuation is can be seen in the TL computed by the energy-conservation method at the range of 9*km*. The result is mainly caused by the first order finite difference in calculate the stress T_{zz}. While, the high order finite difference is used in the result of the coordinate mapping method.

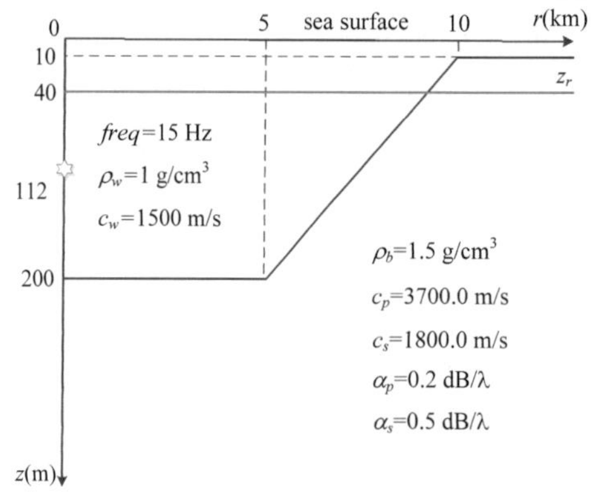

Fig. 2. An ocean waveguide with an elastic upslope bottom.

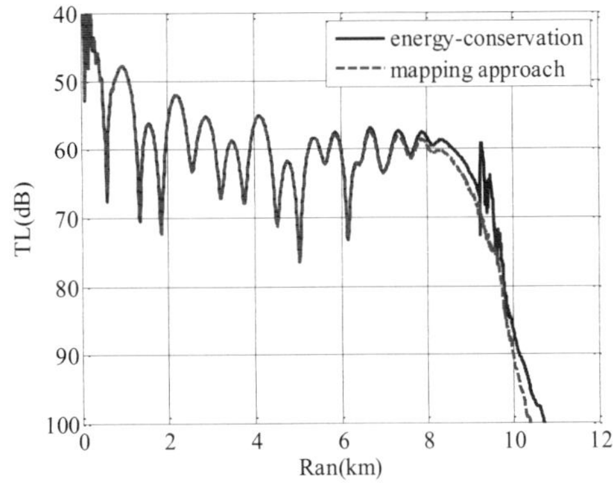

Fig. 3. Sound field in the waveguide with an elastic bottom

4. The analysis of multi-layered sea bottom

4.1. The effect in different frequency and sediment thickness cases

The effect caused by the multi-layered bottom to the propagation is obvious related to the sound frequency (wavelength) and the thickness of the sediment. To evaluate the influence, we consider a range-independent case with a fluid sediment covering an elastic basement. The schematic of the problem is shown in Fig. (4). Figure (5) shows the TL at different frequencies (20Hz, 40Hz, 50Hz and 100Hz) with sediment in different thickness ($0m$, $10m$, $20m$ and $50m$). As shown in Fig. (5), the sediment can be considered as the supplement of the water, and the transmission ability of the LF sound energy is enhanced in general. When the frequency increasing, the effect caused by the sediment will weaken, and how the sediment influence the propagation will vary. For example, at 50Hz, when the sediment is sufficient thick enough, very little sound energy penetrate to the basement, so the sediment can be seen as a half-space slow-speed bottom. This would cause a larger TL at far field.

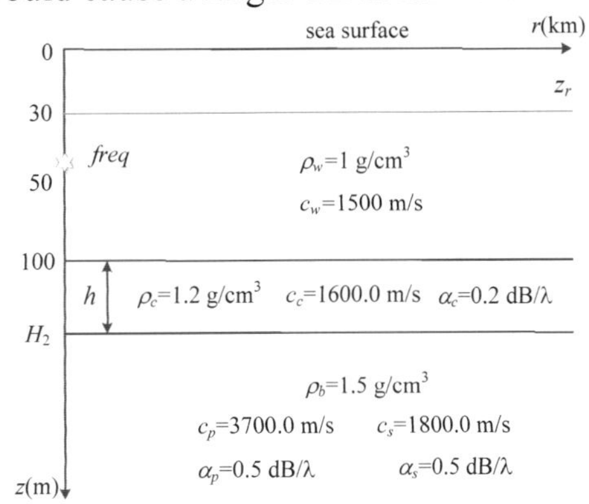

Fig. 4. Schematic of a range-independent shallow water waveguide with a fluid sediment

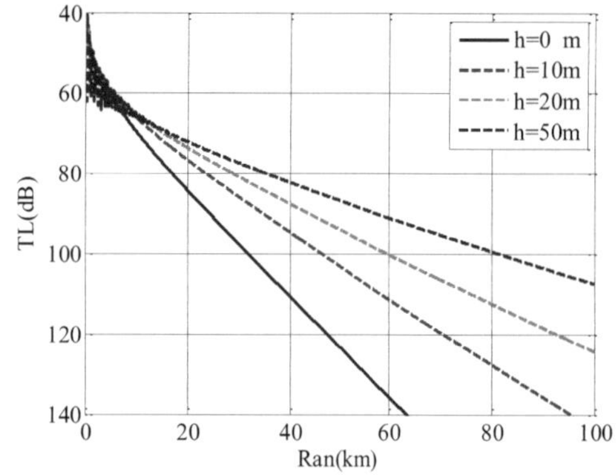

(a) The case of freq=20Hz

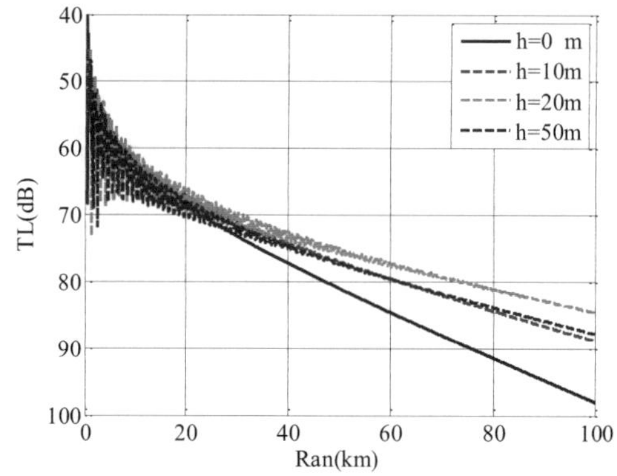

(b) The case of freq=40Hz

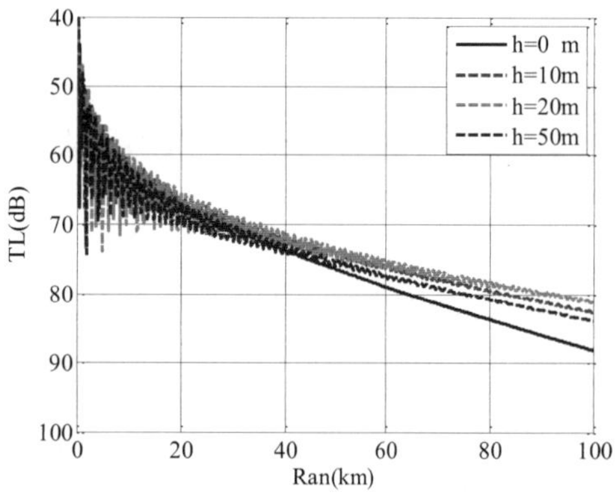

(c) The case of freq=50Hz

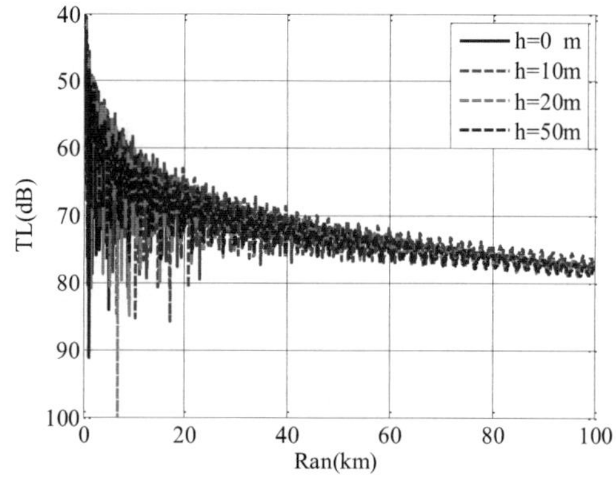

(d) The case of freq=100Hz

Fig. 5. Transmission loss at different frequencies with sediment in different thickness.

4.2. Sound propagation in the reefs environment

Reefs and their adjacent areas often have stable multi-layered bottom because of the geologic structure and the motion of the sea. The reef environment used is shown as Fig. (6), and the sound fields in the waveguide with different sediment thickness h are calculated. The result is appeared in Fig. (7).

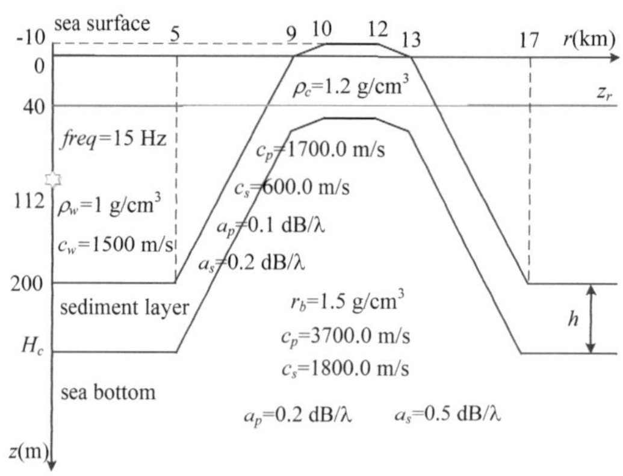

Fig. 6. The reef environment used for simulation.

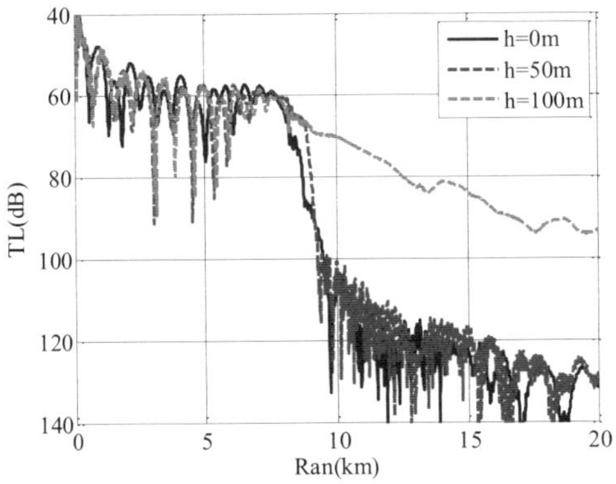

(a) TL at the receive depth

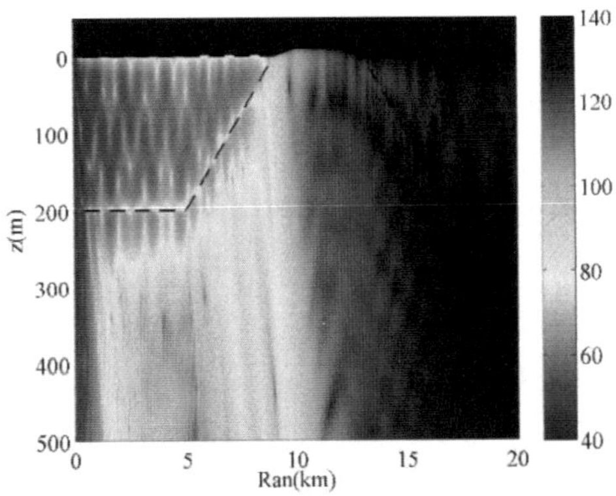

(b) The sound pressure when h=0m

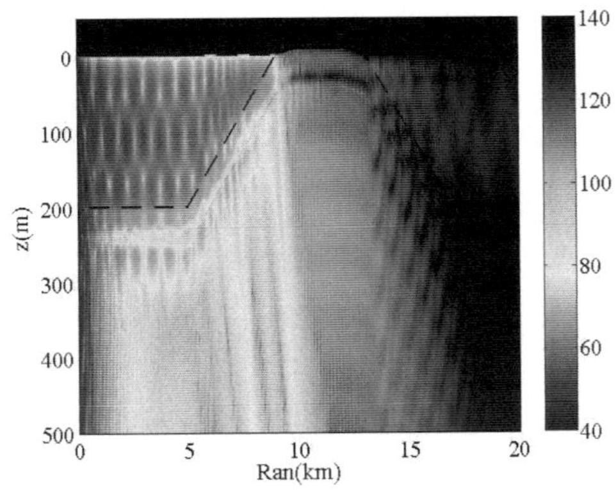

(c) The sound pressure when h=50m

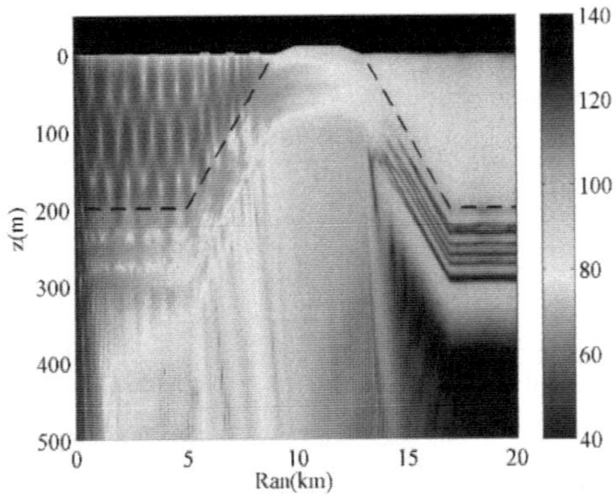

(d) The sound pressure when h=100m

Fig. 7. The sound field in reef waveguides with sediment for different thickness.

Compared with half-infinite sea bottom, the acoustic energy can be transmitted by the path of multi-layered bottom and especially when the sediment thickness is greater than one wavelength. The sound energy penetrates more to the sediment as the ocean becoming shallower, and the acoustic signal can be received on the areas after reefs. The results in Fig. (7) can also suggest that the interfacial energy is stronger at the elastic to elastic interface.

5. Summary

The mapping solution has been implement in the $[\Delta, w]$ in water and $[u_r, w]$ in elastic column formulation to obtain an approach for accurately solving a large class of ocean-acoustic problems involving layered elastic sediments. The sound field computation model based on coordinate mapping parabolic equation method can deal with elastic multi-layered bottom properly and the program is more stable and efficient.

Based on the model, the effect caused by multi-layered bottom is analyzed. This effect is related to the thickness of the sediment and the frequency. And only at VLF, the effect is proportional to the thickness of the sediment. At VLF, the acoustic energy can be propagated more efficiently in the waveguide made up of multi-layered bottom because sediment can be described as the supplement of the water. Especially in the beach or reefs environment, due to the existence of the multi-layered sea bottom, the acoustic signal can be received on the shore or after reefs. What's more, the intensity of interface wave between elastic layers is higher than that between liquid-elastic layers.

Acknowledgments

This work was supported by the National Natural Science Foundation of China (Grant No. 11804360), and the IACAS Young Elite Researcher Project (Grant No. QNYC201703).

References

[1] B. E. McDonald, "Bathymetric and volumetric contributions toc ocean acoustic mode coupling," *J. Acoustic. Soc. Am.*, **100**(1) (1996), 219-224.
[2] Y. X. Mo, S. C. Piao, H. G. Zhang and L. Li, "Mode coupling and energy transfer in a range-dependent waveguide," *Acta. Phys. Sin.*, **63**(21) (2014), 214302.
[3] M. D. Collins, "A single-scattering correction for the seismo-aciustic parabolic equation," *J. Acoustic. Soc. Am.*, **131**(4) (2012), 2638-2642.
[4] J. Tang, S. C. Piao and H. G. Zhang, "Three-dimensional parabolic equation model for seismo-acoustic propagation: Theoretical development and preliminary numerical implementation," *Chinese Physics B.*, **26**(11) (2017), 114301.
[5] L. C. Lu and L. Ma, "Acoustic characteristics of the seabed," *Physics*, **43**(11) (2014), 717-722.
[6] F. B. Jensen, W. A. Kuperman, M. B. Porter and H. Schmidt, "Computational Ocean Acoustics," *New York: Springer*, (2011), 643-647.
[7] H. G. Zhang, S. C. Piao and S. E. Yang, "Propagation of seismic waves caused by underwater infrasound," *J. Harb. Eng. Univ.*, **31**(7) (2010), 879-887.
[8] M. D. Collins and W. L. Siegmann, "Treatment of a sloping fluid-solid interface and sediment layering with the seismo-acoustic parabolic equation," *J. Acoustic. Soc. Am.*, **137**(1) (2015), 492-497.
[9] M. D. Collins and D. K. Dacol, "A mapping approach for handling sloping interfaces," *J. Acoustic. Soc. Am.*, **107**(4) (2000), 1937-1942.

Estimation of Sediment Parameter Based on Supervised Machine Learning: Preliminary Results from at-sea Data

Haiyan Ni[1], Wenbo Wang[1], Qunyan Ren [2*], Licheng Lu[2], and Li Ma [2]

1, Key Laboratory of Underwater Acoustic Environment, Institute of Acoustics, Chinese Academy of Sciences, University of Chinese Academy of Sciences, Beijing,
100190, China

2, Key Laboratory of Underwater Acoustic Environment, Institute of Acoustics, Chinese Academy of Sciences,
Beijing, 100190, China
renqunyan@mail.ioa.ac.cn

In this study, the feasibility of artificial neural networks in sediment classification and parameter estimation has been discussed. In 2018, an experiment was conducted by simultaneously using a single-beam echo sounder and a multibeam sonar system in Qingdao sea area, China. The mean angular response extracted from the multibeam backscattered data was exploited as the input parameter in backpropagation neural networks (BPNN) to estimate the sediment properties. The neural network mines the connection between the input parameters and label information, and then used to predict the mean grain size value of the surface sediment. The estimated index of mean grain size from single-beam data inversion was utilized as a training label corresponding to the input multibeam data in neural networks, consistent with the ground-truth information. The preliminary results from at-sea data demonstrate that the maximum prediction accuracy of the neural-network-based method is 97% with an absolute error tolerance of 0.1 with respect to the mean grain size prediction.

Keywords: Sediment characterization; acoustic echo-sounding; artificial neural network

1. Introduction

Clearly understanding the structure and properties of the ocean sediment is crucial for hydrographic surveying and underwater sound propagation. Therefore, sediment classification and characterization are extensively studied using multiple acoustic sonar systems, including single-beam echo sounders (SBESs), side-scan sonars (SSSs), and multibeam echo sounders (MBESs) [1, 2, 3]. SBESs have been extensively used for many years and can typically obtain strong echo signals from a small location due to the narrow beam coverage, which cannot satisfy the demand for large areas in survey research. As a supplementary tool, MBESs, renowned for their large coverage and narrow beam angles, make fine seafloor imaging and measurement possible. The backscatter data collected using the MBESs demonstrate differences observed in case of different sediment types, which are exploitable for seafloor classification and parameter estimation.

Artificial neural networks (ANNs), which are data-driven, have been gradually applied to sediment classification and characterization. As a kind of supervised machine learning method, ANNs can be used to automatically learn a mapping relation from the input to output (or labels) data pairs [4]. With respect to sediment analysis, the backscatter data obtained from an MBES system can be utilized as the input data, and the specific sediment type or property parameters are the corresponding training labels in an ANN. The neural network intelligently mines the connection between the input parameters and label information when it is being trained; thus, the ANN can predict the surface sediment parameter values if trained properly. However, because of the limitation of the sampling method, the real-time properties of the seafloor sediment are difficult to obtain directly. Therefore, an alternative method has been proposed in this study. When combined with the analysis results of the SBES systems, the mean grain size (M_z) values are utilized as the ground-truth information to label multibeam backscatter data, which are representative parameters of the surficial sediment obtained from the SBES geoacoustic inversion.

2. Data for Sediment Characterization

2.1. Training Data

In 2018, an experiment was conducted offshore Qingdao, China [5], a single-beam echo sounder and a multibeam sonar system were simultaneously used in this experiment. The backscatter data obtained using the MBES demonstrate different responses when the incident angle changes under different sediment-type conditions. This intrinsic physical phenomenon can be used to classify the sediment type and predict the sediment properties. Thus, the mean angular response curves extracted from the backscatter data were used as the input data during the ANN training process.

2.2. Label

M_z, typically in units of φ, is the negative logarithm of the grain diameter of the sediment substrates, as presented in Eq. (2.1). According to approximate classification, the sediment type can be classified as gravel, sand, and mud. Their corresponding M_z values have been approximately presented in Table (1) [6]. However, the actual distribution of M_z is much more complicated because of the broad range of grain sizes in coarse sediments. Although there is no one-to-one correspondence between M_z and the sediment type, M_z can be used to represent and create a general classification of the substrate.

$$M_z = -\log(d) \tag{2.1}$$

Note that the grain diameter d is presented in millimeters.

The traditional method to obtain M_z, typically based on the drilling sampling methods, is extremely expensive and time consuming. In addition, the sampling methods generally target single discrete points; therefore, it is difficult to continuously describe the sediment information for the whole ship route in this experiment. Thus, in the proposed method, the inverted parameters of the surficial sediment from SBESs are utilized as the ground-truth information to label the multibeam backscatter data. M_z is obtained using a model-based inversion scheme as illustrated in [5]. Figure 1 presents the inverted values along the whole ship track.

Table 1. The Wentworth sediment classification scheme [6]

Grain diameter range (in φ unit)	Detailed Classification	Coarse Classification
< -8	Boulder	Gravel
-8 –6	Cobble	Gravel
-6 –2	Pebble	Gravel
-2 –1	Granule	Gravel
$-1 - 0$	Very coarse sand	Sand
0-1	Coarse sand	Sand
1-2	Medium sand	Sand
2-3	Fine sand	Sand
3-4	Very fine sand	Sand
4-8	Silt particle	Mud
>8	Clay particle	Mud

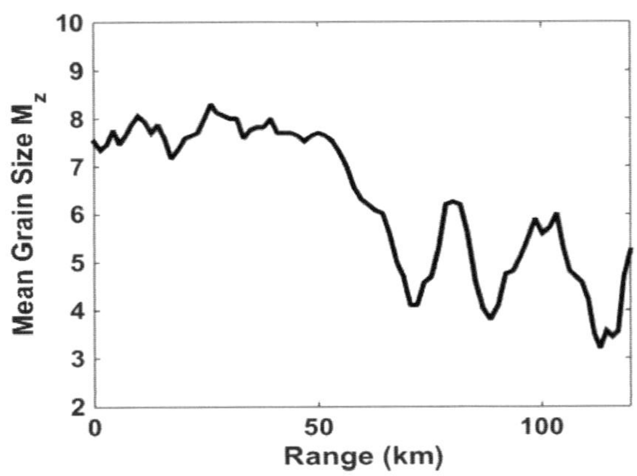

Fig. 1. The mean grain size M_z inverted from the SBES envelopes [5].

3. Artificial Neural Networks

3.1. M-P Neuron Model

The most fundamental part of neural networks is the M–P neuron model [7], which is obtained based on the biological neural structures. In this model, a neuron receives an input signal x_k from other neuron as presented in Fig. 2. Weighted by connections, these input signals z are transferred using a nonlinear activation function f to obtain the neuron output y.

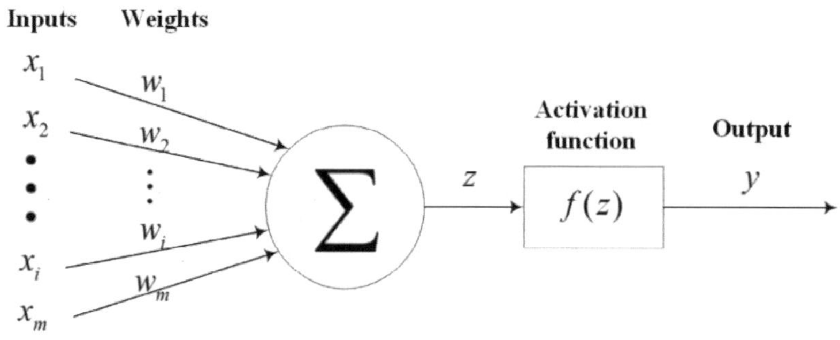

Fig. 2. The M–P neuron model

In this model, the informational flow from input to output is expressed using Eqs. (3.1) and (3.2), where x_k and w_k denote the input and connection weight from the kth neuron, respectively. In addition, b represents the biases or threshold value.

$$z = \sum_{k=1}^{m} w_k x_k + b. \tag{3.1}$$

$$y = f(z). \tag{3.2}$$

3.2. Neural Networks

A neural network can be obtained by connecting many M–P neurons in a certain hierarchical structure. Such a network is essentially a parametric model obtained by nesting the nodes in each layer transmitted in a layer-by-layer manner. In each layer, the neuron output can be obtained by weighting and activating the output value of the upper layer node. For a multilayer neural network, the output of the lth layer can be expressed as a matrix (Eq. (3.3)). Here, the forward propagation process of the neural network uses several weight coefficient matrices $\mathbf{W}$ and bias matrices $\mathbf{b}$ to perform a series of linear and activation operations based on the input value vector $\mathbf{X}$.

$$\mathbf{X}^{(l)} = f(\mathbf{z}^{(l)}) = f(\mathbf{W}^{(l)}\mathbf{X}^{(l-1)} + \mathbf{b}^{(l)}) \tag{3.3}$$

The forward propagation process establishes the mapping relation from input to output. However, this process is not complete until the backward propagation of errors in neural networks is complete. Here, the error backpropagation algorithm is the most important tool for optimizing and upgrading the network parameters.

The backpropagation algorithm transmits the error between the output value and the real value of the network from the back to the front. The initial step is to calculate the loss function between the network output X and the real value y as shown in Eq. (3.4) Here, the performance function is the mean squared error (MSE). In the second step, the gradient of the loss function of each layer parameter is calculated to get the weight correction Δw (Eq. (3.5)). η denotes the learning rate. Finally, the connection parameters in the neural networks are updated (Eq. (3.6)).

$$J = mse\left(X^l - y\right) \tag{3.4}$$

$$\Delta w = -\eta \frac{\partial J}{\partial w} \tag{3.5}$$

$$w \leftarrow w + \Delta w \tag{3.6}$$

4. Application and Results

4.1. Application

The mean angular response curves obtained from the multibeam backscattered data are used as the input parameters in the BPNN to estimate the surface sediment M_z values. The M_z values are the training labels of the input multibeam data in the training process and the output of the neural networks in the testing process. In the training process, the neural network establishes a connection between the input multibeam data and the label M_z values. Subsequently, the developed relation can be used to predict the M_z value of the multibeam backscatter test data.

Further, the multibeam backscatter data on the entire ship track are divided into the training (80%) and testing (20%) datasets. Using Levenberg–Marquardt, which is an improved BP training algorithm, the neural network is adapted for parameter estimation.

4.2. Results

The accuracy of the estimated M_z values was evaluated by comparing the MSE values, the correlation coefficient (R), and the accuracy rate within the absolute error tolerance. These values were obtained based on the estimated values and the actual label values of the mean grain size during the training and testing processes. As presented in Table 2, the small estimation error and high accuracy rate obtained using the testing dataset denote the high prediction accuracy.

Table 2. The performance evaluation criteria

Criteria	Testing	Testing
MSE Error	0.00098	0.0010
Correlation Value	0.99978	0.9998
Accuracy Rate (error tolerance of 0.1)	———	97.84%
Accuracy Rate (error tolerance of 0.25)	———	100%
0.99978	0.999	

5. Conclusion

Herein, we discussed the application of ANNs in sediment characterization. The mean angular response curves of the MBES backscatter data were utilized as the input data, and the corresponding M_z values of the surficial sediment were used as labels during the ANN training process, obtained based on SBES inversion. During the testing process, the trained neural network model provided the estimated M_z values of different MBES backscatter data as the output. Furthermore, the small estimation error and high accuracy rate demonstrate the feasibility of applying ANNs for sediment parameter estimation.

Acknowledgments

The authors are thankful for the support of project 11604360 funded by the National Science Foundation of China.

References

[1] Siemes, K, M Snellen, A. R Amiri-Simkooei, D. G Simons, and J. P Hermand, "Predicting Spatial Variability of Sediment Properties From Hydrographic Data for Geoacoustic Inversion." IEEE Journal of Oceanic Engineering 2010. 35 (4) 766-778.
[2] Berthold, T., A. Leichter, B. Rosenhahn, V. Berkhahn, and J. Valerius, "Seabed sediment classification of side-scan sonar data using convolutional neural networks." IEEE Symposium Series on Computational Intelligence (SSCI), 27 Nov.-1 Dec. 2017.
[3] Parnum, Iain M, and Alexander N Gavrilov. "High-frequency multibeam echo-sounder measurements of seafloor backscatter in shallow water: Part 2 – Mosaic production, analysis and classification." Underwater Technology the International Journal of the Society for Underwater 2011. 30 (1):13-26(14).
[4] Bianco, Michael J., Peter Gerstoft, James Traer, Emma Ozanich, and Weichang Li, "Machine learning in acoustics: a review". 2019.
[5] Licheng Lu, Haiyan Ni, Wenbo Wang, Li Ma, JianChun Huang, Qunyan Ren, "Experimental results of sediment characterization by processing backscatter envelope of single-beam Sonar," Procc. Of OCEANS '19 Marseille, 2019.
[6] Chotiros N P, Acoustics of the Seabed as a Poroelastic Medium[M]. Springer International Publishing, 2017.
[7] Zhou Zhihua, Machine learning[M], Tsinghua University Press, 2015.

Influence of Periodic Corrugated Surfaces on the Generation and Propagation of Scholte Wave

Minshuai Liang[1],Gaokun Yu[1],Linhui Peng[1]

1, Department of Marine Technology , Ocean University of China, 266100, Qingdao, Shandong, China

Liang_0719@126.com

gky@ouc.edu.cn

penglh@ouc.edu.cn

This paper studies influence of periodic corrugated surfaces on the generation and propagation of Scholte wave. The coupling relation between parameters of periodic surfaces and the generation frequency of Scholte wave is studied through theoretical analysis which includes the theoretical derivations on dispersive velocity equation of Scholte wave and scattering coefficient equations of periodic corrugated surfaces,and also the calculation model has been set up by using finite element method, and numerical calculations prove that theory is correct. Through comparing results of theoretical calculations and numerical simulations, conclusions can be obtained that periodic corrugated surfaces play a role in the generation of Scholte wave, the finite-length periodic corrugated surfaces and hard seabed are the key factors for the generating long-range Scholte wave.

Keywords: Periodic corrugated surfaces; Scholte wave.

1. Introduction

The very-low-frequency(VLF) sound has a very small attenuation in seawater, and it can propagate for a long distance underwater, so it is playing a significant role in ocean detections and communications[1]. In fact, ocean is a natural waveguide environment, especially in some shallow water areas where there will low-frequency cutoffs, making it difficult to measure signals of VLF sound in sea water. In recent years, some studies have shown that the Scholte wave on the surface of seabed probably is a way for long-distance propagation of VLF sound.[2][3][4][5][6]

Studies on Scholte wave have shown that the phase velocity of Scholte wave is lower than the velocity in water, lower than longitudinal and shear wave in solid, it means the wavenumber of Scholte wave is large[7], so when the flat "fluid-solid" surface is used in the study model, a strong Scholte wave can be generated only when the sound source is close to the surface of seabed[8].

In fact, the surface of seabed is rough. Scatterings on corrugated seabed can compromise the distribution of sound field on the seabed[9][10], and eventually affect the generation and propagation of Scholte wave[11]. This means a strong Scholte wave can also possibly be generated with a source far away from the surface of seabed. Therefore, the characteristics of corrugated surface are considered in the study model of Scholte wave, and influence of periodic corrugated surfaces on the generation and propagation of Scholte wave is studied in this paper.

2. Theoretical Analysis

2.1. Theoretical relationship of generation of Scholte wave on horizontal surface

The horizontally stratified structure is used to study the generation of Scholte wave on horizontal surface. The calculation model is shown in Fig(1).

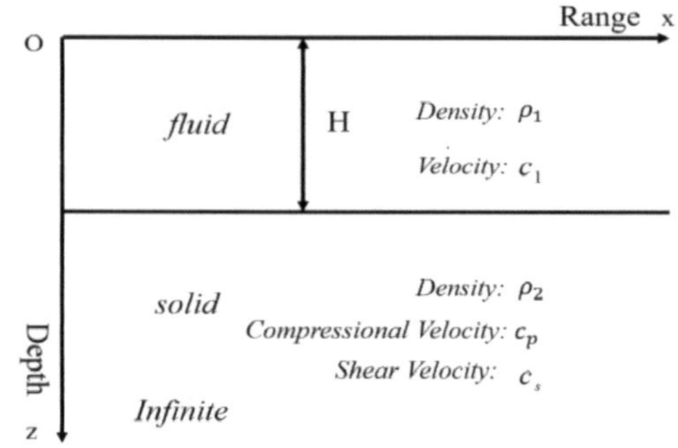

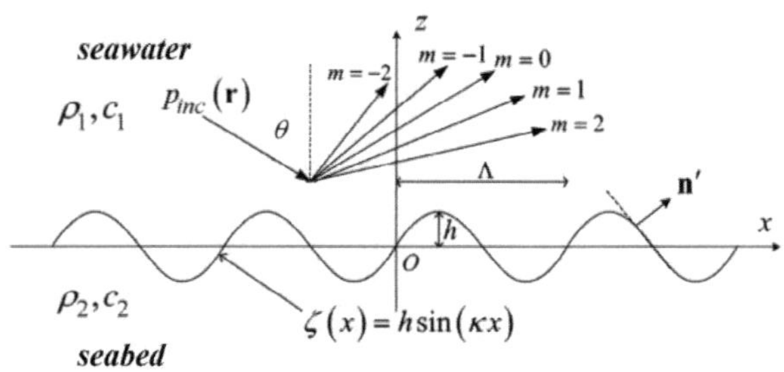

Figure 1 Clculation model of horizontal surface Figure 2 The surface of sinusoidal periodic corrugated seafloor

The upper layer is seawater, the depth is H and the lower layer is infinite elastic seabed According to boundary condition: when z=0, sound pressure is 0; when z=h, stress and normal displacement are continuous. The velocity equation of Scholte wave can be obtained.

$$\left(2-\frac{c^2}{c_s^2}\right)^2-4\sqrt{1-\frac{c^2}{c_s^2}}\sqrt{1-\frac{c^2}{c_p^2}}+\frac{c^4}{c_s^4}\frac{\sqrt{1-\frac{c^2}{c_p^2}}}{\sqrt{1-\frac{c^2}{c_1^2}}}\frac{\rho_1}{\rho_2}\tanh\left(\frac{\omega}{c}\sqrt{1-\frac{c^2}{c_1^2}}H\right)=0 \tag{2.1}$$

It can be obtained that the establishment of this equation is related to the frequency of source and the depth of seawater H. Therefore, it can be obtained that the Scholte wave on the surface has dispersive characteristics in this case.

2.2. Theoretical Relationship of Generation of Scholte Wave on Periodic Corrugated Surfaces

2.2.1. Reflection and transmission coefficient

Study the case where the seabed is a sinusoidal periodic corrugated surface, and the theoretical analysis is based on the Rayleigh hypothesis.

The sinusoidal periodic corrugated surfaces are shown in Fig.(2).The upper layer is infinite seawater, and the lower layer is infinite elastic seabed.According to the boundary condition: stress and normal displacement are continuous on the seabed surface. In this case, the surface is sinusodial, the stress in x and y direction is continuous respectively.

The normal displacement can be expressed as follows:

$$\vec{u}_w \cdot \nabla g = \vec{u}_b \cdot \nabla g \tag{2.2}$$

$$-f'(x)u_w + v_w = -f'(x)u_b + v_b \tag{2.3}$$

And the stress can be expressed as:

$$\left[(\nabla g)_x \quad (\nabla g)_z\right]\begin{bmatrix} T_{xxw} & T_{xzw} \\ T_{zxw} & T_{zzw} \end{bmatrix} = \left[(\nabla g)_x \quad (\nabla g)_z\right]\begin{bmatrix} T_{xxb} & T_{xzb} \\ T_{zxb} & T_{zzb} \end{bmatrix} \tag{2.4}$$

According to wave equation and boundary condition, coefficient equations can be obtained.

$$\sum_m A_m^r \frac{I_{p-m}\left(k_{1z}^m\right)}{k_{1z}^m}\left[k_1^2 - k_x^m k_x^p\right] - \sum_m A_m^t \frac{I_{p-m}\left(k_{2z}^m\right)}{k_{2z}^m}\left[k_2^2 - k_x^m k_x^p\right] - \sum_m B_m^s I_{p-m}\left(k_{sz}^m\right)k_x^p + \frac{I_p\left(k_z^{inc}\right)}{k_z^{inc}}\left[k_1^2 - k_x^{inc}k_x^p\right] = 0 \tag{2.5}$$

$$-\rho_1\left(k_x^p - k_x^{inc}\right)\frac{I_p\left(k_z^{inc}\right)}{k_z^{inc}} - \rho_1\sum_m A_m^r\left(k_x^p - k_x^m\right)\frac{I_{p-m}\left(k_{1z}^m\right)}{k_{1z}^m} + \rho_2\sum_m A_m^t\frac{I_{p-m}\left(k_{2z}^m\right)}{k_{2z}^m}\left[\left(k_x^p - k_x^m\right) - \frac{2\left(k_2^2 - \left(k_x^m\right)^2\right)\left(k_x^p\right)}{k_s^2}\right]$$

$$-\rho_2\left[+\sum_m B_m^s I_{p-m}\left(k_{sz}^m\right)\left(\frac{2k_x^m k_x^p}{k_s^2} - 1\right)\right] = 0 \tag{2.6}$$

$$\rho_1 I_p\left(k_z^{inc}\right) + \rho_1\sum_m A_m^r I_{p-m}\left(k_{1z}^m\right) - \rho_2\sum_m A_m^t I_{p-m}\left(k_{2z}^m\right)\left(1 - \frac{2k_x^p k_x^m}{k_s^2}\right)$$

$$+\rho_2\sum_m B_m^s\left(k_x^p - k_x^m\right)\frac{I_{p-m}\left(k_{sz}^m\right)}{k_{sz}^m}\left[2\frac{\left(k_x^m\right)^2}{k_s^2} - 1\right] + \rho_2\sum_m B_m^s I_{p-m}\left(k_{sz}^m\right)\frac{2\left(-k_{sz}^m\right)k_x^m}{k_s^2} = 0 \tag{2.7}$$

According to these equations, the reflection and transmission coefficient can be solved in this case.

Studies have shown that the hard seabed is more conducive to the generation of Scholte wave[12], so this paper is focusing on the study of hard seabed. Fig.(3) shows the results of the normal incidence of sound wave, the medium parameters and the sinusoidal surfaces parameters are shown in the table1.

Table 1 parameters of medium and surfaces

water density (kg/m³)	water velocity (m/s)	seabed density (kg/m³)	longitudinal wave velocity (m/s)	shear wave velocity (m/s)	surface period (m)	surface height (m)
1000	1500	1500	3800	1800	75	4

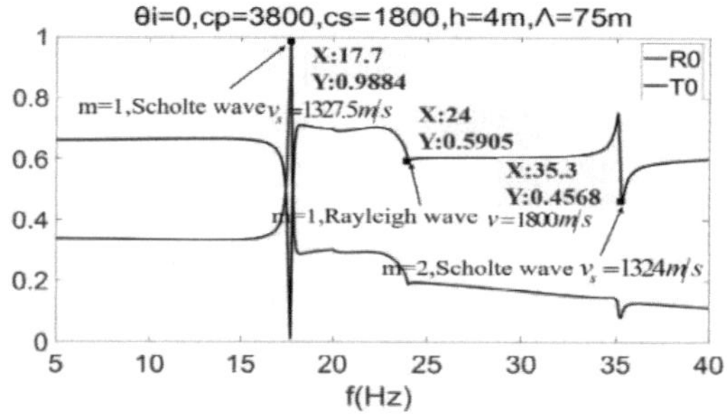

Figure 3 Reflection and transmission coefficients

Through calculation, it can be obtained that the coefficients will have a series of jump points as the frequency changes. The frequencies of these points equal to the value of WOOD[13] anomaly point and the velocities at 17.7Hz and 35.3Hz is close to the velocity of Scholte wave that are calculated in Eq.(2.1). Therefore, according to the principle of sound velocity matching, it can be considered that 17.7Hz and 35.3Hz are the generation frequencies of the Scholte wave.

2.2.2. Bragg scattering equation

According to the calculation results of coefficients above, there is a connection between the periodic corrugated surfaces and the generation of the Scholte wave. Normally, Bragg scattering will occur when sound wave propagate to the corrugated surface, so here the Bragg scattering of surfaces may play a role. To further understand this connection, the relation between the Bragg scattering of surfaces and the generation of the Scholte wave has been established below. The theoretical relation of Bragg scattering when the sound waves propagate to the surface at a fixed angle is:

$$\frac{\sin\theta_m^d}{\lambda^d}-\frac{\sin\theta^i}{\lambda^i}=\frac{m}{\Lambda}, m=\pm 1,2...,n \tag{2.8}$$

θ^i is incidence angle, θ_m^d is scattering angle, λ^i is incident wavelength, λ^d is scattering wavelength, Λ is surface period, m is order. Assuming that the scattered sound wave is a Scholte wave, the following transformation can be made.

$\lambda^i = c_i/f$, $\lambda^d = c_{sw}/f$, $\theta_m^d = \pm 90^\circ$,where c_{sw} is the velocity of Scholte wave, which can be calculated from the dispersive equation of Scholte wave.

Then the coupling relationship between Bragg scattering and the generation of Scholte wave can be obtained:

$$f=\frac{m}{\Lambda(-\frac{\sin\theta^i}{c_i}\pm\frac{1}{c_{sw}})}, m=\pm 1,2...,n \tag{2.9}$$

The matching generation frequency of Scholte wave can be obtained from this equation, and its physical interpretation is the matching of horizontal wavenumber.

3. Results of numerical calculation

3.1. The model of calculation

The array of point acoustic sources shown in Fig.(4) are used as source in this paper. The distance between two point sources: $d < \lambda/2$, the length of array: $L > \lambda/2$, and the intensity of point sources is set according to Gaussian distribution. Eg, when frequency of sources is 19.86Hz, the distance $d = 30m$.

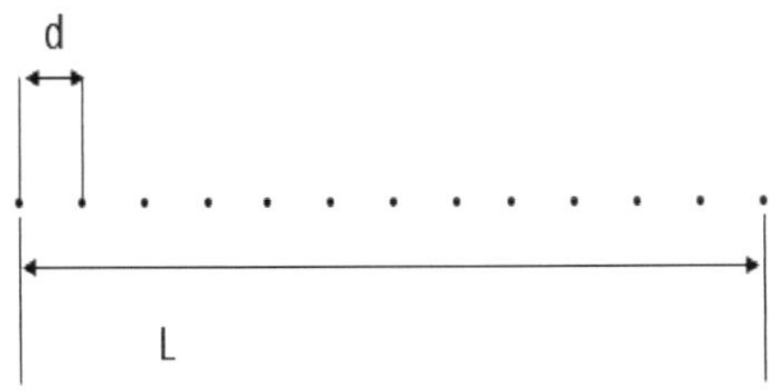

Figure 4 Point sources array

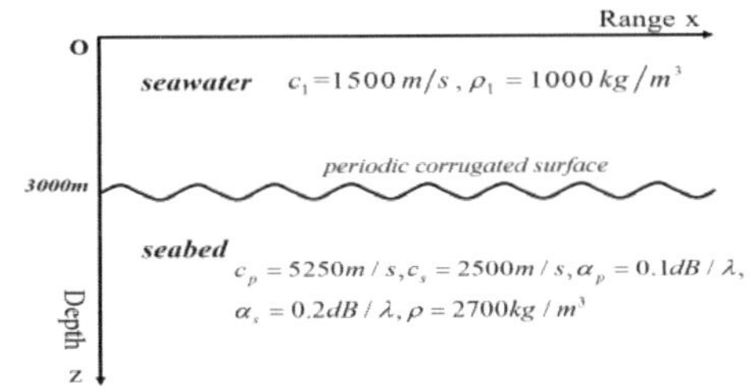

Figure 5 Environmental model

Environmental parameters are set as shown in Fig.(5), depth of water is 3000m, height of periodic corrugated surfaces is $H = 4m$,period is $\Lambda = 75m$.

According to the results of geological exploration[14][15][16], the main substance of ocean crust is basalt, so the parameters of basalt are used in environment model.

Taking those parameters into the dispersive Eq.(1), the dispersive curve of Scholte wave can be obtained, the result is shown in Fig.(6).

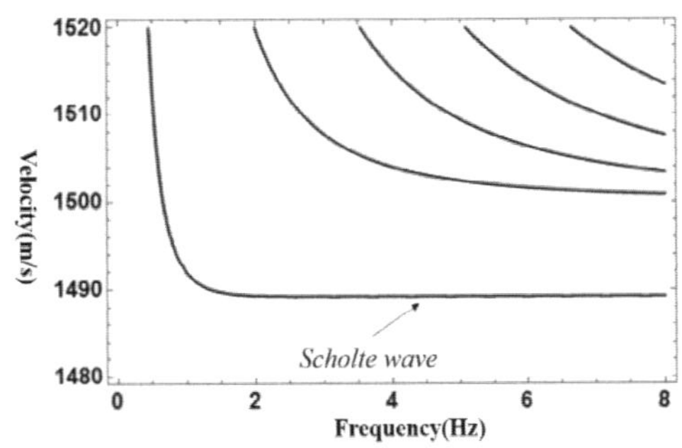

Figure 6 Dispersive curve of Scholte wave

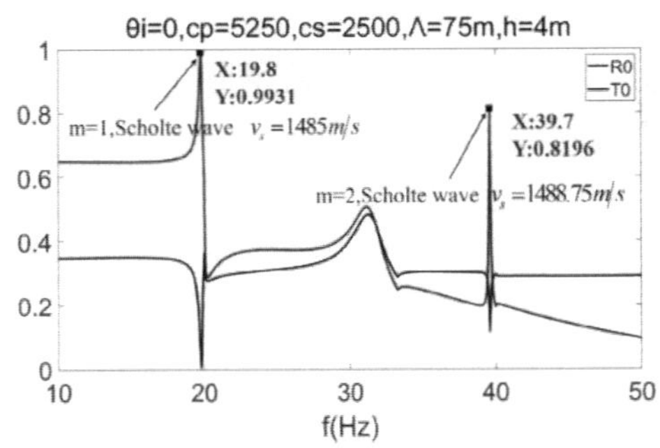

Figure 7 Reflection and transmission coefficients

According to the dispersive curve of Scholte wave, the velocity of the Scholte wave doesn't increase anymore when the frequency is higher than 2Hz, the stable velocity of the Scholte wave is $c_{sw} = 1489.26\,m/s$.

Taking the parameters of media and corrugated surface into Eqs.(5)(6)(7), and the relation of the reflection and transmission coefficients can be obtained, and the results are shown in Fig.(7).

The jump points of the reflection and transmission coefficients can be obtained, they are 19.8Hz and 39.7Hz.

Another way, taking the stable velocity of Scholte wave and parameters of corrugated surfaces into Eq.(9), the results are $\mathrm{m}=\pm 1$, $f \approx 19.86Hz$; $\mathrm{m}=\pm 2, f \approx 39.71Hz$. From above calculations, it can be found that the frequency at the jump points of reflection and transmission coefficient s equal to the result of Bragg scattering formula, and the generation frequencies of the first and second order Scholte wave is 19.8Hz and 39.7Hz, respectively. Generally, the intensity of the first-order Scholte wave is stronger than that of higher order, so the subsequent study will focus on the first-order Scholte wave.

3.2. Results of numerical calculations

The main purpose of this study is to address the issue that a strong Scholte wave can only be generated when the source is close to the surface of seabed, so the depth of sources array is set at 100m in this study, it's far away from the seabed.

3.2.1.Generation frequency

the frequency of sources is 19.8Hz, the acoustic intensities of the flat surface and periodic corrugated surfaces are calculated, respectively. The results of simulation are shown below. In order to facilitate the observation and comparison on numerical calculation results, a local enlarged view near the surface is given below.

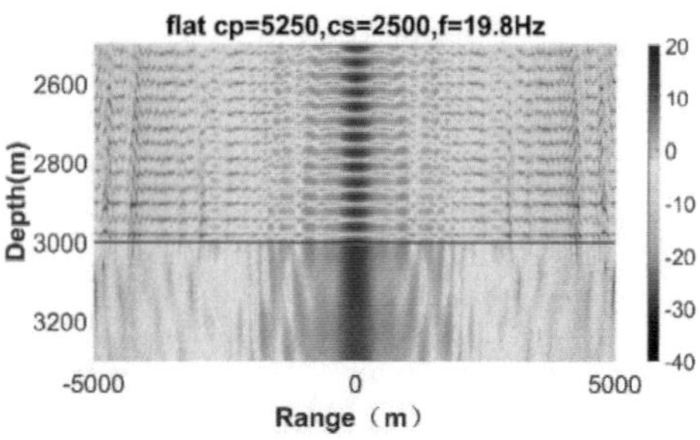

Figure 8 Intensity of flat surface

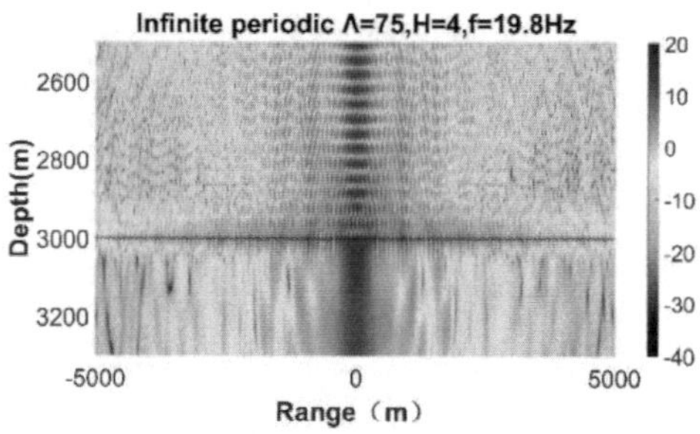

Figure 9 Intensity of periodic surface

By comparing Figs.(8)(9), it can be obtained that when the frequency of sound wave is 19.8Hz, there is an obvious generation of Scholte wave on the periodic surfaces, and when the surface is flat, the energy is transmitted into the sea bottom, and there is no generation of Scholte wave on the surface.
The frequency of sound wave is changed to 11 Hz, and the parameters of periodic corrugated surfaces are unchanged. The results are shown in Fig.(10).

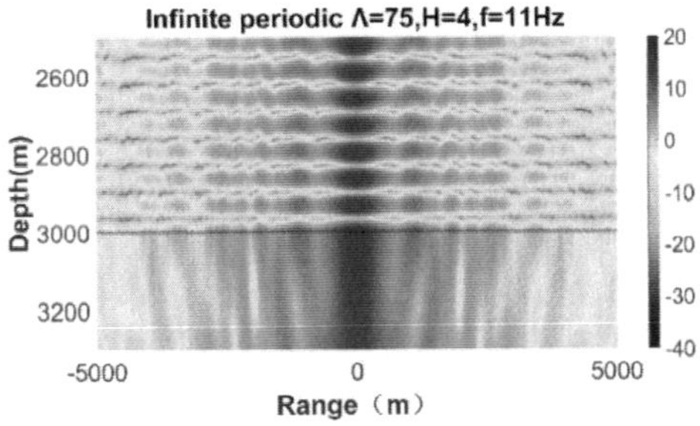

Figure 10 Intensity of periodic surface

Comparing Figs.(9)(10), it can be obtained that when the frequency of source is changed to 11 Hz, there is no generation of Scholte wave on the periodic corrugated surfaces.

From the above calculation results, it can be obtained that the periodic corrugated surfaces play a role in the generation of Scholte wave, but a strong Scholte wave can be generated only when wavenumber in water is matching with wavenumber of Scholte wave.

3.2.2. Periodic corrugated surfaces with finite length

Considering the scattering of periodic surfaces may affect the propagation of the Scholte wave, the periodic corrugated surfaces with finite length will be considered here. The parameters of periodic corrugated surfaces are set as these: height: $H=4m$, period $\Lambda=75m$.

The intensity of 2 cycle lengths and 4 cycle lengths is calculated respectively. The numerical simulation results are shown in the following figures:

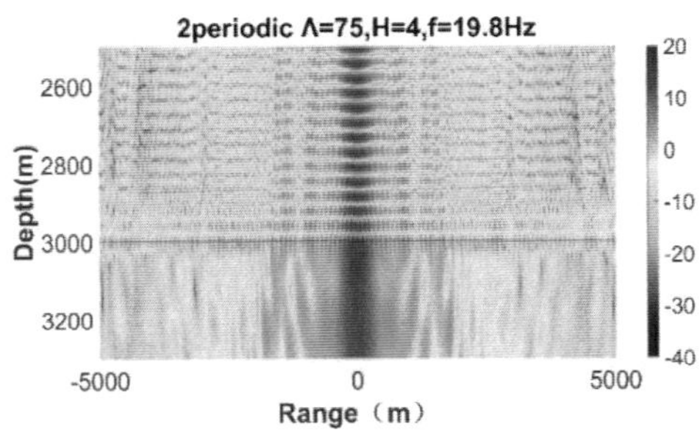

Figure 11 Intensity of 2 cycles

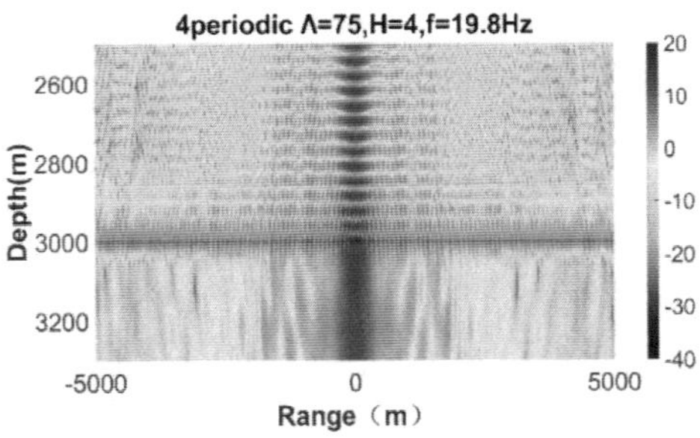

Figure 12 Intensity of 4 cycles

By comparing Figs.(11)(12)(9), it can be obtained that there is obvious generation of Scholte wave on the surface when two cycles are used; the intensity of the Scholte wave is obviously stronger than that of the infinite length of period corrugated surfaces in the case of four cycles. It means that the periodic corrugated surfaces aren't conducive to the propagation of Scholte wave due to its scattering. Therefore, judging from combination of these two factors above, the periodic corrugated surfaces of finite length is playing an important role here.

3.2.3. Long-distance propagation of Scholte wave

The influence of the periodic corrugated surfaces on the generation and propagation of Scholte wave has already been studied in the section above. In fact, it has more important practical significance only when the generated Scholte wave can propagate for a long distance.

Therefore, the condition of finite length will still be used to verify whether the Scholte wave can propagate for a long distance.
The calculation environment is set as follows, the depth of source is 100m, the depth of water is 3000m, and the frequency of source is 19.8Hz (the matching frequency of first-order Scholte wave). Due to the amounts of calculation, the max distance of numerical calculation is set to 20km. The intensity of the 4 cycles and the infinite length of periodic corrugated surfaces is calculated respectively. The calculation results are shown as follows.

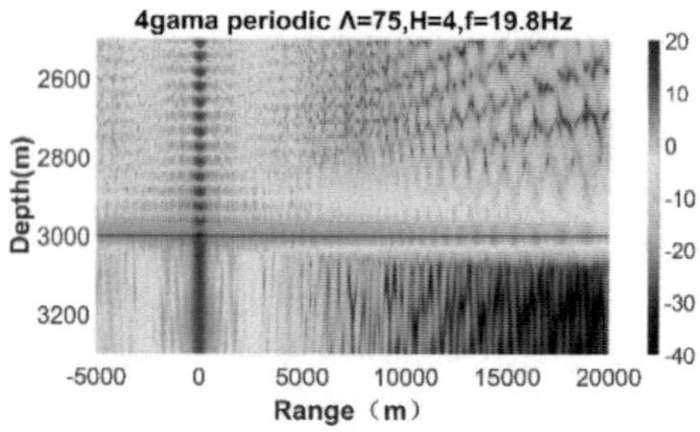

Figure 13 Intensity of 4 cycles

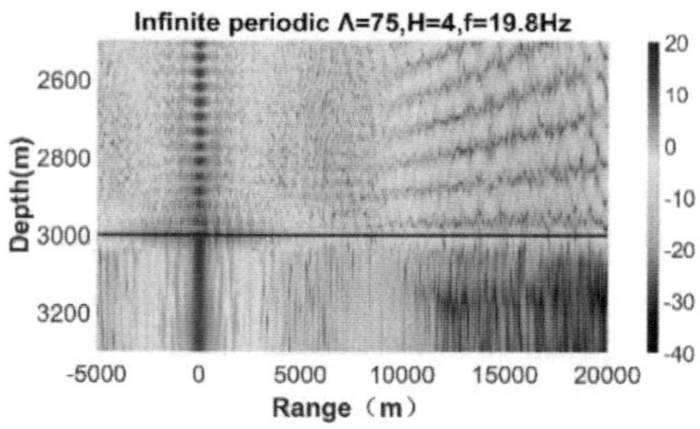

Figure 14 Intensity of periodic surface

By comparing Figs.(13)(14), it can be obtained that the intensity of the Scholte wave generated by four periods at 20km is stronger than that of the infinite-length condition, and the intensity of Scholte wave is stronger than the intensity of sound in water. Therefore, it can be obtained that then finite length of periodic corrugated surfaces is an important factor in the generation of long-distance Scholte wave.

4. Conclusions

The theoretical relation of generation of Scholte wave on periodic corrugated surfaces is derived based on the theoretical relation of generation of Scholte wave on horizontal surface, the distributions of sound field at different surfaces of seabed are calculated by finite element method and the law of influence of periodic corrugated surfaces on the generation and propagation of Scholte wave is obtained.
The velocity of sound at the frequencies of jump points of reflection and transmission coefficients and the velocity of the Scholte wave are calculated in equations. The coupling relation between Bragg scattering and Scholte wave on the periodic corrugated surfaces is established by the matching of horizontal wavenumber, and then, the coupling relation between the parameters of periodic corrugated surfaces and the matching frequencies is obtained in theory, the coupling relation is the matching of horizontal wavenumber.
By comparing the results of numerical calculations and theoretical analysis, it can be concluded that the periodic corrugated surfaces are conducive to the generation of Scholte wave, and the finite-length periodic corrugated surfaces and the hard seabed are the key factors for generation of long-distance Scholte wave.

References

[1] Yang shi e. Principles of Underwater Acoustic Propagation (in Chinese). First Edition. Harbin

Engineering University Pres, 1994 :1

[2] Dale D. Ellis and D. M. F. Chapman, A simple shallow water propagation model including shear wave effects, J. Acoust. Soc. Am. 78 (6), December 1985.

[3] John Northrop, Low-frequency sound propagation off Mission Beach, California, J. Acoustic. Soc. Am. 67:1598-1602 ,1980

[4] J. G. Scholte. The range of existence of Rayleigh and Stoneley waves. Monthly Notices, Roy. Astronomical Soc, 1947(5):120-126.

[5] Michael K. Broadhead. Scholte Wave Attenuation Estimates from Two Diverse Test Sites. IEEE, 1993(2).

[6] James A. TenCate, Thomas G. Muir, Andrea Caiti, Age Kristensen, Jason F. Manning, Jack A. Shooter, Robert A. Koch, and Enzo Michelozzi, Beamforming on Seismic Interface Waves with an Array of Geophones on the Shallow Sea Floor, IEEE JOURNAL OF OCEANIC ENGINEERING, VOL. 20, NO. 4, OCTOBER 1995.

[7] D. Rauch. Seismic interface waves in coastal waters: A review. La Spezia, Italy: SACLANTCEN Report SR-42,NATO SACLANT Undersea Research, 1980.

[8] Zhang Hai-gang, Piao Sheng-chun, Yang Shi-e. Propagation of seismic waves caused by underwater infrasound. Journal of Harbin Engineering University, Jul.2010, 31(7):879-887

[9] R. J. Urick, Principles of Underwater Sound, McGraw–Hill, New York, 1983.

[10] J. L. Uretsky, The scattering of plane waves from periodic surfaces. Annals of physics, 33, 400-415,1965.

[11] Zheng Y, Fang X, Liu J, et al. Scholte waves generated by seafloor topography. Physics, 2013.

[12] Zhang Hong-xing, Wang Meng, Zhang hai-gang, Research on Rule of Seismic Wave Propagation Caused by Underwater Source in Elastic Bottom. Technology Acoustics, Oct.2011, 30(5):45-47.

[13] R. W. Wood, "On a remarkable case of uneven distribution of light in a diffraction grating spectrum," Philos. Mag. 4, 396–402 (1902).

[14] J. G. Heacock, The Earth's Crust: its Nature and Physical Properties. Beijing: Earthquake Publishing House1983.07.

[15] Kennett J. P., Marine Geology. Beijing:The OceanPublishing Company, 1992.

[16] Zhu Erqin Editor, Modern Marine Geology(in Chinese). Qingdao:Qingdao Ocean University Press, 1991.

Anomalous Transmission Loss due to Bathymetry Variation

LICHENG LU, QUNYAN REN, SHENGMING GUO, LI MA

Key Laboratory of Underwater Acoustic Environment,
Institute of Acoustics, CAS, Beijing, 100190, China
luce_1983@mail.sina.com
renqunyan@mail.ioa.ac.cn
guoshengming@mail.ioa.ac.cn
mali@mail.ioa.ac.cn

An acoustic propagation experiment was conducted in the East Sea in July 2017. Two types of explosive sources detonated at depths of 25 m and 50 m were used to calculate the transmission loss (TL) along ranges. The TL at the depth of 50 m explosive source are found largely anomalous in the frequency band of 300Hz-500Hz at range about 40 km, while only minor anomalies of the TL at the depth of 25 m is observed. It is well known that, the sound propagation in shallow water is greatly influenced by the properties of the seabed, such as bathymetry and sediment acoustic parameters, which may cause anomalous TL. This paper compares the results of the experiment with the prediction using a range-dependent sound propagation model. Numerous synthetic simulations have been calculated to replicate the experimental results. From these simulations, it has been demonstrated that the bathymetry variation can affect the TL in specific frequency band.

Keywords: Transmission loss; Normal mode; Bathymetry variation.

1. Introduction

Underwater acoustic environment including sound speed profile (SSP), the seabed bathymetry and sediment properties have a great effect on acoustic propagation, especially in shallow water. The impact of water depth variation as one main factor on acoustic propagation has received much attention in the past several decades. The changes of the sound propagation and the sound intensity due to the water depth variation have been studied analytically, numerically and experimentally [1-7]. Evans *et al* [1-2] established a coupled normal mode solution for acoustic propagation in a waveguide with water depth variations of a penetrable bottom. Collins *et al* [4-5] used the parabolic equation method to solve the range-dependent acoustic propagation problem. Porter *et al* [5] applied the Gaussian beam tracing in the ray method for computing ocean acoustic field. There is also a mass of experiment data to test and verify the truth that the water depth can change the acoustic propagation greatly. Dosso *et al* [6] found the TL over a continental slope decreased about 15dB than a flat seabed in the west costal of Canada. Northrop *et al* [7] investigated in an experiment conducted in American California ocean area that the TL would decrease due to the slope of bathymetry.

Most of the research above focuses on large-scale variation of water depth on acoustic propagation, while in shallow water some seafloor has small-scale fluctuation, such as sand dune. This kind of bathymetry is also appealed to some underwater researchers. Linus *et al* [7-8] investigated the criterion for adiabatic invariance of normal mode based on the sand dune which is found in the northern South China Sea and the normal incidence measurement error due to bathymetry. This paper presents the result of an acoustic propagation experiment conducted in the East Sea in July 2017, where the water depth is changed along the acoustic propagation track. Numerous synthetic simulations using a range-dependent sound propagation model have been calculated to replicate the experiment results. From these simulations, it has been demonstrated that the bathymetry variation can affect the TL in specific frequency band.

2. Transmission Loss Measurement

2.1. Description of East Sea

One primary goal of this experiment, which was carried out in the East Sea in July 2017, is to invert a broad-band geoacoustic model. There are four transmission loss tracks in an area of about 60km × 60km, and only the track B-O3 was analyzed. A vertical line array of 32 elements was anchored at O3 position to receive signals. Two types of explosive sources detonated at depths of 25 m and 50 m were used to calculate the TL. The thermometer chain was also set in the same O3 position to measure the temperature profile during the experiment. A conductance, temperature and depth (CTD) sensor was used before the survey. And as the ship sailed along the track, expendable bathythermograph (XBT) was used to measure the temperature profile.

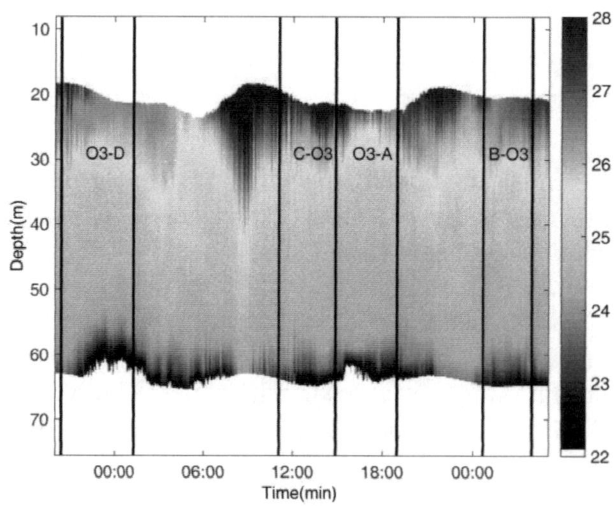

Fig. 1 Temperature profile by the thermometer chain during the experiment

Fig. (1) and (2) show the time varying temperature profile during the experiment and sound speed profile at different ranges. Spatial varying is obvious and the time varying is neglected, so the water volume is modeled as frozen and range-dependent during the experiment track B-O3. Fig. (3) shows the bathymetry of the track.

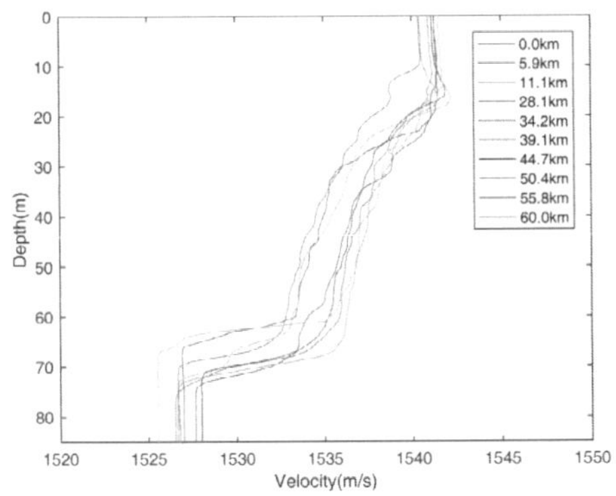

Fig. 2 Sound speed profile along the track B-O3

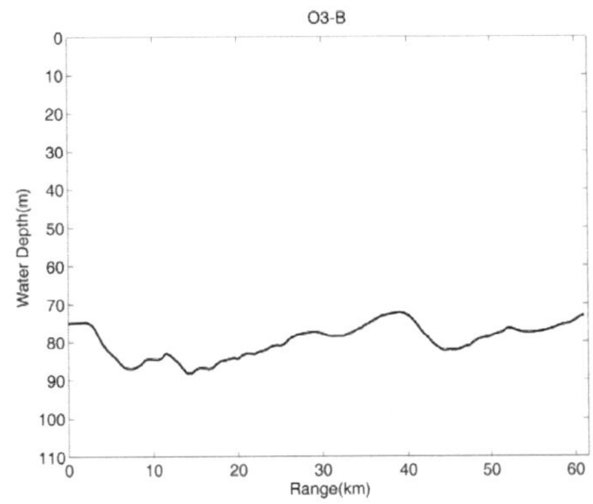

Fig. 3 Water depth along the track

2.2. Modeling of the TL

To accurately predicate the TL, underwater acoustic environment model should be properly applied. In order to simulate the reality of acoustic environment, the SSP is interpolated every 2km as shown in Fig. (4). MFP geoacoustic inversion method and core sample were used to get the geoacoustic model.

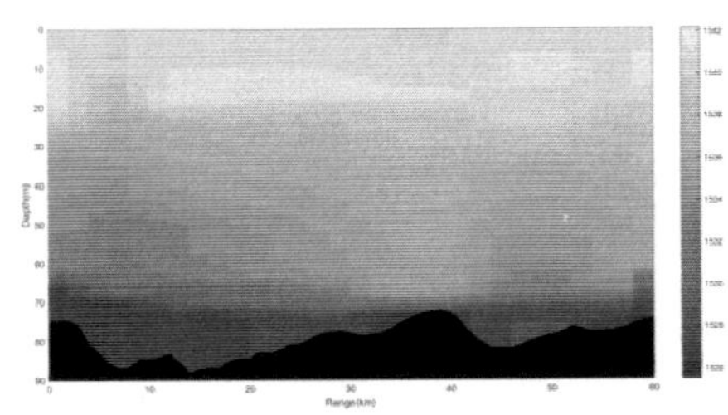

Fig. 4 Interpolated SSP along the whole track

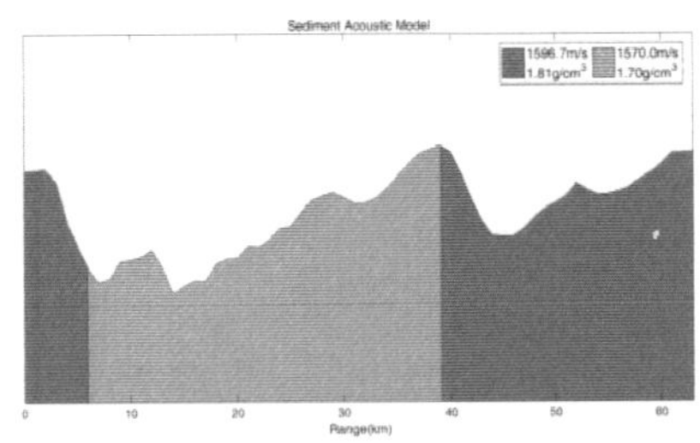

Fig. 5 Range-dependent geoacoustic model

A soft sediment is deposited in the pit of bathymetry, and a range-dependent geoacoustic model is employed. A semi-infinite layer geoacoustic model is assumed for acoustic field calculation. Fig. (5) gives the seabed acoustical parameters of velocity and density. The attenuation coefficient forum is as follows:

$$\alpha = 0.15 \cdot (f/1000)^{1.57} dB/m \qquad (2.1)$$

As underwater acoustic environment model is established, TL can be calculated by the Parabolic Equation (PE) method. RAM [5,9] is based on the split-step Padé solution of parabolic Equation, which allows large range steps and is the most efficient PE algorithm. The formal solution of outgoing wave equation is:

$$p(r + \Delta dr) = \exp\left(ik_0 \Delta r (1 + X)^{1/2}\right) p(r, z) \qquad (2.2)$$

where Δr is the range step, and $k_0 = \omega / c_0$, c_0 is a representative phase speed, X is depth operator

$$X = k_0^{-2} \left(\rho \frac{\partial}{\partial z} \frac{1}{\rho} \frac{\partial}{\partial z} + k^2 - k_0^2 \right) \qquad (2.3)$$

The exponential function is approximated using an n-term rational function to obtain an equation that can be solved numerically.Acoustic field calculated from the RAM are averaged in 1/3 octave frequency band to get the TL. As acoustic field satisfies the reciprocity principle, so four elements of the vertical line array can be taken as the sources and the explosive source depth can be taken as the receiver depth. The simulated TL and the experimental TL are compared at different depths and frequencies. Fig. (6) and (7) show comparisons of the simulated TL and the experimental TL for two types of explosive sources respectively at frequencies from 125Hz to 630Hz.

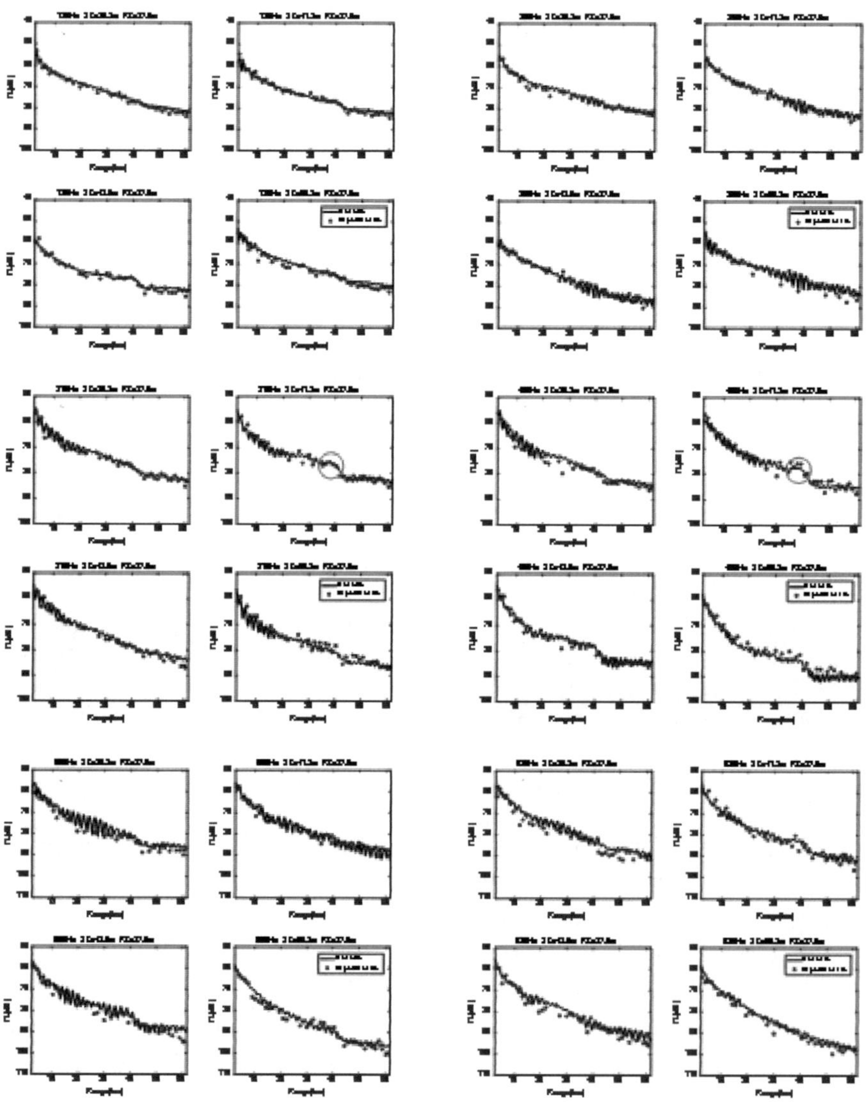

Fig. 6Comparisons of simulated TL and experimental TL, and green cycles indicate anomalous TL (The nominal Source depth is 25m, and the actual source depth is 27.6m)

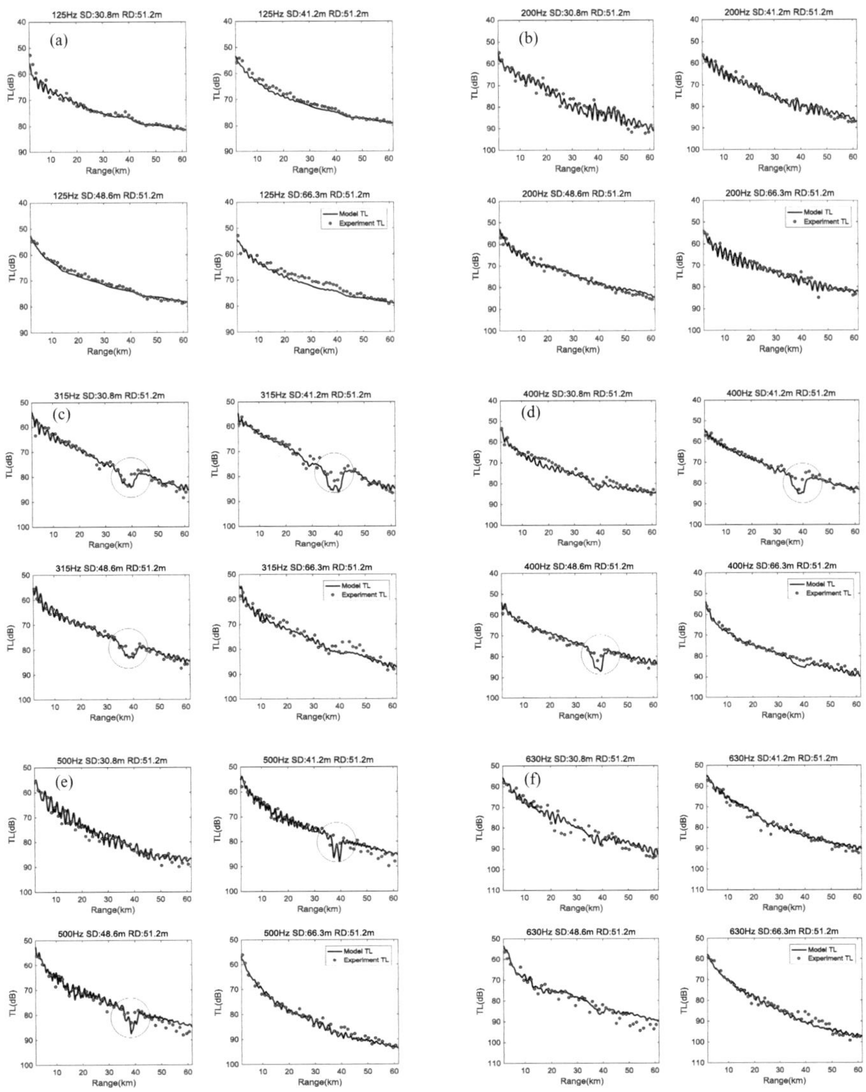

Fig. 7 Comparisons of simulated TL and experimental TL
(Red cycles indicate anomalous TL. The nominal source depth is 50m. The actual source depth is 51.2m)

The TL of the explosive sources detonated at the depth of 50 m are found largely anomalous in the frequency band of 300Hz-500Hz at range about 40 km (Fig. 7 (c) (d) (e), red circles), while only minor anomalies of the TL of the explosive sources detonated at the depth of 25 m is observed (Fig. 6 (c) (d) (e), green circles).

3. Interpretation of Anomalous TL

The adiabatic approximation of normal mode theory is employed to explain what happens to the anomalous TL. A modified adiabatic formula is

$$p(r,z) = \frac{i\exp(-\frac{i\pi}{4})}{\rho(z_s)\sqrt{8\pi}} \sum_{m=1}^{\infty} \Psi_m(z_s)\Psi_m(r,z) \frac{\exp(i\int_0^r k_{rm}(r')dr')}{\sqrt{\int_0^r k_{rm}(r')dr'}} \tag{3.1}$$

where $\Psi_m(r,z)$ is the local normal mode shape. The acoustic field is mainly dominated by a specific number of normal mode which excites at source location and the local normal mode. Fig. (8) shows the TL for sources at 315Hz with the depth being 30m, 40m and 50m respectively. The dashed lines are the local 2nd normal mode shapes and the red points are nodes of the 2nd normal mode. As the seabed bathymetry varies along acoustic propagation path, the 2nd normal mode shape changes the position of the normal mode node. At the range of 40km, the normal node is compressed to about 50m depth. So the TL becomes large at the depth of 51.2m, while it is not obvious at the depth of 27.6m.

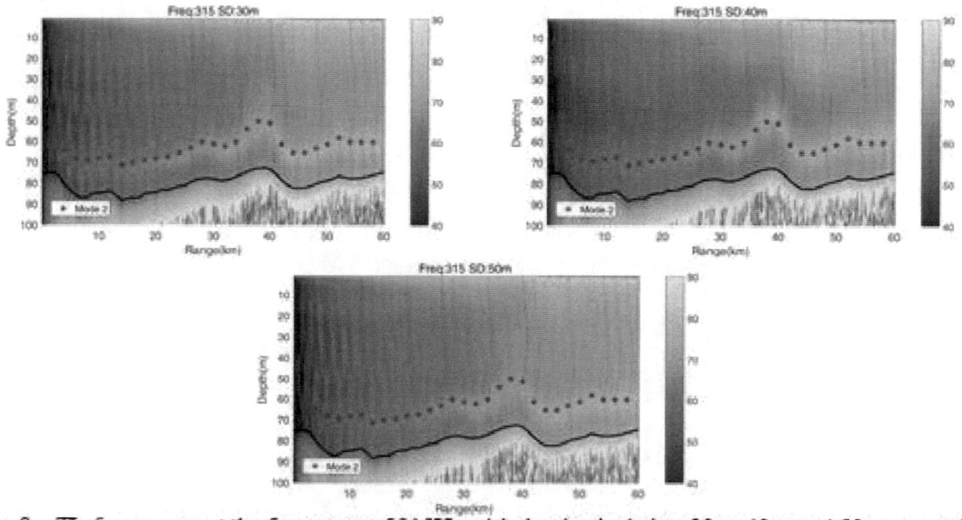

Fig. 8 TL for sources at the frequency of 315Hz with the depths being 30m, 40m and 50m respectively (The dashed lines are the local 2nd normal mode shapes every 2km)

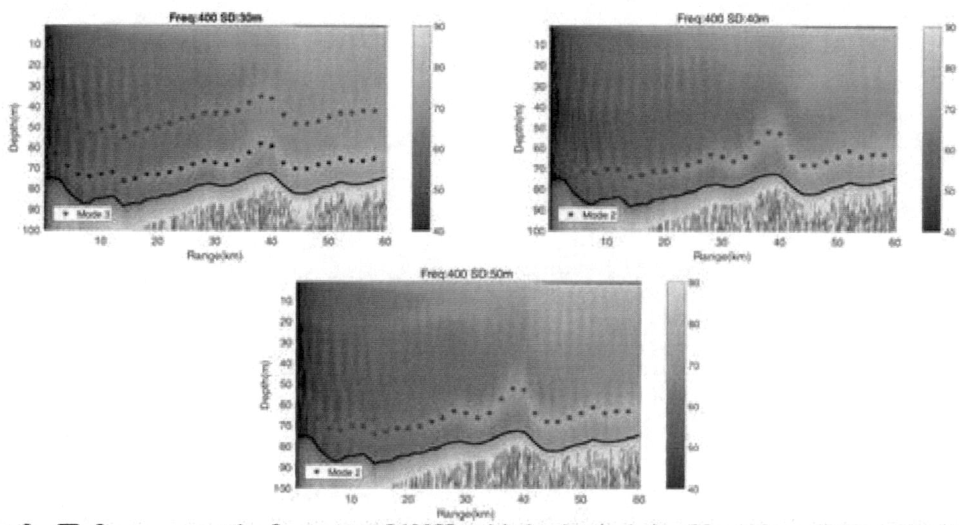

Fig. 9 TL for sources at the frequency of 400Hz with the depths being 30m, 40m and 50m respectively (The dashed lines are the local 3rd normal mode shapes for (a) and local 2nd normal mode shapes for (b) (c) every 2km)

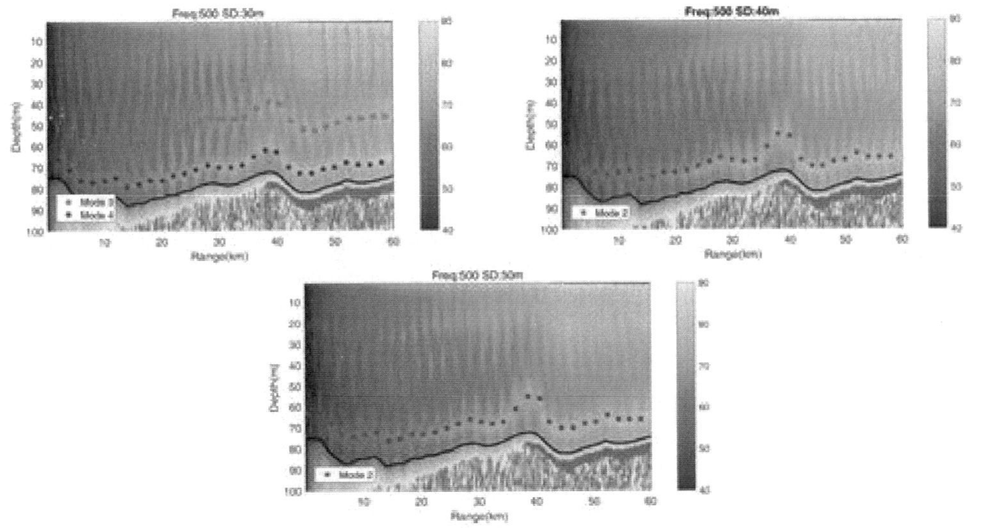

Fig. 10 The TL for sources at the frequency of 500Hz with the depths being 30m, 40m and 50m respectively

Fig. (9) and(10) show the TL for sources at the frequency of 400Hz and 500Hz with the depths being 30m, 40m and 50m respectively. Fig. (9a) gives the 3rd normal mode shape. Although the shape is compressed at range of 40km, TLs at 27.6m and 51.2m are slightly affected. Fig. (9b) and Fig. (9c) give the local 2nd normal mode shapes and the red points are nodes of the 2nd normal mode. Just as the TL at the frequency of 315Hz, the TL at the frequency of 400Hz also becomes large at the depth of 51.2m, while that at the depth of 27.6m is not obvious. The anomalous TL is found at the depth of 60m. Fig. (1 a) gives the 3rd and 4th normal mode shapes and TL becomes large at the depth of 60m. Fig. (10b) and Fig. (10c) is the same as Fig. (8), Fig. (9b) and Fig. (9c). The lower frequency acoustic field has few normal modes and the 1st normal mode is dominant for sources at middle depth of water, so TL is not obviously anomalous as the seabed bathymetry changes. The higher frequency acoustic field has more normal modes and interference of different modes blurs anomalous TL.

4. Conclusion

Sound propagation in shallow water is greatly influenced by bathymetry, which may cause the anomalous TL. Numerous synthetic simulations have been calculated to replicate the experimental results. Bathymetry variation can affect the TL as much as 5-8dB in specific frequency band. The adiabatic approximation of normal mode theory is employed to explain the anomalous TL. The normal mode shape is compressed as water depth becomes small. And the normal node is ascending and causes the TL large.

References

[1] Evans, R. B., "A coupled mode solution for acoustic propagation in a waveguide with stepwise depth variations of a penetrable bottom,"J. Acoust. Soc. Am, 74(1) (1983), 188-195.

[2] Evans, R. B., Gilbert, K. E.,"The periodic extension of stepwise coupled modes," J. Acoust. Soc. Am, 77(3), (1985), 983-988.

[3] Collins, M. D., Westwood, E. K.,"A higher-order energy-conserving parabolic equqation for range-dependent ocean depth, sound speed, and density,"J. Acoust. Soc. Am, 89(3) (1991), 1068-1075.
[4] Collins, M. D.,"A split-step Padé solution for the parabolic equation method," J. Acoust. Soc. Am 93 (1993), 1736-1742.
[5] Porter M. B., Bucker H. P.,"Gaussian beam tracing for computing ocean acoustic fields," J. Acoust. Soc. Am, 82 (1987), 1349-1359.
[6] Dosso S E, Chapman N R.,"Measurement and modeling of downslope acoustic propagation loss over a continentalslope," J. Acoust. Soc. Am,81 (1987), 258-268.
[7] Northrop J, Lougbrid M S, Werner E W., "Effects of near-source bottom conditions on long range sound propagation in the deep ocean," J Geophys Res.73 (1968), 3905-3908.
[8] Linus Y.S. Chiu, and D.Benjamin Reeder, "Acoustic mode coupling due to subaqueous sand dunes in the South China Sea," J. Acoust. Soc. Am 134(2) (2016), EL198-EL204.
[9] Linus Y.S. Chiu and Andrea Y. Y. Chang, "Normal incidence measurement in a subaqueous sand dune field in the South China Sea," J. Acoust Soc. Am 136(5) (2016), EL376-EL382.
[10] M. D. Collins, "Generalization of the split-step Padé solution," J. Acoust. Soc. Am (96) (1993), 382-385.

Simulation of the Three-Dimensional Effect of Ocean Ambient Noise Field in Seamount Area·

Shan Yuanchun[1,2] Lin Jianheng[1] Yi Xuejuan[1] Jiang Pengfei[1] Sun Junping[1] Li Na[1]

1, Qingdao Acoustics Laboratory, Institute of Acoustics, Chinese Academy of Sciences.
Qingdao, China;
2, University of Chinese Academy of Sciences.
Beijing, China.
shanyuanchun@mail.ioa.ac.cn

Abstract: The three-dimensional effect is a key point of ocean ambient noise research, because it can have an obvious influence on the performance of sonars. Seamount is a main factor causing the three-dimensional effect of ocean ambient noise. A large scale seamount and sources randomly distributing on an infinite plane under ocean surface are assumed in this paper. Some characteristics of ambient noise field were simulated using ray method and compared in two condition: one considered horizontal refraction and the other not. The results showed that the energy diffused around seamount when ray horizontal refraction was considered, and the ambient noise level was higher than the condition without considering ray horizontal refraction. The difference of ambient noise level, vertical correlation and vertical directionality caused by horizontal refraction was much obvious, especially in different bearings and ranges.

Keywords: Ocean ambient noise; Three-dimensional; Vertical directionality

1. Introduction

Ocean ambient noise is the resident acoustic field in the ocean, as an important factor which can affect sonar performance, ambient noise carries a lot of information about the ocean environment and weather information. Ocean ambient noise was originally investigated during World War II [1][2]. In 1990s, researchers began to focus attention on the three-dimensional effects of ambient noise[3], establishing an appropriate 3D noise model became more and more urgent.

2. Theoretical model

The three-dimensional model of ocean ambient noise includes two parts: noise source model and propagation model. Ray theory is often used to calculate the sound field in deep ocean and large scale ocean environment[4].

For simplicity of calculation, noise sources are assumed to be uniformly distributed on an infinite plane below the sea surface at depth z_S [5][6]. Furthermore, divide horizontal azimuth angle into J equal parts, $\theta_j = j * \Delta\theta (j = 1 \cdots J)$

divide horizontal distance into L equal parts, $r = r_0 + l * \Delta r$, as shown in figure 1. Then, the area of each sector ring is $S_l = r_l \Delta\theta \Delta r$[7]. Assume the sound intensity of per unit area on surface is $I_{l,j} = ns_{l,j}^2 = 10^{NSL_{l,j}/10}$. NSL is empirical formula of sound intensity level.

$$NSL = 55 - 6log_{10}\left[\left(\frac{f}{400}\right)^2 + 1\right] + (18 + \frac{v}{4})log_{10}(\frac{v}{10})^{[8]} \tag{1}$$

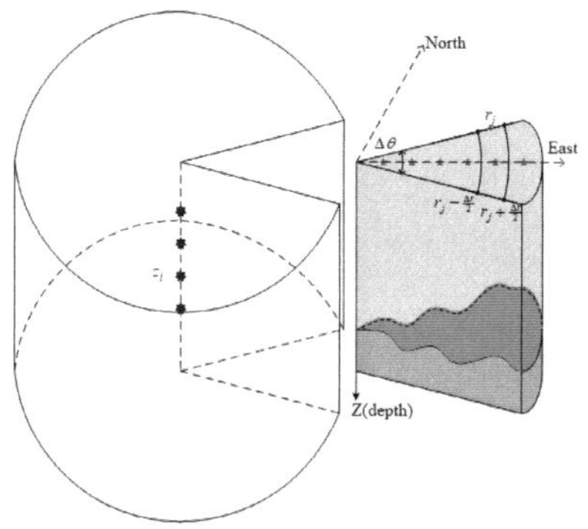

Fig. 1 Geometry for ambient noise model

Vertical arrays of receivers are located in the center of the water column, apply the three dimensional propagation code to calculate the sound field at each receiver caused by the noise sources in per sector ring, and compare the difference between the calculation results using 3D algorithm and N×2D algorithm.

Consider $P(z_1, r_l, z_S, \theta_j)$ as sound pressure received at depth z_1, generated by noise source which is located at depth z_S, horizontal range is r_l, horizontal azimuth is θ_j, if noise sources are uncorrelated, the noise cross-spectral density would be

$$C(z_1, z_2) \cong \sum_{j=1}^{J} \sum_{l=1}^{L} ns_{l,j}^2 S_j P(z_1, r_l, z_S, \theta_j) P^*(z_2, r_l, z_S, \theta_j)^{[3]} \tag{2}$$

2.1. Vertical directionality and vertical correlation

Vertical directionality and vertical correlation of ocean ambient noise are two typical factors which can reflect the characteristics of propagation process and seabed environment.

$$\vec{q}(\alpha, \beta) = \exp(-i\vec{k} \cdot \vec{x_n}) \tag{3}$$

This formula is sound direction vector which is used for calculating the vertical directionality, $\vec{k}$ is vector of plane wave, α, β are elevation angle and azimuth angle respectively.

So, the vertical directionality is

$$\vec{q}^H \cdot C \cdot \vec{q}^{[4]} \tag{4}$$

Same as the formula of vertical directionality, vertical correlation can also be expressed by SPL, sound pressure level.

$$C_{12} = \frac{C(z_1,z_2)}{\sqrt{C(z_1,z_1)C(z_2,z_2)}} \text{[9]} \tag{5}$$

In this formula, z_1 and z_2 are different depth of receivers.

3. Calculation results and analysis

The calculation parameters are as follows: the radius of seamount is 20 km, radius for calculation is 80 kilometers; the ocean depth is 5684 meters, the depth of seamount top is 196 meters; assume receiving array are located at 10 kilometers from seamount center with three depth scopes: 200 m - 229 m, 1290 m - 1319 m, 2000 m - 2029 m, the element spacing is 1 m.

Calculation frequency is 100Hz, calculate results of frequency is 1000Hz for comparing, number of elements is 30,but the spacing distance of every elements is 0.3 meters when calculation frequency is 1000Hz, wind speed is 6m/s. Sound speed profile is assumed Munk profile.

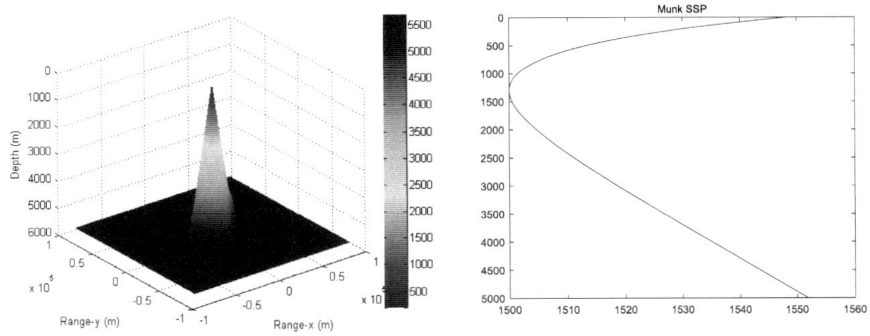

Fig. 2 Seamount seabed and Munk SSP

3.1. Calculation results of vertical directionality

Fig. 3 (a). (b) are vertical directionality of ocean ambient noise at 100Hz and 1000Hz for flat bottom when depth of top receiver is 1290 m respectively, X-axis is azimuth angle, Y-axis is elevation angle. There are typical manifestation of vertical directionality, the notch appears at elevation angle of 0 degree, with the change of azimuth angle, the notch will not disappear or be filled, and the value gradually increase with the increase of elevation angle.

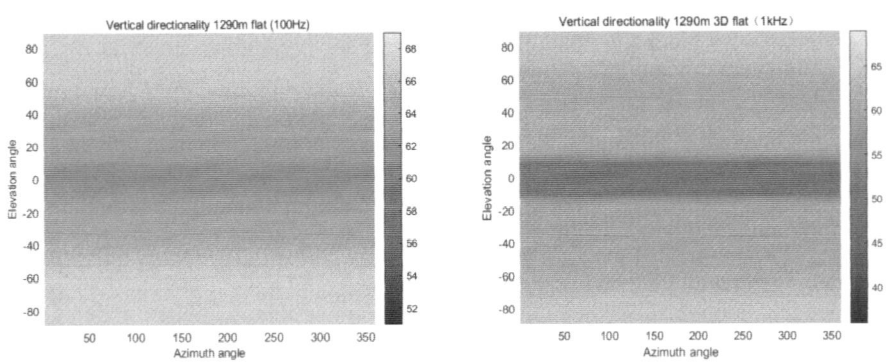

(a) (b)

Fig. 3 Vertical directionality of ocean ambient noise for flat bottom

3.1.1. Frequency is 100Hz

Fig. 4 (a),(c),(e) are vertical directionality of ocean ambient noise calculated by 3D model when the depth of top receiver are located at 200 m,1290 m and 2000 m respectively; (b),(d),(f) are calculated by N×2D model in the same condition.

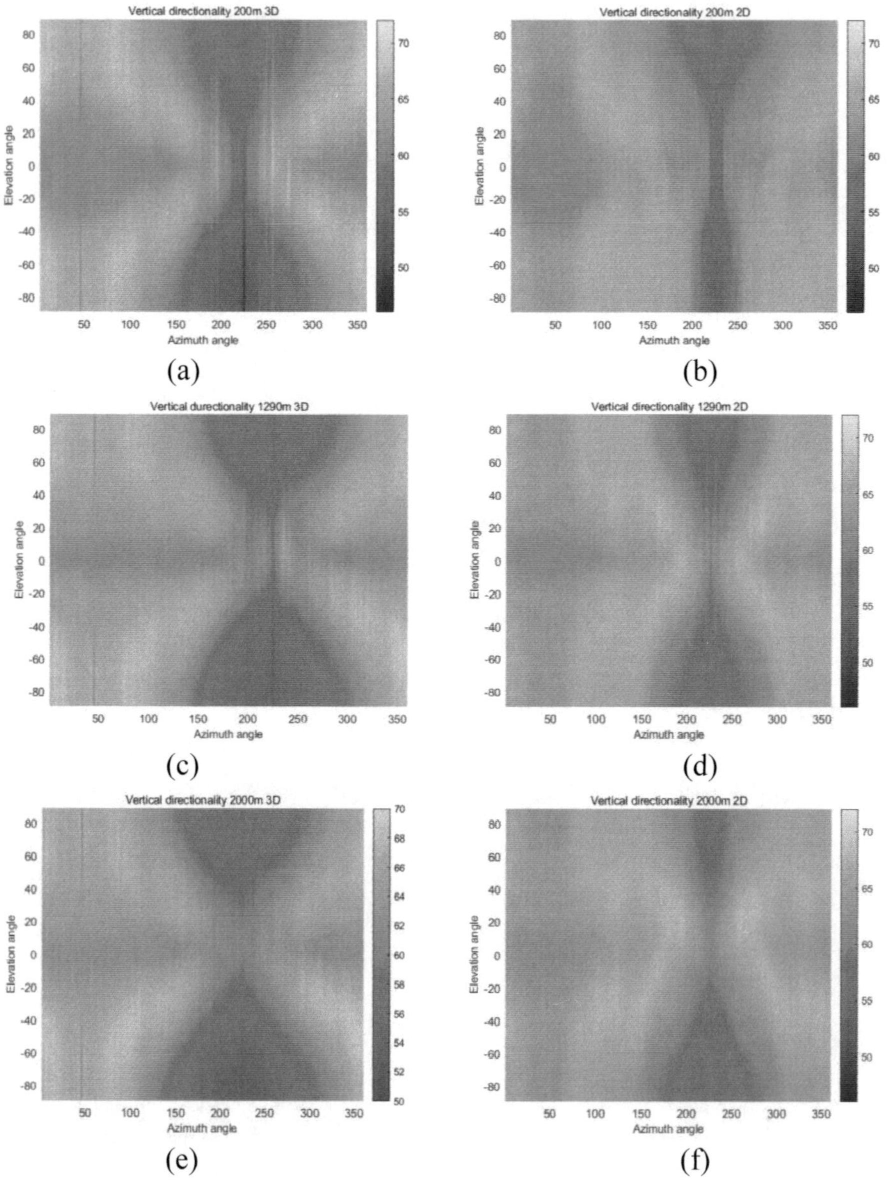

Fig. 4 Vertical directionality of noise calculated by 3D model and N×2D model at three depths (100Hz).

Different from the results for flat bottom, whether 3D results or N×2D results, although noise notches all appear at elevation angle of 0 degree, however, with the horizontal angle gradually close to the direction of seamount which are angles between 150 degrees and 300 degrees, the notch may be filled even disappear, especially at horizontal angles between 200 degrees and 250 degrees, which are the right side to the seamount.

Comparing the results of 3D model with N×2D model, the noise notches calculated by 3D model are more distinct than those of N × 2D model. Formula (4) shows that vertical directionality of noise also reflects the difference of sound pressure level in different models, which means the results calculated by 3D model have wider energy diffusion area than those of N×2D model at horizontal angle, because 3D model considers the influence of horizontal refraction of rays.

3.1.2. Frequency is 1000Hz

As in fig. 4, Fig. 5 (a),(c),(e) are results of 3D model, the first array element are located at 200 meters, 1290 meters and 2000 meters respectively, (b),(d),(f) are results of N×2D model at same depths, the results of the two frequencies are somewhat similar, however, there are some different.

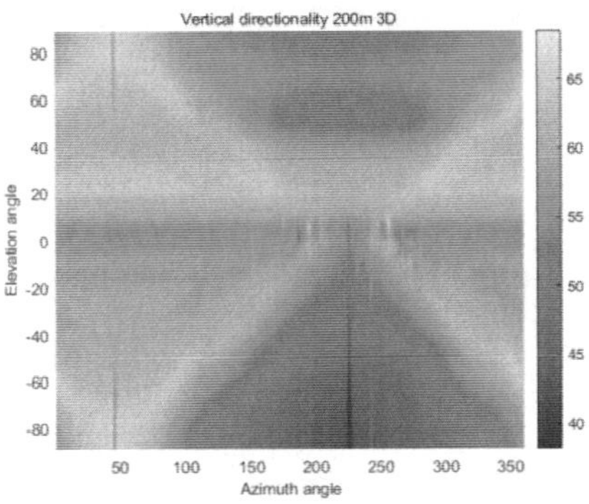

(a)

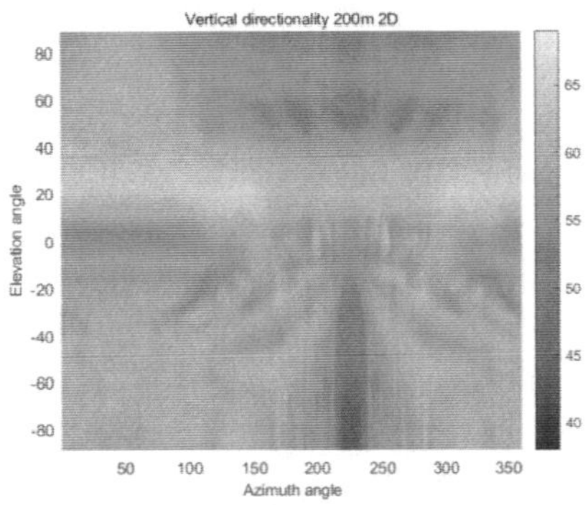

(b)

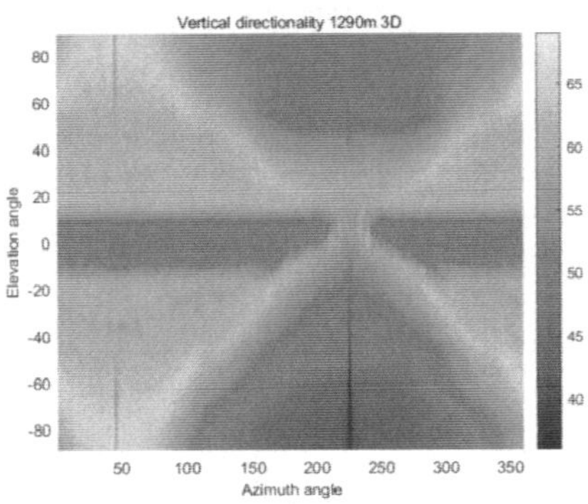

(c)

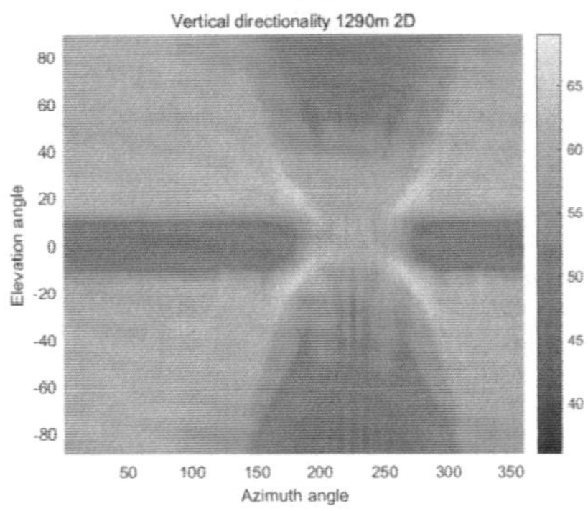

(d)

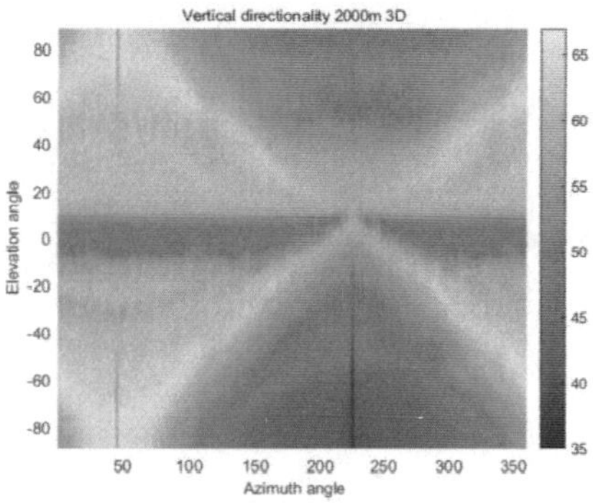

(e)

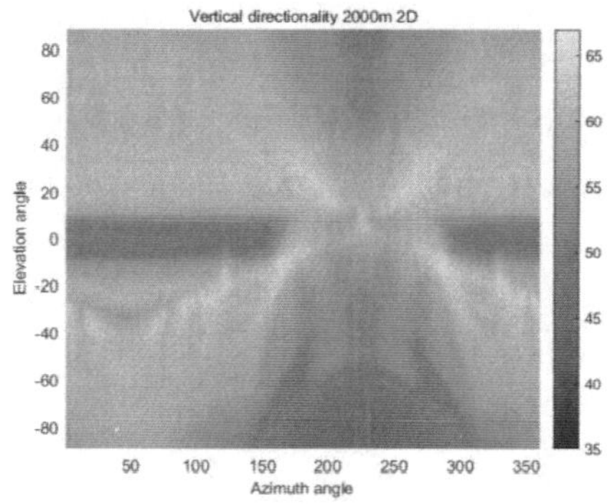

(f)

Fig. 5 Vertical directionality of ocean ambient noise calculated by 3D model and N×2D model at three depths (1000Hz).

The similarity between the results of the two frequencies is that the notches all appear at elevation angle of 0 degree, the notch may disappear or be filled in the seamount direction, the results for 3D model have wider energy diffuse area in azimuth angle.

Also there is some difference compare with that at frequency of 100Hz, especially when the depth is 200 m, it's difficult to distinguish the noise notch of N×2D model in the direction of seamount, maybe it's because the depth of seamount top is smaller than receiver depth of 1290 meters or 2000 meters, hence, it have different reflection to different wave length.

It should be noted that the results of 3D model at three depths are similar to each other than N×2D model.

3.2. Correlation

Vertical correlation is also an important property of ocean ambient noise, we simulated and compared the influence of different frequencies, different depths and different kinds of seabed on vertical correlation of ocean ambient noise.

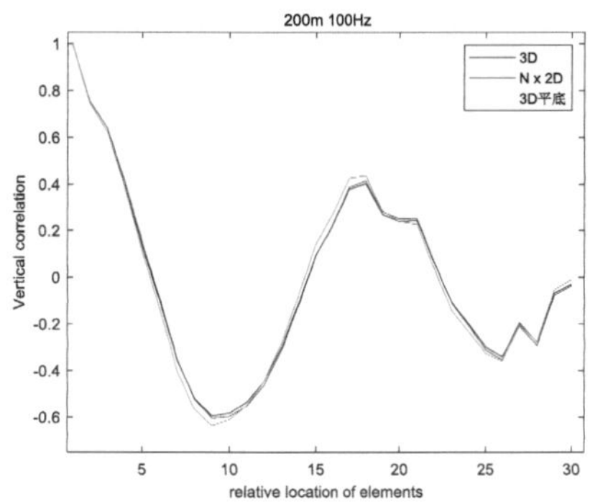

(a)

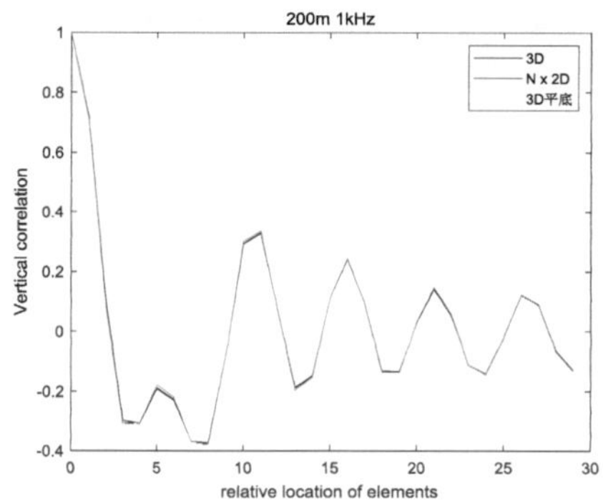

(b)

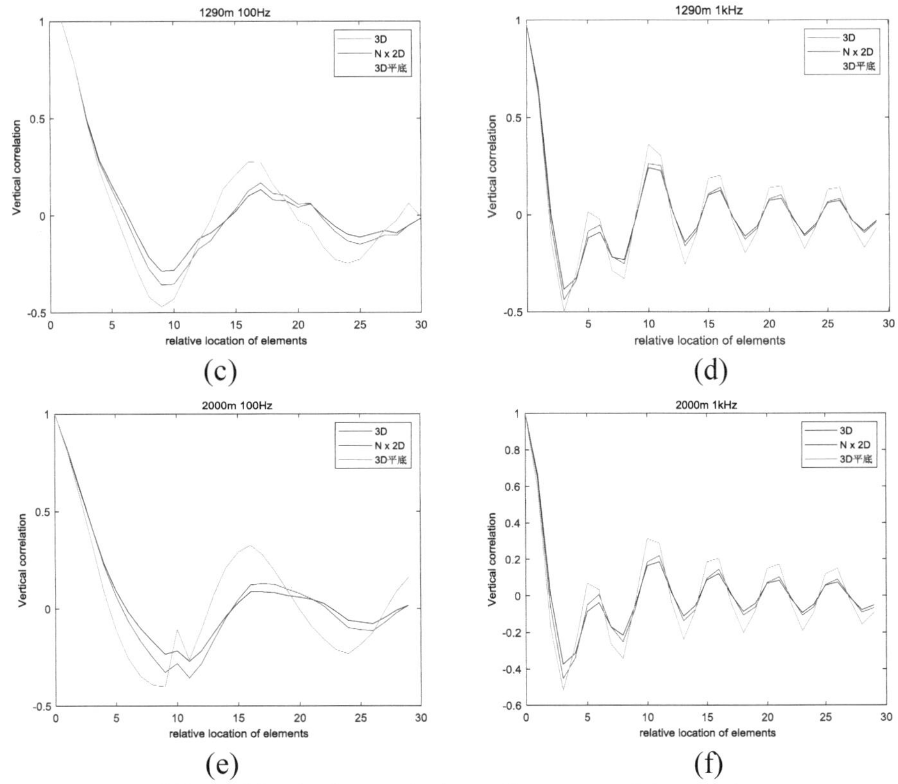

Fig. 6 Vertical correlation of ocean ambient noise

Fig. 6 are the simulation results of vertical correlation of ocean ambient noise in three cases: the depth of top receiver are 200 m, 1290 m and 2000 m respectively, red curve is result of 3D model, blue curve is result of N×2D model, green curve is result of 3D model in flat bottom, (a), (c), (e) are results of noise vertical correlation when frequency is 100Hz, (b), (d), (f) are those when frequency is 1000Hz, X-axis is relative location of array elements, Y-axis is vertical correlation of noise.

Whether frequency is 100Hz or 1000Hz, seamount cannot influence the trend of correlation, however, with the increase of depth, the difference of noise vertical correlation between flat bottom and seamount seabed becomes more and more obvious.

4. Summary

By developing the theoretical model to calculate the vertical directionality and correlation of ocean ambient noise at different depths, frequencies and different kinds of seabed with 3D algorithm and N×2D algorithm, we can conclude that seamount could influence the vertical directionality of ocean ambient noise, because horizontal refraction of rays would cause energy diffusion to other side, as a result, the notch of vertical directionality which should appear at elevation angle of 0 degree will be filled, even disappear.

Different from vertical directionality, seamount cannot influence the trend of vertical correlation of ocean ambient noise a lot, while when receiver elements are located at the deep ocean, there are still some difference of value between seamount seabed and flat seabed.
To verify the accuracy of this model, we will make the simulation environment more close to real environment, and compare the simulation results with measured data to correct the parameters and propagation process of this model.

References

[1] Knudsen V O, Alford R S, Emling J W. Underwater ambient noise. J. Marine Res.,1948;7(3):410-429.

[2] Wenz G M. Acoustic ambient noise in the ocean: spectra and sources. J Acoust Soc Am., 1962;34(12):1936-1956.

[3] Perkins J S, Kuperman W A, Ingenito F, Fialkows L T,Glattetre John. Modeling ambient noise in the three dimensional ocean environment. J. Acoust.Soc.Am., 1993;93(2):739-752.

[4] Harrison C H. Noise directionality for surface sources in range-dependent environment. J Acoust. Soc.Am.,1997;102(5):2622-2655;

[5] Yang T C, Kwang Yoo. Modeling the environment influence on the vertical directionality of ambient noise in shallow water. J. Acoust. Soc. Am., 1997;101(5):2541-2554.

[6] Michael J.Buckingham, Nichola M. Carbone. Source depth and the spatial coherence of ambient noise in the ocean. J. Acoust.Soc.Am.,1997;102(5):2637-2644.

[7] Yi Xuejuan, Lin Jianheng, Yin Baoyou, Jiang Pengfei. Ambient noise analysis of arbitrary sound speed profile in slope bottom. Technical Acoustics. 2008;27(5):90-91.

[8] Jiang Dongge, Li Zhenglin, Qin Jixing, Peng Zhaohui, Hao Shao. Characterization and Modeling of Wind-Dominated Ambient Noise in South China Sea. Sci.China-Phys. Mech. Astron.60, 124321 (2017). DOI:10.1007/s11433-017-9088-5.

[9] Wang Jing-yan, Li Feng-hua. Research on the vertical correlation of ambient noise in deep sea. Technical Acoustics., 2016;35(2):109-113.

Detection and Localization of Indo-Pacific Humpback Dolphin's Whistle Signal with multiple PAM stations in the vicinity of Taichung Harbor

Wei-Yen Chu [1] Wei-Lun Li [1] Chi-Fang Chen[1]

1, Department of Engineering Science and Ocean Engineering, National Taiwan University

r06525012@ntu.edu.tw

chifang@ntu.edu.tw

For a nuclear-free homeland in 2025 and considering their international carbon reduction commitment, Taiwan's government is developing an independent green industry. The development of offshore wind farms along the western coast currently is the government's main energy policy. Nevertheless, the wind farm is adjacent to the China White Dolphin reservation zone. A passive acoustic monitoring system for cetaceans will be established as a development priority in the future wind farm operation.
This study deployed four hydrophone stations near Taichung Harbor. To testify this system's capability, this study used a human-made dolphin whistle signal to imitate a real dolphin's call, and used a self-developed whistle detector to capture the signal. Moreover, we used the time difference of arrivals (TDOA) method to compute the localization of signal sources. This TDOA experiment was conducted near Taichung Harbor. The result showed that the average of the positioning errors was 150m due to the long range hydrophone array. Over all, this study provides initial reference directions for key technologies of the PAM used in Taiwan.

Keywords: Passive Acoustic Monitoring; Whistle Detector; TDOA.

1. Introduction

Nowadays, most of Taiwan's energy raw materials are imported, and this has made a huge and immediate impact on the environment. Therefore, the government is developing green energy positively, and offshore wind farms have been established. Nevertheless, most of the site for the offshore wind farms overlaps with the Indo-Pacific Humpback Dolphin reservation zone. In order to avoid the noise impact to the cetaceans caused by the construction and operation of the wind turbine, the establishment of a monitoring system is a priority. PAM (Passive Acoustic Monitoring) is used widely and its efficiency is much higher, so we use PAM to monitor the ocean background noise and the cetacean call. In addition to making up for the defects of the visual method, it also can understand the relationship between the two. This study deployed several PAM stations near Taichung harbor and recorded the cetaceans call. Moreover, the study tries to localize the call's position.
The study of the cetacean whistle is quite vigorous. In the algorithm of catching the cetacean whistle, in order to distinguish different cetacean species, Alexandre Gannier [1] used the regression tree to group the characteristics of the cetacean whistle on the time spectrogram

(whistle length, beginning frequency, ending frequency, maximum frequency and minimum frequency). L. Y. Zhong [2] turned the characteristics of the whistle on the spectrogram into eigenvectors, and used the support vector machine to perform cetacean whistle clustering. In addition, S.Datta [3] used the Hidden Markov Model (HMM) to group signature whistles. From the identification of "category," further grouping "individuals," the signature whistle is the whistle of some species of dolphins, unique to a single individual, so the whistle algorithm mentioned above is specific and targeted. It is necessary to group a specific archive segment into a certain cetacean group and individuals. T. H. Lin [4] wrote a non-targeted algorithm on the Matlab 2013 platform. It can help users to grasp the position of the whistle in a large number of audio files, which is convenient for the research team to further process. The whistle has a narrow frequency on the spectrogram and a high continuity in the time domain. T. H. Lin [5] also first denoised the spectrogram and detected the whistle with characteristics. The algorithm of this study, the whistle detector, includes some concepts from T. H. Lin's works.

2. Method

2.1. Detection - Whistle Detector

With the popularization of underwater acoustic recorders, Passive Acoustic Monitoring is used widely in marine monitoring. There is massive recorded data generated under long-term measurement, and it requires high-efficiency algorithms to assist researchers in finding the required file segments. This study used the algorithm called Whistle Detector [6,7,8], written on Matlab and Python, which is used to detect the characteristics of the whistle on the spectrogram. The algorithm has no specific object, and the frequency range determines which specific species will be detected. The general idea of the algorithm is smoothing, denoising, removing single-point noise, limiting the whistle bandwidth, and verifying the continuity of the whistle in the time domain. A detail flow chart is shown in Fig. 1

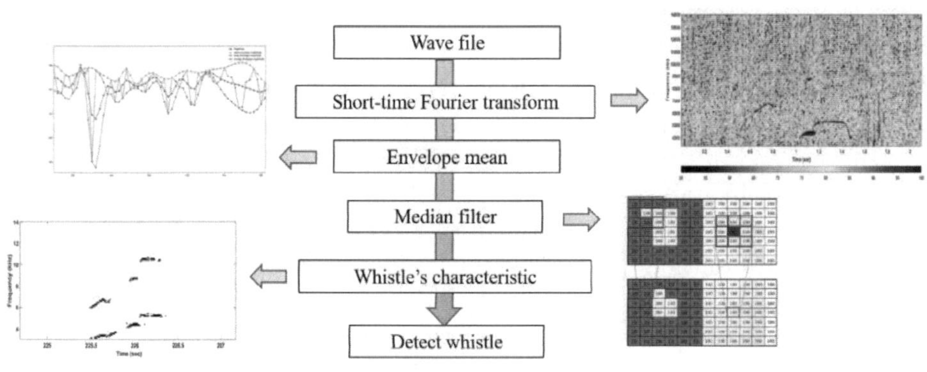

Fig. 1. Whistle Detector Flow Chart

Fourier Transform converts a periodic continuous signal from the time domain into frequency domain and does not provide information in the time domain. Therefore, this study used Short Time Fourier Transform, which added a window function to obtain the frequency domain information changed by the time domain. This establishes a frame to slide on the time domain signal and extracts the signal in the frame, which convolves with the window function to perform the Fourier Transform. After that, this information is used to produce the spectrogram. For the smoothing method, this study considers the whistle to be a random signal, so we chose a local smoothing method, envelope mean, to highlight the position of the whistle. First, find the local maxima value of the sequence, connect it to the upper envelope by curve interpolation, and find the local minima value of the sequence to obtain the envelope. Finally, the upper and lower envelopes are averaged into a new sequence, and the new sequence is subtracted from the original sequence. For denoising, we used the median filter, which is often used for image processing and is a technique for nonlinear signal processing. It is particularly significant for removing salt-and-pepper noise and speckle noise in images. The median filter is easy to implement in the algorithm. The spectrum is regarded as an energy matrix and divided into several small matrices. The median in the small matrix is found sequentially to replace the energy of the intermediate elements of the small matrix. To separate one whistle from another, the signal we capture must have these two whistle characteristics: 1) Narrow frequency band, with bandwidth less than 300 Hz, and 2) high continuity in the time domain.

2.2. Localization - TDOA

TDOA, short for Time Difference of Arrival, often is used in signal source positioning. It only requires the time the signal was received and the speed that the signal travels. Once the signal is received at two receiving stations, the difference in arrival time can be used to draw the hyperbola of possible location by the equation shown below. If we have three receiving stations, it can produce at least 2 hyperbolas, as shown in Fig. 2 Their intersection will be the signal source location. To achieve this hypothesis, the receiving stations must have accomplished time synchronization. In this study, before deploying the hydrophones, we used metal to produce a loud, momentary sound, and considered this sound to be the benchmark for correcting the time.

$$\sqrt{(x-x_1)^2+(y-y_1)^2}-\sqrt{(x-x_3)^2+(y-y_3)^2}=c(t_1-t_3)$$
$$\sqrt{(x-x_2)^2+(y-y_2)^2}-\sqrt{(x-x_3)^2+(y-y_3)^2}=c(t_2-t_3)$$

t1, t2 and t3 are the times when the same signal arrives at different hydrophones. (x, y) is the position of the unknown signal source. c is the sound speed from the local sound speed profile.

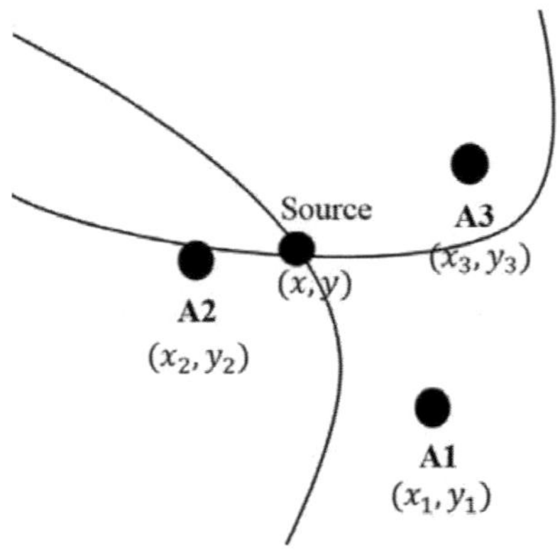

Fig. 2. TDOA schematic figure

3. Taichung Harbor TDOA Experiment

3.1. Experimental Configuration

This study deployed four hydrophone stations near Taichung Harbor. The reason we choose Taichung harbor is, according to Prof. Chou [9], Taichung Harbor is one of the hot spots for witnessing the Chinese white dolphin. The location of the hydrophones is shown in Fig. 3. The detailed latitude and longitude is shown in Table. 1.

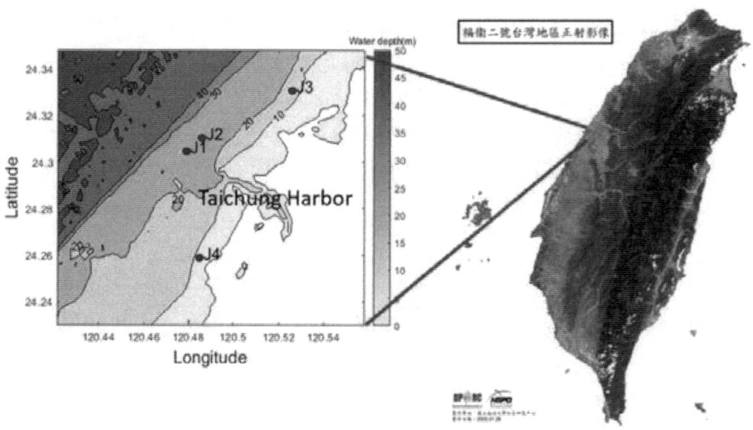

Fig. 3. Hydrophone Stations Location

Table. 1 Hydrophone Stations latitude and longitude

Station	Latitude(N)	Longitude(E)	Depth(m)
J1	24.3045°	120.4788°	8.0
J2	24.3101°	120.4861°	28.7
J3	24.3305°	120.5259°	29.1
J4	24.2588°	120.4851°	11.0

The hydrophone instrument uses the SoundTrap ST500 at the J1 point and the Wildlife Acoustics SM3M at the J2~J4 point, and they are deployed using the bottom mounted method. The sampling frequency was set to 96 kHz. To simulate a real Chinese white dolphin's whistle, which has frequency range from 3kHz to 9kHz, this study used three kinds of artificial sound signals, which are rising frequency (5 kHz~9 kHz), decreasing frequency (9 kHz ~ 5kHz), and U type (9 kHz - 5 kHz - 9 kHz), with a time length of one second. According to L. H. Guo [10], the Chinese white dolphins often live about 5 meters below sea level. Therefore, the sound drum SQS-23 was placed at 5m water depth, as shown in Fig. 4. The artificial sound signals were played every 10 seconds for 10 minutes in the 15 spots (T1-T15) outside the Taichung Harbor, as shown in Fig. 5.

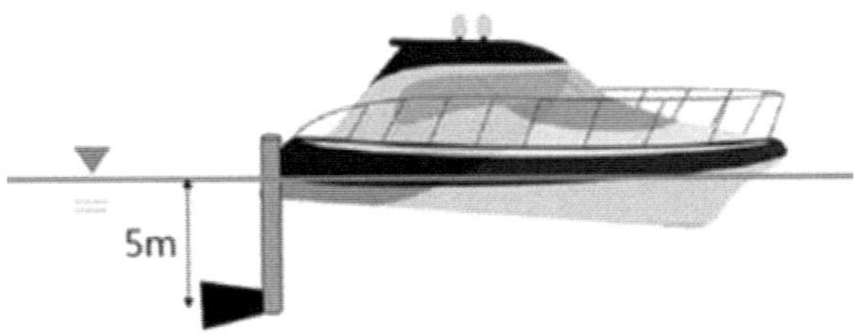

Fig. 4. Sound drum set schematic figure

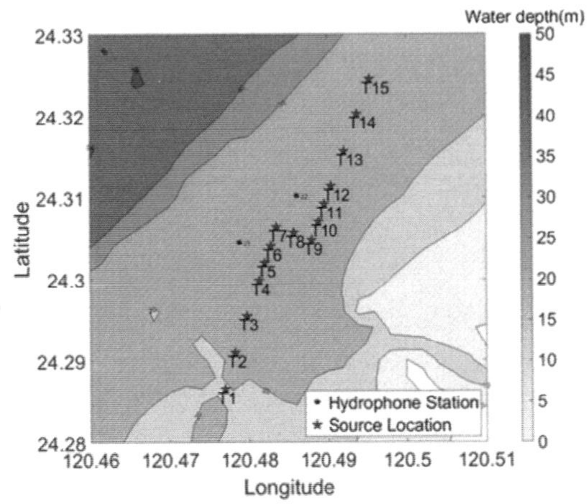

Fig. 5. Signal source location

3.2. Experimental Data Analysis Method

In this study, after the short-distance Fourier transform is performed on the sound file recorded by the hydrophones, a complex matrix is obtained. After that, we use Whistle Detector to capture the time segment of the artificial whistle signal received. For more accurate time measurement of when the hydrophones received the signal, cross-correlation analysis with the original artificial signal and the received signal is performed to get more precise arrival time. Then, the time points of each hydrophone receiving the signal are compared to acquire the time difference. Finally, the Time Difference of Arrival method is used to obtain the location of the signal source.

3.3. Experimental Result

The positioning method of this study uses the time difference of arrival (TDOA) method. Basically, as long as there are three signal receiving stations, two sets of hyperbolic curves can be drawn to generate the intersection of the sound source, and the sound source position is recorded according to the experimental ship GPS positioning system. Finally, we compare the positioning accuracy of the two. In order to ensure the success of the experiment, a total of four sets of hydrophones were placed in this experiment. When the intersection of hyperbolic curves is plural, the center point is taken as the final judgment location.

The first experiment is the rising frequency (5 kHz~9 kHz) signal, where the blue dot is the hydrophone station position (J1, J2), the red dot is the signal source position of the experimental ship's GPS record, and the green star is the TDOA positioning result. As shown in Fig. 6 the sound source near the center position J1 and J2 of the whole group of hydrophone stations has a high positioning accuracy. The nearest positioning point T5 to T12 has an average positioning error of 47.2 meters. The overall positioning error comes to 191.1 meters, which is affected by the lower accuracy of the outer point.

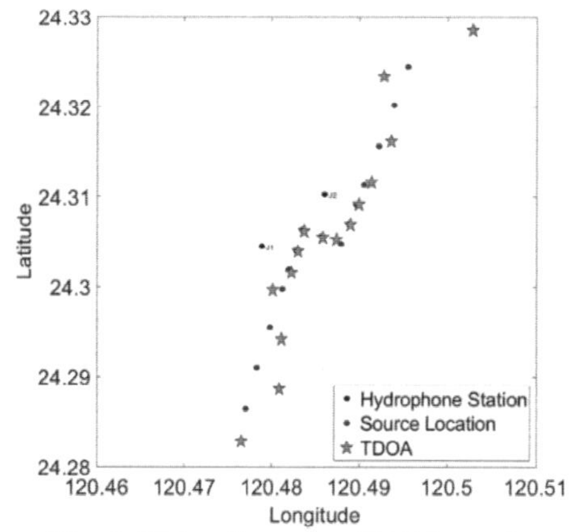

Fig. **6**. Rising frequency TDOA result

The second experiment is the decreasing frequency (9 kHz~5 kHz), and its positioning trend is similar to the rising frequency signal. It also has higher positioning accuracy when the signal source is close to the J1 and J2 station, which is the center position of the whole group of hydrophone stations. The average positioning error of T5 to T12 is larger than the rising frequency signal, which is 86.5 meters, and the overall positioning error comes to 196.5 meters.

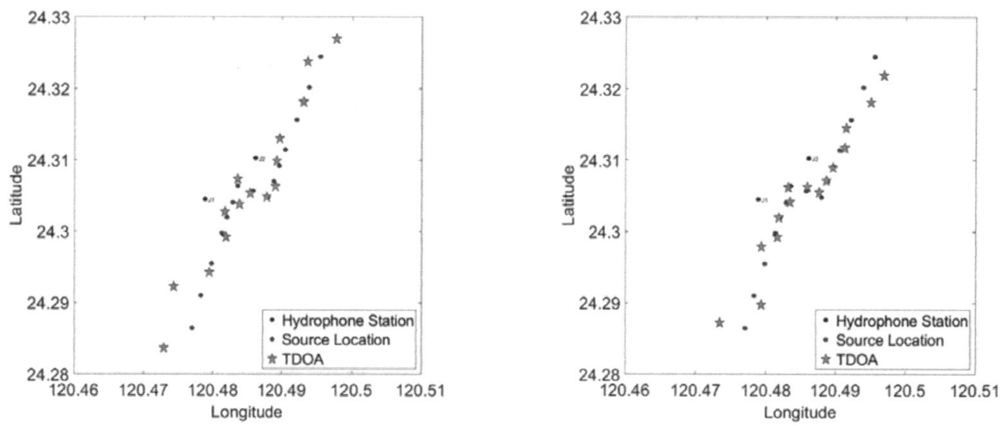

Fig. 7. Right side is the decreasing frequency signal TDOA result; left side is the U-shape signal TDOA result

Finally, the U-shaped (9 kHz-5 kHz-9 kHz) signal also displays the same trend as the aforementioned signals. The average positioning error of T5 to T12 is 51.8 meters, but the overall positioning error is the smallest of the three signals. It is 134.8 meters. Further comparison between the position of the signal source's distance between J1 and J2 and the three kinds of signals' positioning error is shown in Fig. **8** The result is clearer. As the signal

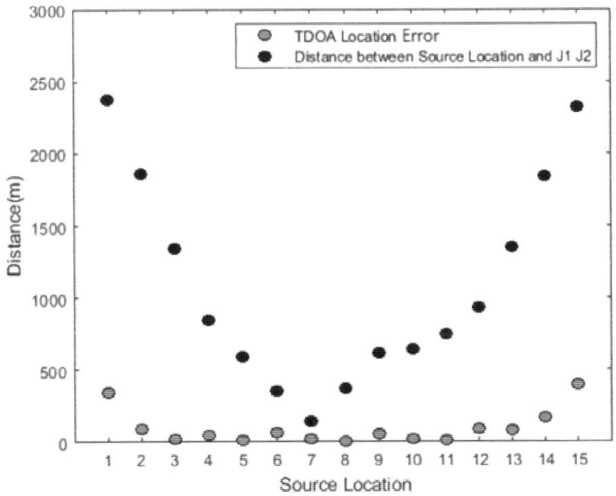

source is far from the J1, J2 station, the positioning error is higher.

Fig. 8. TDOA location error compared to the distance between signal source to J1, J2 stations

4. Conclusion

With the Whistle Detector and TDOA method, the method can achieve basic localization. According to the experimental results, the trend of the three kinds of signal positioning errors is about the same, and the accuracy of the sound source positioning near the J1 and J2 points is relatively high. It is presumed that low signal strength results in low signal to noise ratio due to the greater distance between the sound source and the J1 and J2 point. J1 and J2 are used as the two receiving stations in the calculation. Although the Whistle Detector still can capture the time segment when the hydrophones received the signal, the deviation of receiving time is generated due to low SNR when we used cross-correlation analysis. In addition, it can be estimated that the range of the signal frequency does not affect the positioning accuracy. The main factor is the signal-to-noise ratio.

References

[1] A. Gannier, S. Fuchs, P. Quèbre, and J. N. Oswald, "Performance of a contour-based classification method for whistles of Mediterranean delphinids," Applied Acoustics, vol. 71, no. 11, pp. 1063-1069, 2010.

[2] J. Allen, "Short term spectral analysis, synthesis, and modification by discrete Fourier transform," IEEE Transactions on Acoustics, Speech, and Signal Processing, vol. 25, no. 3, pp. 235-238, 1977.

[3] S. Datta and C. Sturtivant, "Dolphin whistle classification for determining group identities," Signal processing, vol. 82, no. 2, pp. 251-258, 2002.

[4] T.-H. Lin, " The Application of Passive Acoustic Monitoring for Studying Indo-Pacific Humpback Dolphin Behavior and Habitat Use off Western Taiwan," Master thesis, Homepage of Institute of Ecology and Evolutionary Biology, National Taiwan University, pp. 1-150, 2013

[5] T.-H. Lin, L.-S. Chou, T. Akamatsu, H.-C. Chan, and C.-F. Chen, "An automatic detection

algorithm for extracting the representative frequency of cetacean tonal sounds," The Journal of the Acoustical Society of America, vol. 134, no. 3, pp. 2477-2485, 2013.

[6] Wei-Lun Li, Chi-Fang Chen, " Study of Dolphin Whistle Detection " Master thesis, Department of Engineering Science and Ocean Engineering, National Taiwan University, 2018

[7] Wei-Lun Li, Wei- Yen Chu, Chi-Fang Chen, "Apply passive acoustic monitoring for Sousa chinensis," 2nd OCEANOISE ASIA, Hakodate, Hokkaido, Japan, 2018

[8] Wei-Lun Li, Wei- Yen Chu, Chi-Fang Chen, " Dolphin Whistle Detection," The 6th PACIFIC RIM UNDERWATER ACOUSTIC CONFERENCE, Taipei/Hualien, Taiwan, 2018

[9] Lien-Siang Chou et al., "Population Ecology and Estuary Habitat Monitoring for Chinese White Dolphin (Sousa chinensis)(II)", Forestry Bureau, Council of Agriculture, Executive Yuan, Taiwan, 2019

[10] [Lien-Han Kuo, " Statistical Analysis of Whistle and Ambient Noise of Summer in the Habitat of Indo-Pacific Humpback Dolphin (Sousa chinensis) ", Master thesis, Institute of Undersea Technology, National SunYat-sen University, 2014

Statistical Model of High Density Ships in Port and its Application in Ambient Noise Spatial Distribution

GUOLI SONG [1] XINYI GUO [2]

1, Institute of Acoustics, Chinese Academy of Sciences, No.21, North 4th Ring Road,
Beijing, Haidian District, China
songguoli@mail.ioa.ac.cn
2, Key Laboratory of Underwater Acoustic Environment, No.21, North 4th Ring Road,
Beijing, Haidian District, China
guoxinyi@mail.ioa.ac.cn

This paper presents a model of high-density ships in port and based on which studying on the spatial distribution of ocean ambient noise. Firstly, the distribution form of average acoustic energy is analyzed under statistical conditions. And then an equivalent model of high-density ship noise sources is established using the same technology as the former, which shows that the effect on the far field of multiple ships in a small area can be approximated as a point source with increased intensity. After that, a method is proposed to study spatial distribution difference in different positions based on the model presented before, which shows that the noise level difference of two stations is linearly correlated with the transmission loss difference. Finally, the validity of this method is verified by experimental data, and the result shows that the correlation coefficient between the two mentioned above is nearly 0.79 in the band of 50~500Hz.

Keywords: Ocean ambient noise; statistical model; spatial distribution difference.

1. Introduction

The spatial distribution of ocean ambient noise is irregular and changes with the environment to a great extent. The analysis and research on the spatial distribution of ocean ambient noise need to be carried out from two aspects: noise sources and sound propagation [1-2].

In terms of noise sources, E. Tsang-Hin-Sun et al. obtained the low-frequency ocean ambient noise in six sea areas of the South Indian Ocean, and gave the conclusion that the noise level (NL) difference between different positions was caused by the biological noise and the glacier activities[3]. Wiggins analyzed the ambient noise in the Gulf of Mexico. It was found that the NLs in the deep sea, the continental shelf and the edge of the continental shelf were different, considering that it was caused by human activities[4]. In the aspect of inherent transmission conditions of ocean acoustic channels, there are also lots of researches on it. By research on the NL in different position in the eastern coast of Korea, Byoung-Nam Kim pointed out that the existence of deep-sea underwater acoustic channel is a favorable condition for the noise propagation along the continental slope[5]. Ingenito and Wolf investigated the NLs of the shallow water in different areas, and revealed that the acoustic channel was one of the main factors which led to the noise spatial distribution difference[6]. And the conclusion was confirmed by Knoble using the results of deep-sea ambient noise and the wind-driven noise in high sea conditions in shallow water[7].

In this paper, a noise source model of high-density ships under statistical condition is established. Combined with the transmission conditions, a method is proposed to analyze the ambient noise spatial distribution. Results show that the noise level difference (NLD) between two stations can be described by transmission loss (TL) and the number of ships.

2. Core Theory

2.1. Statistical processing method of ocean ambient noise

Ocean ambient noise is a broadband random signal, but in practical application, it is always truncated in time domain and narrowband filtered so that it can be regarded as a stationary narrowband random process. And now record an acoustic pressure signal with a bandwidth Δf and lasts for ΔT as $P(t)$, its analytical formal is recorded as $\tilde{P}(t)$,

$$\tilde{P}(t)=P(t)+j\hat{P}(t). \tag{2.1}$$

where $\hat{P}(t)$ is the Hilbert transformation of $P(t)$. After multiplying the factor $e^{-j\omega_0 t}$ on the equation, it changes to

$$\begin{aligned}\tilde{P}(t)e^{-j\omega_0 t} &=\left[P(t)\cos\omega_0 t+\hat{P}(t)\sin\omega_0 t\right]+j\left[-P(t)\sin\omega_0 t+\hat{P}(t)\cos\omega_0 t\right]\\ &=a(t)+jb(t)\\ &=A(t)e^{j\varphi(t)}.\end{aligned} \tag{2.2}$$

where

$$\begin{aligned}&a(t)=P(t)\cos\omega_0 t+\hat{P}(t)\sin\omega_0 t,\ b(t)=-P(t)\sin\omega_0 t+\hat{P}(t)\cos\omega_0 t.\\ &A(t)=\sqrt{a^2(t)+b^2(t)},\ \varphi(t)=\arctan\left(b(t)/a(t)\right).\end{aligned} \tag{2.3}$$

So,

$$\tilde{P}(t)=A(t)e^{j(\omega_0 t+\varphi(t))}. \tag{2.4}$$

Where ω_0 is carrier frequency, which can be regarded as the center frequency of narrowband noise. $A(t)$ and $\varphi(t)$ are the envelopes and phases of noise respectively.

It should be pointed out that $a(t)$ and $b(t)$ are stochastic processes with the same expectation and variance. Namely

$$E\left[a(t)\right]=E\left[b(t)\right]=0,D\left[a(t)\right]=D\left[b(t)\right]=\sigma^2. \tag{2.5}$$

For stationary narrowband Gaussian noise, $a(t)$ and $b(t)$ are band-limited Gaussian processes. This paper takes Gaussian noise as an example to analyze the significance of statistical processing.

The NL is sound power in unit Hertz. And the acoustic power can be expressed as follows,

$$I=1/T\int_0^T\left|\tilde{P}_T(t)\right|^2dt=1/\Delta T\int_0^{\Delta T}1/N\sum_{i=1}^N\left|\tilde{P}_i(t)\right|^2dt. \tag{2.6}$$

Denote $1/N\sum_{i=1}^{N}\left|\tilde{P}_i(t)\right|^2$ by p^2, which presents the average acoustic energy of N segments with duration ΔT,

$$p^2 = 1/N\sum_{i=1}^{N}\left|\tilde{P}_i(t)\right|^2 = \sigma^2/N\sum_{i=1}^{N}\left(\left(a_i(t)/\sigma\right)^2+\left(b_i(t)/\sigma\right)^2\right). \tag{2.7}$$

And it can be expressed in the form of chi-square distribution, with mathematical expectation and variance as follows,

$$E\left(p^2\right)=2\sigma^2, D\left(p^2\right)=4\sigma^4/N. \tag{2.8}$$

Therefore, the mathematical expectation of average acoustic energy remains unchanged with sectional treatment, but the variance decreases with the increase of segment numbers, which indicates that statistical method makes the acoustic energy more stable.

Similarly, statistical method eliminates the influence of unstable factors and makes the NL tend to be stable. Take the weak-Gaussian noise into consideration, the NL processed statistically represents the average level under stable conditions.

2.2. Statistical model of high-density ships

Processing ship noise sources in the same way. For high-density ships in a port of same or similar types, the number of it is a random variable $M(t)$ about port area S and ship's density ρ,

$$M(t)=\int_S \rho(t)ds. \tag{2.9}$$

Corresponding to the noise processing method, sampling the ship's number every ΔT for totally N times,

$$\bar{M} = 1/N\sum_{i=1}^{N} M_i(t). \tag{2.10}$$

When N is big enough, the statistical average value tends to be the mathematical expectation, namely,

$$\bar{M} = E(M). \tag{2.11}$$

Therefore, dealing with ambient noise statistically is equivalent to averaging the effect of noise sources. Generally speaking, the density of ships in port area is much greater than that in surroundings, namely $M_{port} >> M_{other}$. Under far field condition, the "geometric radius" of the port area is very small relative to the propagation distance of noise.

Therefore, under statistical average condition, the influence of port ships on the far-field can be approximately equivalent to a point source with the number of $E(M)$.

2.3. Spatial distribution difference analysis of ambient noise

Using the simplified model of high-density ships mentioned above to analyze the spatial distribution of ambient noise under the influence of ships in different ports. As shown in Fig. (1), P1 and P2 are two ports, N1 and N2 are noise collection stations, which are affected by ship radiation noise at ports P1 and P2 respectively.

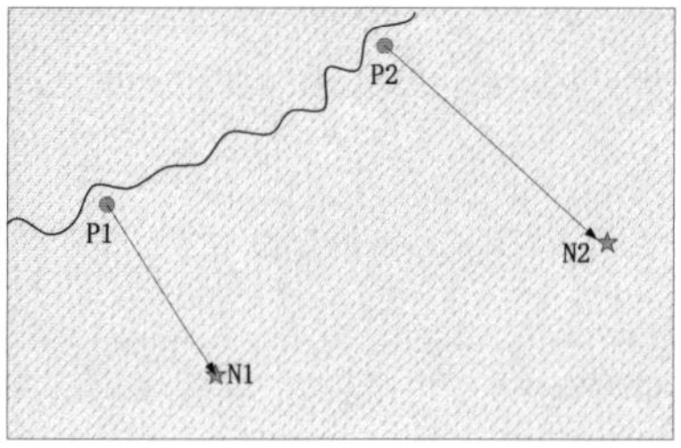

Fig. 1. Noise collection station schematic diagram.

Ideally, the ship type at each port is alike and concentrated in a certain area. Let $E(M_1)$ be the mathematical expectation of the number of ships in port P1 during a statistical time T, s_1 be the effective sound pressure of a single ship, H_1 be the transfer function of sound field from P1 to N1. Correspondingly, variables at N2 are represented by footnote "2". Because the radiated noise between ships is incoherent, the ship noise source levels (SLs) at ports P1 and P2 can be expressed as follows respectively (ignoring the reference sound pressure)

$$SL_1 = 10\lg E(M_1) + 10\lg s_1^2, SL_2 = 10\lg E(M_2) + 10\lg s_2^2. \tag{2.12}$$

So affected by single ship, the NLs of stations N1 and N2 can be expressed as follows

$$NL_1 = 10\lg E(M_1) + 10\lg H_1^2, NL_2 = 10\lg E(M_2) + 10\lg s_2^2 \tag{2.13}$$

Here the transfer function of sound pressure presents the TL. Recorded as

$$TL_1 = -10\lg H_1^2, TL_2 = -10\lg H_2^2. \tag{2.14}$$

Therefore, the NLD between two stations is equivalent to the following equation,

$$NL_1 - NL_2 = 10\lg E(M_1)/E(M_2) + (10\lg s_1^2 - 10\lg s_2^2) - (TL_1 - TL_2). \tag{2.15}$$

Note NLD, transmission loss difference (TLD), and noise source level difference (SLD) of single ship as

$$\Delta NL = NL_1 - NL_2, \Delta TL = (TL_1 - TL_2), \Delta SL_0 = 10\lg s_1^2 - 10\lg s_2^2. \tag{2.16}$$

so Eq. (2.15) equivalent to Eq. (2.17)

$$\Delta NL = 10\lg E(M_1)/E(M_2) + \Delta SL_0 - \Delta TL. \tag{2.17}$$

In actual ocean environment, noise will be inevitably affected by some unknown sources, such as wind, discrete ships and marine organism and so on, their existence will also cause the difference of noise spatial distribution. Under statistical condition, these unstable factors can be eliminated as far as possible, so that the ocean environment of the same area in the same season is a relatively stable system. Using "other" to represent the influence of this part of sources, it can be considered that

$$(SL_{other} - TL_{other})_{N1} \approx (SL_{other} - TL_{other})_{N2} + c. \tag{2.18}$$

So, under the consideration of other sources, Eq. (2.17) extends to

$$\Delta NL = 10\lg E(M_1)/E(M_2) + \Delta SL_0 - \Delta TL + c. \tag{2.19}$$

When the ship type of the two ports are the same, Eq. (2.19) can be reduced to

$$\Delta NL = 10\lg E(M_1)/E(M_2) - \Delta TL + c. \tag{2.20}$$

So a conclusion is reached that the NLD and TLD is linearly correlated. The noise spatial distribution difference can be analyzed by TLD, source level, and the number of ships. This method reduces the influence of unstable noise sources, and avoids the consideration of absolute value but the relative value, which eliminates the influence of uncertainties.

3. Data Verification

To verify the method here, ocean ambient noise data is acquired from the northern area of the South China Sea. During the experiment, noise was measured at two stations named N1 and N2, S1 and S2 represent the two ports with high-density ships. The stations are affected by the two port ships respectively. For N2 station, the measurement lasts for 5 days before the fishing moratorium, but for N1 station, it is during the fishing moratorium.

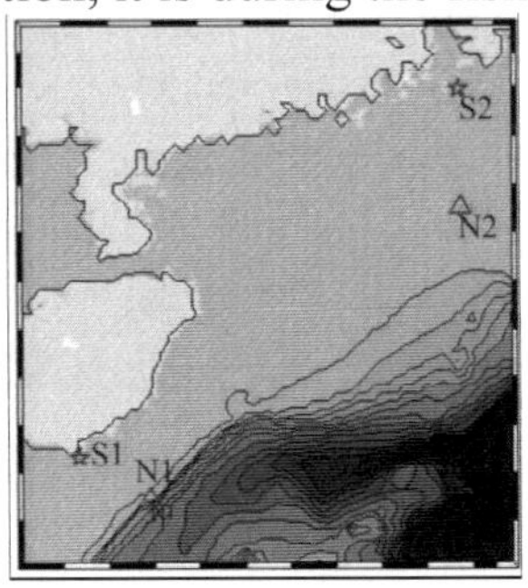

Fig.2. The measurement stations and ports.

During this period, the weather and sea conditions of two stations did not change much, and the wind speed is about 5 to 6 meters per second. The sound speed profiles are measured by CTD (conductivity-temperature-depth), as shown in Fig. (3). As for the sea depth profile, S1N1 is a typical continental shelf steep slope, the depth changes from 30m to 280m. For S2N2, the depth ranges from 30m to 87m, which changes slowly.

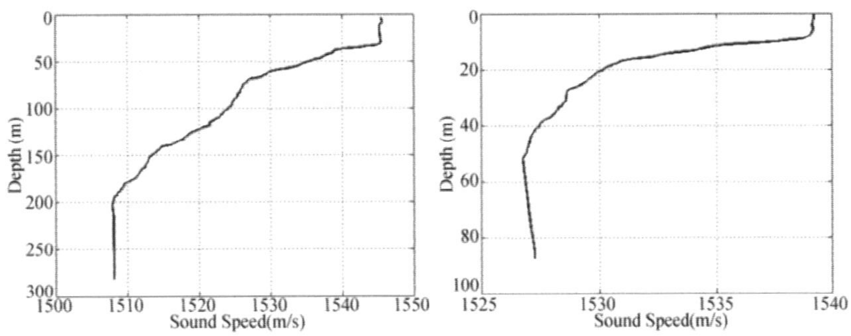

Fig.3. Sound speed profile of N1and N2 (left: N1 right: N2).

Considering the frequency range of ship noise, the ambient noise data are processed in one-third octave frequency band in 50Hz-1000Hz. And the NL at same moment of the two stations are compared in Fig. (4). The NL of N2 station is higher than that of N1 station nearly in the whole frequency. The following work is to analyze the spatial difference using the model and method proposed before.

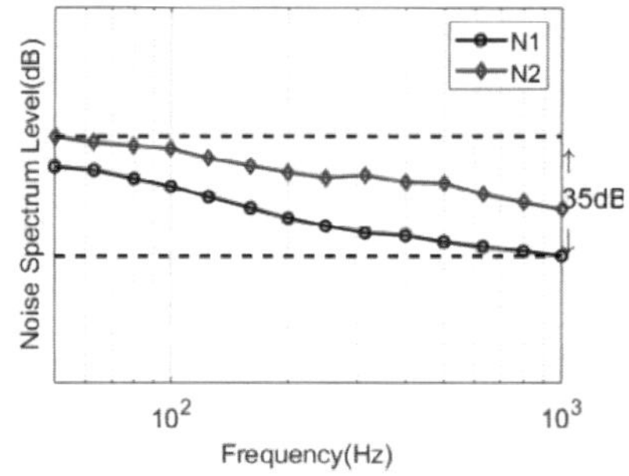

Fig.4. Noise spectrum level comparison for N1 and N2 stations.

According to Eq. (2.20), TLD between S1N1 and S2N2 is needed, so the acoustic field simulation analysis is carried out using the RAM (Range-dependent Acoustic Model[8] according to the environmental condition. Environmental parameters used in RAM are shown in the table below. They are set up according to actual measurement data and related theories of the sea area over the years[9-10].

Table 1. Environmental parameters used in RAM.

Schedule	S1N1	S2N2
Ship source depth	7m	7m
Submarine sound speed	1600 m/s	1630 m/s
Sediment density	1.8 g/cm^3	1.8 g/cm^3
Absorption coefficient	$\alpha = 0.39 f^{1.5}$dB/m	$\alpha = 0.39 f^{1.5}$dB/m

Figure (5) show the distribution of acoustic energy of 200 Hz. It can be seen that the acoustic energy is propagating along the continental slope to the deep water area, so the bottom moored measurement buoy can be affected by the noise of the ships.

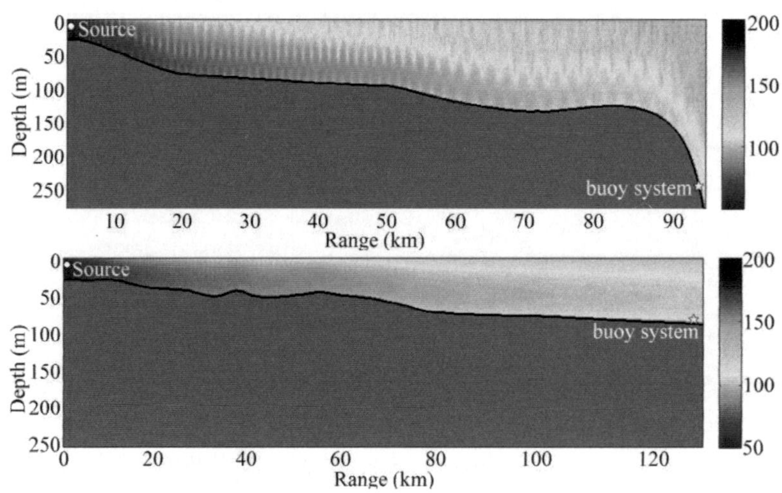

Fig.5. TLs of 200Hz for stations N1 and N2 (up: N1 down: N2).

Smoothing TL values in one-third octave frequency with a bandwidth of 1Hz and averaged it in depth, the variation of TL with frequency is got and compared, as shown in Fig. (6). It can be seen that nearly in the whole band, the TL of S1N1 path is smaller than that of S2N2 path and the difference between the two TL decrease with frequency increasing.

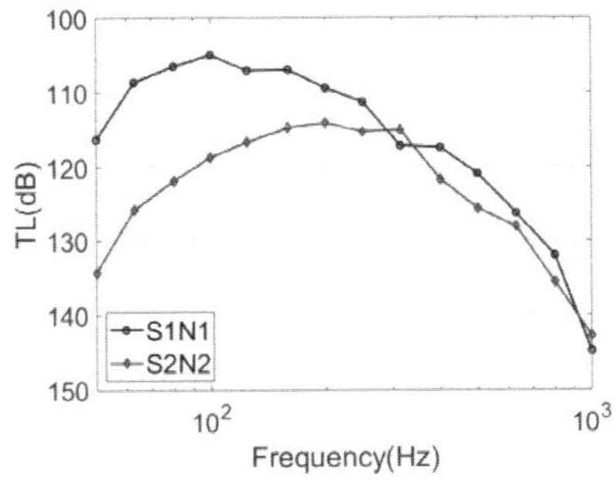

Fig. 6. The TL variation of two stations.

As so far, the NLD and TLD are got and Figure (7) is the result of the two. Here the dotted line represents the opposite value of NLD and the solid line represents the TLD. Obviously, a similar trend can be found from the figure. The correlation coefficient of NLD and TLD is 0.788 in 50Hz~500Hz, which means the spatial distribution difference between the two station is closely related to the propagation channel from the port to the noise measurement station.

In addition, the range of the sum of the two tends to be a constant, which is about -18 dB to -26 dB. This indicates the number of ships at S2 is far more than that at S1, which is consistent with the measurement background. As for the fluctuation, it is explained in Ref. (11).

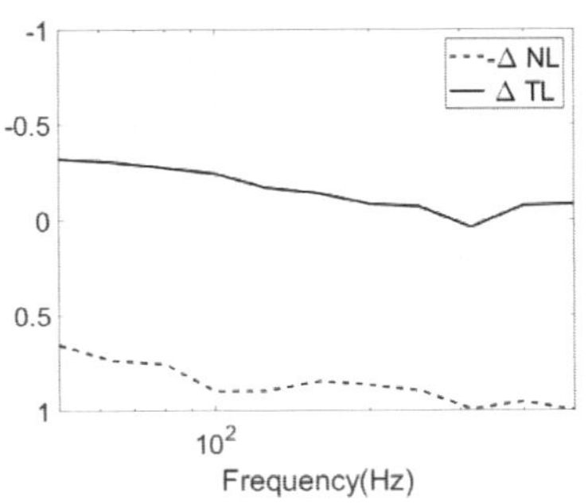

Fig. 7. The NLD (negative value) and TLD at 12:00.

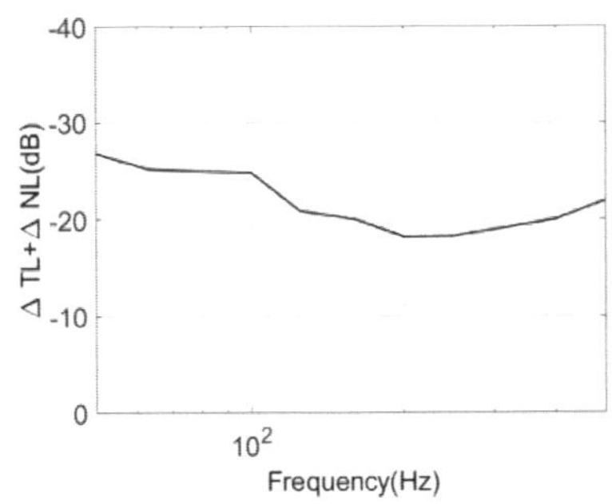

Fig. 8. Sum of NLD and TLD.

In a word, the spatial distribution difference between two stations is caused by the high-density ships and the transmission channel.

4. Conclusion

In combination with statistical processing method of ocean ambient noise, a statistical model of high-density ships in port is proposed. The number of ships obtained by statistical average eliminates the unstable change of ships and makes them tend to stable value. Therefore, the influence of port ships on the far-field can be approximately equivalent to a point source with high-density. Under this condition, the ambient noise spatial distribution difference caused by port ships can be characterized by the transmission loss difference, the source level difference and the number of ships.

References

[1] J. A. Hildebrand, "Anthropogenic and natural sources of ambient noise in the ocean," Mar. Ecol.-Prog. 395(12) (2009), 5–20.
[2] M. A. McDonald, J. A. Hildebrand, and S. M. Wiggins, "A 50 year comparison of ambient ocean noise near San Clemente Island: a bathymetrically complex coastal region off Southern California," J. Acoust. Soc. Am., 124(4) (2008), 1985–1992.
[3] Tsang-Hin-Sun E, J. Y. Royer, and E. C. Leroy, "Low-frequency sound level in the Southern Indian Ocean," J. Acoust. Soc. Am., 138(6) (2015), 3439–3446.
[4] S. M. Wiggins and M. H. Jesse, "Gulf of Mexico low-frequency ocean soundscape impacted by airguns," J. Acoust. Soc. Am., 140(1) (2016), 176–183.
[5] B. N. Kim, B. K. Choi, and S. H. Kim et al, "Effect of underwater sound channel on variation of ambient noise level in eastern sea of Korea," Jpn. J. Appl. Phys., 53(7S) (2014), 07KG04-1–07KG04-5.
[6] F. Ingenito and S. N. Wolf, "Site dependence of wind-dominated ambient noise in shallow water," J. Acoust. Soc. Am., 85(1) (1989), 141–145.
[7] D. P. Knoble, S. M. Joshi and R. D. Gaul et al, "Analysis of wind-driven ambient noise in a shallow water environment with a sandy seabed," J. Acoust. Soc. Am., 124(3) (2008), EL157–162.
[8] M. D. Collins, "A split step Pade solution for parabolic equation method," J. Acoust. Soc. Am., 93(4) (1993), 1736–1742.
[9] LONG Jianjun and LI Ganxian, "Theoretical relationship between sound velocity and the physical properties of submarine sediment," Chinese Journal of Acoustics, 34(4) (2015), 401–412.
[10] Ji-Xun Zhou and Xue-Zhen Zhang, "Low-frequency geoacoustic model for the effective properties of sandy seabottoms," J. Acoust. Soc. Am., 125(5) (2009), 2847–2866.
[11] S. Guoli, G. Xinyi, M. Li and Z. Qianchu. "Analysis on spatial difference of ocean ambient noise spectrum in the northern South China Sea," Chinese Journal of Acoustics, 38(1) (2019), 49–61.

Underwater noise simulation of impact pile driving with the noise mitigation technology for offshore wind farm in Taiwan

Chiu-Kuan Shih, Yin-Ying Fang, Wei-Chun Hu, Chi-Fang Chen
Department of Engineering Science and Ocean Engineering,
National Taiwan University
chifang@ntu.edu.tw
r06525035@ntu.edu.tw

In recent years, the international community actively has promoted green energy. As wind power has become one of the major development projects, piling noise also has become an important research topic. In this study, a finite element (FE) model was built using COMSOL Multiphysics software to calculate the sound field of piling noise. In Taiwan, coastal waters suitable for developing offshore wind energy are close to the main habitats of endangered marine mammals. Piling produces considerable low-frequency noise that may seriously affect the ecological environment. In addition, underwater noise regulations and monitoring standards must be observed during construction. This study also uses noise mitigation techniques (balloon curtains) to create an integrated piling noise prediction and mitigation system. The simulation results are compared with the actual piling noise measured from a bottom-mounted recorder. The piling energy mainly is distributed between 100 Hz and 500 Hz. The results show that the piling noise can be predicted in the finite element model and display the effect of the mitigation system.
This research is funded by the Ministry of Science and Technology under Project No. MOST
107-3113-E-002 -006 -CC2

Keywords: Finite Element; Pile Driving Noise; Noise Mitigation; Balloon Curtains

1. Introduction

1.1. Background

International attention to environmental issues is increasing, and renewable energy has become a topic of great importance. In Taiwan, the geographic environment and wind source are suitable for developing wind energy. Because of the potential of offshore wind energy, Taiwan is actively promoting the "Thousand Wind Turbines" Project and has set two goals: first is 520 MW offshore wind power prior to 2020 and second is 3000 MW offshore wind power prior to 2025. Unfortunately, the location for potential offshore wind farms is close to the habitat of the endangered marine "Chinese White Dolphin". Pile driving noise may cause behavior disturbance and even auditory damage to them. If we can predict the pile driving noise in advance, we can assess whether we need to do noise mitigation or not. This study simulates the pile driving noise to estimate the noise intensity generated by it, and it adds the balloon curtain noise mitigation system to carry out the complete simulation to analyze and predict the pile driving noise.

Offshore Wind Power Planning	
Schedule	Capacity
2015~2020	520MW
2015~2025	3GW
2025~	10~17GW

(Bureau of Energy, 2017)

區域	遴選容量	比例
桃園	350 MW	9.1%
苗栗	378 MW	9.9%
彰化	2400 MW	62.6%
雲林	708 MW	18.4%
總計	3836MW	100%

註:上述結果係依評選序位及台電公司公告之併網容量所分配結果，惟已獲得分配申請案，後續如依「離岸風力發電規劃場址容量分配作業要點」規定放棄獲配容量，則上述分配容量將隨之調整。

Fig.1. Offshore wind farm locations in Taiwan

1.2. Methodology

1.2.1. Pile driving noise simulation

The main physical mechanism of the pile driving is the normal wall displacement caused by the compressional wave propagation in the pile along the axial direction by means of the Poisson contraction of solid. We can see the strike is applied to the top of the pile and generates a compression wave, which will be transmitted to the bottom and reflect, causing the Poisson contraction and sound radiation. This process may cause Mach waves to radiate from the pile into the water and sediment surrounding the pile. The right figure below is the hammer strike we used in the finite element model. As the analysis is in the frequency domain, first we need to transform our hammer strike energy from the time domain to the frequency domain. The impact force signal is given as an exponential function.

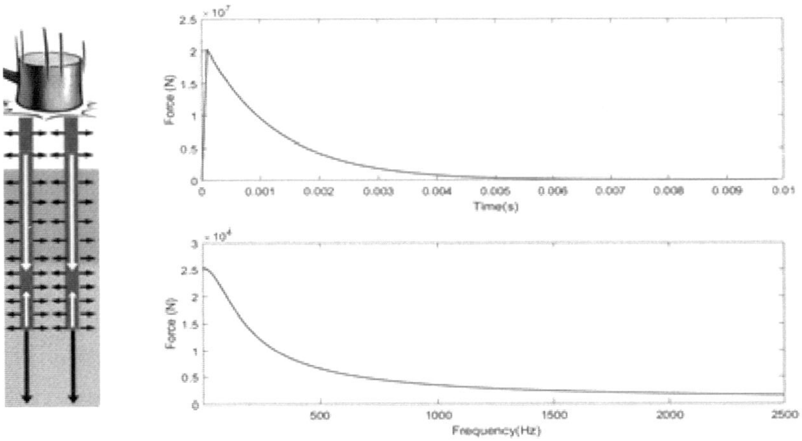

Fig. 2. Pile driving force.

The common numerical method is finite element (FE) model and is mostly linear and axisymmetric. In addition, the bottom is viewed as fluid with equivalent sound attenuation to reduce the computation time and complexity. In this paper, a detailed linear axisymmetric FE model in the frequency domain was applied for solving the acoustic field. To investigate the acoustic radiation from a pile strike, a finite element (FE) model with frequency domain analysis was used. The model used commercial software COMSOL Multiphysics.

1.2.2. Noise mitigation with balloon curtain

The water noise mitigation system added in the simulation of this study is a balloon curtain, which is a balloon screen noise reduction technology developed by the National Taiwan University Underwater Acoustics Laboratory. In 2016, there was a real sea area noise reduction system experiment, which has been patented. The system reduces the noise using the balloon to resonate with the sound wave under water and using the balloon curtain to reduce the noise by surrounding the pile. In the 2016 sea area experiment, the noise mitigation effect of the piling frequency band from 40 to 500 Hz is about 15 to 20 dB and the center frequency of 100 to 200 Hz is the best frequency band for noise mitigation. In order to achieve the prediction of piling noise and the possible effect of noise mitigation, this study calculates the possible noise reduction effects in the finite element simulation with the balloon curtain system.

Fig. 3. Balloon curtain 2016

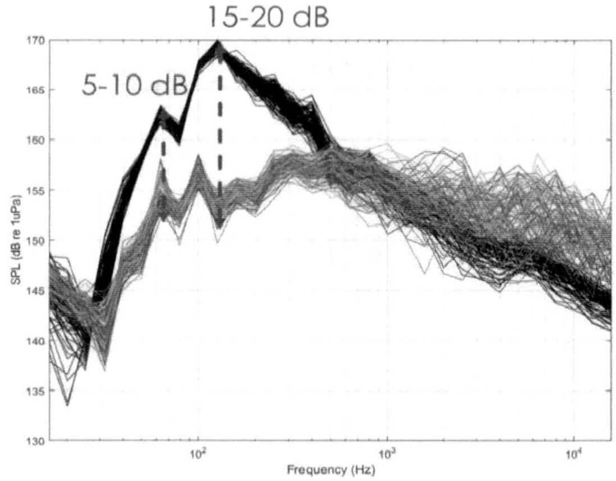

Fig. 4. Mitigation effect of balloon curtain

2. Pile driving simulation

2.1. Setting

The computational domain consists of piles, water, and sediment, and it is axisymmetric and is truncated by a perfectly matched layer (PML). PML can adjust the scale factor and the ratio PML curvature to prevent the reflected wave from reaching the boundary parameters. PML increase factor values can improve resolution near the physical boundary wavelength and attenuation. The pile was modeled as a linear elastic hollow steel, *i.e.*, the Young's modulus was E = 210 GPa, the Poisson's ratio was $\mu = 0.3$, the density $\rho = 7850$ kg/m^3, pile length was about 65 m, diameter was 5.8 m, and wall thickness was 0.065 m. The environmental variables were set to a water depth of 20 m and a sediment depth of 100 m. Unlike other studies, we used thick, uneven deposits to consider some sound waves that are transmitted to the deeper bottom layer and reflected back into the water. The energy loss mechanism of piling is the friction caused by the interaction between the embedded portion of the pile and the deposit. The influence of steel damping itself is small, and the estimated value of the empirical formula of compression wave damping and shear wave damping reference 1.5 dB and 3 dB per wavelength. The finite element model was solved and increased to 1403 Hz in 1 Hz increments at 40 Hz. The mesh element has a maximum size of 0.2 m.

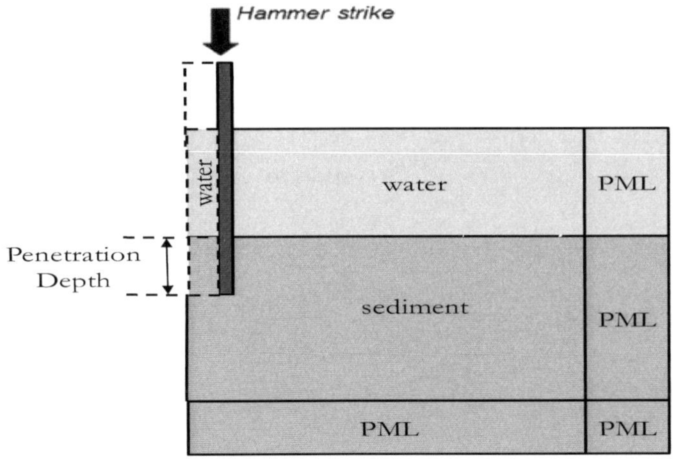

Fig. 5. Pile driving model

2.2. 3D piling model

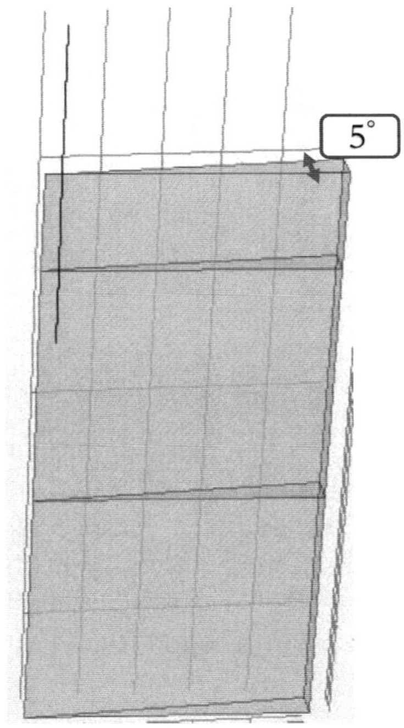

Fig. 6. 3D model.

At the beginning of this simulation, a 3D piling model was established. Since the 3D model is more traditional than the traditional model, it requires more computational grid and computation time. Therefore, the 3D simulation calculation range is reduced to 50 meters from the pile and the angle chosen for calculation was 5 degrees.

To ensure that the simulation is not distorted, the maximum mesh length cannot be greater than one-sixth of the wavelength. I tried two boundary conditions with the same pile driving power 1082 kj, the hard field (reflection) and the perfectly matched boundary (PML). The difference between the two is very large. The hard field boundary reflects the sound energy into the water, causing the measured sound pressure intensity to significantly exceed the expected value. The perfectly matched boundary (PML) makes the sound pressure energy too divergent, and it results in deviation of the calculation result.

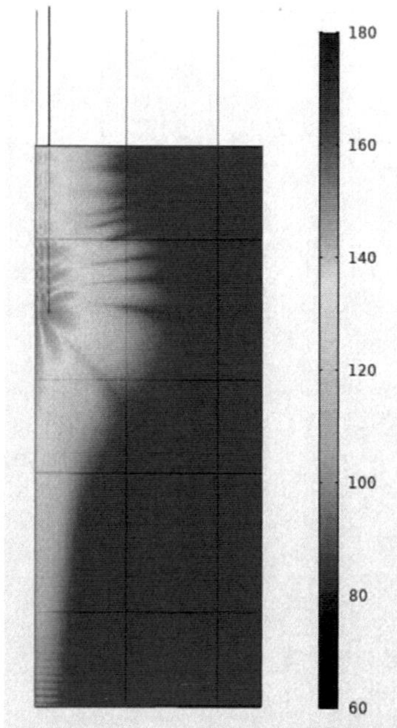

Fig. 7. Perfectly matched boundary.

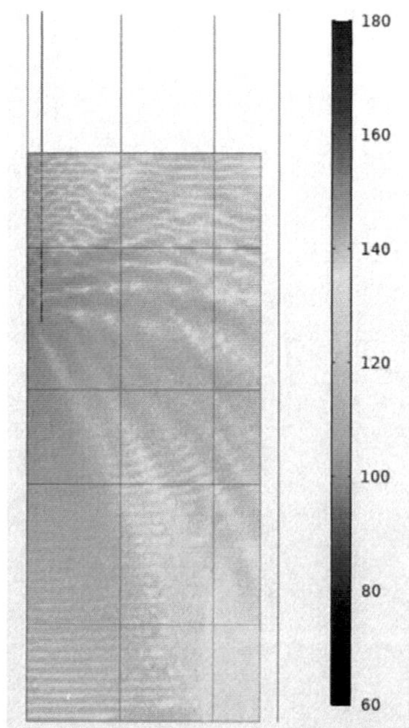

Fig. 8. Hard field boundary.

Too small a calculated angle results in a boundary condition that greatly affects the outcome and may be a major factor in the simulation results. In order to solve the problem of boundary condition interference results, change the simulation angle to thirty degrees to increase the calculation range, and reduce the stimuli caused by the boundary conditions.
This still requires some future work to overcome, the biggest difficulty being that the calculation time is too long and the calculation is too large, so it requires a stronger computer.

2.3. 2D model

Based on the current situation, I chose a two-dimensional axisymmetric model to simulate piling noise. The FEM method is used to model the near-field region around the pile, which is solved in the frequency domain and preprocessed and post-processed via Matlab. The pile material is set to a linear elastic material and the entire model is axially symmetrical. The pressure release boundary condition is applied to the top of the pile, the energy loss caused by the friction between the pile and the sediment needs to be considered in the model, and it is assumed that the water and the sediment are fluid substances. In the fluid domain, sound attenuation in the water column and equivalent sound attenuation in the deposit are considered. Resolve the reflection problem of the boundary by coating the outer side of the model with a perfect matching layer (PML)
The simulation results have the largest sound level at 125 HZ, and the 500 HZ sound waves more obviously display the sound wave transmission. This can be seen from the calculation results that the acoustic energy of 125 HZ and the results displayed by 500 HZ exceed the limit values specified in the current regulations. It can be seen in this case under the piling during construction. If the power and energy of pile driving do not change, the noise pressure energy will be out of specifications, so noise mitigation measures must be carried out for the project.

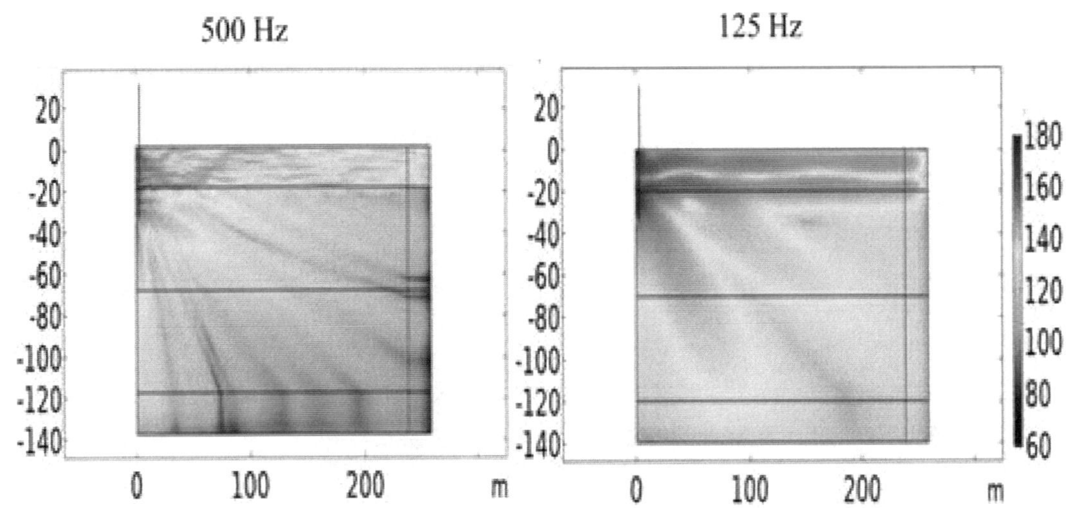

Fig. 9. Sound pressure level @500Hz & @125Hz (original)

3. Pile driving simulation with noise mitigation system

3.1. Settings

In this chapter, the second chapter 2D simulation is added to the noise mitigation system. The boundary conditions and model settings are the same. The balloon model is added at a distance of 3 meters from the piling. The radius ranges from 0.05 meters to 0.75 meters. In the model, the balloon dimension is a single layer, and the water surface cloth is placed on the bed. A total of 145 balloons are used. The resonance between the balloon and the sound wave reduces the noise energy of the pile driving.

In the calculation of the finite element method model added to the noise reduction system, the sound pressure intensity noticeably is reduced in the simulation results. The sound wave and energy transfer trends from 500HZ and 125HZ are the same as the original. Nevertheless, there is a significant reduction in energy intensity after adding balloon curtains to reduce noise.

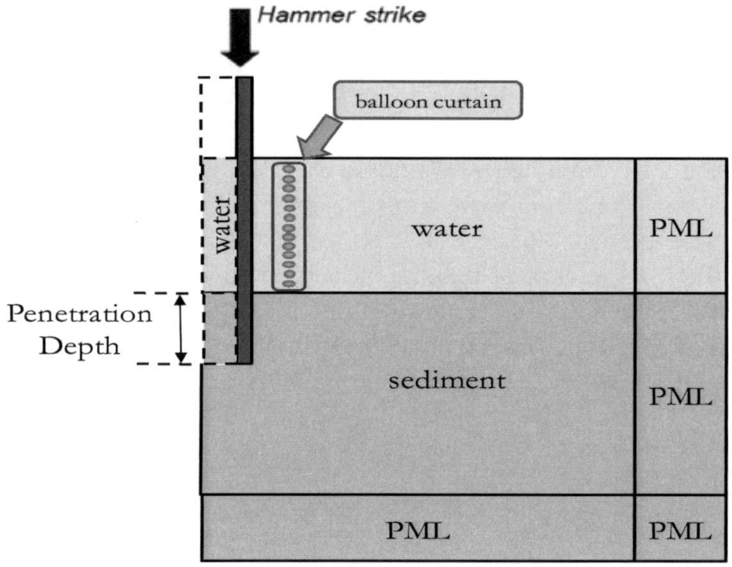

Fig. 10. 2D Axial symmetric simulation model with balloon curtain

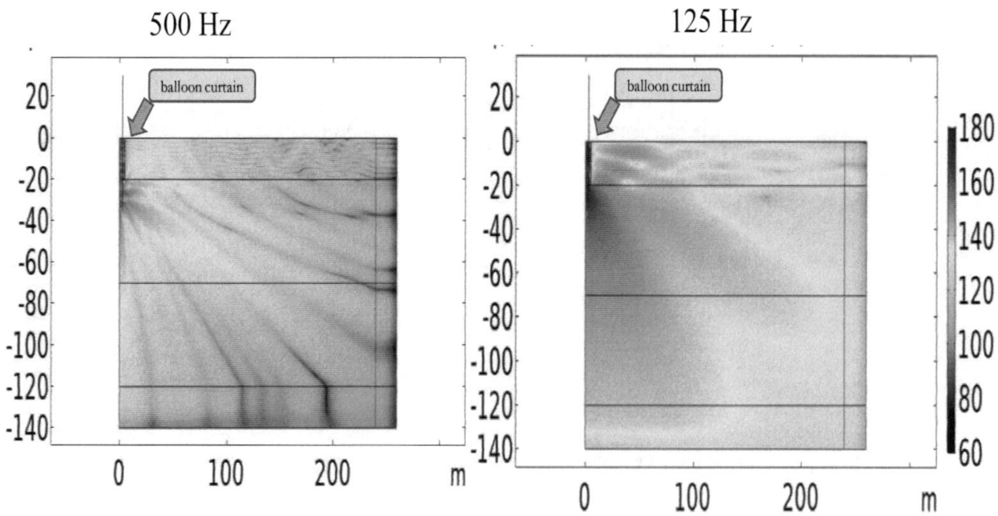

Fig. 11. Sound pressure level @500Hz & @125Hz (with balloon curtain)

4. Conclusion

Comparing the results of the simple piling simulation and the noise mitigation system in the simulation results, the acoustic exposure values are calculated at 5 m and 230 m from the piling extension. The water depths are 5 m, 10 m, 15 m, and 20 m.

The results show that there is a considerable acoustic exposure near the bed. It is speculated

	Without @5m	With @5m	Without @230m	With @230m
Water depth 5 m	190dB	177dB	177dB	163dB
Water depth 10 m	191dB	179dB	178dB	165dB
Water depth 15 m	190dB	178dB	178dB	164dB
Water depth 20 m	193dB	182dB	178dB	165dB

Fig. 12. Comparison of sound exposure level (SEL) for one second

that the reason may be the energy transmitted from the sediments and the sound pressure energy also being attenuated with distance.

Using 2D simulation to analyze and add noise reduction systems can show a 15-20dB noise level reduction. This simulation not only predicts piling noise, but also helps us estimate the noise level using a noise reduction system. This study has practical significance for the improvement and development of the next noise reduction technology and the prediction and evaluation before the pile foundation construction. Nevertheless, it still is necessary to continue to overcome the difficulty of 3D piling simulation calculation, and to carry out 3D simulation and analysis to further improve and verify the reliability of your piling prediction model.

.

References

[1] The prediction benchmark case of underwater noise emissions from impact pile driving has been built. (Stephan Lippert, Marten Nijhof, Tristan Lippert…,2016)

[2] Underwater noise simulation of impact pile driving for offshore wind farm in Taiwan (Yin-Ying Fang, Chi-Fang Chen,…,2019)

[3] Study of Pile Driving Noise and Mitigation Mechanism (Wei-Chieh Wang, Chi-Fang Chen,2016)

Multi-mode Excitation of Frequency Modulated Signals in Shallow Water

XIAO-FENG YI[12] DA-YONG PENG[1†] JUAN ZENG[1] LI MA[1]

1, Institute of Acoustics, Chinese Academy of Sciences
Key Laboratory of Underwater Acoustic Environment, Chinese Academy of Sciences
No. 21 North 4th Ring Road, Haidian District, Beijing 100190, P. R. China
† pengdayong@mail.ioa.ac.cn
2, University of Chinese Academy of Sciences, No. 19(A) Yuquan Road, Shijingshan District, Beijing 100149, P. R. China

A multi-mode sound field excitation method of frequency modulated (FM) signals using a vertical source array (VSA) in shallow water is proposed. The eigenvalues and eigenfunctions of the low-order modes are calculated using the carrier frequency based on the normal mode theory. Then, by adjusting the weight coefficients of the VSA to stack the low-order modes in the same phase at a specific position, the sound field focusing effect can be obtained within a certain space around the specific position. The simulations of multi-mode excitation of FM signals in Pekeris waveguide show that using the first three modes can obtain a robust focusing effect at most water depths when the bandwidth is much less than the carrier frequency. In addition, by scanning the focusing depth using the multi-mode excitation method, target depth discrimination can be realized according to the target echo strength of different focusing depths, which indicates that the multi-mode excitation method of FM signals has a broad application prospect in active detection.

Keywords: Multi-mode excitation; sound field focusing; target depth discrimination.

1. Introduction

Vertical source array (VSA) has been used in spatial focusing of signal energy for shallow water active sonar applications because of its ability to form directivity and spatial gain. Currently, single-mode excitation and time-reversal mirror (TRM) are well-developed technologies in field focusing. Single-mode excitation technology exploits the orthonormality of normal modes to excite selected single modes in an acoustic field by adjusting the weight vector of the VSA. It has the advantage of suppressing multi-path and reverberation [1-2]; however, it also has a limitation related to target detection because of its single depth distribution of the acoustic field. On the other hand, TRM is a process of transmitting a received signal in a time-reversed order. It uses a source/receiver array (SRA) to refocus the received signal transmitted by a probe source (PS) on the initial position of the PS [3-4]. However, it has a limitation related to active detection because of the lack of PS around the real target.

In this paper, a multi-mode excitation method is proposed, which concentrates the wave energy on several lower modes and utilizes them to obtain the focusing effect at the desired position. It realizes a compromise between single-mode excitation and TRM technologies because single-mode excitation only uses a single mode while TRM uses all of the modes to focus the wave energy. The paper is organized as follows. Section 2 introduces the theory of multi-mode excitation and shows the simulation results of single-frequency excitation. Section 3 discusses the multi-mode excitation method of frequency modulated signals. Finally, Sec. 4 summarizes the results and conclusions from the work.

2. Multi-mode Excitation

2.1. Theoretical analysis

In horizontally stratified ocean waveguide, the normal mode theory states that the far-field from a point source is given by

$$p(r,z;z_s)=\frac{\mathrm{i}}{\sqrt{8\pi}}\sum_{m=1}^{\infty}\frac{\varphi_m(z_s)\varphi_m(z)e^{\mathrm{i}(k_m r-\pi/4)}}{\rho(z_s)\sqrt{k_m r}}, \tag{2.1}$$

where z_s and z are the depths of the source and the receiver, respectively; r is the range between the source and the receiver; $\rho(z_s)$ is the density of water at z_s; and k_m and φ_m represent the eigenvalue (modal wavenumber) and eigenfunction (mode function), respectively. The mode functions form an orthogonal complete set that satisfies

$$\int_0^{\infty}\frac{\varphi_m(z)\varphi_j^*(z)}{\rho(z)}\mathrm{d}z=\delta_{mj}, \tag{2.2}$$

$$\sum_{m=1}^{\infty}\frac{\varphi_m(z)\varphi_m^*(z_s)}{\rho(z_s)}=\delta(z-z_s), \tag{2.3}$$

where the density $\rho(z)$ takes an appropriate value in each layer and δ_{mj} is the Kronecker delta function.

We assume that there is a VSA of N transducers at the origin located at depths $z_1,z_2,\cdots,z_N$. Furthermore, we assume that only a finite number of modes M propagate to the point (r,z) in the field. Hence, by applying Eq. (2.1), the pressure field at the point (r,z) to the VSA is written as

$$p_N(r,z;z_1,z_2,\cdots,z_N)=\frac{\mathrm{i}}{\sqrt{8\pi}}\sum_{n=1}^{N}w_n\sum_{m=1}^{M}\frac{\varphi_m(z_n)\varphi_m(z)e^{\mathrm{i}(k_m r-\pi/4)}}{\rho(z_n)\sqrt{k_m r}}, \tag{2.4}$$

where $w_1,w_2,\cdots,w_N$ are the weight coefficients for each of the N transducers in the VSA. Single-mode excitation sets the weight coefficients as the conjugate of the eigenfunction corresponding to the jth mode sampled at the source depths

$$w_n=\varphi_j^*(z_n),\ n=1,2,\cdots,N. \tag{2.5}$$

On the other hand, TRM excites the SRA sources by the complex conjugate of the Green's function

$$w_n=G^*(r_0,z_n;z_0). \tag{2.6}$$

where the Green's function $G(r_0,z_n;z_0)$ is the received field at the SRA at range r_0 from the PS with source/receive elements at depths z_n given by

$$G(r_0, z_n; z_0) = \frac{\mathrm{i}}{\sqrt{8\pi}} \sum_{m=1}^{M} \frac{\varphi_m(z_0)\varphi_m(z_n)e^{\mathrm{i}(k_m r_0 - \pi/4)}}{\rho(z_0)\sqrt{k_m r_0}}. \tag{2.7}$$

When there is no PS, the Green's function can be estimated based on the normal mode theory. This needs *a priori* knowledge of the environmental parameters to calculate the eigenvalues and eigenfunctions. However, the environmental parameters especially the geo-acoustic parameters cannot be obtained accurately, resulting in estimating errors for the k_ms and φ_ms. Generally, the higher the modal order m is, the larger the estimating errors for k_m and φ_m are. As a result, the VSA cannot focus the acoustic energy at the desired position because of the estimating error of the Green's function.

To reduce the estimating errors and improve the robustness, we only choose J $(1 < J < M)$ lower modes to estimate the Green's function, written as Q

$$Q(r_0, z_n; z_0) = \frac{\mathrm{i}}{\sqrt{8\pi}} \sum_{j=1}^{J} \frac{\varphi_j(z_0)\varphi_j(z_n)e^{\mathrm{i}(k_j r_0 - \pi/4)}}{\rho(z_0)\sqrt{k_j r_0}}. \tag{2.8}$$

Then, we set the weight coefficients as the conjugate of Qs

$$w_n = Q^*(r_0, z_n; z_0). \tag{2.9}$$

Substituting Eq. (2.8) and Eq. (2.9) into Eq. (2.4), the pressure field at (R, z) is

$$P_N(R, z; z_1, z_2, \cdots, z_N) \approx \frac{1}{8\pi} \sum_{j=1}^{J} \frac{\varphi_j(z)\varphi_j^*(z_0)e^{\mathrm{i}k_j(R-r_0)}}{\rho(z_0)k_j\sqrt{Rr_0}}. \tag{2.10}$$

and the acoustic field at (r_0, z_0) becomes

$$P_N(r_0, z_0) \approx \frac{1}{8\pi} \sum_{j=1}^{J} \frac{|\varphi_j(z_0)|^2}{\rho(z_0)k_j r_0}. \tag{2.11}$$

Equation (2.11) illustrates that the J lower modes stack in the same phase at (r_0, z_0) rather than all of the M modes. In other words, it neglects the $M - J$ higher modes and utilizes the J multiple modes to obtain the focusing effect at (r_0, z_0); hence, calling it "multi-mode excitation".

2.2. Simulations of single-frequency excitation

Figure (1) shows the focusing effects of multi-mode excitation of single-frequency signals in Pekeris waveguide when $J = 2, 3, 5, 7$. The parameters used are as follows: water depth $H = 50$ m, sound speed in water $c_0 = 1500$ m/s, density of water $\rho_0 = 1.0$ g/cm^3, sound speed in sediment $c_b = 1600$ m/s, density of sediment $\rho_b = 1.5$ g/cm^3, and attenuation in sediment $\alpha_b = 0.2$ dB/λ. The VSA with element number of 32 and element spacing of 1.5 m transmits at a single frequency of 750 Hz. The focusing range r_0 is 10 km and the focusing depths z_0 are 12, 25, and 38 m. The figure shows that several focusing areas are formed in the acoustic field. This is the consequence of the interference effects of the J lower modes at different ranges. At the desired focusing position, when $J = 2$, it can focus well on the upper and lower halves of the water layer but cannot focus well on the middle of the water layer; hence, $J = 2$ is not suitable for depth scanning. When $J \geq 3$, it can focus well on most depths of the water layer but higher modes have higher sensitivities to environmental mismatch and larger grazing angel; hence, in order to improve the robustness and reduce the reverberation, $J = 3$ is more suitable for depth scanning using multi-mode excitation in Pekeris waveguide.

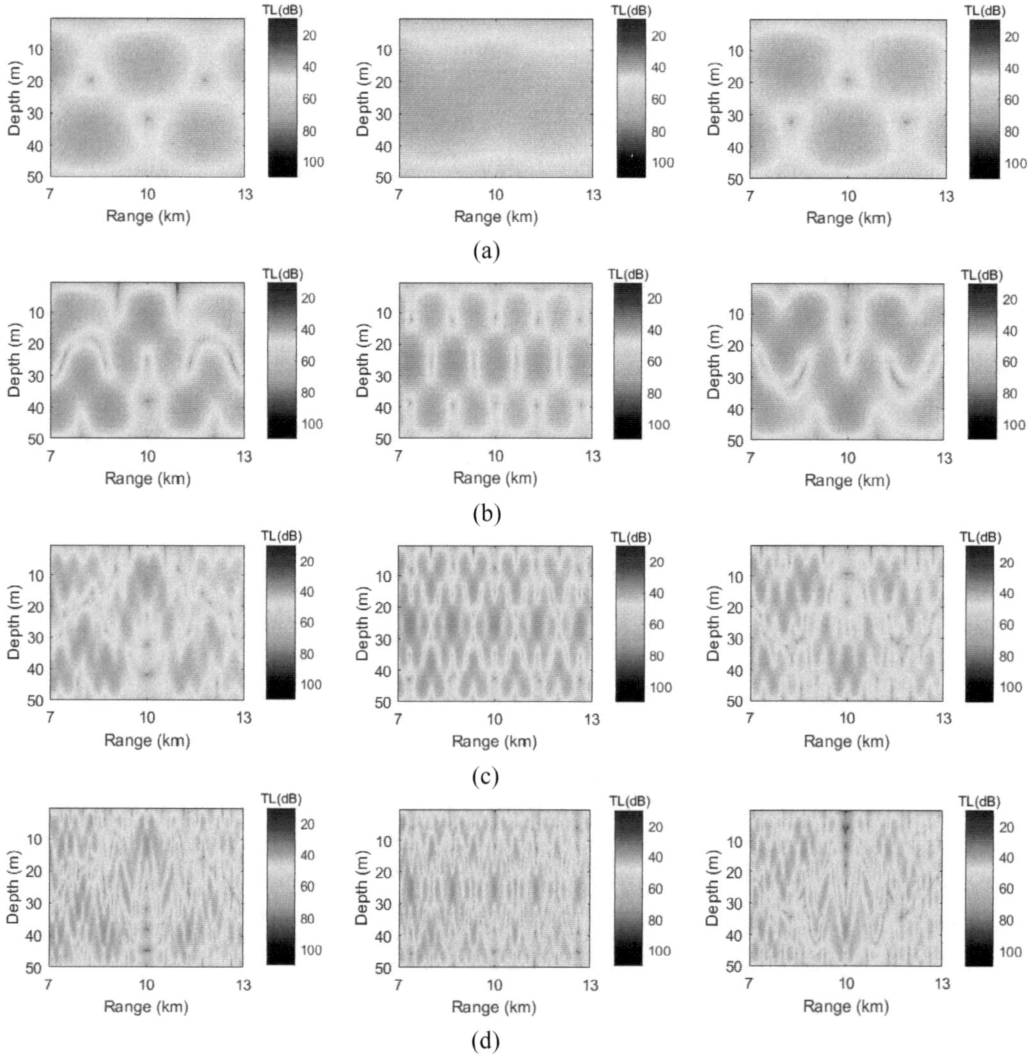

Fig. 1. Focusing effects of multi-mode excitation. The focusing range is 10 km and the focusing depth from left to right is 12 m, 25 m, and 38 m, respectively. (a) $J = 2$, (b) $J = 3$, (c) $J = 5$, and (d) $J = 7$.

3. Multi-mode Excitation of FM Signals

3.1. Theoretical analysis

The theory described in Sec. (2) is based on a single-frequency signal, but FM signals, such as linear frequency modulated (LFM) and hyperbolic frequency modulated (HFM) signals, are also commonly used in active detection. To realize the multi-mode excitation of FM signals, we use the carrier frequency f_0 to calculate the multi-mode weight coefficients

$$w_n = \sum_{j=1}^{J}[\frac{\mathrm{i}}{\sqrt{8\pi}}\frac{\varphi_j(z_0)\varphi_j(z_n)e^{\mathrm{i}(k_j r_0-\pi/4)}}{\rho(z_0)\sqrt{k_j r_0}}]^*. \quad (3.1)$$

Then, substituting Eq. (3.1) into Eq. (2.4), the multi-mode acoustic field of FM signal is

$$P_N(R,z;f) \approx \frac{1}{8\pi}\sum_{j=1}^{J}\frac{\varphi_j^f(z)\varphi_j^*(z_0)e^{\mathrm{i}(k_j^f R-k_j r_0)}}{\rho(z_0)\sqrt{k_j^f R}\sqrt{k_j r_0}}, \quad (3.2)$$

where k_j and $\varphi_j(z)$ represent the jth eigenvalue and eigenfunction at the carrier frequency f_0, respectively. At other instantaneous frequencies f of the FM signal, the jth eigenvalue and eigenfunction are represented by k_j^f and $\varphi_j^f(z)$, respectively.

Hence, the multi-mode acoustic field of FM signal at (r_0,z_0) is

$$P_N(r_0,z_0;f) \approx \frac{1}{8\pi}\sum_{j=1}^{J}\frac{\varphi_j^f(z_0)\varphi_j^*(z_0)}{\rho(z_0)\sqrt{k_j^f k_j r_0}}e^{\mathrm{i}(k_j^f-k_j)r_0}. \quad (3.3)$$

Compared to Eq. (2.11), there is an extra phase term $\exp[\mathrm{i}(k_j^f-k_j)r_0]$ in Eq. (3.3); thus, the J modes cannot stack in the same phase.

3.2. Simulations

The environmental parameters are the same as those used in Fig. (1). The transmitting signal is an LFM signal. The carrier frequency f_0 is 750 Hz, the bandwidth B is 150 Hz, the pulse width T is 1 s, and the focusing position (r_0,z_0) is $(10\ \mathrm{km}, 25\ \mathrm{m})$. Figure (2) shows the envelope energy of the received signals at 10 km when $J=3,5,7$. At the desired focusing depth, it only focuses well on the limited bandwidth around the carrier frequency. However, at other instantaneous frequencies, the real focusing depth changes, which contributes to a high level of energy distribution at the entire depth, and large J worsens the focusing effect.

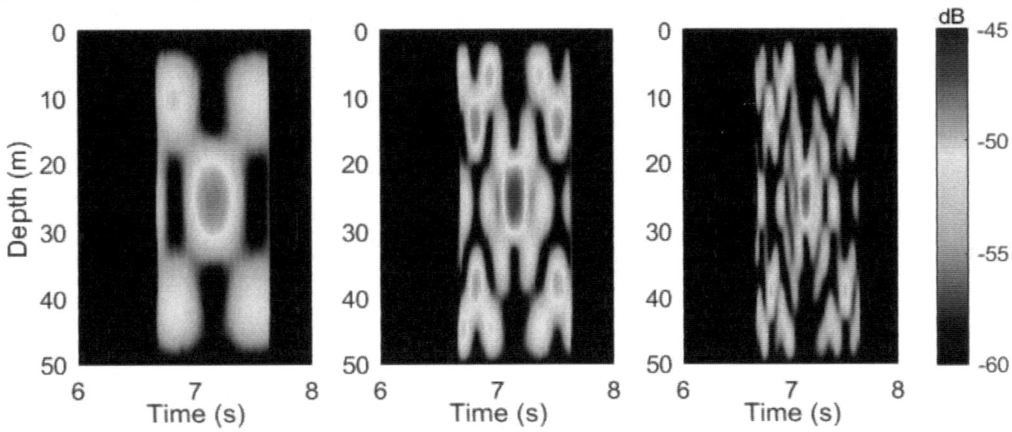

(a) (b) (c)

Fig. 2. Envelope energy of the received signals. (a) $J=3$, (b) $J=5$, and (c) $J=7$.

Figure (3a) shows the envelope energy of the received signal at (r_0,z_0) when $J=5$. We define the available bandwidth as the difference between the upper and lower frequency bounds, where the upper/lower frequency bounds are the positions when the intensity is 6 dB lower than the carrier frequency (see Fig. 3a). Figure (3b) shows the relationship between the available bandwidth and J. It illustrates that the larger J is, the narrower the available bandwidth is at the same focusing range.

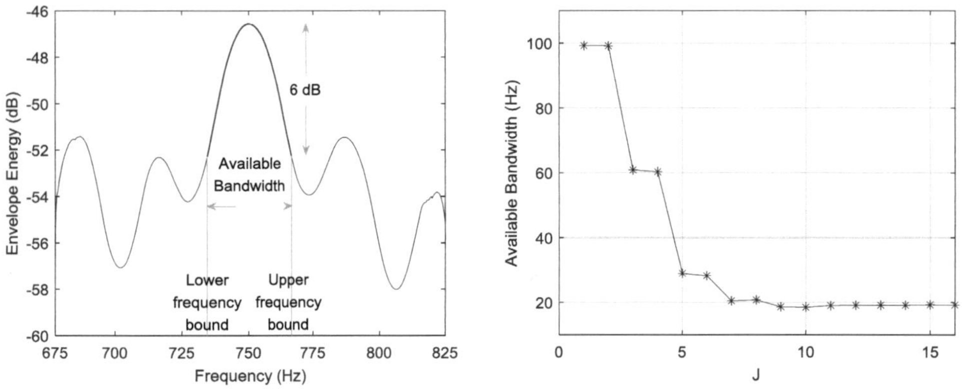

(a) (b)

Fig. 3. (a) The envelope energy of received signal at (r_0, z_0) when $J=5$. (b) The available bandwidth for different Js.

Figure (4) shows the focusing effect of the LFM signal with the available bandwidth when $J=3,5,7$. The bandwidths used are 61, 29, and 20 Hz. The other parameters are the same as those used in Fig. (2). Figures 4 indicates that using the available bandwidth can obtain the desired focusing effects with different Js.

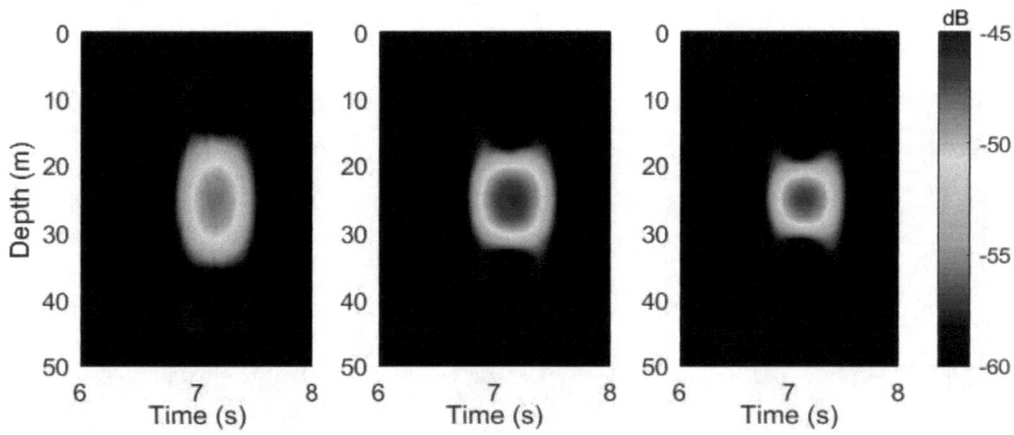

(a) (b) (c)

Fig. 4. Focusing effect of LFM signal with the available bandwidth. (a) $J=3$, $B=61$ Hz, (b) $J=5$, $B=29$ Hz, and (c) $J=7$, $B=20$ Hz.

As for active detection, the signal processing gain is $G=2BT$, where B and T are the bandwidth and pulse width of the signal, respectively. As Fig. (3b) indicates, the smaller the J is, the wider the available bandwidth is. Therefore, to improve the signal processing gain, a smaller J must be chosen. For Pekeris waveguide, we use $J=3$ for multi-mode excitation of FM signals because it cannot focus well on the middle of the water layer when $J=2$.

3.3. Target depth discrimination

We assume that there is a rigid sphere target with a radius of 5 m located at (10 km, 20 m). We choose J = 3 to excite the multi-mode focusing field using the LFM signal with the available bandwidth. Depth scanning is realized by changing the focusing depth at 5, 15, 25, 35, and 45 m. Then, after pulse compression of echo signals, the envelope outputs are obtained, as shown in Fig. (5). At the time around 13.3 seconds, which corresponds to the target range of 10 km, the pulse compression outputs are much larger than the others when z_0 is 15 or 25 m. Hence, we conclude that the target depth is between 15 and 25 m. The simulation results suggest that multi-mode excitation of FM signals can realize target depth discrimination in shallow water.

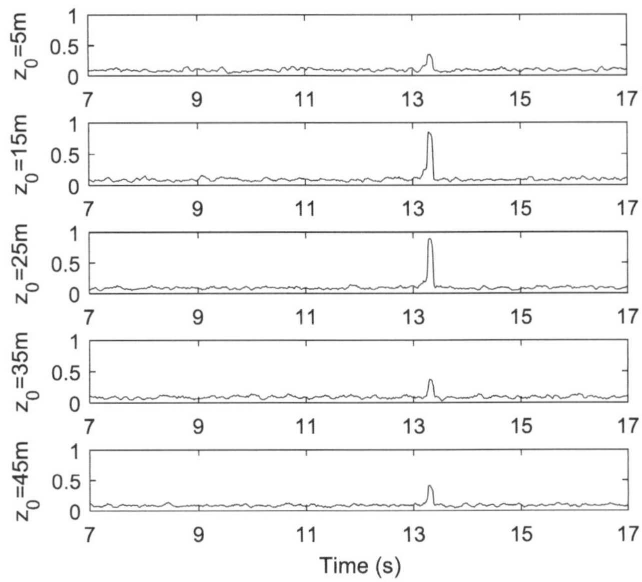

Fig. 5. Pulse compression outputs of echo signals with different focusing depths.

4. Summary

Single-mode excitation and TRM have limitations related to target depth discrimination. In this paper, we introduced the multi-mode excitation theory of single-frequency signal, which is a compromise method for robust field focusing between single-mode excitation and TRM. Based on single-frequency excitation, we introduced the multi-mode excitation method of FM signals. The weight coefficients were calculated by the carrier frequency of the FM signal, and we showed that a desired focusing effect with the available bandwidth can be obtained. Because a smaller J is related to a wider available bandwidth, we used J = 3 to improve the signal processing gain and to realize the focusing depth scanning in Pekeris waveguide. The simulations showed that using multi-mode excitation can achieve target depth discrimination, which indicates that it could be applied to active detection in the future.

Acknowledgments

This work was supported by the National Natural Science Foundation of China under Grant No. Y211071131.

References

[1] M. Ajtai, J. Komlos, and E. Szemeredi, "An O(nlogn) sorting network," Proc. 15th ACM Symp. Theory Comput., ACM Press, 1983, pp. 1–9. D. F. Gingras, "Single mode excitation, attenuation, and backscatter in shallow water," J. Acoust. Soc. Am., 103(1) (1998), 195–204.

[2] J. Zeng, W. Y. Zhao, and D. Y. Peng, "Measurements of ocean bottom low-angle backscattering by single-mode reverberation," J. Acoust. Soc. Am., 136(6) (2014), 2976–2986.

[3] W. A. Kuperman, W. S. Hodgkiss, and H. C. Song, "Phase conjugation in the ocean: Experimental demonstration of an acoustic time-reversal mirror," J. Acoust. Soc. Am., 103(1) (1998), 25–40.

[4] S. Kim, W. A. Kuperman, and W. S. Hodgkiss, "Robust time reversal focusing in the ocean," J. Acoust. Soc. Am., 114(1) (2003), 145–157.

© ICTCA2019 14th International Conference on Theoretical and Computational Acoustics

Sequential source localization using unscented particle filter under circumstances of highly nonlinear time-evolving sound speed profiles

Su Lin [1] Guo Shengming[2] Ren Qunyan[3], Ma Li[4]

1, Key Lab. Of Underwater Environment, Institute of Acoustics, Chinese Academy of Sciences
No. 21 North 4th Ring Road, Haidian District
Beijing, 100190, China
sulin807@mail.ioa.ac.cn

2, Key Lab. Of Underwater Environment, Institute of Acoustics, Chinese Academy of Sciences
No. 21 North 4th Ring Road, Haidian District
Beijing, 100190, China
guoshengming@mail.ioa.ac.cn

3, Key Lab. Of Underwater Environment, Institute of Acoustics, Chinese Academy of Sciences
No. 21 North 4th Ring Road, Haidian District
Beijing, 100190, China
renqunyan@mail.ioa.ac.cn

4, Key Lab. Of Underwater Environment, Institute of Acoustics, Chinese Academy of Sciences
No. 21 North 4th Ring Road, Haidian District
Beijing, 100190, China
mary1968@tom.com

Ocean dynamic processes such as sea waves, rainfall, and internal waves lead to modeling mismatches and influence the performance of source localization of matched-field processor (MFP). Based on empirical orthogonal functions (EOFs) and the state-space model, which describe the evolution characteristics of sound speed profile (SSP), source range and depth are estimated via the acoustic array data simulated by the measured SSPs and prior seabed acoustic properties. In consideration of the characteristics of nonlinear systems and non-Gaussian distributions in the underwater acoustic channel, an algorithm for the unscented particle filter (UPF) is implemented for the tracking of moving source under the circumstances of time-evolving sound speed profiles. The validity and practicality are demonstrated by the simulation, which indicate that the proposed scheme enables the continuous tracking of the moving source.

Keywords: time-evolving sound speed profiles; empirical orthogonal function (EOF); sequential source localization; solitary internal wave.

1. Introduction

A popular approach for source localization is matched-field processing (MFP), which has suggested some enabling capabilities and was a great research topic at the intersection of underwater acoustics and signal processing. However, MFP does not perform well in mismatch environments[1]. In particular, the sound speed profile (SSP) in water column is highly variable in time and space and cannot be accurately known among measurement periods in coastal water. These factors lead to modeling mismatches and influence the performance of source localization of the matched-field processor.

The significant temporal evolution characteristics of the SSP provide a feasible inspiration for the sequential estimation algorithm. The possibility of sequential tracking of source range and depth under the circumstances of time-evolving sound speed profiles is discussed in this paper. Some scholars had introduced sequential filtering method into acoustic inversion problems. Candy[2] first introduced extended the Kalman filtering algorithm into marine acoustic inversion. Nonlinear Kalman filters (KF), such as the ensemble Kalman filter (EnKF), have been pioneered in a series of papers to estimate the time-evolving ocean sound velocity field[3,4,5]. EnKF is also used to track the moving source in a range-dependent environment[3]. Because of the nonlinear characteristics of underwater acoustic channel transmission function, nonlinear Kalman filters are used in the aforementioned studies. These studies show that EnKF is efficient for large parameter vectors.

However, the highly nonlinear features of time-evolving SSP require numerical methods for the calculation of posterior probability distribution functions (PDF). These approaches are termed particle filter (PF) approaches, which are more suitable for highly nonlinear systems and have been encountered in ocean acoustic applications[7,8,9]. In this study, improved PF methods are applied to the sequential source localization problem under the circumstances of time-evolving SSP; this technique is more favorable than traditional MFP methods. Moreover, the introduction of unscented Kalman filters can improve the tracking capabilities of sequential filters. This method also shows better performance than that of the EnKF algorithm when compared in terms of source localization accuracy.

2. Background

2.1. Empirical orthogonal function representation of SSP

SSP is usually expressed as a matrix array of depth and distance for better research, but this approach requires a lot of parameters. Scholars put forward an empirical orthogonal function (EOF) representation method[10], which can greatly reduce the number of inversion parameters. Once the basis function is determined, SSP can be reconstructed using a limited number of EOF coefficients. Therefore, the EOF method is widely used in the inversion of SSP, ocean acoustic tomography, and acoustic inversion to improve the efficiency and robustness of the inversion algorithm.

The background SSP $\bar{\boldsymbol{c}}(\boldsymbol{d})$ can be obtained via the mean of N SSP data sets.

$$\bar{\boldsymbol{c}}(\boldsymbol{d}) = \frac{1}{N}\sum_{i=1}^{N}\boldsymbol{c}_i(\boldsymbol{d}) \tag{2.1}$$

The fluctuation of every SSP is expressed as

$$\Box \boldsymbol{c}_i(\boldsymbol{d}) = \boldsymbol{c}_i(\boldsymbol{d}) - \bar{\boldsymbol{c}}(\boldsymbol{d}),\ i = 1,\ 2,\ \cdots, N \quad . \tag{2.2}$$

Suppose each SSP is discretized to M depths. N $\Box \boldsymbol{c}_i(\boldsymbol{d})$ can then form an M×N fluctuation matrix $\boldsymbol{C}$. The eigenvalue decomposition of the covariance matrix of $\boldsymbol{C}$ is performed:

$$\frac{1}{N}\boldsymbol{C}\boldsymbol{C}^{\mathrm{T}}\boldsymbol{U} = \boldsymbol{U}\boldsymbol{l} \quad , \tag{2.3}$$

where $\boldsymbol{U} = [\boldsymbol{u}_1(d)\ \ \boldsymbol{u}_2(d)\ \ \mathrm{L}\ \ \boldsymbol{u}_M(d)]^{\mathrm{T}}$ is the eigenfunction matrix, and

$\boldsymbol{l} = diag(l_1\ \ l_2\ \ \mathrm{L}\ \ l_M)$ is the eigenvalue vector. SSP can then be expressed as

$$\boldsymbol{c}(\boldsymbol{d})\ ?\ \bar{\boldsymbol{c}}(\boldsymbol{d})\ \ \mathring{a}_{m=1}^{g}\ a_m \boldsymbol{u}_m(\boldsymbol{d}). \tag{2.4}$$

Generally, once the background SSP data and the EOF basis function are extracted, Eq. (2.4) can describe SSP accurately.

2.2. State-space model

Sequential filtering is the problem of sequentially estimating the states of a system as a set of observations becomes available on-line. The state-space model is used to describe the problem. Current SSP and source position can be estimated according to the estimated value at the previous moment and the current observation value. The time evolution of the EOF coefficient is considered as a first-order random walk process. The state equation and measurement equation are then written as

$$\begin{aligned} x(t) &= x(t-1) + \omega(t) \\ y(t) &= H[x(t)] + v(t) \end{aligned} \ , \tag{2.5}$$

where $x(k) = [\alpha_1(k), \alpha_2(k), \alpha_3(k), r(k), z(k), \mathrm{vel}(k)]^T$ is the parameter to be estimated, including the first three EOF coefficients: source range, source depth, and source moving velocity; H is the observation matrix, representing the acoustic propagation model; $\boldsymbol{y}(t)$ is the signal received by an L -element vertical line array at time t ; and the Gaussian random sequences $\boldsymbol{\omega}(t)$ and $\boldsymbol{v}(t)$ are the process noise and measurement noise, respectively.

3. Nonlinear sequential filtering algorithm

The underwater column is a nonlinear and non-Gaussian system for sound propagation. Particle filter is a good approach to handling the nonlinear and non-Gaussian estimation problem. PF uses the Monte Carlo method to simulate the posterior probability density distribution, which does not require too many constraints on the probability density of state variables and can obtain a better filtering effect in the state estimation of nonlinear systems. However, the variance of particle weight will increase with time iteration, and a large amount of computing resources will be consumed on useless particles, leading particle degradation. Extended particle filter (EPF) and unscented particle filter (UPF) use Kalman filters to guide particle distribution and prevent particle degradation.

3.1. Improved particle filter algorithm

The flowchart of EnKF algorithm has been elaborated in literatures 7 and 11 and will not be repeated here. This paper introduces mainly the procedure for the UPF algorithm.

Particle filters allow us to approximate the posterior density $p(X_t | Y_t)$ using a set of N weighted particles. $X_t = \{x_1, x_2, \ldots, x_t\}, Y_t = \{y_1, y_2, \ldots, y_t\}$, x_t represent the system state at time t, and y_t represents the observed value. Each particle has a weight of $w_t^{(i)}$. The posterior distribution at time t can then be approximated as $p(X_t | Y_t) \approx \sum_{i=1}^{N} w_t^{(i)} \delta(X_t - X_t^{(i)})$.

Generally, the posterior probability distribution function cannot be obtained directly. Bayesian importance sampling theorem firstly samples from a known reference distribution, $q(X_t | Y_t)$, that is easy to sample, and then approximates the posterior probability by weighting the sampling particle points of the reference distribution. In this case, the particle weight can be expressed as $w_t^{(i)} \propto \frac{p(X_t^{(i)} | Y_t)}{q(X_t^{(i)} | Y_t)}$. When the characteristics of time-series recursive estimation are considered, it is assumed that the system state conforms to the first-order Markov process; that is, each observation is independent, and the current state does not depend on future observations. When sampling at time $t-1$, we calculate the importance weight in the form of recursion, with the sample set of the past state sequence remaining unchanged. The reference distribution can then be written as

$$q(X_t | Y_t) = q(X_{t-1} | Y_{t-1}) q(x_t | X_{t-1}, Y_t) \quad . \tag{3.1}$$

The particle $x_t^{(i)} \sim q(X_t^{(i)} | Y_t)$ can be estimated via proposal distribution $x_{t-1}^{(i)} \sim q(X_{t-1}^{(i)} | Y_{t-1})$ and update state $x_t^{(i)} \sim q(X_t^{(i)} | Y_t)$. Through the drawing of samples from proposal distribution, the importance weights can be estimated recursively using Eq. (3.2).

$$w_t^{(i)} \propto w_{t-1}^{(i)} \frac{p(y_t | x_t^{(i)}) p(x_t^{(i)} | x_{t-1}^{(i)})}{q(x_t^{(i)} | X_{t-1}^{(i)}, Y_t)} \tag{3.2}$$

The choice of proposal distribution is one of the most critical issues in the design of a particle filter. The most popular choice in the standard particle algorithm is the transitional prior $q(x_t | X_{t-1}, Y_t) = p(x_t | x_{t-1})$, which does not incorporate the most recent observation, which will otherwise make it heavily dependent on the model. Therefore, it is important to move the particles toward regions of high likelihood; this simply requires that the proposal distribution must include support of true posterior distribution and most recent observations. The proposal distribution can be approximated by incorporating the most current measurement via Gaussian approximation, such as EKF and UKF. Considering the nonlinearity of the system, we propose the use of unscented Kalman filter for proposal generation. UKF is based on the unscented transform (UT). UT is a function used to estimate the result of applying a given nonlinear transformation to a probability distribution, which can achieve accurate to the 3rd order for Gaussians and get higher-order errors scaled by choice of transform parameters. UPF, which combines PF and UKF, has two superior properties. Firstly, it incorporates the latest available information, and secondly, it has heavy tails.

3.2. Weight calculation in UPF

Weight calculation is the core problem of the particle filtering algorithm. Based on the particle weight, high-quality particles can be copied in large quantities and inferior particles can be eliminated. Therefore, it is important and difficult to keep the balance of the past and current data ratio according to the proposal distribution and the latest status update weights. As mentioned before, the conventional particle filter uses $p(x_t \mid x_{t-1})$ as a prior, which is a sub-optimal choice but relatively easy to operate. The UPF algorithm updates the particle weight by introducing the latest observation into the importance density function. The particle state at time t is denoted as $x_t^{(i)}$, the prediction of observation value of each particle at time t is denoted as $\vec{Y}_{pre}^{(i)}(t)$, and the sensor measurement value at time t is denoted as Y_t.

Probability density distribution of multidimensional data is involved for array data. We have to make assumptions that the array data are Gaussian, and then the likelihood function is expressed as Eq. (3.3).

$$p(Y_t \mid x_t^{(i)}) = \frac{1}{(\sqrt{2\pi})^N \mid C \mid^{1/2}} \exp(-\frac{1}{2}[\vec{Y}(t) - \vec{Y}_{pre}^{(i)}(t)]^H C^{-1} [\vec{Y}(t) - \vec{Y}_{pre}^{(i)}(t)]) \quad (3.3)$$

where C is the covariance matrix. If it is assumed that the acoustic data received by N elements are statistically independent and have the same variance, then the covariance matrix can be written as $C = v^2 I$. Substituting it into Eq. (3.3), we can obtain

$$p(Y_t \mid x_t^{(i)}) = \frac{1}{(\sqrt{2\pi})^N v^N} \exp(-\frac{1}{2}[\vec{Y}(t) - \vec{Y}_{pre}^{(i)}(t)]^H v^{-2} [\vec{Y}(t) - \vec{Y}_{pre}^{(i)}(t)]) \quad (3.4)$$

It should be noted that Eq. (3.4) is only an approximation because the acoustic data received by the array are usually not statistically independent. Therefore, N is often selected as the effective normal wave number.

According to the maximum likelihood estimation criterion $\frac{\partial p}{\partial v} = 0$, we can obtain

$$v^2 = \frac{\left|\vec{Y}(t) - \vec{Y}_{pre}^{(i)}(t)\right|^2}{N} \quad . \quad (3.5)$$

The likelihood function can be obtained by substituting Eq. (3.5) into Eq. (3.4).

$$p(Y_t \mid x_t^{(i)}) = \frac{\sqrt{N}}{(\sqrt{2\pi})^N \left(\left|\vec{Y}(t) - \vec{Y}_{pre}^{(i)}(t)\right|^2\right)^{2/N}} \exp(-\frac{N}{2}) \quad (3.6)$$

Similarly, assuming the prior state distribution to be Gaussian, each statistic is independent and has the same variance, and the prior distribution probability can be obtained via Eq. (3.7).

$$p(x_t^{(i)} \mid x_{t-1}^{(i)}) = \frac{\sqrt{U}}{(\sqrt{2\pi})^U \left(\left|\vec{x}(t)^{(i)} - \vec{x}(t-1)^{(i)}\right|^2\right)^{2/U}} \exp(-\frac{U}{2}) \quad (3.7)$$

where U is the number of sigma-point sets.

If the mean value $\bar{x}^{(i)}$ and covariance $P^{(i)}$ of sigma-point sets obtained through UT transformation are assumed to be Gaussian, the distribution probability can be written as

$$q(x_t^{(i)} \mid X_{t-1}^{(i)}, Y_t) = \frac{1}{(\sqrt{2\pi})^U \mid P^{(i)} \mid^{1/2}} \exp(-\frac{1}{2}[\vec{x}^{(i)}(t) - \bar{x}^{(i)}]^H P^{(i)-1}[\vec{x}^{(i)}(t) - \bar{x}^{(i)}]) \quad (3.8)$$

Through the substitution of equations Eq. (3.6), Eq. (3.7), and Eq. (3.8) into Eq. (3.3), the weight of each particle can be obtained.

4. Numerical simulation

4.1. Introduction to the simulation test

The ocean environment model and experimental arrangement are shown in Fig. 6. The depth of water was about 90 m. The sediment layer was 10 m thick with a density of 1600 kg/m³, sound speed of 1575 m/s, and sound absorption coefficient of 0.2 dB/λ. The seabed layer had a density of 1700 kg/m³, sound speed of 2000 m/s, and sound absorption coefficient of 0.2 dB/λ. The receivers were on a vertical line array spanning the water column from 15 m to 60 m; there were a total of 32 phones with uniform spacing of 1.5 m. The source was 5 km from the VLA (vertical line array) in the initial state and at depth of about 30 m, the source frequency was from 280 Hz to 320Hz. We assumed the source was moving in a constant speed at about 2.5 m/s.

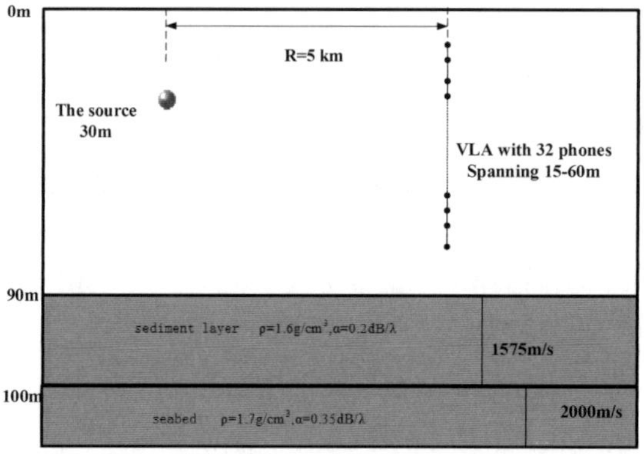

Fig. 6. Ocean model for the simulation experiment. All parameters are range-independent. A vertical array consisted of 32 elements with the uppermost element at a depth of 15 m and an element spacing of 1.5 m.

Fig. 7(a) shows that the sound speed profiles lasted about 20 hours; these profiles were measured in the South China Sea in the summertime. In this study, we selected the two-hour period between the two red lines to test our algorithm. The EOF function was obtained via the first ten hours of SSP. Interval waves are added in Fig. 7(b) to simulate highly nonlinear time-evolving sound speed profiles. Notice that a range-independent assumption is made, which may not be always true; thus, it is a suboptimum choice for checking the tracking ability of our algorithm at jump time for the nonlinear underwater channel.

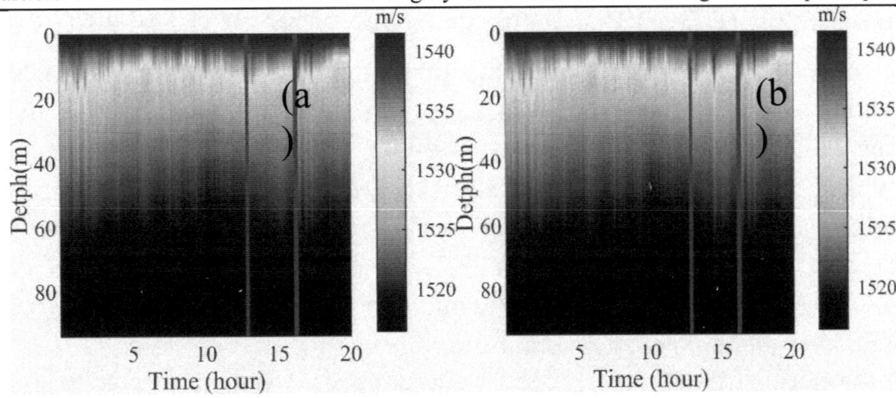

Fig. 7. (a) SSP measured in the South China Sea in the summertime (b) soliton internal wave with max amplitude of eight meters is added to the period between the two solid lines (lasted two hours) in Fig. 2(a).

4.2. Sensitivity analysis

The pre-condition of sequential inversion and localization through sound field data is that the estimated parameters are sensitive to the objective function. The normalized objective function used here is similar in Refs. 12 and 13 and is given as

$$\mathbf{F}(x) = 1 - \frac{1}{\boldsymbol{y}_t^{\mathrm{H}}\boldsymbol{y}_t}\left\| \boldsymbol{y}_t - \frac{\boldsymbol{d}(x_t)^{\mathrm{H}}\boldsymbol{y}_t}{\left\|\boldsymbol{d}(x_t)\right\|^2}\boldsymbol{d}(x_t) \right\|^2 . \tag{4.1}$$

Fig. 8 is plotted by varying one parameter at time t while the other five parameters are assigned the true values. The objective function is given for three different frequencies: at 280Hz, 300Hz, and 320Hz, respectively. Note that $\mathbf{F}(x)$ for the 2nd EOF coefficient and source velocity is less sensitive than the other parameters.

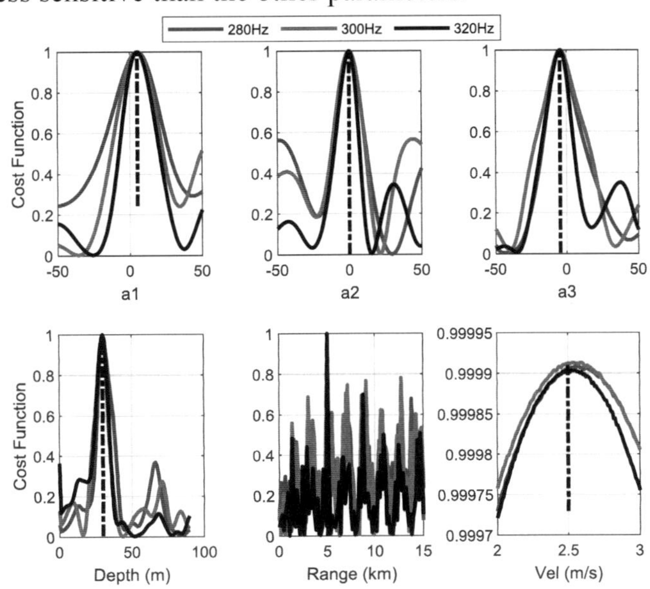

Fig. 8. Normalized objective functions of six estimated parameter at three frequencies. The cost function for each parameter is obtained by fixing all other parameters to their true values (dashed line).

4.3. Sequential tracking of time-varying SSP and moving source

In this part, time-evolving SSPs and source position information are estimated via the acoustic array data simulated by the measured SSPs and prior seabed acoustic properties described in Sec. 4.1. The evolution of the six parameters by UPF 500, EnKF-1000, and EnKF-2000 at five frequencies (280, 290, 300, 310, and 320 Hz) are given in Fig. 9. All three filters are sensitive to the six parameters. The 2nd EOF coefficient and source velocity start to diverge after jump at t=60 min for EnKF-1000 and EnKF-2000 because the two parameters are less sensitive to the objective function. Meanwhile, UPF-500 can track the six parameters perfectly even after the rapid changes at time 60 min.

Notice that the track of the 2nd EOF coefficient and source velocity becomes less noisy as the number of particles increased in EnKF. However, even if we increase the number of particles to 7000, there will still be significant divergence after the mutation.

The estimated errors of SSP can be evaluated by the depth-integrated root mean square error (RMSE) metric4 which is defined by

$$C_{\text{RMS}} = \sqrt{\frac{1}{N}\sum_{i=1}^{N}\left|c(d_i) - \hat{c}(d_i)\right|^2}\,. \tag{4.2}$$

As shown in Fig. 9, the divergence of SSP estimated in the EnKF filters can be seen more obviously by calculating the RMSE evolution.

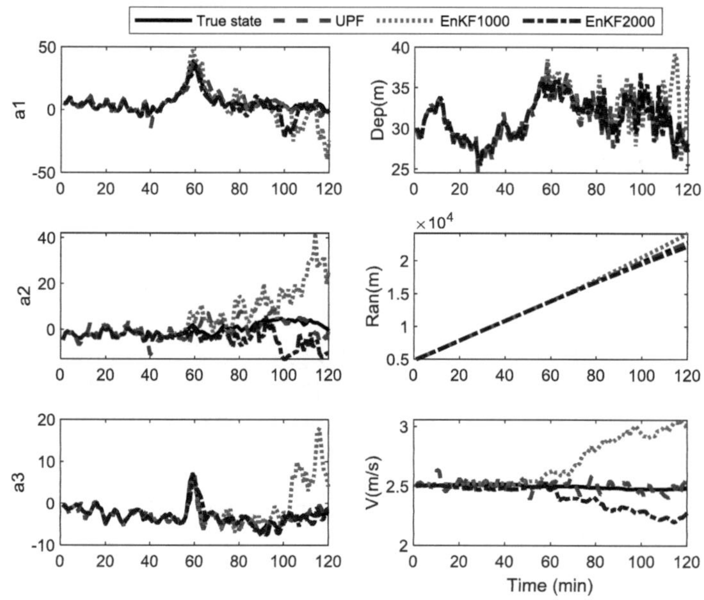

Fig. 9. Tracking result of UPF500 (red dashed line), EnKF 1000 (pink dotted line), and EnKF2000 (blue dot-dashed line) for the six parameters in Eq. (2.5).

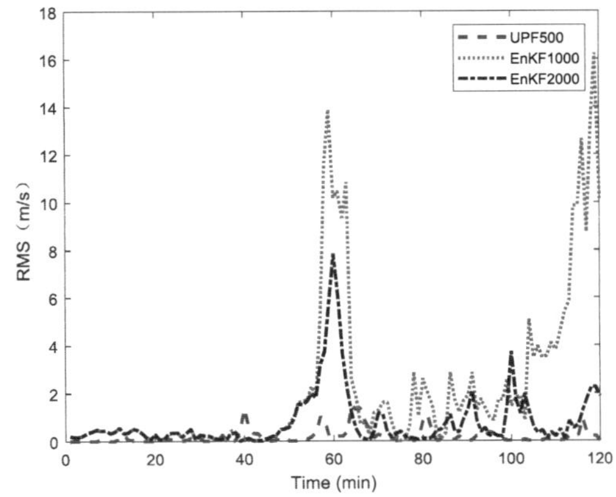

Fig. 10. Depth-integrated RMSE of UPF500 (red dashed line), EnKF 1000 (pink dotted line), and EnKF2000 (blue dot-dashed line).

The relative error ratios of source range estimation and source depth estimation are also shown in Fig. 11. The sequential localization error is also compared with that of the traditional MFP as a reference, which takes no consideration of environmental changes during the two hours. MFP failed to localize the moving source at jump time because of model mismatch, whereas sequential filters performed better. As mentioned before, the source velocity is the parameter where there is marked difference between UPF and EnKF. Although it is less sensitive to the objective function, UPF performs well after the jump, which indirectly leads to more accurate range estimation.

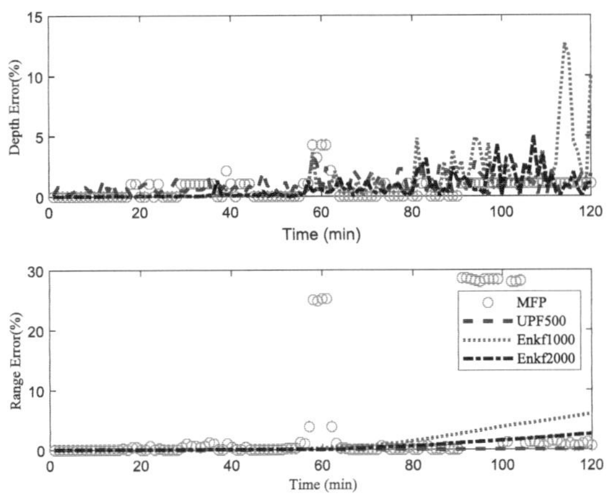

Fig. 11. Relative error ratio in source range and depth estimation of MFP (green circle), UPF500 (red dashed line), EnKF 1000 (pink dotted line), and EnKF2000 (blue dot-dashed line).

5. Summary

Considering the nonlinear characteristics of SSP time evolution, we propose an improved particle filter-UPF based on EOF model and state space model to track the time-evolving SSP and source position sequentially. Numerical simulation using measured SSP with interval wave added and prior seabed acoustic properties verifies the effectiveness of the proposed algorithm. Results show that: (1) The sequential filters outperform MFP for source localization in time-evolving environments, especially when the ocean environment parameters change dramatically. (2) UPF combining standard particle filter and unscented Kalman filter with enough particles is proved to be superior to EnKF in the case of highly nonlinearity, even for the parameter (e.g., source velocity) that is less sensitive to the objective function.

However, the simulation experiment presented in this paper is used only for algorithm verification. The actual situation is much more complex. For example, the range-dependent effect brought by the internal waves may have greater influence on acoustic propagation. In addition, if the EOF function itself has changed, the performance of the algorithm will be greatly reduced. In subsequent research work, the algorithm will be further optimized, and adding the ocean dynamics mode into the state equation, to overcome the tracking errors caused by the inaccuracy of the equation of state and the change of the EOF function, will be considered.

Acknowledgments

The work was supported by the National Natural Science Foundation of China (Grant NO. 11704396).

References

[1] H. P. Bucker, “Use of calculated sound fields and matched field detection to locate sound sources in shallow water.” The Journal of the Acoustical Society of America, 59(2) (1976), 368–373.

[2] J. V. Candy and E. J. Sullivan, “Model-based environmental inversion: A shallow water ocean application.” The Journal of the Acoustical Society of America, 98(3) (1995), 1446–1454.

[3] Carrière, J. P. Hermand, J. C. LeGac et al., “Full-field tomography and Kalman tracking of the range-dependent sound speed field in a coastal water environment.” Journal of Marine Systems, 78(1) (2009), S382–S392.

[4] Carrière, J. P. Hermand, and J. V. Candy, “Inversion for time-evolving sound-speed field in a shallow ocean by ensemble Kalman filtering.” IEEE Journal of Oceanic Engineering, 34(4) (2009), 586–602.

[5] L. L. Jin, J. L. Li, and W. Xu, “Tracking of time-evolving sound speed profiles with an auto-regressive state-space model.” Chinese Journal of Acoustics, 36(43) (2017), 302–312.

[6] X. L. Guo, K. D. Yang, Y. L. Ma et al., “Tracking-positioning of sound speed profiles and moving acoustic source in shallow water.” Chinese Journal of Acoustics, 36(4) (2017), 439–453.

[7] C. Yardim, P. Gerstoft, and W. S. Hodgkiss. “Tracking of geoacoustic parameters using Kalman and particle filter.” The Journal of the Acoustical Society of America, 125(2) (2009), 746–760.

[8] T. Lin and Z. H. Michalopoulou. “Sound speed estimation and source localization with linearization and particle filtering.” The Journal of the Acoustical Society of America, 135(3) (2014), 1115–1126.

[9] B. Ristic, S. Arulampalam, and N. Gordon, Beyond the Kalman Filter: Particle Filters for Tracking Applications. Boston, London: Artech House Publishers, 2004.

[10] L. R. LeBlanc and F. H. Middleton, “An underwater acoustic sound velocity data model.” The Journal of the Acoustical Society of America, 67(6) (1980), 2055–2062.

[11] P. J. van Leeuwen, “An efficient variance-minimizing filter (and smoother!) for large-scale problems.” Monthly Weather Review, 131(9) (2003), 2071–2084.

[12] P. Gerstoft and C. F. Mecklenbrauker, “Ocean acoustic inversion with estimation of a posteriori probability distributions.” The Journal of the Acoustical Society of America, 104(2) (1998), 808–819.

[13] C.-F. Huang, P. Gerstoft, and W. S. Hodgkiss, "Uncertainty analysis in matched-field geoacoustic inversions," The Journal of the Acoustical Society of America, 119(2) (2006), 197–207.

Source Depth Estimation Based on Mode Phase Matching in Shallow Water

CAO HUAIGANG[1,2,3] , ZHAO ZHENDONG[1,2], GUO SHENGMING[1,2], MA LI[1,2]

1, Institute of Acoustics, Chinese Academy of Sciences, Beijing 100190, China
2, Key Laboratory of Underwater Acoustic Environment, Chinese Academy of Sciences, Beijing 100190, China
3, University of Chinese Academy of Sciences, Beijing 100190, China
caohuaigang16@mails.ucas.edu.cn

Aiming at the problem of passive continuous source depth estimation in shallow water waveguides, a passive source depth estimation method with a vertical line array processing is proposed in this paper. The method estimates the source depth through matching the phase of modes. In this method, the signal received from a vertical line array is used to get normal mode coefficients by mode decomposition processing which relies on a normal-mode propagation model, and thus requires prior knowledge of the mode characteristics. After mode decomposition processing, the phase relation can be obtained from the specific value of adjacent normal mode coefficient. According to phase relation of different modes, the depth of source can be estimated. Comparing with traditional matched mode processing, this method has lower requirements for the hydrophone spacing of the vertical line array. Simulation and experimental results show that the depth of the source can be estimated even if the depth sampling is not sufficient and the decomposition of normal waves is not ideal.

Keywords: Source depth region discrimination; mode filtering; mode Phase relation; vertical line array

1. Introduction

In underwater acoustics, the ability to estimate the source depth could serve in many applications. And it is also an important and difficult problem. The matched-field processing (MFP) relies on accurate environment parameters and acoustic field calculation model, which need large calculation [1,2]. Matched-mode processing (MMP)---based on mode filtering---is an effective method and widely used in the past few years for source locating [3-5]. It can work without complete acoustic field data and environment information. However, MMP may get a poor source depth estimating result when SNR is too low or the vertical line array (VLA) does not sample enough. Premus studied a mode subspace projections method, also on the basis of mode filtering [6]. The approach exploits the phenomenon of mode trapping, wherein a shallow acoustic source cannot excite the lowest order waveguide modes due to its evanescent amplitude dependence near the surface. Conan proposed an approach for source depth discrimination where the tested hypotheses are formulated in terms of the source depth and involve a user-chosen discrimination depth [7,8]. These two methods are particularly applied to a downward-refracting shallow water environment and couldn't work in iso-velocity cases.

Yu proposed a method that using active component of sound pressure cross-spectral for source depth region discrimination in vector field [9]. Liu proposed that using relation formula warping transform for source depth discrimination in shallow water [10]. Weng proposed that using the interference cycles of sound intensity based on a single hydrophone in deep water [11]. Rakotonarivo studied that using interference of normal mode and waveguide invariant for source locating [12].

In this paper, a new robust method for source depth region discrimination based on the phase relation of adjacent normal modes is proposed. The method fits for constant or slowly varying sound speed profile. It can work when the depth sampling is insufficient or the mode filtering result is not ideal.

2. Mode Filtering With a Vertical Line Array

For a layered media, the sound pressure generated by a single-frequency source can be expressed as the summation of the normal modes in the far field.

$$p(r,z)=\sum_{m=1}^{M}\sqrt{2\pi}\frac{1}{\sqrt{k_m r}}\psi_m(z_s)\psi_m(z)e^{ik_m r+i\pi/4} \tag{2.1}$$

Where k_m, ψ_m and z_s are respectively the horizontal wave-number, the depth-dependent mode function of mode *m*, and the source depth. Take no account of absorption and leave out time factor $e^{-i\omega t}$, Eq. (2.1) can be expressed as

$$p(r,z)=\sum_{m=1}^{M}\psi_m d_m(r,z_s) \tag{2.2}$$

where

$$d_m(r,z_s)=\sqrt{2\pi}\frac{1}{\sqrt{k_m r}}\psi_m(z_s)e^{ik_m r+i\pi/4} \tag{2.3}$$

is the normal mode coefficient containing information of source location.

For an *N*-element VLA at range *r*, sampling the water column at depths z_1, z_2, …, z_N, the received signal can be expressed as:

$$\mathbf{p}=\begin{bmatrix}p(r,z_1)\\ \vdots\\ p(r,z_N)\end{bmatrix}=\begin{bmatrix}\psi_1(z_1) & \cdots & \psi_M(z_1)\\ \vdots & \ddots & \vdots\\ \psi_1(z_N) & \cdots & \psi_M(z_N)\end{bmatrix}\begin{bmatrix}d_1(r,z_s)\\ \vdots\\ d_m(r,z_s)\end{bmatrix} \tag{2.4}$$
$$\equiv\mathbf{\Psi d}$$

where $\mathbf{\Psi}$ is a $N\times M$ matrix of the sampled mode functions and **d** is a $M\times 1$ vector of the modal amplitudes. **d** can be expressed as

$$\mathbf{d}=\mathbf{\Psi}^{+}\mathbf{p} \tag{2.5}$$

where "+" denotes the generalized inverse of matrix. This is the general inverse algorithm of mode filtering.

3. Depth region discrimination

3.1. Principle and algorithm

Taking the Pekeris waveguide model shown in Fig. 1 as an example, the model parameters are as follows: water depth is 70m, the sound speed in water column is 1500m/s, and the density 1.026g/cm^3, the sound speed of seabed is 1770m/s, and the density 2.0g/cm^3, the absorption coefficient is 0.1dB/λ. The source frequency is 200Hz.

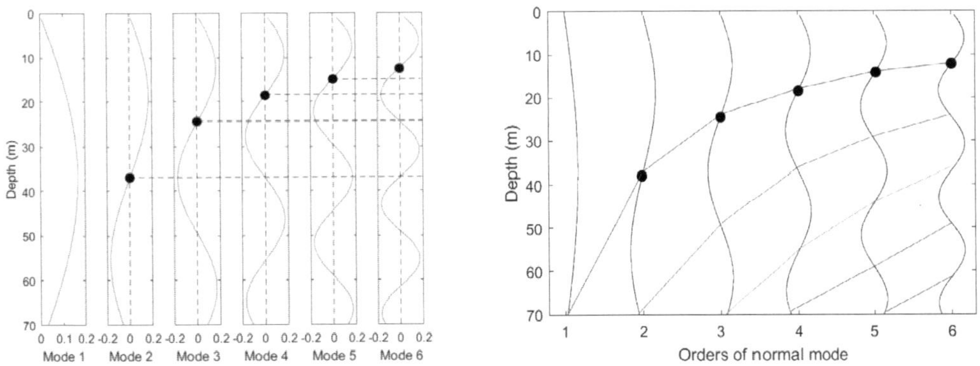

(a) The first 6 normal modes. (b) Division of phase regions.

Fig. 1 The first 6 normal modes are generated by a single source of 200Hz.

Through Fig.1 we can see that the eigenfunction of normal modes have different phase at different depth. Fig. 1 (b) shows the connection lines of zero amplitude points. The lines divide the normal modes into different regions. Different normal modes are in-phase in a given region. It is obvious that only the surface sources can excite normal modes which are in-phase. The blue line in Fig. 1(b) is the boundary separating surface region and submerged region. It can be seen that the boundary is more close to the surface as the orders of normal modes increases. The boundary of surface and submerged sources is the black point in Fig. 1. Through mode filtering processing, we can get normal mode coefficient $d_m(r,z_s)$. To determine whether adjacent normal modes are in-phase, in this paper we define a specific value of the adjacent normal modes coefficient.

$$\frac{d_{m+1}(r,z_s)}{d_m(r,z_s)} = \sqrt{\frac{k_m}{k_{m+1}}}\frac{\psi_{m+1}(z_s)}{\psi_m(z_s)}e^{i(k_{m+1}-k_m)r} = Q_m e^{i(k_{m+1}-k_m)r} \tag{3.1}$$

where $Q_m = \sqrt{\frac{k_l}{k_m}}\frac{\psi_{m+1}(z_s)}{\psi_m(z_s)}$. The value of Q_m determines whether the eigenfunction of adjacent normal modes are in-phase. If $Q_m > 0$, the adjacent normal modes (ψ_m and ψ_{m+1}) are in-phase; while if $Q_m < 0$, the adjacent normal modes are out-phase. Q_m in Eq. (3.1) can be expressed as

$$Q_m = \frac{d_{m+1}(r,z_s)}{d_m(r,z_s)}e^{-i(k_{m+1}-k_m)r} \tag{3.2}$$

In Eq. (3.2) k_m and k_{m+1} can be calculated through environment coefficients, and r is treated as known in prior with error δr,

$$(k_{m+1} - k_m)\delta r << \pi \tag{3.3}$$

Eq. (3.3) is not a critical condition in most practical situations [13]. That means the error in range has little influence and the sign of Q_m obtained by Eq. (3.3) is accurate.

4. The numerical simulation

4.1. Simulation of method feasibility

In order to verify the feasibility of the abovementioned method, a numerical simulation is performed using the KRAKEN code firstly. The environment model shown in Fig. 1 is used in the following analysis. A 32-element VLA with a 2m inter-element spacing is used for receiving. Two sources respectively at the depth of 5m and 65m are analyzed. Choose the first four normal modes for discrimination. The decision depth is $z_{\lim} = 18m$ (the black point on the fourth normal mode in Fig. 1). The attenuation of higher order normal modes with propagation distance is not considered. Environment noise is not taken into simulation. Q_m in Eq. (3.1) is used to calculate the relationship of adjacent modes, its sign can be expressed as

$$B_m = \frac{Q_m}{|Q_m|} \tag{4.1}$$

$B_m = 1$ means the adjacent normal modes are in-phase; $B_m = -1$ means the adjacent normal modes are out-phase. The simulation results are shown in Fig. 2. The normal modes in Fig. 2(a) are in-phase thus the corresponding sources are surface ones, which fits the settings. The normal modes in Fig. 2(b) are out-phase, thus they are submerged sources, which also agrees with the settings.

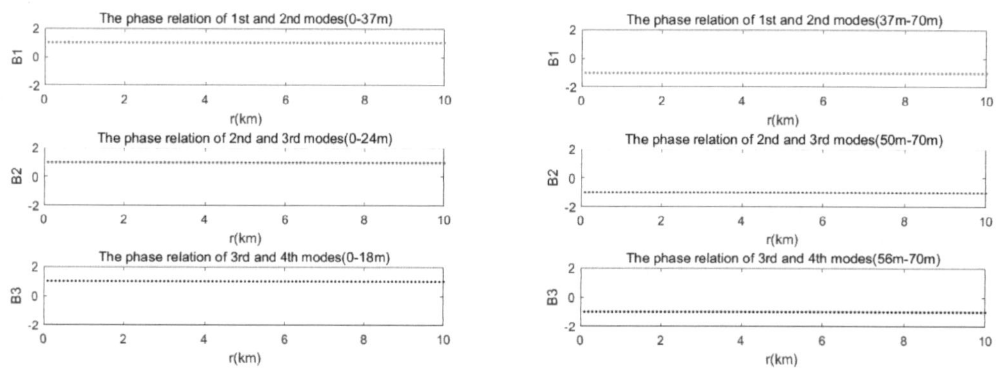

(a) Z_s=10m (b) Z_s=65m

Fig. 2 The phase relation of adjacent normal modes. (B_m=0 indicates the boundary position)

4.2. Simulation of depth sampling insufficient

To prove the method can still work when the depth sampling is insufficient. We will use an 8-element VLA to simulate. The environment parameters are as same as Fig. 2. In this case, the simulation result is shown in Fig. 3.

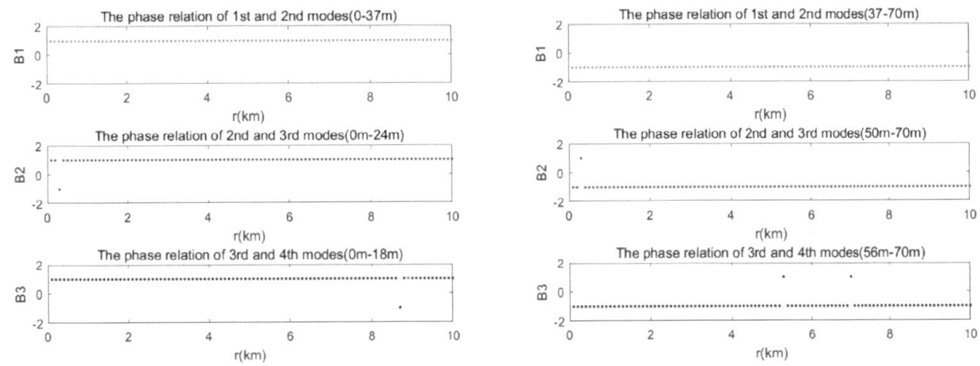

(a) Z_s=10m (b) Z_s=10m

Fig. 3 The phase relation of adjacent normal modes when the depth sampling is insufficient. (B_m=0 indicates the boundary position)

As shown in Fig. 2 and Fig. 3, even if the number of array elements is reduced, the source depth region can still be estimated accurately. It proves that the method can still discriminate the source depth region when the depth sampling is not so sufficient.

5. Application to experimental data

5.1. Experiment description

Now we demonstrate this method by processing the data from a shallow water propagation experiment, which was conducted in the Yellow Sea in January 2018. The average water depth is 41m. The sound speed increases slowly with depth. Two ships are used in this experiment, respectively for transmitting and receiving. The receiving ship suspends a 32-element VLA with 1m inter-element spacing. The transmitting ship moves close to the array with a constant speed of 11km/h. The average depth of the explosive sources is about 7m. The narrow-band average method is used to select the frequency of the source. The center frequency f_0=440Hz is selected for mode filtering, and the bandwidth is 10Hz.

6. Experimental data results

6.1. Discrimination results with a 32-element VLA

The depth of the explosive sources is about 7m, which are surface sources when the selected normal modes are the first three modes. In Fig. 4, when only two orders of normal mode are selected, sources within 20km can be accurately discriminated and the discrimination accuracy reaches 100%. However, at this time, the boundary of surface and submerged sources is not accurate enough, which is 21m. When three orders of normal mode are selected, due to the attenuation of normal mode increase, the error discrimination points have increased. But the boundary is greatly improved compared with two orders of normal mode, which is 14m. The discrimination results in Fig. 4 are in good agreement with the reality.

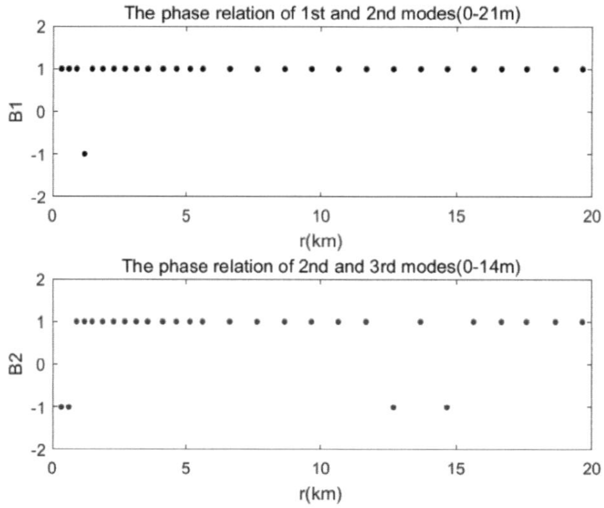

Fig. 4 The phase relation of the adjacent normal modes with a 32-element VLA. (B_m=0 indicates the boundary position)

6.2. Discrimination results with 8-element and 4-element VLA

Next, we verify the discrimination under the condition of sparse depth sampling. 8 and 4 from the 32 elements are selected respectively to form an 8-element array and a 4-element array with equal spacing, and the data received by these two re-formed arrays are respectively used for processing. The central frequency is 440Hz, and the discrimination results are shown in Fig. 5.

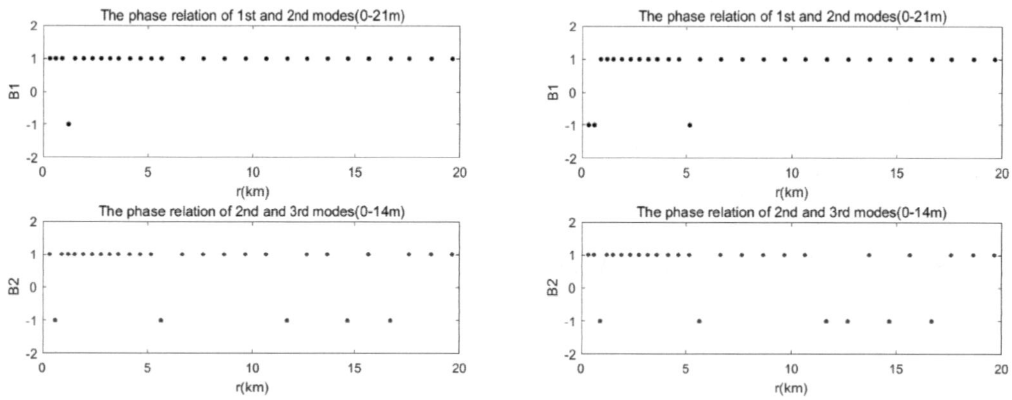

(a) 8 elements (b) 4 elements

Fig. 5 The phase relation of adjacent normal modes when source depth is not sufficient. (B_m=0 indicates the boundary position)

Through Fig. 5, it can be seen that the discrimination results of the first three modes are relatively accurate within 11km. It proves that the method can still work when depth sampling is insufficient or the mode filtering result is not ideal.

7. Conclusions

In shallow water, the source depth has a great relationship with the phase of normal modes.

The phase relation is different at different depths, especially near the water surface, different normal modes are in-phase. Therefore, the source depth region can be estimated by using the phase relation of normal modes. This paper using mode filtering to get the normal mode coefficient, the phase relation of adjacent modes can be obtained after processing the normal modes coefficient. The feasibility of the method is verified by simulation and experiment data. The method can still work in the situation when the source depth sampling is insufficient.

References

[1] H. P. Buker, "Use of calculated sound fields and matched-field detection to locate sound sources in shallow water," Journal of the Acoustical Society of America, 59(2) (1976), 368-373.

[2] A. B. Baggeroer, W. A. Kuperman, P. N. Mikhalevsky, "An overview of matched field methods in ocean acoustics," IEEE Journal of Oceanic Engineering, 18(4) (1993), 401-424.

[3] E. C. Shang, C. S. Clay, and Y. Y. Wang, "Passive harmonic source ranging in waveguides by using mode filter," Journal of the Acoustical Society of America, 78(1) (1985), 172-175.

[4] T. C. Yang, "A method of range and depth estimation by modal decomposition," Journal of the Acoustical Society of America, 82(5) (1987), 1736-1745.

[5] J. R. Buck, J. C. Preising, and K. E. Wage, "A unified framework for mode filtering and the maximum a posteriori mode filter," Journal of the Acoustical Society of America, 103(4) (1998), 1813-1824.

[6] V. E. Premus, and D. Backman, "A matched subspace approach to depth discrimination in a shallow water waveguide," Proceedings of the 41st Asilomar Conference on Signals, Systems and Computers, Asilomar, America, 2007, 1272-1276.

[7] E. Conan, J. Bonnel, T. Chonavel, and B. Nicolas, "Source depth discrimination with a vertical line array," Journal of the Acoustical Society of America, 140(5) (2016), 434-440.

[8] E. Conan, J. Bonnel, B. Nicolas, and T. Chonavel, "Use of trapped energy ratio for source depth discrimination with a horizontal line array: Theory and experimental results," Journal of the Acoustical Society of America, 142(5) (2017), 2776-2786.

[9] Y. Yu, J. Y. Hui, Y. Chen, and G. C. Sun, "Research on target depth classification in low frequency acoustic field of shallow water," Acta Physica Sinica, 58(9) (2009), 6335-6343.

[10] Z. T. Liu, L. H. Guo, C. Yan, "Source depth discrimination in shallow water based on relation formula warping transform," Acta Acoustic, 44(1) (2019), 28-38.

[11] J. B. Weng, Y. M. Yang, "A passive source range and depth estimation method by single hydrophone in shadow zone of deep water," Acta Acoustic, 43(6) (2018), 905-914.

[12] S. T. Rakotonarivo, W. A. Kuperman, "Model-independent range localization of a moving source in shallow water," Journal of the Acoustical Society of America, 132(4) (2012), 2218-2218.

[13] E. C. Shang, "Source depth estimation in waveguides," Journal of the Acoustical Society of America, 77(4) (1985), 1413-1418.

Underwater Positioning Study of Flight Recorder

Wen-Yang Liu[1] Richard Jih[2] Chi-Fang Chen[1]

1, Department of Engineering Science and Ocean Engineering,
National Taiwan University
chifang@ntu.edu.tw
r06525035@ntu.edu.tw
2, Investigation Lab, Aviation Safety Council,
Republic of China
richard@asc.gov.tw

A flight recorder, which is also called the "black box," is installed on each airplane, and it records the process of every flight. If the airplane crashes into water, the underwater locater beacon (ULB) of the flight recorder will be activated and emit ultrasonic sound at 37.5 kHz for 30 days. We propose using underwater acoustic detection simulation to enhance the search process by identifying the location with acoustic data assimilation and transmission loss simulation. The ULB of NA-706 Black Hawk Helicopter in the tragedy in February 2018 was salvaged successfully, and the location was close to the estimated location based on the scheme of the acoustic data assimilation and transmission loss simulation proposed in this paper. Aircraft manufactured from now on must be equipped with an 8.8 kHz flight recorder. This study compares the detection ranges of these two types of flight recorders. It can be found that the detection range of the 8.8 kHz recorder is greater. This is helpful to reduce the time required for search and rescue.

Keywords: Flight Recorder; Transmission Loss; Underwater Positioning; Detection Range

1. Introduction

The flight recorder is an avionics device on the aircraft, commonly known as the "black box." Its actual color, however, is orange-red so it can be spotted clearly during search operations. It is installed on aircraft and commonly is used for aviation accident investigation and flight test purposes. Since the air crash usually occurs in an instant, if the captain and all passengers were to be killed, the investigation of the accident would become difficult. The flight recorder can provide investigators with the moment and the time of the crash, the flight status of the aircraft, the operation of the equipment on board, etc. The cockpit call recorder helps people analyze the cause of the accident based on various conversations between the crew to make a correct conclusion about the accident.

A cylindrical buzzer is attached to the outside of the flight recorder. As soon as it hits the water, the water will short-circuit its line. The buzzer will emit a 37.5 kHz frequency signal for 30 days. A salvage ship will expand the scope of the planned reentry line in the sea area where the aircraft had an accident. The intensity of the sound signal collected along the line using an omnidirectional hydrophone during the voyage is shown in Fig 1. Using the collected information to draw the sound signal intensity map of the area, indicating the hot zone of the flight recorder (P5-P7) is shown in Fig 2. The salvage manufacturer then sails to the location and uses the ROV to visually confirm the location of the flight recorder and start salvage operations.

Air Combat Team No. NA-706 Black Hawk Helicopter was sent on a patient service from Taitung to Orchid Island on February 5, 2018. About one to two minutes after takeoff on the return flight, an accident occurred in the sea two miles from Orchid Island. Aviation Safety Council immediately contacted our laboratory to provide information on the intensity of the sound signal detected by the salvage vessel. These data were simulated for sound transmission loss to assist the investigation team in determining the location of the flight recorder.

2. Challenges in Underwater Search for Flight Recorder

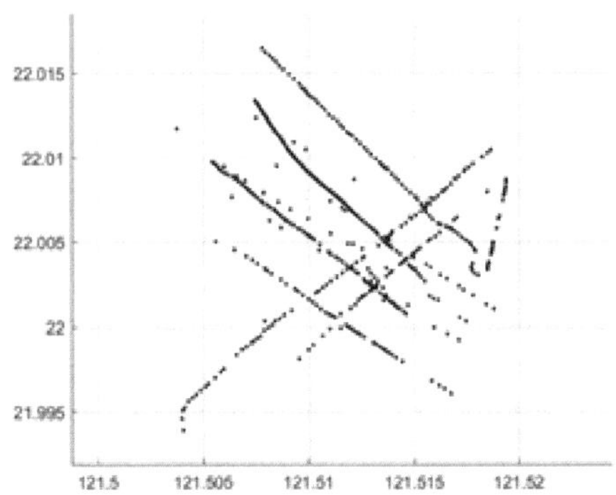

Fig. 1. Receiving points of hydrophone.

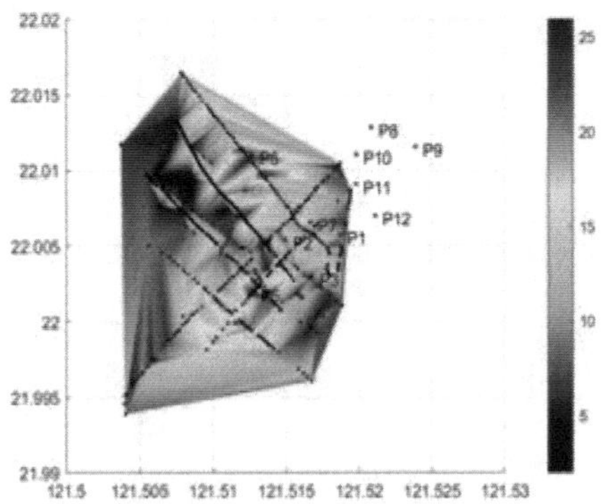

Fig. 2. Simulation Points (Hot zone and

The initial accident investigation of a flight accident is the search and salvage of the flight recorder. There have been accidents where a plane crashed in the Taiwan Strait, where the water is shallow. This time, the plane crashed on the East Coast, where the water is deep. In the NA-706 accident, the search and rescue team used an omnidirectional hydrophone along the line in the sea area around the wreck collecting the intensity of the sound signal, drawing the intensity map of the sound signal in the area, and marking the possible position of the flight recorder under the water. There was no way to choose the hot zone, and the cost of manpower, time, and money for each salvage attempt is very high. Nevertheless, the underwater positioning transmitter on the flight recorder only lasts about 30 days. After 30 days, the signal will be lost due to insufficient power, which highlights the urgency of the investigation and positioning of the flight recorder.

The directional hydrophone of the ASC and the omnidirectional hydrophone of the partner are limited by the depth of the hydrophone. It could only receive signal in shallow waters (depth about 5 to 30 meters), but the flight recorder often falls on the seabed. Looking at the speed of sound distribution caused by refraction, as shown in Fig. 3, a simulation of sound trace propagation of a flight recorder beacon in shallow waters (depth about 60 meters) on the seabed shows that the sound rays are densely distributed in shallow water and that it is easy to receive signals. On the contrary, as shown in Fig. 4, a simulation of sound trace propagation of a flight recorder in deep waters (depth about 1550 meters) on the seabed shows the distribution of sound rays in shallow water is sparse, making reception difficult.

xTherefore, the hydrophone only receiving in shallow water, is the limitation of current search operations in deep water. As far as the sound ray simulation is concerned, when the flight recorder is located in deep water, there is also a chance to receive the signal in the shallow water. The chances of receiving the flight recorder signal in the shallow water,however, are much smaller. Therefore, if there is an omnidirectional and directional underwater microphone that can be placed deeper, it will improve the chance of receiving signals from the flight recorder. Therefore, the general practice is to use an omnidirectional underwater microphone, which is placed at different depths for reception. If the directional direct-water microphone or horizontal array with adjustable depth can be placed after the received signal is determined, the position detection can be performed. Nevertheless, the current directional hydrophone of ASC only can work in shallow water and cannot be hoisted into deep waters.

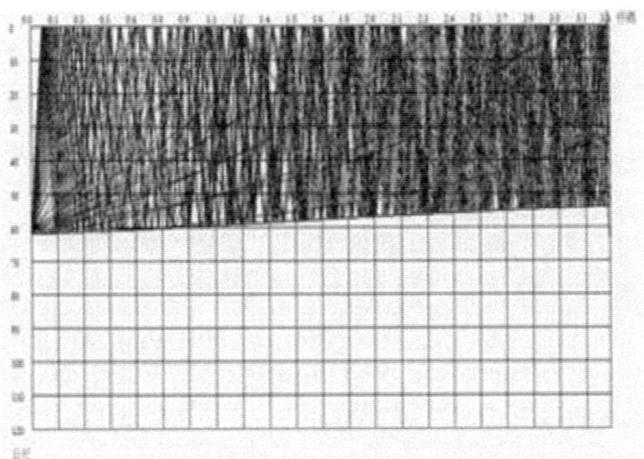

Fig. 3. Sound ray propagation in shallow waters.

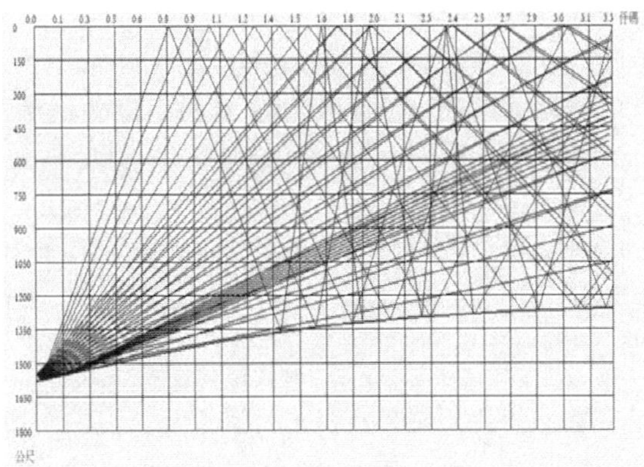

Fig. 4. Sound ray propagation in deep waters.

3. Simulation

3.1. Settings

This study simulates the possible location of the flight recorder of the Black Hawk helicopter on February 5, 2018, as the sound source point. Since the flight recorder is likely to sink to the bottom of the sea, the depth of the sound source is set on the seabed. The frequency is set to 37.5 kHz, the slap angle is set to omnidirectional, and the calculated distance is shown in Table 1. The receiving point is a handheld hydrophone used by the investigation team, and the depth is set to 5 meters. The hydrological data used in the simulation was extracted from the laboratory hydrological database for February. The terrain used for the simulation is the topographic data measured by the side scan sonar provided by the ASC. In order to reduce the calculation time, the simulation setting of the shooting angle will be calculated every 2 degrees.

Table 1. Distance from Hot zone to Hydrophone (m)

	P5	P6	P7
P1	870	740	220
P2	670	450	220
P3	1000	430	400
P8	890	1470	820
P9	1180	1570	930
P10	760	1250	600
P11	790	1080	430
P12	1000	1040	460

3.2. Transmission Loss

Transmission loss simulation is shown from the hot zone (P5) to the hydrophone in Fig 5. The black line is the distance between the towed sonar and the suspected location of the helicopter. Mark the transmission loss value in the figure, and output the transmission loss, as shown in Table 2. From the simulation results, it can be found that the transmission loss value at the P7 point is lower than the transmission loss values at the other two points, thereby estimating that the flight recorder is more likely to be at the P7 point.

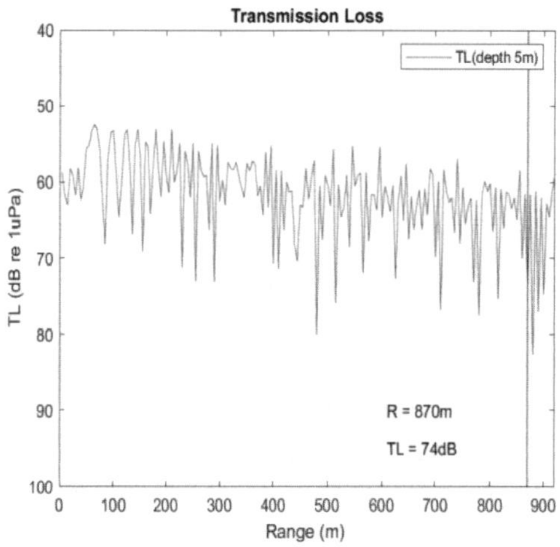

Fig. 5. P5 to P1 Transmission loss

Table 2. TL value from each hot zone to hydrophone (dB)

	P5	P6	P7
P1	74	59	57
P2	60	54	56
P3	63	57	61
P8	61	76	60
P9	75	63	58
P10	61	64	52
P11	62	66	59
P12	61	59	54

3.3. TL Simulation with Range Averaging

When using acoustic mode simulation, the sound source usually is set to use a harmonic wave. This sound source is a continuous wave that causes spatial interference. The sound source and sonar used in the experiment are broadband signals. Using the center frequency to add adjacent frequencies to generate wide-band signals can reduce spatial interference effects. The simulation single-frequency signal may be caused by spatial interference. If the bandwidth of the simulation sound source is increased, the interference effect in the distance will be compressed to approach zero. Therefore, it can be seen that the average of the frequency can be roughly equal to the average of the distance.

Regarding the average of the frequencies, we can use a sliding pane where width varies with distance to make the range average. The bandwidth is defined as α times the center frequency, and α is multiplied by the calculated distance as the size of the change pane. Transmission loss simulation from the hot zone (P5) to the hydrophone is shown in Fig 6. The blue line is the transmission loss that has not been subjected to range averaging. It can be found that there is still a large jitter guessing as a single frequency to cause spatial interference. After 0.2 times the distance, the average transmission loss is shown by the red line. The trend of sound transmission loss can be observed clearly. The black line is the distance between the towed sonar and the suspected position of the helicopter. Mark the transmission loss value (red line) in the figure, and output the transmission loss, as shown in Table 3. From the simulation results, it can be found that the transmission loss value by range average at the P7 point is lower than the transmission loss values by range average at the other two points, thereby estimating that the flight recorder is more likely to be at the P7 point.

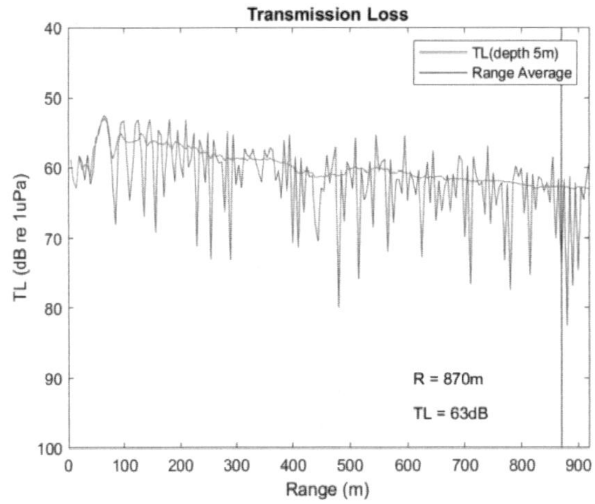

Fig. 6. P5 to P1 Transmission loss by range average.

Table 3. TL value from each hot zone to hydrophone (dB)

	P5	P6	P7
P1	63	59	56
P2	62	58	57
P3	63	59	60
P8	59	65	60
P9	63	66	61
P10	59	65	58
P11	61	62	57
P12	63	61	58

4. Detection Range

In Taiwan, the water depth difference between the East Coast and the West Coast is very large. The East Coast has a water depth of more than a kilometer and is very steep; the West Coast has a very shallow and flat water depth of about 50 meters. This simulation will compare the detection ranges of the 8.8 kHz and 37.5 kHz flight recorders through different water depths and topography.

On the West Coast, the detection range of 8.8 kHz is 19.8 km and the detection range of 37.5 kHz is 3.8 km (as shown in Fig. 7). We can find that the detection range is about 5 times worse. On the East Coast, the detection range of 8.8 kHz is 16.2 km, and the detection range of 37.5 kHz is 2.3 km (as shown in Fig. 8). From this result, we can find that the detection distance of 37.5 kHz is much smaller than 8.8 kHz, which makes it difficult to accomplish search and rescue today. Therefore, it is reasonable to add 8.8 kHz signal to the black box.

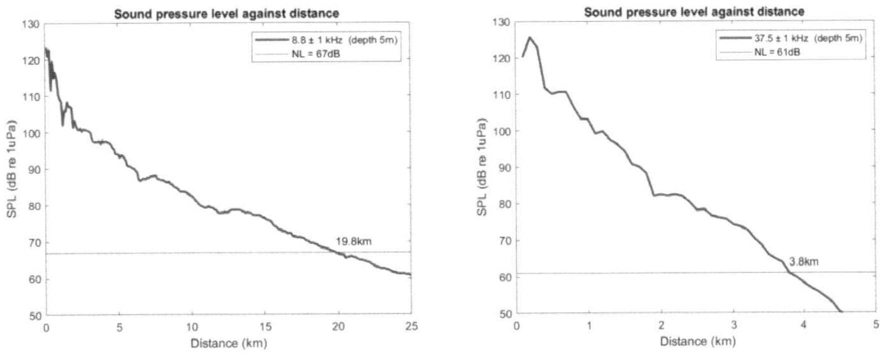

Fig. 7. Detection range on West Coast.

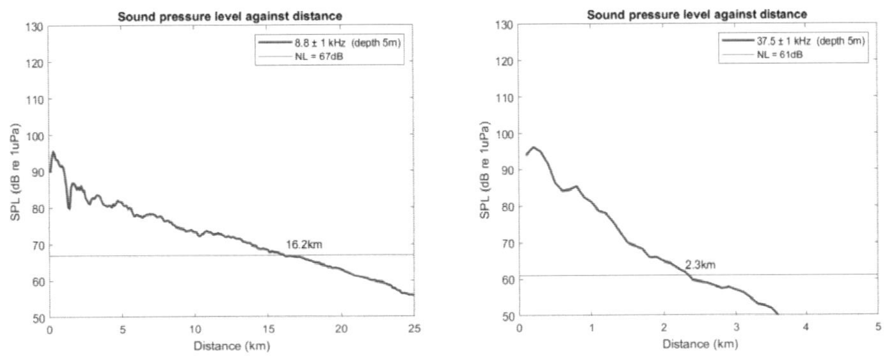

Fig. 8. Detection range on East Coast.

5. Summary

This study uses the sound signal strength data detected by the fishing boat provided by ASC to carry out calculation simulations to assist the investigation team in determining the location of the flight recorder. Preliminary results show that the simulation results are close to the actual position of the flight recorder. In the future, this simulation can be used to assist in determining the location of the sound source when needed.

After different frequency simulation (detection range) in this study, one can see that it is reasonable for the aviation administrator to decide to use low frequency ULB in the aircraft fuselage. The 8.8 kHz ULD attached to the structure of the aircraft would decrease the time needed to search any given area because of the increased range due to the lower frequency.

Acknowledgement

This work was supported by Aviation Safety Council. We are grateful to the survey team that assisted the ship survey for their contribution to the success of this simulation.

References

[1] Liu Mengyu, "Study on the Three-dimensional Ocean Sound and Seabed Sand Dunes Effect" , Master's Thesis, Institute of Engineering Science and Ocean Engineering, National Taiwan University, 2014.

[2] Yuan Meijun, " Study on the Uncertainty Analysis and Detection Efficiency of Underwater Sound Transmission in Shallow Waters," Ph.D. Thesis, Institute of Engineering Science and Ocean Engineering, National Taiwan University, 2007 .

Acoustic Relaxation Spectral Gas Detection Based on Deep Learning

Wei Zheng[1], Xue Wang[2], Junyu Ren[2], Ming Zhu[2]*
1, State Grid Corporation of China Australia Representative Offce,
Sydney, 2000/NSW, Australia
wei-zheng@sgcc.com.cn
2, School of Electronic Information and Communications, HuaZhong University of Science and Technology,
Wuhan, 430074/Hubei , China
zhuming@mail.hust.edu.cn

Traditional gas detection method is to analyze acoustic gas spectral mathematically, which is not practical for complicated components due to its complexity. So we established a one-dimensional convolutional neural network (1D CNN) for acoustic spectral classification. We verified that the 1D CNN could extract acoustic spectrum characteristic automatically and classify these characteristic frequency points with high accuracy. Furthermore, an acoustic relaxation gas detection Web application has been designed and tested. We provide an interactive and visualize simulation platform for acoustic relaxation spectral gas detection.

Keywords: Gas detection; Deep learning; Acoustic relaxation.

1. General Appearance

Acoustic absorption in gases consists of classic absorption and relaxation absorption, the former can be calculated by mature theories long since 1960s[1]. Yet the research on the latter has gone through a long and tortuous process, the application of molecular relaxation to gas mixture laid foundation for study on relaxation absorption in gas mixture[2][3]. And the deduction of acoustic relaxation absorption spectra[4][5] made it possible to qualitatively analyze gas mixture component with relaxation absorption[6][7].

It's impractical to specify the contribution every gas component made to the whole relaxation process by investigation relaxation spectra with mathematical method due to its complexity. So the spectrum-based gas detection methods are limited to mixtures of background components are known. Beyond that, existing ultrasonic transducers can only send fixed frequency signals, measuring the spectrum by intensity sampling is costly. The urgent demand of acoustic relaxation gas detection is an efficient approach to extract characteristic parameters from the sound spectra which can identify gas components. Due to the limitations of traditional mathematical methods, wavelet transform was used to extract sound spectra characters and support vector machine (SVM) model undertook the classification work[8]. However, considering the small sample volume and low detection accuracy, this scheme is not suitable for more complex multi-component gas detection.

Inspired by the great success of deep learning, this article proposed a one-dimensional convolutional neural network for acoustic relaxation gas detection. Compared with typical conventional machine learning models (e.g., SVM, KNN), the CNN can automatically learn features from raw input data. Moreover, CNN is an end-to-end deep network jointly learn features and classify in one model, offers better performance.

2. Method for Acoustic Relaxation Gas Detection Based on Deep Learning

2.1. Analysis of gas acoustic spectra

From the thermodynamic energy relaxation equation[9], the effective isochoric molar heat (IMH) of a gas mixture with W kinds of molecules including N types of vibrational modes:

$$C_V^{eff} = C_{mix}^{\infty} + \sum_{q=1}^{N} a_q C_q^{vib} \frac{dT_q^{vib}}{dT}, \tag{2.1}$$

$$C_{mix}^{\infty} = \sum_{l=1}^{W} a_l C_l^{\infty}, \sum_{l=1}^{W} a_l = 1, \tag{2.2}$$

where C_{mix}^{∞} is the external IMH of the mixture, C_l^{∞} is the external IMH of molecule l, a_l is the mole fraction of molecule l; T and T_q^{vib} are the instantaneous temperatures of the external degree of freedom and vibrational mode q respectively. C_q^{vib} is the vibrational IMH of mode q. If molecule l contains N_l vibrational modes, these N_l modes share the same mole fraction as a_l.

The effective acoustic wave number k^{eff} can be given in terms of the effective thermodynamic sound speed c_e or the frequency-dependent phase speed $c(\omega)$ and relaxation absorption $a_r(\omega)$,

$$\begin{aligned} k^{eff}(w) &= \frac{\omega}{c_e(\omega)} - w\sqrt{\frac{p_0}{\rho_0}\frac{C_V^{eff}+R}{C_V^{eff}}}, \\ &= \frac{\omega}{c(w)} - ia_r(\omega), \end{aligned} \tag{2.3}$$

where $\omega = 2\pi f$ is the acoustic angular frequency, ρ_0 and P_0 are the equilibrium density and pressure respectively, R is the universal gas constant.

Therefore, the sound speed c and the dimensionless relaxation absorption coefficient $a_r\lambda$ can be written as:

$$c = \frac{1}{\text{Re}(c_e^{-1})}, \tag{2.4}$$

$$a_r\lambda = \frac{-2\pi - \text{Im}(c_e^{-1})}{\text{Re}(c_e^{-1})}. \tag{2.5}$$

Based on Eqs. (2.4) and (2.5), the precise relaxation absorption spectra can be obtained. In this paper, 5 common gases (CH_4、Cl_2、CO_2、H_2、N_2) were experimented on. In Fig. (1), the acoustic relaxation absorption spectra between 10^3~10^7Hz of these 5 common gases under temperature 288K and 1atm are shown. At room temperature and pressure, the acoustic relaxation absorption spectra of most excitable gases distributed in 10~10^8Hz[10][11]. But in Fig. (1.b), the acoustic relaxation absorption spectral peak of N_2 located around 10^{-2}Hz. Gas detection based on the locations of spectral peak[7] is reasonable, but unpractical. Since the spectral peak of weak relaxation gases is too inconspicuous to be detected when mixed with strong relaxation gases.

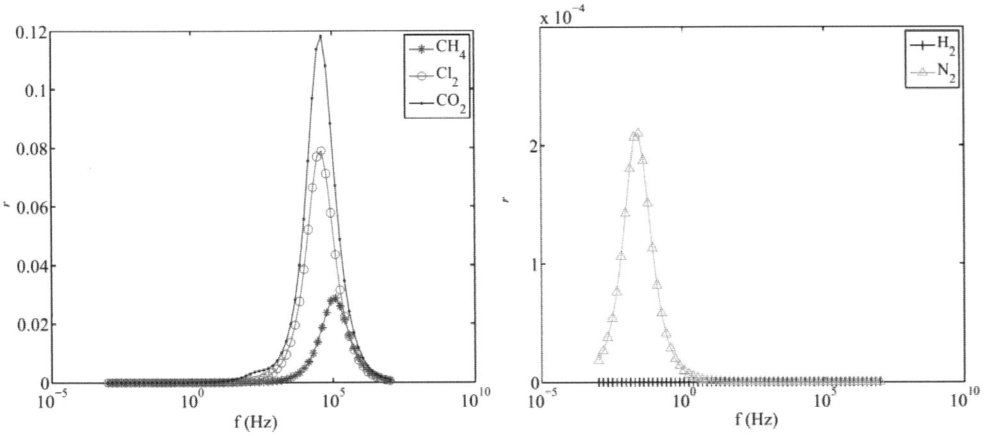

(a) (b)

Fig. 1. Acoustic relaxation absorption of several gases. (a)Strong relaxation gases, (b)weak relaxation gases.

Acoustic classic absorption in gases depends on viscosity and heat conduction,

$$a_c = \frac{2\pi^2}{r\lambda} \cdot [\frac{4}{3}\eta + (\frac{\gamma-1}{C_p}) \cdot k] \cdot \frac{f}{p}, \tag{2.6}$$

where λ is acoustic wave length, f is sound frequency, C_P is the specific heat at constant pressure, η is the viscosity of gas, k is Bolzmann constant, P is pressure. The acoustic classic absorption spectra of 5 gases at 288K are in Fig. (2). As shown in Fig. (2), for most gases, the acoustic classic absorption is relatively weak and embodies little difference compared with relaxation absorption. But some gases like H_2 are more distinguishable in acoustic classic absorption spectra.

According to Eqs. (2.3), (2.4) and (2.5), the sound speed can be obtained as:

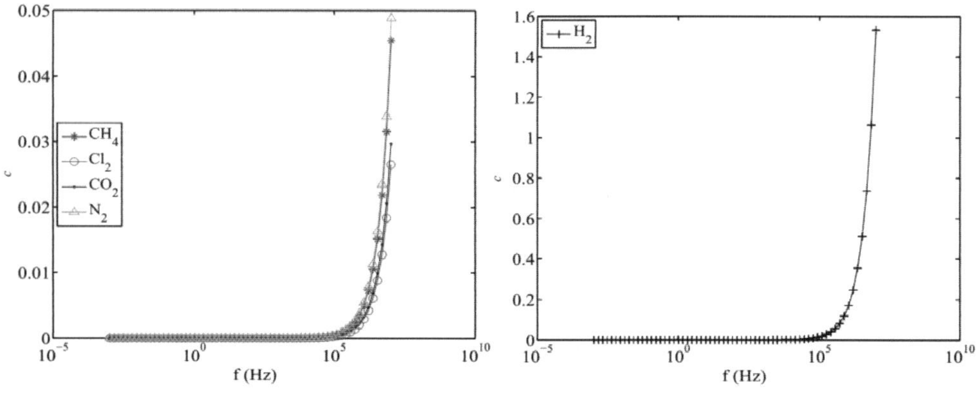

(a) (b)

Fig. 2. Acoustic classic absorption spectra of several gases. (a) Classic absorption spectra are similar with low amplitude. (b) the classic absorption of H 2 is obviously stronger in 10^5~10^7Hz.

$$c = \frac{c_0}{\sqrt{\gamma}} \sqrt{\frac{C_V^{eff} + R}{C_V^{eff}}}, \tag{2.7}$$

when $\omega \to 0$, the sound speed is written as c_0. c_0 represents the classic sound speed. The sound speed varying with frequency is called dispersion, dispersion is quite feeble as shown in Fig. (3). The lighter the molecular weight, the faster the velocity of sound. Sound speed can reflect the difference in gas components and fractions, so as to detect gas in quality and quantity[12]. However, through sound speed spectra may not obtain right judgement for two mixtures with same average molecular weight.

2.2. Proposed scheme

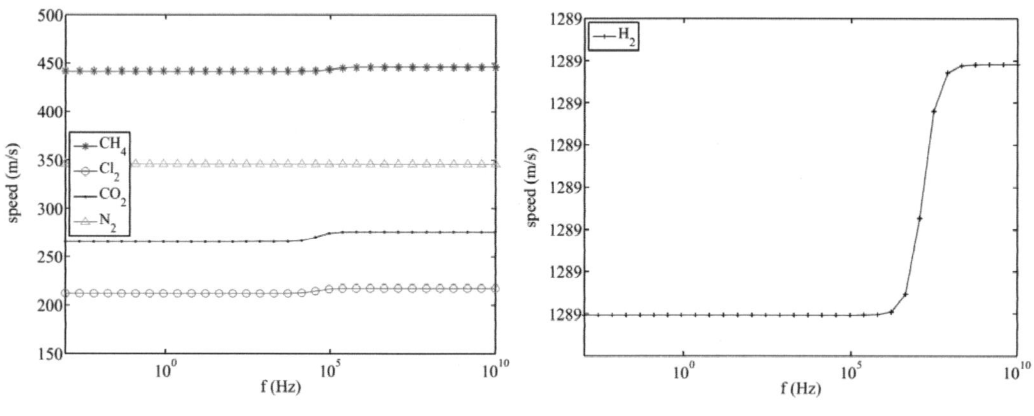

(a) (b)

Fig. 3. Sound speed spectra of several gases.

As analyzed in 2.1, gas composition information can be provided by acoustic relaxation spectra, acoustic classic spectra and sound speed spectra, but not sufficient by either one. So, gas detection was implemented by combination these three kinds of spectra in this paper. The acoustic relaxation absorption and acoustic classic absorption was combined by additive operation, and acoustic absorption spectra was obtained. Data for one kind of gas were sampled on its' acoustic absorption spectrum and sound speed spectrum, 64 points on each curve. Each gas sample is a random mixture of 5 components at 288K and 1atm, the volume of dataset is 10,000. All data were standardized by Z-Score method before training and testing. The model was used is a one-dimensional CNN model. It begins with an input layer, which accepts a feature tensor with the shape of 128 * 1. Then convolutional layer is applied in order to exact useful and highly representative features, LeakyRelu activates the output of convolutional layers. Each Max-pooling layer with stride of 3 reduces the output length to 1/3. Finally, the model ends with several fully connected layer with Softmax activation. Cross-entropy was used for loss calculation, and the error is 0 for perfectly classifying during the test. Failing this, error between 0 and 1 were counted as punishment for misclassifications.

$$L(y,\hat{y}) = -\sum_{i=1}^{c} y_i \log \hat{y}_i \,, \tag{2.8}$$

where y is the truth label for input X, and $\hat{y}$ is prediction generated by the classifier, C is sample volume.

In this paper, Adam was used as optimization method, which provides efficient stochastic optimization and requires little memories. This method computes individual learning rates for different parameters from estimates of first and second moments of gradients.

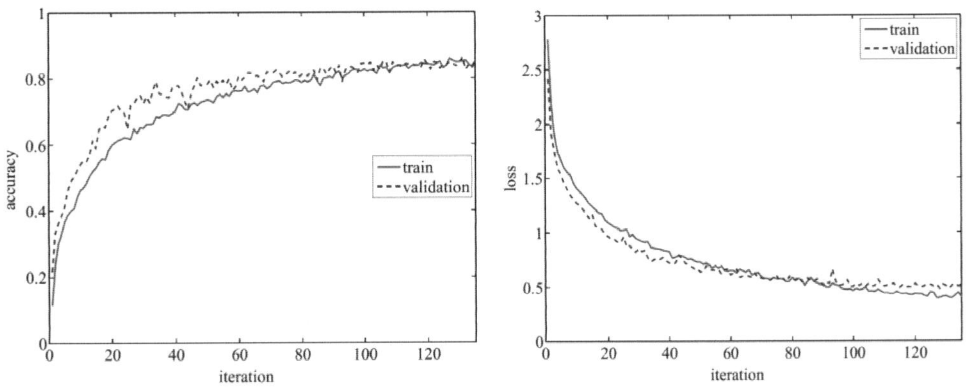

(a) (b)

Fig. 4. (a)Accuracy curve for qualitative detection of CH_4, (b) Loss curve for qualitative detection of CH_4

Learning curves are one of the most important evaluation measures for machine/deep learning algorithms. As can be seen in Fig. (4.a), training accuracy and validation accuracy for qualitative detection of CH_4 in five-gas mixture maintain a steady increase as the number of training iterations increases. Similarly, in Fig. (4.b), it can be seen that training loss and validation loss continue to decrease as the number of epochs goes up. Based on the learning curves, it can be concluded that we didn't incur an "overfitting" or "underfitting" phenomenon.

2.3. Performance of recognition

The sample gases are composed of target gas with concentration gradient 5% and the random mixture of last 4 components. Recognition accuracies for qualitative detection of five gases are list in Table 1. As a contract, the wavelet and multi-classification SVM (MSVM) scheme was also used for gas detection experiment. According to Table 1, compared with "shallow learning", one-dimensional CNN model can reach higher recognition accuracy without tedious manual exaction for spectra features.

Table 1. Detection Accuracy of 5 common gases.

Target Gas	1D CNN	MSVM
CH_4	82.5%	35.2%
Cl_2	95.0%	34.5%
CO_2	91.5%	33.2%
H_2	92.1%	31.7%
N_2	84.5%	34.7%

2.4. Frequency points of high impact

In order to exact respective points from acoustic spectra, mean impact value (MIV) method was used to analyze the correlation between input and classification results. The average fluctuations of model output were measured in case each input point were increased or decreased by 10% respectively. The points corresponding to the greater fluctuations are of high impact to classification result. The standardized acoustic spectra of a gas synthesized from the average concentration of each component in the sample dataset are marked by frequency points of high impact as Fig. (5). The results show that the convolutional neural network has the ability to extract the inflection points of sound spectrum. And gas detection based on small amount of significant frequency points is practical and effective, since these points affect gas recognition to a great extent.

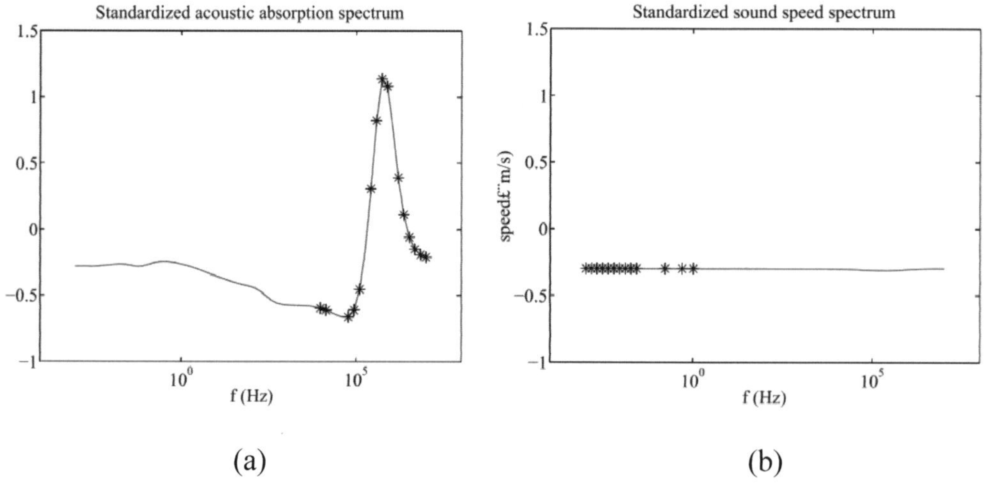

Fig. 5. Standardized sound spectra marked by frequency points of high impact.

2.5. Acoustic relaxation gas detection simulation platform

Guided by acoustic relaxation theory and deep learning method provided above, an acoustic relaxation gas detection simulation experimental system was built under the Django framework. It realized cross-platform and interactive acoustic spectral simulation. TensorFlow.js was used to implement the visualization of deep learning process on the browser side. It can be accessed through the website http://203.195.153.225/.

3. Conclusion

In this work, we analyzed gas acoustic spectra and proposed a CNN model for gas spectra classification. Compared with conventional SVM method, the deep learning scheme provided in this article was proved to be more efficient and accurate. By use of MIV method, small amount of influential spectra feature points were extracted. Which means gas detection can be conduct by sparse sampling on gas acoustic spectra in practice.

Acknowledgments

This work was supported by the National Natural Science Foundation of China under Grant 61571201, the National Key Technologies R&D Program under Grant 2016YFC0201101, and the Science & Technology Project of STATE GRID Corporation of China: "The research on defect detection technology and diagnostic method of high voltage shunt reactor based on acoustic vibration signal" under Grant 52199919000A.

References

[1] Shields, and F. Douglas . "Tube Corrections in the Study of Sound Absorption." The Journal of the Acoustical Society of America, 29(4) (1957), 470.

[2] Dain, Y , and R. M. Lueptow . "Acoustic Attenuation in Three-component Gas Mixtures--Theory." The Journal of the Acoustical Society of America, 109(1) (2001), 1955.

[3] Petculescu, Andi G., and Richard M, Lueptow. "Synthesizing Primary Molecular Relaxation Processes in Excitable Gases Using a Two-Frequency Reconstructive Algorithm." Physical review letters, 94(23) (2005), 238301.

[4] Ming Zhu, Tingting Liu, Xiangqun Zhang, et al. "A simple measurement method of molecular relaxation in a gas by reconstructing acoustic velocity dispersion." Measurement Science and Technology, 29 (2018), 015109.

[5] Ming Zhu, Tingting Liu, Shu Wang, et al. "Capturing molecular multimode relaxation processes in excitable gases based on decomposition of acoustic relaxation spectra." Measurement Science and Technology, 28 (2017), 085008.

[6] Petculescu, Andi , and Richard M, Lueptow. "Quantitative Acoustic Relaxational Spectroscopy for Real-time Monitoring of Natural Gas: A Perspective on Its Potential." Sensors and Actuators B (Chemical) 169(7) (2012), 121-127.

[7] Yi Hu, Shu Wang, Ming Zhu, et al. "Acoustic absorption spectral peak location for gas detection." Sensors and Actuators B: Chemical, 203(11) (2014), 1-8.

[8] Yaqiong Jia. "Construction of Gas Ultrasonic Spectra and Its Application in Gas Detection." Huazhong University of Sicience and Techonology, 2013.

[9] Lingzi Zhu. "Support Vector Machine and Signal Matching Algorithm in the Gas Detection of Sound spectrum." Huazhong University of Sicience and Techonology, 2016.

[10] Tingting Liu, Shu Wang, and Ming Zhu. “Decomposition of effective specific heat of molecular relaxation for gas detection in a mixture.” The Journal of the Acoustical Society of America, 141(3) (2017), 1844.
[11] Yi Hu, Shu Wang, Ming Zhu. “A relaxation times coupling method to construct acoustic relaxation calibration for two-frequency measuring gas compositions.” Applied Acoustics, 113 (2016), 102–108.
[12] Xiangqun Zhang, Shu Wang, Ming zhu, et al. “Decoupling Multiple Rotational Relaxations of Hydrogen to Detect Gas Mixtures.” IEEE ACCESS, 7 (2019), 115774.

Carbonate Reservoir Characterization by Joint Seismic Attributes

FAN LI[1], JING BA[1], CUN YU[1], WEI QIAN[1]

1, School of Earth Sciences and Engineering, Hohai University, Nanjing, 211100, China

1037053385@qq.com

jba@hhu.edu.cn

Conventional interpretation methods are challenged to effectively identify carbonate oil/gas reservoirs in China. This is because those carbonate reservoirs in China are generally deep and situated in a complex sedimentary environment. Furthermore, they demonstrate low porosity, low permeability, and strong heterogeneity. In this paper, we developed a new prediction method based on joint seismic attributes. The proposed method combines seismic attenuation and seismic instantaneous phase properties to construct a joint indicator, which can be used to characterize the pore-permeability features and thereby identify gas-bearing rocks in complex carbonates reservoirs.

Keywords: Attenuation; Instantaneous phase; Carbonates; Properties.

1. Introduction

Seismic attributes refer to various indicators which characterize seismic responses derived from mathematical transformations (Yin., 2006; Du., 2004). Seismic attribute analysis can be used to predict reservoir oil and gas properties. It's primary use is for reservoir performance and hydrocarbon-bearing evaluation (Wang., 2013). It can indicate seismic reflection intensity and stratigraphic occurrence. It also provides information on lithologic changes. However, single attribute leads to prediction ambiguities (Shi., 2007). Therefore, integration of multi-attributes is necessary to reduce the ambiguity. In China, multi-attributes analysis has been developed for many oilfields under a great variety of geological environments. Many cases have been studied and published, such as the beach dam sand body of Shengli Oilfield, Honghaoershute depression, Tazhong carbonate fracture cave, Subei oilfield, and Liaohe oilfield (Gong et al., 2007; Hong et al., 2007; Wen et al., 2007; Xu., 2010; Qu et al., 2012; Liu et al., 2013; Yao et al., 2013). Xu Zhandong (Xu., 2010) has conducted a qualitative prediction for the reservoirs of the Nantun Formation in the Wunan sub-dove, using root mean square (RMS) root-amplitude and average reflection intensity. Xie Lihua(Xie., 2013) used seismic facies technology to analyze the favorable reservoir facies in Wudong slope zone. He finds that the anomaly of RMS amplitude reflects the structural changes in this area.

In this study, we aim at the complex diagenesis of carbonate gas reservoirs. The reservoir has high anisotropy, low porosity, and permeability. We have developed a joint index for two seismic properties of high lateral resolution. This joint index is used to identify gas bearing area of the complex carbonate reservoirs.

2. Principle of the method

The theoretical assumption of the improved frequency shift method suggest that seismically estimated Q can effectively reduce the effect of noise. In our method, the quality factor Q is estimated as follows:

$$Q = \frac{\sqrt{\pi^5} t f_{c2} f_{c1}^2}{16(f_{c1}^2 - f_{c2}^2)} . \tag{2.1}$$

where, t is travel time, f_{c1} and f_{c2} are the centroid frequency before and after attenuation.
The instantaneous phase is affected by the fluid content in reservoir rocks. Generally, when the seismic signal transmits through a reservoir interface, the seismic reflection coefficients change and phase features are therefore reversed. Therefore, the instantaneous phase is capable to detect the lithologic boundary and achieve a good recognition effect. It can be estimated as:

$$IP(t) = \arctan \frac{g(t)}{f(t)} \tag{2.2}$$

where, g(t) is the imaginary part of Hilbert transform of the seismic record, and f(t) is the real part. We combine the normalized attenuation attribute and instantaneous phase to construct indicator Q_p:

$$Q_p = mQ_g + (1-m)IP_g \cdot \tag{2.3}$$

where, m is the weight coefficient, Q_p is the normalized parameter of Q , and IP_g is the normalized parameter of IP , which can be decided based on vertical resolution of target reservoir and the actual reservoir thickness. The Q_p indicator not only preserves the horizontal distinguishing capability of the attenuation attribute for the stratum, but also incorporates the vertical resolution, therefore it can be used for a relatively complete prediction for reservoir quality.
The new joint attribute is used for characterizing complex carbonate reservoirs from west China. Q_p shows its effectiveness of identifying the reservoirs, which reveals the true thickness of the reservoir, and simultaneously distinguishes hydrocarbon-bearing rocks from brine-saturate ones.

3. An application example

3.1. Work area

The Longwangmiao carbonate gas reservoir in the Moxi area of the Anyue gas field is one of the oldest and most productive carbonate gas reservoir in China. It is located in central Sichuan paleo-uplift and has great oil/gas potential. The lithology of the Longwangmiao formation is basically carbonate rock. It is mainly dissolved dolomite or grain dolomite. The reservoir space mainly consists of pores, karst cavities and fractures. The intergranular and intercrystalline dissolved pores are dominant. The continuity of the reservoir is good with lateral connectivity reaches up to 3 - 4 km, and gas-bearing area more than 800 square kilometers. The proven reserves are more than 400 billion cubic meters, indicating a great potential for exploration and development (Wang et al., 2016; Zhang et al., 2015). The first survey line passes through 3 wells, the second survey line passes through 2 wells (Fig. 1). Workflow chart of the proposed seismic attribute analysis technique as Fig. 2.

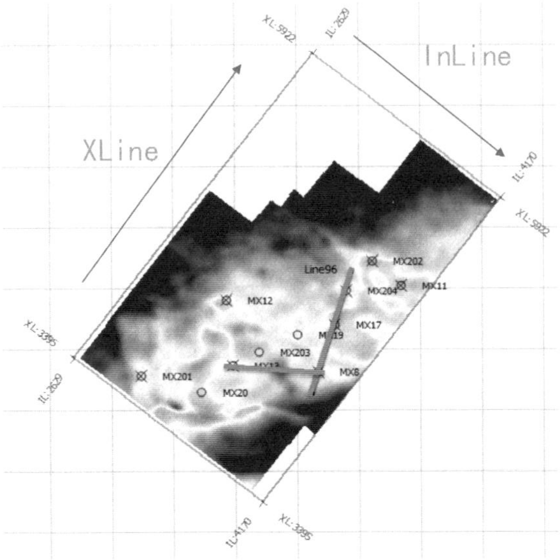

Fig. 1. Seismic coverage.

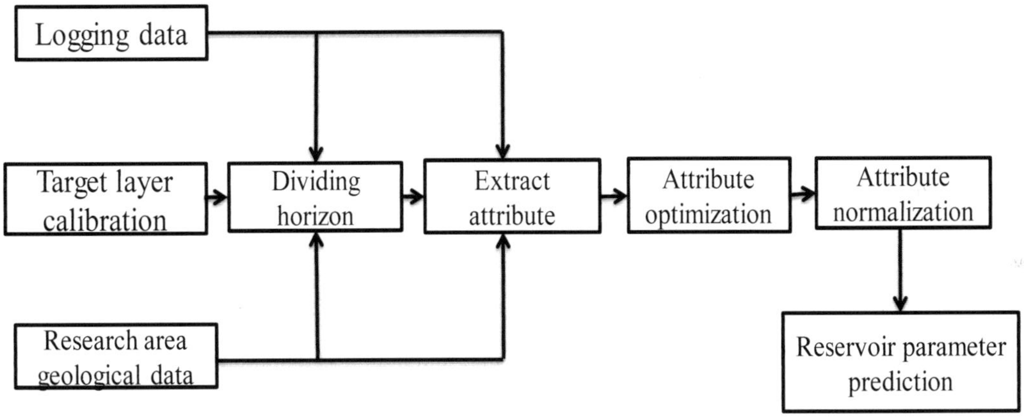

Fig. 2. Workflow chart of the proposed seismic attribute analysis technique

3.2. Joint index

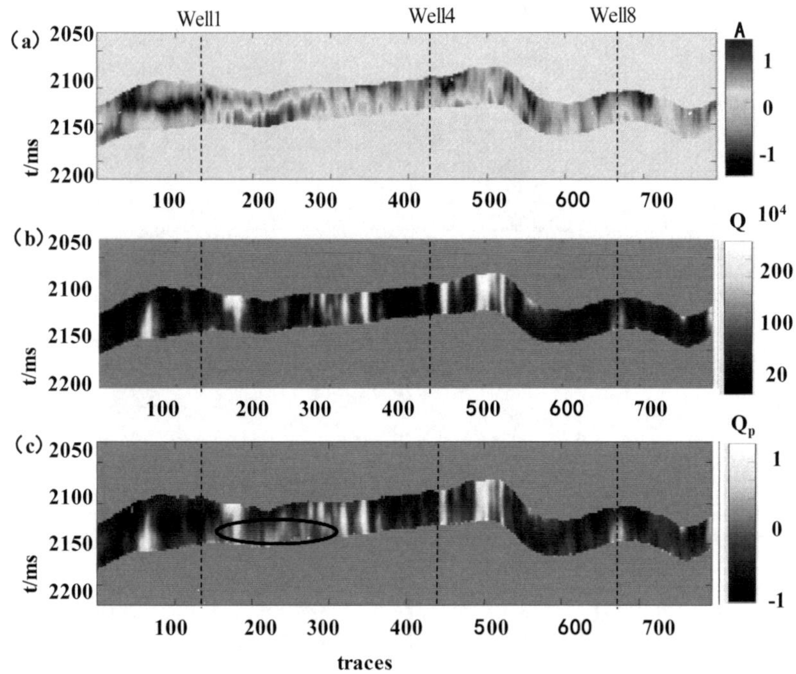

Fig. 3. (a) Instantaneous phase section; (b) Q- section; (c) Section of the joint index Q_p

As shown in Fig. 3 (a), the instantaneous phase for the target layer has high resolution for the horizontal direction. Its positive angle characteristic is presumed to be the upward displacement of the lower stratum due to a set of normal fault. Compared with the Q-value, the Q_p is effectively compensated in horizontal direction, and the thin inter-beded layers in the southern Well 1 are successfully identified. Well 4 shows the thinnest reservoirs among three low-Q wells, and it also corresponds to the areas with the lowest porosity and permeability.

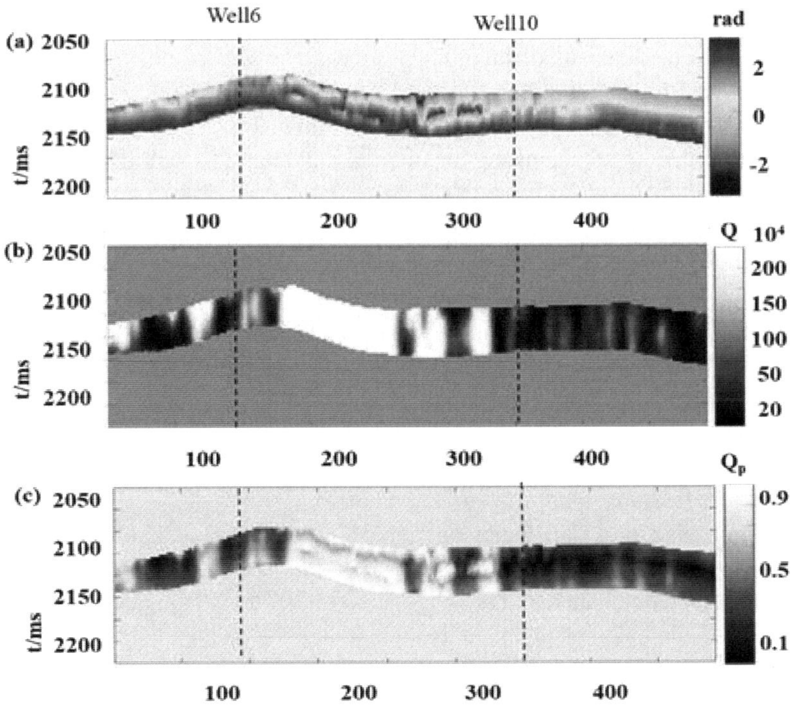

Fig. 4. (a) Instantaneous phase section; (b) Q- section; (c) Section of the joint index Q_p

From Fig. 4 (a), for the instantaneous phase, we can see the boundary of a low-amplitude thin layer. It reflects a lithological change of the target formation. Although the Q_p value is small, it demonstrates a continuous pattern in the well 10 area, which is an ideal location for oil and gas reservoirs.

4. Conclusion

- The attenuation extraction method and the attenuation-instantaneous phase joint index method have a significant effect on the prediction of high-quality reservoirs.
- The instantaneous phase can compensate well for the problem of insufficient attenuation in the longitudinal resolution, and Q_p is shown to identify the reservoirs, which contains the true thickness information of the reservoir, and simultaneously distinguishes hydrocarbon-bearing rocks from the brine-saturate ones.

Acknowledgments

The National Natural Science Foundation of China (grant no. 41974123, 41704109), Jiangsu Innovation and Entrepreneurship Plan, Specially-Appointed Professor Plan of Jiangsu Province and the Fundamental Research Funds for Central Universities, China (grant no. 2016B13114) all funded this study.

References

[1] Shitong Du. "Seismic attribute analysis." *Petroleum Geophysics*, 2004, 2 (4) : 19-30

[2] Fisher R A. "The foundations of theretical statistics." *Philosophical Transactions of the Royal Society a Mathematical Physical & Engineering Sciences*,1992.222(1) : 309-368.

[3] Lanting Shi, Qinlin Yang, Dinghong Yi, "Sedimentary evolution and reservoir-cap rock assemblages of palaeogeue in dawangzhang area, raoyang sag, central Hebei provience." *Journal of East China University of Technology(Natural Science)* , 2007 (2) : 132 - 136

[4] Kaiyan Wang, Qingyan Xu, Guifang Zhang. "Summary of seismic attribute analysis." *Progress in Geophysics*,2013,28(2):815-823

[5] Zecheng Wang, Tongshan Wang, Long Wen. "Basic geological characteristics and accumulation conditions of Anyue giant gas field, Sichuan basin." *China Offshore Oil and Gas*, 2016, 28 (2) : 45-52

[6] Zhandong Xu. "Study on reservoir prediction of Nantungroup in southern area of wuerxun hollow." *Daqing Petroleum Institute*,2010. (In Chinese).

[7] Xingyao Yin, Wengong Han, Zhenchun Lu. "New developments in seismic technology." *Journal of China University of Petroleum*,2006

[8] Jianyong Zhang, Wenjun Luo, Jingao Zhou. "Main Origins of High Quality Reservoir of Lower Cambrian Longwangmiao Formation in the Giant Anyue Gas Field, Sichuan Basin, SW China." *Natural Gas Geoscience*, 2015, 26 (11) : 2063-2074

Characteristics of Waves in Gas Hydrate-Bearing Sediments

LIN LIU[1,2,3] XIU-MEI ZHANG*[1,2,3] XIU-MING WANG[1,2,3]

1, State Key Laboratory of Acoustics, Institute of Acoustics, Chinese Academy of Sciences,
Beijing, China
2, University of Chinese Academy of Sciences,
Beijing, China
3, Beijing Engineering Research Center of Sea Deep Drilling and Exploration,
Institute of Acoustics, Chinese Academy of Sciences, Beijing, China
liulin@mail.ioa.ac.cn
zhangxiumei@mail.ioa.ac.cn
wangxm@mail.ioa.ac.cn

The analysis of the effects of frequency, gas hydrate saturation and clay content on the velocity and attenuation of body waves are the basis for identifying hydrate reservoirs and estimating hydrate saturation. In this paper, the improved LCA model is used to study the propagation characteristics of elastic waves in gas hydrate-bearing sediments, where the friction coefficient between two solids proposed by Geurin is included, and also the elastic modulus of skeleton are those from Lee's simplified three-phase Biot model. Variations of phase velocities and attenuation of different type of body waves with frequency, gas hydrate saturation, clay content, etc. are analyzed. The investigations give comprehensive relations of the velocity and attenuation with varies parameters. In particular, the features of these waves in the frequency range of seismic exploration and acoustic logging are studied. The analyses show that the P1 and S1 waves are nondispersive at seismic or acoustic logging frequency range, while their phase velocities increase with the increase of gas hydrate saturation. In seismic exploration frequency range, P2, S2, and P3 waves are dispersive, and the attenuation of them is significant. In acoustic logging frequency range, however, P2, S2, and P3 waves are nondispersive when the gas hydrate saturation is low. Clay reduces the phase velocities of P1 and S1 waves significantly and has almost no effect on phase velocities of S2 and P3 waves. In the frequency range of seismic exploration, the phase velocity of P2 wave is not sensitive to clay content but sensitive in the frequency range of acoustic logging. Clay decreases the attenuation of P1 wave, and the attenuation of S1, P2, S2 and P3 waves is not affected by clay content.

Keywords: Gas hydrate-bearing sediments; phase velocity; attenuation; gas hydrate saturation.

1. Introduction

With the increasing consumption of petroleum resources and the tension of energy supply, it is essential to find new alternative resources. Gas hydrate is abundant in reserves but challenging to exploit. As clean energy, gas hydrate has become a research hotspot. The study of velocity and attenuation characteristics of gas hydrate-bearing sediments is the basis of accurate identification and quantitative evaluation of gas hydrate.

In order to quantitatively evaluate gas hydrate saturation, many scholars have proposed physical models for calculating P-and S-wave velocity of hydrate-bearing sediments, such as cementation theory, equivalent medium model, K-T equation, Biot-Gassmann model, etc. These models can estimate hydrate saturation to a certain extent, but they simplify the hydrate reservoir, which is not consistent with the real situation. In 1994, Leclaire put forward the theory of three-phase porous media on the basis of Biot model, and analyzed the wave propagation in frozen porous media (frozen or permafrost). It is pointed out that when waves propagate in porous media with two solids and one liquid, three compressional waves and two shear waves can be excite. But Leclaire assumes that there is no direct contact between solid grains and ice in the model. In 2001, Carcione improved the Leclaire model, assuming that hydrate is part of the solid skeleton, considering there is contact between solid grains and the ice, and calculating the skeleton modulus of solid grains and gas hydrate by K-T theory. Wang and others called this model Carcione-Leclaire model or LCA model. However, many parameters involved in the LCA model are not clearly expressed, which limits its practical application. In 2005, Geurin defined the expression b_{13} of the friction coefficient produced by the contact between solid grains. To study the velocity and attenuation of gas hydrate-bearing sediments, Lee proposed a simplified three-phase Biot model with a simpler and more effective method for calculating skeleton modulus. But the velocity calculation in Lee's model is based on the low frequency, and he ignored the shear modulus. In this paper, the expressions of dissipation coefficient b_{13} and the skeleton bulk modulus are added to the LCA model to increase the theoretical integrity, which is called the improved LCA model.

2. Wave and Dispersion Equation

Based on Biot theory, Laclaire deduced the motion equation of three-phase porous media.

$$\boldsymbol{\rho}\ddot{\mathbf{u}} + \mathbf{A}\dot{\mathbf{u}} = \mathbf{R}\,\mathrm{grad}\,\mathrm{div}\,\mathbf{u} - \boldsymbol{\mu}\,\mathrm{curl}\,\mathrm{curl}\,\mathbf{u}\,. \tag{2.1}$$

In Eq. (2.1), $\boldsymbol{\rho}$, $\mathbf{A}$, $\mathbf{R}$, and $\boldsymbol{\mu}$ are the matrixes of density, friction coefficient, bulk and shear modulus respectively. After deductions, the formulas for calculating the phase velocity and inverse quality factor of five body waves are obtained as Eq. (2.2) and Eq. (2.3).

$$V_j = \omega / \left|\mathrm{Re}\left(k_j\right)\right| \tag{2.2}$$

$$1/Q = 2\left|\mathrm{Im}\left(k_j\right)\right| V_j / \omega,\ j\text{=P1, P2, P3, S1, S2} \tag{2.3}$$

3. Numerical Simulation and Analysis

According to the dispersion equation, there are three kinds of P-wave and two kinds of S-wave in Gas hydrate-bearing sediments. They are P1 wave, P2 wave, P3 wave, S1 wave and S2 wave. The relationship between the phase velocity and attenuation obtained from the analytical solution and frequency, hydrate saturation and clay content are discussed. The physical parameters are shown in Table 1.

Table 1. Parameters Used in the Model

Parameter	Value
Grain density (kg/m^3)	2650
Water density (kg/m^3)	1040
Hydrate density (kg/m^3)	910
Clay density (kg/m^3)	2580
Sand bulk modulus (GPa)	36
Sand shear modulus (GPa)	45
Shale bulk modulus (GPa)	21.2
Shale shear modulus (GPa)	6.67
Pore fluid bulk modulus (GPa)	2.29
Hydrate bulk modulus (GPa)	6.41
Hydrate shear modulus (GPa)	2.54
Sand permeability κ_{sand} (m^2)	5×10^{-11}
Hydrate permeability κ_{io} (m^2)	1×10^{-5}
Grain/hydrate friction coefficient (kg m^{-3} s^{-1})	2.2×10^{8}
Water viscosity (kg m^{-1} s^{-1})	1.8×10^{-3}

3.3. Influence of frequency and gas hydrate saturation

Firstly, the phase velocities and attenuation characteristics of five kinds of body waves without clay are studied.

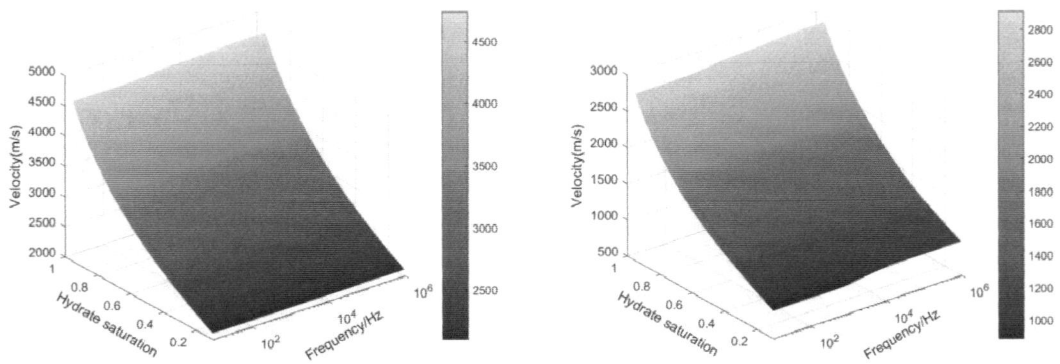

(a) (b)

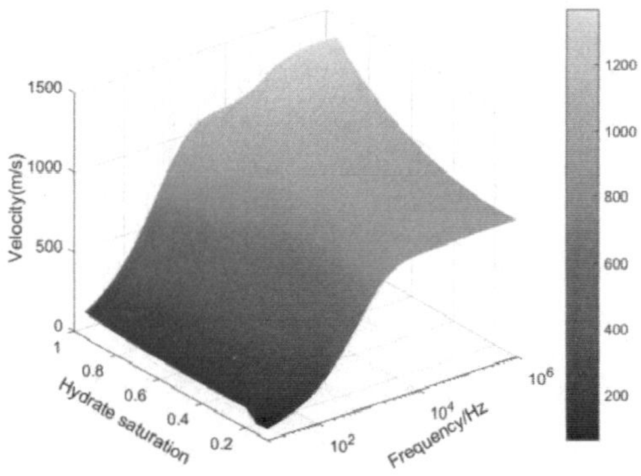

(c)

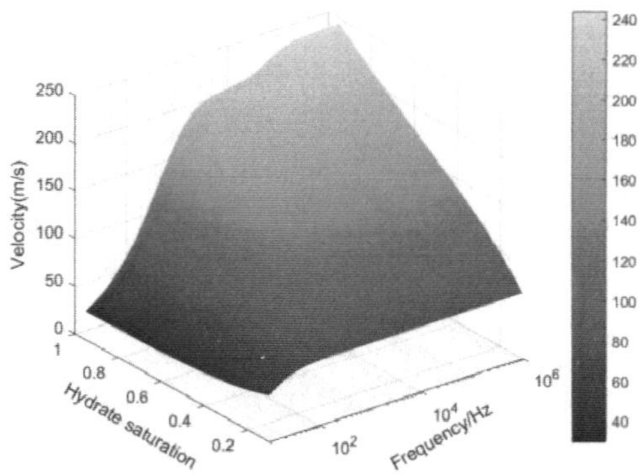

(d)

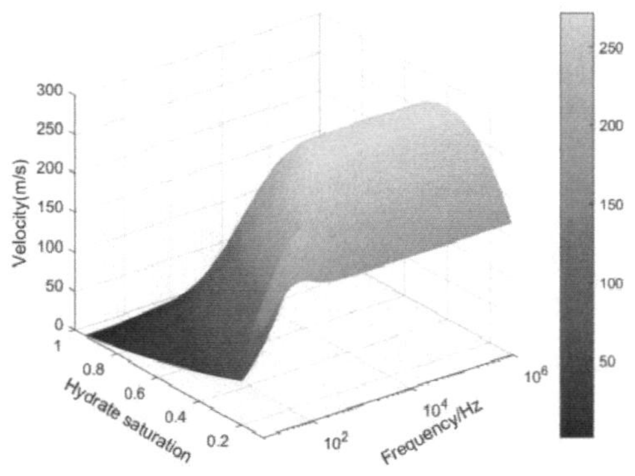

(e)

Fig. 1. Effects of frequency and hydrate saturation on phase velocity of five body waves (a) P1 wave; (b) S1 wave; (c) P2 wave; (d) S2 wave; (e) P3 wave

Figure. 1 shows the variation of phase velocity of five body waves with frequency and hydrate saturation when the porosity is 0.5. The frequency coordinates in the figure are logarithmic. From the Figs. (a) and (b), it can be seen that there is no dispersion of P1 and S1 waves in the seismic exploration (10-100Hz) and acoustic logging (1kHz-20kHz) frequency range, the velocity of these two waves increase with the increase of hydrate saturation. From Figs. (c)-(e), it can be seen that the velocity of P2, P3 and S2 waves is slow, and these three waves are dispersive at low frequency range, while there is no dispersion at high frequency range. With the increase of gas hydrate saturation, the transition bands of the low and high frequency of P2, S2, and P3 waves move towards high frequency. The phase velocity of P2, S2 and P3 waves is smaller than that of P1 and S1 waves. With the increase of gas hydrate saturation, the phase velocity of P2 wave decreases first and then increases, the velocity of S2 wave increases, and the velocity of P3 wave increases first and then decreases.

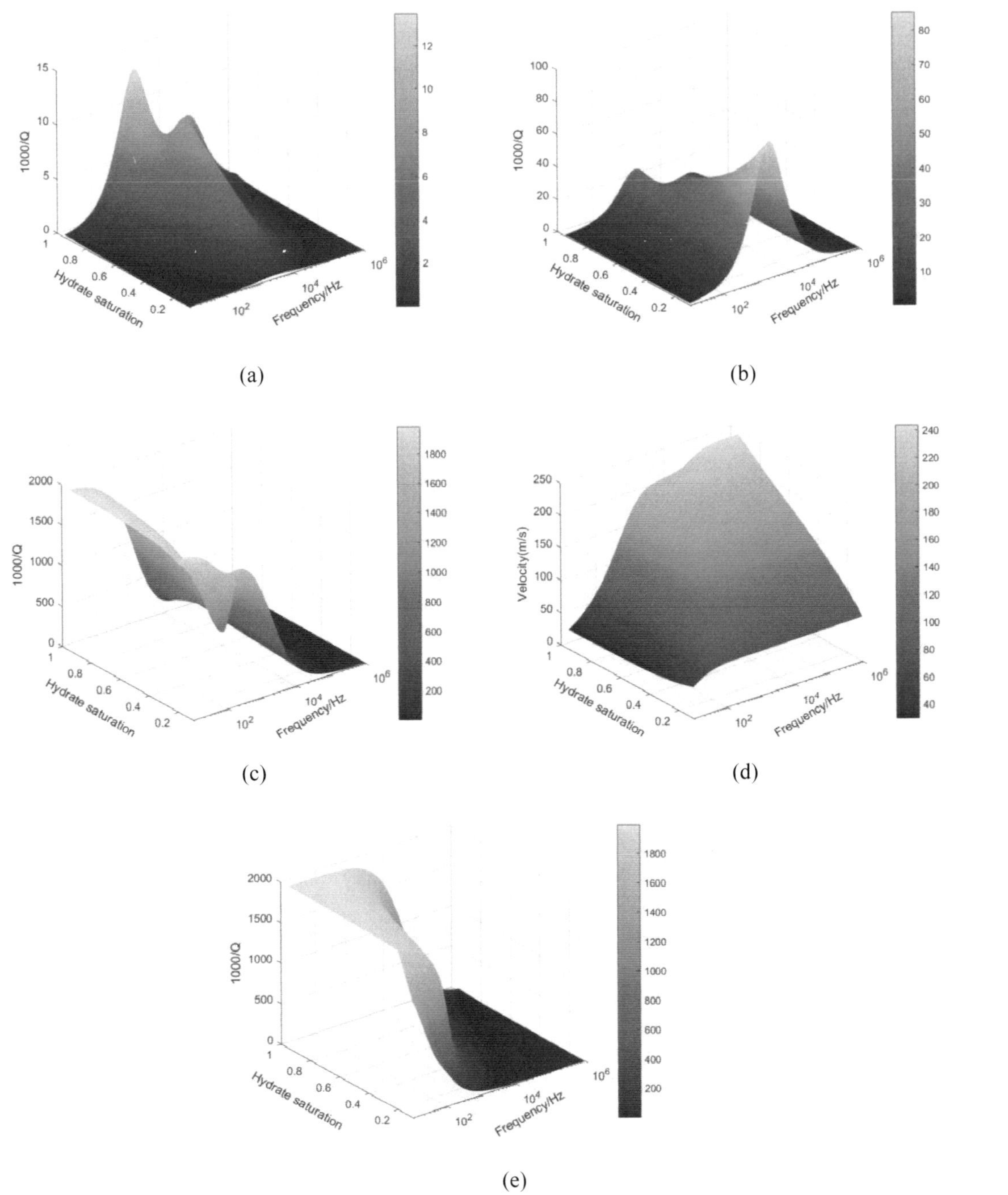

Fig. 2. Effects of frequency and hydrate saturation on attenuation of five body waves (a) P1 wave; (b) S1 wave; (c) P2 wave; (d) S2 wave; (e) P3 wave

Figure. 2 shows the variation of attenuation of five body waves with frequency and gas hydrate saturation when the porosity is 0.5. It can be seen that the attenuation characteristics of the waves are similar to those in two-phase porous media: the attenuation of P1 wave is the smallest, the attenuation of S1 wave is small but more substantial than that of P1 wave. There are attenuation peaks of P1 and S1 waves. The attenuation of P2, S2 and P3 waves is larger and has the same order of magnitude. These three waves have large dispersion and corresponding attenuation, which is consistent with the conclusions of Dvorkin and Uden. Because the velocity of P2, S2 and P3 waves is small and the attenuation of them is large at low frequency range, these three waves are difficult to be observed in the frequency range of seismic exploration, which is similar to the case of Biot medium. But the three slow waves also carry part of the energy and decay quickly. Therefore, the effect of slow waves on attenuation should be considered when processing actual seismic data.

3.4. The influence of clay

Solid phase in porous media is usually composed of a variety of substances, and a small amount of clay can affect the compressional and shear waves. Geurin and others believe that clay content decreases linearly with the increase of gas hydrate content. Natural gas hydrate mostly exists in sandstone reservoirs with small clay content. In this paper, a relationship between clay content and gas hydrate content is proposed, in which clay content is controlled within 20%.

$$\beta = 0.20 - 0.20\phi_h \cdot \tag{3.1}$$

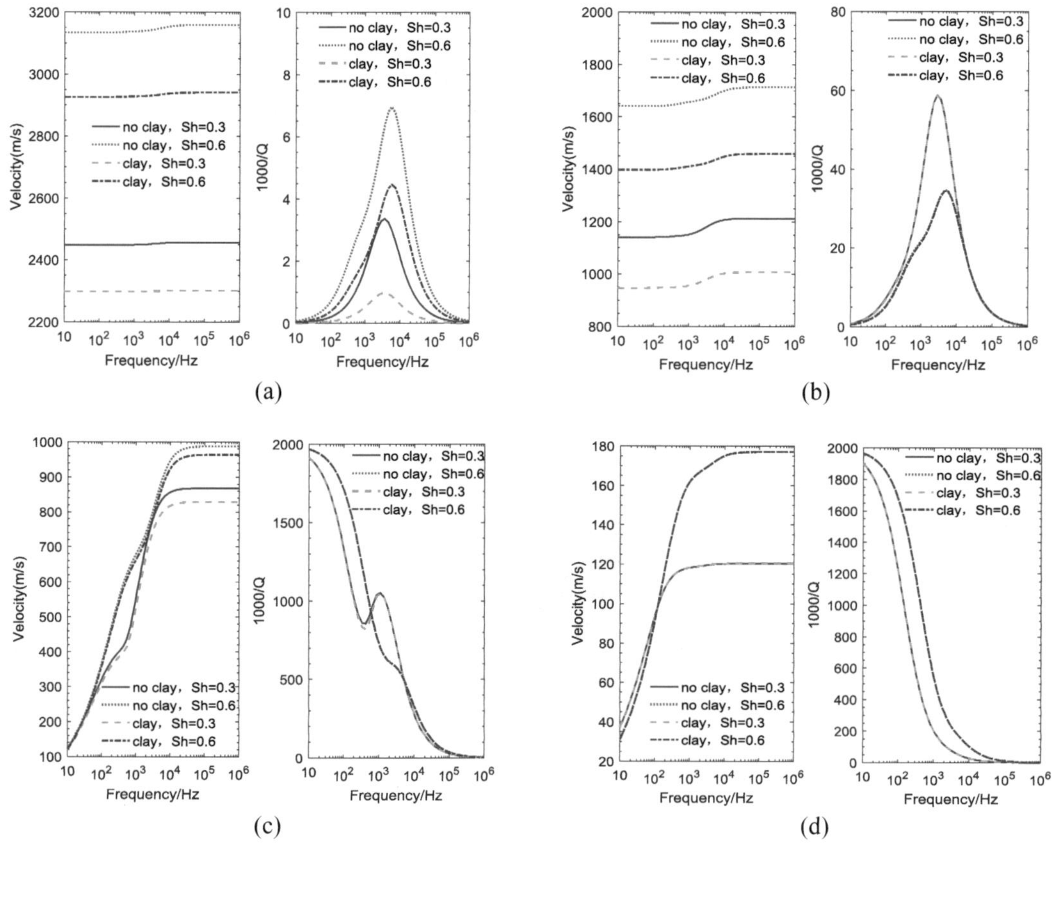

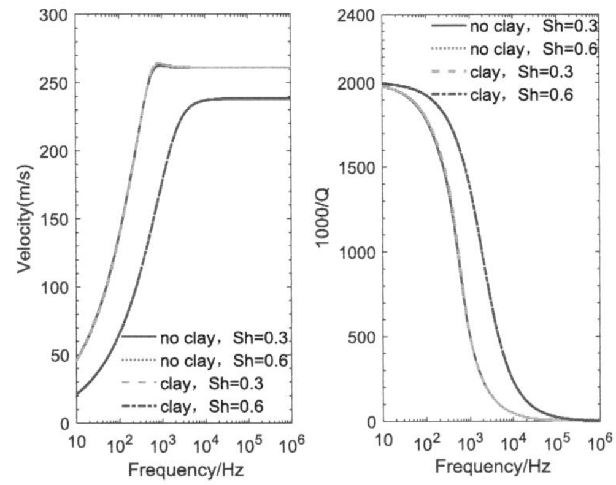

(e)

Fig. 3. Effects of frequency and saturation on velocity and attenuation in the presence of clay (a) P1 wave; (b) S1 wave; (c) P2 wave; (d) S2 wave; (e) P3 wave

Figure .3 shows the effect of clay on the phase velocity and attenuation of five body waves when the porosity is 0.5 and the gas hydrate saturation is 0.3 and 0.6 respectively. Since the presence of clay makes the shear modulus of the frame decrease, the phase velocity of P1 and S1 waves decrease with the increase of clay content. This phenomenon can be validated in experiments conducted by Han. The phase velocity of S2 and P3 waves, however, are not sensitive to clay content at all. In the frequency range of seismic exploration, clay has little impact on the phase velocity of P2 wave, while reduces the phase velocity of P2 wave obviously in the frequency range of acoustic logging. This is because clay mainly affects the skeleton phase of solid particles, P1 and S1 waves are related to the skeleton of solid particles, P2 wave is related to the coupling between the skeleton of solid particles and natural gas hydrate, S2 wave is related to natural gas hydrate, the energy of P2 and S2 waves is mainly concentrated in the hydrate phase, and P3 wave is related to the skeleton of solid particles and pore fluid. The energy of P3 wave is mainly concentrated in the fluid phase. Therefore, the presence of clay has little effect on the phase velocities of P2, S2 and P3 waves. Clay decreases the attenuation of P1 wave, but doesn't change the attenuation of S1, P2, S2 and P3 waves.

4. Conclusions

By using the improved LCA model, the effects of frequency, hydrate saturation and clay content on the phase velocity and attenuation of the theoretical predicted five body waves are analyzed in detail. The findings are listed below:

It shows that there are five kinds of body waves (three compressional waves and two shear waves) in gas hydrate-bearing sediments. The phase velocity and attenuation of five kinds of body waves are significantly affected by frequency and gas hydrate saturation. P1 and S1 waves have no dispersion in the frequency range of seismic exploration and acoustic logging. The P1 wave velocity and S1 wave velocity increase with the increase of gas hydrate saturation. With the increase of gas hydrate saturation, the transition bands of the low and high frequency of P2, S2 and P3 waves move towards high frequency. Clay reduces the phase velocities of P1 and S1 waves and has no significant effect on the phase velocities of S2 and P3 waves. In the low frequency range, the phase velocity of P2 wave is not affected by clay content. In the high frequency range, clay reduces the phase velocity of P2 wave. The attenuation of the waves are not sensitive to clay except for P1.

Acknowledgments

The work is sponsored by the National Natural Science Foundation of China (Grant Nos. 11974018, 11734017, 91630309)

References

[1] De-hua Han, A. Nur, D. Morgan, "Effects of porosity and clay content on wave velocities in sandstones," *Geophysics*, **51**(11) (1986), 2093-2107.
[2] G. Guerin, D. Goldberg, "Modeling of acoustic wave dissipation in gas hydrate-bearing sediments," *Geochemistry Geophysics Geosystems*, **6**(7) (2005), 1-16.
[3] J. Dvorkin, R. Uden, "Seismic wave attenuation in a methane hydrate reservoir," *The Leading Edge*, **23**(8) (2004), 730-732.
[4] José M. Carcione, Géza Seriani, "Wave Simulation in Frozen Porous Media," *Journal of Computational Physics*, **170**(2) (2001), 676-695.
[5] M. A. Biot, "Generalized theory of acoustic propagation in porous dissipative media," *The Journal of the Acoustical Society of America*, **34**(9A), (1962), 1254-1264.
[6] M. A. Biot, "Mechanics of Deformation and Acoustic Propagation in Porous Media," *Journal of Applied Physics*, **33**(4) (2004), 1482-1498.
[7] M. W. Lee, W. F. Waite, "Estimating pore-space gas hydrate saturations from well log acoustic data," *Geochemistry Geophysics Geosystems*, **9**(7) (2008), 1-8.
[8] Ph. Leclaire, "Extension of Biot's theory of wave propagation to frozen porous media," *The Journal of the Acoustical Society of America*, **96**(6) (1994), 3753.

Theoretical Modeling on Compressional Wave Velocity Variation with Temperature in Fluid-saturated Rocks

HUI QI[1] JING BA[1] CONG LUO[1] RUPENG MA[1]

1, School of Earth Sciences and Engineering, Hohai University, Nanjing, 211100, China

1073564193@qq.com

Understanding the influence of temperature on the physical and mechanical properties of rocks is important to investigate the deep oil and gas resources, geothermal resources and other exploration projects. In this paper, we utilize the Batzle-Wang equations to establish the fluid model at different temperatures, and then analyze the wave response characteristics of rocks based on the double-porosity media model. Therefore, a model for characterizing the relationship between seismic properties and reservoir fluid temperature is proposed. Comparison of the predicted P-wave velocity with the measurements of the basalt rock samples showed that the P-wave velocity-temperature curves predicted by the model agree well with the experimental data. Finally, the model proposed in this paper can better describe the dependence of P-wave velocity on temperature, and it can provide a basis for predicting reservoir seismic wave velocity changes in actual geothermal exploration.

Keywords: Temperature; Saturated fluid rock; P-wave velocity; Rock physics model.

1. Introduction

With the increase of resource consumption, the exploitation depth of oil and gas resources has been increasing, and the influence of thermodynamic environment (pressure and temperature) on rock properties has become more and more prominent. The thermodynamic environment is also an important factor in the mining and drilling of geothermal reservoirs. Studying the effect of temperature on various physical and mechanical parameters of rock, especially on wave response characteristics, is of great significance for geothermal exploration and other projects.

Wang and Nur (1988) observed that the P wave velocity decreases as the temperature rises to 100 °C in sandstone samples. Many scholars have analyzed the effects of temperature on different lithologic rocks and found that high pressure and high temperature affect the thermal stress, mineral expansion and mineralogical properties of rocks (Kern et al., 1978; Motra and Stutz, 2018).

However, there is the scarce studies about the wave propagation features of the saturated fluid rocks under different temperature conditions (Cermak et al., 1990; Kristinsdottir et al., 2010;). Gassmann (1951) established firstly the relationship between the bulk modulus of fluid-saturated rock and fluid, which provides a method to predict the variation of seismic wave velocity with pore fluid. Batzle and Wang (1992) analyzed the seismic properties of pore fluids and studied the effects of temperature on these properties. Spencer et al. (2013) found that the P-wave velocity in bitumen saturated sandstone decreased significantly with increasing temperature at different frequencies, while the S-wave velocity is almost no change, demonstrated that the decrease of P-wave velocity is mainly contributed to the change in fluid bulk modulus with temperature. Jaya et al. (2010) performed rock physical experiments on geothermal rock samples of Iceland under in-situ reservoir conditions, and analyzed the effects of temperature on seismic velocity and attenuation using a modified Gassmann relationship.

In order to infer reservoir properties from measured seismic velocity, the establishment of an effective rock physical model is essential. The rock physical model is employed to predict the thermophysical effects of saturated pore fluids on seismic properties. Therefore, based on the double-porosity media model and the Batzle-Wang equations, we propose a model to characterize the relationship between seismic properties and reservoir fluid temperature. The model is used to analyze the influence of pore fluid on seismic wave velocity at different temperatures.

2. Theoretical model

2.1. Fluid model

Pore fluids, including density, viscosity, bulk modulus, etc., are closely related to pressure and temperature. When the pore fluid is subjected to changes in pressure and temperature, its physical properties vary greatly, which may cause drastic changes in the whole physical properties of the rock. Hence, in this paper, we use Batzle and Wang (BW) (1992) to establish an empirical formula between different fluid properties and temperature (T), pressure (P), as follows:

The density of pure water ρ_w is

$$\rho_w = 1 + 10^{-6} \times (-80T - 3.3T^2 + 0.00175T^3 + 489P$$
$$-2TP + 0.016T^2P - 1.3\times10^{-5}T^3P - 0.333P^2 - 0.002TP^2) \quad (2.1)$$

The velocity of pure water V_w is

$$V_w = \sum_{i=0}^{4}\sum_{j=0}^{3}\omega_{ij}T^iP^j \quad (2.2)$$

Where ω_{ij} are the constants which are given in Batzle and Wang (1992).

Water viscosity η

$$\eta = 0.1 + 0.333S + (1.65 + 91.9S^3)e^{-[0.12(S^{0.8} - 0.17)^2 + 0.045]T^{0.8}} \quad (2.3)$$

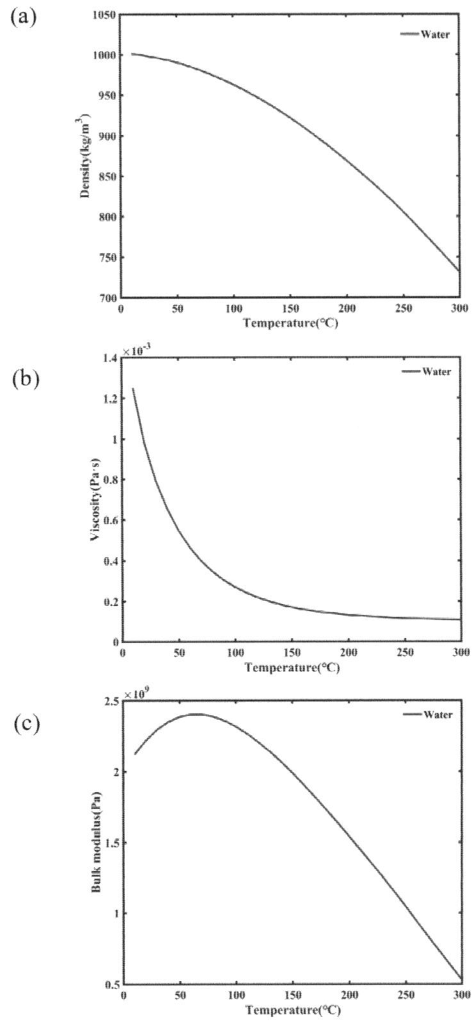

Fig. 1. (a) The density of water as a function of temperature at 50 bar pore fluid pressure. (b) The viscosity of water as a function of temperature at 50 bar pore fluid pressure. (c) The bulk modulus of water as a function of temperature at 50 bar pore fluid pressure.

Figure. (1) shows the fluid properties based on the BW Eqs. (2.1)-(2.3). For a constant pore fluid pressure, the density, viscosity and bulk modulus of water vary in an apparently different manner with temperature. Water density smoothly decreases from 0 to 300 ℃. Instead, water viscosity, decreases rapidly to 75 ℃ and then more slowly to over 250 ℃. Moreover, bulk modulus of water increases slightly to 75 ℃ and decreases speedily from 75 to 300 ℃. On account of the presence of the fluid, the effect of temperature on P-wave velocity is closely related to the thermophysical characteristics of the fluid.

2.2. Double-porosity media model of rock matrix

Considering the complex pore structure inside the actual rock, this paper employed the BR equations, which can describe the heterogeneous porous rock, to investigate wave response characteristics in a double porosity medium. The wave control equations are derived based on the Hamilton's principle, and the local fluid flow is introduced (Ba et al., 2011). Hence, the equations are as follows:

$$N\nabla^2\mathbf{u}+(A+N)\nabla\varepsilon+Q_1\nabla\left(\zeta^{(2)}-\phi_1\varsigma\right)$$
$$=\rho_{11}\ddot{\mathbf{u}}+\rho_{12}\ddot{\mathbf{U}}^{(1)}+\rho_{13}\ddot{\mathbf{U}}^{(2)}+b_1\left(\dot{\mathbf{u}}-\dot{\mathbf{U}}^{(1)}\right)+b_2\left(\dot{\mathbf{u}}-\dot{\mathbf{U}}^{(2)}\right), \tag{2.4}$$

$$Q_1\nabla\varepsilon+R_1\nabla\left(\zeta^{(1)}+\phi_2\varsigma\right)=\rho_{12}\ddot{\mathbf{u}}+\rho_{22}\ddot{\mathbf{U}}^{(1)}-b_1\left(\dot{\mathbf{u}}-\dot{\mathbf{U}}^{(1)}\right), \tag{2.5}$$

$$Q_2\nabla\varepsilon+R_2\nabla\left(\zeta^{(2)}-\phi_1\varsigma\right)=\rho_{13}\ddot{\mathbf{u}}+\rho_{33}\ddot{\mathbf{U}}^{(2)}-b_2\left(\dot{\mathbf{u}}-\dot{\mathbf{U}}^{(2)}\right), \tag{2.6}$$

$$\phi_2(Q_1\varepsilon+R_1(\zeta^{(1)}+\phi_2\varsigma))-\phi_1\left(Q_2\varepsilon+R_2\left(\zeta^{(2)}-\phi_1\varsigma\right)\right)$$
$$=\frac{1}{3}\rho_f\ddot{\varsigma}R_{12}^2\frac{\phi_1^2\phi_2\phi_{20}}{\phi_{10}}+\frac{1}{3}\frac{\eta\phi_1^2\phi_2\phi_{20}}{\kappa_1}\dot{\varsigma}R_{12}^2, \tag{2.7}$$

.

3. Model prediction comparison

Based on the proposed model, we simulated the P-wave velocity with temperature in rock samples. Figure. (2) shows that when the temperature is below 100 ℃, the P-wave velocities slightly increase with the increasing temperature. However, the P-wave velocities sharply drop when the temperature is more than 100 ℃. Because the effect of temperature on seismic velocities is closely related to the thermophysical properties of the pore fluid. The temperature increase causes the thermal expansion of rock minerals, which promotes the development of microcracks in rocks, and then leads to the rapid decreases of P-wave velocities.

(a)

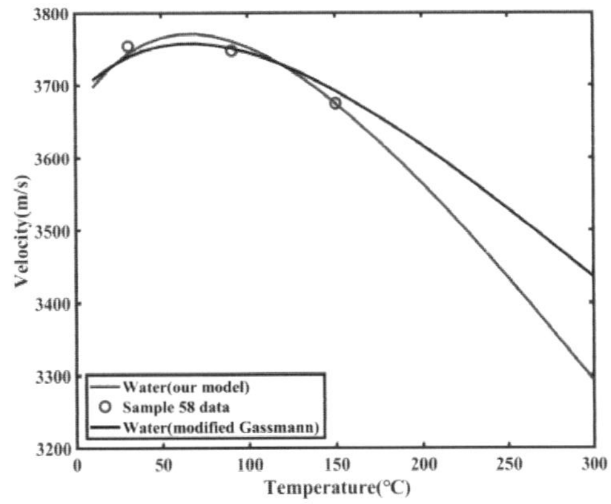

(b)

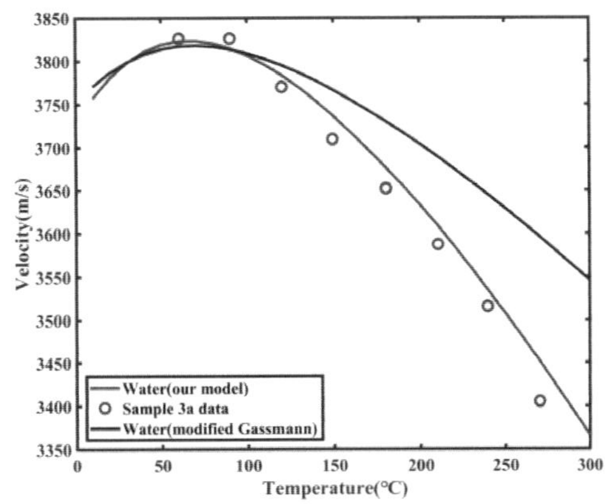

Fig. 2. Temperature-dependent P-wave velocities for water, compared with the modified Gassmann equation (blue line) (a: sample 58 at 19 bar pore fluid pressure; b: sample 3a at 50 bar pore fluid pressure).

The basalt and hyaloclastite rock samples are collected from Krafla and Hengill, Iceland. The porosities and densities of samples are 20% and 20.7%, 2.37g/cm^3 and 2.15g/cm^3, respectively. The experimental measurements are performed by Jaya et al (2010) on the samples at the temperature range of 0~300℃. We analyze these experimental data of the water-saturated rock samples by the proposed model. Figure. (2) shows that the predicted P-wave velocities agree well with the experimental data, which indicates that the model, to some extent, can effectively describe the variation of P-wave velocity with the temperature of basalt and hyaloclastite. The predicted results of the model are also compared to that of the modified Gassmann equation (MG) by Jaya et al (2010) proposed. The MG results have relatively lower consistency, especially at high temperature. Because of the hard texture of basalt and hyaloclastite, the hard pores within the rock gradually soften with the temperature increases, which causes the change of rock pore structure and further changes the fluid flow channel. Therefore, compared with our model, the MG method ignores the changes of the complex pore structure at high temperature.

4. Conclusion

This paper has studied on the effect of temperature on the P-wave velocity, based on the temperature-dependent fluid property equation and the double porosity medium model. The simulated results show that the predicted P-wave velocity of basalt and hyaloclastite samples decreases with the increase of temperature, and the P-wave velocity in the saturated state increases slightly at lower temperature.

In contrast to previous model, our proposed model provides a relatively reliable method for predicting seismic properties as a function of temperature, especially at higher temperatures. In addition, it helps explaining the effect of rock pore fracture and fluid bulk modulus on velocity as a function of temperature. Hence, the proposed model has great potential applicability in geothermal reservoirs and deep reservoirs exploration and exploitation.

Acknowledgments

The National Natural Science Foundation of China (grant no. 41974123, 41704109), Jiangsu Innovation and Entrepreneurship Plan, Specially-Appointed Professor Plan of Jiangsu Province, and the Fundamental Research Funds for the Central Universities, China (grant no. 2016B13114).

References

[1] J. Ba, J. M. Carcione, J. X. Nie, "Biot-Rayleigh theory of wave propagation in double-porosity media," *Journal of Geophysical Research: soild earth* **116**(B6) (2011), B06202.

[2] J. Ba, W. H. Xu, L. Y. Fu, et al., "Rock anelasticity due to patchy saturation and fabric heterogeneity: A double double-porosity model of wave propagation," *Journal of Geophysical Research: Solid Earth* **122**(3) (2017), 1949-1976.

[3] M. L. Batzle, Z. J Wang, "Seismic properties of pore fluids," *Geophysics* **57**(11) (1992), 1396-1408.

[4] V. Cermak, L. Bodri, L. Rybach, G. Buntebarth, "Relationship between seismic velocity and heat production: comparison of two sets of data and test of validity," *Earth Planet. Sci. Lett* **99**(1–2) (1990), 48–57.

[5] F. Gassmann, "Elastic waves through a Peaking of spheres," *Geophysics* **16** (1951), 673-682.

[6] M. S. Jaya, S. A. Shapiro, L. H. Kristinsdóttir, D. Bruhn, H. Milsch, E. Spangenberg, "Temperature dependence of seismic properties in geothermal rocks at reservoir conditions," *Geothermics* **39**(1) (2010), 115–123.

[7] H. H. Kern, "The effect of high temperature and high confining pressure on compressional wave velocities in quartz-bearing and quartz-free igneous and metamorphic rocks," *Tectonophysics* **44** (1978), 185–203.

[8] L.H. Kristinsdóttir, Ó. Flóvenz, K. Árnason, D. Bruhn, H. Milsch, E. Spangenberg, J. Kulenkampff, "Electrical conductivity and P-wave velocity in rock samples from high-temperature Icelandic geothermal fields," *Geothermics* **39**(1) (2010), 94–105.

[9] H. B. Motra, H. H. Stutz, "Geomechanical Rock Properties Using Pressure and Temperature Dependence of Elastic P- and S-Wave Velocities," *Geotech Geol Eng* **36** (2018), 3751–3766.

[10] J. W. Spencer, "Viscoelasticity of Ells River bitumen sand and 4D monitoring of thermal enhanced oil recovery processes," *Geophysics* **78**(6) (2013), D419-D428.

Pre-stack Seismic Inversion of Tight Sandstone Reservoirs based on Levenberg-Marquardt Algorithm

Shuang Xiao [1] Jing Ba *[1] Qiang Guo [2] Tiansheng Chen [3]

1, School of Earth Sciences and Engineering, Hohai University, Nanjing, China
1124611557@qq.com
2, School of Information Engineering, China Jiliang University, Hangzhou, China

3, Sinopec Petroleum Exploration and Production Research Institute, Beijing, China

The Levenberg-Marquardt (LM) and simulated annealing (SA) are two commonly-used optimization algorithms in solving pre-stack inversion problems. However, conventional LM has premature convergence given poor initial models, while SA suffers from slow and even unstable convergence. To address the problems, a new inversion strategy is purposed in this paper. In specific, the damping factor autoregulator and the memory are added to achieve higher convergence effect in the Levenberg-Marquardt algorithm. Besides, the objective function, the disturbance equation and the cooling strategy are improved to have faster and stable convergence in simulated annealing algorithm. Then the proposed method was applied to the real data from the western Sichuan depression to test its validity, and was also compared with the conventional LM algorithm.
Keywords: Levenberg-Marquardt algorithm; Simulated annealing algorithm; Pre-stack inversion.

1. Introduction

The original seismic information may be affected by the post-stack processing, which in turn affects the subsequent seismic interpretation and reservoir prediction. The pre-stack seismic data preserves the full information lied in the characteristics of amplitude variations versus offset (AVO), from which the compressional wave, shear wave, and density information can be estimated. Since the sensitivities of compressional wave and shear wave to reservoir fluid are different, and the different elastic parameters can be calculated by the combinations of three parameters (P- and S-wave velocities and density), which can effectively describe the subsurface rock physical properties.

The establishment of the Zoeppritz formula laid the foundamental theory for pre-stack AVO inversion (Zoeppritz, 1919). According to the optimization algorithm, pre-stack AVO inversion is divided into linear inversion and nonlinear inversion. The damped least squares, also called Levenberg-Marquardt (LM) method proposed by K. Levenberg and D.W. Marquardt (1963) is a commonly-used algorithm for solving linear inversion problems. However, since the method highly relies on the initial model, the damping factor is difficult to be determined in the inversion process, resulting in low inversion accuracy. Rothman (1986) initially introduced simulated annealing (SA) into geophysical research. SA is a nonlinear optimization algorithm featured by being avoided falling into local minima. However, conventional SA has low computational efficiency and slow convergence. The optimization parameters are unstable and the application is limited in multi-parameter pre-stack AVO inversion.

The exact Zoeppritz equation is used as the forward model in order to avoid calculation errors. In order to achieve better inversion results, the damping factor automatic regulator and memory are introduced to improve the LM method, and the cooling method and the disturbance equation are added to the memory to improve the SA method. The two types of methods were tested seperately, and then a random line of prestack data from the western Sichuan depression was selected for inversion, and the two types of inversion results were compared and analyzed.

2. Methodologies

2.1. Pres-tack AVO forward equation

In order to avoid errors in the calculation of the reflection coefficient and improve the stability of the inversion, the exact Zoeppritz equation(F Q Zhang, 2013) is selected as forward equation.

$$\begin{bmatrix} \sin\theta_1 & \cos\phi_1 & -\sin\theta_2 & -\cos\phi_2 \\ \cos\theta_1 & -\sin\phi_1 & \cos\theta_2 & -\sin\phi_2 \\ \cos 2\phi_1 & -\frac{V_{S1}}{V_{P1}}\sin 2\phi_1 & -\frac{\rho_2}{\rho_1}\frac{V_{P2}}{V_{P1}}\cos 2\phi_2 & \frac{\rho_2}{\rho_1}\frac{V_{S2}}{V_{P1}}\sin 2\phi_2 \\ \sin 2\theta_1 & \frac{V_{P1}}{V_{S1}}\cos 2\phi_1 & \frac{\rho_2}{\rho_1}\frac{V_{S2}^2 V_{P1}}{V_{S1}^2 V_{P2}}\sin 2\theta_2 & \frac{\rho_2}{\rho_1}\frac{V_{S2}V_{P1}}{V_{S1}^2}\cos 2\phi_2 \end{bmatrix} \begin{bmatrix} R_{PP} \\ R_{PS} \\ T_{PP} \\ T_{PS} \end{bmatrix} = \begin{bmatrix} -\sin\theta_1 \\ \sin\theta_1 \\ -\cos 2\phi_1 \\ \sin 2\phi_1 \end{bmatrix} \tag{2.1}$$

Where R_{PP} is the longitudinal wave reflection coefficient, R_{PS} is the shear wave reflection coefficient; T_{PP} is the longitudinal wave transmission coefficient; T_{PS} is the transverse wave transmission coefficient.

2.2. Pre-stack Seismic Inversion based on Levenberg-Marquardt Algorithm

Among the linear inversion algorithms, Levenberg-Marquardt (R R WANG, 2015) algorithm method is one of the best algorithms currently known to solve the optimization problem. Due to the introduction of the damping factor, the singularity in the inversion process is reduced, which makes it greatly used in the actual inversion process. It is iterative equation (Y Du, 1992) is

$$(J^{(l)T}J^{(l)}+\lambda I)\ \delta_M = J^{(l)T}(y-F^{(l)}) \tag{2.2}$$

here δ_M is the iterative correction; λ is the damping factor; J is the Jacques matrix.

It is difficult to determine the damping factor in the LM algorithm inversion. The damping factor in the conventional LM method is usually obtained based on trial testing, which lead to great randomness in the inversion. In this paper, the damping factor automatic regulator proposed by R. Fletcher (1971) is used to improve the conventional LM method. Because the damping factor of the next iteration based on the information of the iteration can be predicted, the randomness of the selection of the damping factor are avoided, and the convergence speed is improved. The damping factor in the improved LM algorithm can be determined as follows:

$$R = \frac{\phi(x^{(l)}) - \phi(x^{(l)} + \delta\lambda^{(l)})}{\phi(x^{(l)}) - \hat{\phi}(x^{(l)} + \delta\lambda^{(l)})} \tag{2.3a}$$

$$\hat{\phi} = \sum_{i=1}^{n}[\sum_{j=1}^{m}\frac{\partial F_i^{(l)}}{\partial p_j} - (y_i - F_i^{(l)})]^2 \tag{2.3b}$$

Where R scale factor. ρ and σ are domain limits, if R<ρ, increasing λ; if R>σ, decreasing λ; if ρ ≤ R ≤ σ, keeping the λ of the previous iteration.

As can be seen from Figure 1, the optimal solution is not directly accepted after the end of each iteration. Therefore, a memorizer which records each result is set during the inversion process. After the iterative process ends, the result obtained by the algorithm is compared with the solution in the memory, and then the best one is taken as the final output.

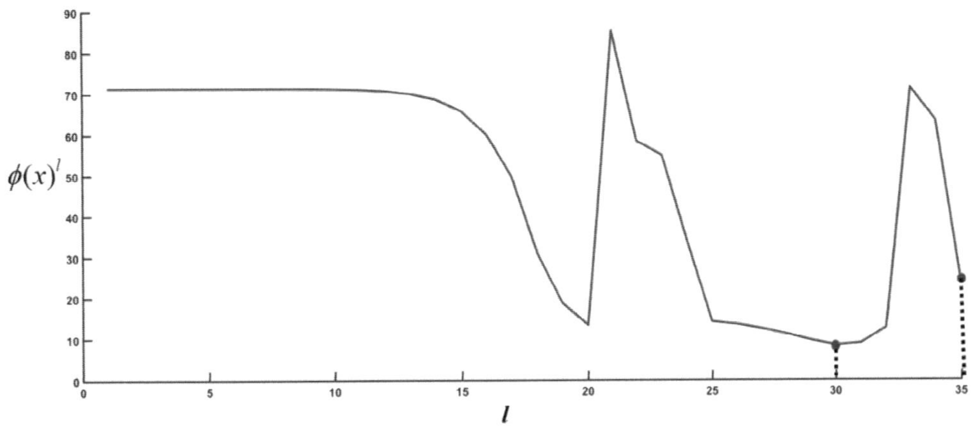

Fig. 1. Single-trace inversion: Objective Function $\varphi(x)^l$ – Number of iterations l

In order to verify this method, we conduct a synthetic test. Figure 2 is the test invert results. The inversion results of each parameter (dash red) show good agreement with the trend of the real model (solid black).

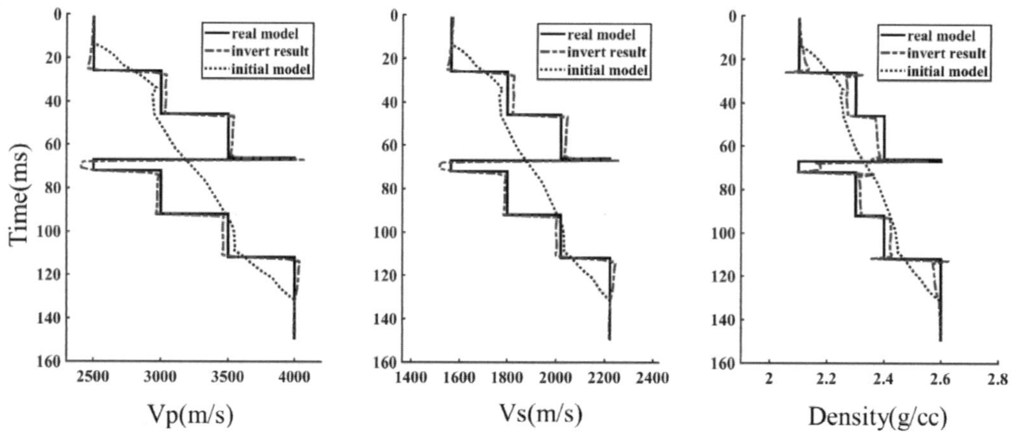

Fig. 2. Single theoretical seismic trace model test

2.3. Pre-stack Seismic Inversion based on Simulated Annealing Algorithm

Geophysical inverse problems are generally characterized by multiple parameters and nonlinearity. Although linear optimization algorithms show high robustness and computational efficiency, but it strongly relied on the quality of the initial model, and needs to solve complex large matrices in the inversion process, which limited its application effect (S. Kirkpatrick, 1983). With the development of computer technology, nonlinear inversion has gained its popularity because it does not rely on the initial model, especially for nonlinear inversion problems. As one of the excellent nonlinear inversion algorithms, SA algorithm has achieved good results in practical applications.

There are two main problems in conventional SA inversion: operational efficiency and stability of inversion parameters. The inversion objective function established in this paper not only reflects the fitting degree of the model synthetic seismic record and the measured seismic record, but also considers the normalization of the amplitude to avoid normalizing the forward record and the actual seismic record in each iteration, processing to improve the efficiency of the inversion operation. Therefore, the objective function is built as follows

$$E(x)=\sum_{i=1}^{M}\left[\frac{d_i}{W_d}-\frac{g_i(x)}{W_t}\right]^2 \tag{2.4}$$

Where

$$W_d=\frac{1}{M}\sum_{i=1}^{M}|d_i| \qquad W_t=\frac{1}{M}\sum_{i=1}^{M}|g_i(x)| \tag{2.5}$$

Where W_d indicates the strength of the measured amplitude response, Wt indicates the strength of the theoretical amplitude response.

The traditional perturbation equation directly perturbs the parameters, resulting in unstable shear wave velocity and density inversion, and low inversion accuracy. Based on the logistic statistical relationship between Vp and Vs, Vp and density, this paper establishes constraints based on statistical parameter fitting, stabilizing the disturbance of Vs and density, and thereby improving the stability and accuracy of the inversion. The disturbance of Vp is proposed by Ingber (1989).

$$m_i = m_i + y_i(B_i - A_i)$$
$$y_i = T\,\mathrm{sgn}(u-0.5)[(1+\frac{1}{T})^{|2u-1|}-1] \tag{2.6}$$

Where m_i is new model; B_i-A_i is the variation range. Based on the logistic statistical relationship between Vp and Vs, Vp and density, the way to create Vp and Vs is as follows.

$$V_S(i) = K_1V_P(i) + b_1 + y_i|b_{11} - b_{12}| \tag{2.7a}$$

$$\rho(i) = K_2V_P(i)^2 + K_3V_P(i) + b_2 + y_i|b_{21} - b_{22}| \tag{2.7b}$$

In order to verify the proposed method, we conduct a synthetic test. Figure 3 is the test invert results. The inversion results of each parameter are in line with the trend of the real model.

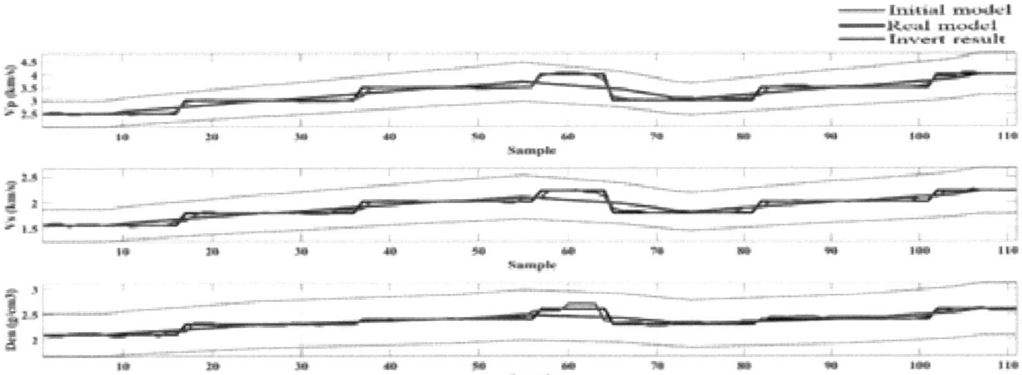

Fig. 3. Single theoretical seismic trace model test

3. Example Application Comparison

In order to further verify the inversion algorithm, the seismic data of the Xujiahe Formation in western Sichuan were tested. The study area is a tight sandstone gas layer. A two-dimensional arbitrary line seismic section in Area A of the western Sichuan depression was selected, with a total of 101 CDPs. The two wells are located at CDP 13 (well 1) and CDP 89 (well 2).

This is the vp inversion based on Levenberg-Marquardt Algorithm.

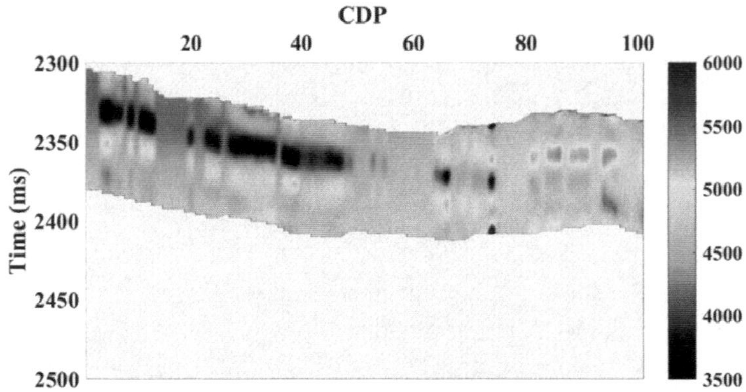

Fig. 4. Vp inversion result based on L-M Algorithm

From figure 4, we find some problems: the inversion results have poor horizontal continuity (by trace inversion), which is less stable and too different from the logging data. After analysis, we know that it is difficult to establish initial model with better effect and constrain multiple parameters in the inversion process.

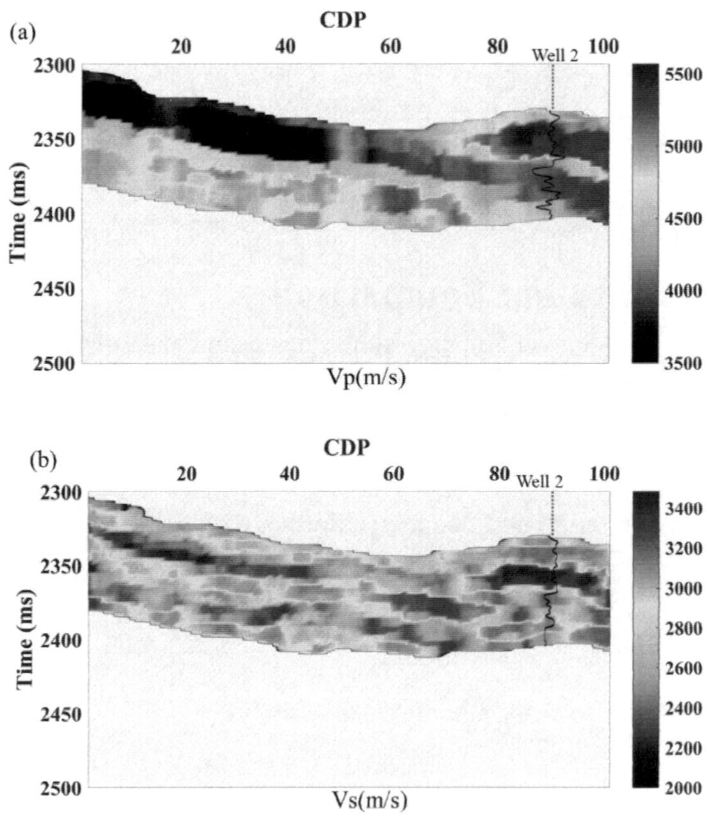

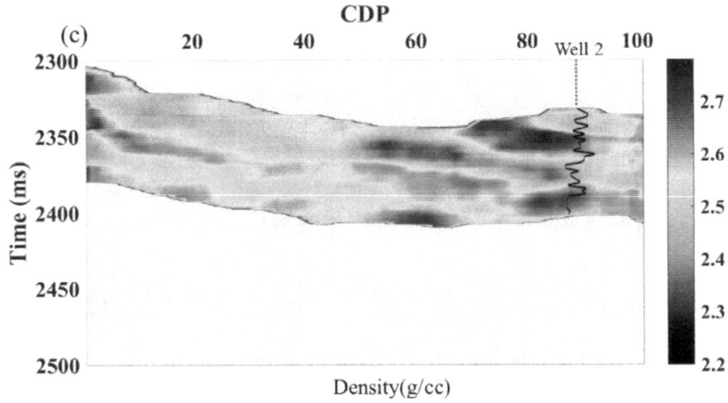

Fig. 5. Inversion result based on S-A Algorithm

By comparison, figure 5 is the inversion result based on SA Algorithm. Taking vp and vs profile as examples, the inversion results can generally indicate the gas-bearing low-velocity layer (blue mark), which is basically consistent with the logging data. The density profile basically indicates the gas-bearing layer. At the gas-bearing layer of the well, there is a significant low value, while some high-frequency information is missing. There is some errors in comparison with the well log curve because the density is not sensitive to the amplitude change. All in all, according to the inversion profile, the inversion resolution is up to the expectation, and the variation trend is in line with the reality. The inversion results are in good agreement with the well logging data at the well.

4. Conclusion

Compared with the conventional Levenberg-Marquardt algorithm, the damping factor autoregulator and the memory are added to make it have higher convergence effect; Compared with the conventional simulated annealing algorithm, the objective function, the disturbance equation and the cooling method are improved to have faster converge faster and the better convergence effect. Through comparison of results, the nonlinear inversion has higher resolution and precision in practical applications.

Acknowledgments

The National Natural Science Foundation of China (grant no. 41974123, 41704109), Jiangsu Innovation and Entrepreneurship Plan, Specially-Appointed Professor Plan of Jiangsu Province, and the Fundamental Research Funds for the Central Universities, China (grant no. 2016B13114).

References

[1] K. Zoeppritz. "On the reflection and penetration of seismic waves through unstable layers." *Goettinger Nachr*, (1919), pages 66-84.

[2] D.M. Marquart, "An algorithm for Least squares estimation of non-linear parameters." *SIAM* J. (1963), **11**, pp. 431-441.

[3] D.H Rothman. "Automatic estimation of large residual statistics correction." *Geophysics*, (1986), **51**(2):323-346.

[4] F Q Zhang, F J Wei, et al. “Generalized linear AVO inversion with the priori constraint of trivariate Cauchy distribution based on Zoeppritz equation.” *Geophys (in Chinese)*. (2013). **56**(6) :2098-2115.

[5] R R WANG, DAI Y S, LI C, et al. “An evaluation criterion on the accuracy of time-varying wavelet extraction based on singular value decomposition.” *Geophysical Prospecting for Petroleum*, (2015), **54**(5) :531-540.

[6] Y Du, Segall P, Aydin A. “Comparison of various inversion techniques as applied to the determination of a geophysical deformation model for the 1983 Borah Peak earthquake.” *Bulletin of the Seismological Society of America,* (1992), **82**(4):1 840-1866.

[7] R. Fletcher, “A modified Marquardt Subroutine for non-linear least squares.” *UKAEA Research Group Report AERF R*. (1971),6799.

[8] S. Kirkpatrick, C. D. Jr Gclatt, and M. P. Vecchi, “Optimization by simulated an-nealing.” *Scicncc*, (1983), **220**, 671-680.

[9] L. Ingber. “Very fast simulated re-annealing.” *Mathematical and Computer Modeling*. (1989), **12**(8): 967-993.

Analytical solutions of borehole acoustic fields for an eccentric drill collar in the monopole acoustic LWD

YUNJIA JI[1] XIAO HE[2] ZHIFENG SUN[3] HAO CHEN[4] XIUMING WANG[5]

1,2,4,5, State Key Laboratory of Acoustics, Institute of Acoustics, Chinese Academy of Sciences,
Beijing, 100190, P. R. China,
University of Chinese Academy of Sciences,
Beijing, 100049, P. R. China
jiyunjia@mail.ioa.ac.cn[1]
hex@mail.ioa.ac.cn[2]
chh@mail.ioa.ac.cn[4]
wangxm@mail.ioa.ac.cn[5]
3, China Oilfield Services Limited
Beijing, 065201, P. R. China
sunzhf3@cosl.com.cn

Analytical solutions of acoustic fields are derived for the case of an eccentric drill collar inside a fluid-filled borehole, which often troubles us a lot during logging while drilling due to complex string movements. With this method, the borehole wavefields in such condition are investigated excited by a monopole source with the center frequency of 8 kHz. The effects of varying tool eccentricity on the waveforms at different azimuths, are analyzed. The results reveal that the wavefields properties in some direction are closely related to the thickness of the fluid annulus between the collar and the formation toward that azimuth, especially for collar waves and Stoneley waves. In addition, based on the two-dimensional spectrum technique, the coupling of multipole modes is revealed, when the drill collar is off center. Particularly, in the case of severe eccentricity, the flexural mode can be strong enough that it may interfere the recognition of Stoneley waves. These studies will be helpful for tool design and data processing.

Keywords: Acoustic logging while drilling; analytical solutions; two-dimensional spectrum technique.

1. Introduction

In recent years, the acoustic problem of an eccentric steel collar in a fluid-filled borehole has attracted a great deal of attention, because of applications of acoustic logging while drilling (LWD) technology in oil reservoir exploration.

Considerable researches are involved in LWD acoustic responses when the collar is centered in the borehole. However, the tool is mostly deviated in a harsh LWD environment. Understanding of the effects of tool eccentricity on the LWD data will benefit the interpretation and evaluation. Huang *et al.*[1] and Zheng *et al.*[2] respectively used the finite-difference method (FDM) and the finite-element method (FEM) to investigate the effects of the LWD tool eccentricity on dispersion features of borehole acoustic fields. Their numerical results indicated that the collar deviation will lead to generating more modes as well as changing their dispersion properties. Pardo *et al.*[3] made a comparison of acoustic responses between wireline logging and LWD for the monopole case. Wang *et al.*[4] studied LWD wavefields of a multipole tool in horizontal and deviated wells and further proposed a method to quantify the extent of tool eccentricity. However, almost all the above studies adopted numerical approaches such as FDM or FEM. Although the full wave can be obtained by performing these methods, it's hard to reveal the characteristics of each component in borehole acoustic fields when the collar is off center. Besides, few numerical studies involved the severely eccentric case since the grid size must be small enough resulting in much time cost. Haugland developed an analytical method for an off-center solid mandrel in a borehole[5,6]. Yet he did not further evaluate how the mandrel eccentricity influence the wave propagation. Also, his physic model far differed from true LWD we state, as the LWD tool is a fluid-filled cylinder.

In this paper, the acoustic LWD model with an eccentric monopole tool are first established. Then an analytical method is developed based on two cylindrical coordinate systems related by the translational addition theorem. With this approach, the borehole wavefields with varying tool eccentricity are investigated. Finally, by analyzing waveforms received at different azimuths and two-dimensional spectra with varying tool eccentricity, some interesting conclusions are drawn.

2. Formulations

The theoretical acoustic LWD model with an off-center collar is shown in Fig. (1). In Fig. (1b), these four cylindrical layers from inside to outside are the inner fluid, the collar, the outer fluid, and the formation, respectively. A monopole normal-stress source is directly mounted on the outer surface of the collar.

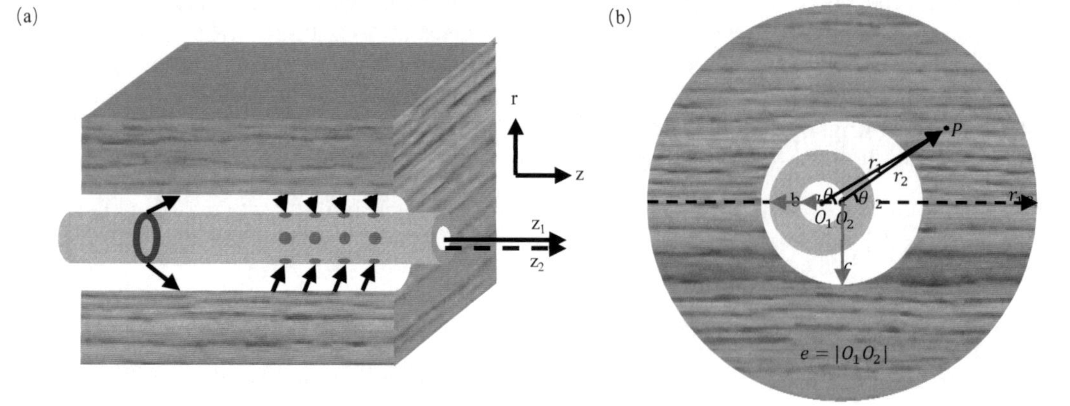

Fig. 1. The radially layered model for acoustic logging while drilling with the eccentric collar at the (r, θ, z) cylindrical coordinates. (a) Front view of the model. (b) Side view of the model.

Two cylindrical coordinate systems (r_1, θ_1, z_1) and (r_2, θ_2, z_2), are employed to describe the acoustic fields involved, as depicted in Fig. (1). Here the first and the second coordinate systems are respectively based on the collar and the borehole. a, b and c in Fig. (1b) respectively represent the internal and external radii of the collar as well as the radius of the borehole. The cylinder axes of the collar and the borehole are parallel, and the origin-to-origin separation is $e = |O_1O_2|$, which is the collar offset.

First, with leaving out the term $e^{i(kz-\omega t)}$, the displacement potentials of each layer, may respectively be written with regard to their relevant cylindrical coordinate systems as

$$\bar{\varphi}(r_1,\theta_1,k,\omega)=\sum_{n=-\infty}^{\infty}\left[a_n I_n(\beta r_1)+b_n K_n(\beta r_1)\right]\cos(n\theta_1), \quad (2.1a)$$

$$\bar{\psi}(r_1,\theta_1,k,\omega)=\sum_{n=-\infty}^{\infty}\left[c_n I_n(\xi r_1)+d_n K_n(\xi r_1)\right]\sin(n\theta_1), \quad (2.1b)$$

$$\bar{\chi}(r_1,\theta_1,k,\omega)=\sum_{n=-\infty}^{\infty}\left[e_n I_n(\xi r_1)+f_n K_n(\xi r_1)\right]\cos(n\theta_1), \quad (2.1c)$$

$$\bar{\phi}_{in}(r_1,\theta_1,k,\omega)=\sum_{n=-\infty}^{\infty} g_n I_n(\eta^f r_1)\cos(n\theta_1), \quad (2.2)$$

$$\bar{\phi}_{ex}(r_1,\theta_1,k,\omega)=\sum_{n=-\infty}^{\infty}\left[h_n I_n(\eta^f r_1)+i_n K_n(\eta^f r_1)\right]\cos(n\theta_1), \quad (2.3)$$

$$\bar{\varphi}_F(r_2,\theta_2,k,\omega)=\sum_{v=-\infty}^{\infty} j_v K_v(\beta_m r_2)\cos(v\theta_2), \quad (2.4a)$$

$$\bar{\psi}_F(r_2,\theta_2,k,\omega)=\sum_{v=-\infty}^{\infty} k_v K_v(\xi_m r_2)\sin(v\theta_2), \quad (2.4b)$$

$$\bar{\chi}_F(r_2,\theta_2,k,\omega)=\sum_{v=-\infty}^{\infty} l_v K_v(\xi_m r_2)\cos(v\theta_2). \quad (2.4c)$$

where I and K are the modified Bessel functions of the first and the second kinds, respectively; ω is the angular frequency; t is the time; k is the axial wavenumber; β and ξ are the compressional and shear radial wavenumbers in the steel collar, respectively; η^f is the compressional radial wavenumber in the inner and outer fluids; β_m and ξ_m represent the compressional and shear radial wavenumbers in the formation, respectively; $a_n - i_n$ and $j_v - l_v$ are the unknown excitation coefficients of each layer; the subscript number n and v denotes the circumferential periodic numbers in both coordinate systems, respectively.

To determine the above unknown coefficients, the relevant boundary conditions at the three liquid-solid interfaces must be applied, which are the continuity radial displacements and radial stresses as well as no tangential forces. For example, at the inter surface of the collar, the following equations can be obtained[7]

$$\left(a_n V_{1n}^{[1]}+b_n V_{1n}^{[2]}+c_n V_{2n}^{[1]}+d_n V_{2n}^{[2]}+e_n V_{3n}^{[1]}+f_n V_{3n}^{[2]}\right)\Big|_{r_1=a}-g_n\left.\frac{\partial I_n(\eta^f r_1)}{\partial r_1}\right|_{r_1=a}=0, \quad (2.5a)$$

$$\left(a_n S_{1n}^{[1]} + b_n S_{1n}^{[2]} + c_n S_{2n}^{[1]} + d_n S_{2n}^{[2]} + e_n S_{3n}^{[1]} + f_n S_{3n}^{[2]}\right)\Big|_{r_1=a} + \rho_f \omega^2 g_n I_n\left(\eta^f a\right) = 0\,, \tag{2.5b}$$

$$\left(a_n S_{4n}^{[1]} + b_n S_{4n}^{[2]} + c_n S_{5n}^{[1]} + d_n S_{5n}^{[2]} + e_n S_{6n}^{[1]} + f_n S_{6n}^{[2]}\right)\Big|_{r_1=a} = 0\,, \tag{2.5c}$$

$$\left(a_n S_{7n}^{[1]} + b_n S_{7n}^{[2]} + c_n S_{8n}^{[1]} + d_n S_{8n}^{[2]} + e_n S_{9n}^{[1]} + f_n S_{9n}^{[2]}\right)\Big|_{r_1=a} = 0\,. \tag{2.5d}$$

where V and S the function of variables ω and k. Similar equations can be derived at the outer surface of the collar.

However, at the borehole wall, the field components in the outer fluid and the formation are written in terms of different coordinate systems. A transformation needs to be performed to make them in the same coordinate system through the translational addition theorem. The theorem for cylindrical Bessel functions can be expressed as[8]

$$I_n\left(\eta^f r_1\right)\begin{Bmatrix}\cos(n\theta_1)\\ \sin(n\theta_1)\end{Bmatrix} = \sum_{v=-\infty}^{\infty} I_{n-v}(\eta^f e) I_v\left(\eta^f r_2\right)\begin{Bmatrix}\cos(v\theta_2)\\ \sin(v\theta_2)\end{Bmatrix}, \tag{2.6a}$$

$$K_n\left(\eta^f r_1\right)\begin{Bmatrix}\cos(n\theta_1)\\ \sin(n\theta_1)\end{Bmatrix} = \sum_{v=-\infty}^{\infty} (-1)^{n-v} I_{n-v}(\eta^f e) K_v\left(\eta^f r_2\right)\begin{Bmatrix}\cos(v\theta_2)\\ \sin(v\theta_2)\end{Bmatrix}. \tag{2.6b}$$

Through the above Eqs. (2.6a) and (2.6b), Eq. (2.3) can be written in the second coordinate system as below

$$\bar{\varphi}_{ex}\left(r_2, \theta_2, k, \omega\right) = \sum_{v=-\infty}^{\infty}\left[H_v I_v\left(\eta^f r_2\right) + \tilde{I}_v K_v\left(\eta^f r_2\right)\right]\cos(v\theta_2) e^{i(kz-\omega t)}\,, \tag{2.7a}$$

$$H_v = \sum_{n=-\infty}^{\infty} h_n I_{n-v}\left(\eta^f e\right),\quad \tilde{I}_v = \sum_{n=-\infty}^{\infty} i_n (-1)^{n-v} I_{n-v}\left(\eta^f e\right). \tag{2.7b}$$

Therefore, equations at the wellbore can be set, like Eqs. (2.5a) – (2.5d).

Combining all equations at the three interfaces, an infinite-order linear system will be established, which contains $a_n - i_n$ and $j_v - l_v$, with $n, v = 0, \pm 1, \ldots, \pm\infty$. In practical simulations, it is truncated by setting $n, v = 0, \pm 1, \ldots, \pm N$. Consequently, one can obtain the following systems of finite linear equations

$$\mathbf{D}_N \mathbf{x}_N = \mathbf{b}_N\,, \tag{2.8}$$

where $\mathbf{D}_N$ is a square matrix, whose elements are the function of variables ω and k; $\mathbf{x}_N$ is the column vector of unknown coefficients; $\mathbf{b}_N$ is contributed by the source.

After evaluating $\mathbf{x}_N$, all field components can be totally determined. For example, the pressure of the outer fluid in the space and time domains can be written as

$$\bar{p}_{ex}(t) = \frac{1}{2\pi}\int_{-\infty}^{\infty} \rho_f \omega^2 \int_{-\infty}^{\infty} \sum_{n=-N}^{N}\left[h_n I_n\left(\eta^f r_1\right) + i_n K_n\left(\eta^f r_1\right)\right]\cos(n\theta_1) \mathrm{S}(\omega) \mathrm{e}^{-i\omega t} \mathrm{U}(k) \mathrm{e}^{ik} dk d\omega\,, \tag{2.9}$$

where $\mathrm{S}(\omega)$ and $\mathrm{U}(k)$ depict the features of the acoustic source in the frequency and wavenumber domains, respectively[9]. Further, taking the parts of the square brackets in Eq. (2.9) out separately, the two-dimensional spectra of acoustic fields can be expressed as below[10]

$$P_n(f, v) = h_n I_n\left(\eta^f r_1\right) + i_n K_n\left(\eta^f r_1\right). \tag{2.10}$$

By analyzing spectra, the effects of tool eccentricity on the dispersion features of borehole wavefields will be revealed.

3. Simulation Results

In this section, with the above theoretical analyses, characteristics of borehole wavefields with varying tool eccentricity are investigated. Table 1 lists a set of parameters of the model. To describe the extent of collar deviation quantitatively, we define a normalized eccentricity coefficient (*Ecc*) as following

$$Ecc = \frac{e}{(b-a)} \times 100\%, \tag{2.11}$$

where e represents the collar offset; $(b-a)$ is the thickness of the fluid annulus originally.

Table 1. Model parameters for the simulations

Material	P velocity (m/s)	Q_P	S velocity (m/s)	Q_S	Density (kg/m^3)	Radius (m)
Inner Fluid	1470	100	–	–	1000	0.027
Metallic Collar	5860	30	3130	40	7800	0.090
Outer Fluid	1470	100	–	–	1000	0.117
Formation	3972	50	2455	60	2320	∞

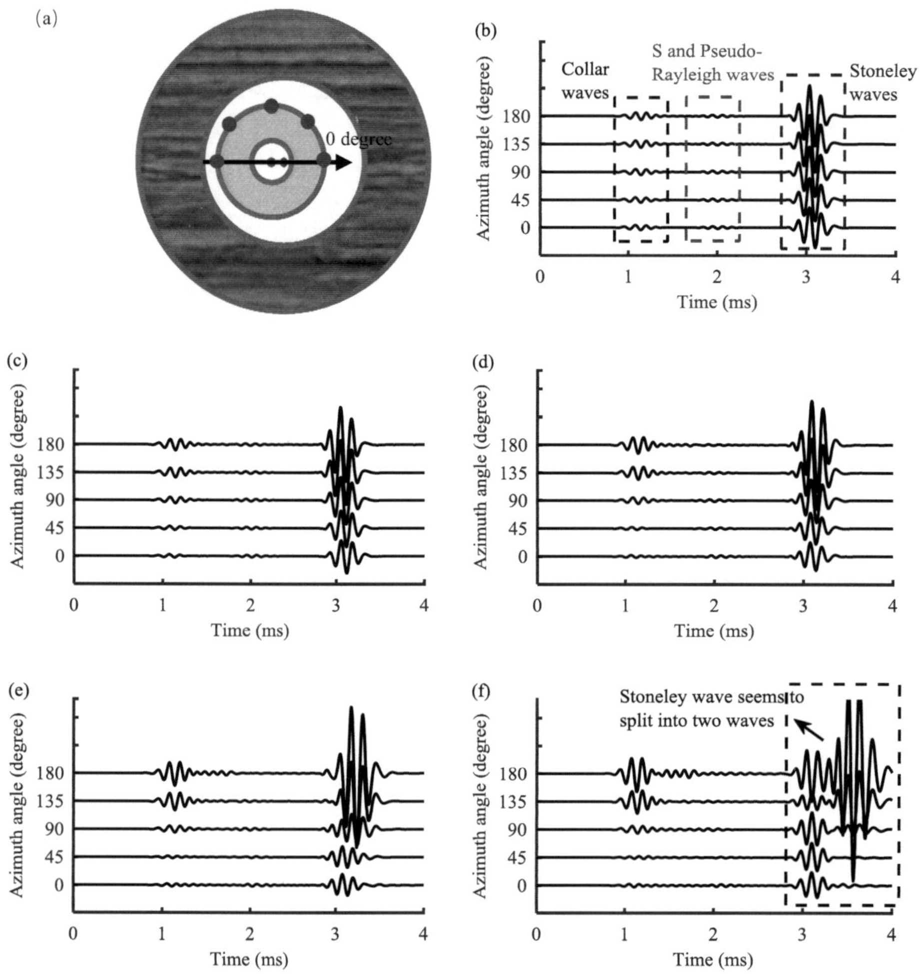

Fig. 2. (a) The schematic diagram of receivers (red dots) at different azimuths. The synthetic waveforms received at different azimuths with varying tool eccentricity. (b) $Ecc = 10\%$. (c) $Ecc = 30\%$. (d) $Ecc = 50\%$. (e) $Ecc = 70\%$. (f) $Ecc = 90\%$.

3.1. Waveforms

In this part, we focus on how the waveforms at different azimuths change with tool eccentricity by evaluating Eq. (2.9). The receiving azimuth angles are 0°, 45°, 90°, 135° and 180°, respectively, as shown in Fig. (2a). Figs. 2(b) – (2f) illustrate the full waveforms at the above five azimuths with varying eccentricity. The receiver-to-source distance is 4 m in the z- direction. In Fig. (2b), the collar is deviated slightly and hence the performances of these waveforms are similar to those with no eccentricity. The three prominent wave groups of each waveform in Fig. (2b) are collar waves, formation S wave and pseudo-Rayleigh waves, and Stoneley waves[9]. Next, focusing on Figs. (2b) – (2f), two types of comparisons are performed. One is that we fix the eccentricity unchanged and compare the waveforms at different azimuths. The other is that fixing the azimuth angle unchanged and analyzing differences of the relevant waveforms with varying *Ecc*. The results reveal that the wavefields properties in some direction are closely related to the thickness of the fluid annulus toward that azimuth, especially for collar waves and Stoneley waves. Besides, there are two obvious wave groups after 2.9 ms, which is not discovered in Figs. (2b) –(2e). It seems that the Stoneley wave splits into two individual waves. To distinguish the Stoneley wave from other modes, a signal processing based on the two-dimensional spectrum technique is necessary, which will be discussed below.

3.2. Two-dimensional spectra

Figs. (3a) – (3f) present the two-dimensional spectra with varying *Ecc* by evaluating Eq. (2.10). Notice the brightness indicates the intensity. First, in Fig. (3a), which represents no deviation, there are four modes. The top two modes are associated with the drill collar, which need to be paid no attention. And we mainly focus on the other two modes, pseudo-Rayleigh waves and Stoneley waves, because from which one can obtain the formation information. Through comparisons, near pseudo-Rayleigh waves, there appear other modes as *Ecc* increases. These newly generated waves are unwanted noises and can obstruct the determination of formation S velocity. Besides, in the Stoneley wave area, there gradually appears a discontinuous gap at about 2 kHz with *Ecc* increasing. In fact, there are two curves in this area, which can be easy to be recognized in Fig. (3e) or (3f). In order to answer where these modes come from, we combine Figs. (3f) and (3g) to make a theoretical analysis. Fig. (5g) illustrates dispersion curves of normal modes with the monopole, dipole and quadrupole case when the collar is centered. By comparing Figs. (3f) and (3g), it is revealed that the multipole modes with cross points in Fig (3g) are coupled with each other, when the collar is off center. The curves seem to repel each other near the crossing points to avoid crossing. In particular, the coupling of the lowest-order monopole and dipole modes is most obvious in the case of severe eccentricity. Therefore, in Fig (3f), the faster one of the above two modes presents the properties of Stoneley waves within 2 kHz and flexural waves beyond 2 kHz. Performances of the slower one is exactly opposite. Note that when *Ecc* is not great enough, the excitation of the flexural wave part of the faster mode is very weak and the velocity difference of the two modes is also not clear, hence leading to only one wave group observed in the waveforms. It's evident the faster mode presents a relatively weak intensity; while the excitation of the slower one is relatively large beyond about 2 kHz, according to brightness levels. This is in good agreement with the simulation results of the waveforms.

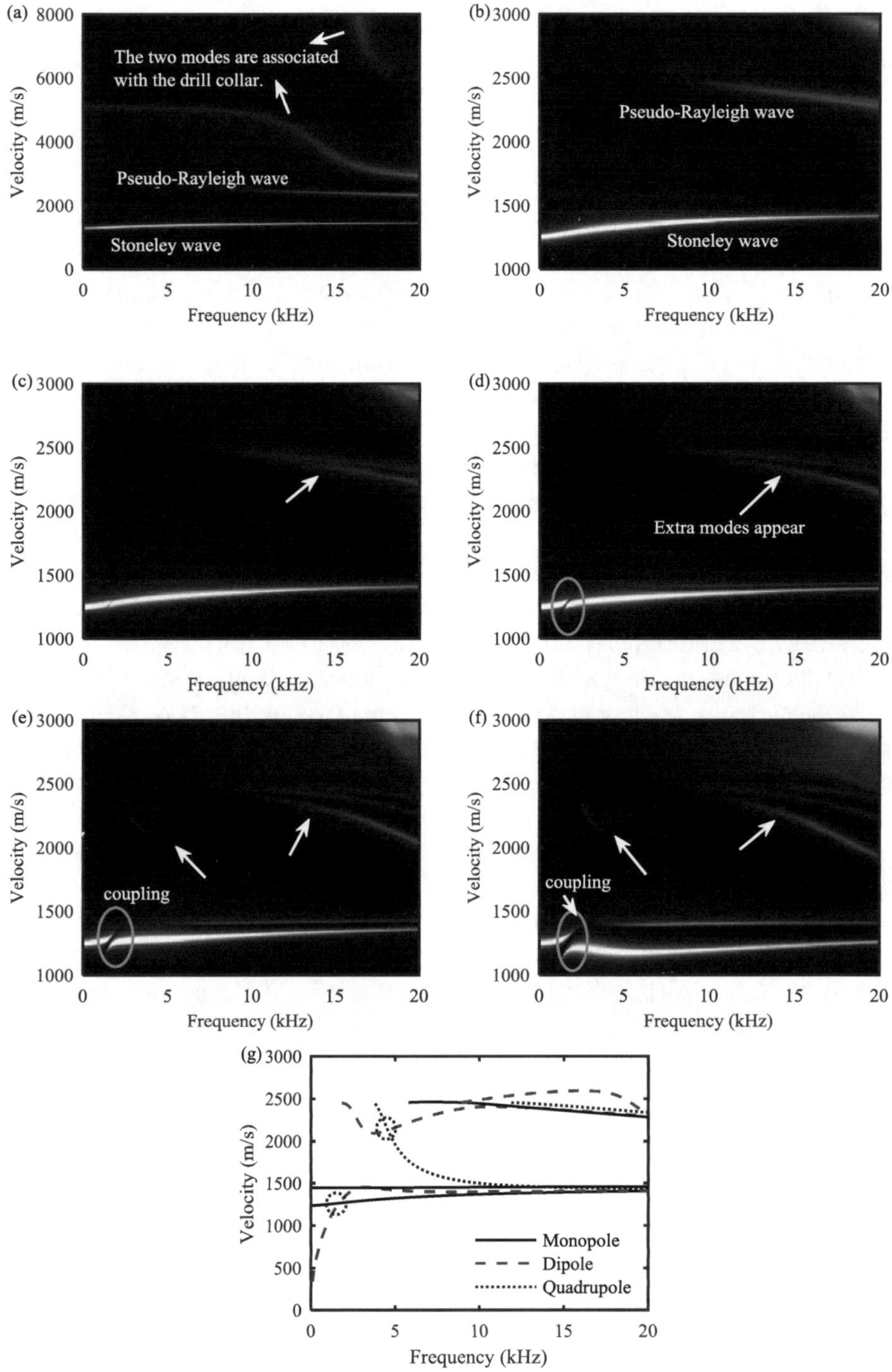

Fig. 3. The two-dimensional spectra in the frequency and the phase velocity domains with varying tool eccentricity. (a) *Ecc* = 0%. (b) *Ecc* = 10%. (c) *Ecc* = 30%. (d) *Ecc* = 50%. (e) *Ecc* = 70%. (f) *Ecc* = 90%. (g) The dispersion curves of the monopole, dipole and quadrupole modes when the collar is centered.

4. Conclusions

In this work, an analytical method is developed to investigate acoustic responses when the LWD tool is no longer centralized in the borehole. By analyzing the synthetic waveforms received at different azimuths with varying tool eccentricity, it is revealed that the borehole wavefields are closely related to the thickness of the fluid annulus toward that azimuth, especially for collar waves and Stoneley waves. Furthermore, by means of the two-dimensional spectrum technique, it is revealed that multipole modes appear, and their dispersion features have changed when the collar is off center. In the case of severe eccentricity, the newly generated waves have a significantly negative effect on the useful signals we need. Particularly, the flexural mode is strong enough that it interferes with the identification of Stoneley waves. Therefore, more caution should be required for processing and utilizing such LWD data. For example, using Stoneley waves to inverse formation permeability may not be a wise choice in such condition.

Acknowledgments

This study is supported by the National Natural Science Foundation of China (Grant Nos. 11774373, 11734017, and 11574347).

References

[1] X. Huang, Y. Zheng, and M. N. Toksöz, "Effects of tool eccentricity on acoustic logging while drilling (LWD) measurements," *74th SEG Annual Meeting*, 2004, pp. 290–293.

[2] Y. Zheng, X. Huang, and M. N. Toksöz, "A finite element analysis of the effects of tool eccentricity on wave dispersion properties in borehole acoustic logging while drilling," *74th SEG Annual Meeting*, 2004, pp. 294–297.

[3] D. Pardo, P. J. Matuszyk, I. Muga, C. Torres-Verdín, A. Mora, and V. M. Calo, "Influence of borehole-eccentered tools in wireline and LWD sonic logging measurements," *Geophys. Prospect.* **61**(s1) (2013), 268–283.

[4] H. Wang, G. Tao, and K. Zhang, "Wavefield simulation and analysis with the finite-element method for acoustic logging while drilling in horizontal and deviated wells," *Geophysics* **78**(6) (2013), D525–D543.

[5] S. M. Haugland, "Mandrel eccentricity effects on acoustic borehole-guided waves," *74th SEG Annual Meeting*, 2004, pp. 282–285.

[6] S. M. Haugland , "Analytical solution for an eccentric mandrel in a fluid-filled borehole," The acoustic case," *74th SEG Annual Meeting*, 2004, pp. 330–333.

[7] S. M. Hasheminejad, and H. Mousavi-Akbarzadeh, "Three dimensional non-axisymmetric transient acoustic radiation from an eccentric hollow cylinder," *Wave Motion* **50**(4) (2013), 723–738.

[8] G. N. Watson, *A Treatise on the Theory of Bessel Functions*, Cambridge University Press, 1944.

[9] Z. W. Cui, Theoretical and numerical study of modified Biot's models, acoustoelectric well logging and acoustic logging while drilling excited by multipole acoustic sources, Ph.D. dissertation, Jilin University, 2004,

[10] J. G. Shen, *Applied acoustic basis: integral on the real line and two-dimensional technique*, Tianjin University Press, 2004.

Discrete Differential Forms for the Numerical Solution of Helmholtz Equations

G. WIMMER[1] S. LANGE[2]

1, University of Applied Sciences Würzburg-Schweinfurt, Ignaz-Schön-Str. 11, Schweinfurt, 97421, Germany
georg.wimmer@fhws.de[§]
2, Bundeswehr Research Institute for Protective Technologies and CBRN Protection,
Munster, 29633, Germany
sebastian1lange@bundeswehr.org

Partial differential equations that arise in computational electromagnetics and acoustics can be written with the common operators grad, div and curl. However the methodology of differential forms allows to formulate the partial differential equations in a compact and elegant way. It is also shown that the common procedure of Galerkin discretization can also be applied to that new formulations. Furthermore the implementation should also follow that concept to mimic the behaviour and properties of differential forms. Examples prove the validity of the implementation by using the method of manufactured solutions.

Keywords: Electromagnetics; Differential Forms; Eigenvalue Problem.

1. Introduction

It is quite convenient to write Maxwell's equations and derived partial differential equations using the mathematical notation of differential forms. The theory of differential forms is a mature theory and often used in theoretical physics and mathematics. However this notation is not only for the beauty of mathematics. It can be shown that using overloading of functions and polymorphism of an object oriented programming language such as C++ the behavior of differential forms can be put into a computer code. Also using different basis functions for different physical quantities is essential.

2. Formulation

Electrostatic, magnetostatic or dc conduction field equations can be reduced to the Poisson equation

$$-\operatorname{div}\left(\varepsilon \cdot \operatorname{grad} u\right) = f \text{ in } \Omega,\ u = u_D \text{ on } \partial\Omega. \tag{2.1}$$

Here, Ω is an open bounded subset of $\square^{2}$ and $\partial\Omega$ denotes the boundary of Ω . Other boundary conditions or mixed boundary conditions are possible. For convenience of representation only Dirichlet boundary conditions on $\partial\Omega$ are used. The quantity u represents the electric or magnetic vector potential, ε a material parameter and f are the sources such as charge density or current density.

Time harmonic solutions of the wave equation known as Helmholtz type equations occur in computational acoustics and electromagnetics and can be written as

$$\operatorname{curl}\operatorname{curl} E - k^2 E = 0 \text{ in } \Omega_{3D} \text{ or } \Delta E_z + k^2 E_z = 0 \text{ in } \Omega_{2D}, \tag{2.2}$$

$$\Delta p + k^2 p = 0 \text{ in } \Omega_{3D} \text{ or } \quad p + k^2 p = 0 \text{ in } \Omega_{2D} \tag{2.3}$$

in a 3-dimensional or 2-dimensional bounded domain with smooth boundary Ω_{3D} or Ω_{2D} . Here E denotes the electric field, E_z the $z-$ component of the electric field for electromagnetic applications as an accelerator induction cell and p denotes the pressure in acoustic applications. These equations are well investigated from a theoretical point of view and numerical techniques as the Finite Element method has been used for the numerical solution. However it is important to understand that the electric field E is a vector quantity related to a line. However E_z and p are quantities related to a vertex.

3. Physical Quantities and Differential Forms

A 0-form describes a continuous, scalar quantity as the electrostatic potential. Fig. (1) shows the electrostatic potential of an insulator. The 0-form's properties are continuity in every direction, evaluation or integral at one point and the derivative is the gradient.

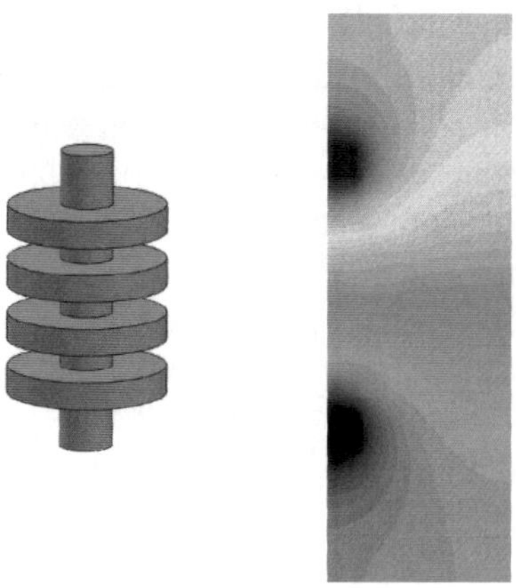

Fig. 1. Model (left) and electrostatic potential in a plane (right).

Fig. (2) shows the electric field that is generated by a voltage drop. The lower, horizontal line is put to 0 V and the upper, horizontal line is put to 10 V. All other edges are set to homogenous Neumann or natural boundary condition. The properties of a 1-form is tangential continuity across edges and evaluation or integral along a line. The derivative is the curl. Also

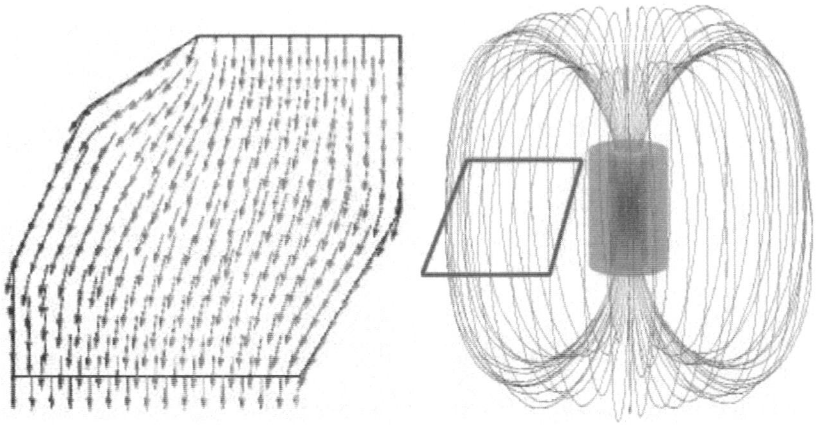

Fig. 2. Electric field from voltage drop (Left). Magnetic flux density lines from a current in a coil (Right).

the unity [V/m] of the electric field shows clearly that it is related to a line.
Fig. (3) shows the magnetic flux density as a vector field that was generated by a current in a coil. The magnetic flux density represents a 2-form which is normal continuous and the evaluation or integral can be done over a surface. The derivative is divergence div. Also from the units [T/m*m] it can be seen that the magnetic flux density is related to a surface.
Overall the properties of 0-, 1-, 2-forms are depicted in Table (1).

Table 1. Properties of 0-, 1-, 2-forms.

Form	Example	Continuity	Integral	Derivative
0-form	Electrostatic potential	total	point	grad
1-form	Electric field	tangential	line	curl
2-form	Magnetic flux density	normal	surface	div

4. Differential Forms

A differential form ω of order k (k-form) in is a mapping $\omega : \Omega \to \bigcup_{p\in\Omega} \Lambda^k T_p^*(\Omega)$ with $\omega(p) \in \Lambda^k T_p^*(\Omega)$ for all $p \in \Omega$. Here $T_p^*(\Omega)$ denotes the space of alternating linear mappings to □ on the cotangential space $T_p^*(\Omega)$. The k-form ω can be written in coordinate representation uniquely as $\omega = \sum_{i_1<...<i_k} f_{i_1}...f_{i_k} dx_{i_1} \wedge dx_{i_k}$ with unique functions

$f_{i_1}...f_{i_k} : \Omega \to \mathbb{R}$ and $\wedge$ denoting the wedge product. The integral $\int \omega$ of a 0-form is defined as $\omega := \omega(p)$ which is simply the evaluation of ω at point p . The electrostatic potential is an example for a 0-form which can be evaluated at any point $p \in \Omega$. The integral $\int \omega$ of a 1-form is defined as

$$\int_{\alpha} \omega = \int_{t=a}^{b} \langle \omega(\alpha(t)), \dot{\alpha}(t) \rangle \mathrm{d}t = \int_{t=a}^{b} \sum_{i=1}^{n} f_i(\alpha(t)) \cdot \dot{\alpha}_i(t) \mathrm{d}t \tag{4.1}$$

with $\alpha : [a,b] \to \Omega \in C^1$. The electric field as an example for a 1-form which can be evaluated along α which gives the potential difference between the starting and end point of α . If the functions $f_{i_1...i_k}$ are C_1 then ω is said to be C_1 and the

derivative $d\omega$ of ω is defined as $d\omega := \sum_{1<...<i_k}^{n} df_{i_1}...f_{i_k} \wedge dx_{i_1} \wedge dx_{i_k}$. The derivative is

also refered to as exterior derivative. Since a 0-form ω is just a real function f on Ω, it can be shown that the derivative of ω is $d\omega(p)v = df(p)v = \langle \mathrm{grad}\, f(p), v \rangle$. Hence the derivative of a 0-form is the gradient of a real function on Ω . Furthermore it can be shown that the derivative of a 1-form is the curl operator and the derivative of a 2-form for $n = 3$ is the div operator. As a result the integral of k-form and its derivative can be written in a unique manner as $\int \omega$ and $d\omega$. A detailed description about differential forms can be found in [1]. It is the idea to put the discrete differential forms into a computer code using object oriented programming which follow the mathematical notation above. Another requirement for the basis functions representing discrete k-forms should be the specific continuity property along element interfaces which is shown in Table (1). For the electric scalar potential or heat distribution the ordinary nodal finite elements might be suitable. However for the electric field H(curl)-conforming finite elements or edge elements are more convenient as they model properly the discontinuity jump across element interfaces while enforcing tangential continuity. Edge elements were introduced by Nédélec[4], [5] A generalized framework for constructing conforming finite element spaces following the idea of differential forms is to be found in [3]. Let $(-1)^k d*_{\alpha} du = \rho,\ T_D(u) = u_D$ with u being a $(k-1)$ -form, ρ a $(3-k+1)$ -form on Ω , $*_{\alpha}$ the Hodge operator and du denoting the exterior derivative of u and T_D the trace operator. Equation (1) results for $k = 1$. A weak form of (12) is obtained by using standard techniques. However calculus of differential forms as multiplication using the wedge product needs to be used instead. Multiplication of eq. (12) by v , a $(k-1)$ -form, and integration yields $\int_{\Omega} (-1)^k d*_{\alpha} du \wedge v = \int_{\Omega} \rho \wedge v$. Integration by parts using the formula $\int_\Omega d\omega \wedge v + (-1)^k \int_\Omega \omega \wedge dv = \int_{\partial\Omega} \omega \wedge v$ results finally in

$\int_\Omega *_\alpha du \wedge dv = \int_\Omega \rho \wedge v + \int_{\partial\Omega} *_\alpha du \wedge v$. The left side of (15) yields the bilinear form and the right side of (15) yields the linear form. The implementation is following this idea as proposed in [2]. The k-form class contains methods to evaluate the k-form or evaluate its derivative as depicted in Table II for k = 0. The general k-form class contains the same methods. However the implementation should be different. The implementation of these classes also depend on the geometry (triangle, quadrilateral or other polyhedral) and the exact location of the Lagrangian interpolatory points in the reference triangle. That means that from a pure virtual class other classes with specific implementation of methods are derived.

5. Method of Manufactured Solutions

The method of manufactured solutions (see [6]) implies that the exact solution $u = u(x, y)$ is given and $f = f(x, y)$ and $u_D(x, y)$ are calculated such that (1.1) is fulfilled. The errors

$$e_L(u_h) := \sqrt{\int_\Omega (u - u_h)^2 \, \mathrm{d}\Omega}, e_Q(u_h) := \sqrt{\int_\Omega (\nabla u - \nabla u_h)^2 \, \mathrm{d}\Omega} \quad (5.1)$$

are investigated with u_h denoting the numerical solution for polynomial shape functions of

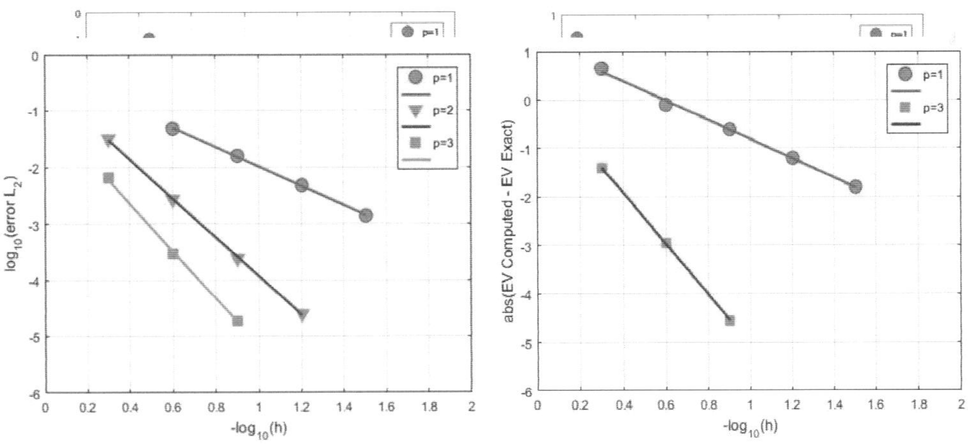

Fig. 5. Errors on different meshes and shape functions for the eigenvalue problem.

degree p on a triangular mesh with size h . Fig. (4) shows the errors on logarithmic scale and the linear least squares straight line for $u(x, y) = \sin(2\pi x)\cos(2\pi y)$ solved on the unit square in 2D. The negative slopes represents the convergence order and the results are 1.98, 3.00, 3.98, 4.97 for e_L and 0.99, 1.98, 2.98, 3.97 for e_Q which perfectly matches the theoretical result.

Similarly the numerical solution of $\Delta u + k^2 u = 0,\ u_D = 0$ is $u(x,y) = \sin(n_x \pi x) \cdot \sin(n_y \pi y)$ with $k^2 = \pi^2 (n_x^2 + n_y^2)$. Discretization leads to the generalized eigenvalue problem $Az = k^2 \cdot Bz$ with A the stiffness matrix and B the mass matrix. Left Fig. (5) shows the error e_L on a logarithmic scale and right Fig. (5) shows the error of the smallest eigenvalue for different meshes and shape function degrees.
The negative slopes in Fig. 5 are 1.70, 3.44, 4.20 for e_L and 1.99 and 5.23 for the smallest eigenvalue error.

6. Conclusion

It is convenient to write partial differential equations using the methodology of differential forms. It is the aim to mimic the behavior of discrete differential forms on a mesh in a computer code. Most suitable are object oriented languages which provide overloading and derivative of classes. Convergence results on different meshed and shape function degrees are provided for Poisson equation and Helmholtz equation.

References

[1] D. Arnold, R. Falk, and R. Winther. "Finite element exterior calculus, homological techniques, and applications", Acta Numerica, (2003), 1-155.
[2] P. Castillo, J. Koning, R. Rieben, M. Stowell, and D. White. "Discrete
[3] Differential Forms: A Novel Methodology for Robust Computational Electromagnetics", Lawrence Livermore National Laboratory, 2003.
[4] R. Hiptmair. "Canonical construction of finite elements", Math. Comp., 228 (1999), 1325–1346.
[5] J. C. Nédélec. "Mixed finite elements in r3", Numer. Math., 35 (1980), 315–341.
[6] J. C. Nédélec. "A new family of mixed finite elements in r3". Numer. Math., 50 (1986), 57–81.
[7] P. J. Roache. "Code verification by the method of manufactured solutions". Journal of Fluids Engineering, 124(1) (2002), 4–10.

Microseismic Location Based on Interferometric Imaging and Hilbert-Huang Transform

TING-TING ZHAN[1,2,3] HAO CHEN*[1,2,3]

1, State Key Laboratory of Acoustics, Institute of Acoustics, Chinese Academy of Sciences,
Beijing, China

2, University of Chinese Academy of Sciences,
Beijing, China

3, Beijing Engineering Research Center of Sea Deep Drilling and Exploration, Institute of Acoustics, Chinese Academy of Sciences, Beijing, China

zhantingting@mail.ioa.ac.cn

chh@mail.ioa.ac.cn

For microseismic monitoring, the inaccurate microseismic source location will inevitably lead to misjudgment of the fracture geometry, thus reducing the reliability of microseismic monitoring. The location accuracy is greatly affected by the noise. Therefore, it is necessary and important to improve the accuracy and the robustness of the source location algorithm under the low SNR condition. Considering the non-stationarity of microseismic signals with strong random noise, a new microseismic event location approach based on interferometric imaging and Hilbert-Huang transform (HHT) is proposed. First, the synthetic microseismic signals are processed to the instantaneous energy spectrums and the Hilbert spectrums by HHT. Then, these two spectrums are respectively used as the characteristic functions of interferometric imaging method for microseismic source location and two different location methods are obtained. Finally, in homogeneous medium, the imaging results of the traditional approach and the proposed approach on synthetic low SNR datasets are analyzed and compared. The results demonstrate that the proposed approach can effectively suppress random noise and improves the location accuracy under the low SNR condition. These studies are of great significance to real time microseismic monitoring, especially for the surface monitoring.

Keywords: Source location; interferometric imaging; Hilbert-Huang transform.

1. Introduction

With the increasingly severe energy situation in the world, the focus of oil and gas exploration has gradually shifted from conventional to unconventional oil and gas fields. The unconventional oil and gas fields are characterized by tight and low permeability and they are mainly explored by the hydraulic fracturing technology. In order to achieve safe and effective development of oil and gas resources, microseismic monitoring technology is used to monitor the fracturing effect. However, microseismic data have the characteristics of the complex polarity change, low intensity and low SNR, which make it challenging to pick event first arrivals, especially for the surface monitoring. All these factors will lead to low precision location result and then misjudge the fracture trend.

Therefore, researchers have done a lot of studies on the microseismic location. In 2004, Kao and Shan proposed a diffraction-stack location method, using the absolute values of raw amplitudes. Then, many different processing ways to raw amplitudes were developed. Such as, envelopes(Kao and Shan, 2007), squared values(Gajewski *et al.*, 2007), ratios of short-term average to long-term average(STA/LTA) (Drew *et al.*, 2013) and kurtosis values(Langet *et al.*, 2014). They are named as the characteristic functions which not only can highlight the effective signal but also can correct the waveform polarity. However, simple stack methods are challenged with high amplitude values which usually appears in the form of noise in microseismic data. Instead, researchers gradually began to use the similarity and coherency of the waves to locate the source. In 2010, Chambers *et al.* located the source by the semblance of waveforms. This coherence location method can overcome the above shortcoming. However, all above methods need to determine the original time and source location at the same time which will limit the location accuracy. In 2015, Li *et al.* used interferometric imaging method to decouple the original time from the location algorithm which reduce the impact of seeking the original time on location results and improve the location accuracy. But the traditional characteristic functions are sensitive to noise, especially for the STA/LTA. So, in recent years, signal analysis methods are applied to microseismic location to reduce noise impact, especially for interferometric imaging. In 2018, Huang *et al.* considered the non-stationarity of the microseismic signal and the strong randomness of the noise and applied cross wavelet transform to interferometric imaging, which can give a more reliable result. Meanwhile, a new time-frequency signal analysis method called Hilbert-Huang transform is gradually used in microseismic monitoring(Li *et al.*, 2019).

In this study, we focus on improving location accuracy at low SNR conditions and propose a new location approach, based on HHT and interferometric imaging. The numerical simulation results show that the proposed approach is more accurate and robust under low SNR conditions.

2. Basic Principles

2.1. Interferometric Imaging

For microseismic source location, the essence is to invert seismic source parameters according to weak seismic signals of one or more seismic events to each station. Figure. (1) shows the schematic diagram of the interferometric imaging based source location.

First, the target space is divided into uniform grids. Second, solving the eikonal equation with given velocity model compute the theoretical traveltime $t^{P}_{i,\vec{x}}$ of the P-waves from each node $\vec{x}$ to each receiver(i-th). Third, the cross-correlogram C^{ij}_{s} is carried out on seismograms from two arbitrary receivers(i-th, j-th) as

$$C^{ij}_{s}(\tau)=\sum_{t=0}^{t_{\max}} CF^{i}(t)CF^{j}(t+\tau). \tag{2.1}$$

Where $CF^{i}(t)$ and $CF^{j}(t)$ are the characteristic functions about the i-th and j-th traces, $t_{\max}$ is the length of the raw waveform and τ is the time parameter. Fourth, using the time difference

$d_{ij,\vec{x}}$ to migrate every cross-correlogram and the final source imaging profile $S(\vec{x})$ is obtained by stacking all migration profiles as

$$S(\vec{x}) = \sum_{\substack{i=1 \\ j=i+1}}^{N} C_s^{ij}(\mathrm{d}\tau_{ij,\vec{x}}) = \sum_{\substack{i=1 \\ j=i+1}}^{N} C_s^{ij}(\tau_{i,\vec{x}}^{p} - \tau_{j,\vec{x}}^{p}). \tag{2.2}$$

Where N is the number of the receivers. Only the correct location has a high value in the imaging profile.

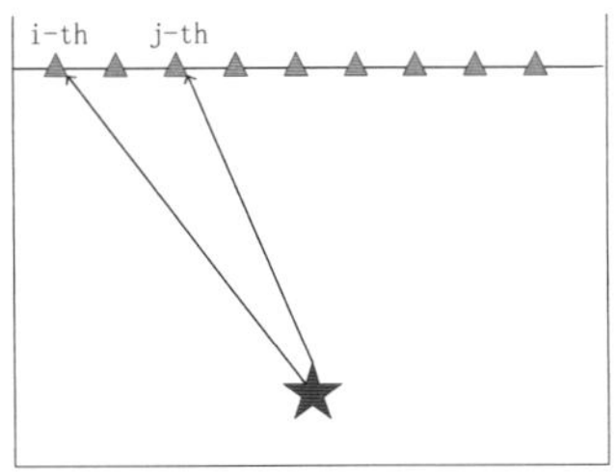

Fig. 1. The schematic diagram of the interferometric imaging based microseismic source location.

2.2. Hilbert-Huang Transform

HHT method is developed for non-stationary signals by Huang *et al.* in 1998. It consists of two parts: Empirical mode decomposition(EMD) and Hilbert transform.
The EMD is used to decompose the given signal $x(t)$ into n intrinsic mode functions(IMFs) $C_i(t)$ and a residue $r_n(t)$ as

$$x(t) = \sum_{i=0}^{n} C_i(t) + r_n(t). \tag{2.3}$$

These IMFs can directly solve instantaneous parameters.
Then the Hilbert transform processes each IMF to obtain the corresponding instantaneous parameters and Hilbert spectrums. All these Hilbert spectrums are added to obtain the Hilbert amplitude spectrum $H(t,w)$ of the raw signal as

$$H(t,w) = \mathrm{Re}\sum_{i=1}^{n} a_i(t)e^{j\varphi_i(t)} = \mathrm{Re}\sum_{i=1}^{n} a_i(t)e^{j\int w_i(t)dt}. \tag{2.4}$$

Where $a_i(t)$, $\varphi_i(t)$ and $w_i(t)$ are respectively the instantaneous amplitude, instantaneous phase and instantaneous angular frequency for i-th IMF.
The Hilbert energy spectrum $|H(t,w)|^2$ can be got by squaring the Hilbert amplitude spectrum. Then, integrating the frequency of the Hilbert energy spectrum obtain the instantaneous energy spectrum $h(t)$ as

$$h(t) = \int |H(t,w)|^2 dw. \tag{2.5}$$

3. Numerical experiments

A simple 2D numerical experiment using a homogeneous medium model is adopted because we mainly focus on the impact of noise on the proposed location approach. The velocity model and source-receiver geometry are shown in Fig. (2). The receivers with spacing of 10m are arranged at the plane of Z=0 to simulate the surface monitoring. Meanwhile, the first-order velocity-stress equation and the finite difference method based on staggered grid are used to simulate the microseismic wave filed. Some key parameters are shown in Table 1. Source excitation mode is the common explosion source in exploration seismology. The point source excitation is applied in two normal stress directions and only excite the compressive wave.

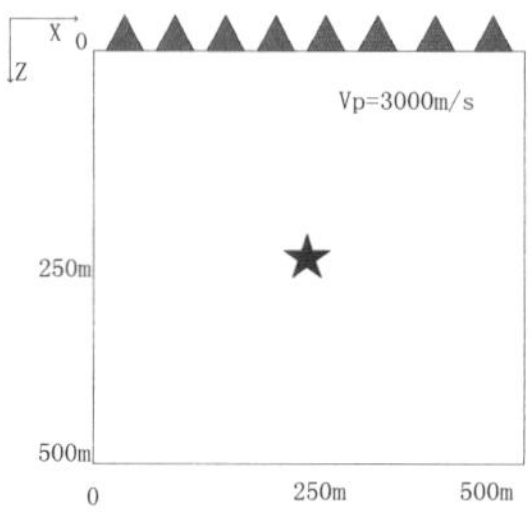

Fig. 2. Two-dimension uniform medium and source-receiver geometry.

Table 1. Parameters of two-dimensional uniform model

Name of parameter	Value	Name of parameter	Value
Model size	500m×500m	Space interval	2.5m
V_P	3000m/s	Time interval	0.5ms
V_P/V_S	1.67	Source location	(250m,250m)
Density	3000kg/m^3	Source wavelet	60Hz Ricker wavelet

Then, the corresponding Hilbert energy spectrums and instantaneous energy spectrums are obtained by HHT. In Fig. (3), the effective part is clearly displayed while the noise is evenly distributed throughout the Hilbert spectrum. As for the instantaneous energy spectrum, shown in Fig. (4), the energy distribution of the waveform with time corresponds to the amplitude distribution and meanwhile, the polarity of the waveform has been corrected. However, the instantaneous energy spectrum represents the sudden release of energy at a certain moment. So, the energy distribution with time is more obvious for the effective part. In other words, the effective signal of the waveform has been strengthened and the ambient noise and distributing signals have been overwhelmed.

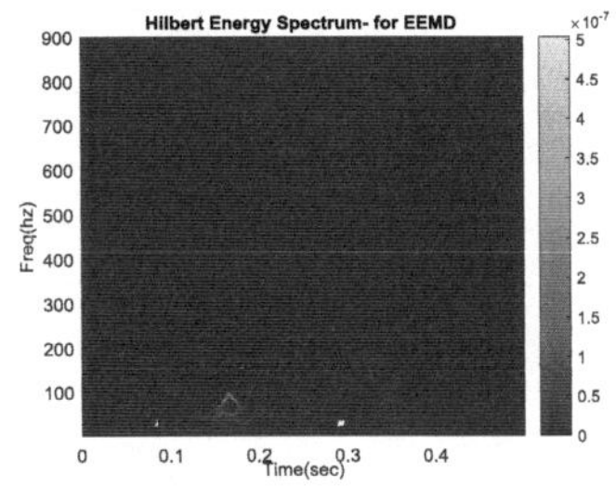

Fig. 3. The Hilbert energy spectrum of the 1st V_Z component.

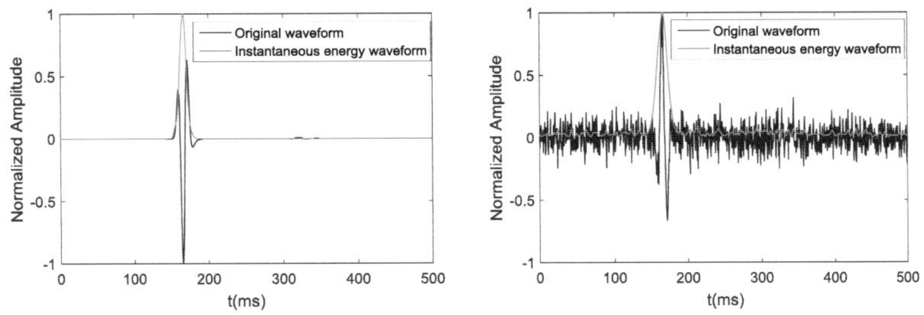

(a) (b)

Fig. 4. The 51th V_X component under noise-free condition(a) and the 1st V_Z component under noise condition(b).

So, there are two processing ways for the proposed location approach and they can be described as flows. The Hilbert spectrum and the instantaneous energy spectrum are used as the characteristic function *CF* in Eq. (2.1), respectively. Only the V_Z component is used to locate the source for convenience in the following study.

3.1. The Hilbert Energy Spectrum

The first processing way is using Hilbert energy spectrum to improve the location method. The characteristic function *CF* in Eq. (2.1) is $|H(t,w)|^2$, and then integrate the frequency.

Figures. (5)(a) and (5)(b) show the location results under noise-free condition and noise condition, which the SNR is 1.5dB. They both only have a 2.5 meters location error. The corresponding results of traditional location method which is based on STA/LTA and interferometric imaging are shown in Figs. (5)(c) and (5)(d). They both have location errors of up to 7.5 meters to 10 meters in vertical direction.

The location results are improved to some extent. Because only when the effective signals in the i-th and j-th spectrum coincide, the value of cross correlogram reaches the maximum. It uses the correlation between the effective signals in two spectrums. However, because the screening process in EMD is largely dependent on the interpolation of the maximum and minimum values, the final result has some stability problems in the presence of noise. So, the energy distribution varies in Hilbert energy spectrum with each treatment and these can lead to different location results. It is a waste of time for processing the signal several times by HHT to obtain a correct location result.

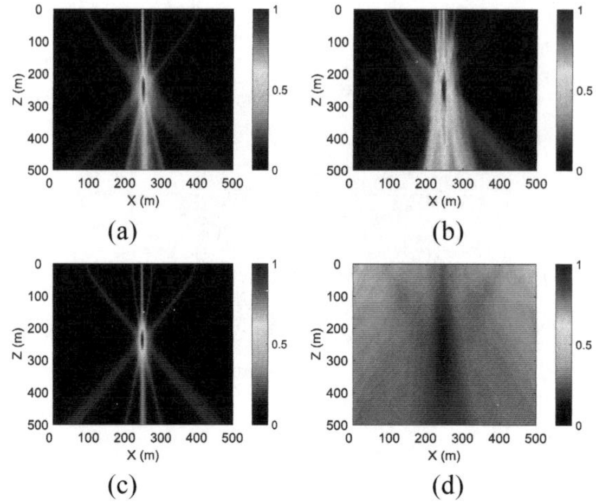

Fig. 5. The location profiles based on Hilbert energy spectrum under noise-free condition(a) and noise condition(b). The location profiles based on STA/LTA under noise-free condition(c) and noise

3.2. The Instantaneous Energy Spectrum

The second processing way is using instantaneous energy spectrum. The characteristic function *CF* in Eq. (2.1) is $h(t)$. Gaussian white noise was added to noise-free data to simulate different SNR conditions and the location results are shown in Fig. (6).

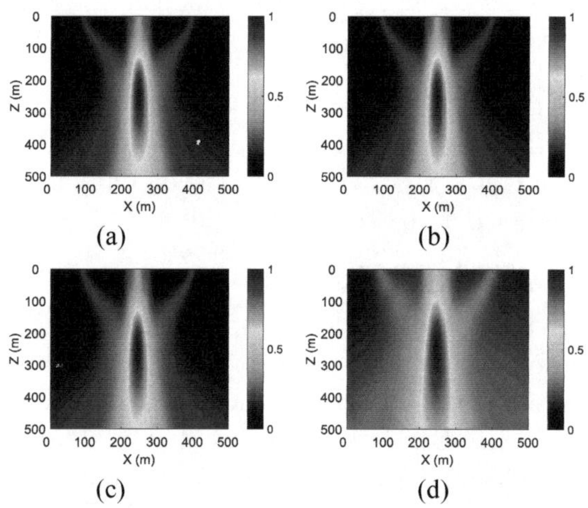

Fig. 6. The imaging profiles based on instantaneous energy spectrum under noise condition. The SNRs are 30dB(a), 20dB(b), 10dB(c) and 1.5dB(d), respectively.

The location results of the traditional location method are also shown in Fig. (7) at the same SNR conditions, to make a contrast with the proposed method.

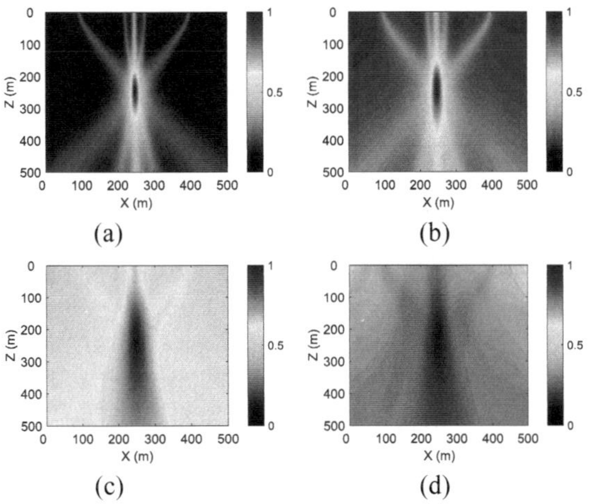

Fig. 7. The location profiles based on STA/LTA under noise condition. The SNRs are 30dB(a), 20dB(b), 10dB(c) and 1.5dB(d), respectively.

Then, the location errors of two location methods are shown in Fig. (8) and we can clearly see that the proposed method has fewer location errors than the traditional location method. This is because when random noise and high frequency pulse appear in the data, these high peaks will affect the accuracy of picking first arrivals of STA/LTA and even generate pseudo peaks in STA/LTA traces, which can lead to wrong source location. However, the instantaneous energy spectrum can suppress the noise and enhance the energy of the effective signal. So, the proposed location method can get more accurate locations result at low SNR conditions.

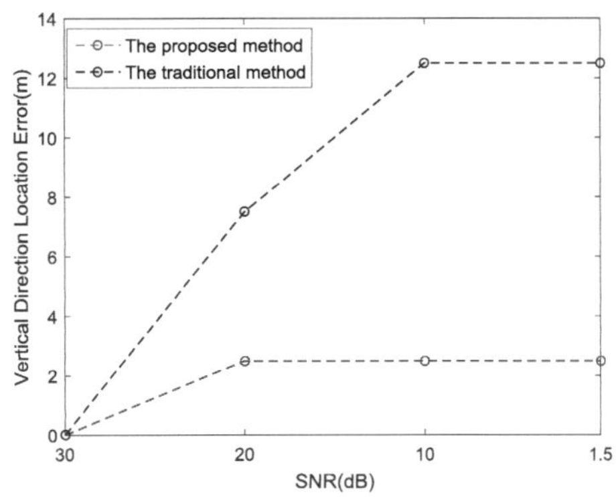

Fig. 8. The comparison diagram.

4. Conclusions

A source location approach based on the interferometric imaging and Hilbert-Huang transform is proposed. We use a simple 2D homogeneous medium and simulate different SNR conditions to text the anti-noise performance of the proposed approach. Through the above analysis, the proposed approach can significantly improve the accuracy and the robustness of the location algorithm under different SNR conditions, especially based on the instantaneous energy.

Acknowledgments

The work is sponsored by the National Natural Science Foundation of China (Grant Nos. 11574347,11734017 and 11774373).

References

[1] D. Gajewski, D. Anikiev, B. Kashtan, et al., "Localization of seismic events by diffraction stacking." *77th Ann. Soc. Expl. Geophys. Mtg.*, Expanded Abstracts, 2007, 1287–1291.

[2] H. Kao, and S. J. Shan, "The source-scanning algorithm: Mapping the distribution of seismic sources in time and space," *Geophysical Journal International*, **157**(2) (2004), 589–594.

[3] H. Kao, and S. J. Shan, "Rapid identification of earthquake rupture plane using source-scanning algorithm," *Geophysical Journal International*, **168**(3) (2007), 1011–1020.

[4] J. Drew, R. S. White, F. Tilmann, et al., "Coalescence microseismic mapping," *Geophysical Journal International*, **195**(3) (2013), 1773–1785.

[5] K. Chambers, J. M. Kendall, S. Brandsberg-Dahl, et al., "Testing the ability of surface arrays to monitor microseismic activity," *Geophysical Prospecting*, **58**(5) (2010), 821–830.

[6] L. Li, H. Chen, X. M. Wang, "Weighted-elastic-wave interferometric imaing of microseismic source location," *Applied Geophysics*, **12**(02) (2015), 221-234.

[7] L. Q. Huang, H. Hao, X. B. Li, et al., "Source identification of microseismic events in underground mines with interferometric imaging and cross wavelet transform," *Tunnelling and Underground Space Technology*, **71**(2018), 318–328.

[8] N. Langet, Maggi, A., Michelini, A., et al., "Continuous Kurtosi-Based Migration for Seismic Event Detection and Location, with Application to Piton de la Fournaise Volcano, La Réunion," *Bulletin of the Seismological Society of America*, **104**(1) (2014), 229–246.

[9] N. Li, B. X. Huang, X. Zhang, et al., "Characteristics of microseismic waveforms induced by hydraulic fracturing in coal seam for coal rock dynamic disasters prevention," *Safety Science*, **115**(2019), 188-198.

[10] N. E. Huang, Z. Sheng, S R .Long, "The empirical mode decomposi-tion and hilbert spectrum for non-linear and non-stationary time series analysis," *Proceeding of the Royal Society of London, Series A*, **454**(1971) (1998), 930-995.

Simulation of Reflection and Scattering Waves in Acoustic Logging While Drilling

YUE PAN[1,2,3] XIAO HE*[1,2,3] HAO CHEN[1,2,3]

1, State Key Laboratory of Acoustics, Institute of Acoustics, Chinese Academy of Sciences, Beijing 100190, China

2, University of Chinese Academy of Sciences, Beijing 100049, China.

3, Beijing Engineering Research Center of Sea Deep Drilling and Exploration, Institute of Acoustics, Chinese Academy of Sciences, Beijing 100190, China

panyue@mail.ioa.ac.cn

hex@mail.ioa.ac.cn

chh@mail.ioa.ac.cn

To extract the reflection signals from the logging while drilling (LWD) data for the goal of geo-steering, it was significant to investigate the propagation of those arrivals separately. Yet the reflection responses which are produced by the medium discontinuity at the drill bit and the bottom of borehole, could cover the signals we need. In this work, we investigated the wave fields generated by the scattering effects, which confirmed that the collar and the Stoneley waves produced a strong reflections of the Stoneley and the collar waves at the bottom of the well, respectively, through the finite difference modeling. In the LWD model of the heterogeneous formation in front of the drill bit with infinite borehole, the reflect collar waves were received, revealing that the energy of the collar wave could propagate along the well. According to the simulation results, we suggested one install the receivers below the transmitter, which was better for separation of the direct waves and reflect waves by the *f-k* filtering.

Keywords: Logging while drilling; acoustic logging; finite difference in time domain.

1. Introduction

Acoustic logging while drilling (LWD) is a rapidly developing measurement technique for oil reservoir exploration nowadays. As one of the most advanced technologies used in exploration geophysics and petroleum engineering, it can provide elastic parameters of the formation in real-time drilling (Aron et al., 1997). With the increasing demands for LWD as well as the acoustic geo-steering, it is essential to develop the imaging techniques for near-borehole structures. Tang and Cheng (2007) pointed out the feasibility and potential application value of geo-steering using acoustic LWD data. Chen et al. (2012) ,Wang et al. (2014), Wang et al. (2015), Cao et al. (2016) did the relevant simulations using different sources. Nevertheless, previous scholars mainly focused on the measurement of formation acoustic velocity and the propagation of mode waves in LWD. Therefore, infinitely long borehole models are generally adopted, ignoring the influence of bottom hole and drill bit.

In this paper, mode conversion between collar and Stoneley waves is analyzed, because of the existing of the bottom of the borehole. In the numerical simulation example, the infinite borehole and the finite borehole in the homogeneous formation are compared, and the reflection characteristics generated by the bottom of the well are quantitatively analyzed. Secondly, heterogeneous formation with horizontal hard formation in front of the drill bit is simulated. We aim at revealing mode conversion between collar and Stoneley waves. And the energy of the collar propagating along the formation around the well which can reflect at the interface is also proved.

2. Fundamental principles of remote acoustic LWD

The acoustic logging model can be described by a radio acoustic model. Figure 1 is a schematic diagram of an acoustic logging while drilling. Conventional acoustic logging method uses wellbore refracted waves and guided waves to measure formation parameters propagating along the borehole, including refracted (sliding) formation longitudinal waves, refracted (sliding) formation transverse waves, and guided waves (pseudo Rayleigh wave and Stoneley wave). Later, far-detected acoustic logging was developed, not only using waves propagating at the interface, but also the source in the well radiating P and S wave deep into the formation surrounding the wellbore. These outwardly radiated energy can be reflected back into the well by the acoustic impedance discontinuous interface beside the well or refracted back into the well by mode switching and received by the receiving probe. The acoustic impedance discontinuous interface or reflective interface may be due to cracks, salt domes, or formation interfaces in the ground. By receiving and processing these reflected signals and mode-switching signals, the orientation and position of the reflector can be obtained, so that the formation cracks can be evaluated and even small geologic structures can be imaged. Apply this far-detection technique to the environment of acoustic LWD, as shown in Fig. 1. Below the acoustic emission transducer is a drill bit that is in contact with the bottom of the well. Then, the acoustic signal emitted by the transmitting transducer is reflected at the bottom of the well, and the resulting bottom reflection response affects the signal of the formation reflection wave and the well detection signal in front of the drill bit.

It's difficult to calculate the LWD model with geological interface beside the borehole by an analytical method, and the finite difference (FD) method is a useful tool for seismic wave propagation modeling(Wang and Tang, 2003; Huang, 2003; Sinha et al., 2009; Yang et al., 2016). Due to the cylindrical structure of the wellbore, the calculation using the cylindrical coordinate system is more direct and natural. The three-dimensional problem can be simplified into a two-dimensional problem when the acoustic field is axisymmetric especially, thereby greatly improving the calculation efficiency. Therefore, in this paper, the two-dimensional cylindrical coordinate finite difference method is used to simulate to reduce the calculation amount and operation time. The LWD model can be described by a cylindrical radial layered model, as shown in Figure 2. The media in the radial direction from the inside to the outside are the inner fluid layer (water), the drill collar layer (steel), the outer fluid layer (water) and the formation. The formation outside the wellbore is an infinite solid medium. The drill collar is located in the center of the wellbore, and the lower part is in contact with the bottom of the well. The inner and outer spaces of the drill collar are filled with water. The media parameters are shown in Table 1 and Table 2.

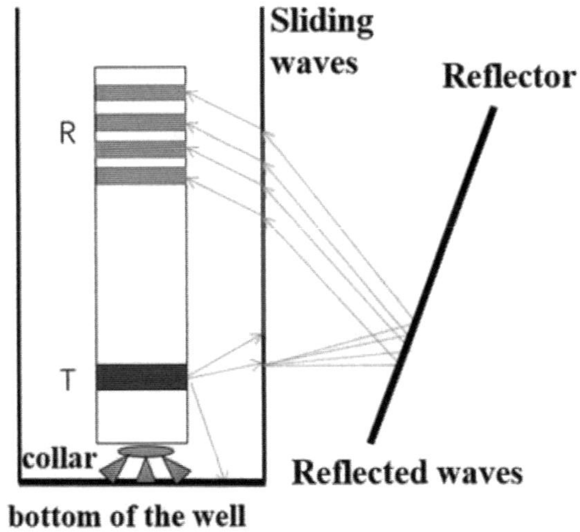

Fig. 1. Schematic diagram of the sonic logging model while drilling.

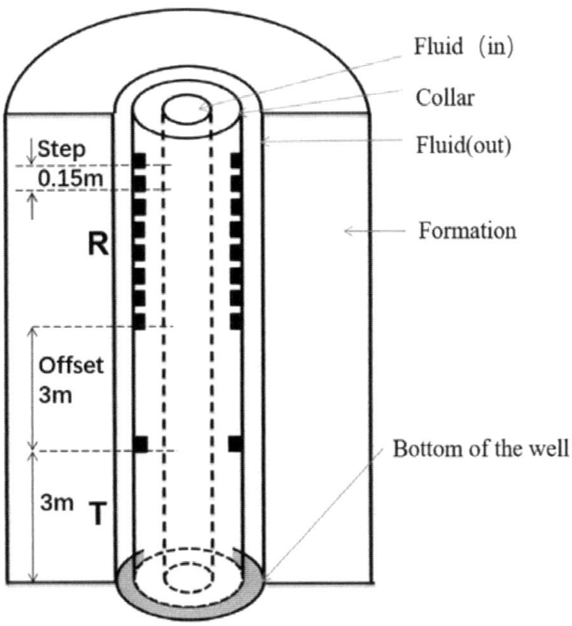

Fig. 2. Radial stratification of the well.

Table 1. Stratigraphic parameters

Parameters	P-wave velocity (m/s)	S-wave velocity (m/s)	Density (kg/m^3)
Formation 1	2500	1800	2320
Formation 2	5200	3800	2600

Table 2. Parameters of the internal and external fluids of the drill collar and the drill collar

Parameters	P-wave velocity (m/s)	S-wave velocity (m/s)	Density (kg/m^3)	Outer radius (m)
Internal fluid	1600	0	1000	0.025
Drill collar	5900	3220	7800	0.09
External fluid	1600	0	1000	0.12

3. Simulation Results

3.1. Simulation Results of Homogenous Medium

In order to study the characteristics of the bottom reflection and the reflection response of the pre-drilling formation, it is explored whether the reflection at the bottom of the well will affect the effective signal of the far-detection. This paper simulates two sets of models as shown in Fig. 3. Model A is a model used by previous researchers to study the remote exploration while drilling. The wellbore and the drill collar are infinitely long, and the wellbore formation is homogeneous. The media parameters are shown in Table 1. In contrast, the model B is closer to the real environment of the acoustic LWD, the emission source is 3m from the bottom of the well, the well formation is also a uniform formation, and the medium parameter is the parameter of the formation 1.

In order to analyze of the response due to the action of the bottom hole, the model B and the received waveform of the model A are subtracted, the resulting waveform is the response generated by the bottom of the well, as shown in Fig. 4. Combined with the above analysis, a, c, and d are the reflected borehole waves generated by the drilling and boring waves reflected at the bottom of the well, and the internal and external Stoneley waves are reflected. It can be analyzed that the drill wave propagates outward while continuously scattering, and once it reaches the discontinuous interface of the bottom of the well, it will produce reflection. Any point of reflection can be seen as a new "scattering sound source" and can generate drill collar waves, (internal and external) Stoneley waves into the well. Similarly, the Stoneley wave propagates along the fluid-solid interface and reaches the discontinuous interface at the bottom of the well. It can also be regarded as a “scattering sound source”, and can also stimulate the reflected drilling wave in the well (b), (inside and outside) Stoneley wave (e, f).

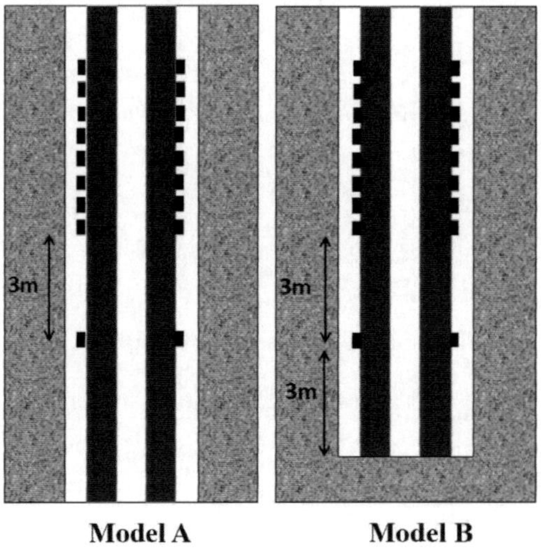

Fig. 3. Comparison models with infinite and finite borehole in homogenous formation.

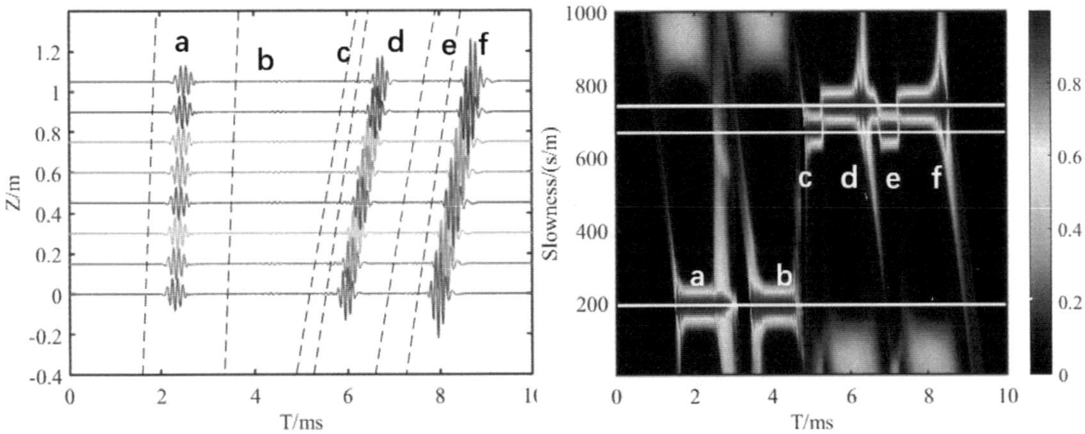

Fig.4. Reflection analysis of the well bottom.

3.2. Simulation Results of Heterogeneous Medium

Figure 5 shows the acoustic reflection LWD model, with discontinuous formation in front of the drill bit. There is a high velocity hard formation below as shown in the model C, and the acoustic signal will reflect when it encounters the interface. The comparison of the received waveform with slowness-time coherence process (STC) (Kimball and Marzetta, 1984) of model C is shown in Fig. 6. Combined with velocity analysis, a, b are direct drilling waves and Stoneley waves, c is the external Stoneley wave generated by the drilling wave reflection in the formation, and d is the Stoneley wave generated by Stoneley wave reflection in the formation. The parameters are shown in the parameters of the formation 2 in Table 1. As a comparison, the model D has both the bottom of the well and the formation interface with discontinuous wave impedance. The distance between the source and the bottom of the well is 3m. By subtracting the received waveform of model C from the received waveform of the same parametric model in a uniform formation, the reflected response of the well-site interface can be obtained. Comparing the bottom hole reflection wave in model D with the reflected wave at the well perimeter interface, the influence of the bottom hole on the well detection can be discussed.

In the model D, both the well bottom and the formation interface generate reflect waves, and the comparison of the received waveform and the STC is shown in Fig. 7. a, c are direct collar wave and Stoneley wave, b, d, e, f, g, h are the bottom hole reflected waves. Here, i and j are the reflected waves generated by the formation, which are caused by the internal and external Stoneley waves. Comparing the STC graphs of Fig. 6 and Fig. 7, it can be found that there is only the out-Stoneley wave in the STC diagram of the model C, and there is no in-Stoneley wave. The second model D generate both in-Stoneley and out-Stoneley wave.

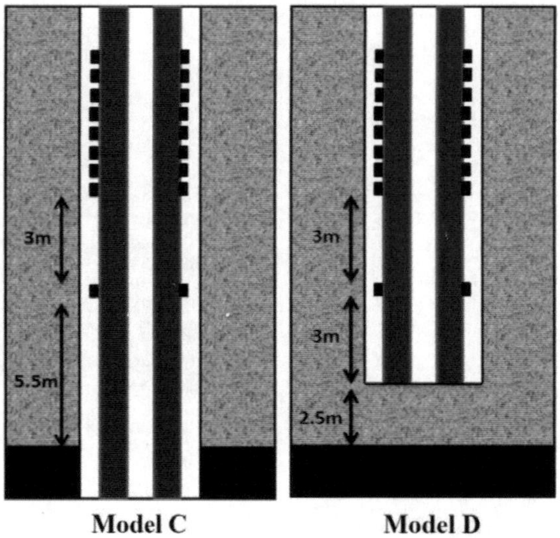

Fig. 5. Comparison models with infinite and finite borehole in heterogeneous formation.

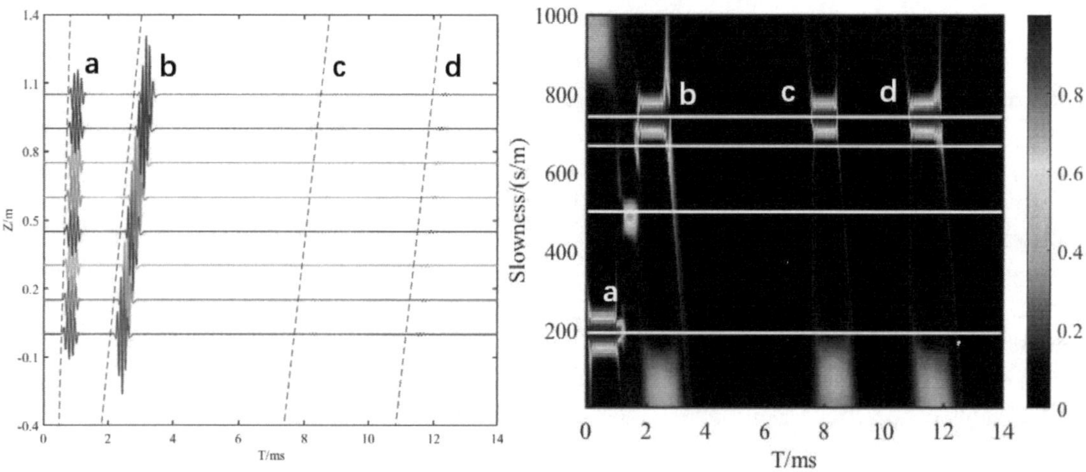

Fig. 6. Waveform and STC diagram of model C.

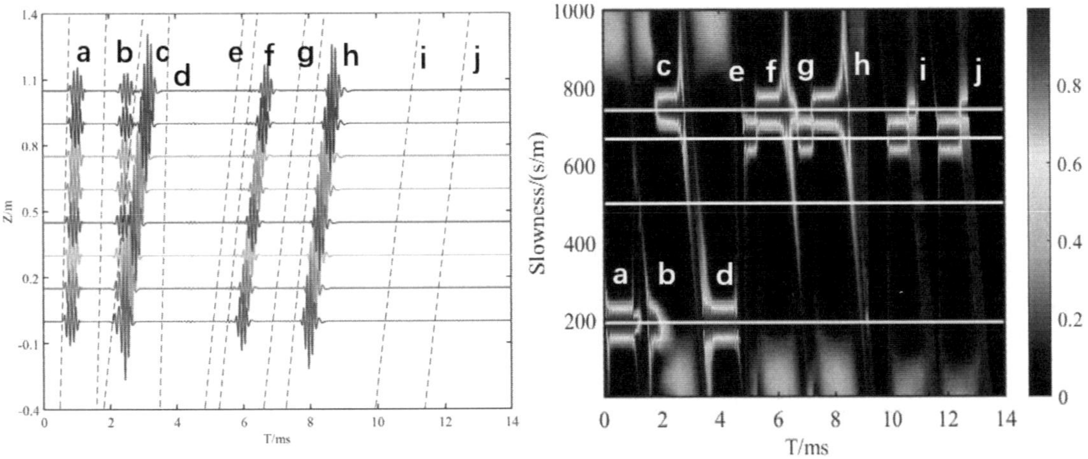

Fig. 7. Waveform and STC diagram of model D.

4. Conclusions

In this paper, the 2D FDTD is implemented to simulate the acoustic fields of LWD models, and the influence of bottom reflection on the pre-drilling formation detection is discussed. The main conclusions are as follows:

1. The collar wave and Stoneley wave spread along the wellbore, each of which will separately generate strong reflection of the Stoneley wave and the collar wave at the bottom of the well. The bottom of the well can be equivalent to new scattering sources, which can generate collar waves and Stoneley waves propagating backwards.
2. During propagation, the energy of the collar wave is continuously leaking outwards. It can be proved that parts of the energy radiate the formation and reflect at a discontinuous interface.
3. It is recommended that for the acoustic LWD tools, installing the transmitters above the receiver arrays is an optimized design to reduce the effect of well bottom reflection.

Acknowledgments

This study is supported by the National Natural Science Foundation of China (Grant Nos. 11774373, 11734017, and 11574347).

References

[1] Aron, J., S. Chang, D. Codazzi, R. Dworak, K. Hsu, T. Lau, G. Minerbo, and E. Yogeswaren, "Real-time sonic logging while drilling in hard and soft rocks," *Presented at SPWLA 38th Annual Logging Symposium*, 1997.

[2] Byun J., Toksöz M. N., "Analysis of the Acoustic Wavefields Excited by the Logging-While-Drilling (LWD) Tool," *Geosystem Engineering,* 2003, **6**(1): 19-25.

[3] Cao J. J., Tang X. M., Su Y. D., et al., "Radiation characteristics of the single-well imaging field in while-drilling logging using an acoustic dipole source," *Chinese J. Geophys,* (in Chinese), 2016, **59**(09):3503-3513.

[4] Chen X. L., Wei Z. T., "Numerical simulation of single-pole acoustic reflection logging while drilling", *Acta Petrolei Sinica,* (in Chinese), 2012, **33**(5): 835-840.

[5] Cui Z. W., *Theoretical and numerical study of modified Biot's models, acoustoelectric well logging and acoustic logging while drilling excited by multipole acoustic sources*: PhD Thesis, Jilin University, 2004.

[6] Huang X. J., *Effects of tool positions on borehole acoustic measurements: A stretched grid finite difference approach*: PhD Thesis, Massachusetts Institute of Technology, 2003.

[7] He X., Hu H. S., Guan W., "Fast and slow flexural waves in a deviated borehole in homogeneous and layered anisotropic formations," *Geophysical Journal International*, 2010, **181**(1): 417-426.

[8] He X., *Simulations of acoustic logs in transversely isotropic formations and researches on permeability inversion*: PhD Thesis, Harbin Institute of Technology, 2010.

[9] He X., Wang X. M., Chen H., "Theoretical simulations of wave field variation excited by a monopole within collar for acoustic logging while drilling," *Wave Motion*, 2017, **72**:287-302.

[10] Kimball C. V., Marzetta T. L., "Semblance processing of borehole acoustic array data," *Geophysics*, 1984, **49**(3):274-281.

[11] Sinha B. K., Simsek E., Asvadurov S., "Influence of a pipe tool on borehole modes," *Geophysics*, 2009, **74**(3): E111-E123.

[12] Tang, X.M., Zheng, Y., Patterson, D., 2007, "Processing array acoustic-logging data to image near-borehole geologic structures," *Geophysics*, **72** (2), E87–E97.

[13] Wang R. J., Qiao W. X., "Numerical simulation of 3D Drilling Acoustic Imaging Logging," *Chinese J. Geophys*, (in Chinese) , 2015, **58**(6): 2201-2209.

[14] Wang R. J., Qiao W. X., Che X. H., "A phased arc array acoustic LWD transmitter constructed by arcuate piezoelectric vibrators," *Chinese J. Geophys*, (in Chinese) , 2015, **58**(1): 327-337.

[15] Wang T., Tang X. M., "LWD Finite-difference Modeling of elastic wave propagation: A nonsplitting perfectly matched layer approach," Geophysics, 2003, 68(5):1749-1755.

[16] Yang Y. F., Guan W., Cui N. G., et al., "FDTD simulation and analysis of the collar wave propagation in acoustic logging while drilling," Chinese J. Geophys, (in Chinese), 2016, 59(1):368-380.

Anisotropy Inversion Using a Small-diameter Acoustic Logging Tool with Separated Cross-dipole Sources

CHAO LI[1,2], HAO CHEN[1,2], XIAO HE[1,2], XIU-MING WANG[1,2], FU-QIANG ZENG[3]

1, Beijing Engineering and Technology Research Center for Deep Drilling Exploration and Measurement, No. 21 North 4th Ring Road, Haidian District, Beijing, 100190, China
chaoli@mail.ioa.ac.cn
2, State Key Laboratory of Acoustics, Institute of Acoustics, Chinese Academy of Sciences,
No. 21 North 4th Ring Road, Haidian District, Beijing, 100190, China
3, State Key Laboratory of Petroleum Resources and Prospecting, China University of Petroleum-Beijing,
No.18 Fuxue Road, Changping District, Beijing, 102249, China

Cross-dipole acoustic logging is commonly used to obtain the azimuth anisotropy in the HTI (Horizontal Transverse Isotropy) formation. We develop an anisotropy inversion method for a small-diameter acoustic logging tool without the two dipole sources assembling in the same position. Additionally, the unmatched property of the fast and slow flexural waves caused by the transmitter and formation is considered. An objective function in frequency domain in consideration of the source-receiver spacing and wave amplitude difference is constructed. Firstly, four-component cross-dipole acoustic logging responses with different source-receiver spacing and source signals are simulated in HTI medium. Then the fast and slow flexural wave slowness and azimuth are inverted with a single dipole source and two separated cross-dipole sources respectively. The results using a single dipole source show that it can acquire anisotropy under favorable conditions. The joint inversion with two separated cross-dipole sources can achieve more accurate results. Finally, the method is used in field data processing which further testify its effectiveness. Therefore, an anisotropy inversion method for separated cross-dipole sources is developed, which could be used both for small-diameter tool and other tools without requiring the cross-dipole sources are collocated.

Keywords: anisotropy inversion; acoustic logging; cross dipole; separated sources.

1. Introduction

Anisotropy is widely existing in the sedimentary rocks. Cross-dipole acoustic logging is commonly used to obtain the azimuth anisotropy in the HTI (Horizontal Transverse Isotropy) formation [1-4]. Since slim hole drilling technology has been utilized in oil and mining industry, the corresponding diameter of logging devices should also be reduced. In such cases, it would be a challenge to design a cross-dipole acoustic logging tool with the two dipole sources assembling in the same position.

In this research, we develop an anisotropy inversion method for a small-diameter acoustic logging tool with separated cross-dipole sources. Additionally, the unmatched property of the fast and slow flexural waves caused by the transmitter and formation is considered. An objective function in frequency domain in consideration of the source-receiver spacing and wave amplitude difference is constructed. The method is used in both synthetic and field data processing to testify its effectiveness. Therefore, an anisotropy inversion method for separated cross-dipole sources is developed, which could be used both for small-diameter tool and other tools without requiring the cross-dipole sources are collocated.

2. Method

The schematic diagram of cross-dipole acoustic logging in HTI formation with separated sources is shown in Fig. (1). The cross-dipole acoustic logging includes two orthogonal dipole sources X and Y and two corresponding receiver arrays. In HTI medium, the X-source emit dipole acoustic wave and it will split into the fast-flexural wave and the slow- flexural wave respectively when the source X have an angle θ related to the fast wave symmetric axis of HTI. Then the fast and slow flexural wave will be projected back to the X receiver and named as XX component. Similar principle can be used to obtain the XY, YX and YY components, which are generally called the four components data.

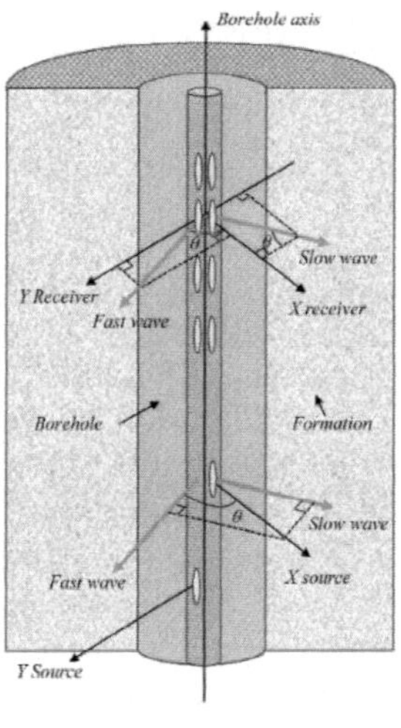

Fig. 1. Schematic diagram of a small-diameter acoustic logging tool with separated cross-dipole sources.

Similar to the time domain method [3], the four components of cross-dipole acoustic logging in frequency domain can be written as follows [4],

$$\begin{cases} U_{XX}(z_n,\omega) = S_X(\omega)G_f(z_n,\omega)\cos^2(\theta) + S_X(\omega)G_s(z_n,\omega)\sin^2(\theta) \\ U_{XY}(z_n,\omega) = \left(S_X(\omega)G_f(z_n,\omega) - S_X(\omega)G_s(z_n,\omega)\right)\sin(\theta)\cos(\theta) \\ U_{YX}(z_n,\omega) = \left(S_Y(\omega)G_f(z_n,\omega) - S_Y(\omega)G_s(z_n,\omega)\right)\sin(\theta)\cos(\theta) \\ U_{YY}(z_n,\omega) = S_Y(\omega)G_f(z_n,\omega)\sin^2(\theta) + S_Y(\omega)G_s(z_n,\omega)\cos^2(\theta) \end{cases}, \tag{2.1}$$

Where $S_X(\omega)$ and $S_Y(\omega)$ are the frequency spectrum for X and Y source respectively. Unlike the time domain method which need the two dipole sources are identical, the frequency domain method can deal with the difference of them. Then the fast and slow wave for them can be obtained,

$$\begin{cases} U_{X,f}(z_n,\omega)=U_{XX}(z_n,\omega)+U_{XY}(z_n,\omega)\tan(\theta) \\ U_{X,s}(z_n,\omega)=U_{XX}(z_n,\omega)-U_{XY}(z_n,\omega)\cot(\theta) \\ U_{Y,f}(z_n,\omega)=U_{YY}(z_n,\omega)+U_{YX}(z_n,\omega)\cot(\theta) \\ U_{Y,s}(z_n,\omega)=U_{YY}(z_n,\omega)-U_{YX}(z_n,\omega)\tan(\theta) \end{cases}, \tag{2.2}$$

The objective function for X and Y source are written as

$$Obj\left(v_f(\omega),v_s(\omega),\theta(\omega)\right)=\sum_{m,n}\left\|U_{X,f}(z_{X,m},\omega)/g_f(z_{X,m},\omega)-U_{X,s}(z_{X,n},\omega)/g_s(z_{X,n},\omega)\right\|^2, \tag{2.3}$$

$$Obj\left(v_f(\omega),v_s(\omega),\theta(\omega)\right)=\sum_{m,n}\left\|U_{Y,f}(z_{Y,m},\omega)/g_f(z_{Y,m},\omega)-U_{Y,s}(z_{Y,n},\omega)/g_s(z_{Y,n},\omega)\right\|^2, \tag{2.4}$$

Where g_f and g_s are the propagation functions, and the source to receiver spacing (TR) for X and Y is z_X and z_Y respectively. Considering the amplitude difference between the fast and slow wave and the two dipole sources, the AR (amplitude ratio) function is defined [4],

$$AR_X(\omega)=\sum_n abs\left(U_{X,s}(z_n,\omega)\right)\Big/\sum_n abs\left(U_{X,f}(z_n,\omega)\right), \tag{2.5}$$

This function is defined for source X and similar form for source Y can also be obtained. The average function for them is written as

$$\overline{AR}(\omega)=\frac{1}{2}\left(AR_X(\omega)+AR_Y(\omega)\right), \tag{2.6}$$

The joint objective function of X and Y source is defined as

$$Obj\left(v_f(\omega),v_s(\omega),\theta(\omega)\right)=\sum_{m,n}\left(\|C\|/\|D\|\right)^2+\sum_{m,n}\left(\|E\|/\|F\|\right)^2, \tag{2.7}$$

$$\begin{cases} C=\overline{AR}(\omega)U_{X,f}(z_{X,m},\omega)/g_f(z_{X,m},\omega)-U_{X,s}(z_{X,n},\omega)/g_s(z_{X,n},\omega) \\ D=\overline{AR}(\omega)U_{X,f}(z_{X,m},\omega)/g_f(z_{X,m},\omega)\cos^2(\theta)+U_{X,s}(z_{X,n},\omega)/g_s(z_{X,n},\omega)\sin^2(\theta) \\ E=\overline{AR}(\omega)U_{Y,f}(z_{Y,m},\omega)/g_f(z_{Y,m},\omega)-U_{Y,s}(z_{Y,n},\omega)/g_s(z_{Y,n},\omega) \\ F=\overline{AR}(\omega)U_{Y,f}(z_{Y,m},\omega)/g_f(z_{Y,m},\omega)\sin^2(\theta)+U_{Y,s}(z_{Y,n},\omega)/g_s(z_{Y,n},\omega)\cos^2(\theta) \end{cases} \tag{2.8}$$

3. Synthetic Examples

A time domain finite difference method is used to simulate the acoustic responses of cross-dipole acoustic logging in HTI formation (c11, c12, c22, c44 and c55 are 25.59, 3.13, 43.45, 12.9 and 11.23 GPa respectively). To simulate the worst situation, two different source functions are used. As shown in Fig. (2), the amplitude of two sources are normalized.

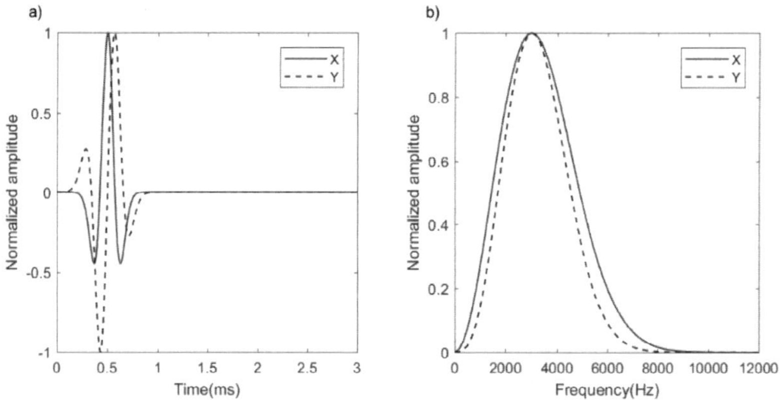

Fig. 2. (a) X and Y source signals and (b) their frequency spectrum.

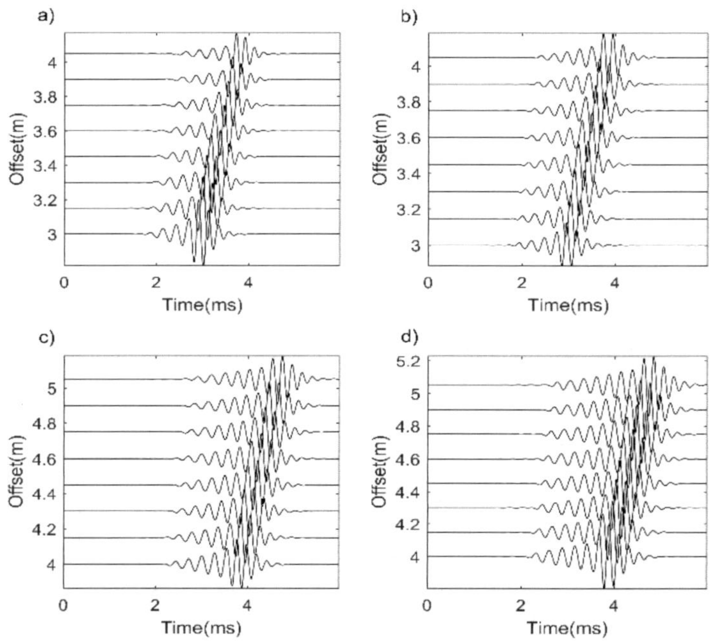

Fig. 3. Synthetic four component waveforms. (a) and (b) are XX and XY waves (TR=3m). (c) and (d) are YX and YY waves (TR=4m).

The four component waveforms are shown in Fig. (3), different waveform characteristics can be observed because different source functions and different source to receiver spacing are used. The inversion results using Eq. (2.3), (2.4) and (2.7) are plotted together in Fig. (4). The results indicate that both the X and Y source waveforms can be used for inversion but the joint inversion result is more accurate and stable.

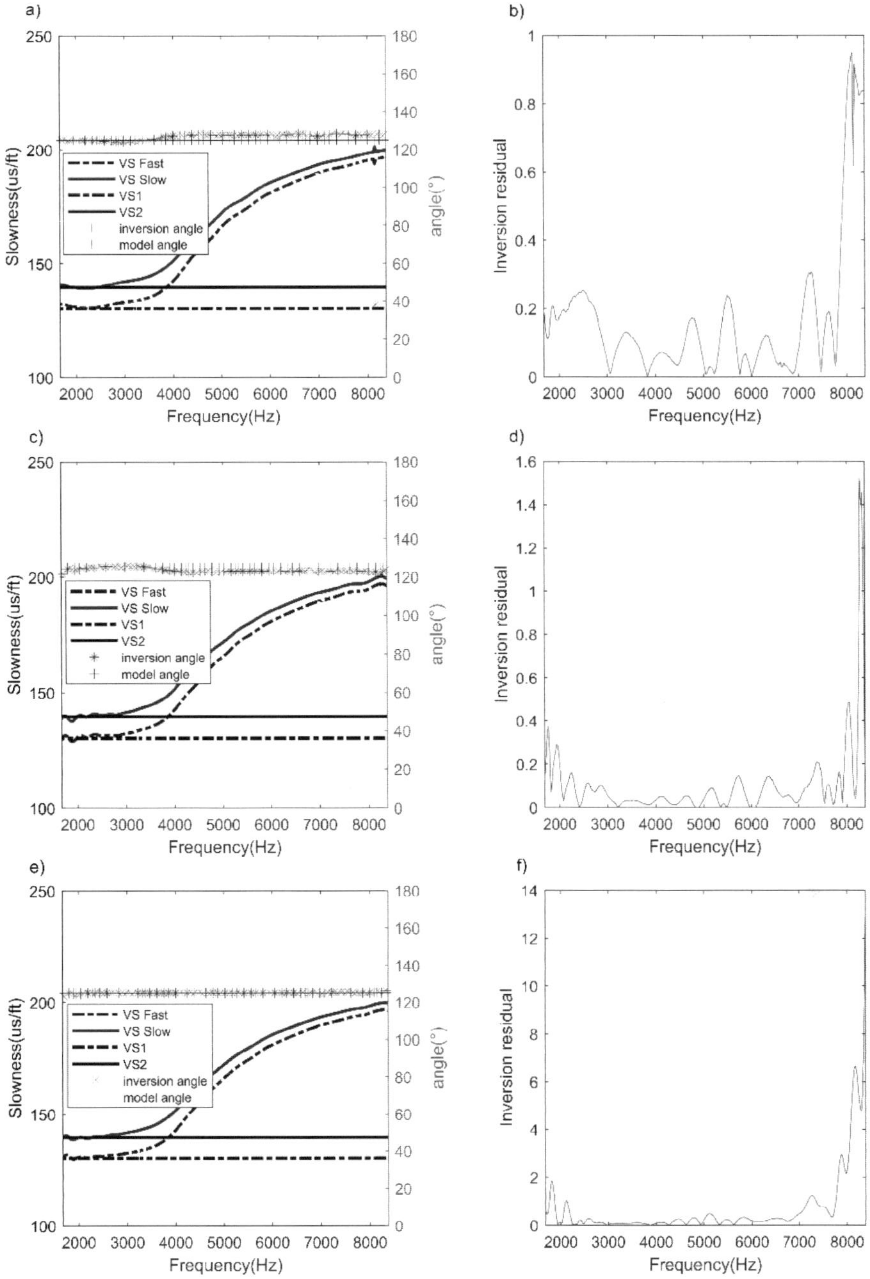

Fig. 4. The inversion results with different objective functions. (a) and (b) are the result and inversion residual using Eq. (2.3). (c), (d) and (e), (f) are the results using Eq. (2.4) and (2.7) respectively.

The inversion residual in (b), (d) and (f) of Fig. (4) can also be used as a quality indicator for the inversion.

4. Field Data Examples

A field data example is shown in Fig. (5) to testify the applicability of the method. Although the high frequency dispersion curve is distorted due to the existing of noise, the low frequency slowness and inverted anisotropic azimuth is flat and stable.

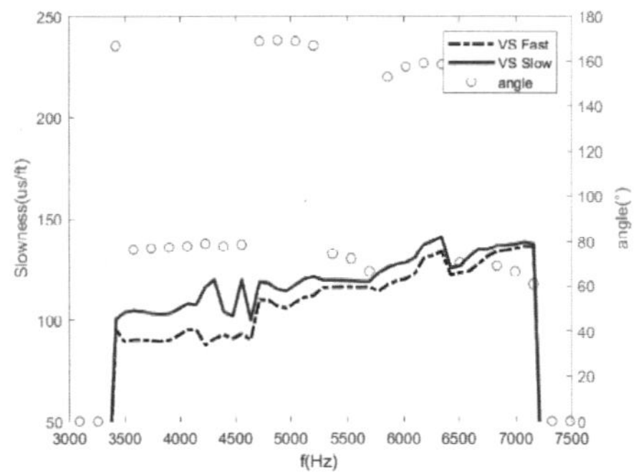

Fig. 5. Field data inversion result.

5. Conclusions

An anisotropy inversion method for a small-diameter acoustic logging tool with separated cross-dipole sources is developed, which could be used both for small-diameter tool and other tools without requiring the cross-dipole sources are collocated. The unmatched property of the fast and slow flexural waves caused by the transmitter and formation is considered. An objective function in frequency domain in consideration of the source-receiver spacing and wave amplitude difference is constructed. The results using a single dipole source indicate it can acquire anisotropy under favorable conditions. The inversion with two separated cross-dipole sources can achieve more accurate results.

Acknowledgments

This work is supported by the National Natural Science Foundation of China (Grant No. 11774373, 11734017, 11574347 and 91630309).

References

[1] Alford, R. M., "*Shear data in the presence of azimuthal anisotropy*", 56th Annual International Meeting, SEG Technical Program Expanded Abstracts, 1986, 476–479.

[2] Bose, S., Sinha, B.K., Sunaga, S., Endo, T., and Valero, H.P., "*Anisotropy processing without matched cross-dipole transmitters*", 77th Annual International Meeting, SEG Technical Program Expanded Abstracts, 2007, 114-118.

[3] Tang, X. M., and R. K. Chunduru, "*Simultaneous inversion of formation shear-wave anisotropy parameters from cross-dipole acoustic-array waveform data*", Geophysics 64, 1999, 1502–1511.

[4] Zeng F., Yue W., Li C., "*Anisotropy inversion in the frequency domain for flexural waves with unmatched sources*", IEEE Geoscience and Remote Sensing Letters, 2018, no.10, 1530-1534.

Asymptotic ray tracing on seismic velocity models parameterized by sigmoidal shape functions for wave propagation modeling

SAULO P. OLIVEIRA[1,*], JUAREZ S. AZEVEDO[2], WILSON M. FIGUEIRÓ[3], RODRIGO A. GUIMARÃES[1], ANDRESSA DE OLIVEIRA[1], WINICIUS J. SILVA[1]

1, Centro Politécnico, Universidade Federal do Paraná
Curitiba-PR, 81531-980, Brazil
saulopo@ufpr.br, rodrigo98ag@gmail.com, andressa.obmep@gmail.com; winiciusgeo@gmail.com

2, Instituto de Ciências, Tecnologia e Inovação, Universidade Federal da Bahia
Camaçari-BA, 42802-721, Brazil
jdazevedo@ufba.br

3, Instituto de Geociências, Universidade Federal da Bahia
Salvador-BA, 40170-115, Brazil
figueiro@ufba.br

Acoustic modeling methods based on asymptotic ray theory have a lower computational cost than full wave-equation methods but require a smooth velocity field, though discontinuities may be handled by imposing reflection and transmission conditions across the interfaces. We propose to approximate discontinuous velocity fields with model parameterizations based on smooth, rapidly varying functions known as sigmoidal functions. We have implemented the proposed technique on rectangular grids using the wavelet theory formalism. Numerical experiments with two-dimensional, initial-value ray tracing in layered structures illustrate the proposed approach.

Keywords: Ray tracing; sigmoidal functions; velocity field parameterization.

1. Introduction

Numerical methods based on asymptotic ray theory are useful tools for qualitative modeling of wave propagation phenomena [2]. These methods usually have a lower computational cost than others based on a full wave-equation, such as finite-difference and finite-element methods. On the other hand, they are very sensitive to the velocity field representation.

In particular, ray tracing is not a trivial task in complex, discontinuous velocity fields. Perhaps the best currently available approach in this case is to proceed as follows: 1) decompose the velocity field into subdomains such that the velocity is smooth within each subdomain; 2) starting from a source point, perform ray tracing until the ray strikes an interface; 3) through a reflection, transmission, or conversion condition, establish an initial condition for the continuation of ray propagation in the same subdomain or in the outer, adjacent subdomain; 4) repeat steps 2 and 3 until the ray reaches the global model boundary, or until some other stopping criteria is met. Such an approach becomes cumbersome when a large number of subdomains is needed to represent the velocity field.

There have been efforts to develop globally smooth models that are capable of representing complex velocity fields. One of the earliest approaches in this direction was the generalized smoothing cubic spline technique [8]. Later on, B-spline [7] and natural spline [1] interpolation have also been considered. Other approaches involve least-squares fitting, for instance locally weighted regression [4] and global polynomial fitting [9].

In this paper, we parameterize velocity fields by sigmoidal functions [3] that allows sharp variations of material properties without losing continuity and does not need domain decomposition. As in wavelet theory, the basis functions are generated by scaling and shifting a single sigmoidal function (except at the borders), leading to simple velocity field models in one-dimensional and rectangular grids.

2. Ray tracing

Let us consider the following Hamiltonian system from asymptotic ray theory [2] for two-dimensional acoustic wave propagation:

$$\begin{cases} \frac{d\boldsymbol{x}}{ds} = \frac{1}{|\boldsymbol{p}|}\boldsymbol{p}, \\ \frac{d\boldsymbol{p}}{ds} = \nabla\left(\frac{1}{V(\boldsymbol{x})}\right), \\ \frac{dT}{ds} = \frac{1}{V(\boldsymbol{x})}. \end{cases} \tag{2.1}$$

Herein, $\boldsymbol{x}(s) = [x(s), z(s)]$ denotes the position of the ray trajectory, while $\boldsymbol{p}(s) = [p_1(s), p_2(s)]$ represents the slowness vector, and $T(s)$ is the travel time, parameterized by the arc length s along the ray. Vector $\boldsymbol{p}$ is related to the velocity field through the eikonal equation $|\boldsymbol{p}|^2 = 1/V^2(\boldsymbol{x})$. System (2.1) can be written in vector form as

$$\frac{d\boldsymbol{y}}{ds} = \boldsymbol{f}(s, \boldsymbol{y}(s)), \tag{2.2}$$

where $\boldsymbol{y} = [x, z, p_1, p_2, T]$, $\boldsymbol{f} = [p_1/|\boldsymbol{p}|, p_2/|\boldsymbol{p}|, -\partial_x V/V^2, -\partial_z V/V^2, 1/V]$, while $\partial_x V$ and $\partial_z V$ are the partial derivatives of V with respect to x and z, respectively. We discretize system (2.2) using the fourth-order Runge-Kutta method with step length Δs, finding $\boldsymbol{y}(n\Delta s) \approx \boldsymbol{y}_n$, where

$$\boldsymbol{y}_{n+1} = \boldsymbol{y}_n + \frac{1}{6}(\boldsymbol{k}_1 + 2\boldsymbol{k}_2 + 2\boldsymbol{k}_3 + \boldsymbol{k}_4), \tag{2.3}$$

$$\begin{cases} \boldsymbol{k}_1 = \Delta s \boldsymbol{f}(s_n, \boldsymbol{y}_n), \\ \boldsymbol{k}_2 = \Delta s \boldsymbol{f}\left(s_n + \frac{1}{2}\Delta s, \boldsymbol{y}_n + \frac{1}{2}\boldsymbol{k}_1\right), \\ \boldsymbol{k}_3 = \Delta s \boldsymbol{f}\left(s_n + \frac{1}{2}\Delta s, \boldsymbol{y}_n + \frac{1}{2}\boldsymbol{k}_2\right), \\ \boldsymbol{k}_4 = \Delta s \boldsymbol{f}(s_n + \Delta s, \boldsymbol{y}_n + \boldsymbol{k}_3). \end{cases} \tag{2.4}$$

For the initial condition we assume the ray leaves a source point located at $\boldsymbol{x}_s = [x_s, z_s]$ with take-off angle θ with respect to the z-axis, i.e., $\boldsymbol{y}_0 = [x_s, z_s, \sin(\theta)/V_0, \cos(\theta)/V_0, 0]$, where $V_0 = V(\boldsymbol{x}_s)$ [2, Sec. 3.2.1].

3. Model Parameterization

Let us first describe the sigmoidal parameterization in one spatial dimension, which provides the key ingredients for more general cases. We define the sigmoidal functions

$$\phi_L(x) = \frac{e^{-a(x-1)}}{1+e^{-a(x-1)}},\quad \phi(x) = \frac{1}{1+e^{-ax}} - \frac{1}{1+e^{-a(x-1)}},\quad \phi_R(x) = \frac{1}{1+e^{-ax}} \tag{3.1}$$

where the parameter a controls the transition between plateaus, which may be smooth or sharp if a is small or large, as shown in Fig. (1).

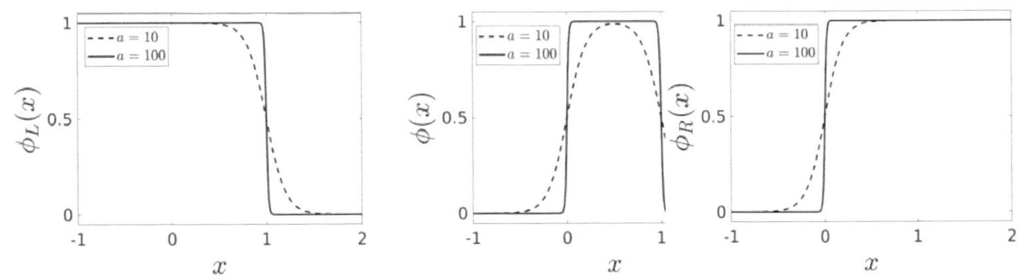

Fig. 1. Sigmoidal functions ϕ_L (left), ϕ (center), and ϕ_R (right) with slope parameters $a = 10$ and $a = 100$.

Noting that $\phi(x)$ resembles the Haar scaling function $\phi_H(x) = \chi_{[0,1)}(x)$, where $\chi_I(x)$ is the characteristic function over the interval I, we borrow from wavelet theory the idea of decomposing a signal into a sum of scaled and shifted versions of a generating function, usually the scaling or the mother wavelet [5]. In particular, let $z_n = nh$ with $0 \leq n \leq N$ and $h=L/N$ define a grid over the domain $[0,L]$ and let $v(z)$ be a piecewise-constant function defined as $v(z)=v_n$ for $z \in [z_n,z_{n+1})$ and $0 \leq n \leq N-1$. We approximate $v(z)$ as follows:

$$\tilde{v}(z) = \sum_{n=0}^{N-1} v_n \phi_n\left(\frac{z}{h} - n\right),\quad \phi_n(z) = \begin{cases} \phi_L(z)\,, n = 0, \\ \phi(z)\ \ , 0 < n < N-1. \\ \phi_L(z)\,, n = N-1. \end{cases} \tag{3.2}$$

Functions ϕ_L and ϕ_R are suited to the left and right endpoints of the domain, respectively. As illustrated in Fig. (2), approximation (3.2) is convenient for representing velocity fields with abrupt changes. For practical calculations, $\phi_n(z/h-n)$ should decay to zero away from the interval $[z_n, z_{n+1}]$. To guarantee that

$$\phi_n\left(\frac{z}{h} - n\right) \leq \varepsilon,\quad z \notin [z_{n-1}, z_{n+2}], \tag{3.3}$$

i.e., if z is not in $[z_n, z_{n+1}]$ or the adjacent intervals, we impose $\phi_R(-1) \leq \varepsilon$, *i.e.*, $a \geq \ln(1/\varepsilon - 1)$. For instance, if the desired tolerance is $\varepsilon = 10^{-4}$, then one should use $a \approx 9$ or larger.

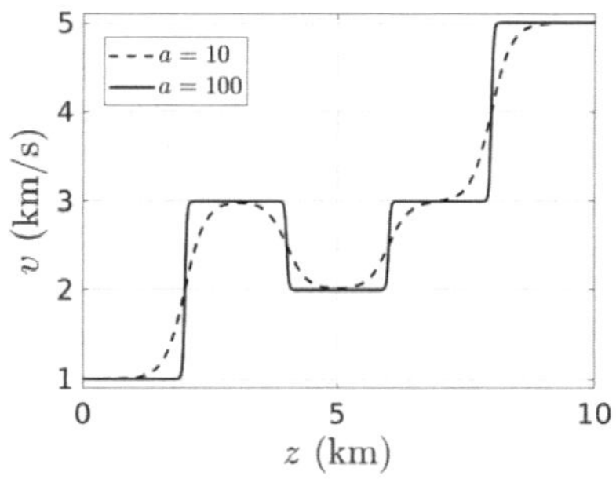

Fig. 2. Sigmoidal approximation of a 1D velocity field for $a = 10$ and a 100.

Approximation (3.2) can be easily extended to a rectangular domain $[0, L_x]\times[0, L_z]$ with grid points $(x_m, z_n) = (mh_x, nh_z)$, $0 \leq m \leq N_x$ and $0 \leq n \leq N_z$, by the following tensor-product expansion:

$$\tilde{v}(x,z) = \sum_{n=0}^{N_z-1} \sum_{m=0}^{N_x-1} v_{m,n}\phi_m\left(\frac{x}{h_x} - m\right)\phi_n\left(\frac{z}{h_z} - n\right). \tag{3.4}$$

By choosing a such that (3.3) holds with ε sufficiently small, we have that the above expansion can be approximated as follows:

$$\tilde{v}(x,z) \approx \sum_{i=-1}^{1} \sum_{j=-1}^{1} v_{m+i,n+j}\phi_{m+i}\left(\frac{x}{h_x} - (m+i)\right)\phi_{n+j}\left(\frac{z}{h_z} - (n+j)\right), \tag{3.5}$$

where $(x, z) \in [x_m, x_{m+1}]\times[z_n, z_{n+1}]$ and the summation limits may be modified to guarantee $0 \leq m+i \leq N_x$ and $0 \leq n+j \leq N_z$.

4. Results and discussion

The proposed parameterizations will now serve as input data to the ray tracing algorithm described in Section 2.

The first example emphasizes the relevance of handling discontinuities for ray tracing. Let us consider the elementary model of two horizontal layers of thickness L and velocities v_1 and v_2, with a single surface source at the origin. The velocity below the second layer is v_3. For simplicity, we consider the rays that (i) are reflected by the first interface and (ii) are first transmitted to the second layer and then reflected once, as depicted in Fig. (3).

For a take-off angle θ the rays in case (i) reach the surface at $x_r = 2L\tan(\theta)$ with travel time $T = 2L\sec(\theta)/v_1$, while in case (ii) they arrive at $x'_r = x_r + 2L\tan(\theta')$ with travel time $T = T + 2L\sec(\theta')/v_2$, where $\theta' = \sin^{-1}(\sin(\theta)\, v_2/v_1)$. The latter case is restricted to $\theta \leq \theta_c$, where $\theta_c = \sin^{-1}(v_2/v_1)$ is the critical angle.

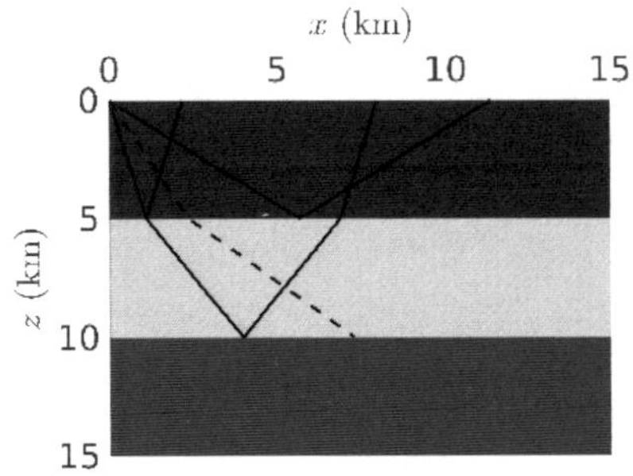

Fig. 3. A simple two-layer model with rays that are reflected by the first and second interfaces. The critical angles are indicated by dashed lines. The velocities are v_1=1.5 km/s in the first layer, v_2=3.5 km/s in the second layer, and v_3=5 km/s below the second layer.

Fig. (4) shows some of the ray paths and the travel times obtained with the representation of the velocity field shown in Fig. (3) by the sigmoidal expansion (3.5) with a =100. We have shot 200 rays with take-off angle θ uniformly distributed in [0, π/2[. The sigmoidal approach automatically selects either the transmitted of the reflected ray, depending approximately on the critical angle θ_c, and has been able to detect reflections from both the first and second layers.

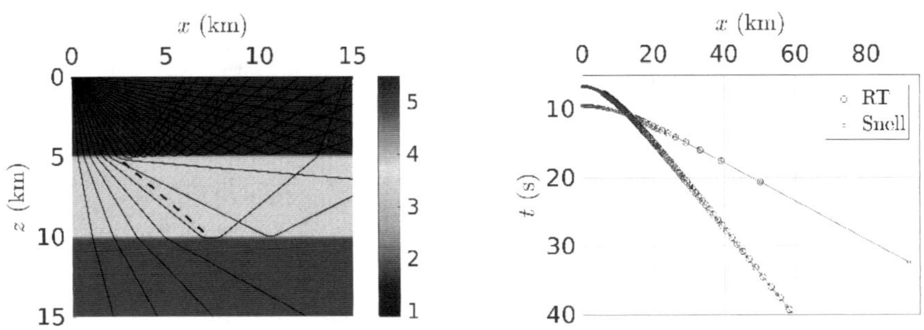

Fig. 4. Reflected P-wave rays (left) and travel times found by asymptotic ray tracing (RT) from sigmoidal models (right). The narrow and wide hyperbolas (Snell) are predicted travel times due to reflections by the first and second interfaces, respectively.

In the second experiment, we illustrate the sigmoidal representation of a laterally heterogeneous velocity field over a rectangular grid with 24×48 cells, shown in Fig. (5).

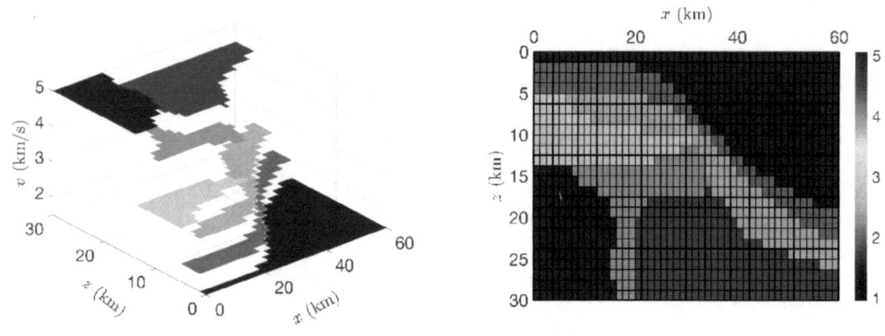

Fig. 5. A piecewise constant velocity model defined in a rectangular grid.

As in Figs. (1)-(2), we select the slope parameters $a = 10$ and $a = 100$, which lead to smoother and sharper models, respectively (Fig. (6)). The influence of the parameter a is further noted in Fig. (7), where 51 rays are traced with take-off angle θ uniformly distributed in $[-\pi/4, \pi/4[$ from a single surface source located at $x_s = 20$ km. The smoother model yields mostly curved rays as in classical analytical models, whereas the rays in the sharper model are nearly straight and are reflected or transmitted depending on the incidence angle, as expected from Snell's law.

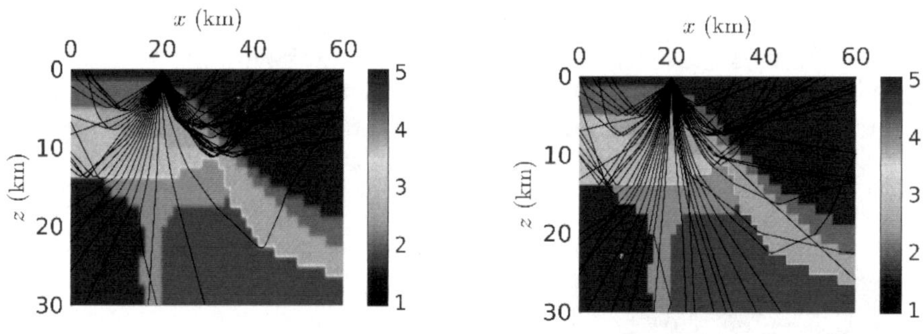

Fig. 6. Velocity model defined in a rectangular grid with sigmoidal functions for $a = 10$ and $a = 100$.

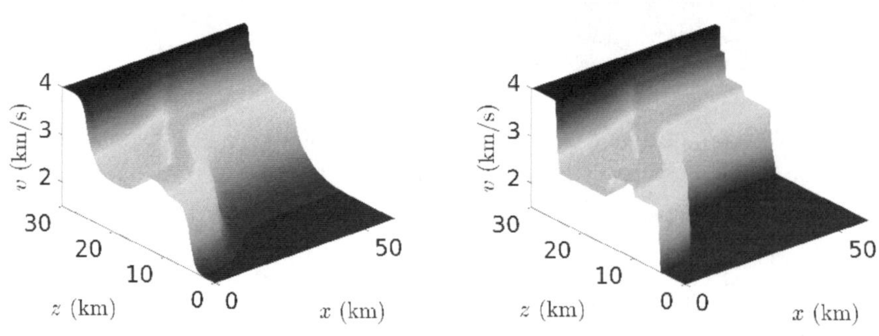

Fig. 7. Reflected P-wave rays from the velocity models in Fig. (6).

Finally, we have applied our parameterization to the Marmousi benchmark model [10]. We have used the data available in the CREWES toolbox [6] with spacing $\Delta x = \Delta z = 10$ m and velocity field ranging from 1.5 km/s to 5.5 km/s. We present in Fig. 8 the rays traced through the Marmousi model from the shot point at (6.0 km, 2.8 km) with take-off angle θ uniformly distributed in $[\pi/2, 3\pi/2[$. We have used a total of 51 rays and selected the sigmoid parameters a =10 and a =100.

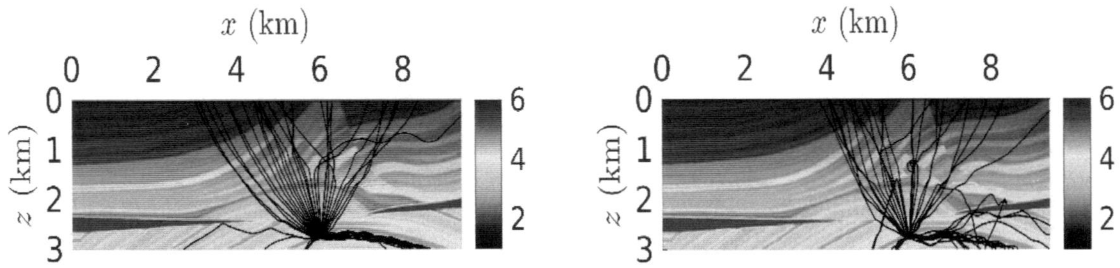

Fig. 8. Reflected P-wave from the sigmoidal representation of the Marmousi model for $a = 10$ and $a = 100$.

5. Conclusions

In this work we have proposed a technique that conciliates the simplicity of ray tracing with smoothed velocity fields with the accuracy of multi-domain ray tracers. We believe that the proposed parameterization has great potential not only in 2-D or 3-D ray tracing, but also in conjunction with other algorithms for wave propagation modeling and inversion.

Some limitations of the sigmoidal parameterization are readily noticed. Only a unique event (reflection or transmission) can be identified over a potential discontinuity. In elastic media, conversions from P- to S- waves and vice-versa are likely to be missed.

Acknowledgments

This work has been developed under the framework of the Brazilian consortium INCT-GP/CNPq/MCT, which has provided fellowships to R. A. Guimaraes and W. J. Silva. A. de Oliveira has been supported by the UFPR-TN fellowship and S. P. Oliveira acknowledges the receipt of a fellowship from the ICTP Programme for Training and Research in Italian Laboratories (Trieste, Italy), and from CNPq (grant 313100/2017-9). He is also grateful to the National Institute for Oceanography and Experimental Geophysics (INOGS, Trieste, Italy) for supporting his participation in ICTCA 2019.

References

[1] P. Bulant and L. Klimeš, "3-D velocity models – transformation from general to natural splines," *Stud. Geophys Geod.* **63**(1) (2019), 137–146.

[2] V. Červený, *Seismic Ray Theory*, Cambridge University Press, 2001.

[3] D. Costarelli and R. Spigler, "Constructive approximation by superposition of sigmoidal functions," *Anal. Theory Appl.* **29**(2) (2013), 169–196.

[4] H. J. Grubb and A. T. Walden, "Smoothing seismically derived velocities," *Geophys. Prospect.* **43**(8) (1995), 1061–1082.

[5] S. Mallat, A Wavelet Tour of Signal Processing: The Sparse Way, Academic Press, 2008.

[6] G. F Margrave and M. P Lamoureux, *Numerical methods of exploration seismology: with algorithms in MATLAB*. Cambridge University Press, 2019.

[7] A.Michelini and T. V. McEvilly, "Seismological studies at Park field. I. Simultaneous inversion for velocity structure and hypocenters using cubic B-splines parameterization," *Bull. Seismol. Soc. Am.* **81**(2) (1991), 524–552.

[8] V. Pretlová, "Bicubic spline smoothing of two-dimensional geophysical data," Stud. Geophys. Geod. **20**(2) (1976), 168–177.V. G. Santos and W. M. Figueiró, "Seismic ray tomography using L1 integral norm," Rev. Bras. Geofis. **29**(2) (2011), 347–358.

[9] R. J. Versteeg, "The Marmousi experience: Velocity model determination on a synthetic complex data set," Lead. Edge **13**(9) (1994), 927–936.

Experimental Verification of Acoustic Source Localization Technique in Heterogeneous Plates

SHENXIN YIN[1,2] JIA FU[1] TRIBIKRAM KUNDU[2] ZHIWEN CUI[1]

1, Department of Acoustics and Microwave Physics, College of Physics, Jilin University, 2699Qianjin Street,
Changchun, Jilin130012, China
cuizw@jlu.edu.cn

2, Department of Civil and Architectural Engineering and Mechanics, University of Arizona, 1209 E 2nd St,
Tucson, AZ 85719, USA

Acoustic source localization (ASL) in a structure by analyzing the recorded signals at the receivers is an important process in nondestructive testing for various applications. In spite of recent research advances on this topic some challenges still remain when the plate becomes heterogeneous. Heterogeneous structures are found in natural materials as well as in engineered synthetic materials. The wave propagation direction deviates from a straight line when it propagates through a heterogeneous structure due to refraction at the interface. This paper combines the law of refraction and TDOA technique to localize the acoustic source. No complicated nonlinear equation solution is required and thus it avoids the problem of multiplicity and wrong solution. The process of acoustic emission source localization is fast and easy for structural health monitoring. Positioning a set of sensor clusters in every one of different media media constituting the heterogeneous structure is required. It enables acoustic source localization in a heterogeneous plate of unknown material properties. The technique works well for homogeneous and multi-layered heterogeneous plate structures. The experiment results show that the new acoustic source localization technique of heterogeneous plate can localize the acoustic source accurately.

Keywords: Source localization; refraction; heterogeneous media; time difference of arrival

1. Introduction

The acoustic source localization technique has extensive and important applications in the fields of underwater sonar navigation [1], mobile communications [2], multimedia [3], global positioning system [4] and so on. As a nondestructive testing (NDT) method, the acoustic source localization technique also plays an indispensable role in structural health monitoring (SHM) [5,6]. Deformation and cracking of materials when under stress can initiate the structural failure. Such crack formation can act as the acoustic emission source. Acoustic source localization can protect or decrease the damage of the structure by taking remedial action to arrest the crack after knowing its location before catastrophic failure of the structure.

Several acoustic source localization techniques for different situations have been proposed by various investigators over last few decades [7-13]. The acoustic source localization in heterogeneous materials is complex especially when the acoustic emission source and the receiving sensors are in different media. The acoustic waves during propagation through different media reflect and refract at the interfaces according to Snell's Law. The propagation path from the acoustic source to the sensors is a straight line in a homogeneous medium. When they are in different media then the waves deviate from the straight line propagation [14]. To avoid cumbersome iteration algorithm, a large number of sensor arrays and *a priori* knowledge of structural properties are required by other available techniques. The time difference method used in this paper considers the refraction correctly. Experiments show that this method can predict the acoustic source location better than traditional average velocity method that ignores the refraction at different interfaces.

2. Formulation

"L" shaped sensor cluster with a distance *d* from the middle sensor S_1 (x_1, y_1) to the end sensors S_2 (x_2, y_2) and S_3 (x_3, y_3) in orthogonal directions can give the direction of the acoustic source as shown by Kundu [15-18] through TDOAs (time difference of arrivals), see Fig. (1).

$$\tan\alpha_1 = \frac{\Delta t_{13}}{\Delta t_{12}}. \tag{2.1}$$

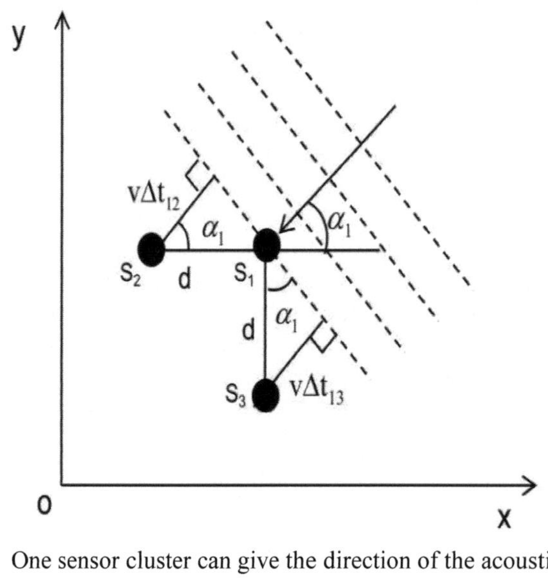

Fig. 1. One sensor cluster can give the direction of the acoustic source.

The location of the sensor clusters and the interface should be known. That means the height of the interface ya is known. So it's easy to find the intersection point coordinates (*xa, ya*) by the time difference of arrivals at receivers as shown in Fig. (2).

$$\tan\alpha_1 = \frac{ya - y_1}{xa - x_1}. \tag{2.2}$$

The straight line folds at the interface when the source and the sensor clusters are in different media as shown in Fig. (2) following snell's law:

$$\frac{\sin(\theta_1)}{c_1} = \frac{\sin(\theta_2)}{c_2}. \tag{2.3}$$

The direction of the acoustic source after refraction can be obtained if the wave velocities in the two media are known. A line through the acoustic source can be drawn from the time difference values in one cluster and the space information after considering refraction. One more line through the acoustic source can be obtained in the same process from one more cluster. If the third line still goes through the intersection point of the first two lines. Then the prediction can be concluded reliable and accurate. Otherwise, these three lines will give a triangular space indicating the acoustic source region. Two or three sensor clusters can predict the localization of the acoustic source regardless of the number of layers of heterogeneous material as long as the velocities in all layers that do not have sensor clusters are known.

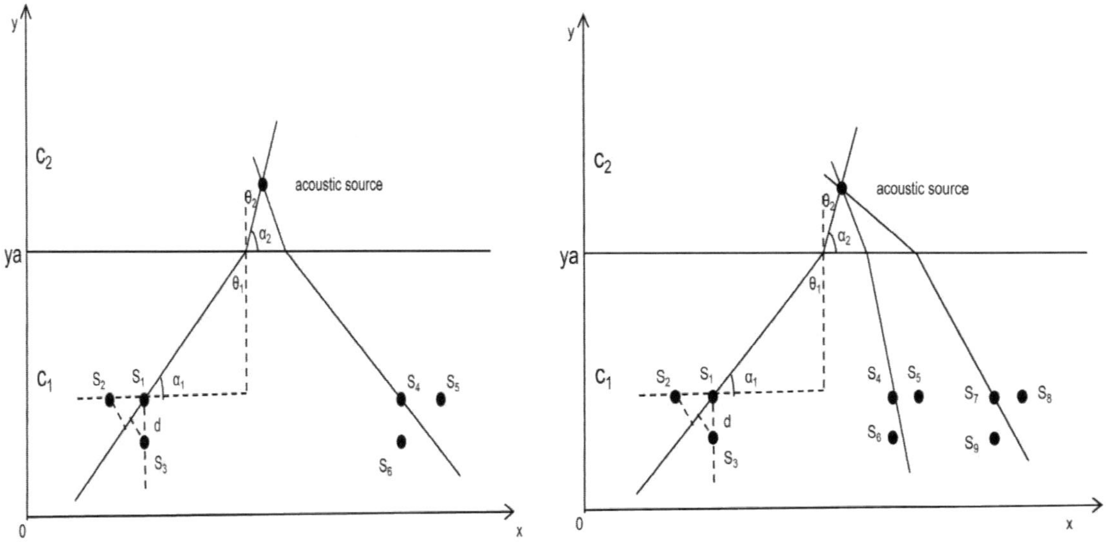

Fig. 2. Two clusters give two lines that go through refraction. The intersection of two lines indicates the predicted acoustic source position in the left picture. The third cluster will give the third line to check the localization accuracy as shown in right picture.

When the velocity is unknown then the wave velocity in each layer can be calculated from the time difference of arrivals in different sensors in a cluster.

$$c_1 = \frac{d}{\sqrt{t_{12}^2 + t_{13}^2}}. \tag{2.4}$$

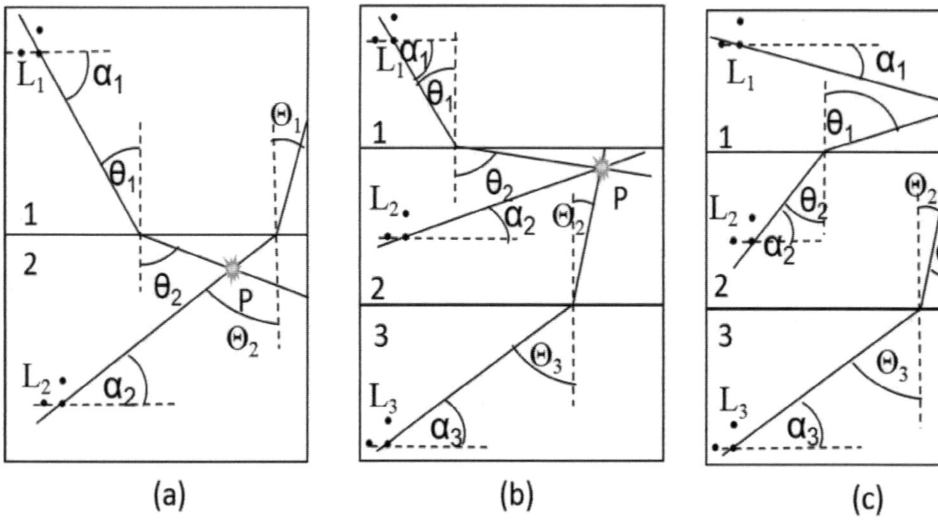

Fig. 3. Tracing the acoustic source location in 2-layered and 3-layered structures from L-shaped sensor clusters without knowing the material properties of individual layers.

A cluster is attached in each layer to locate acoustic source. When the acoustic event occurs in the structure of three or more different layers, this acoustic localization technique is also effective.

3. Experimental investigation

A heterogeneous plate having two different material properties was constructed for the experimental investigation. The heterogeneous plate is formed by a porous natural rock plate and soaking half of the plate in water as described by Qu *et al* (2018) [19]. The acoustic wave velocity of some natural rock changes when it is water saturation. Half of the plate was soaked in the water for a long time until the wave velocity in the wet part of the rock plate became a steady value. Different acoustic properties in water soaked part of the plate and the dry plate made the sample a heterogeneous plate. In absence of a multi-channel oscilloscope in the laboratory, this experiment had to be carried out in a more innovative way with the available simple devices. The experiment was conducted using a single channel ultrasonic emission unit, an oscilloscope and two 150 kHz ultrasonic transducers as shown in Fig. (4). Experimentally measured average guided wave speeds of the sample plate was c_1=2908m/s in the dry part as reference. The velocity of the water saturated part was c_2=3204m/s. The time difference of arrival of the first peaks at the 3 sensors in a cluster as shown Fig. (4) is Δt. The zero-axis is shifted vertically upward for a clearer view of the time history plots.

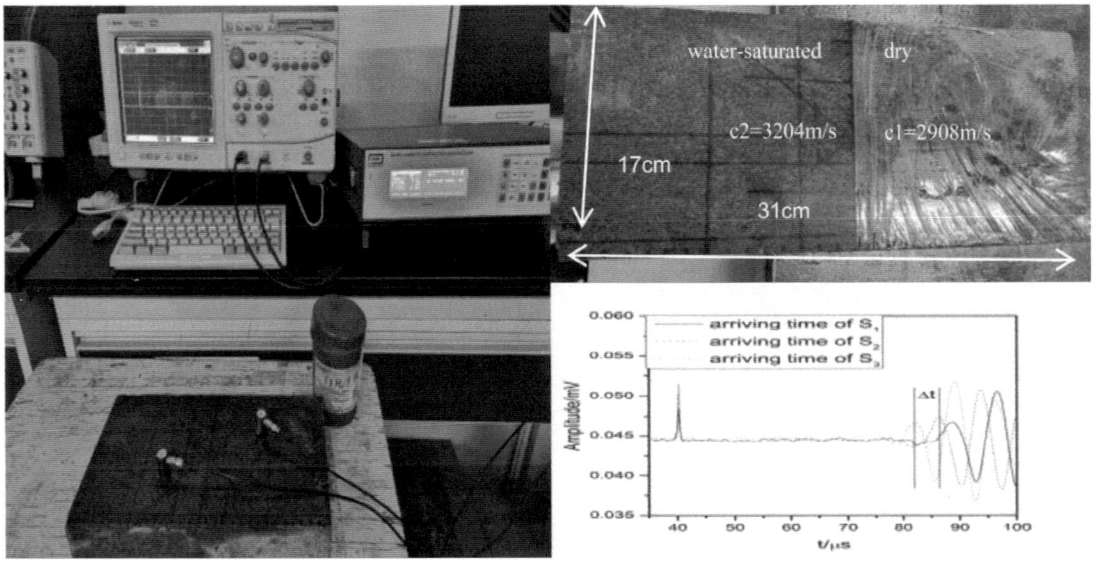

Fig. 4. The experiment is performed by two sensors as transmitter and receiver, respectively. The sample plate is formed by partially water-saturated natural rock. The time difference at any two sensors in a cluster is obtained by measuring the time shift of a recognizable peak.

First, six receiving sensors locations of two L-shaped cluster configurations on a 310 mm × 170 mm × 15 mm sample plate were marked. One ultrasonic sensor acting as the transmitter is placed at a specific location on the plate while the other one acting as the receiver is placed in one of the marked positions - S_1, S_2, S_3 and S_4, S_5, S_6. The experiment is repeated six times for the six positions. The travel times of the acoustic wave from the source to the individual receivers are recorded. Then the time differences of arrival for different sensor pairs are obtained simply by subtracting from one another the wave propagation times to those sensor pairs.

The acoustic source was localized using the theory presented above. The velocity of dry part of the plate is c_1 and that of the wet part is c_2. The calculated velocities obtained from Eq. (2.4) are shown in Fig. (5).

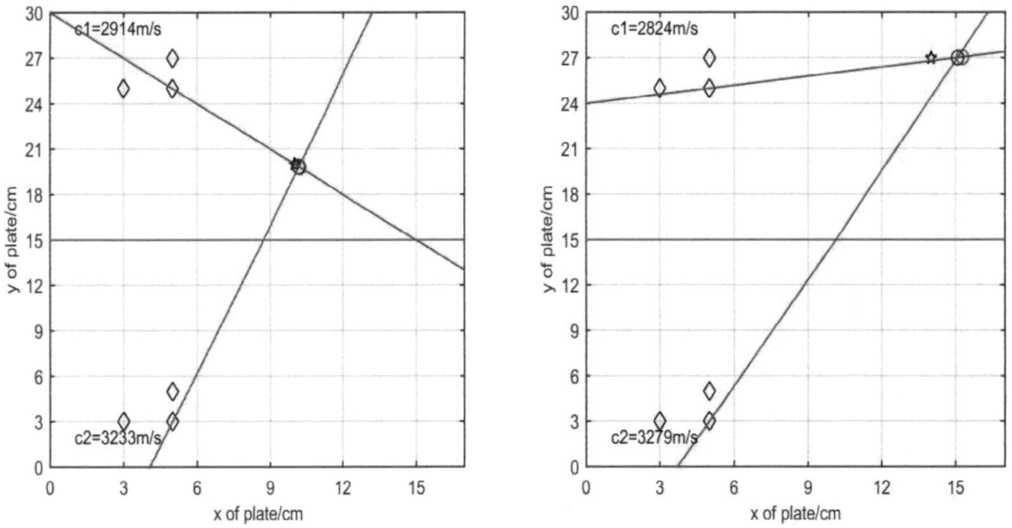

Fig. 5. Experimental results - the predicted source locations (intersection points of the two lines) and exact source locations (shown by the star markers) . The experimentally obtained (using Eq. 2.4) wave velocities c_1 and c_2 *accor*ding to Eq. (2.4) are also shown in the figure for every source location.

Final predicted results for four different source locations are shown in Table 1. Acoustic sources are localized by both considering and ignoring the heterogeneity. The error for each case is calculated from Eq. (3.1) and shown in the table.

$$error = \sqrt{(xx - xp)^2 + (yy - yp)^2}\ . \tag{3.1}$$

Table 1. True and predicted source locations for a 2-layered structure.

Exact source location (cm)	Predicted point considering refraction at the interface (cm)	Error considering refraction	Predicted point ignoring refraction at the interface (cm)	Error ignoring refraction
(10.20)	(10.17, 19.82)	0.2476	(10.34, 19.55)	0.5640
(14.27)	(14.96, 26.92)	0.9633	(15.08, 26.61)	1.1482
(10.17)	(10.40, 16.92)	0.4079	(10.58, 16.79)	0.6168
(14.08)	(13.57, 7.83)	0.5948	(13.44, 7.61)	0.6824

Note that for every case even for such small heterogeneity the error is reduced when the new algorithm for source localization in a heterogeneous structure is adopted.

4. Conclusion

Since heterogeneous layered structures are widely used, the acoustic emission source localization in such non-homogeneous structures is important. When the acoustic signal propagates through different layers in a non-homogeneous plate, it is refracted at the interfaces following Snell's law. In this paper the source localization technique is extended to the heterogeneous structures considering the refraction phenomenon. In the proposed new technique no complicated nonlinear equation solution is required which avoids the problem of multiplicity and wrong solution. Only six sensors give two lines for acoustic emission source localization considering refraction in a heterogeneous plate made of two materials.

The process of acoustic emission source localization is fast and easy for structural health monitoring. The new technique works even when the wave velocities in different layers are unknown and when the heterogeneous plates are made of three or more different layers. Good matching between predicted and actual acoustic source locations were observed in the experimental investigation.

Acknowledgments

This work was supported by the China Scholarship Council (201806170164, 201806170278), Science and Technology Research Planning Project of Education Department of Jilin Province, China (Grant No. JJKH20190182KJ) and MOHRSS: Homeland-Serving Action Plan for Overseas Chinese, China (Grant No. GDW20182200133).

References

[1] Le Chevalier, F., *Principles of Radar and Sonar signal Processing*, Artech House, 2002.

[2] Gustafsson, F. and Gunnarsson, F., "Mobile positioning using wireless networks: Possibilities and fundamental limitations based on available wireless network measurements," *IEEE Signal Process. Mag.* **22** (2005), 41–53.

[3] Valin, J. M, et al. "Robust sound source localization using a microphone array on a mobile robot." *Ieee/rsj International Conference on Intelligent Robots and Systems IEEE*, **2** (2016), 1228-1233.

[4] Hofmann-Wellenhof, B., Lichtenegger, H., and Collins, J., *Global Positioning System: Theory and Practice*, Springer Science & Business Media, 2013.

[5] Giurgiutiu, Victor. "Lamb wave generation with piezoelectric wafer active sensors for structural health monitoring." *Smart Structures and Materials 2003: Smart Structures and Integrated Systems International Society for Optics and Photonics*, 2003, 111-122.

[6] Tribikram Kundu, Samik Das, Kumar V. Jata, "Health Monitoring of a Thermal Protection System using Lamb Waves", *Structural Health Monitoring: An International Journal* **8**(1) (2009), 29-45.

[7] T. Kundu, Acoustic source localization, *Ultrasonics*, **54**(1) (2014), 25-38.

[8] Ebrahimkhanlou, S. Salamone, Acoustic emission source localization in thin metallic plates: A single-sensor approach based on multimodal edge reflections, *Ultrasonics*, **78** (2017), 134-145.

[9] Z.L. Zhou, Y.C. Rui, J. Zhou, L.J. Dong, X. Cai, Locating an Acoustic Emission Source in Multilayered Media Based on the Refraction Path Method, *IEEE Access*, **6** (2018), 25090-25099.

[10] Z. L. Zhou, J. Zhou, L. J. Dong, X. Cai, Y. C. Rui, C.T. Ke, Experimental study on the location of an acoustic emission source considering refraction in different media. *Scientific Reports*, **7** (1) (2017), 7472.

[11] Park, W.H., Packo, P. and Kundu, T, "Acoustic source localization in an anisotropic plate without knowing its material properties–a new approach", *Ultrasonics*, **79** (2017), 9-17.

[12] Sen, N. and Kundu, T, "A new wave front shape-based approach for acoustic source localization in an anisotropic plate without knowing its material properties." *Ultrasonics*, **87** (2018), 20-32.

[13] Yin, S., Cui, Z. and Kundu, T., "Acoustic source localization in anisotropic plates with "Z" shaped sensor clusters", *Ultrasonics*, **84** (2018), 34-37.

[14] Yin, S., Cui, Z., Fu, J., & Kundu, T. Acoustic source localization in heterogeneous media. Ultrasonics, 99, (2019). [105957].

[15] Kundu, T., Das, S. and Jata, K. V., "Point of Impact Prediction in Isotropic and Anisotropic Plates from the Acoustic Emission Data", *Journal of the Acoustical Society of America*, **122**(4) (2007), 2057-2066.

[16] Kundu, T., Das, S. and Jata, K. V., "Impact Point Detection in Stiffened Plates by Acoustic Emission Technique", *Smart Materials & Structures*, **18** (2009), Article 035006.

[17] Kundu, T., Das, S., Martin, S.A., and Jata, K.V., "Locating point of impact in anisotropic fiber reinforced composite plates", *Ultrasonics*, **48**(3) (2008), 193-201.
[18] Kundu, T., Nakatani, H. and Takeda, N. "Acoustic source localization in anisotropic plates", *Ultrasonics*, **52**(6) (2012), 740-746.
[19] Qu Y., Liu J., Cui Z. and Lv W. "Third-Order Elastic Moduli of the Dry and Water Saturated Rocks", *In Proceedings of the International Workshop on Environment and Geoscience*, **1** (2018), 428-433.

Finite Element Model Coupled With Lumped Parameter Elements

DANIEL GERT NIELSEN[1] JAKOB SØNDERGAARD JENSEN[2,3] VICENTE CUTANDA HENRIQUEZ[2,1] FINN THOMAS AGERKVIST[1]

1, Acoustic Technology, Dept. of Electrical Engineering, Technical University of Denmark
Ørsteds Plads 352, Kgs. Lyngby, 2800, Denmark
dgniel@elektro.dtu.dk
2, Centre for Acoustic-Mechanical Micro Systems, Technical University of Denmark
Ørsteds Plads 352, Kgs. Lyngby, 2800, Denmark
3, Solid Mechanics, Dept. of Mechanical Engineering, Technical University of Denmark
Nils Koppels Allé, Kgs. Lyngby, 2800, Denmark

This paper presents a numerical modelling technique for loudspeakers in which a finite element model is coupled with a lumped parameter model. Our approach includes the electric motor system of the loudspeaker in the numerical simulation without increasing the computational cost. This is achieved by considering the motor system as a lumped component, furthermore, parts of the mechanical system are also included in the lumped parameter model. Lastly, initial results are presented, where we illustrate the effect of including the electric motor system by comparing the proposed model with an acoustic-mechanical finite element model.

Keywords: Lumped parameter model; Acoustic-structure interaction; Loudspeaker design

1. Introduction

Moving-coil loudspeakers are a challenging task to model, due to the fact that many engineering areas of expertise are to be combined to create an accurate model of the loudspeaker. The physics that are to be computed are strongly coupled which means that the accuracy of the solution will depend on the modelling choices made.

One could include everything in a finite element (FE)-model and accept a large number of degrees of freedom (DOFs), which could cause infeasible computational times. This leads to the usage of much simpler models such as the lumped parameter models (LPMs). These types of models are 1 degree of freedom (DOF) models that represents the co-dependent physics in simple electric circuits.

The accuracy of these models decreases as the excitation frequency increases [4]. This is due to the fact that above the first mechanical resonance frequency the vibration pattern of the loudspeaker starts to deviate from the piston-like movement it exhibits below the first resonance frequency and thereby making the LPM inaccurate.

In-order to accurately capture the high frequency vibration pattern of a loudspeaker FE-models or similar computational tools are necessary. Furthermore, with a FE-model of the loudspeaker, structural optimization can be utilized [1].

The purpose of this paper is to develop a simplified generic numerical model of a loudspeaker that can be modelled with an in-house numerical framework, which in the future can be used for structural optimization of selected parts of the transducer, in this paper we focus on the diaphragm. In this paper we explicitly describe the necessary steps to implement and use this method. It should be noted that a similar method exist for users of the commercial simulation tool Comsol [5]. An optimization schemes is an iterative procedure, where the numerical is solved for each iteration, thus, it is desired to be able to solve it as efficiently as possible. Therefore, this paper proposes a hybrid method in which the advantages of LPM and FE-models are utilized.

2. Theory

This paper deals with two simplifications, the first is to consider the FE model problem as 2D-axisymmetric, this method is well known and thoroughly described in [3]. The second simplification is an approach in which the entire electrical motor system and parts of the mechanical components are lumped, thus only spending computational resources on modelling the diaphragm and the acoustic waves radiating from the diaphragm. The proposed method makes it possible to include the lumped system in the actual finite element matrices, thus no post-processing of the numerical results are required since all equations are solved at once.

Figure 1 shows a 2D sketch of a generic loudspeaker. The following sections will be used to establish the system of equations for both the FE-model and the lumped parameter model and describe how these two system can be combined.

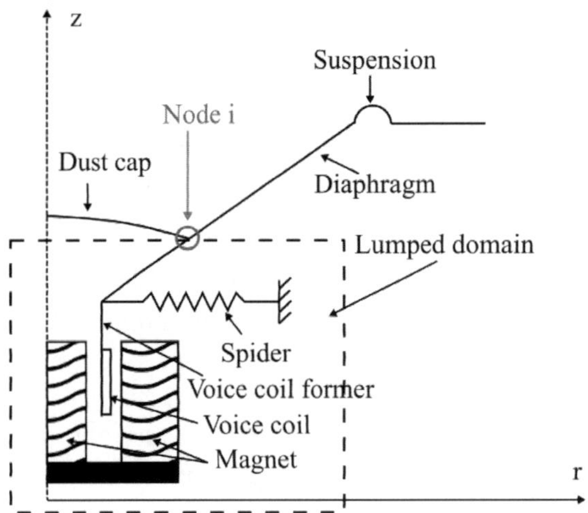

Fig. 1. sketch of the 2D axisymmetric model problem, everything inside the boxed region is contained in the lumped model, the rest is modelled with a FE-model.

2.1. Finite element model

The finite element model consists of a structural mechanics part and an acoustic domain. The governing equation for a mechanical elastic body subject to a time harmonic force is

$$(\mathbf{K} - \omega^2\mathbf{M})\mathbf{u} = \mathbf{f}\,, \tag{2.1}$$

where the capital bold letters indicate that it is a matrix, small bold letters are vectors, ω is the excitation frequency, **M** is the structural mass matrix, **K** is the structural stiffness matrix **u** is the solution vector containing the structural displacements and **f** is the externally applied time harmonic force. Damping is included as a structural loss factor η, such that $\mathbf{K} = \mathbf{K}(1 + j\eta)$, where j is the imaginary number.

In the acoustic domain we solve the Helmholtz equation to obtain the nodal pressure. The loudspeaker is radiating into free-space. Perfectly Matched Layers (PMLs) are therefore used [2]. This results in a frequency dependent matrices in the acoustic domain

$$(\mathbf{K}_a(\omega) - \omega^2\mathbf{M}_a(\omega))\mathbf{p} = \mathbf{f}_\mathrm{a}\ . \tag{2.2}$$

Here $\mathbf{M}_\mathrm{a}$ is the acoustic mass matrix, $\mathbf{K}_\mathrm{a}$ is the acoustic stiffness matrix, **p** is the solution vector containing the nodal pressures and $\mathbf{f}_\mathrm{a}$ is the vector containing acoustic sources, which will be regarded as a zero vector for the remainder of this paper.

The coupling between the two domains is defined such that when the mechanical structure vibrates it acts as an acoustic source, furthermore the pressure acting on the mechanical structure is accounted for. This is included in the coupling matrix **S**, the entire system of equations for the FE-model are [3]

$$\left(\begin{bmatrix} \mathbf{K} & -\mathbf{S}^T \\ \mathbf{0} & \mathbf{K}_\mathrm{a}(\omega) \end{bmatrix} - \omega^2 \begin{bmatrix} \mathbf{M} & \mathbf{0} \\ \rho_a\mathbf{S} & \mathbf{M}_\mathrm{a}(\omega) \end{bmatrix}\right)\begin{Bmatrix} \mathbf{u} \\ \mathbf{p} \end{Bmatrix} = \begin{Bmatrix} \mathbf{f} \\ \mathbf{0} \end{Bmatrix}\ . \tag{2.3}$$

We choose to write eq. (2.3) in compact form

$$\left(\widetilde{\mathbf{K}} - \omega^2\widetilde{\mathbf{M}}\right)\begin{Bmatrix} \mathbf{u} \\ \mathbf{p} \end{Bmatrix} = \begin{Bmatrix} \mathbf{f} \\ \mathbf{0} \end{Bmatrix}\ . \tag{2.4}$$

2.2. Coupled system

As shown on Fig. 1. parts of the mechanical system and the entire electric motor system are lumped. The lumped systems are represented by simple electrical circuits as shown in Fig. 2. The left circuit corresponds to the electrical part of the motor system, in which e_g is the applied voltage, i_c is the current, R_E is the resistance of the voice coil, L_E is the inductance of the voice coil and e_c describes the back induced voltage from the mechanical system. In the expression for e_c the product of the force factor, Bl, and the velocity, $\dot{u}$, appears from the mechanical structure in the coupling node. The right circuit corresponds to the partly lumped mechanical system, the force on the mechanical system, F^{elek} is proportional to the electrical current, M_{lump} is the mass of the lumped components, R_{lump} is the damping coefficient of the lumped system, C_{lump} is the compliance of the mechanical components and finally the finite element model is included as an equivalent impedance.

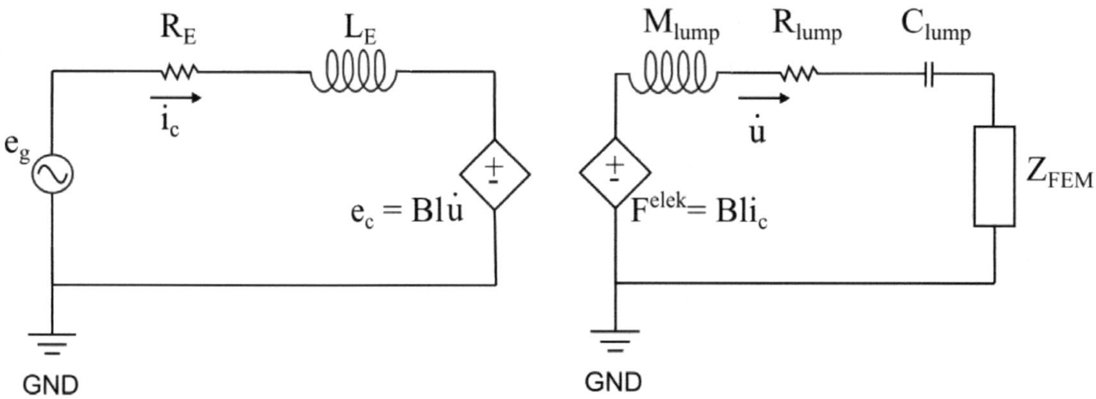

Fig. 2. The lumped system model, including the contribution from the FE-model as an impedance.

The scalar equation cast in the frequency domain for the electrical motor system in Fig. 2.

$$e_g = R_E i_c + j\omega L_E i_c + j\omega Blu \ , \qquad \text{s}(2.5)$$

and this equation is to be included in the finite element equation.

The equation for the partly lumped mechanical system, including the FE-model is

$$Bli_c(t) = -\omega^2 M_{lump} u + j\omega R_{lump} u + \frac{1}{C_{lump}} u + j\omega u Z_{FEM} \ , \qquad (2.6)$$

where Z_{FEM} is the impedance of the mechanical part of the finite element model, which is utilized to provide an expression for the mechanical force in the FE-model

$$Z_{FEM} = \frac{F_i}{j\omega u_i} \qquad (2.7)$$

where sub *i* refers to the value in the coupling node *i* of a FE vector. Inserting into eq. (2.6) yields

$$Bli_c(t) = -\omega^2 M_{lump} u + j\omega R_{lump} u + \frac{1}{C_{lump}} u + F_i \quad . \qquad (2.8)$$

This addition to the FE-model in node *i* is most easily done by indicator matrices as shown in eq. (2.9). Let $\mathbf{I}_{iz}$ be a zero matrix with size of the entire system of equations with an entry of value 1 in its diagonal corresponding to the DOF for the r-direction at node *i* and similarly, let $\mathbf{I}_{iz}$ have one entry in the DOF for the z-direction of node *i*. $\mathbf{J}_{iz}$ is a zero matrix with one unit entry in the bottom row in the column corresponding to the DOF for the z-direction in node *i*, finally $\mathbf{L}$ is defined as a zero matrix with one unit entry in the last DOF of the diagonal.

$$\mathbf{I}_{ir} = \begin{bmatrix} 0 & \cdots & \mathbf{0} & \cdots & 0 \\ \vdots & \ddots & & & \vdots \\ \mathbf{0} & & i_{dofr} & & \mathbf{0} \\ \vdots & & & \ddots & \vdots \\ 0 & \cdots & \mathbf{0} & \cdots & 0 \end{bmatrix}, \quad \mathbf{I}_{iz} = \begin{bmatrix} 0 & \cdots & \mathbf{0} & \cdots & 0 \\ \vdots & \ddots & & & \vdots \\ \mathbf{0} & & i_{dofz} & & \mathbf{0} \\ \vdots & & & \ddots & \vdots \\ 0 & \cdots & \mathbf{0} & \cdots & 0 \end{bmatrix}, \qquad (2.9)$$

$$\mathbf{J}_{\mathrm{iz}} = \begin{bmatrix} 0 & \cdots & \mathbf{0} & \cdots & 0 \\ \vdots & \ddots & & & \vdots \\ \mathbf{0} & & \mathbf{0} & & \mathbf{0} \\ \vdots & & & \ddots & \vdots \\ 0 & \cdots & i_{dofz} & \cdots & 0 \end{bmatrix}, \mathbf{L} = \begin{bmatrix} 0 & \cdots & \mathbf{0} & \cdots & 0 \\ \vdots & \ddots & & & \vdots \\ \mathbf{0} & & \mathbf{0} & & \mathbf{0} \\ \vdots & & & \ddots & \vdots \\ 0 & \cdots & \mathbf{0} & \cdots & 1 \end{bmatrix}.$$

Adding one equation to the FE equations of eq. (2.4) and the indicator matrices from eq. (2.9) the system of equations for the hybrid FE-LPM model is

$$\begin{aligned} \Bigg(\bigg(\begin{bmatrix} \tilde{\mathbf{K}} & \mathbf{0} \\ \mathbf{0} & 0 \end{bmatrix} + \frac{1}{C_{lump,x}}\mathbf{I}_{\mathrm{ir}} + \frac{1}{C_{lump,y}}\mathbf{I}_{\mathrm{iz}} + R_E\mathbf{L} - Bl\mathbf{J}_{\mathrm{iz}}^T\bigg) + j\omega\big(R_{lump}\mathbf{I}_{\mathrm{iz}} + Bl\mathbf{J}_{\mathrm{iz}} + L_E\mathbf{L}\big) \\ - \omega^2\bigg(\begin{bmatrix} \tilde{\mathbf{M}} & \mathbf{0} \\ \mathbf{0} & 0 \end{bmatrix} + M_{lump}\mathbf{I}_{\mathrm{iz}}\bigg)\Bigg)\begin{Bmatrix} \mathbf{u} \\ \mathbf{p} \\ i_c \end{Bmatrix} = \begin{Bmatrix} \mathbf{0} \\ \mathbf{0} \\ e_g \end{Bmatrix}, \end{aligned} \tag{2.10}$$

where $\mathbf{J}_{\mathrm{iy}}^T$ is the transpose of $\mathbf{J}_{\mathrm{iy}}$. One should notice that the compliance has a contribution in the stiffness matrix in both r- and z-direction, whereas all other lumped parameters are assumed to only have a contribution in the direction of the applied force. The stiffness is assumed to be equal size, so in the next section C_{lump} refers to the compliance in both r- and z-direction.

3. Numerical Modelling

Figure 4 shows a sketch of the model problem that is used to test the implementation. Essentially, the sketch shows a flat piston (Ω) connected to a rigid wall via a rubber surround (Ω_s). The piston is connected to the lumped system in node *i*. The piston radiates sound into free field, which is the domain Ω_F, the PMLs are present in Ω_A regions.

Table 1 and 2 shows the data used in the simulations.

Tab. 1. Simulation data used in the FE-model

Mechanical FE-Data				
	E [GPa]	ρ $[kg/m^3]$	υ	η
Surround	0.03	1400	0.45	0.25
Cone/Dustcap	10	1300	0.3	0.3

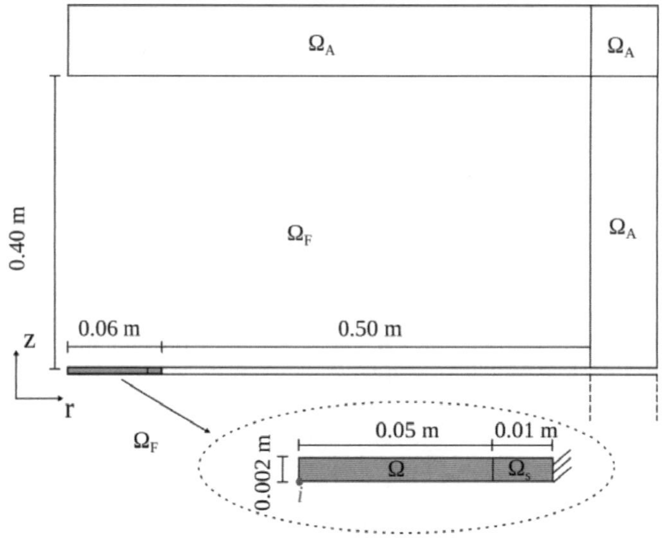

Fig. 3. Sketch of the model problem which is a piston with a radius of 5 cm connected to a rigid wall (infinite baffle) via a 1 cm rubber surround.

Tab. 2. Simulation data used in the LPM

Lumped Model Data						
$M_{lump}[kg]$	$C_{lump}[m/N]$	$Bl\ [Tm]$	$L_E[mH]$	$R_{lump}[N * s/m]$	$R_E[\Omega]$	$e_g[V]$
0.004	$369 * 10^{-6}$	7.0	1.22	1.85	3.3	2.83

4. Numerical Results

This section will showcase the initial results obtained with the proposed FE-LP method. This section will highlight the benefits of the approach by comparing the results to a regular FE-model without LPM i.e. only a mechanical structure exited by a frequency independent time harmonic force. The compared data is obtained in node *i* as shown on Fig. 3.

Figure 4 compares the FE-LPM model to a FE-model excited by a constant time harmonic force. It can be observed that at the first mechanical resonance frequency there is a clear discrepancy between the two models. That is due to the fact that for the FE-LPM the total electrical impedance increases at the resonance frequency, this is opposed to the FE-model in which the force acting on the structure is constant which amplifies the resonant behavior of the structure.

The effect of the inductance is mostly observed for higher frequencies when using the FE-LPM. The displacement shows a 2nd order decay which means that the acceleration of the loudspeaker is almost constant at higher frequencies. For the model without a LPM we observe that the acceleration is not constant at higher frequencies which implies that the pressure in the far-field will increase with frequency. One could include this high frequency behavior in a regular acoustic-mechanical FE-model by scaling the force inversely with frequency, this approach would however not capture the behavior around the mechanical resonances, to capture this effect one must consider the electrical motor system.

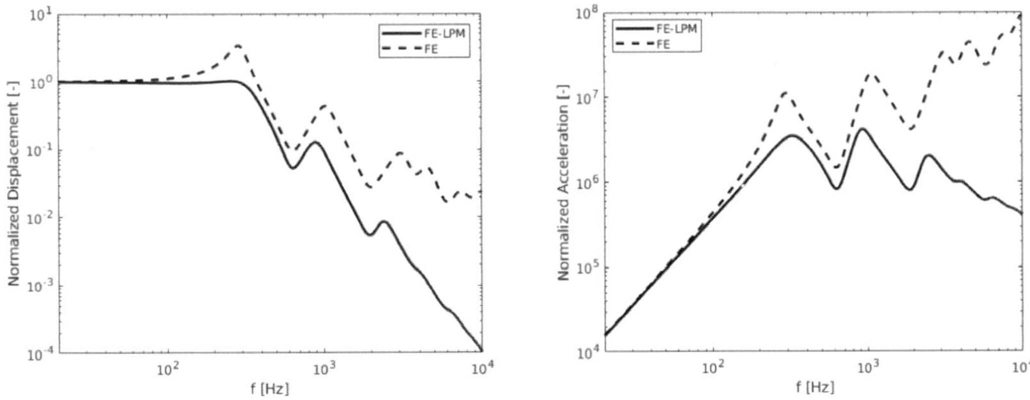

Fig. 4 (top left) normalized displacement for the FE-LPM and FE-model, (top right) normalized acceleration for the FE-LPM.

Another advantage of using the proposed FE-LPM model is that the impedance of the voice coil can now easily be obtained. This quantity can be used to compare the numerical model of a transducer or an optimized transducer with datasheets from bookshelf loudspeakers

$$Z_{VC} = \frac{e_g}{i_c}. \tag{4.1}$$

Figure 5 shows the impedance of the voice coil for the simple test example in Fig. 3, which essentially shows the influence of the loudspeaker on the electrical motor system. From the impedance curve it is possible to identify the first and second mechanical resonance, furthermore, one can observe the impact of the inductance when the excitation frequency increases.

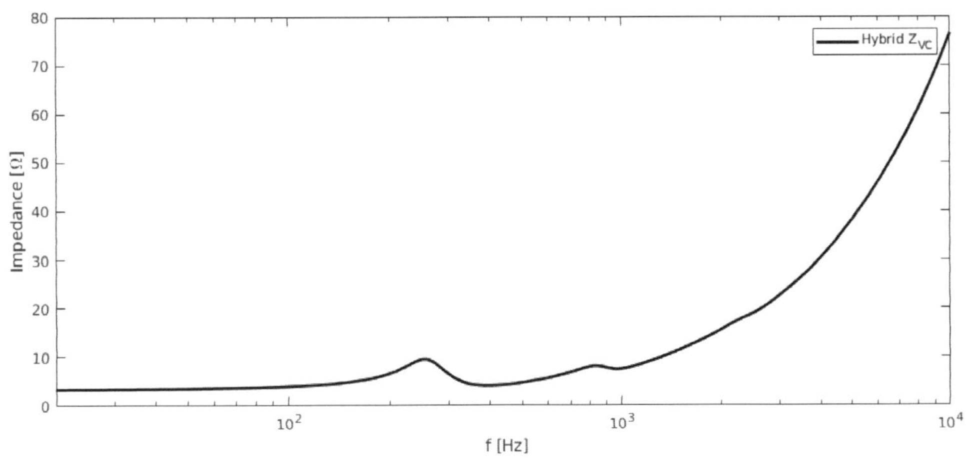

Fig. 5. The electrical impedance of the voice coil as a function of frequency.

5. Conclusion

A method containing the advantages of FE and LPM has been exploited to create a hybrid FE-LPM numerical model. Modelling of the diaphragm with a FE-model ensures accuracy for high frequency excitations. By considering the electromagnetic system of the loudspeaker it is possible to fully capture the physics in the loudspeaker.

By including the LPM in the FE equations by the proposed manner the implementation can readily be used for optimization of the mechanical components of the loudspeaker, as a significant speed up is achieved by lumping parts of the transducer.

It is the intention of the authors to extend the LPM to include losses in the electric motor system, which implies that the resistance and the inductance of the voice coil should be frequency dependent. It should be noted that the frequency dependency also can be included in the mechanical components such that viscoelastic effects can be accounted for.

References

[1] M. P. Bendsøe, O. Sigmund, "Topology Optimization: Theory, Methods and Applications", Springer Verlag, 2004

[2] A.Bermúdez, L. H. Nieto, A. Prieto, R. Rodríguez, "An Optimal Finite-Element/PML Method for the Simulation of Acoustic Wave Propagation Phenomena", Variational Formulations in Mechanics: Theory and Applications, 2006

[3] R. D. Cook, D. S. Malkus, M. E. Plesha, R. J. Witt, "Concepts and Applications of Finite Element Analysis", John Wiley and Sons, 4th edition, 2002.

[4] W. M. Leach, Jr, "Introduction to Electroacoustics & Audio Amplifier Design", Kendal/Hunt Publishing Company, 3rd edition, 2003.

[5] P. Marttila, M. J. H. Jensen, "A Hybrid Electroacoustic Lumped and Finite Element Model for Modeling Loudspeaker Drivers", AES 51st International Conference, 2013

Flexural Wave Bandgap Property in Thin Plates with Periodic Partial-Constrained-Layer Damping Coverage

Qi Qin*, Mei-Ping Sheng†, Fan Zhao‡, and Zheng Fang††

School of Marine Science and Technology, Northwestern Polytechnical University,
127 Youyixilu, 710072 Xi'an, P. R. China
Research & Development Institute of Northwestern Polytechnical University in Shenzhen,
25 Gaoxin Nan Sidao, 518057 Shenzhen, P. R. China
*34231@mail.nwpu.edu.cn
†smp@nwpu.edu.cn
‡1017086974@qq.com
††fangzheng@mail.nwpu.edu.cn

Traditional theory on partial-constrained-layer damping (PCLD) is mainly focused on vibration damping and system loss factors. Bandgap analysis is introduced in thin plates with periodic PCLD coverage. The bandgap dispersion relation is studied first, with the periodic cell consisting of a base plate lattice and the attached structure of certain scales. Each attached structure includes the constraining layer and the viscoelastic layer. Multiple resonant modes of the attached structure make the band-structure curves abundant, and there appear bandgaps within which flexural waves are forbidden to propagate into the plate. Vibration transmission response in the finite structure is also calculated, and the transmission gaps are in good agreement with the bandgaps. Furthermore, by applying the damping characteristic to viscoelastic layers, the vibration attenuation band can be broadened. To illustrate vibration suppression effects of periodic PCLD coverage, together with another two finite models, the transverse vibration transmittances are compared, including a plate attached with periodic lumped resonators, and a sandwich plate with monolithic constrained-layer damping coverage. Results show that much broader attenuation bands are achieved in the plate with periodic PCLD coverage. The bandgap analysis in plates with periodic PCLD coverage can give guidance on suppression of structural vibration.

Keywords: Periodic partial-constrained-layer damping; bandgap property; vibration transmission; broad attenuation band.

1. Introduction

Constrained layer damping (CLD) treatment has been regarded as an effective way to suppress structural vibrations and sound radiation. In the early time, most works have been dealt with full CLD coverage[1,2]. Owing to the constraints of cost and weight in most cases, partial constrained layer damping (PCLD) treatment is more practical, where the base structure is partially covered with CLD instead of full coverage. No matter full CLD or PCLD coverage, however, the efforts are mainly focused on the improvement of system damping performance[3-5].

It is obvious that the case of pieces of PCLD coverage periodically distributed on the base structure can be classified into periodic structures. In the past few decades, the extraordinary properties of periodic structures have attracted a great deal of interest[6,7]. It is well known that specific frequency ranges called bandgaps may be observed in periodic structures, within which the propagation of waves is forbidden, while waves outside the bandgap frequencies can propagate freely without attenuation. Wave propagation in 1D or 2D structures is studied a lot, where scattering units or locally resonant units are periodically placed in the host medium[8-13]. A number of methods have been developed for calculating the bandgaps and wave transmission characteristics[14-17], among which finite element method (FEM) is a flexible method for solving the problem of wave propagation in periodic structures[18,19].

In this paper, flexural wave bandgap property in thin plates with periodic PCLD coverage is analyzed. Following the introduction, the theoretical model of the plate lattice with PCLD coverage is presented in Sec. 2. In Sec. 3, the bandgap property and vibration transmission of the corresponding finite plate are investigated. Furthermore, there also compare vibration suppression effects of the plate with periodic PCLD coverage, the plate with periodic lumped resonant elements, and the sandwich plate with monolithic viscoelastic core. Finally, the conclusions are summarized in Sec. 4.

2. Model and Theory

The periodic element considered here consists of the base layer (BL) attached with the viscoelastic layer (VL) and the constraining layer (CL), both of which have the same size, smaller than the base plate lattice, as shown in Fig. 1. The finite element method (FEM) combined with the Bloch periodic boundary conditions is used to investigate the band structures. According to Bloch's theory[11], the wave motion can be described as

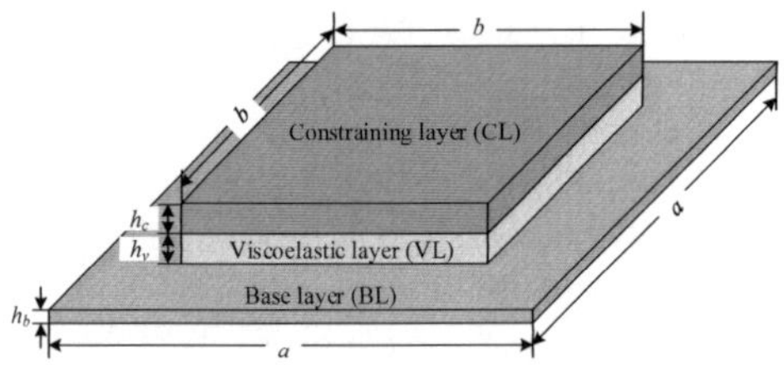

Fig. 1. Schematics of the periodic element composed of BL attached with VL and CL.

$$\mathbf{u}(\mathbf{r})=\mathbf{u}_k(\mathbf{r})e^{-\boldsymbol{\mu}\cdot\mathbf{r}}, \tag{2.1}$$

where $\mathbf{u}(\mathbf{r})$ represents the elastic displacement at the location $\mathbf{r}=(x, y, z)$, and $\mathbf{u}_k(\mathbf{r})$ is a periodical vector function with the same periodicity as the periodic element, and $\boldsymbol{\mu}$ is the propagation constant. The Bloch-Floquet boundary conditions can be obtained according to Eq. (2.1)

$$\mathbf{u}(\mathbf{r}+\mathbf{a})=\mathbf{u}(\mathbf{r})e^{-\boldsymbol{\mu}\cdot\mathbf{a}}, \tag{2.2}$$

where $\mathbf{a}$ is the periodicity lattice vector. For a 2D periodic structure, via the determination of various combinations of propagation constants $\boldsymbol{\mu}=(\mu_x, \mu_y)$ in the x and y directions, the frequency values where free wave propagation occurs can be evaluated[12]. While

$$\mu_x = \delta_x + ik_x,\ \mu_y = \delta_y + ik_y, \tag{2.3}$$

where the real and imaginary parts of the propagation constants are denoted as 'attenuation' and 'phase' constants respectively. If μ_x and μ_y are purely imaginary, then the waves are free to propagate; if μ_x or μ_y is purely real or complex, then the waves are attenuated as they propagate from one cell to another.

By applying the Bloch-Floquet boundary conditions, the eigenvalue problem in FEM form can be expressed as

$$\left|\mathbf{K}(\mu_x, \mu_y) - \omega^2\mathbf{M}(\mu_x, \mu_y)\right| = 0, \tag{2.4}$$

where $\mathbf{M}$ and $\mathbf{K}$ are the mass and stiffness matrices respectively.

The software of Comsol Multiphysics is applied to solve the eigenvalue problem without considering the structural damping, which means that the attenuation constants δ_x and δ_y are set to 0. Solving the determinant for a given $\mathbf{k}=(k_x, k_y)$ on the boundary $M\Gamma XM$ of the irreducible first Brillouin zone can reach an $\omega(\mathbf{k})$, thus the band structures of the plate with PCLD coverage can be obtained.

Then the forced response of a finite plate made up of limited periodic elements is considered. The transverse vibration transmittance is defined as

$$T = 20\log_{10}\left|v_r/v_e\right|, \tag{2.5}$$

where v_e and v_r are the average velocities of the excitation area and the response area.

3. Numerical Results and Discussions

Using the numerical model described in Sec. 2, bandgap property of a thin plate with periodic PCLD coverage and vibration transmission of the corresponding finite plates are studied in this section. A reference configuration of the base plate lattice with PCLD coverage is shown in Table 1, including geometrical and material parameters. The parameters are not changed in the following work unless otherwise stated.

Table 1. Parameters of reference configuration of the base plate lattice with PCLD coverage.

	Geometrical parameters		Material parameters	
BL	BL length	$a = 0.1$ m	Young's modulus	$E_b = 210$ GPa
	BL thickness	$h_b = 0.004$ m	Density	$\rho_b = 7800$ kg/m^3
			Poisson's ratio	$\upsilon_b = 0.3$
VL	VL length	$b = 0.06$ m	Young's modulus	$E_v = 10$ MPa
	VL thickness	$h_v = 0.005$ m	Density	$\rho_v = 1100$ kg/m^3
			Poisson's ratio	$\upsilon_v = 0.49$
CL	CL length	$b = 0.06$ m	Young's modulus	$E_c = 40.8$ GPa
	CL thickness	$h_c = 0.006$ m	Density	$\rho_c = 11340$ kg/m^3
			Poisson's ratio	$\upsilon_c = 0.37$

3.1. Bandgap properties

Figure 2 shows the band structure curves of the plate with periodic PCLD coverage of the designed parameters in Table 1. The band structure curves of the uniform plate are also shown in Fig. 2(a) for comparison. As can be seen from the curve intersections, no bandgap appears and flexural waves can propagate freely in the uniform plate at all frequencies. When PCLD coverage is applied, more modes appear and band structure curves become more complicated. Shown in Fig. 3 are the mode shapes corresponding to the modes 'a'-'f' labeled in Fig. 2(b). Fig. 3(a)-(b) show two modes where only in-plane wave motions of the base plate are observed. Note that only flexural wave bandgaps are considered here for the reason that flexural waves are of the greatest significance in the process of structure-fluid interaction at audio frequencies[20]. Therefore, influences of in-plane waves in bandgap regions are ignored. Fig. 3(c)-(f) show some of flexural wave motions in which PCLD coverage is deformed vigorously. Multiple modes of PCLD coverage are induced, leading to multi-bandgap property. Bandgaps are generated between the flexural wave curves, including complete bandgaps (CBs) and directional bandgaps (DBs), as shown in Fig. 2(b). Two CBs are [1683 – 1944] Hz and [2536 – 2695] Hz. The DBs along the ΓX direction are [649 – 819] Hz, [1683 – 2181] Hz, [2456 – 3036] Hz, and [3126 – 3178] Hz. It can be seen that the bandwidth of all the DBs are wider than that of CBs, which means that the PCLD coverage on the plate could be more effectively suppresssing the flexural wave propagation along the ΓX direction.

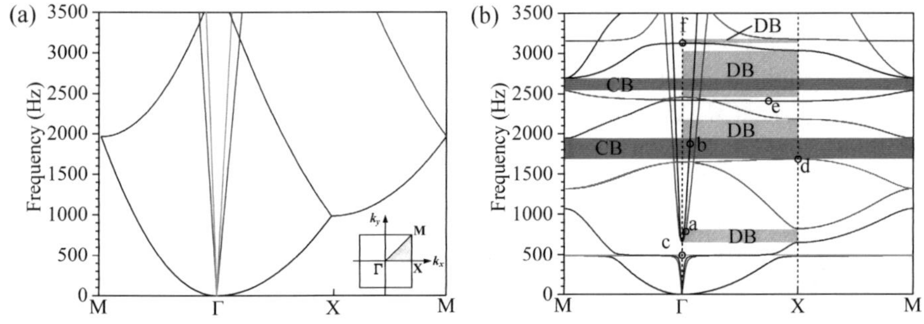

Fig. 2. Band structure curves of (a) the uniform plate and (b) the plate with periodic PCLD coverage. The shaded areas are bandgaps labeled by CB and DB.

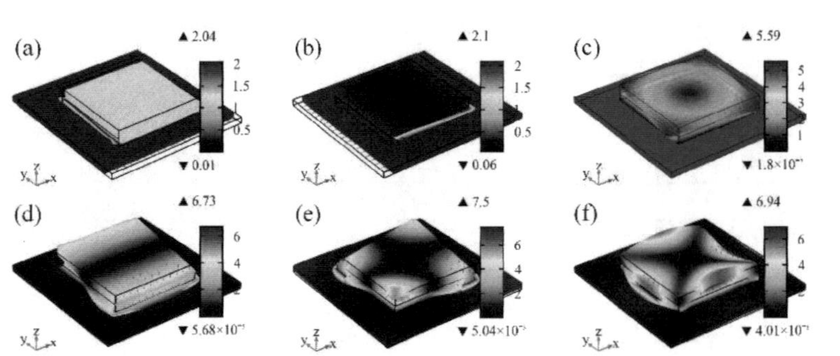

Fig. 3. Displacement fields of the modes labeled as 'a'-'f' in Fig. 2(b) for the plate with PCLD coverage.

By FEM with the software of Ansys, Fig. 4 shows the finite element model applied to calculate the transverse vibration transmission of the plate with periodic PCLD coverage. The base plate measures $1.5\,\text{m}\times 0.7\,\text{m}\times 0.004\,\text{m}$, with 13×7 periodic elements distributed uniformly in the middle part of the length 1.3 m. The geometrical and material parameters of each periodic element are all shown in Table 1. Besides PCLD coverage distribution area, two homogeneous areas, excitation area and response area, are reserved on both sides along x direction of the base plate. One area of the same size in the middle part is chosen as transmitted area. By substituting the average velocities of excitation area and transmitted area, or response area on the plate into Eq. (2.5), the transverse vibration transmittances can be obtained. Line force excitation and point force excitation are respectively applied on the specific locations of the base plate to see the flexural wave transmission.

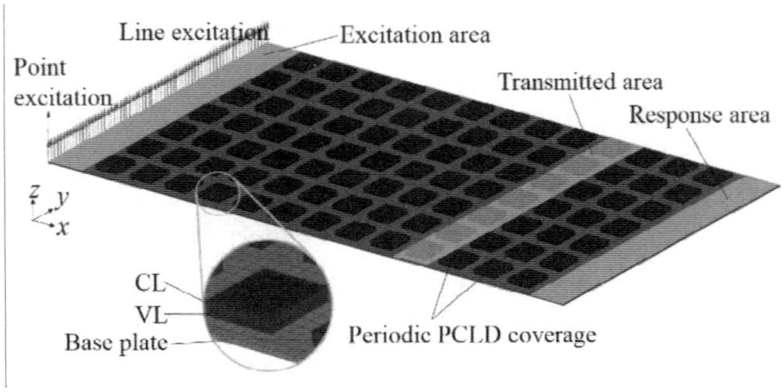

Fig. 4. FEM model of the base plate with PCLD coverage of 13×7 periodic elements distributed uniformly in the middle part. The vibration transmittances of transmitted area and response area are calculated.

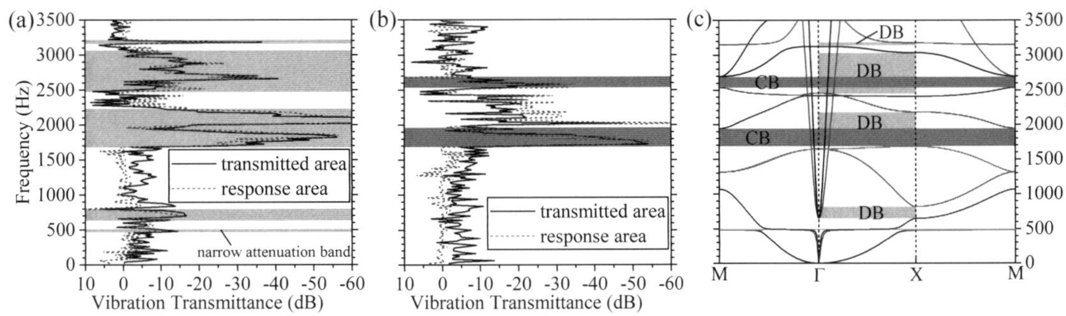

Fig. 5. The transverse vibration transmittances of transmitted area and response area under (a) line excitation; (b) point excitation. (c) The band structure curves with the bandgaps labeled as DB and CB.

Shown in Fig. 5(a) and (b) are the transverse vibration transmittances of transmitted area and response area under line excitation and point excitation, respectively. The band structure curves are replotted in Fig. 5(c) for comparison. Four attenuation frequency ranges are obviously observed in Fig. 5(a), and they are in good agreement with the DBs. Actually, there also exists one narrow attenuation band at 480 Hz, not easily identified as other four attenuation bands. It seems no bandgap is formed at 480 Hz; however, the modes on two adjacent band structure curves are changing from in-plane wave motions to out-of-plane wave motions as the increase of k_x along the ΓX direction. The narrow frequency range is

[477 – 485] Hz, where the mode shapes behaves in-plane wave motion. It is in accordance with the attenuation band at 480 Hz in Fig. 5(a).

As shown in Fig. 5(b), two frequency ranges of the same widths of CBs are sketched. The flexural waves in both frequency ranges are attenuated sharply, while the transverse vibration transmittances in the frequency range between the two CBs also show effective attenuation property. Shown in Fig. 6 are two displacement results of the base plate at 2000 Hz and 2360 Hz between the two CBs. It can be seen form the displacement distributions, given the designed parameters in this paper, flexural waves mainly propagate along x direction, which means that the DBs along the ΓX direction play a leading role in controlling the attenuation property in this frequency range.

(a) (b)

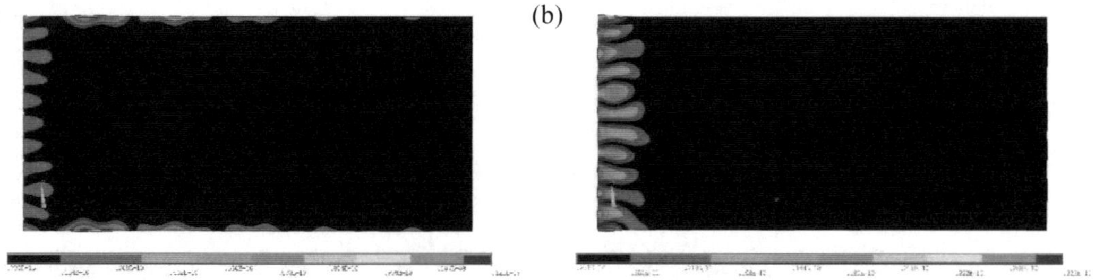

Fig. 6. Displacement responses of the base plate at (a) 2000 Hz and (b) 2360 Hz within the frequency range [1944 – 2536] Hz between the two CBs.

3.2. Effect of VL damping and vibration suppression comparisons

In order to clearly observe the bandgap property, the above band structures are calculated without considering damping. It is well known that damping characteristic in engineering can reduce the peak values and smooth the dynamic response curves, thus in the following discussion, the damping loss factor (here, independent of frequency) of VL material is induced. Other parameters are set the same as the above finite structures.

Figure 7 show the transverse vibration transmittances of the response area on the plate with PCLD coverage with damping loss factor. The damping loss factor of the VL is set as 0, 0.05, and 0.2, respectively. For the case of line excitation in Fig. 7(a), when considering the damping characteristic of VL, it has little influence on vibration response in lower frequency range. However, the attenuation band is substantially broadened with frequency increasing. As the increase of damping loss factor, the transverse vibration transmittance curve become almost a smooth curve in higher frequency range, and the attenuation band covering the latter three DB frequency ranges gets much wider. Similarly with the appearance in Fig. 7(a), the attenuation band covers the two CBs and adjacent DBs under point excitation in Fig. 7(b), while not all the DBs influence the attenuation band, such as the second one.

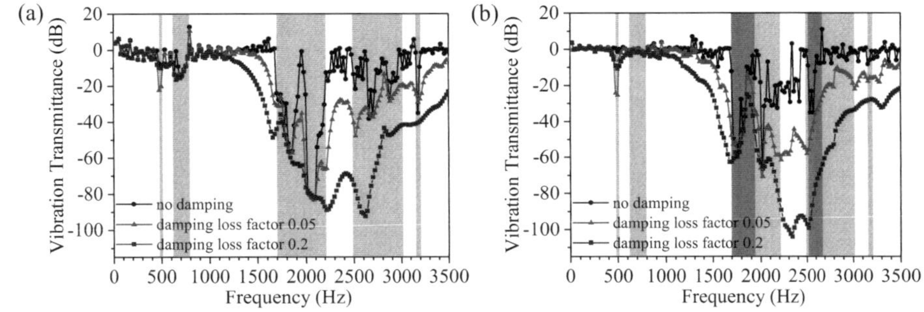

Fig. 7. Attenuation band broadening on the transverse vibration transmittance of response area with damping loss factors of the VL set 0, 0.05, and 0.2, respectively, under (a) line excitation; (b) point excitation.

To illustrate superior suppression effects of designed periodic PCLD coverage, another two finite models for comparison are selected to calculate the transverse vibration transmittances, including a plate attached with periodic lumped resonators, and a sandwich plate with monolithic constrained-layer damping (CLD) coverage, as shown in Fig. 8(a) and (b). Both models are using the same base plate with the above finite plate. There are 26×14 lumped resonators attached periodically on the base plate. Each lumped resonator consists of a viscoelastic block (0.02 m×0.02 m×0.01125 m) with a cap of heavy block (0.02 m×0.02 m×0.0135 m), of which the materials are identical to VL and CL listed in Table 1. The monolithic CLD on the sandwich plate is composed of viscoelastic core and constrained layer, of which lengths are 1.3 m, and widths are 0.7 m, and heights are kept the same as PCLD coverage. The material parameters are shown in Table 1.

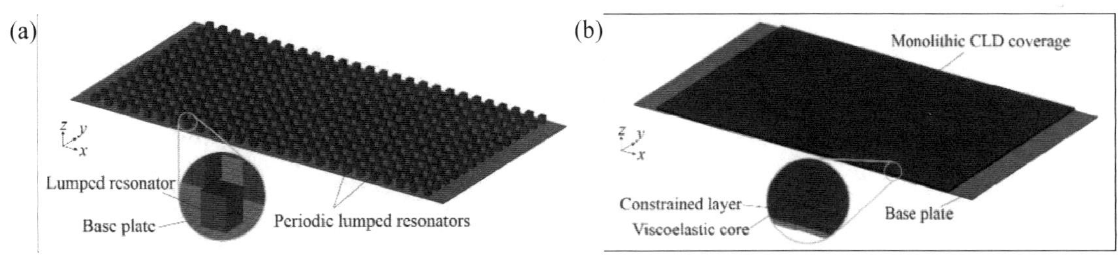

Fig. 8. Finite element model of a finite base plate with (a) periodic lumped resonators; (b) with monolithic CLD coverage.

The damping loss factors of viscoelastic material are set as 0.2 in all the three comparable models. The comparison among transmission curves of the three models is shown in Fig. 9. For the case of line excitation in Fig. 9(a), an attenuation band around 500 Hz appears for the base plate with periodic lumped resonators. Periodically distributed lumped resonators lead to the formation of a locally resonant (LR) bandgap. The valley of the attenuation band based on the LR mechanism can be deep enough, while the transmission in other frequency ranges changes little. For the sandwich plate, an attenuation band can be observed above 1800 Hz, while its bandwidth is not as wide as that of the plate with periodic PCLD coverage, and the depth of the valley is not as deep as that of the other two models. Similar phenomenon could be seen in Fig. 9(b) in the case of point excitation applied on the three comparable models.

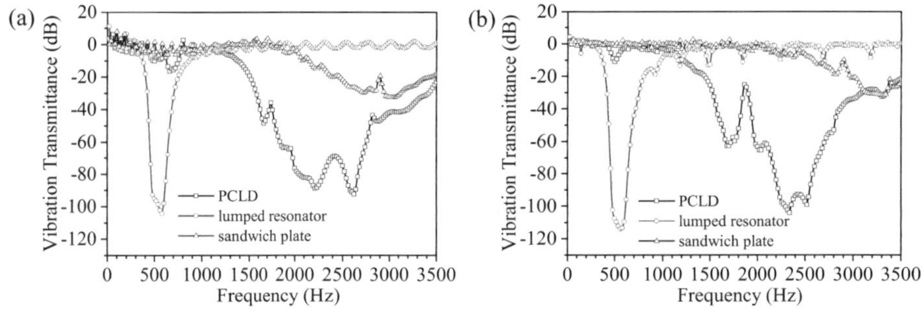

Fig. 9. The transverse vibration transmittances of response area on the base plate in the three different comparable models, under (a) line excitation; (b) point excitation.

4. Conclusions

In this paper, flexural wave bandgap property in thin plates with periodic PCLD coverage is analyzed. Utilizing FEM, band structure curves are simulated with the designed parameters. Compard with the uniform plate, when PCLD coverage is applied on the plate, CBs and DBs are generated among the flexural wave curves, while the bandwidth of all the DBs are wider than that of CBs. By simulating the transverse vibration transmission, attenuation frequency ranges are in good agreement with the bandgaps, for both cases of line excitation and point excitation. Besides, the DBs along the ΓX direction play a leading role in controlling the attenuation property. When considering the damping characteristic of VL, the attenuation band is substantially broadened. As the increase of damping loss factor, the attenuation band covering the bandgap frequency ranges gets much wider. Moreover, the transverse vibration transmittances of a plate attached with periodic lumped resonators, and a sandwich plate with monolithic constrained-layer damping coverage are calculated. Results show that a narrower LR bandgap appears, while the transmission out of the LR bandgap frequency range changes little; meanwhile, the attenuation bandwidth of the sandwich plate is not wide and deep enough as that of the plate with periodic PCLD coverage. The superior suppression effect of periodic PCLD coverage application can give guidance on structural vibration control.

References

[1] E.M. Kerwin, "Damping of flexural waves by a constrained viscoelastic layer," *J Acoust Soc Am*, **31**(7) (1959), 952–962.

[2] D.J. Mead, and S. Markus, "The forced vibration of a three-layer damped sandwich beam with arbitrary boundary conditions," *J Sound Vib*, **10**(2) (1969), 163–175.

[3] J.L. Marcelin, P. Trompette, and A. Smati, "Optimal constrained layer damping with partial coverage," *Finite Elem Anal Des*, **12**(3–4) (1992), 273–280.

[4] Y.C. Chen, and S.C. Huang, "An optimal placement of CLD treatment for vibration suppression of plates," *Int J Mech Sci*, **44**(8) (2002), 1801–1821.

[5] H. Zheng, and C. Cai, "Minimization of sound radiation from baffled beams through optimization of partial constrained layer damping treatment," *Appl Acoust*, **65** (2004), 501–520.

[6] L. Rayleigh, "XVII. On the maintenance of vibrations by forces of double frequency, and on the propagation of waves through a medium endowed with a periodic structure," *The London, Edinburgh, and Dublin Philosophical Magazine and Journal of Science*, **24**(147) (1887), 145–149.

[7] D.J. Mead, "Wave propagation in continuous periodic structures: research contributions from Southampton, 1964–1995," *J Sound Vib*, **190** (1996), 495–524.

[8] G.S. Gupta, "Natural flexural waves and the normal modes of periodically-supported beams and plates," *J Sound Vib*, **13**(1) (1970), 89–101.

[9] W. Xiao, G.W. Zeng, and Y.S. Cheng, "Flexural vibration band gaps in a thin plate containing a periodic array of hemmed discs," *Appl Acoust*, **69**(3) (2008), 255–261.

[10] L. Dai, S. Jiang, Z. Lian, H. Hu, and X. Chen, "Locally resonant band gaps achieved by equal frequency shunting circuits of piezoelectric rings in a periodic circular plate," *J Sound Vib*, **337** (2015), 150–160.

[11] J. Hsu, "Local resonances-induced low-frequency band gaps in two-dimensional phononic crystal slabs with periodic stepped resonators," *J Phys D: Appl Phys*, **44**(5) (2011), 055401.

[12] Y. Song, L. Feng, J. Wen, D. Yu, and X. Wen, "Reduction of the sound transmission of a periodic sandwich plate using the stop band concept," *Compos Struct*, **128** (2015), 428–436.

[13] Q. Qin, and M. Sheng, "Analyses of multi-bandgap property of a locally resonant plate composed of periodic resonant subsystems," *Int J Mod Phys B*, **32**(24) (2018), 1850269.

[14] W. Jung, Z. Gu, and A. Baz, "Mechanical filtering characteristics of passive periodic engine mount," *Finite Elem Anal Des*, **46**(9) (2010), 685–697.

[15] J. Huang, and Z. Shi, "Attenuation zones of periodic pile barriers and its application in vibration reduction for plane waves," *J Sound Vib*, **332**(19) (2013), 4423–4439.

[16] G. Wang, J. Wen, and X. Wen, "Quasi-one-dimensional phononic crystals studied using the improved lumped-mass method: application to locally resonant beams with flexural wave band gap," *Phys Rev B*, **71**(10) (2005), 104302.

[17] C. Qiu, Z. Liu, J. Mei, and M. Ke, "The layer multiple-scattering method for calculating transmission coefficients of 2D phononic crystals," *Solid State Commun*, **134**(11) (2005), 765–770.

[18] D.J. Mead, "The forced vibration of one-dimensional multi-coupled periodic structures: an application to finite element analysis," *J Sound Vib*, **319**(1–2) (2009), 282–304.

[19] K. Manktelow, R.K. Narisetti, and M.J. Leamy, "Finite-element based perturbation analysis of wave propagation in nonlinear periodic structures," *Mech Syst Signal Process*, **39**(1–2) (2013), 32–46.

[20] F.J. Fahy, and P. Gardonio, *Sound and Structural Vibration: Radiation, Transmission, and Response, 2nd edition*, Elsevier, 2007.

High-order Solution of Nonlinear Acoustic Wave Equation for Isotropic Solids Using Perturbation and Finite Difference Methods*

WENHAN LYU[1,2] XIANMEI WU[1,2] WEIJIANG XU[3] JIAYI CHEN[1,2]

1, State Key Laboratory of Acoustics, Institute of Acoustics, Chinese Academy of Sciences,
Beijing, 100190, China
wuxm@mail.ioa.ac.cn§
2, University of Chinese Academy of Sciences,
Beijing, 100049, China
3, Université Polytechnique Hauts-de-France, IEMN-DOAE,
59313 Valenciennes Cedex 9, France; CNRS, UMR 8520, F-59650 Villeneuve d'Ascq, France

Nonlinear acoustic wave equation with Murnaghan parameters in isotropic solids is usually resolved by perturbation method. High-order harmonics are obtained by expanding the equation in one linear and a series of nonlinear equations. It is found that errors in harmonics will accumulated when the order is increased. To estimate these errors at high-order harmonics, numerical method of finite difference in time domain (FDTD) was employed and the solutions were compared to those obtained by perturbation method. Computational parameters from steel were used as an example. Results show that perturbation solutions of fundamental wave and the second-order harmonics are in good agreements with the solutions in FDTD, relative errors are no more than 10%. While for higher order harmonics, relative errors increase heavily, especially for solutions at longer propagation distance or with higher driving amplitude, the difference is up to 50%, or even higher.

Keywords: High-order perturbation; finite difference in time domain (FDTD); nonlinear wave in isotropic solids.

1. Introduction

Acoustic wave equation is nonlinear for finite amplitude vibration in isotropic solids. Waveform is distorted due to the existence of harmonic signals during its propagation. Solving nonlinear wave equation with higher precision and efficiency is a way for obtaining the propagation properties of nonlinear acoustic waves in solids[1-2]. Perturbation method with the second-order expansion were ever used to get a simple analytical solution, which are usually applied to evaluate the weak nonlinearity in liquids or solid materials[3]. In this method, the nonlinear effect is assumed to be small so that the energy transforming from fundamental wave to high-order harmonics is ignored. However, the cumulative character of nonlinear acoustic field often leads to considerable waveform distortions, and even formation of shock waves, which means that initial assumption of weak high-order harmonics for perturbation method becomes invalid. Therefore, it is necessary to get high-order solutions. Green function method was introduced by Jones and McCall to obtain high-order cumulative solutions of nonlinear equations in solids[4]. Using this method, nonlinear term in the equation is assumed small enough to be ignored in order to get a linear solution and this solution is substituted in nonlinear terms to get the next order solution. Therefore, this method is suitable for solving equations with very small nonlinear terms.

In our work, high-order perturbation method is applied to separate the nonlinear wave equation in isotropic solids. Mach number is chosen as the perturbation term in the assumed solution. Factoring the nonlinear equation with the order of Mach number, one linear equation and a series of nonlinear equations are obtained, then each order equation can be resolved with iterative method. High-order analytical solution can be obtained with this perturbation method. However, its accuracy depends greatly on the expansion orders. Higher order makes much more complexity. Some researches[5] derived FEM equations and programmed codes to analyze the nonlinear wave propagation in liquids. But in solids, it may spend too much time and space to get a good convergence. For finite difference method, first-order difference scheme was commonly used[6], with which method the wave equation must be transformed in the form of stress and velocity for decreasing orders. In our work, the second-order difference scheme is applied to solve the nonlinear longitudinal wave equation in isotropic solids. Central difference form was applied to the second-order terms in nonlinear equation. With the difference equation, solution of each step can be obtained while a driving source is given. Computational parameters of steel[7] were given to solve the nonlinear longitudinal wave equation with two methods, which can estimate the relative errors of solutions obtained with perturbation method.

2. Formulation

Nonlinear wave equations with Murnaghan parameters[8] in a certain direction x can be expressed as follows:

$$\begin{cases} \frac{1}{c^2}\frac{\partial^2 u}{\partial t^2} - \frac{\partial^2 u}{\partial x^2} = \frac{3\lambda+6\mu+2l+4m}{\lambda+2\mu}\left(\frac{\partial u}{\partial x}\frac{\partial^2 u}{\partial x^2}\right) + \frac{\lambda+2\mu+m}{\lambda+2\mu}\left(\frac{\partial v}{\partial x}\frac{\partial^2 v}{\partial x^2} + \frac{\partial w}{\partial x}\frac{\partial^2 w}{\partial x^2}\right) \\ \frac{1}{c^2}\frac{\partial^2 v}{\partial t^2} - \frac{\partial^2 v}{\partial x^2} = \frac{\lambda+2\mu+m}{\mu}\left(\frac{\partial u}{\partial x}\frac{\partial^2 v}{\partial x^2} + \frac{\partial v}{\partial x}\frac{\partial^2 u}{\partial x^2}\right) \\ \frac{1}{c^2}\frac{\partial^2 w}{\partial t^2} - \frac{\partial^2 w}{\partial x^2} = \frac{\lambda+2\mu+m}{\mu}\left(\frac{\partial u}{\partial x}\frac{\partial^2 w}{\partial x^2} + \frac{\partial w}{\partial x}\frac{\partial^2 u}{\partial x^2}\right) \end{cases}. \quad (2.1)$$

where λ, μ are the Lame constants and l, m, n are nonlinear parameters. Assuming that $v = v(x,t)$, $u = w = 0$, which means the driving source is transverse wave. Then, Eq. (2.1) becomes:

$$\frac{1}{c^2}\frac{\partial^2 u}{\partial t^2} - \frac{\partial^2 u}{\partial x^2} = \frac{3\lambda+6\mu+2l+4m}{\lambda+2\mu}\left(\frac{\partial u}{\partial x}\frac{\partial^2 u}{\partial x^2}\right). \quad (2.2)$$

which is one-dimensional nonlinear longitudinal wave equation in isotropic solids.

3. Methods

3.1. Perturbation method

To solve Eq. (2.2), high-order perturbation method is applied firstly to get an analytical solution. Assuming the following solution form, which is expanded with Mach number,

$$u = \sum_{i=1}^{n} M^i u_i. \tag{3.1}$$

where $M = V_0/c$ is Mach number, V_0 is the amplitude of the vibration velocity and $c = \sqrt{\frac{\lambda+2u}{\rho_0}}$ is the wave propagation velocity in the material, ρ_0 is the mass density of the material. Substituting Eq. (3.1) into Eq. (2.2), where $\beta = \frac{3\lambda+6\mu+2l+4m}{\lambda+2\mu}$,

$$\frac{1}{c^2}\frac{\partial^2}{\partial t^2}\left(\sum_{i=1}^{n} M^i u_i\right) = \frac{\partial^2}{\partial x^2}\left(\sum_{i=1}^{n} M^i u_i\right) + \beta\frac{\partial}{\partial x}\left(\sum_{i=1}^{n} M^i u_i\right)\frac{\partial^2}{\partial x^2}\left(\sum_{i=1}^{n} M^i u_i\right). \tag{3.2}$$

Factoring the above equation in terms of M^i,

$$M^1: \frac{1}{c^2}\frac{\partial^2 u_1}{\partial t^2} = \frac{\partial^2 u_1}{\partial x^2}, \tag{3.3}$$

$$M^2: \frac{1}{c^2}\frac{\partial^2 u_2}{\partial t^2} = \frac{\partial^2 u_2}{\partial x^2} + \beta\frac{\partial u_1}{\partial x}\frac{\partial^2 u_1}{\partial x^2}, \tag{3.4}$$

$$M^{\cdots}: \quad \cdots\cdots \tag{3.5}$$

Eq. (3.3) is a linear equation and its solution can be resolved using the method of separation variables. Considering a linear driving wave propagating in the positive x direction,

$$u_1 = A_0\cos(kx - \omega t), \tag{3.6}$$

where A_0 is wave amplitude at initial position (usually a driving source), k is wave number and ω is angular frequency. Substituting Eq. (3.6) into Eq. (3.4),

$$\frac{1}{c^2}\frac{\partial^2 u_2}{\partial t^2} - \frac{\partial^2 u_2}{\partial x^2} = \frac{1}{2}\beta {A_0}^2 k^3\sin(2kx - 2\omega t). \tag{3.7}$$

Whose solution can be found to be,

$$u_2 = \frac{1}{8}\beta {A_0}^2 k^2 x\cos(2kx - 2\omega t). \tag{3.8}$$

and so on, with the same method:

$$u_3 = \beta^2\left[-\frac{1}{32}{A_0}^3k^4x^2\cos(kx-\omega t) - \frac{3}{32}{A_0}^3k^3x\sin(kx-\omega t) + \frac{1}{32}{A_0}^3k^4x^2\cos(3kx-3\omega t) + \frac{5}{96}{A_0}^3k^3x\sin(3kx-3\omega t)\right]. \tag{3.9}$$

$$u_4 = \beta^3\left[\left(-\frac{1}{96}{A_0}^4k^6x^3 + \frac{1}{12}{A_0}^4k^4x\right)\cos(2kx-2\omega t) - \frac{33}{512}{A_0}^4k^5x^2\sin(2kx-2\omega t) + \left(\frac{1}{96}{A_0}^4k^6x^3 - \frac{11}{512}{A_0}^4k^4x\right)\cos(4kx-4\omega t) + \frac{5}{128}{A_0}^4k^5x^2\sin(4kx-4\omega t)\right]. \tag{3.10}$$

The first two order solutions permit the next order one, therefore, $u_5, u_6, \dots\dots, u_n$ can be obtained with the same method. Substituting all the solutions into Eq. (3.1) and integrating the terms having same harmonic frequency, there is

$$u = \sum_n A_n\sin\left(nkx - n\omega t + \tanh^{-1}\frac{c_n}{s_n}\right). \tag{3.11}$$

where $A_n = \sqrt{{s_n}^2 + {c_n}^2}$, and $\tanh^{-1}\frac{c_n}{s_n}$ (for $n = 1,2,3,4,\ldots$) is amplitude and phase of the nth harmonic wave component, respectively. A_n, s_n, c_n are functions of propagation distance x and wave amplitude A_0 at initial position.
The first four orders are given as following:

$$s_1 = -\frac{3}{32}M^3\beta^2{A_0}^3k^3x, c_1 = A_0M - \frac{1}{32}M^3\beta^2{A_0}^3k^4x^2, \quad (3.12)$$

$$s_2 = -M^4\beta^3\frac{33}{512}{A_0}^4k^5x^2, c_2 = \frac{1}{8}M^2\beta{A_0}^2k^2x + M^4\beta^3\left(-\frac{1}{96}{A_0}^4k^6x^3 + \frac{1}{12}{A_0}^4k^4x\right), \quad (3.13)$$

$$s_3 = \frac{5}{96}M^3\beta^2{A_0}^3k^3x, c_3 = \frac{1}{32}M^3\beta^2{A_0}^3k^4x^2, \quad (3.14)$$

$$s_4 = \frac{5}{128}M^4\beta^3{A_0}^4k^5x^2, c_4 = M^4\beta^3\left(\frac{1}{96}{A_0}^4k^6x^3 - \frac{11}{512}{A_0}^4k^4x\right), \quad (3.15)$$

Where, the Mach number $M = V_0/c = \omega A_0/c$.

3.2. Finite difference in time domain method

FDTD method was commonly used for solving first-order linear elastic wave equations expressed with stress and velocity. But for nonlinear equations, it is hard to get their first-order form due to the existence of nonlinear terms. Therefore, the second-order FDTD form was tried to solve this problem in our work, as shown in Eq. (2.2), which has been proved to have good convergence and accuracy in solving some other similar problems[9].
Integrating the above equation.

$$u_i^{n+1} = 2u_i^n - u_i^{n-1} + \Delta T^2\left(\frac{u_{i+1}^n - 2u_i^n + u_{i-1}^n}{\Delta h^2}\right) + \beta\Delta T^2\left(\frac{u_{i+1}^n - u_{i-1}^n}{2\cdot\Delta h}\right)\left(\frac{u_{i+1}^n - 2u_i^n + u_{i-1}^n}{\Delta h^2}\right). \quad (3.16)$$

The stability condition should be satisfied:

$$V_{max} = \frac{du}{dt} < \frac{\Delta h}{\Delta T}\ . \quad (3.17)$$

where $V_{max} = \frac{du}{dt}$ is the maximum amplitude of the vibration velocity in the computational model.
With the above equations, codes can be programmed by MATLAB to obtain the numerical results. Once a diving source u is given at the initial time and position, the displacement at the next time and space step could be computed. Then, the newly obtained solution becomes the driving source to resolve the next step. Finally, displacement at each step can be obtained with continuous iteration process.

4. Results and Discussions

From both Eq. (3.11) and Eq. (3.16), the displacement of nonlinear acoustic wave during its propagation can be obtained with a driving source. Results in isotropic steel are given as an example and the relevant parameters[7] are shown in Tab. 1.

Tab. 1. Computation parameters

Parameters	Perturbation method	FDTD
λ	11.58GPa	11.58GPa
μ	7.99GPa	7.99GPa
l	-24.8GPa	-24.8GPa
m	-62.3GPa	-62.3GPa

f	1MHz	1MHz
c	5900m/s	5900m/s
ρ	7800kg/m^3	7800kg/m^3
ΔT	/	1e-8s
Δh	/	1.18e-4m

A driving source $u = 0.5e^{-6}\sin(2\pi ft)$ is given at the initial position, one propagation direction is considered and the signals received at different position are discussed. Signal received at 400mm far away from the initial position is chosen as an example to observe its variation compared with initial driving source (sine wave) in time domain and frequency domain, respectively, as shown in Fig. 1.

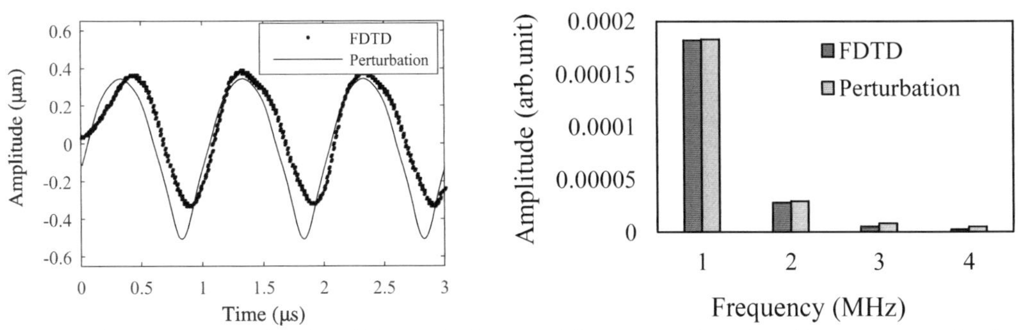

Fig. 1. The signals received at 400mm in time and frequency domain with the two methods

When acoustic wave with finite amplitude propagates, its waveform deforms gradually compared with the initial signal due to the nonlinearity of the material, as shown in Fig. 1. The deformations are a little different for the results of two methods as harmonics components in the solution are limited within the expansion orders for perturbation method while there is no order limitation in FDTD solutions. Waveform deformation means high-frequency harmonics generation, as shown in the spectrum results. Amplitudes of the harmonics obtained by perturbation method are higher than results of FDTD, especially for the third- and fourth-order harmonics.

Wave deformation depends greatly on driving amplitude, propagation distance and material properties. Therefore, harmonics generation of different propagation distance with different amplitude ($0.34, 0.38, 0.42\mu m$) were computed. A_n/A_0 (amplitude ratio of the nth order harmonics and driving source amplitude) is applied to represent harmonics generation efficiency. Results are shown in Fig. 2.

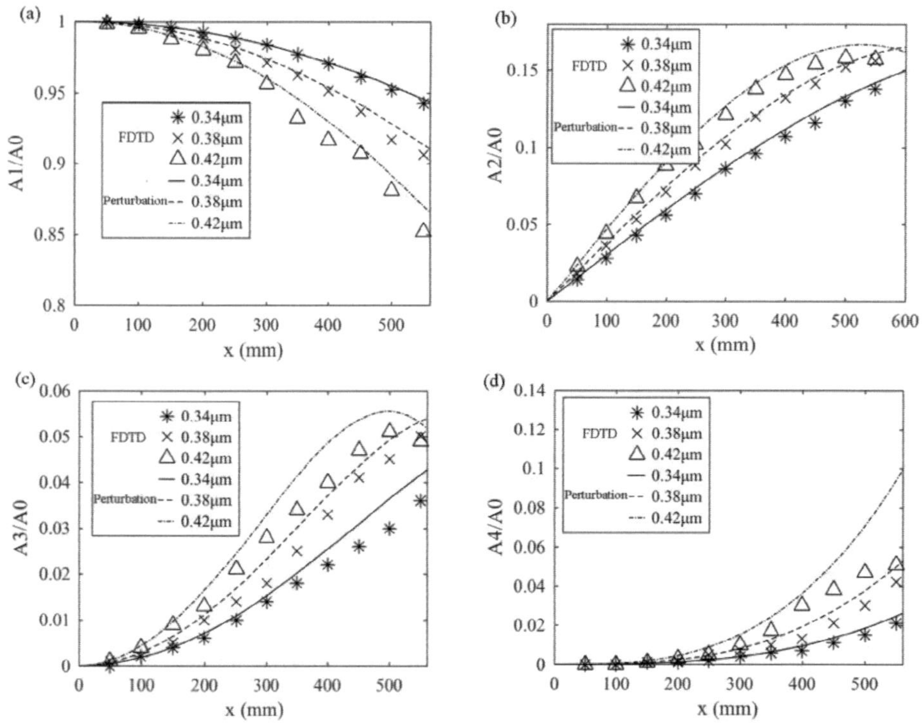

Fig. 2. Harmonics generation efficiency variation of: (a) fundamental waves (A_1/A_0); (b) the second-order (A_2/A_0); (c) the third-order (A_3/A_0); (d) the fourth-order harmonics (A_4/A_0) with propagation distance under different driving source amplitude.

For fundamental wave, as shown in Fig. 2(a), its amplitude decreases gradually with the increase of propagation distance under a certain driving source amplitude and it falls faster while driving source amplitude is higher. For the second- and third-order harmonics, as shown in Fig. 2(b) and (c), their value both increase firstly and then drops down during its propagation. Therefore, there is a turning point in each curve and higher amplitude of the driving source leads to the earlier coming of the turning point. Because signals with lower-orders are the energy source of higher-orders, nonlinear phenomenon is accumulated during waves propagation. So the components of harmonics become richer for longer propagation distance. More energy will be transferred from lower order to higher order harmonics during propagation. Therefore, amplitude of the fundamental wave drops and other higher order harmonics cannot increase all the time. As the energy of the fourth-order harmonics is very weak, as shown in Fig. 2(d), its amplitude will drop down for much longer distance or with higher driving amplitude.

Results in both methods are in good agreements for fundamental and the second-order harmonics. While for the third- and fourth-order harmonics, the errors of the perturbation method become much more obvious. The relative errors of each order harmonics obtained with perturbation method compared with FDTD, are given in Fig. 3.

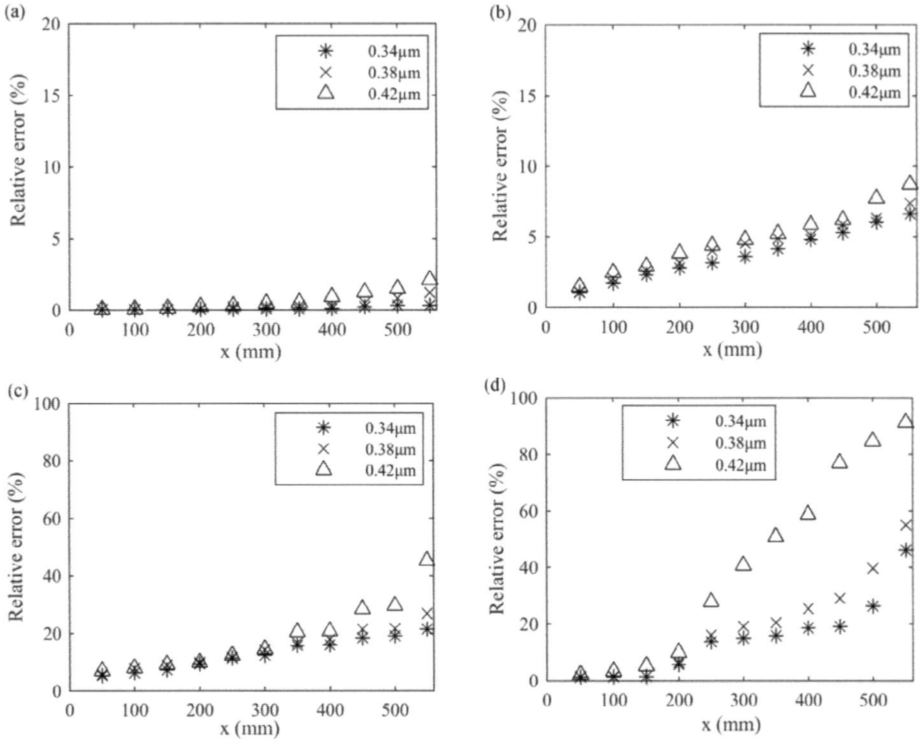

Fig. 3. The relative errors of: (a) fundamental waves (A_1); (b) the second-order (A_2); (c) the third-order (A_3); (d) the fourth-order (A_4) harmonics in perturbation method compared with FDTD.

Compared with numerical solution, the relative errors of perturbation solution increase gradually with the harmonics' order. For the solution of fundamental wave and the second-order harmonics, relative errors are no more than 10%, as shown in Fig. 3. (a) and (b). While for higher order harmonics, relative errors increase heavily, especially for solutions at longer propagation distance or with higher driving amplitude, errors are up to 50%, or even higher, as shown in Fig. 3. (c) and (d). Because expansion orders limit the harmonics orders of the perturbation method, so energy exchanged among the harmonics is also limited, especially for the third-, fourth- or higher order harmonics. For longer propagation distance and higher driving source, nonlinear phenomenon becomes much more obvious, so that the relative errors are much bigger. Therefore, perturbation method is commonly used to provide an estimated analytical solution, which is effective under some conditions, such as weakly nonlinearity for the second-order harmonics or higher-order harmonics with lower energy input and short propagation distance.

5. Conclusion

Perturbation and FDTD methods were used to solve the nonlinear wave equation in isotropic solids. High-order perturbation method provides an analytical solution, from which mathematic relationships among the parameters, such as driving source amplitude, propagation distance and nonlinear coefficients, can be obtained. However, the accuracy of the solution depends greatly on the expansion orders. Much higher order makes much more complexity. FDTD method gives a numerical solution, which provides a general relationship among the relevant parameters. It has good convergence even for high nonlinearity and no limitation of solution orders compared with perturbation method.

Perturbation solutions of fundamental wave and the second-order harmonics are in good agreements with solutions of FDTD, relative errors are no more than 10%. While for higher order harmonics, relative errors increase heavily, especially for solutions at longer propagation distance or with higher driving amplitude, the errors are up to 50%, or even higher.

References

[1] Gurbatov, S.N., I.Y. Demin, and N.V. Pronchatov-Rubtsov, *Bispectral analysis in inverse nonlinear acoustics problems.* Acoustical Physics, 2017. **63**(6): p. 637-641.

[2] Naugolnykh, K.A. and I.B. Esipov, *The propagation of a nonlinear sound wave in an unconsolidated granular medium.* Acoustical Physics, 2005. **51**(6): p. 713-718.

[3] Wallace, K.D., et al., *Finite Amplitude Measurements of the Nonlinear Parameter B/A for Liquid Mixtures Spanning a Range Relevant to Tissue Harmonic Mode.* Ultrasound in Medicine and Biology, 2007. **33**(4): p. 620-629.

[4] McCall, K.R., *Theoretical study of nonlinear elastic wave propagation.* Journal of Geophysical Research: Solid Earth, 1994. **99**(B2): p. 2591-2600.

[5] Campos-Pozuelo, C., B. Dubus, and J.A. Gallego-Juárez, *Finite-element analysis of the. nonlinear propagation of high-intensity acoustic waves.* The Journal of the Acoustical Society of America, 1999. **106**(1): p. 91-101.

[6] Wang, X., et al., *Finite-difference time-domain scheme for nonlinear acoustic waves in solids.* Mechanical Systems and Signal Processing, 2018.

[7] Egle, D.M. and D.E. Bray, *Measurement of acoustoelastic and third-order elastic constants for rail steel.* The Journal of the Acoustical Society of America, 1976. **60**(3): p. 741-744.

[8] Murnaghan, F.D., *Finite Deformation of an Elastic Solid.* 1951, John Wiley: New York. p. 60-66.

[9] Yan, H., L. Yang, and X.-Y. Li, *Optimal staggered-grid finite-difference schemes by combining Taylor-series expansion and sampling approximation for wave equation modeling.* Journal of Computational Physics, 2016. **326**: p. 913-930.

Optimal Design on SAW Strain Sensing Device at High Temperature Employing AlN Piezoelectric Thin-film*

Shuyao Fan[1,2] Wen Wang[1] Xueling Li[1,2] Yana Jia[1, 2]
1, Institute of Acoustics, Chinese Academy of Sciences,
Beijing, 100190, China
2, University of Chinese Academy of Sciences, School of Electronic, Electrical and Communication Engineering
Beijing, 100049, China
fanshuyao@mail.ioa.ac.cn
1, Institute of Acoustics, Chinese Academy of Sciences,
Beijing, 100190, China
wangwenwq@mail.ioa.ac.cn§
1, Institute of Acoustics, Chinese Academy of Sciences,
Beijing, 100190, China
lixueling@mail.ioa.ac.cn
1, Institute of Acoustics, Chinese Academy of Sciences,
Beijing, 100190, China
jiayana225@163.com

Sensing strain of high-temperature components in the fields of aerospace and nuclear power is of great significance to ensure accurate operation and safe production of equipment. To obtain strain information at extreme high temperature environment, a SAW strain sensing device employing composite structure of Al_2O_3/IDTs/AlN/Metal/Diamond was proposed. Al_2O_3 is filled between the IDT electrodes to increase electrode reflectivity, allowing reduction of acoustic losses and improvement of device temperature stability. Obviously, high performance as Q-value and low insertion loss of the sensing chip is the key for achieving successful wireless strain sensing system. In this work, the SAW propagation characteristics in multi-layered composite structures was analyzed by using finite element method (FEM), and corresponding simulation parameters in coupling of modes (COM) model was extracted theoretically. High Q-value and excellent temperature stability were achieved from the proposed SAW sensing device structure using the determined design parameters.
Keywords: AlN Piezoelectric Film; High Temperature Strain Sensor; Finite Element Method; SAW.

1. Introduction

Sensing strain of high-temperature components in the fields of aerospace and nuclear power is of great significance to ensure accurate operation and safe production of equipment. Therefore, the extreme high-temperature environmental strain online monitoring technology has become a research hotspot in recent years. Surface acoustic wave (SAW) based device has attracted great interests for sensing strain at extreme temperature because it features small size, low cost, fast response, mass production and their ability to operate wirelessly and passively by deriving all the measurement energy from an incident radio frequency (RF) signal. Actually, some mature applications for sensing gas, temperature, and pressure were realized by using the SAW devices with various structures. However, as for the construction of the sensing device towards high temperature sensor, the SAW devices still suffer from the piezoelectric crystals and metal electrodes for high temperature.

(i) Typical piezoelectric crystals used for the SAW devices were quartz and Lithium. The piezoelectric properties of these substrates will be deteriorated at high temperature because of their low Curie temperature. Obviously, exploitation of new high-temperature-resistant materials should be the focus of high temperature sensing device. Till present, there some new piezoelectric materials were exploited. Among the available materials, Aluminum Nitride (AlN) features excellent characteristics of high-temperature-resistant over 1150°C[1]. Also, high temperature electrode in sensing device is a problem to be solved. Platinum (Pt) and Pt alloy becomes a suitable candidate for high-temperature sensing device because of their excellent properties such as high-temperature resistance, high strength, oxidation resistance and corrosion resistance. So, the sensing device employing AlN thin-film and Pt electrodes provides a solution for sensing strain at extreme high temperature.

(ii) It is well-known that the device property determines directly the sensor performance. Especially, high Q-value and low insertion loss of the sensing chip is the key for achieving successful wireless strain sensing system. Hence, the optimal design towards the sensing device allowing excellent performance is very important prior to device fabrication, but, it is rarely reported in previous literatures.

(iii) In this work, the optimal design on SAW strain sensing device at high temperature was conducted by using the finite element method (FEM) and coupling of modes (COM). The composite structure of Al_2O_3/IDTs/AlN/Metal/Diamond was used to build the sensing device[2], in which, the Al_2O_3 acts as the protective layer to suppress the agglomeration of the metal electrode at high-temperature.

(iv) Using the FEM, the SAW propagation along the multilayer composite structure of Al_2O_3/IDTs/AlN/Metal/Diamond was investigated, and corresponding COM parameters were extracted. On this basis, the optimal design on the SAW high-temperature strain sensing device was realized.

2. Coupling of Modes Theory and Simulation

The AlN multilayer composite structure was used to build the high-temperature strain sensing device. So, the FEM analysis was performed to investigate the SAW propagation characteristics in multilayer composite structures of Al_2O_3/IDTs/AlN/Metal/Diamond, and corresponding COM simulation parameters were extracted theoretically.

2.1. Modeling and meshing

First, the FEM modeling was conducted to demonstrate the acoustic wave propagation along the layered structure. Figure 1 depicts the meshing picture of the proposed strain sensing device using the layered structure of Al_2O_3/IDTs/AlN/Metal/Diamond. It is well-known that the displacement distribution of SAW is confined into the crystal surface, and the displacement component in Y-direction can be neglected. For simplification, the hypothesis of continuous periodicity is set in the calculation. Addtionally, the Diamond is used as the perfect matching layer (PML) to reduce the thickness of the substrate and suppress the spurious waves from the interface reflection.

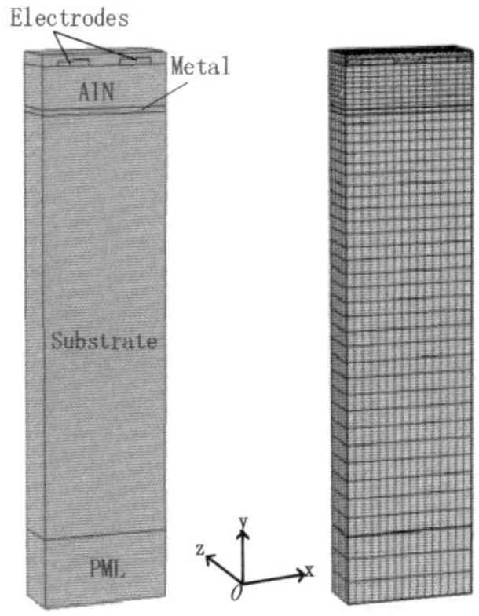

Fig.1 Period model for the Al_2O_3/IDTs/AlN/Metal/Diamond SAW high-temperature strain Sensor.

The AlN material constants are taken from reference[3]. Metal plate and electrode are made by high-temperature resistant Pt. Corresponding material constants used in the simulation are listed in Table 1.

Table 1. The materials parameters

Materials	Parameters Q	Q_0 at room temperature
Pt	ρ(kg/m³)	21450
T_0=25℃	E (N/m²)	168e9
	μ	0.38
Diamond (100)	ρ(kg/m³)	3515
T_0=25℃	ε(10−11F/m²)	4.51
	E (N/m²)	105e10
	μ	0.1
Al_2O_3	ρ(kg/m³)	3965
T_0=25℃	ε(10−11F/m²)	5.05
	E (N/m²)	400e9
	μ	0.22

2.2. Coupling of modes modeling

First, the modal analysis towards acoustic wave propagation in layered structure of Al_2O_3/IDTs/AlN/Metal/Diamond can be well conducted, and corresponding SAW natural frequencies was obtained. Following the modal analysis, the appropriate frequency scanning range is selected. Harmonic response analysis is carried out by setting electrical boundary conditions for the device model. Finally, the static analysis was performed to the multilayer composite structure to obtain the static electric field energy, and hence, the static capacitance can also be determined.

Based on the typical COM theory, corresponding COM parameters defined by Eq. (2.1-2.3)[4] for device simulation can also be extracted. Here, parameters of v, κ, α and Cn are defined by propagation velocity, coupling coefficient, excitation coefficient, and normalized static capacitance, respectively. f_{sc+}, f_{sc-}, f_{oc+}, and f_{oc-} denote the up and down boundary frequency of the stopband in periodic shorted grating and open grating. W and λ are the acoustic aperture and corresponding wavelength, respectively. W_e is the static electric field energy.

$$\begin{cases} v = \lambda \dfrac{(f_{sc+} + f_{sc-})}{2}, \\ |\kappa|\lambda = 2\pi \dfrac{f_{sc+} - f_{sc-}}{f_{sc+} + f_{sc-}}. \end{cases} \tag{2.1}$$

$$\begin{cases} |\alpha_n| = \sqrt{\omega C_n \lambda \pi \left(\dfrac{f_{oc+} + f_{oc-}}{f_{sc+} + f_{sc-}} - 1 \right)}, \\ \cos\left(\angle\alpha^2/\kappa\right) = \dfrac{(f_{oc+} - f_{oc-})^2 - (f_{sc+} - f_{sc-})^2 - \left[(f_{oc+} + f_{oc-}) - (f_{sc+} + f_{sc-})\right]^2}{2(f_{sc+} - f_{sc-})\left[(f_{oc+} + f_{oc-}) - (f_{sc+} + f_{sc-})\right]}. \end{cases} \tag{2.2}$$

$$C_n = \frac{W_e}{(\Delta V)^2 W}. \tag{2.3}$$

The resonance and anti-resonance frequencies, f_r and f_a, respectively, are determined by the calculated input admittance towards the different acoustic wave modes, and their effective electromechanical coupling factor K_e^2 can also be deduced by Eq. (2.4)[5].

$$K_e^2 = \left(\frac{\pi f_r}{2 f_a}\right) \cot\left(\frac{\pi f_r}{2 f_a}\right) \tag{2.4}$$

3. Simulation Analysis

Based on the theoretical model, the propagation characteristics in layered structure of Al_2O_3/IDTs/AlN/Metal/Diamond composite structure are investigated. Wavelength λ used in the calculation is set to 13.688um, and the metal plate thickness and the electrode thickness are both set to 0.02λ, respectively.

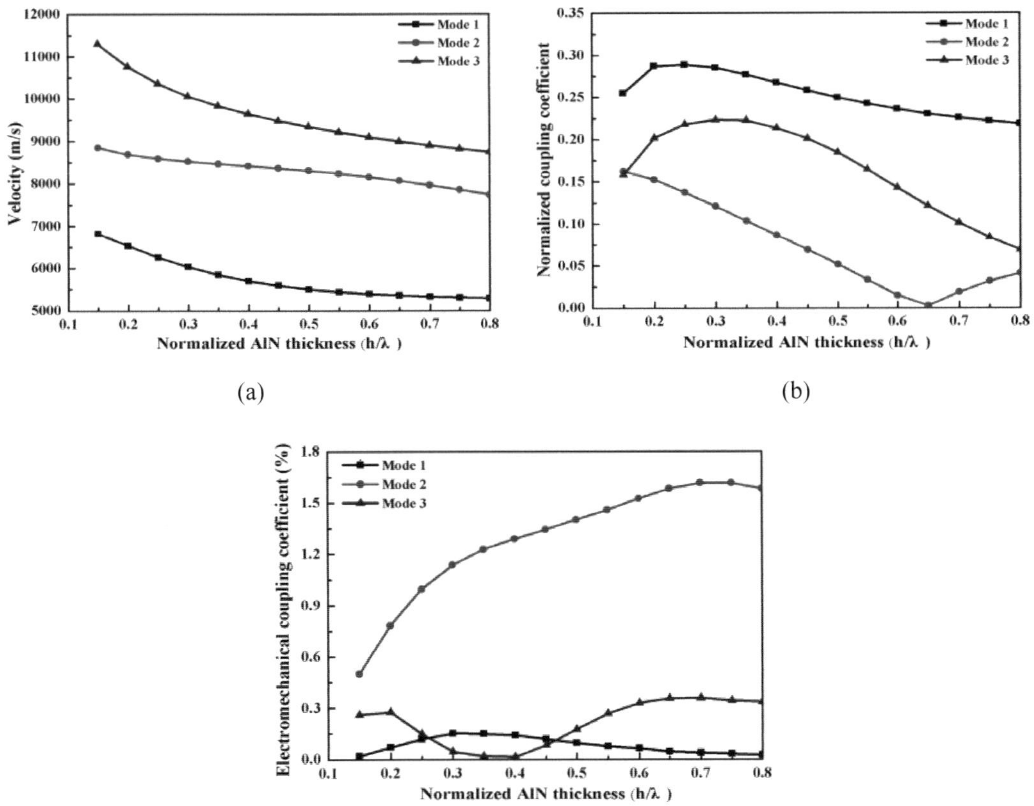

(a) (b)

(c)

Fig. 2. Variation of v (a), κ_p (b), K_e^2 (c) with h_{AlN}/λ.

Figure 2 offers COM parameters of v, κ_p and K_e^2 varying with AlN thickness of h_{AlN}/λ, where h_{AlN} is the AlN thickness. Multiple acoustic modes exist and are marked in the order of their phase velocities. Mode 1, mode 2 and mode 3 are Rayleigh wave, Sezawa wave[7] and Lamb wave, respectively. As illustrated in Fig. 3(a), the acoustic velocity of all modes decreases as the AlN thickness increases because the acoustic wave velocity in AlN is less than that in diamond. As shown in Fig. 3(b), the coupling coefficients of mode 1 and mode 3 increases first with increases in AlN, and then decreases. Obviously, there occurs a maximum value of coupling coefficient varying with the AlN thickness. For mode 1, the largest coupling coefficient of 0.286 was observed at AlN thickness of 0.25λ. Corresponding maximum value of 0.223 in coupling coefficient was obtained from mode 3 when AlN thickness is 0.30λ. It is seen that mode 2 is different from the former two, which takes a minimum value of 0.0028 at h_{AlN}/λ=0.65. As shown in Fig. 2(c), the K_e^2 of mode 1 and mode 2 firstly increases, then decreases with h_{AlN}. When AlN thickness is 0.30λ, a maximum K_e^2 is 0.153% for mode 1; Moreover, when AlN thickness is 0.75λ, a maximum K_e^2 of 1.62% for mode 2 is obtained. When AlN thickness is 0.35λ, the K_e^2 of mode 3 is close to 0. The reason is that there are some other acoustic modes near mode 3. It should be noted that the frequency corresponding to the other acoustic modes also changes as the thickness of the AlN increases. Coupling will occur between modes when the frequencies of the two or more acoustic modes are close.

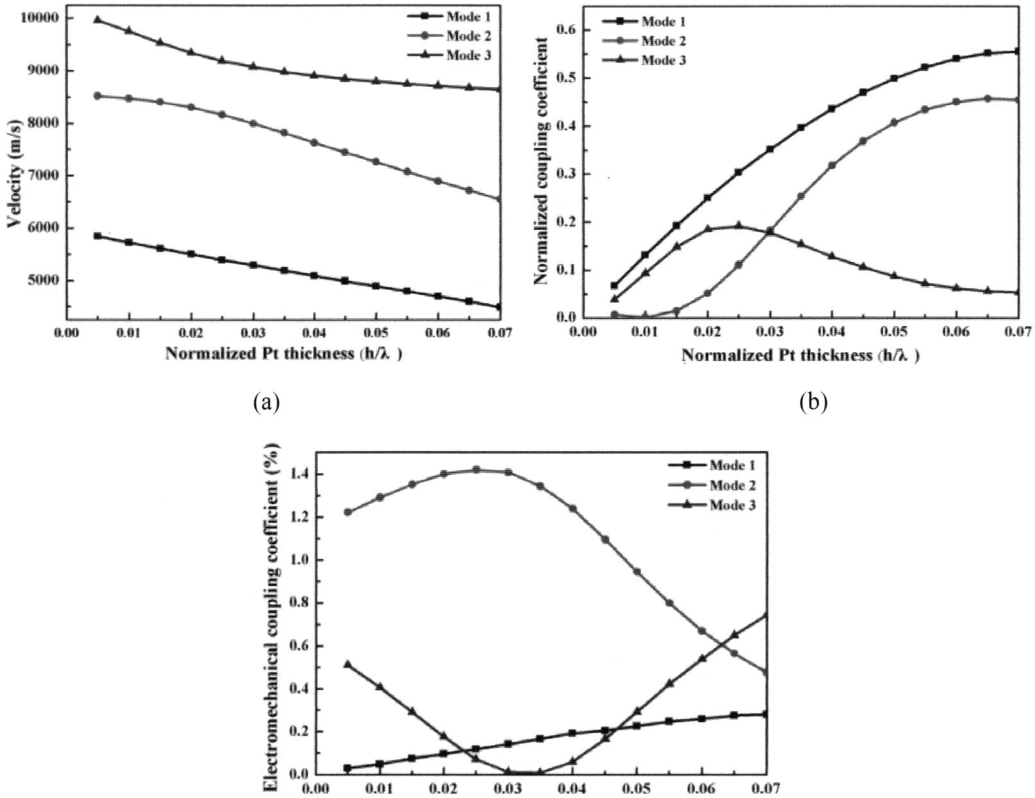

(a) (b)

(c)

Fig. 3. Variation of v (a), κ_P (b), K_e^2 (c) with h_{Pt}/λ.

Considering COM parameters, the AlN thickness is set to 0.50λ and the metal plate thickness is fixed to 0.02λ. Figure 3 shows the changes of v, κ_p and K_e^2 in the structure of Al_2O_3/IDTs/AlN/Metal/Diamond as a function of h_{Pt}/λ, where h_{Pt} is the Pt electrode thickness. The acoustic wave velocity decreases with the increase of the Pt electrode thickness (Fig. 3(a)) because of the mass loading effect. As shown in Fig. 3(b), the coupling coefficient of both acoustic modes firstly increases, then decreases with h_{Pt}. As the electrode thickness increases, more acoustic energy is directed to the surface of piezoelectric material and the area near the electrode. Therefore, the coupling coefficient increases with h_{Pt} within a certain range of electrode thickness. However, when the electrode thickness exceeds a certain value, the coupling coefficient gradually decreases. This is the result of the interaction of electrical load and mechanical load. As shown in Fig. 3(c), the K_e^2 of mode 1 increases with the increase of Pt electrode thickness, and the K_e^2 of mode 2 first increases and then decreases with h_{Pt}. The K_e^2 of mode 3 is opposite to that of mode 2.

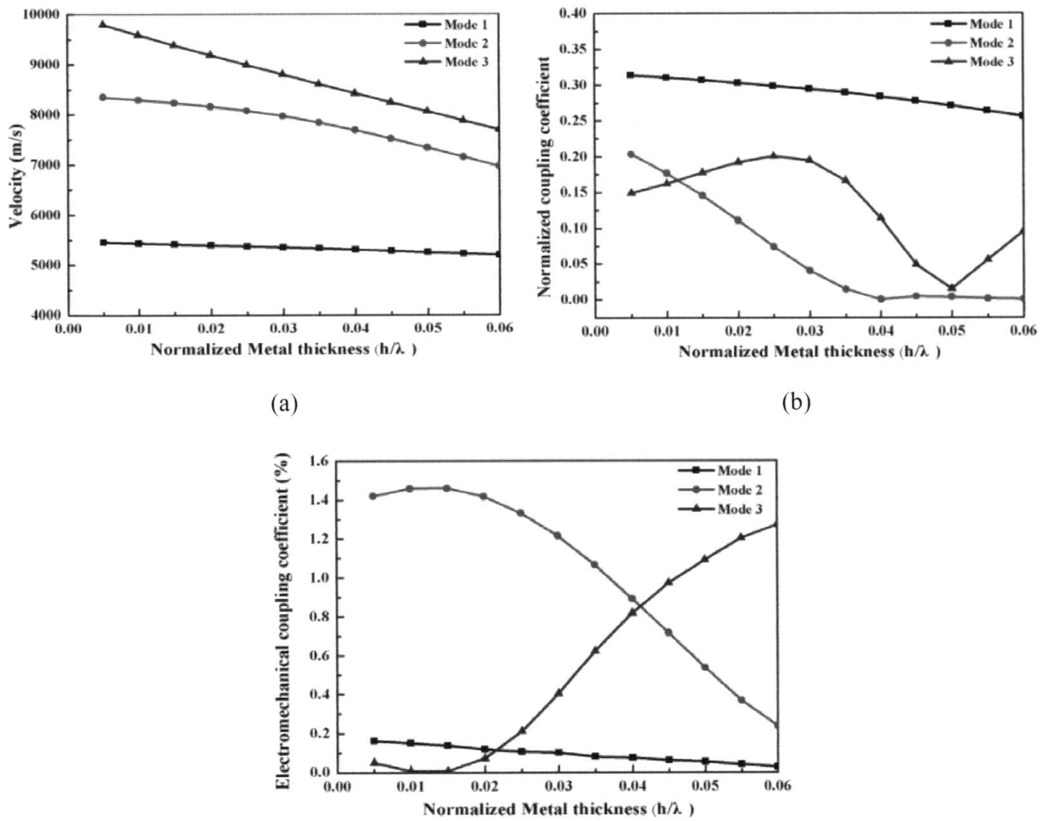

(a) (b)

(c)

Fig. 4. Variation of v (a), κ_p (b), K_e^2 (c) with h_{Pt}/λ.

Considering COM parameters, the AlN thickness is fixed to 0.50λ, and the Pt electrode thickness is set to 0.025λ. Figure 4 shows the estimated v, κ_p and K_e^2 as a function of h_{Metal}/λ, where h_{Metal} is the Pt metal plate thickness. As shown in Fig. 4(a), velocity of all acoustic modes in SAW device decrease with the increase of Pt metal plate thickness. Among them, the velocity of mode 1 is least affected by h_{Metal}. As shown in Fig. 4(b), the coupling coefficients of mode 1 and mode 2 decrease gradually with h_{Metal} until they become stable. The change trend of coupling coefficient of mode 3 is different from the former two, which is more complex. Because mode 3 will gradually transformed into the Lamb wave with h_{Metal}. As shown in Fig. 4(c), we can see that the K_e^2 of mode 1 decreases with h_{Metal}. The K_e^2 of mode 2 increases first and then decreases with the increase of metal plate thickness, while K_e^2 of mode 3 decreases first and then increases with h_{Metal}. It should be noted that the K_e^2 of the mode 1 is very small. This finding implies that the electric field generated by the IDT fit well with the other modes, and thus the mode 1 is not efficiently excited.

4. Conclusions

In this paper, the 3-D model of Al_2O_3/IDTs/AlN/Metal/Diamond composite structure is established, and the FEM analysis was performed to describe the SAW propagation characteristics in multi-layer composite structure. Then, the corresponding COM parameters and K_e^2 are extracted theoretically for different acoustic modes. The simulation results show that the thickness of AlN piezoelectric film, the thickness of Pt electrode and the thickness of metal plate have certain influence on the propagation characteristics of SAW in multilayer composite structures. In addition, the high acoustic velocity mode is helpful to decrease the technique difficulty of SAW devices.

References

[1] Lin Shu, *Characteristics of wireless sensing with surface acoustic waves resonator for high temperature application[D]*, Ph.D thesis, University of Electronic Science and Technology, 2016.

[2] Talbi A, Soltani A, Mortet V, et al, *Theoretical study of Lamb acoustic waves characteristics in a AlN/diamond composite membranes for Super High Frequency range operating devices[J]*, Diamond and Related Materials, 2012, 22:66-69.

[3] Tsubouchi K, Mikoshiba N, *Zero-Temperature-Coefficient SAW Devices on AlN Epitaxial Films[J]*. IEEE Transactions on Sonics and Ultrasonics, 2005, 32(5):634-64.

[4] Wang W, Fan SY, Liang Y, et al, *Enhanced Sensitivity of a Love Wave-Based Methane Gas Sensor Incorporating a Cryptophane-A Thin Film, Sensors 2018*, Sensors 2018, 18(10), 3247.

[5] Tang G , Han T, Teshigahara A, et al, *Enhancement of effective electromechanical coupling factor by mass loading in layered SAW device structures[C]*, Frequency Control Symposium & the European Frequency & Time Forum. IEEE, 2015.

[6] Tang G, Han T, Teshigahara A, et al, *Enhancement of effective electromechanical coupling factor by mass loading in layered SAW device structures[C]*, Frequency Control Symposium & the European Frequency & Time Forum. IEEE, 2015.

Optimization of LGS based Surface Acoustic Wave Device for Sensing High Temperature

Xueling Li[1,2] Wen Wang[1] Shuyao Fan[1,2]

1, Institute of Acoustics,Chinese Academy of Sciences,
Beijing, 100049, China
2, University of Chinese Academy of Sciences,School of Electronic, Electrical and Commumication Engineering
Beijing, 100049, China
lixueling@mail.ioa.ac.cn
1, Institute of Acoustics,Chinese Academy of Sciences,
Beijing, 100049, China wangwenwq@mail.ioa.ac.cn§
1, Institute of Acoustics,Chinese Academy of Sciences,
Beijing, 100049, China fanshuyao@mail.ioa.ac.cn

This work contributes a theoretical optimization of LGS based surface acoustic wave (SAW) device structured by Al_2O_3/IDTs/LGS for sensing extreme high temperature in the fields of aerospace vehicles. Referring to the FEM, the SAW transmission characteristics in the layered structure was investigated, and the generation and suppression of clutter modes was explored, and corresponding suppression method was advised. Moreover, the computation parameters for coupling of modes (COM) simulation were extracted. The optimal design parameters of LGS based SAW device employing one-port resonator configuration were determined, leading to significant improvement of Q-value, the key indicator for high temperature sensing. The optimization conducted in this work provides theoretical guidance for development of extreme high temperature sensor.

Keywords: COM; FEM; High temperature sensor; LGS; SAW.

1. Introduction

Traditional sensing technology is difficult to operate at high temperature, high voltage and high rotation due to its active wired sensing mode. Because of their high performance, small size, and high reproducibility, SAW devices have been widely used in aerospace, energy and telecommunication industries. Also because of their high accuracy, SAW devices are suitable for sensor applications such as pressure sensors, biosensors, temperature sensors, and mass sensors. Surface acoustic wave (SAW) monitoring technology enables monitoring signals in a wireless passive manner. Compared with traditional wired active devices, wireless passive sensor has significant advantages especially in harsh environments.

Conventional piezoelectric substrate materials such as quartz are prone to damage in high temperature environments[1]. Langasite (LGS) has been thought as one of the most attractive material in high temperature due to its good temperature stability and large coupling constant K_2 (0.34%), which is two times larger than that of ST-quartz (0.14%) [2]. The LGS orientation Euler angles (0°, 138.5°, 27°) was used in this work. Platinum (Pt) is a good alternative to the commonly used aluminum electrodes because this metal is suitable for high temperature use [600-1000°C] [3]. the Pt film suffers a dewetting process in high temprature, through which the material aggregates into agglomerates in high temperature due to surface tension, disrupting the film uniformity, and finally resulting in a complete loss of electrical continuity[2]. This process may degrade the performance of the SAW device and even damage the device. Therefore, it has been reported in the literature that the multilayer composite structure of Al_2O_3/Pt electrode/LGS can effectively improve the comprehensive high temperature resistance of the sensor device[4]. Obviously, in wireless sensing applications, performance indicators such as sensor component quality factors directly determine the wireless transmission characteristics of the sensing system. However, there have been few optimized designs involving SAW high temperature sensor components to achieve low loss and high quality factors as yet. In this paper, the performance of one port resonator high temperature sensor with Al_2O_3/Pt electrode/LGS multilayer structure is optimized to determine the high-performance device design parameters. The finite element software is used to accurately extract the COM parameters of the resonant device, and the influence of the corresponding electrode thickness is reported in this paper. Combining COM simulation theory to simulate a single-port resonator sensor to determine a high quality factor sensor structure. Provide theoretical guidance for promoting the practical use of high temperature SAW sensing technology.

2. Theoretical research

2.1. COM theory

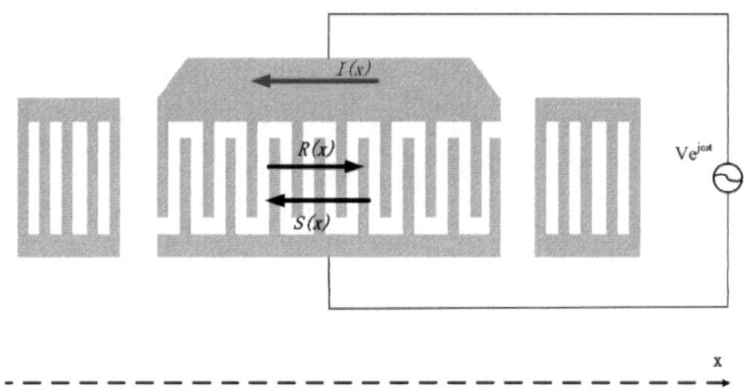

Fig.1 The coupling of modes (COM) model

The coupled mode model (COM) is a theoretical model developed for the needs of low loss SAW devices, providing an effective method for simulating SAW devices of different structures[5]. Figure 1 shows a schematic diagram of the COM model of a typical SAW resonator. The corresponding propagation equation is shown in (2.1)

$$\begin{cases} \dfrac{dR}{dx} = -jkR + j\kappa S\exp(-2jk_0x) + j\alpha V\exp(-jk_0x), \\ \dfrac{dS}{dx} = -j\kappa^* R\exp(2jk_0x) + jkS - j\alpha^* V\exp(jk_0x), \\ \dfrac{dI}{dx} = -2j\alpha^* R\exp(jk_0x) - 2j\alpha S\exp(-jk_0x) + j\omega C. \end{cases} \tag{2.1}$$

R(x) and S(x) represent acoustic waves propagating along the x positive and x negative directions in the periodic structure, respectively, V representing the applied alternating voltage on the bus bar, and I indicating the current flowing into the electrode. The independent COM parameters are the propagation velocity v, the coupling coefficient κ, the excitation coefficient α, the static capacitance C and the attenuation coefficient γ. Since the Rayleigh wave mode propagated in the periodic grid is studied in this paper, the propagation attenuation γ can be ignored. In order to accurately use the COM equation, the extraction of COM parameters is essential. These parameters are calculated by the finite element method(FEM).

2.2. Simulation method

The one port resonator can be divided into several periodic structures, and each component can be characterized by a hybrid (P) matrix. The P-matrix cascading technique is used to obtain the entire device P matrix, thereby obtaining the admittance matrix Y of the whole device. Combined with the expression of the scattering coefficient S_{11}, we can obtain the frequency response of the sensor device. Y_{11} is the admittance of the electrical port of the single-ended resonator, and Y_{01} is the characteristic admittance of the external transmission line of the electrical port, generally taking Y_{01} = 1/50 (S). Then the return loss (RL) is:

$$\mathrm{RL} = 20\log_{10}|S_{11}| = 20\log_{10}\left|\frac{Y_{01} - Y_{11}}{Y_{01} + Y_{11}}\right| (\mathrm{dB}). \tag{2.2}$$

A 3D simulation model was established as shown in Fig. 2. The x direction is an infinite periodic structure. By using the periodic boundary conditions in the x direction, the IDT deposited on the semi-infinite piezoelectric substrate can be simplified into a single-cycle structure. In our simulation model, the wavelength of the SAW device is 6.28 μm. The metallization ratio is 0.5. The thickness of the LGS is 4λ. The acoustic aperture W = λ / 40 can be obtained by using the periodic boundary condition in the y direction to reduce the calculation amount. The boundary conditions in simulation are presented in Table 1.

Table 1. Boundary conditions of the model.

Boundary	Mechanical boundary condition	Electrical boundary condition
Γ_T	Free	Zero Charge
Γ_B	Fixed Ground	Zero Charge
Γ_L, Γ_R	Counter periodical boundary	
Γ_F, Γ_E	Continuity periodical boundary	

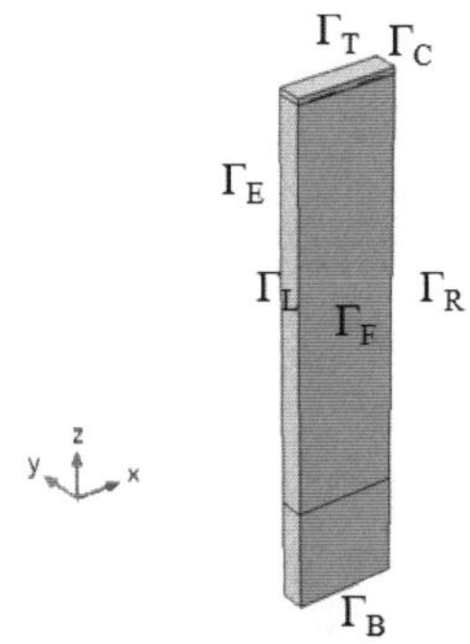

Fig.2 The simulation structure of the model

Analysis is done to determine the eigen-frequency and the acoustic propagation modes in the structures. The natural vibration characteristics of the periodic structure can be obtained by modal analysis. The frequencies corresponding to the two lowest SAW modes are the upper and lower boundary frequencies (fsc+, fsc–) of the periodic short-circuit gratings. Figure. 3 shows the displacement profile corresponding to the SAW mode in a periodic structure, which is the Rayleigh wave mode. The symmetric mode was shown in Fig.3(1), the characteristic frequency is fsc–; Fig. 3(2) is an antisymmetric mode, and the characteristic frequency is fsc+. The magnitude expression of the propagation velocity v and the normalized coupling coefficient $\kappa_n = \kappa\lambda$ in the COM parameter is:

$$\begin{cases} v = \lambda \dfrac{\left(f_{\mathrm{sc}+} + f_{\mathrm{sc}-}\right)}{2}, \\ |\kappa|\lambda = 2\pi \dfrac{f_{\mathrm{sc}+} - f_{\mathrm{sc}-}}{f_{\mathrm{sc}+} + f_{\mathrm{sc}-}}. \end{cases} \tag{2.3}$$

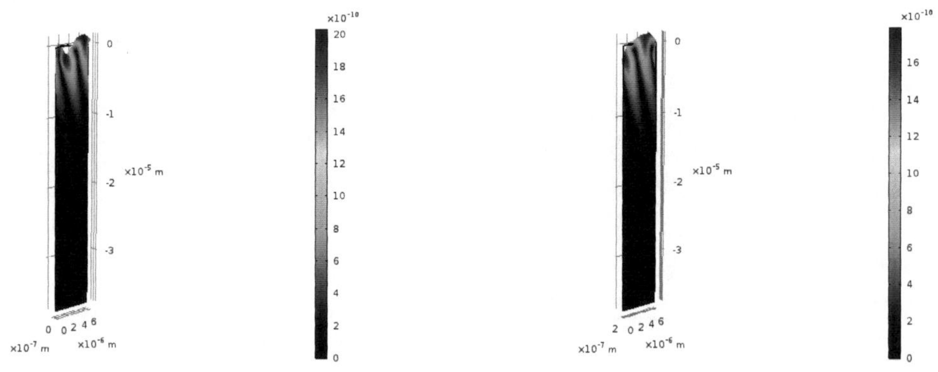

(1) (2)

Fig.3 (1) Symmetric mode (2) Antisymmetric mode

The harmonic response analysis in the frequency band near the boundary frequency obtained by the modal analysis can obtain the harmonic admittance Yin(ω) in the frequency range as shown in Fig.4. By searching for the zero and extreme points of the input admittance Yin(ω), the boundary frequencies of the open-circuit gratings (foc+, foc–) and the boundary frequency of the periodic short-circuit gratings (fsc+, fsc–) can be obtained. Applying an alternating voltage of voltage ΔV = 1V to the IDTs to excite SAW, the logarithmic representation of the normalized input admittance amplitude is shown in Fig.5. The magnitude of the normalized excitation coefficient α_n in the COM parameter and the cosine of the angle between α^2 and κ are expressed as (2.4).

$$\begin{cases} |\alpha_n| = \sqrt{\omega C_n \lambda \pi \left(\dfrac{f_{oc+} + f_{oc-}}{f_{sc+} + f_{sc-}} - 1 \right)}, \\ \cos\left(\angle \alpha^2 / \kappa\right) = \dfrac{\left(f_{oc+} - f_{oc-}\right)^2 - \left(f_{sc+} - f_{sc-}\right)^2 - \left[\left(f_{oc+} + f_{oc-}\right) - \left(f_{sc+} + f_{sc-}\right)\right]^2}{2\left(f_{sc+} - f_{sc-}\right)\left[\left(f_{oc+} + f_{oc-}\right) - \left(f_{sc+} + f_{sc-}\right)\right]}. \end{cases} \quad (2.4)$$

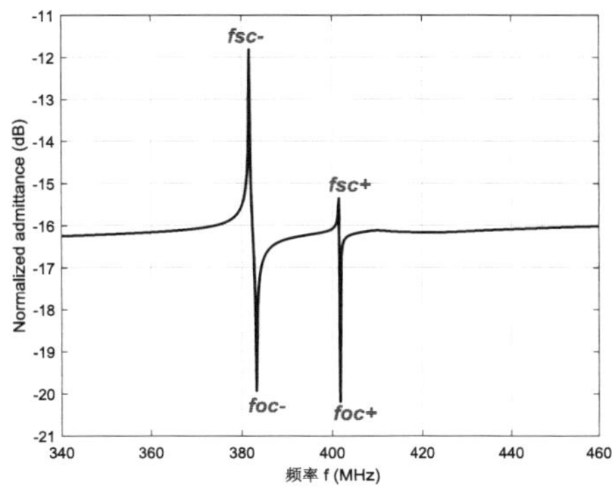

Fig.4 Normalized input admittance

The static analysis is used to obtain the normalized static capacitance C_n, where *We* should be equal to the energy required by the capacitor, and *W* is the acoustic aperture:

$$C_n = \frac{W_e}{(\Delta V)^2 W}. \quad (2.5)$$

The SAW sensor performance is the result of a combination of four COM parameters (propagation velocity v, coupling coefficient κ, excitation coefficient α, and static capacitance C).

3. Simulation results and analysis

This work reported using the finite element method(FEM) to extract the COM parameters of the periodic structure. Different electrode thicknesses will affect the COM parameters. The normalized electrode thickness h/λ of the LGS piezoelectric substrate Pt electrode has been reported in the literature. Simulation studies in the range of 0.5% to 3%, this paper expands the scope of the simulation, normalized electrode thickness h / λ ∈ [0.5%, 6.0%]. The COM parameters of the periodic structure was shown in Fig. 5.

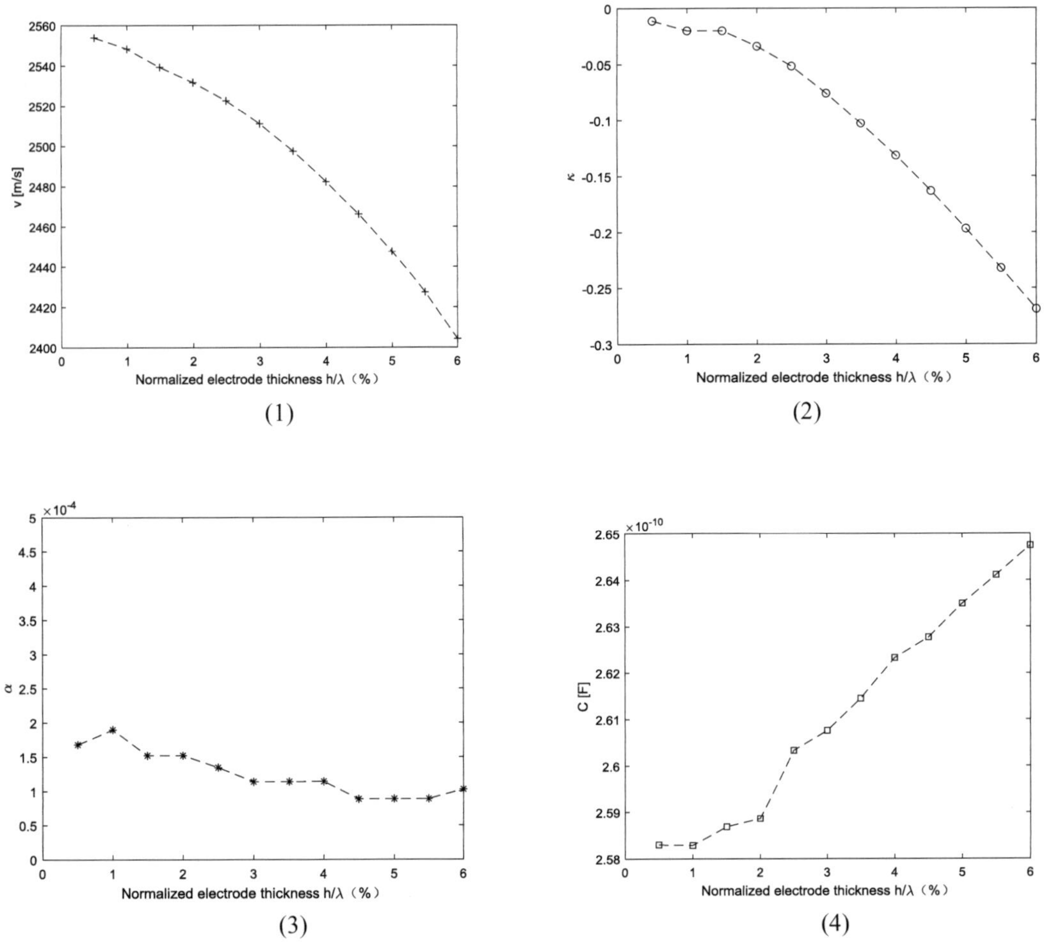

Fig.5 Normalized electrode thickness h/λ COM parameters (1) propagation velocity v (2)coupling coefficient κ (3)excitation coefficient α (4)static capacitance C

Combined with the coupled mode parameters extracted above, the coupled mode theory is used to simulate the one port resonator. The structure was shown in Fig.6 and the structural parameters are shown in Table 2. The simulation results of return loss response with different film thicknesses are shown in Fig.7.

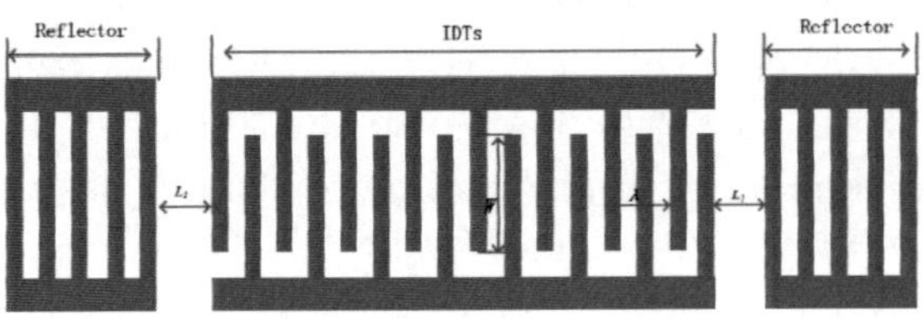

Fig.6 SAW resonator structure

Table 2. SAW resonator structure parameters.

λ (um)	IDT pairs	Reflectors pairs	W	L1	L2
6.28	61	180	111.5λ	0	0.5λ

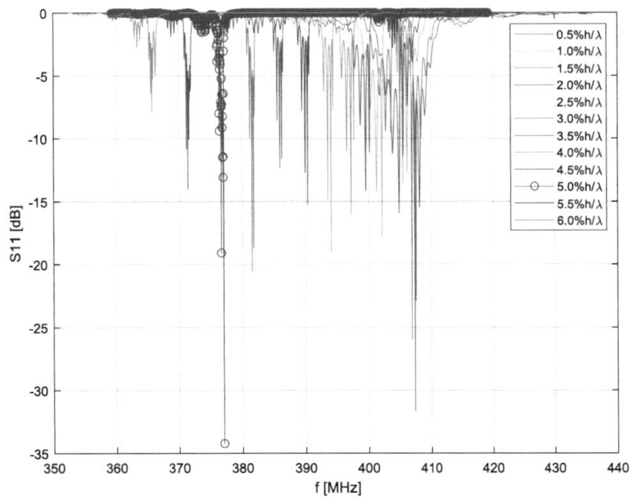

Fig.7 The frequency response of the SAW resonator

The frequency response of the SAW resonator at the thickness of the corresponding finger is calculated according to the COM parameters at different IDTs thicknesses. Figure 7 shows the frequency response of the device with different normalized thickness (h/λ). Obviously, the response of the sensor device is closely related to the thickness of the electrode film, which is mainly due to the migration and change of the acoustic mode under different electrode film thickness conditions. When the normalized film thickness is 5%, the propagation mode of SAW is Rayleigh wave mode, and the device has fewer clutter modes, resulting in lower loss and higher Q.

4. Conclusion

In this paper, the coupling mode parameters of Al_2O_3/Pt electrode/LGS multilayer composite device structure are extracted by finite element method, and the coupled mode theory is used to simulate the re-sponse of high temperature sensor with multi-layer composite structure. The film thickness of Pt electrode is studied. According to the influence of response, the optimized electrode film thickness parameters are extracted to obtain low loss and high Q value, and the optimal design of the sensor device is realized, which provides theoretical guidance for high temperature SAW sensing technology.

References

[1] Mauricio Pereira da Cunha , Thomas Moonlight, et al. High Temperature Sensing Technology for Applications Up To 1000°C, IEEE SENSORS 2008:752-755.

[2] Lin Shu, Yu Wang, bin peng, et al. Research on the LGS SAW sensor coated with AlN film, ICAICTE 2014:48-52.

[3] T. Aubert, F. Sarry, et al. High temperature Pt/LGS SAW sensor: from theory to experiment. IEEE 2011

[4] Thi S. Sakharov, A. Zabelin, S. Kondratiev, et al. Optimization of wafer orientation and electrode materials for LGS high-temperature SAW sensors, IEEE International Ultrasonics Symposium Proceedings 2012:1525-1528
[5] erry AUBERT, Frédéric SARRY, et al.Extraction of COM parameters on Pt/LGS for high temperature SAW sensor, IEEE International Ultrasonics Symposium Proceedings 2008:820-823.

Sensing Mechanism of Love Wave Based Ice Sensor Employing Structure of SiO2/36°YX-LiTaO3

YINING YIN[1,2], WEN WANG [1, §], YANA JIA[1, §]
1, Institute of Acoustics, Chinese Academy of Sciences
Beijing, 100190, China
2, University of Chinese Academy of Sciences
Beijing, 100049, China
yinyining110@163.com
1, Institute of Acoustics, Chinese Academy of Sciences,
Beijing, 100190, China
wangwenwq@mail.ioa.ac.cn[§]
1, Institute of Acoustics, Chinese Academy of Sciences,
Beijing, 100190, China
jiayana225@163.com

In this work, a Love wave based ice sensor configuration was proposed, and corresponding response mechanism was analyzed theoretically. The mass loading induced by the icing process modulate the acoustic wave propagation. By solving the acoustic propagation equations in layered media, the sensing mechanism of the Love wave device employing waveguide structure of SiO_2/36°YX $LiTaO_3$ was investigated and confirmed by the icing experiment. Interesting results were found in the experimental results, that is, in the initial status of icing process with ice-water mixture, a sudden drop was observed in the acoustic wave velocity. While the acoustic wave velocity increases with the completion of the icing process. Obviously, the phenomenon described above provides an effective way to monitor the icing process.

Keywords: Love wave; Ice sensor; Mass loading; Sensing mechanism; SiO_2/36°YX $LiTaO_3$.

1. Introduction

Road icing will bring huge safety hazards to aircraft flight and road safety. Therefore, it is of great significance to use icing sensors to realize early warning of road icing. The traditional available sensing approaches include optical fiber, electrical and mechanical technologies. The measurement accuracy of optical fiber ice sensor is high but suffers from poor anti-interference ability. The electrical ice sensor features simple structure, low cost, but, major flaws are long response time and poor accuracy while the mechanical ice sensor exhibits excellent reliability and stability, but the detection probe is easily damaged[1]. Compared with the available ice sensing technologies, surface acoustic wave (SAW) ice sensor features fast response, simple structure, high sensitivity, small size, low cost and so on[2]. Especially, it can provide a "passive" and "wireless" way for sensing ice. Hence, the SAW based icing technology attracts more interests since from the pioneering work made by Varadan[3]. Kevin.A. Vetelino[4] et al addressed some experimental results employing SAW devices. However, due to the severe longitudinal coupling attenuation of the typical Rayleigh SAW in the liquid phase environment, large acoustic propagation attenuation occurred. To face such issues, the so-called Love wave mode was proposed for sensing icing procedures because of very low acoustic wave propagation attenuation in liquid environment [5]. Gangadharan[6] et al presents a prototype of Love wave device for sensing icing, the experimental results indicated the fast response of the changes from water to ice. Even though some meaningful results were reported, the proposed SAW ice sensing devices still suffered from the sensitivity, and stable sensing structure. One of the reasons lies in the short of the theoretical analysis on sensing mechanism allowing performance optimization.

In this work, the theoretical analysis on sensing mechanism is performed by solving the acoustic propagation equations in layered structure to explore the optimal design parameters. A Love wave device employing SiO_2/36°YX-$LiTaO_3$ waveguide structure was built, and corresponding icing sensing experiment were conducted. The experimental results indicate the proposed sensing device involves the ability of fast and accurate monitor for icing procedures.

2. Theoretical Analysis

2.1. Analysis of propagation characteristics in different layers

A layered structure was established for theoretical analysis as shown in Fig.1, in which, a SiO_2 guiding layer with thickness of h_1 was deposited along the 36°YX-$LiTaO_3$ piezoelectric substrate, and a water layer (h_2) covered over the SiO_2 layer was used to simulate the icing process.

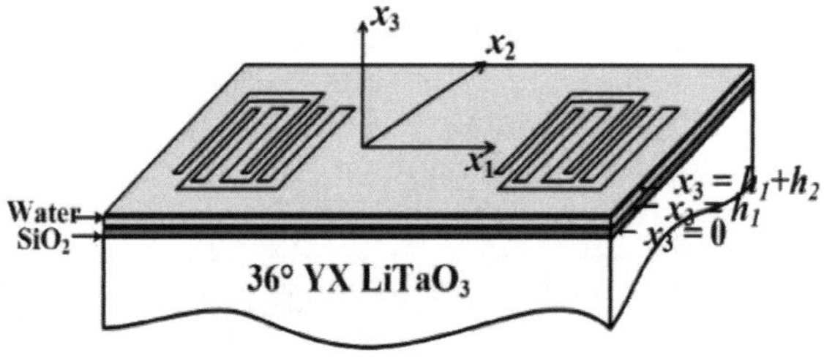

Fig. 1. The coordinate system of semi-infinite piezoelectric substrate

The x_1、x_2、x_3 axis in the Fig.1 are parallel to the SAW propagation direction, the SAW wavefront and the normal direction of the piezoelectric substrate, respectively. To address the acoustic wave propagation along the layered structure, the acoustic wave equation in each medias was solved to achieve the variation of acoustic wave velocity with the water thickness. For simplification, the effective dielectric constant was referred.

First, the the coupled wave equation in piezoelectric substrate is considered as

$$\begin{cases} \rho \dfrac{\partial^2 u_i}{\partial t^2} - c_{ijkl}^{E} \dfrac{\partial^2 u_k}{\partial x_l \partial x_j} - e_{kij} \dfrac{\partial^2 \varphi}{\partial x_k \partial x_j} = 0 \\ e_{jkl} \dfrac{\partial^2 u_k}{\partial x_l \partial x_j} - \varepsilon_{jk}^{S} \dfrac{\partial^2 \varphi}{\partial x_k \partial x_j} = 0 \end{cases} \quad i,j,k,l = 1,2,3 \, . \tag{2.1}$$

where c^E, e, ε^S denote the elastic coefficient, piezoelectric constant and dielectric constant matrix of 36°YX-$LiTaO_3$, respectively. ρ is density, u_i is displacement, and Φ is potential. the solution of the coupled wave equation is assumed as [7]

$$\begin{cases} U_i(x_1,x_3,\omega) = A_i \exp\left[-j(k_s x_1 + \alpha k_s x_3)\right] \\ \Phi(x_1,x_3,\omega) = A_4 \exp\left[-j(k_s x_1 + \alpha k_s x_3)\right] \end{cases}. \tag{2.2}$$

where $k_s = ws$ is the wave vector (assuming that the propagation in the x_1 direction is lossless, then k_s is a real number), v_s is the acoustic wave propagation velocity, $s = 1/v_s$ is the surface wave slowness, and α is the attenuation factor of the acoustic wave in the x_3 direction.

Then, the solution of acoustic wave equation in the SiO_2 waveguide layer is solved by considered the acoustic wave equation as

$$c^L_{ijkl}\frac{\partial^2 u^L_k}{\partial x_l \partial x_j} = \rho^L \frac{\partial^2 u^L_i}{\partial t^2} i,j,k,l = 1,2,3 \cdot \tag{2.3}$$

where, c^L is the matrix of the modulus of elasticity of the SiO_2 film, ρ^L is density and u_i is displacement. Similar to the solution of piezoelectric substrate, the solution of the coupled wave equation in SiO_2 can be denoted by

$$u^L_i(x_1,x_3) = A^L_i \exp\left[j\omega t - j\left(k_s x_1 + \alpha^L k_s x_3\right)\right]. \tag{2.4}$$

According to the Navier-Stokes (N-S) equation, when the viscosity coefficient of a liquid is constant, the wave equation in the liquid layer is represented by [8]:

$$\rho^H \frac{\partial^2 u^H_i}{\partial t^2} = c^H_{ijkl}\frac{\partial^2 u^H_k}{\partial x_l \partial x_k} - \frac{2}{3}\mu jw \frac{\partial}{\partial x_k}\left(\nabla \bullet u^H\right) + \mu jw\left(\frac{\partial^2 u^H_k}{\partial x_j \partial x_j} + \frac{\partial}{\partial x_i}\left(\nabla \bullet u^H\right)\right) i,j,k,l = 1,2,3 . \tag{2.5}$$

where, u^H, ρ^H represent the displacement and liquid density, respectively, c^H is the elastic constant of the ideal liquid, $\nabla \bullet u^H$ is the divergence of the displacement, and μ is the viscosity coefficient of the liquid. In general, a non-viscous liquid refers to a liquid having a viscosity of not more than 0.0015 $P_a \bullet s$, which has a very small viscosity and is negligible in research and analysis[9]. Considering that the viscosity of water is 0.001 $P_a \bullet s$, it can be regarded as an ideal liquid.

Then the equation wave in the water film can be rewritten as:

$$c^H_{ijkl}\frac{\partial^2 u^H_k}{\partial x_l \partial x_j} = \rho^H \frac{\partial^2 u^H_i}{\partial t^2} i,j,k,l = 1,2,3 \cdot \tag{2.6}$$

Because there is no shear stress in the ideal liquid, and the elastic constant is isotropic which can be expressed by:

$$c_{ijkl}^{H}=\begin{bmatrix} c_{11} & c_{11} & c_{11} & 0 & 0 & 0 \\ c_{11} & c_{11} & c_{11} & 0 & 0 & 0 \\ c_{11} & c_{11} & c_{11} & 0 & 0 & 0 \\ 0 & 0 & 0 & 0 & 0 & 0 \\ 0 & 0 & 0 & 0 & 0 & 0 \\ 0 & 0 & 0 & 0 & 0 & 0 \end{bmatrix}. \tag{2.7}$$

where, $c_{11}=\rho_l v_l^2$.

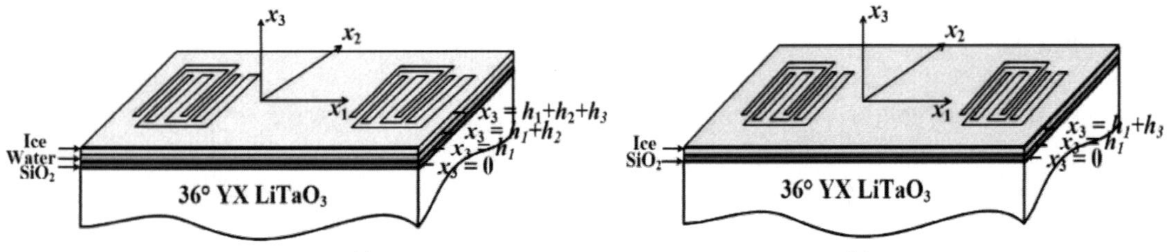

(a) (b)

Fig. 2. (a) layered analysis model with water & ice. (b) layered analysis model with ice.

During the icing process, the physical model can be equivalent to a four-layer structure. As shown in the Fig. 2(a). The ice layer can be regarded as an isotropic film, and the analysis method is similar to the SiO_2. When the water is completely formed into ice, the four-layer structure can be transformed into a three-layer structure (Fig. 2(b)).

Substituting the formal wavelet solution of the coupled wave equation into the wave equation, the corresponding Christoffel equation can be obtained. And the eigenvalue can be calculated from the Christoffel equation. Using the boundary conditions, the solution of the acoustic field distribution was calculated, and corresponding variation of acoustic wave velocity with the water thickness can be addressed.

Next, the surface effective dielectric constant was introduced by

$$\varepsilon_s(s)=\frac{\tilde{\sigma}(s)}{k\tilde{\varphi}(s,x_3)\big|_{x_3=0}}. \tag{2.8}$$

where s is slowness, $s=1/v$, k denotes the wave number, $\tilde{\sigma}(s)$ and $\tilde{\varphi}(s,x_3)$ represent the Fourier transform of the charge density and potential, respectively.

By solving the solution of the field distribution, ε_s can be simplified, the effective dielectric constant curves which demonstrated the change in SAW velocity with different thicknesses of load can be obtained. $\varepsilon_s(s)$ is a complex number which only denoted the function of the material constant. The actual part and the imaginary part varied in the change of the SAW slowness. The slowness s corresponding to the zero crossing of the real part indicates the case where $x_3 = 0$ was free. According to $v_s = s^{-1}$, the SAW phase velocities v_m and v_f at $x_3 = 0$ were calculated, respectively.

Using the theoretical analysis mentioned above, the SAW propagation along the structure of water layer/SiO_2/36°YX-$LiTaO_3$, ice/water layer/SiO_2/36°YX-$LiTaO_3$, and ice/SiO_2/36°YX-$LiTaO_3$ layer structure can be investigated.

2.2. Analysis of calculation results

In Fig. 3, the solid line is the real part of $\varepsilon_s(s)$, and the dashed line is the imaginary part of $\varepsilon_s(s)$. A set of zero (S_{OR}) and extremes (S_{mR}) in the $\varepsilon_s(s)$ curve corresponding to the free surface and metal surface velocities of SAW. As can be seen, there are two modes of wave, the left side is the free surface SH-SAW, and the right side is the Rayleigh wave [8].

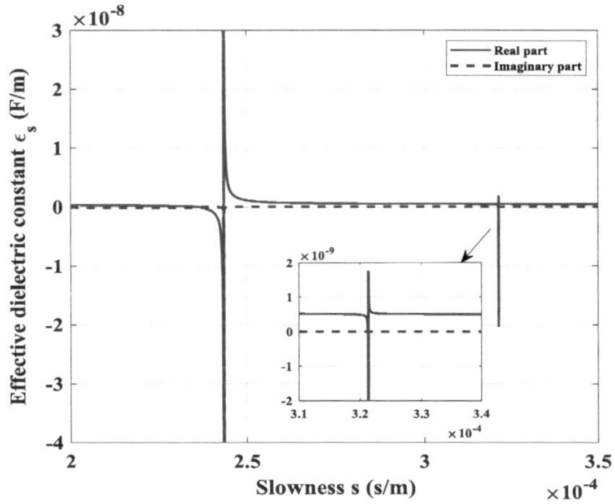

Fig. 3. The effective dielectric constant of 36°YX-LiTaO$_3$.

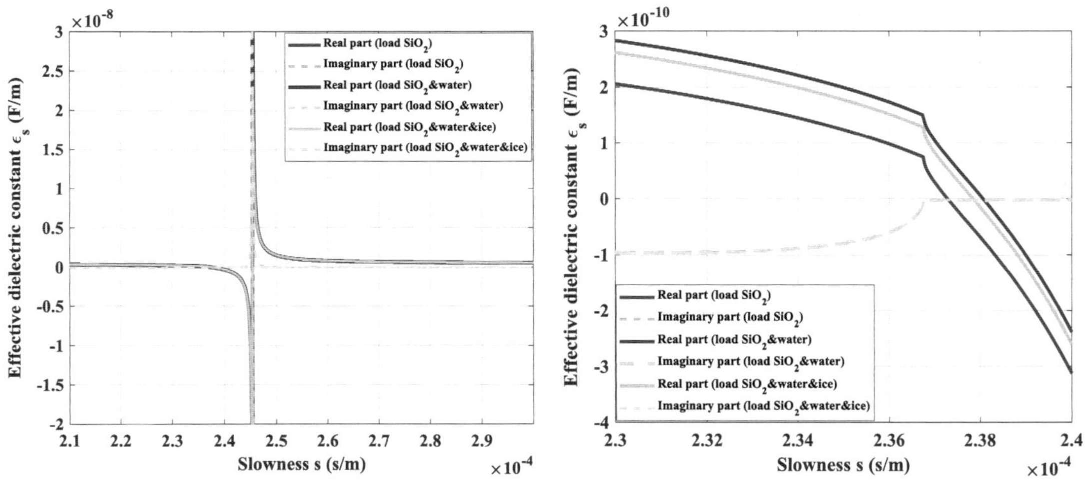

(a) (b)

Fig. 4. (a) the effective dielectric constant of piezoelectric substrates load SiO$_2$, water, and water/ice. (b) the $\varepsilon_s(s)$ curve and the slowness near the zero point

Moreover, the $\varepsilon_s(s)$ curves of piezoelectric substrates load SiO$_2$, water, water ice mixture were depicted, as shown in Fig.4. There only is the SH-SAW mode when covered the waveguide layer SiO$_2$, that is, the Love wave. Love wave is a piezoelectric substrate which supports the SH-SAW propagation. When covered water on the SiO$_2$, the curve shifts to the right and the slowness increases since the mass loading effect. Interestingly, when there is both water and ice, the curve is moving slightly to the left (Fig.4). Obviously, there is no change in the mode of acoustic wave when load SiO$_2$, water, water/ice (Fig. 4(a)), which only exists a single mode. The slowness increases because of the mass load of water, but the variation trend of four-layer water/ice mixture structure is different from the former, it appears that the slowness decreases and the velocity increases due to smaller dielectric constant of ice (Fig. 4(b)).

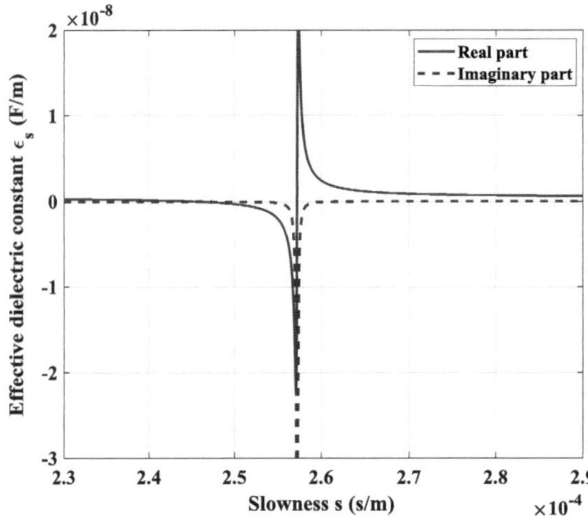

Fig.5. The effective dielectric constant of piezoelectric substrates load ice

Fig. 5 shows that when the load is only thin ice, its surface velocity is also lowered, which is about 4074.7m/s. Because ice can be regarded as an isotropic low-sonic film, when the surface layer has an ice layer, it can be equivalent to a double-waveguide layer.

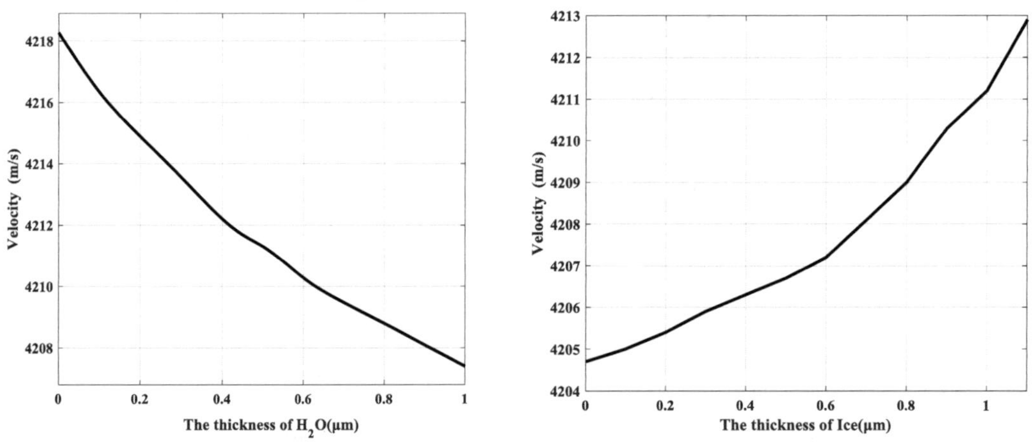

(a) (b)

Fig.6. The phase velocity varying with (a) water thickness and (b) water & ice thickness.

Also, the thickness of the water layer and the change of the free surface velocity at the start of icing was analyzed, as shown in the Fig.6. From Fig. 6(a), the velocity of the Love wave monotonously decreases with the thickness of water layer increases because of the mass loading effect. The velocity of 1μm water is about 4204.7m/s. When the icing starts, as the thickness of the water layer decreases and the thickness of the ice layer increases, the variation trend is different from the former, the velocity of the Love wave gradually increases (Fig. 6(b)). As the water decreases, the ice increases and the velocity can increase to 4212.9m/s. The reason is that the propagation velocity decreases as the water mass loading increases, while the propagation velocity increases due to the smaller dielectric constant of ice when the load becomes a mixture of water and ice. The velocity of surface acoustic wave propagation changes which will cause the frequency of the device to change.

3. Experiments and Discussions

Using the above theoretical derivation, the Love wave delay line device was designed. The device was composed of a SH-SAW delay line pattern on a 36°YX-$LiTaO_3$ substrate and a 1.5μm SiO_2 waveguide layer.

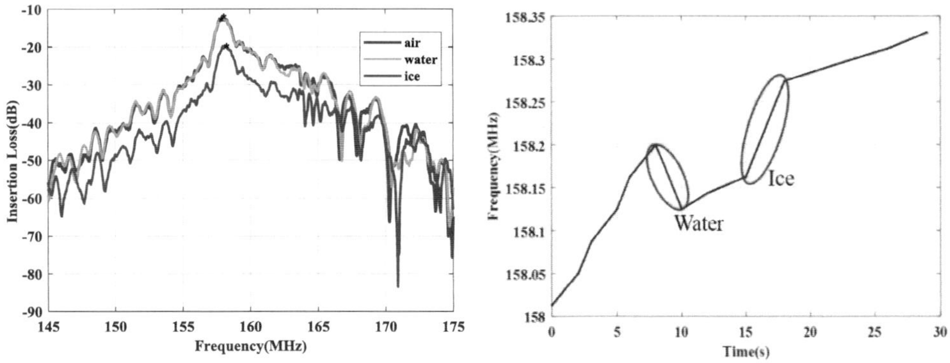

(a) (b)

Fig.7. frequency test result (a) frequency characteristics of the sensor device (b) the center frequency curve of the sensor device

The test experiment was conducted by setting the high-low temperature chamber to -15 °C to ensure that the surface of the sensor device meets the icing conditions. 0.5 μl water was dropped on the surface of the device between the two interdigital transducers and placed in a high temperature chamber. The network analyzer was used to monitor the real time frequency characteristics of the sensor, and the frequency response of the device before and after adding water and icing was compared. The test results are shown in Fig. 8.

Obviously, in the case where the sensor chip was placed in a low temperature state, the center frequency of the sensor chip was lowered for the apparent mass loading during the water addition (as shown in Fig. 7(b).) After the icing starts, the frequency of the sensor increased. In addition, the insertion loss of the sensor increased greatly during the icing process, as shown in Fig. 7(a), the reason may be that the physical properties of the ice caused the acoustic attenuation to cause acoustic leakage. It can be seen from Fig. 7 that the effective discrimination of the ice and water states can be achieved from the frequency response process of the sensor device. The experimental results were in agreement with the theoretical calculations.

4. Conclusion

In this work, a structure of ice sensor based on Love wave was proposed, and the corresponding response mechanism was theoretically analyzed. The mass loading caused by the icing process modulated the acoustic wave propagation. The sensing mechanism of Love wave devices using SiO_2/36°YX-$LiTaO_3$ waveguide structure was described by solving the problem of acoustic propagation in layered media. In the theoretical analysis, it was found that the acoustic wave velocity suddenly decreased in the initial state of the ice-water mixture icing process, and the acoustic wave velocity increased at the end of the icing process, and it was verified in the experimental process. Obviously, the phenomenon indicates the effectiveness of monitoring the icing process.

Acknowledgment

This work was supported by the National Science Foundation of China: No. 11774381.

References

[1] Yin QH, Li J, HU XD. "Application Research on Ice Sensor for Road Safety Warning," *Journal of Wuhan Institute of Technology,* 38(3) (2016),273-276.

[2] Yin YN, Wang W, Jia YN et al. "Development of A Surface Acoustic Wave Delay Line Device for Sensing Ice". *Piezoelectricity, Acoustic Waves, & Device Applications*. 2019

[3] Vijay K. VARADAN and Vasundara V. VARADAN. "IDT, SAW and MEMS sensors for measuring deflection, acceleration and ice detection of aircraft," *Proceedings of SPIE The International Society for Optical Engineering,* 1997.

[4] Kevin A. Vetelino a, Patrick R. Story a, Russell D. Mileham a, David W. "Galipeau b, Improved dew point measurer aents based on a SAW sensor", *Sensors and Actuators B*, 35-36 (1996) 91-98.

[5] Ioannis Nikolaou, Hamida Hallil, et al. "Inkjet-Printed Graphene Oxide Thin Layers on Love Wave Devices for Humidity and Vapor Detection," *IEEE Sensors Journal,* 16(21) (2016) 7620-7627.

[6] HY Wu, HF Zu, QM Wang and H C J Wang. "A love wave biosensor with a phononic wave guiding layer for VEGF detection in selective platelet activation," *IEEE International Ultrasonics Symposium Proceedings*, 2017, pp. 1-4.

[7] John Wiley and Sons, *Auld B A, Acoustic fields and waves in solids-volume 1*, New York, USA, 1973.

[8] Liu JL. "Research on the gas detection apparatus based on GC/SAW. Ph. D. thesis. Institute of Acoustics," Chinese Academy of Sciences, Beijing, China,2010.

[9] Zhang XN. "Research on love wave propagation properties and liquid dielectric constant sensing. Thesis," Nanjing University of Aeronautics and Astronautics, Nanjing, China,2010.

Research on 3D Temperature Distribution Reconstruction Based on Acoustics Tomography

Qian Kong, Genshan Jiang*, Yuechao Liu, Jianhao Sun

North China Electric Power University, Baoding 071003, China

3D temperature field measurement based on acoustic tomography (AT) calculates temperature distributions of the measurement region through multi-path acoustic time of flight (TOF) data. In this paper, a new 3D temperature field reconstruction model based on radial basis function approximation with polynomial reproduction (RBF-PR) is proposed for solving the AT inverse problem. In addition, Discretization of temperature reconstruction inverse problems generally gives rise to very ill-posed systems of algebraic equations, the modified Tikhonov regularization method is presented to improve the reconstruction quality (RQ). Numerical simulations are implemented to evaluate the feasibility and effectiveness of the proposed reconstruction method using 3D different temperature distribution models. To study the anti-noise ability of the modified method, noises are also added to the value of TOF. 3D display of reconstructed temperature fields and reconstruction errors are given. The results indicate that our new method can reconstruct temperature distribution with higher accuracy and better anti-noise ability compared with other popular methods. As a result, an useful approach is introduced for solving the 3D AT inverse problem in this paper.

Keywords: Acoustic tomography, radial basis function approximation with polynomial reproduction, modified Tikhonov regularization, reconstruction quality

1. Introduction

Acoustic tomography (AT) has been widely used and provided an effective means for temperature distribution visualization owing to the advantages of wide measuring range, non-contacting measurement and large measurement space. In recent years, the AT method has been widely used in various application, such as boiler furnaces [1], deep-sea hydrothermal[2], stored grain [3] and atmospheric surface layer[4]. At present, the research on temperature field reconstruction by AT is mainly conducted in two-dimensions [5, 6]. 3D temperature field reconstruction is discussed by only few researchers[7, 8]. So we focus on the method to reconstruct the 3D temperature distribution

AT technology reconstruct the temperature distribution from the acoustic time of flight (TOF)[9], and it is an inversion process. Successful application of the AT measurement greatly depends on reconstruction model. In this paper, an improved 3D reconstruction model based on radial basis function approximation with polynomial reproduction[10] is presented to solve the AT inverse problem. In addition, discretization of temperature reconstruction inverse problems generally gives rise to very ill-posed systems. Truncated singular value decomposition (TSVD)[11] and Tikhonov regularization[12,13] are two popular regularization methods for solving this discrete ill-posed problem. And in this paper we propose a modified Tikhonov regularization reconstruction method for solving the measurement model.

Numerical simulations are conducted to evaluate the effectiveness and feasibility of the proposed method.

2. Acoustic temperature measurement model

2.1. Principle of AT

The theory of AT is based on the relation between the velocity of acoustic and the temperature of gas. The temperature is calculated using the following relation[9]:

$$u(x,y,z) = Z\sqrt{T(x,y,z)} \tag{1}$$

where Z is a fixed constant decided by gas composition.

In the process of acoustic thermometry, when the distance d between the sound receiver and sound transmitter is known, and the time of flight (TOF) is measured, the velocity of sound can be calculated. Combining Eq.(1), the temperature can be measured.

2.2. 3D reconstruction method

A three-dimensional system of $10m \times 10m \times 10m$ being studied is shown in Fig.1. The space in the system is divided into $8 \times 8 \times 8$ blocks. 20 acoustic sensors are arranged on the periphery to form 58 effective flying paths.

When all TOF of the flying paths are obtained, the three-dimensional temperature distribution will be reconstructed by using suitable method.

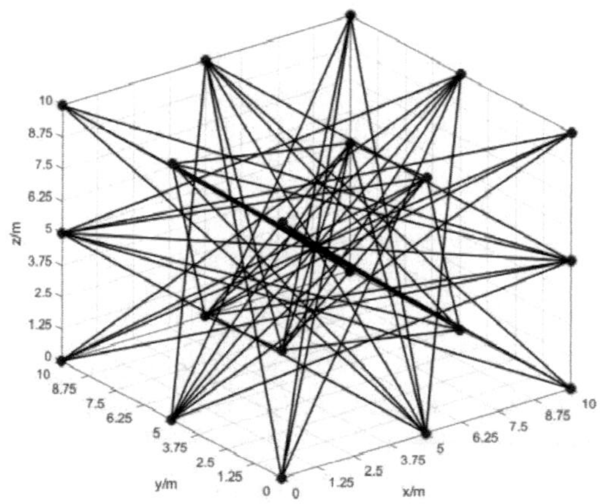

Fig.1 Arrangement of sensors and division of the measure area

Assuming that $v(x,y,z)$ denotes the sound velocity, while $f(x,y,z)$ describes its reciprocal. Then TOF of the kth effective acoustic flying path can be theoretically expressed as:

$$t_k = \int_{l_k} \frac{1}{v(x,y,z)} dl_k = \int_{l_k} f(x,y,z) dl_k \tag{2}$$

Based on radial basis function(RBF) model, the reciprocal of sound speed can be written similarly as

$$f(x,y,z) = \sum_{m=1}^{M} \lambda_m \phi \|(x,y,z) - (x_m, y_m, z_m)\| \tag{3}$$

Where (x_m, y_m, z_m) is the geometric center coordinate of the mth blocks as the sample point, $\|(x,y,z)-(x_m,y_m,z_m)\|$ is the Euclidean norm. ϕ is a basis function, Where $\varphi = \dfrac{1}{\sqrt{(x-x_m)^2+(y-y_m)^2+(z-z_m)^2+C}}$, λ_m is the coefficient for the mth basis function. M is the number of blocks in measured area.

To improve the accuracy and stability of RBF, the RBF approximant is usually extended by a polynomial function

$$f(x,y,z)=\sum_{m=1}^{M}\lambda_m\phi\|(x,y,z)-(x_m,y_m,z_m)\|+\sum_{i=1}^{p}c_i g_i(x,y,z) \tag{4}$$

In this paper, a linear polynomial is used as, So Eq.(5) is became as

$$f(x,y,z)=\sum_{m=1}^{M}\lambda_m\phi_m(x,y,z)+c_x x+c_y y+c_z z+c_0 \tag{5}$$

Then TOF of the kth effective acoustic flying path can be expressed as,

$$\begin{aligned} t_k &= \int_{l_k} f(x,y,z)dl_k = \int_{l_k}\sum_{m=1}^{M}\lambda_m\phi_m(x,y,z)+(c_x x+c_y y+c_z z+c_0)dl_k \\ &= \sum_{m=1}^{M}\lambda_m\int_{l_k}\phi_m(x,y,z)dl_k + c_x\int_{l_k} xdl_k + c_y\int_{l_k} ydl_k + c_z\int_{l_k} zdl_k + c_0\int_{l_k} dl_k \end{aligned} \tag{6}$$

Let $a_{km}=\int_{l_k}\phi_m dl_k$, $g_{k1}=\int_{l_k} xdl_k$, $g_{k2}=\int_{l_k} ydl_k$, $g_{k3}=\int_{l_k} zdl_k$, $g_{k4}=\int_{l_k} dl_k$

and use the matrix notation, we can write

$$\begin{pmatrix} a_{11} & \cdots & a_{1M} & g_{11} & g_{12} & g_{13} & g_{14} \\ \vdots & \ddots & \vdots & \vdots & \vdots & \vdots & \vdots \\ a_{i1} & \cdots & a_{iM} & g_{i1} & g_{i2} & g_{i3} & g_{i4} \\ \vdots & \ddots & \vdots & \vdots & \vdots & \vdots & \vdots \\ a_{K1} & \cdots & a_{KM} & g_{K1} & g_{K2} & g_{K3} & g_{K4} \end{pmatrix} \begin{pmatrix} \lambda_1 \\ \vdots \\ \lambda_M \\ c_x \\ c_y \\ c_z \\ c_0 \end{pmatrix} = \begin{pmatrix} t_1 \\ \vdots \\ t_i \\ \vdots \\ t_K \end{pmatrix}$$

Where K denotes the sum of effective paths.

The equation also can be expressed in the form:

$$A\mathbf{x}=\mathbf{t} \tag{7}$$

Using the singular value decomposition of matrix A and Tikhonov regularization solves the problem (7), we have the following equations,

$$A=U\Sigma V^T,\quad U\in R^{m\times m},\quad V\in R^{n\times n} \tag{8}$$

$$\Sigma = diag(\sigma_1,\sigma_2,\cdots,\sigma_n)\in R^{m\times n},\quad \sigma_1\ge\sigma_2\ge\cdots\ge\sigma_r>\sigma_{r+1}=\cdots=\sigma_n=0$$

$$\min\left\{\|Ax-t\|^2+\mu^2\|Lx\|^2\right\} \tag{9}$$

Where U and V are orthogonal matrices, and r is the rank of A. μ>0 is a regularization parameter and L is referred to as the regularization matrix. The regularization matrix can be given as

$$L_\mu = D_\mu V^T \tag{10}$$

With $D_\mu^2 = diag[\max\{\mu^2-\sigma_1^2,0\},\max\{\mu^2-\sigma_2^2,0\},\cdots,\max\{\mu^2-\sigma_n^2,0\}]$

Then theTikhonov regularization problem(9) can be rewritten as

$$\min\left\{\|Ax-t\|^2+\|L_\mu x\|^2\right\} \tag{11}$$

and we can get the Tikhonov solution given by

$$x_\mu^{Tik} = (A^T A+L_\mu{}^T L_\mu)^{-1}A^T t \tag{12}$$

Substituting Eq.(8) and Eq.(10) into Eq.(12), Eq.(12) is became as

$$x_\mu^{Tik} = V(\Sigma^T\Sigma+D_\mu^2)^{-1}\Sigma^T U^T t \tag{13}$$

Due to $\sigma_k>\mu>\sigma_{K+1}$, then $\Sigma^T\Sigma+D_\mu^2$=diag$[\sigma_1^2,\sigma_2^2,\cdots,\sigma_s^2,\mu^2,\cdots,\mu^2]\in R^{n\times n}$, so we have the solution

$$x_\mu^{TT} = \sum_{i=1}^{r}\lambda_{\mu,i}\frac{u_i^T t}{\sigma_i}v_i \tag{14}$$

Where λ_μ is the filer factors

$$\lambda_{\mu,i} = \begin{cases} 1, & 1\le i\le s \\ \dfrac{\sigma_i^2}{\mu^2}, & s\le i\le r \end{cases} \tag{15}$$

In this paper, we apply the thresold setting to determine the truncation index k and the regularization parameter μ simply.

In practice, once **t** is obtained by actual measurement, Then the reciprocal of acoustic velocity *f(x,y,z)* is known by solving Eq.(7). And the reconstructed temperature distribution will be expressed as

$$T(x,y,z) = \left(\frac{1}{Z\times f(x,y,z)}\right)^2 \tag{16}$$

3. Numerical simulation and discussion

In this section, in order to validate the performance of our proposed method, simulation experiments are carried out, and the results analysis is given. Three kinds of 3D temperature distribution models with different complexity levels, i.e., one-peak symmetry model, one-peak asymmetry model and two-peak model, are chosen.

Model 1: One-peak symmetrical temperature distribution,

$$T(x,y,z) = \frac{2000}{0.05((x-5)^2+(y-5)^2+(z-5)^2)+1} \tag{17}$$

Model 2: One-peak asymmetrical temperature distribution,

$$T(x,y,z)=\frac{2000}{0.05((x-2.5)^2+(y-5)^2+(z-7)^2)+1} \quad (18)$$

Model 3: Two-peak temperature distribution,

$$T(x,y,z)=\frac{2000}{0.05((x-5)^2+(y-1.5)^2+(z-1.5)^2)+1}+\frac{2000}{0.05((x-5)^2+(y-8.5)^2+(z-8.5)^2)+1} \quad (19)$$

The reconstruction quality is given by calculating the mean relative error E_{mean} and root-mean-square percent error E_{rms},

$$E_{mean}=\frac{\sum_{m=1}^{N}\left|\frac{T(m)-T'(m)}{T(m)}\times 100\%\right|}{N} \qquad E_{rms}=\frac{\sqrt{\frac{1}{N}\sum_{m=1}^{N}(T(m)-T'(m))^2}}{T_{mean}}\times 100\% \quad (20)$$

where N is the number of calculated points, $T(m),T'(m)$ are temperatures of point (x_m, y_m) respectively of model one and reconstructed one. T_{mean} is the mean temperature of model. In this section, we generate a noise-vector corresponding to the noise-level α, and the vector **t** can be rewritten as

$$\mathbf{t}=\mathbf{t}\times(1+\alpha\times N_{noise}) \quad (21)$$

where N_{noise} is a standard normal distribution vector, the noise level α is chosen between 0 to 0.1(or 10%).

For convenience, our proposed method is called TT method. Fig.2-4 show us the displays and absolute errors of reconstructed temperature distribution for one-peak symmetrical temperature distribution, one-peak asymmetrical one, two-peak distribution, respectively. The original temperature distributions are shown in Fig2.(a)- Fig4.(a). (b), (c) and (d) of Fig.2-4 are the reconstructed results by using SVD, Tikhonov regulation and the proposed TT methods, respectively. Table 1 lists the reconstruction errors of different methods for these three temperature distributions. In the Tikhonov regulation method, the regularization parameter μ is 0.005.

For simple one-peak symmetrical temperature distribution in Fig.2, the reconstruction temperature fields have been distorted and absolute errors are very large by using the SVD method. By contrast, the results of other methods, Tikhonov regulation and the proposed TT methods have more excellent reconstruction performance than ones of SVD method, and absolute errors of them are small. The absolute errors of TT method are smaller than the ones of Tikhonov regulation methods. In addition, from Table 1 for one-peak symmetrical distribution, the RQ of TT method is high, the, E_{mean} and E_{rms} are 7.97% and 8.27%, which is lower than that of other methods.

For one-peak asymmetrical temperature distribution in Fig.3 and two-peak temperature distribution in Fig.4, in respect of anti-noise, though the reconstructed results of Tikhonov regulation and TT methods also get worse with noise, they present much slighter worsening degree than SVD method. Besides that, the reconstructed temperature fields by proposed TT method are more close to the original fields compared with other methods. From Table.1, the

E_{mean} and E_{rms} of TT method are smaller than the other compared reconstruction methods. The results indicate that the TT method gives a best reflection of temperature distribution and improves the RQ in the AT measurement.

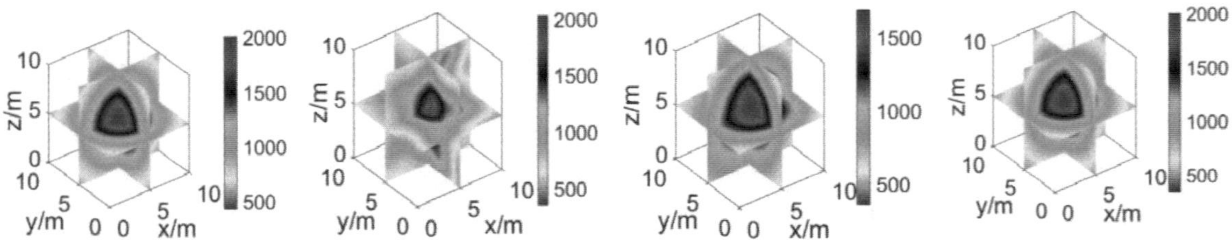

(a)Original distribution (b1) SVD (c1) Tikhonov (d1) TT method

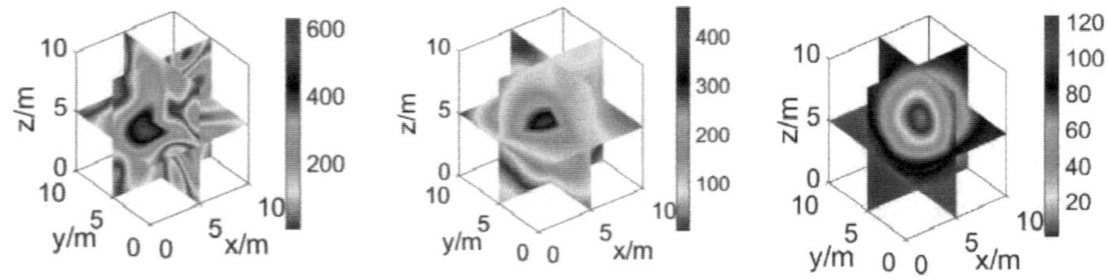

(b2) errors of SVD (c2) errors of Tikhonov (d2) errors of TT

Fig.2 The reconstruction results for one-peak symmetrical temperature distribution

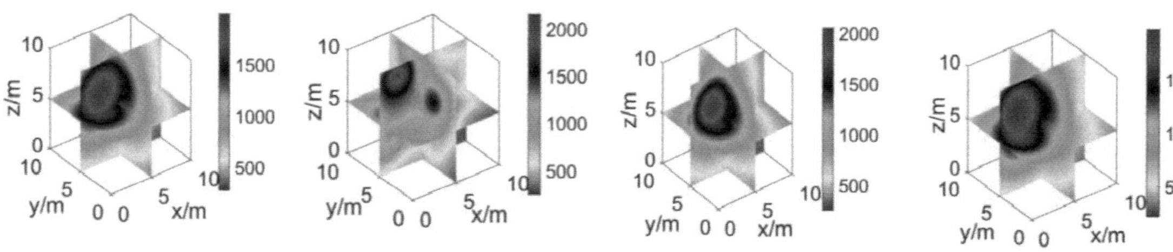

(a)Original distribution (b1) SVD (c1) Tikhonov (d1) TT method

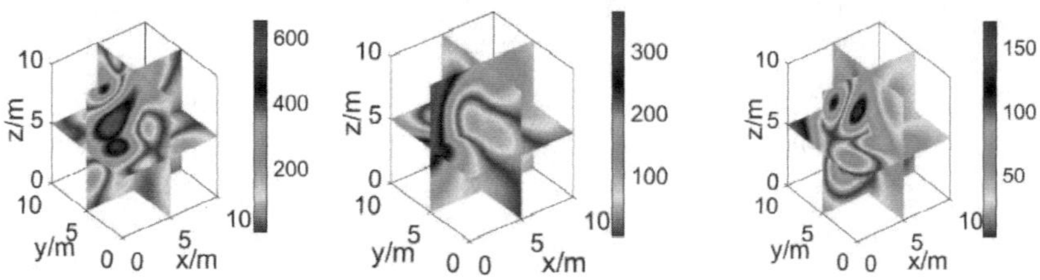

(b2) errors of SVD (c2) errors of Tikhonov (d2) errors of TT

Fig.3 The reconstruction results for one-peak asymmetrical temperature distribution

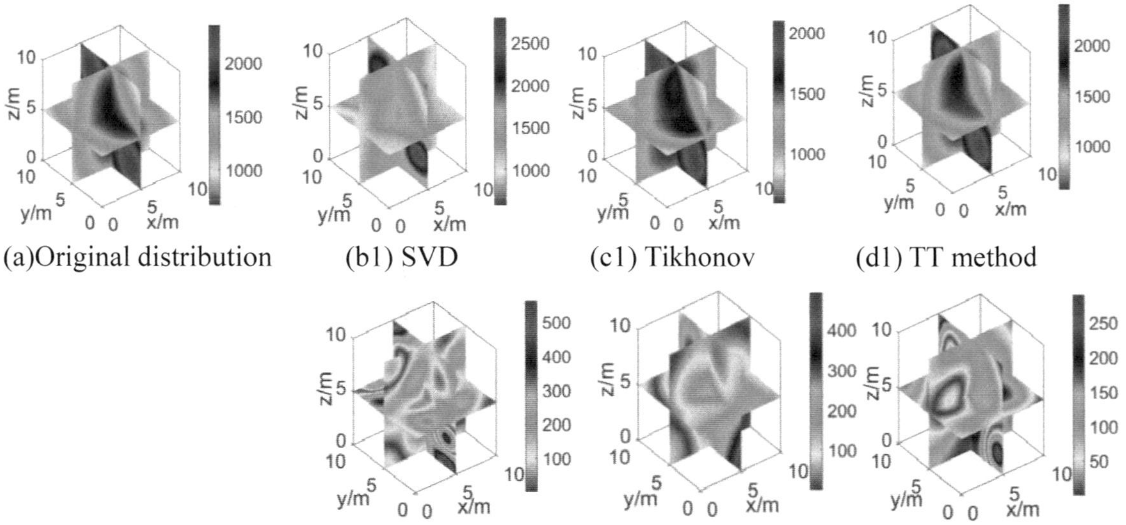

(a)Original distribution (b1) SVD (c1) Tikhonov (d1) TT method

(b2) errors of SVD (c2) errors of Tikhonov (d2) errors of TT

Fig.4 The reconstruction results for two-peak temperature distribution

Table 1 RQ of reconstructed methods for three kinds of temperature distribution

Model	RQ	SVD	Tikhonov	TT
Model 1 (α=0.1)	E_{mean}	14.47%	9.85%	7.97%
	E_{rms}	19.28%	13.54%	8.27%
Model 2 (α=0.1)	E_{mean}	14.80%	10.16%	5.81%
	E_{rms}	19.50%	12.54%	6.13%
Model 3 (α=0.08)	E_{mean}	11.55%	9.02%	7.24%
	E_{rms}	14.95%	11.31%	8.29%

4. Conclusion

In this paper, in order to gain the high-quality 3D reconstruction temperature results in AT measurement, we proposed a new 3D temperature field reconstruction model based on RBF-PR. And the modified reconstruction method was presented to improve RQ and the anti-nosie ability. Numerical simulations were implemented to evaluate the feasibility and effectiveness of the proposed reconstruction method using 3D different temperature distributions. On the basis of the simulation results, we can have the conclusions that the modified reconstructed method can reconstruct temperature distribution with higher accuracy and better anti-noise ability compared with other popular methods in the three temperature distribution models with different complexity.

Acknowledgements

This research is supported by the National Science Foundation of China (No. 11674093 and No. 11474091), and the Fundamental Research Funds for the Central Universities of China

(No. 2018 MS131), and the State Key Laboratory of Acoustics, Institute of Acoustics, Chinese Academy of Science, China (SKLA201808)

References

[1] M. Bramanti, E.A. Salerno, A. Tonazzini, S. Pasini, An acoustic pyrometer system for tomographic thermal imaging in power plant boilers . Instrumentation & Measurement IEEE Transactions on, 45(1996) 159-167

[2] Wei Fan, Ying Chen, Huachen Pan, Ying Ye, Yong Cai, Zhujun Zhang. Experimental study on underwater acoustic imaging of 2-D temperature distribution around hot springs on floor of Lake Qiezishan, China, Experimental Thermal and Fluid Science 34 (2010) 1334–1345

[3] Hua Yan , Guannan Chen, Yinggang Zhou, Lijun Liu. Primary study of temperature distribution measurement in stored grain based on acoustic tomography. Experimental Thermal and Fluid Science 42 (2012) 55–63

[4] W.Y. Tsai, C.F. Huang, T.L. Liao, New implementation of high-precision and instant-response air thermometer by ultrasonic sensors, Sens. Actuators A 117 (2005) 88–94

[5] X.-H. Shen, Q.-Y. Xiong, X Shi, et al. Ultrasonic temperature distribution reconstruction for circular area based on Markov radial approximation and singular value decomposition, Ultrasonic,62(2015) 174-185

[6] P. Holstein, A. Raabe, R. Muller, Acoustic tomography on the basis of travel-time measurement. Measurement Science and Technology, 15(2004)1240-1248

[7] Tong Ma, Yuqian Liu, Chengyu Cao. Neural networks for 3D temperature field reconstruction via acoustic signals. Mechanical Systems and Signal Processing, 126 (2019) 392–406

[8] Hua Yan, Kun Li, and ShanHui Wang. A 3D Temperature Field Reconstruction Algorithm Based on Acoustic Travel-Time Tomography. Advances in Electronic Engineering, Communication and Management Vol.2 2011 , pp 639-644

[9] M. Barth, A. Raabe, Acoustic tomographic imaging of temperature and flow fields in air, Measurement Science & Technology, 22 (2011) 1-13

[10] Qian, Kong, Genshan Jiang, Yuechao Liu. Research on Temperature Field Reconstruction Based on RBF Approximation with Polynomial Reproduction Considering the Refraction Effect of Sound Wave Paths[J], Sound and Vibration, August 2018:8-20.

[11] Enyinda Onunwor, Lothar Reichel. On the computation of a truncated SVD of a large linear discrete ill-posed problem. Numer Algor, 75(2017) 359-380

[12] Xiao-Juan Yang, Li Wang. A modified Tikhonov regularization method. Journal of computational and applied mathematics. 288(2015),180-192

[13] Calvetti, D., Reichel, L. Tikhonov regularization of large linear problems. BIT 43, (2003) 263–283

The CMP stack processing method based on statistical properties of seismic random noise

Guihua Li [1], Jingqi Wang [2], jianguo Feng[3*], Yun Xu[4]

1, College of Earth Science and Engineering,
Shandong University of Science and Technology,Qingdao, China, 266590
skd993914@sdust.edu.cn
2, College of Earth Science and Engineering,
Shandong University of Science and Technology,Qingdao, China, 266590
Wangjingqi_6@163.com
3, College of Earth Science and Engineering,
Shandong University of Science and Technology,Qingdao, China, 266590
skd993875@sdust.edu.cn
4, Retirement office, China University of Geosciences, Beijing, China, 100083

Complex surface conditions and geological structures make seismic records have low signal-to-noise ratio, complex wave fields and difficult to identify effective information, which makes seismic data processing and interpretation difficult. In the field seismic records, some white noises which are not related to the records can be basically eliminated by superposition, but some random interference backgrounds have the characteristics of coherence with CMP gathers, which cannot be eliminated by simple CMP superposition. According to the probability and statistic characteristics and judgment criteria of random disturbance background of seismic records, we analyzed the CMP stacking processing method. The method was applied to simulate the records with random noise which is correlated with seismic records, and the CMP stacking processing of data was carried out, and the ideal results were obtained.

Key words: Seismic random noise; statistical characteristics; CMP stacking.

1. Introduction

With the deepening of oil and gas exploration and the development of exploration technology, the requirement of seismic data accuracy is getting higher and higher. Since digital signal processing technology was introduced into seismic exploration, there is a requirement of high signal-to-noise ratio, high resolution, high fidelity and accurate imaging. High signal-to-noise ratio (SNR) of seismic data is the basis. It is impossible to achieve high resolution and high fidelity without a certain SNR. In potential oil and gas exploration and development zones such as mountainous areas, it

is difficult to process and interpret seismic data because of the existence of random noise which is difficult to remove in seismic records. Random noise is one of the key factors affecting the signal-to-noise ratio of seismic data. The suppression and elimination of random noise is an important link in processing seismic data. In this paper, random noise is removed according to the probability statistical characteristics and judgment criteria of random noise in seismic records.

2. Seismic Statistical Inversion

2.1. Statistical characteristics of seismic forward

Horizontal stacking can suppress regular interference waves, which are dominated by multiple waves. Compared with regular linear interference, random noise has no fixed visual frequency and visual speed, but it follows statistical rules. Therefore, random noise needs to be removed by using the statistical characteristics of multi-channel records.
In the following Eq. (2.1),

$$\xi(t) = m_\xi(t,h,v) + \sum_{i=1}^{N} v_i \varphi_i(t,h,v). \tag{2.1}$$

In Eq. (2.1), $m_\xi(t)$ is the mathematical expectation of $\xi(t)$, and it is regarded as the seismic records without noise; $\sum_{i=1}^{N} v_i \varphi_i(t)$ are the sum of basic random functions, and it is regarded as random noise. The superimposed single trace seismic records in the random sample can be recorded as $\frac{1}{M}\sum_{m=1}^{M}\xi$.

Take a random sample point of ξ, let the sample mean of ξ is $m^*(t_n, h_m, v_j)$, then,

$$m^*(t_n, v_j) = \frac{1}{M}\sum_{m=1}^{M}\xi(t-\tau). \tag{2.2}$$

$$\tau = \sqrt{t_h^2 + \frac{4h_m^2}{v_j^2}}. \tag{2.3}$$

Calculating the mathematical expectation of $m^*(t_n, v_j)$,

$$E[m^*] = \frac{1}{M}E\left[\sum_{m=1}^{M}\xi\right] = \frac{1}{M}\sum_{m=1}^{M}E[\xi] = \frac{Mm_\xi}{M} = m_\xi. \tag{2.4}$$

From the above derivation and central limit theorem, the sample means will surround the overall mean and be normally distributed with a sufficiently large sample size. In other words, the mathematical expectation of the sample mean is exactly equal to the overall mathematical expectation, so the sample mean can be used to estimate the overall mathematical expectation without bias. As far as the seismic record of this paper is concerned, it is essentially stated that the mathematical expectation of ξ is close to the mathematical expectation of the noiseless seismic record. The mathematical expectation of the stacking result after the NMO is the unbiased estimation of the mathematical expectation of the seismic record.

Calculating the variance of a single trace record $\frac{1}{M}\sum_{m=1}^{M}\xi$ in a random sample point.

$$D[m^*] = D\left(\frac{1}{M}\sum_{m=1}^{M}\xi\right) = \frac{1}{M^2}\sum_{m=1}^{M}D\xi = \frac{1}{M^2}M\sigma^2 = \frac{\sigma^2}{M}. \tag{2.5}$$

In Eq. (2.5), σ^2 is the overall variance. Without knowing the overall mathematical expectation m_ξ, only knowing the sample mean m_ξ^*, using

$(\sigma^*)^2 = E\left[\left(\xi - m_\xi^*\right)^2\right] = \frac{1}{M}\sum_{m=1}^{M}(\xi - m_\xi^*)^2$ to estimate the overall variance of the seismic record will produce a bias, calculating the deviation.

$$E[\left(\sigma^*\right)^2] = E[\frac{1}{M}\sum_{m=1}^{M}(\xi - m_\xi^*)^2] = \frac{M-1}{M}\sigma^2 . \tag{2.6}$$

In Eq. (2.6), $(\sigma^*)^2$ is the asymptotic unbiased estimate of the overall variance σ^2 (the unbiased estimate of the overall variance σ^2 when M tends to infinity). Since M cannot tend to infinity in the actual situation, it is a biased estimate and needs to be corrected.

$$\frac{\mathrm{M}}{\mathrm{M}-1}(\sigma^*)^2 = \sigma^2 . \tag{2.7}$$

In other words,

$$\frac{\mathrm{M}}{\mathrm{M}-1}\mathrm{E}\left[\frac{1}{\mathrm{M}}\sum_{\mathrm{m}=1}^{\mathrm{M}}\left(\xi - \mathrm{m}_\xi^*\right)^2\right] = \mathrm{E}\left[\frac{1}{\mathrm{M}-1}\sum_{\mathrm{m}=1}^{\mathrm{M}}\left(\xi - \mathrm{m}_\xi^*\right)^2\right] = \sigma^2 \tag{2.8}$$

Equation (2.8) shows that $S^2 = \frac{1}{M-1}\sum_{m=1}^{M}\left(\xi - m_\xi^*\right)^2$ is an unbiased estimate of the overall variance of seismic records.

2.2. Distribution and hypothesis testing of seismic records with random noise

When the random wave field ξ obeys the normal distribution, whether the number of coverage times M is large or small, the superposition wave field must obey the normal distribution; and according to the central limit theorem, no matter what distribution the overall seismic record obeys, the mean of any sample will surround the overall average value and assume the normal distribution. Therefore the stacking result of random noise must obey normal distribution.

Since the population ξ obeys the normal distribution of parameters m_ξ and σ^2, we can deduce that $\frac{\sqrt{M}}{\sigma}(m_\xi^* - m_\xi)$ obeys the normal distribution from the nature of normal distribution and the Eq. (2.7) and Eq. (2.8). Making $\beta = \frac{\sqrt{M}}{\sigma}(m_\xi^* - m_\xi)$, that is $\beta \sim N(0,1)$.In order to involve only the number of coverage times M and v_j in the calculation, we introduce the χ^2 distribution. Because $\beta \sim N(0,1)$, then $Y = \sum_{m=1}^{M}\beta^2$ obeys the distribution of χ^2 with degree of freedom M. The probability density function is as follows.

$$f(y) = \frac{1}{2^{\frac{M}{2}}}\frac{1}{\Gamma\left(\frac{M}{2}\right)}y^{\frac{M}{2}-1}e^{-\frac{1}{2}y}(y>0) . \tag{2.9}$$

From the nature of χ^2 distribution, we can deduce that $\sum_{m=1}^{M}(\frac{\xi - m_\xi}{\sigma})^2 \sim \chi^2(M)$; when m_ξ is unknown, it can be replaced by m_ξ^*, that is $\frac{(M-1)S^2}{\sigma^2} \sim \chi^2(M-1)$.

At this time, the χ^2 distribution on the right side of the equation does not involve the variance of the overall seismic record, nor its mathematical expectation. It only involves the number of coverage times M and the velocity v_j. From the above derivation, we can conclude that the variance σ^2 of the CMP gather can be estimated by using the χ^2 distribution in the small sample case ($M < 50$).

The hypothesis test in statistics can be used to make statistical inference for suppressing and removing random noise, and the effect of removing random noise can be tested. For the hypothesis test of the total variance σ^2, the χ^2 test method is used as follows.

When m_ξ is known, K^2 is $\sum_{m=1}^{M}(\frac{\xi - m_\xi}{\sigma})^2 \sim \chi^2(M)$, and the rejection fields of K^2 are $(0, \chi^2_{1-\frac{\alpha}{2}}(M))$ and $(\chi^2_{\alpha/2}(M), \infty)$.

When m_ξ is unknown, $(\chi^2_{\alpha/2}(M), \infty)$ is $\frac{(M-1)S^2}{\sigma^2} \sim \chi^2(M-1)$, and the rejection fields of K^2 are $(0, \chi^2_{1-\frac{\alpha}{2}}(M-1))$ and $(\chi^2_{\frac{\alpha}{2}}(M-1), \infty)$.

When the calculation result is in the rejection domain, the hypothesis that has been given should be categorically rejected. That is, there is a big difference between S^2 and σ^2, which is not credible, and the next step is needed to make the effect of removing random noise meet the requirements.

3. Example

Based on the Marmousi model downloaded from SEG, we simulated and processed the seismic records with random noise. The relevant figures are as follows.

Fig. 1 are the simulation CMP gathers (a) without noise and (b) with random noise, number of coverage times: 50; sampling interval: 4msec; trace spacing: 2m. Fig. 2 is Means of CMP gathers based on normal distribution. Fig. 3 Means of CMP gathers based on χ^2 distribution. Comparing Fig.2 and Fig 3, we can get that the means of CMP gathers based on χ^2 distribution is better.

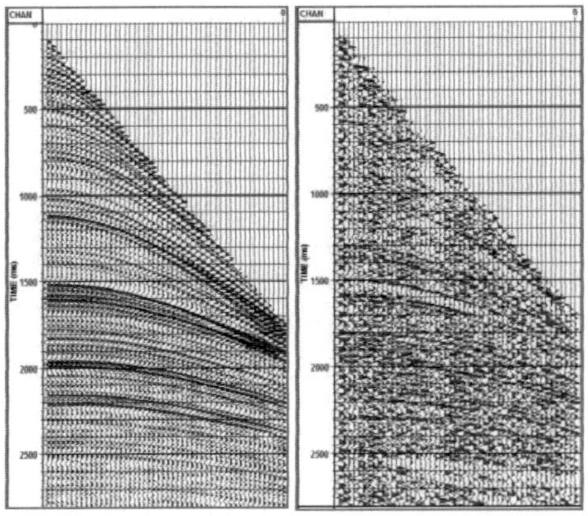

(a) Without noise (b)with random noise

Fig. 1 CMP gathers without random noise and with random noise

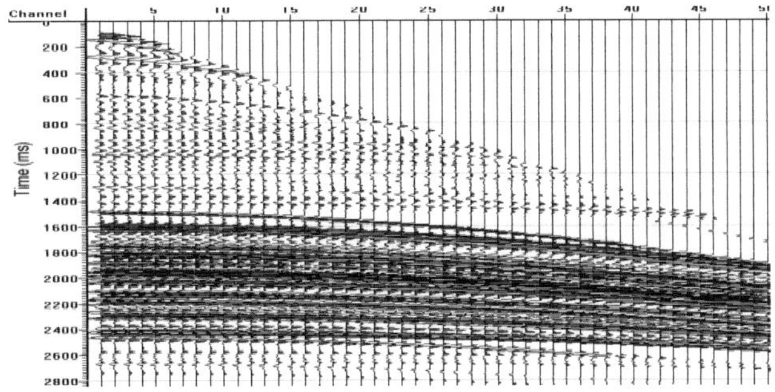

Fig. 2 Means of CMP gathers based on normal distribution

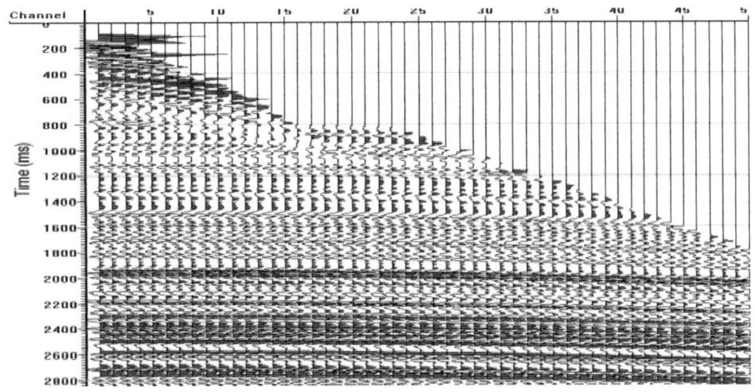

Fig. 3 Means of CMP gathers based on χ^2 distribution

Using the theory of Seismic statistical inversion, we can get the CMP stack profile. Fig. 4 is the CMP stack profile with random noise based on normal distribution. Fig. 5 is the CMP stack profile with random noise based on χ^2 distribution. Comparing the profiles of Fig 4.and Fig 5, Fig 5 is better, and by testing, Fig. 6 is χ^2 test result which is verified reasonable.

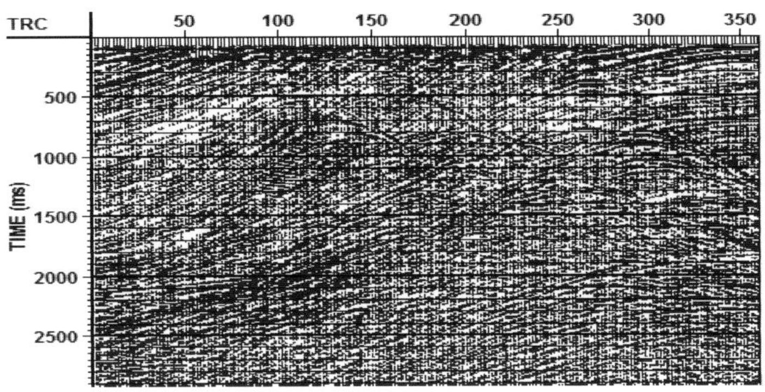

Fig. 4 CMP stack profile with random noise based on normal distribution

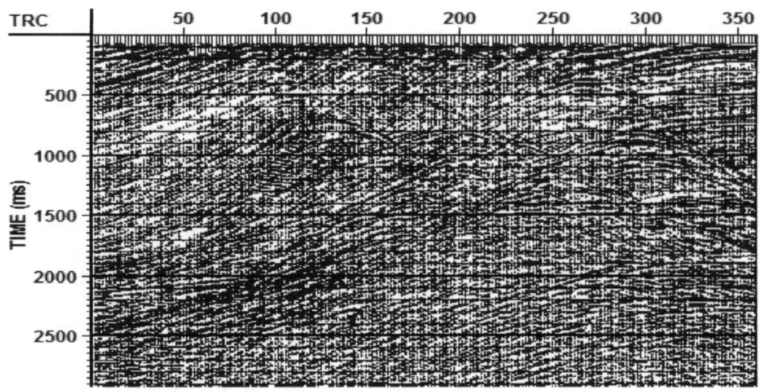

Fig. 5 CMP stack profile with random noise based on χ^2 distribution

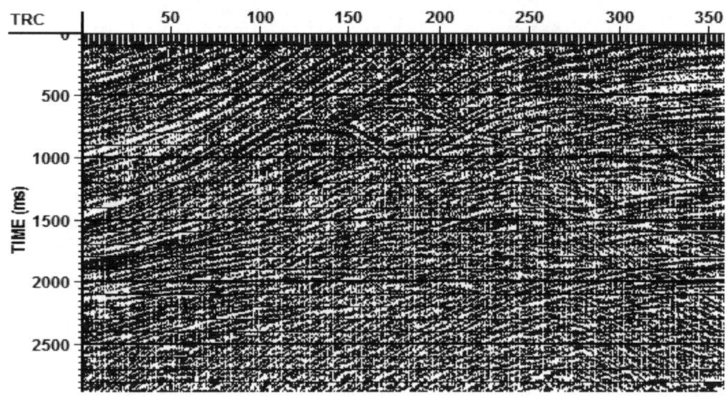

Fig. 6 χ^2 test results

4. Conclusions

Seismic records with random noise are generated based on Marmousi model. The random noise in seismic records is removed by using the statistical characteristics of random noise. When M is large enough, the random noise obeys the normal distribution; when $M < 50$, the random noise also obeys the χ^2 distribution. The effectiveness of the method of removing random noise using statistical features of random noise is verified by χ^2 test.

References

[1] E. C. Wintercheer, Probability Theory, Science and Technology Press, Mingqi Cui, 1961.

[2] Dongmei Wang. Study on Temporal and Spatial Characteristics of Random Noise in Land Seismic Exploration [Ph. D. thesis] (in Chinese).Changchun: Jilin University, 2016.

[3] Tie Zhong. A study on the Characteristics of Land-Seismic-Prospecting random noise based on modern statistical theory [Ph. D. thesis] (in Chinese).Changchun: Jilin University, 2016.

[4] Guanghui Li. The modeling and analysis of seismic exploration [Ph. D. thesis] (in Chinese).

Changchun: Jilin University, 2016.
[5] Kingsbury N. "Complex wavelets for shift invariant analysisand filtering of signals," Applied and Computational HarmonicAnalysis, 10(3) (2001), 234-253.
[6] Diriba Gemechu, Huan Yuan, Jianwei Ma. "Random noise attenuation using an improved anisotropic total variation regularization," Journal of Applied Geophysics, 144(1) (2017), 173-187.
[7] Guo K, Labate D. "The construction of smooth parseval frames of Shearlets," Mathematical Modelling of Natural Phenomena, 8(1) (2013), 82-105.
[8] C. Zhang, Y. Li, H. B. Lin, et al. "Seismic random noise attenuationand signal-preserving by multiple directional time-frequency peakfiltering," Comptes Rendus Geoscience, 347(1) (2015), 2-12.

The Effect of Thin-layer Thickness on Seismic Peak Frequency

Cao Huan[1], Zhao Shuhong[1]

1, The School of Geological Engineering and Geomatics, Chang'an University, Xi'an, Shaanxi, China

970051428@qq.com

Exploration of thin reservoirs is a difficult and key points in today's seismic exploration. In this paper, the thin-layer is divided into four types according to the ratio of reflection-coefficient between the top and bottom of the thin-layer. When the seismic wave is incident vertically, the relation between the peak frequency of the seism and the thickness of the thin-layer is deduced by using the three-layer double-interface time domain model, and the expressions suitable for different thin-layer types are obtained by high-order approximation. Then, the characteristic curves of the peak frequencies of the four thin-layers varying with the thickness are discussed respectively, and the gauge plates with the peak frequencies varying with the thickness are obtained according to the ratio of the reflection coefficients. The thickness of the thin-layers can be read from the gauge plates according to the peak frequencies of the seism, which provides a certain practical reference value for predicting the thickness of the thin-layers. Finally, the model is tested to show its accuracy and reliability.

Keywords: Thin-layer; Thickness; Peak frequency; Thin-layer reflection coefficient combination; Model checking.

1. Introduction

In the actual seismic exploration, the ideal strata of a single medium are very few, often thin reservoirs, so thin-layers and thin interbeds are regarded as the important conquering points of seismic exploration. The definition of thin-layer is relative, the definition of thin-layer has different standards, Widess (1973) defined thin-layer, based on the vertical resolution, generally defined the thickness of less than one-eighth of the seismic wavelength of the reservoir as thin-layer. And the Widess (1973) approximation formula is derived for predicting the thickness of thin-layer. Conventionally, the strata that can not recognize the top-bottom interface are called thin-layers; Li Qing-zhong *et al.* (1994) Defined the thickness of the thin-layer as less than one-fourth of the main wavelength of the seism. In this paper, we will use Li Qing-zhong's (1994) definition of thin-layer, and regard the quarter of the main wavelength as the thickness of thin-layer. And the relationship between the peak frequency of seismic and their thickness has been studied only in recent years, Chung and Lawton (1990, 1995) discussed the relationship between peak frequency and thickness of thin-layers based on a single amplitude characteristic, but a single factor often had many defects and deficiencies. Sun Lu-ping *et al* (2010) deduced the theoretical expression of peak frequency and thickness by means of three-layer double interfaces, established a gauge plate based on different combination of top and bottom reflection coefficients, and gave the variation of peak frequency with thickness , but he did not consider the influence of AVO. Wang Yun-zhuan *et al.* (1997, 2012, 2013, 2017). Analyzed the characteristic response of thin-layer based on forward modeling, simulated thin-layer with different thickness by wave field continuation and depth domain phase shift method (Huang zhen-ping *et al.*, 1997), and proved the quantitative analytical relationship between the main peak frequency and the thickness of thin-layer two-way travel time by theoretical derivation and experimental analysis, which provided an important means for thin-layer thickness prediction (Bai guan-jun *et al.*, 2006; Wang en-hua *et al.*, (1991, 2001)). Starting from the frequency domain, the relation between peak frequency and thickness is approximated by high order approximation, which can be applied to four kinds of thin-layer models (Cheng tian-sheng *et al.,* 2006). The relation between peak frequency and thickness is analyzed. On the basis of this, the gauge plates of the relation between peak frequency and thickness of seismic thin-layer under the combination of the ratio of top and bottom reflection coefficients (Gao jun *et al.*, 2018) of different thin-layers are established.

2. Theoretical Basis of Thin-layer

It is a three-layer dual-interface model, as shown in Fig (1), in which seismic wavelet are incident vertically to that interface after shot-point excitation, and different thin-layer act as filters for the seismic wavelets, and the obtained seismic record is the result of the integrated response of the thin-layer and the seismic wavelets.

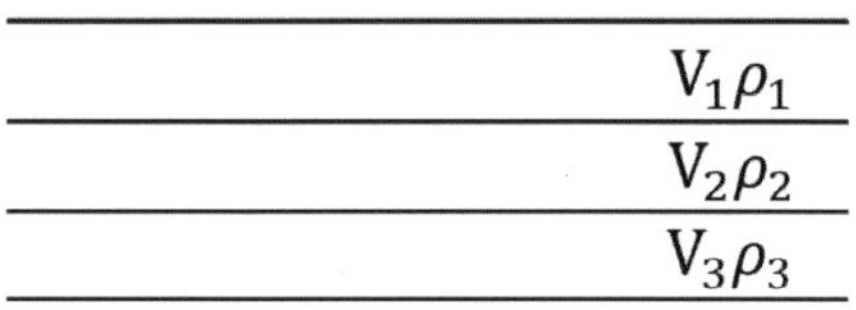

Fig. 1. Three-layer double-interface thin-layer model; $V_1\rho_1$、$V_2\rho_2$、$V_3\rho_3$ represents the velocity and density of the three-layer medium, respectively.

In this paper, the thin-layer is divided into four types according to the ratio of the reflection coefficient (polarity and size) of the top and bottom of the thin- layer (r_1、r_2 are the reflection coefficient of the top and bottom of the thin-layer, respectively, and R is the ratio of the reflection coefficient of the top and bottom), as shown in Table 1:

Table 1. Ratio of reflectance coefficients of four thin films

Thin-layer type	Polarity (r_1)	Size (r_2)	R (r_1/r_2)
Type I	Opposite	Same	-1
Type II	Same	Same	1
Type III	Opposite	Difference	-0.69
Type IV	Same	Difference	0.69

The spectrum of the reflection coefficients of the three-layer dual interface is:

$$R(f) = r_1 e^{-i2\pi f t_1} + r_2 e^{-i2\pi f t_2}. \tag{2.1}$$

Where t_1 and t_2 are the two-way travel time of the thin-layer top-bottom interface, and then the high-order approximate expansion of the thin-layer is performed by means of the Euler formula, and the amplitude spectrum of the thin-layer is taken, then the amplitude spectrum of the reflection coefficient is obtained as follows:

$$A_R(f)=\sqrt{r_1^2+r_2^2+2r_1r_2\cos(2\pi f\Delta t)} \tag{2.2}$$

where $\Delta t = t_2 - t_1$ is the two-way travel time of the thin-layer. Here our seismic wavelet is a Ricker wavelet with a peak frequency of f_m =30 Hz, and its amplitude spectrum is:

$$A_B(f)=\left(\frac{f}{f_m}\right)^2 e^{-\left(\frac{f}{f_m}\right)^2} \tag{2.3}$$

The convolution of seismic Ricker wavelet and thin-layer reflection coefficient is the synthetic seismogram, then according to the Fourier transform characteristic, it is their convolution in time domain and the product of the spectrum of Ricker wavelet and thin-layer reflection coefficient in frequency domain, then the spectrum of seismic synthetic seismogram can be obtained:

$$A(f)=A_B(f)\bullet A_R(f) \tag{2.4}$$

then the value f obtained by deriving the Eq. (2.4) to zero is recorded as the peak frequency, and the following results are obtained:

$$f_p\left[R\pi\Delta t\sin(2\pi f_p\Delta t)\right]=\left[1+R^2+2R\cos(2\pi f_p\Delta t)\right]\left[1-\left(\frac{f_p}{f_m}\right)^2\right] \tag{2.5}$$

As can be seen from that above equation, The seismic peak frequency f_p is not affected by the reflection coefficient at the top and bottom of the thin-layer, and the ratio of reflection coefficient R between top and bottom of thin-layer, when we know the type and thickness of thin-layers and the peak frequency of seismic wavelets, In order to get the expression of the peak frequency and thickness of different thin-layers, we use Euler formula to develop the high-order approximation of the peak frequency and thickness of different thin-layers, and we assume that if the thickness of thin-layers Δt is small enough, there are the following approximations:

$$\sin(2\pi f_p\Delta t)\approx 2\pi f_p\Delta t, \cos(2\pi f_p\Delta t)\approx 1 \tag{2.6}$$

Substituting Eq. (2.6) into Eq. (2.5) gives:

$$f_p \approx f_m\left[1-\frac{R\pi^2\Delta t^2 f_m^2}{(R+1)^2}\right] \tag{2.7}$$

From Eq. (2.7) we can find that the peak frequency of the seismic is related to the type of thin-layer, the thickness and the peak frequency of the wavelet, because we assume that the thickness of the thin-layer is small enough, the formula is not applicable to types I and III. The peak frequency of seismic will have a singular value, especially the type I (R=-1) is completely unsuitable. For the thin-layer of type II and IV, the peak frequency of seismic will decrease with the increase of the thickness, and the magnitude of the decrease is related to the ratio of the reflection coefficient between the top and bottom of the thin-layer.

After the above approximation, we get the thin-layer suitable for type II and IV. In order to get the thin-layer suitable for type I and III, we make a higher-order Eulerian approximation, if the thickness of the thin-layer Δt is small enough:

$$\begin{aligned}&\sin(2\pi f_p\Delta t)\approx 2\pi f_p\Delta t-(2\pi f_p\Delta t)^3/3!\\&\cos(2\pi f_p\Delta t)\approx 1-(2\pi f_p\Delta t)/2!^2\end{aligned} \tag{2.8}$$

according to the Euler approximation, substituting Eq. (2.8) into Eq. (2.5) gives the following:

$$f_p=\left\{\frac{\frac{(R+1)^2}{f_m^2}+6R\pi^2\Delta t^2-\sqrt{\frac{(R+1)^4}{f_m^4}-\frac{4R\pi^2\Delta t^2(R+1)^2}{f_m^2}+36R\pi^4\Delta t^2-\frac{16R\pi^4\Delta t^4(R+1)^2}{3}}}{8R\pi^2\Delta t^2\left(\frac{1}{f_m^2}+\frac{\pi^2\Delta t^2}{3}\right)}\right\}^{\frac{1}{2}} \tag{2.9}$$

For the Eq. (2.9), this formula is applicable to any type, but the disadvantage is that the calculation is large and complicated. In order to get a more accurate and simple formula suitable for type I, we substitute R=-1 into the Eq. (2.9), and then carry out high-order approximation to obtain:

$$f_p\approx\frac{\sqrt{6}}{2}f_m\left(1-\frac{\pi^2\Delta t^2 f_m^2}{6}\right) \tag{2.10}$$

Eq. (2.10) is suitable for the thin-layer type of R=-1. With the increase of the thickness of the thin-layer, the seismic peak frequency decreases.

3. Model Trial Calculation

In order to analyze and discuss the specific change of peak frequency of these four types of thin-layer models with thickness, we use the wedge-shaped thin-layer model as shown in Fig. (2). The parameters for these four types of models are shown in Table 2.

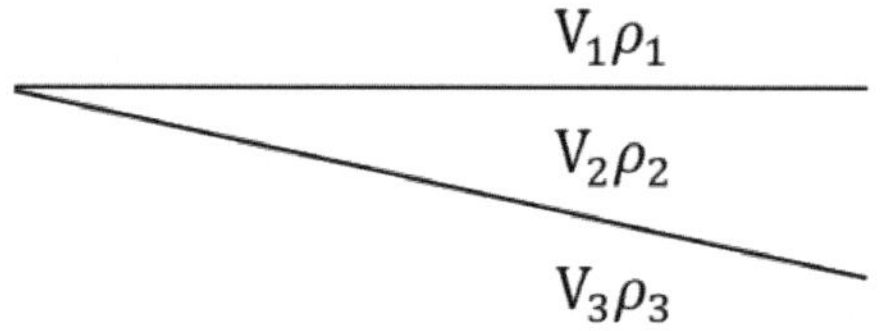

Fig. 2. Thin layer wedge model; $V_1\rho_1$、$V_2\rho_2$、$V_3\rho_3$ represents the velocity and density of the three-layer medium, respectively.

Table 2. Lithologies, layer velocity and layer density for four thin-layers

Thin-layer type	Above Layer	$V_{\rho1}\rho_1$	Middle Layer	$V_{\rho2}\rho_2$	Below Layer	$V_{\rho3}\rho_3$
I	3950	2500	3250	2250	3950	2500
II	2500	2250	3500	2350	3950	2500
III	3750	2400	3250	2250	3950	2500
IV	3250	2250	3450	2400	3950	2500

Using the thin-layer model parameters in the Table 2, the reflection coefficient characteristics of the four types of thin-layers are obtained in Fig. (3). And seismic synthetic record of four types of thin-layers can be obtained in Fig. (4).

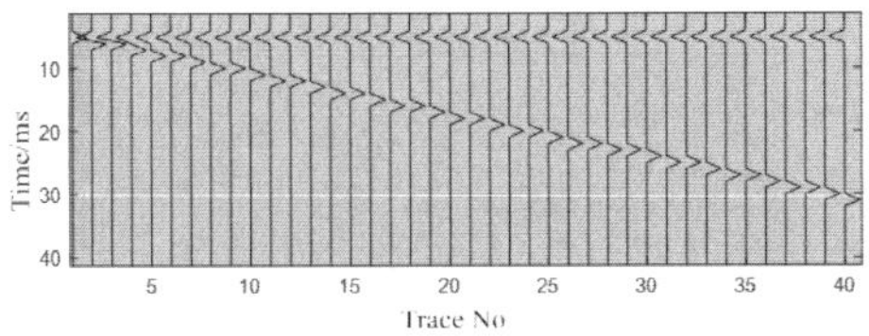

(a) Type I

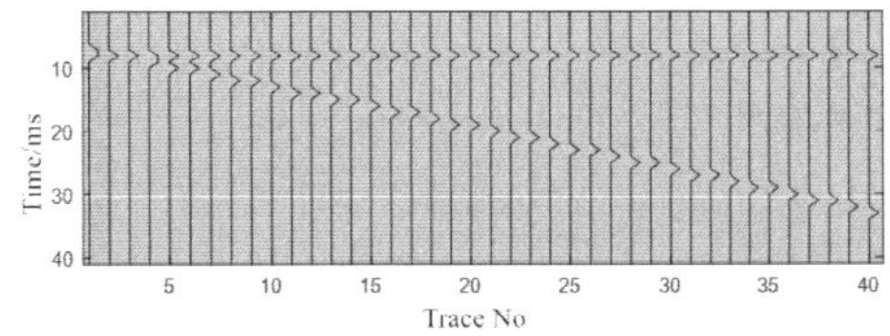

(b) Type II

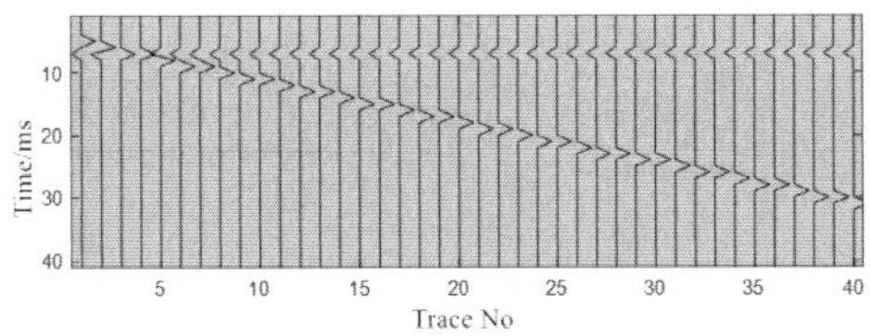

(c) Type III

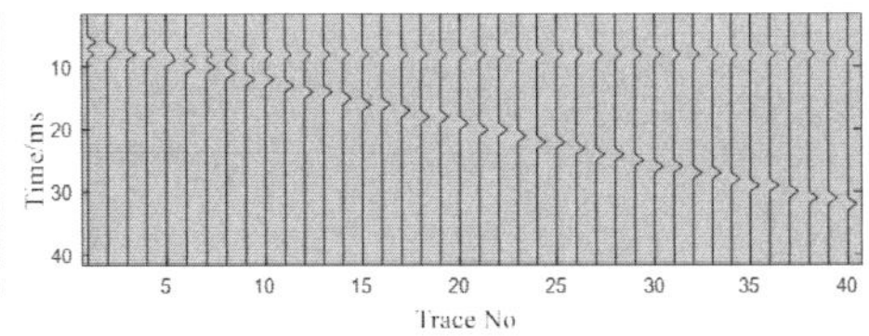

(d) Type IV

Fig 3. Reflectance Coefficients of Four Types of Thin layer; In (a), the ratio of the reflection coefficient at the interface between the top and bottom of the thin layer is -1. In (b), the ratio of the reflection coefficient at the top and bottom of the thin layer is 1. In (c), the ratio of the reflection coefficient at the top and bottom of the thin layer is -0.69. In (d), the ratio of the reflection coefficient at the top and bottom of the thin layer is 0.69.

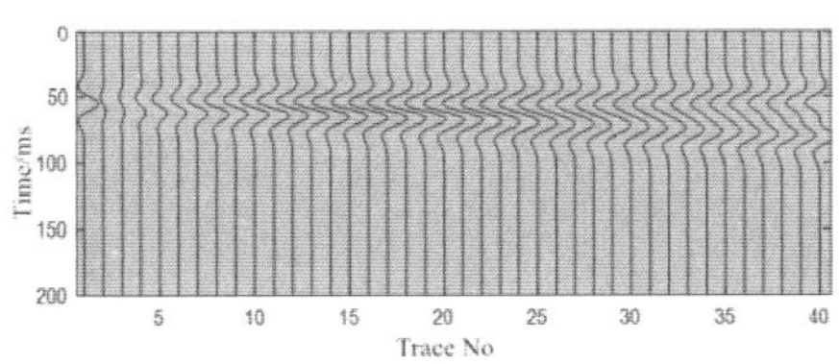

(a) Type I

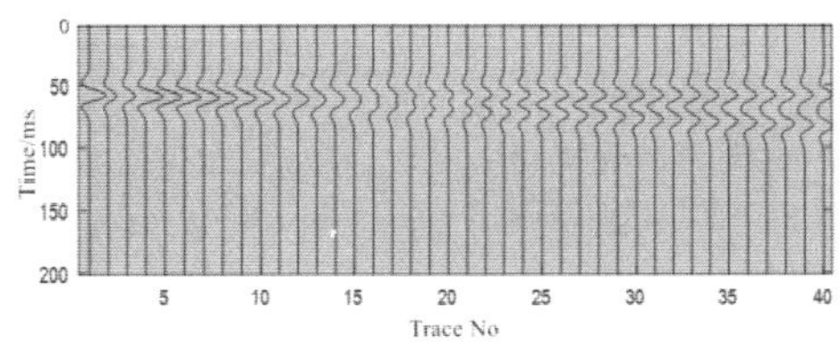

(b) Type II

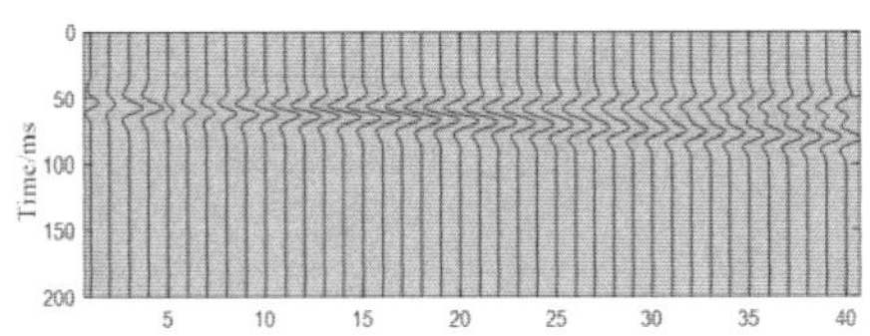

(c) Type III

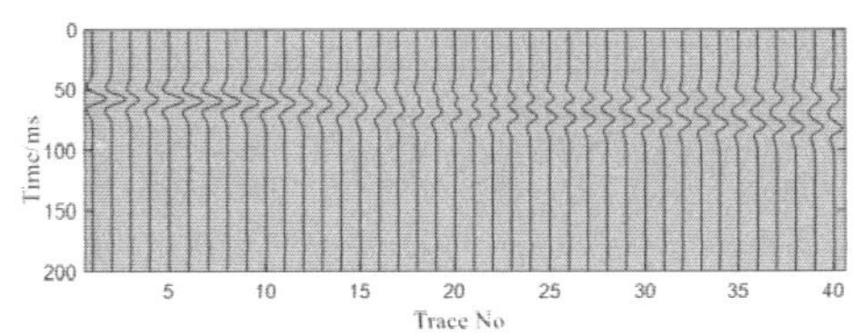

(d) Type IV

Fig. 4. Seismic synthetic record of four types of thin-layers; The Ricker wavelet with f_m=30Hz is convolved with the reflection coefficient of the four thin-layer.

Then use different frequency Ricker wavelets, respectively 10Hz, 20Hz, 30Hz, substituting Eqs (2.5), (2.7), (2.9) and (2.10), extracting the peak frequency of the seismic, we can be found that as the thickness of the thin-layer increases slowly, the peak frequency of the seismic decreases slowly; the higher the frequency of the seismic Ricker wavelet, the more obvious the frequency reduction of the peak frequency of the thin-layer; at the same time, it can also be seen out of the accuracy of the above formula, the accuracy of Eq (2.5) is the highest, and it can be said that the approximation is very close to the true value compared with the high-order approximation formula. The graph below shows the peak frequency as a function of thickness for each type of thin-layer model. The seismic wavelet frequency f_m= 30 Hz at this time.

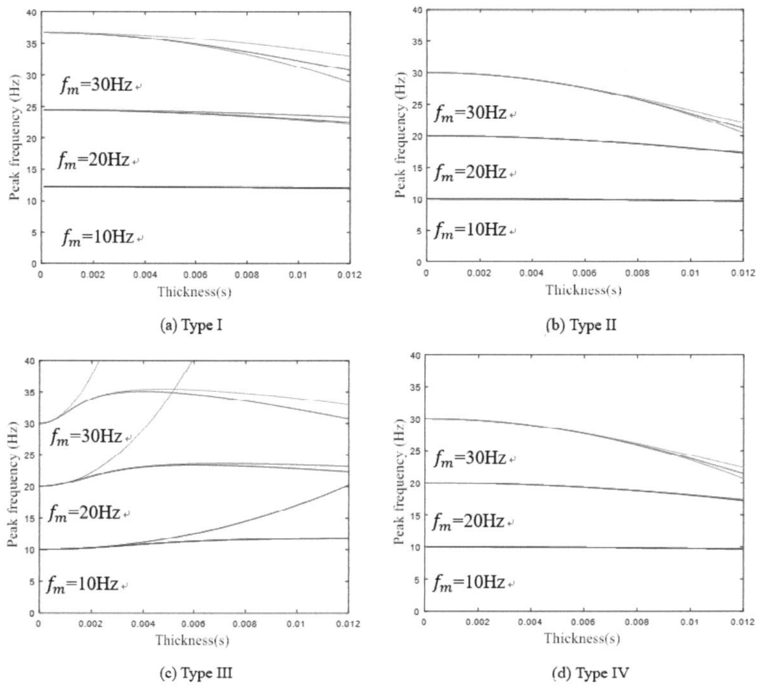

Fig. 5. Variation curve of seismic peak frequency of thin layer with thickness; In (a), Peak frequencies of seismics are extracted by substituting Ricker wavelets of different frequencies (10 Hz, 20 Hz, 30 Hz) into Eqs (2.5), (2.9) and (2.10), respectively. In (b), (c) and (d), Peak frequencies of seismics are extracted by substituting Ricker wavelets of different frequencies (10 Hz, 20 Hz, 30 Hz) into Eqs (2.5), (2.7) and (2.10), respectively.

Figure. (5) (a), (b), and (d), as the thickness of the thin-layer increases slowly, the peak frequencies of the I, II and IV thin-layers are slowly decreasing, and the peak frequency of the Ricker wavelet is higher, the magnitude of the reduction is even greater. This indicates that the thin-layer has a significant frequency-down effect on the higher wavelet frequency. T In the thin-layer of type III, as the thickness of the thin-layer increases slowly, the peak frequency of the seismic first increases and then decreases. In this process, the peak frequency of type III thin-layer appears a maximum value, which is also a feature used to distinguish type III thin-layer.

4. Variation of peak frequency with combination of reflection coefficients at top and bottom of thin-layer

In practical strata, there are various combinations of thin-layer top and bottom reflection coefficients. In this paper, we mainly introduce 40 combinations of R=[-20, 20]. From -20 to 0 and 0 to 20, the step length is 2, while -1 to 1 is 0.1. The following table shows the combinations of reflection coefficients of thin-layers.

Table 3. Combinations of reflection coefficients at top and bottom of different thin-layers

Number	R	Number	R	Number	R	Number	R
...	-∞	11	-1	22	0.1	33	4
1	-20	12	-0.9	23	0.2	34	6
2	-18	13	-0.8	24	0.3	35	8
3	-16	14	-0.7	25	0.4	36	10
4	-14	15	-0.6	26	0.5	37	12
5	-12	16	-0.5	27	0.6	38	14
6	-10	17	-0.4	28	0.7	39	16
7	-8	18	-0.3	29	0.8	40	18
8	-6	19	-0.2	30	0.9	41	20
9	-4	20	-0.1	31	1.0	...	+∞
10	-2	21	0	32	2		

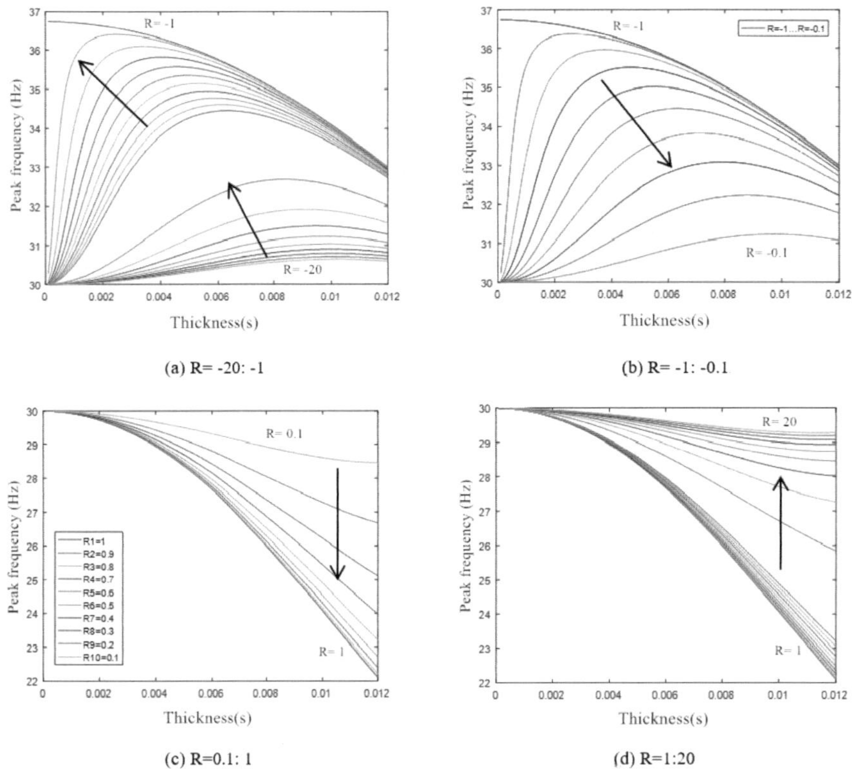

Fig. 6. variation curve of peak frequency with thickness of thin layer; The variation of peak frequency with the thickness of thin layer is obtained by using 30-Hz Ricker wavelet. In (a). R= -20:-1. In (b). R= -1:0. In (c). R=0: 1. In (d). R=1:20; R is the reflection coefficient combination of the top and bottom interfaces of the thin layer.

The variation of peak frequency with the thickness of thin-layer is obtained by using 30-Hz Ricker wavelet , as shown in Fig. (6). From Fig. (6) (a), it can be found that with the increase of the thickness of the thin-layer and the reflection coefficient, the peak frequency of the seismic tends to increase at first and then decrease, and their extreme values decrease along the direction of the thickness of the thin-layer; In Fig. (6) (b), with the increase of the thickness of the thin-layer and the reflection coefficient, the peak frequency of the seismic also tends to increase at first and then decrease, and its extreme value direction follows the direction of the increase of the thickness of the thin-layer; Taken together, it is found that the peak frequency of seismic is always higher than the peak frequency of wavelets when R is negative.

Figure. (6) (c), the seismic peak frequency tends to decrease with the increase of the thickness of the thin-layer and the reflection coefficient; In Fig. (6) (d), the seismic peak frequency tends to increase with the increase of the thickness of the thin-layer and the reflection coefficient, and when R is positive, the peak frequency is always lower than the input wavelet peak frequency.

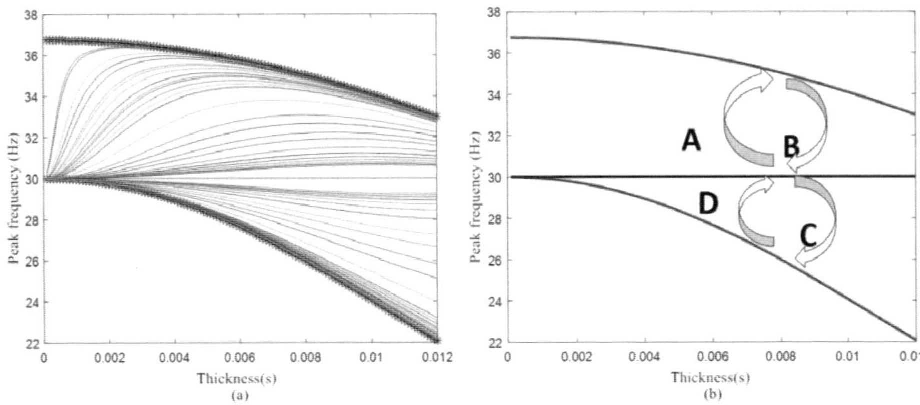

Fig. 7. (a) The relationship between the peak frequency and thickness of different R; (b) Dividing the relationship between peak frequency and thickness of different R into four segments, and dividing the curve cluster into four segments A, B, C and D with the boundaries of R=-1 (upper red), R=1 (lower red) and R=0 (black). A is R= [-20 -1]; B is R= [-1 0]; C segment is R= [0 1]; D is R= [1 20].

Figure (7). (a) is a clust of curves show that peak frequency and thickness of the reflection coefficients at the top and bottom of different thin-layers. For a gauge plate of peak frequency and thickness, the thickness of the thin-layer can be read from the gauge plate for the ratio of the reflection coefficient of the top and bottom of the thin-layer, which provides a new idea for predicting the thickness of the thin-layer. In (b), the curve cluster is divided into four sections A, B, C and D with the bounds of R=-1 and R=1. A is R= [-20 -1]; B is R= [-1 0]; C is R= [0 1]; D is R= [1 20]; As can be seen from that comparison of Fig (7) (a) and (b):

(i) Both segments A and B are distributed in the upper half space of the zero-valued line (R=0), and the whole upper half space is filled with them. The segments C and D are distributed in the lower half space of the zero-valued line (R=0), and the whole lower half space is filled with them. Therefore, we can know that when the thickness of the thin-layer is within the tuning range and R is positive ($R > 0$), the peak frequency of the progressive thin-layer is always lower than the input peak frequency of the wavelet, and when R is negative ($R < 0$), the peak frequency of the rhythmic thin-layer is always higher than the input peak frequency of the wavelet. R=-1 and R=1 in (b)are the most special cases.

(ii) When the thickness of the thin-layer is smaller, the tuning effect of the thin-layer will have more influence on it. In the space of segment A and B, the seismic peak frequency does not increase all the time with the decrease of the thickness of the thin-layer, but increases first and then decreases. When R is closer to -1, the position of the extreme value of their inflection point changes in the direction of the decrease of the thickness of the thin-layer. In the C and D space, the peak frequency does not always increase with the decrease of the thickness of the thin-layer, but decreases first and then increases when R approaches the zero value line, which indicates that the tuning effect is not related to the thin-layer, but to the combination of the reflection coefficient ratio between the top and bottom of the thin-layer, and the tuning effect of the thin-layer is different with different combinations. When the thin-layer Δt is zero, the peak frequency of all R converges to (0, 0), because when the thin-layer Δt is zero, there is no tuning effect without the thin-layer. So the peak frequency of the seismic is equal to the peak frequency of the wavelet.

5. Model Checking

In order to verify the accuracy of the model, the synthetic seismogram is made into Fourier transform (fft), and the peak value of each spectrum is obtained, and the time thickness corresponding to the maximum frequency is found, and the change of peak frequency with the slow increase of time thickness is obtained.

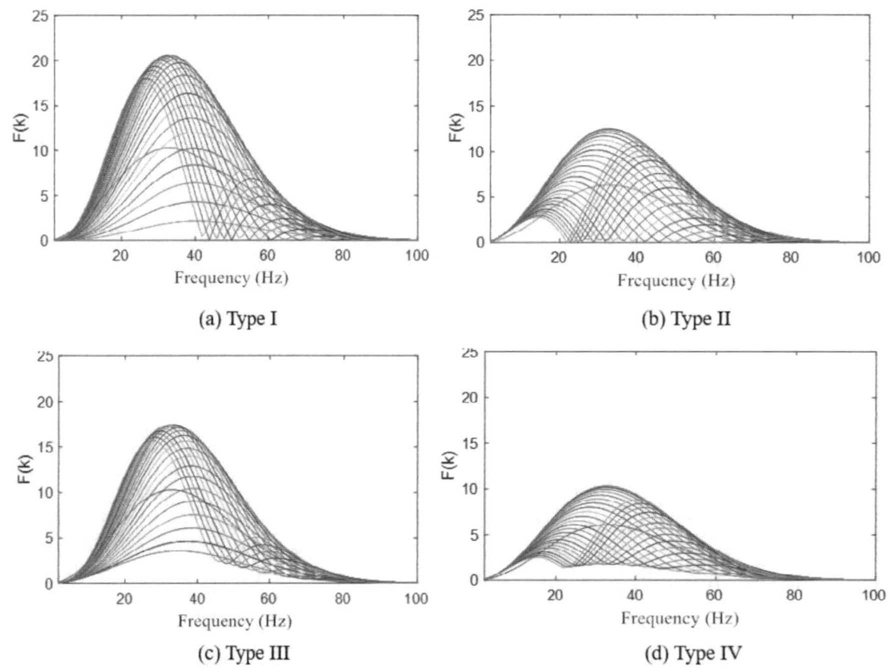

Fig. 8. Spectrum diagram of synthetic seismogram; Four types of thin layers are obtained by Fourier transform, and 40 synthetic seismograms are selected for each type.

As shown in Fig. (8), the spectra of the synthetic seismograms of the four types of thin-layers show the same trend of the type I and III thin-layers, and the same trend of the type II and IV thin-layers, and the peak spectra of each one are basically concentrated in the vicinity of 40 Hz. In fact, the peak frequency of the Rayleigh wavelet is 30 Hz, so we can know that the test value is larger than the actual value, but the trend is the same.

As shown in f Fig (9). , it is the comparison between the actual value and the test value. We find that the actual value and the contrast ratio in Fig (9). (a), (b) and (d) have the same trend and can better reflect the actual situation of the formation. However, the peak frequency of (c) is different from that of the other three types of thin-layers with the change of thickness, which is exactly the characteristic of the third type of thin-layers.

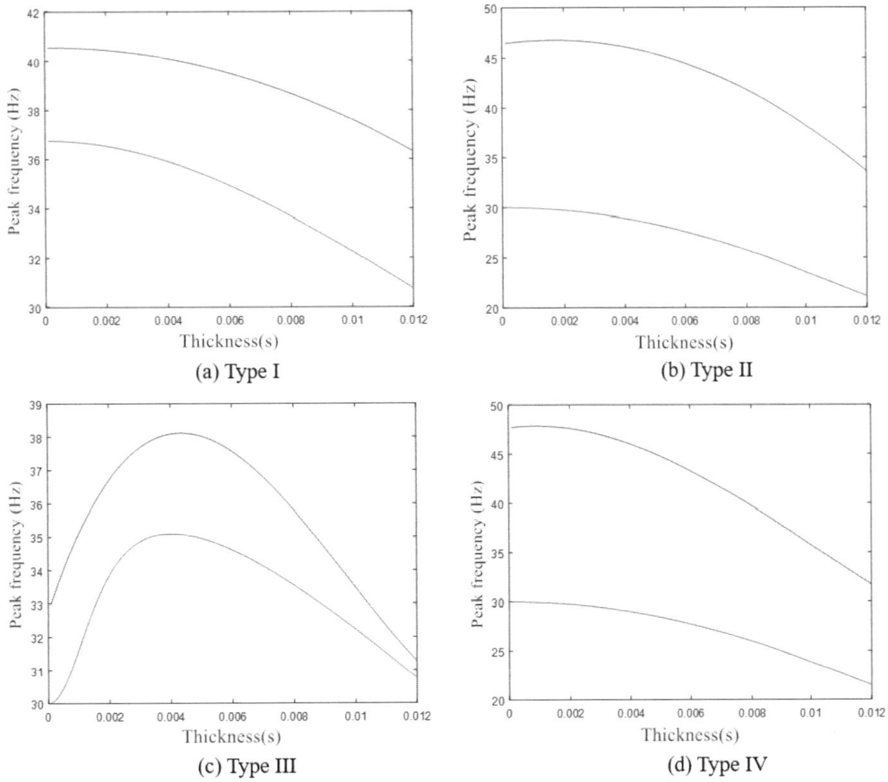

Fig. 9. Synthetic seismogram; The red line is the actual value and the blue line is the inspection value.

6. Conclusion

In this paper, the influence of thin-layer thickness on peak frequency of thin-layer is studied systematically, and the following conclusions are obtained:

(i) In type I, II, III and IV thin-layers, the peak frequency of type I, II and IV thin-layers decreases with the increase of the thickness of the thin-layer, but in type III thin-layers, the peak frequency increases first and then decreases with the increase of the thickness, and the maximum value appears, which is an obvious marker for distinguishing type III thin-layers. At the same time, the expression of the relation between the peak frequency and the thickness of the thin-layer is also compared with the accuracy. The formula obtained by Euler higher order approximation has good accuracy and is suitable for any kind of thin-layer.

(ii) The combination of the ratio of the reflection coefficients at the top and bottom of the seismic thin-layer forms a bounded curve cluster with R=-1 and R=1 in the relation between the peak frequency and the thickness of the seismic layer, Moreover, the seismic peak frequency varies regularly with R. In this process, the thickness of the thin-layer can be read directly according to the response of the seismic peak frequency without knowing the reflection coefficient of the top and bottom of the thin-layer, which provides a certain reference for us to predict the thickness of the thin-layer quantitatively.

(iii) Through the test of the model, we can see that although there are some errors between the actual value and the test value, their change trend is consistent, which can reflect the change law of the actual stratum, and this model has certain feasibility and credibility.

Acknowledgements

The authors would like to express my sincere gratitude to my instructor, Associate Professor Zhao Shu-hong, for providing me with many new ideas and suggestions. In the process, I solved many key problems for me and thanked my tutor again.

References

[1] Bai Guan-guan, WU Han-ning, ZHAO Xi-gang, WANG Jing-hua.Study and application of thin-layer thickness prediction method based on seismic data [J]. Advances in Geophysics, 2006 (02): 554-558.

[2] Chung H M, Lawton D. Amplitude responses of thin beds Sinusoidal approval versus Ricker approval [J]. Geophysics, 199, 60 (L): 223-230.

[3] Chen Tian-sheng, LIU Yang. Thin-layer multiwave AVO based on reflection coefficient spectrum theory [J]. Applied Geophysics, 2006 (01): 27-36 +69.

[4] Frequency characterizations of seismic reflections from this in beds Chung H M, Lawton D. C. Canadian Journal of Exploration Geophysics. 1995Widess M. B. How this is a thin bed [J]. Geophysics, 1973, 38 (6): 1176-1180.

[5] Gao Jun, Cao Siyuan, Lu Xueyan, Ma Yuanyuan, Liu Yaming.Estimation of thin-layer thickness by peak frequency method [J]. Advances in Geophysics, 2018, 33 (01): 204-210.LI Qing-zhong. The Way to Accurate Exploration [M]. Beijing Petroleum Industry Press, 1994.

[6] Huang Zhen-ping, WANG Xiao-hua, WANG Yun-zhuan.Thin-layer seismic attribute parameter analysis and thickness prediction [J]. Petroleum Geophysical Prospecting, 1997 (03): 28-38.

[7] Sun L P, Zheng X D, Shou H et al. The studies on relationship between then in layer seismic peak frequency and its thickness [J]. Oil Geophysical Prospecting (in China), 2010, 45 (2): 254-259.

[8] Wang Yun-zhuan, ZHANG Ying-ying, SHI Ying, KE Xuan. Study on frequency of rake wavelet [J]. Advances in Geophysics, 2017, 32 (05): 2162-2167.

[9] Wang Yun-zhuan, LAN Jin-tao, YU Shu-jie, Study on thin-layer prediction method based on AVO effect [J]. Science Technology and Engineering, 2012, 12 (06): 1366-1368.

[10] Wang Yun-zhuan, GUO Xue-bao, XING Xiao-lin, WANG Kai-yan.Analysis of peak frequency characteristics of thin-layers [J]. Advances in Geophysics, 2013, 28 (05): 2515-2523.

[11] Wang En-hua, HE Zhen-hua, LI Qing-zhong. Forward modeling of thin-layer reflection coefficients [J]. Journal of Chengdu Institute of Technology, 2001 (01): 70-74.

[12] Wang En-hua, HE Zhen-hua, LI Qing-zhong. A new method for calculating thin reservoir thickness [J]. Geophysical and Geochemical Exploration Computing Technology. 2001 (01): 22-25.

[13] Wang En-hua. Spectral formula and model calculation of reflection coefficient for AVO analysis of layered media [J]. Petroleum Geophysical Exploration. 1991, 25 (2): 809.

The Importance of Strain Energy for Interpretation in Exploration Geophysics

Yu-Chiung Teng[1], Zhenxiang Fan[2], Guihua Li[3]

1, Aldridge Laboratory of Applied Geophysics, School of Mines
Columbia University, New York, NY 10027, USA
yt49@columbia.edu

2, Geophysical Research Institute, Geophysical Prospecting Ministry of Petroleum Industry, Zhuo Zhou , Hebei, China

3, College of Earth Science and Engineering,
Shandong University of Science and Technology, Qingdao, China, 266590
skd993914@sdust.edu.cn

The most powerful application of the finite element modeling technology is to simulate the problems with very complex geological structure, particularly for the cases with high contrast wave velocities between media. In this paper, a thin wedged reef model is investigated. With the incorporation of the input parameters provided by well-logged measurements, the numerical results of the two-dimensional finite element model for viscoelastic wave propagation in isotropic media are studied. From the two components of the displacement field, several physical quantities such as dilatation, rotation, strain energy, and kinetic energy can be deduced. Each of these physical quantities lends its support to the others. We found that the magnitudes of the strain energy at the interface of two different media are greater at least 100 times than those in regions of proximity of the interface. Therefore, the snapshot view of wave pattern of the strain energy can sharply delineate the interface of the media. Just as the stress concentration at the interface of two different materials, but of lower order. The display of strain energy possesses higher resolution than that of the displacement fields. Through this analysis, we may have a better understanding of the seismic wave propagation mechanism for the oil-gas bearing strata quantitatively.

Keywords: Viscoelasticity; Finite Element; Strain Energy; Omni-Directional Source

1. Introduction

The numerical methods have become important tools for direct modeling as well as for interpretation in exploration geophysics. In most of the current numerical modeling approaches either the acoustic or the elastodynamic problems for the homogeneous, isotropic media are considered. For example, Teng and Kuo [1983] incorporated the three-dimensional elastodynamic system of equations into their finite element analysis code. Teng [1986, 1989] studied the three-dimentional acoustic problem by means of the finite element method. Fan, Kuo, and Teng [1983] used a statistical approach for the elastic case in their study for the buried reef problem. However, the elastodynamics is still not adequate to describe complex physical phenomena of seismic wave propagation. For example, earth materials are inelastic in their response to a seismic wave. This means a loss of amplitude with distance of travel, since the loss per unit distant is approximately proportional to frequency. For many materials, a seismic wavelet becomes broader as it travels.

In this paper, we implement the viscoelastic equation of motion into the finite element method code. Through this analysis, we may have a better understanding of the seismic wave propagation mechanism for the oil-gas bearing strata quantitatively.

2. The Finite Element Formulation for the Viscoelastic Media

For a two-dimensional (plane strain) homogeneous, isotropic elastic media, we have:

$$\sigma = D\,e \tag{2.1}$$

$$D = \begin{bmatrix} \lambda + 2\mu & \lambda & 0 \\ \lambda & \lambda + 2\mu & 0 \\ 0 & 0 & \mu \end{bmatrix} \tag{2.2}$$

where $e = (e_x,\ e_y,\ e_{xy})^T$ is the strain, $\sigma = (\sigma_x, \sigma_y, \sigma_{xy})^T$ is the stress. D is the elasticity matrix, λ and μ are the Lame's constants. Strain e and displacement U have the relation

$$e = B'U \tag{2.3}$$

where displacement $U = (u, v)^T$. B′ is strain-displacement matrix and has the form of

$$B' = \begin{bmatrix} \frac{\partial}{\partial x} & 0 \\ 0 & \frac{\partial}{\partial y} \\ \frac{\partial}{\partial y} & \frac{\partial}{\partial x} \end{bmatrix} \tag{2.4}$$

However, the earth materials may be regarded as a continuous linear elastic body only when strain of the media does not excess 10^{-5} or 10^{-6} and there is no energy loss. If the Voigt viscoelastic model is to be considered, then the stress consists of two components, the elastic part which is proportional to strain, and the damping force which is proportional to the strain time rate. If in Eq. (2.2), we replace λ and μ by $\lambda + \lambda'\frac{\partial}{\partial t}$ and $\mu + \mu'\frac{\partial}{\partial t}$ respectively, the constitutive relation of Voigt viscoelastic model can be obtained as

$$\sigma = De + D'\dot{e} \tag{2.5}$$

where "." is the derivative with respect to time t. D′ is viscous (or damping) matrix

$$D' = \begin{bmatrix} \lambda' + 2\mu' & \lambda' & 0 \\ \lambda' & \lambda' + 2\mu' & 0 \\ 0 & 0 & \mu' \end{bmatrix} \tag{2.6}$$

By using of the dynamic variational principle (the Hamilton Principle), we obtain the finite element equation for viscoelastic media as

$$M_e U_e + C_e U_e + K_e U_e = R_e \tag{2.7}$$

where M_e is the element mass matrix. C_e *is* the element damping matrix. K_e is the element stiffness matrix; R_e is the column vector of external force and have the expressions as follows:

$$M_e = \int_S \rho N^T N \, ds \tag{2.8}$$

$$C_e = \int_S B^T D' B \, ds \tag{2.9}$$

$$K_e = \int_S B^T D B \, ds \tag{2.10}$$

$$R_e = \int_S N^T \bar{x} \, ds \tag{2.11}$$

The matrices D and D' can then be expressed as

$$D = (N_i T_3 \;\; N_j I_3 \;\; N_k I_3)(D_i \;\; D_j \;\; D_k)^T \tag{2.12}$$

$$D' = (N_i I_3 \;\; N_j I_3 \;\; N_k I_3)(D_i' \;\; D_j' \;\; D_k' \;)^T \tag{2.13}$$

And

$$N_\alpha I_3 = \begin{bmatrix} N_\alpha & 0 & 0 \\ 0 & N_\alpha & 0 \\ 0 & 0 & N_\alpha \end{bmatrix} \qquad \alpha = i.j.k \tag{2.14}$$

$$D_\alpha = \begin{bmatrix} \lambda_\alpha + 2\mu_\alpha & \lambda_\alpha & 0 \\ \lambda_\alpha & \lambda_\alpha + 2\mu_\alpha & 0 \\ 0 & 0 & \mu_\alpha \end{bmatrix}, \quad D_\alpha' = \begin{bmatrix} \lambda_\alpha' + 2\mu_\alpha' & \lambda_\alpha' & 0 \\ \lambda_\alpha' & \lambda_\alpha' + 2\mu_\alpha' & 0 \\ 0 & 0 & \mu_\alpha' \end{bmatrix} \tag{2.15}$$

After the assemblage, we obtain

$$M\ddot{U} + C\dot{U} + KU = R \tag{2.16}$$

where M is the global mass matrix. C is the global damping matrix. K is the global stiffness matrix.

3. Incorporation of the Well-Logged Measurements and the Finite Element System

Currently, the borehole data acquisition can only provide logarithmic decrement value Δ of reflection energy of adjacent formation. In order to establish the relation between the logarithmic decrement values Δ viscoelastic coefficients, we introduce the seismic quality factor Q^{-1} as

$$Q^{-1} = \frac{\Delta}{\pi} = 2V\gamma/\omega, \quad \Delta = ln\frac{A_1}{A_2} \tag{3.1}$$

where A_1 and A_2 are the two successive amplitudes of the time history, γ is the absorption coefficient. However, the quality factor Q_s for transverse wave and quality factor Q_p for compressional wave have different values. Particularly, for a unconsolidated sand, with saturated fluid, the shear speed is very small. Therefore, it is necessary to define Q_p^{-1} and Q_s^{-1} individually. We obtain

$$Q_p^{-1} = \frac{-\frac{(\lambda+2\mu)_x}{(\lambda+2\mu)} - \frac{\omega^2\sqrt{\rho}(\lambda'+2\mu')}{(\lambda+2\mu)^{3/2}}}{\omega\left[\frac{(\lambda'+2\mu')_x}{2(\lambda+2\mu)} + \left(\frac{\rho}{\lambda+2\mu}\right)^{1/2}\right]} \tag{3.2}$$

$$Q_s^{-1} = \frac{-\frac{\mu_y}{\mu} - \frac{\omega^2\mu'\sqrt{\rho}}{\mu^{3/2}}}{\omega\left[\frac{\mu'_y}{2\mu} - \left(\frac{\rho}{\mu}\right)^{1/2}\right]} \tag{3.3}$$

The values of λ' and μ' may be computed from eqs. (3.2) and (3.3), with the values of V_P, V_S, Δ and ρ provided by well logged measurements. Then we may obtain D' and the damping matrix C. If we further make certain assumptions within each layer, then the values of V_p, V_S, γ_p, γ_s, Q_p^{-1} and Q_s^{-1} can be reduced to,

$$V_p \approx \left(\frac{\lambda+2\mu}{\rho}\right)^{1/2} \tag{3.4}$$

$$\gamma_p \approx -\frac{\omega^2\sqrt{\rho}(\lambda'+2\mu')}{2(\lambda+2\mu)^{3/2}} \tag{3.5}$$

$$V_s \approx (\mu/\rho)^{1/2} \tag{3.6}$$

$$\gamma_s \approx -\frac{\omega^2\mu'\sqrt{\rho}}{2\mu^{3/2}} \tag{3.7}$$

$$Q_p^{-1} \approx \frac{\omega(\lambda'+2\mu')}{\lambda+2\mu} \tag{3.8}$$

$$Q_S^{-1} \approx \frac{\omega\mu'}{\mu} \tag{3.9}$$

In finite element analysis, we need to compute the matrices D and D' from equations (2.12) and (2.13)and then calculate the associated stiffness damping matrices. Therefore, by using eqs. (3.4) to (3.9), we can solve the problems for the viscoelastic media by finite element method.

We adopt the combined method, finite element in space and finite difference in time, to solve Eq. (2.16). If the lumped mass approach is used, we have

$$\ddot{U}_n = M^{-1}(R_n - C\dot{U} - KU_n) \tag{3.10}$$

Substituting the following central difference formula

$$h^2\ddot{U}_n = U_{n+1} - 2U_n + U_{n-1} \tag{3.11}$$

$$2h\dot{U}_n = U_{n+1} - U_{n-1} \tag{3.12}$$

$$\ddot{U} = (\dot{U}_{n+1} - \dot{U}_n)/h \tag{3.13}$$

into Eq. (3.10), the displacement U and velocity $\dot{U}$ can be obtained iteratively as

$$U_{n+1} = U_n + h\dot{U}_n + \frac{h^2}{2}M^{-1}(R_e - C\dot{U}_n - KU_n) \tag{3.14}$$

$$\dot{U}_{n+1} = \dot{U}_n + hM^{-1}[R_n - C\dot{U}_n - KU_n] \tag{3.15}$$

where h is the time interval Δt, $U_n = U(n\Delta t)$, $U_{n+1} = U((n+1)\Delta t)$. The two averaging constant strain triangles (2ACST) quadrilateral element is used. The global stiffness matrix is obtained by where h is the time interval Δt, $U_n = U(n\Delta t)$, $U_{n+1} = U((n+1)\Delta t)$. The two averaging constant strain triangles (2ACST) quadrilateral element is used. The global stiffness matrix is obtained by assembling the quadrilateral elements. The damping matrix C is obtained in the same manner as the global stiffness matrix.

4. Numerical Results

Reef model: An interpreted geological section, which includes a wedge shaped thin layer and an irregular shaped inclusion is as shown in Fig. 1. A buried omni-directional (compressional) line source is located at three elements below the free surface. The forcing function used is the Gaussian wavelet with a period of 24 msec. The compressional line source is simulated by superimposing three extra nodal points on the node where the source is applied(Teng and Kuo 1984; 1988 and 1988; Teng 2009). The element size $\Delta x = \Delta y =$ 5m. The time increment is $\Delta t = 0.001$ sec. The parameters used in this calculation are listed in Table I.

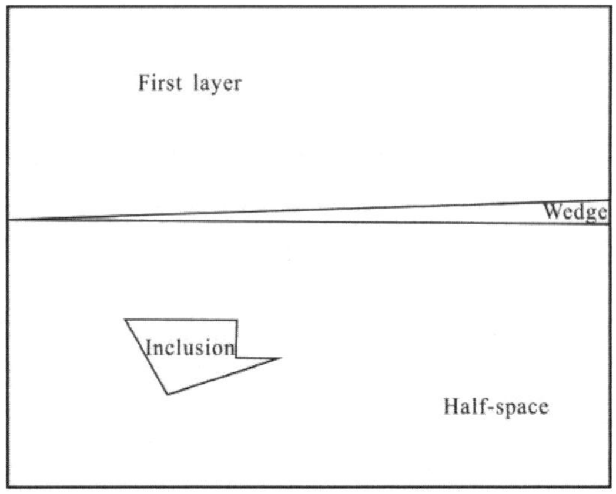

Fig.1 A model includes a wedge and an irregular shaped inclusion to simulate a gas-oil bearing reef

Table I. Physical Parameters of Each Medium for the Reef Model

Item	First layer	Wedge	Half-space	Inclusion
V_p	4,700 m/sec	3,500 m/sec	3,600 m/sec	2,000 m/sec
Vs	2,410 m/sec	2,010 m/sec	2,070 m/sec	1,000 m/ sec
ρ	2.0 g/cm^3	2.0 g/cm^3	2.3 g/cm^3	1.3 g/cm^3
Qp^{-1}	110	50	160	33
Qs^{-1}	115	155	165	33.5

Figure 2 is the snapshot view of the synthetic seismogram of the vertical displacement field at 337.5 msec after the detonation of the plane wave incidence. The characteristics of the wave responses caused by the thin wedge layer can be clearly identified as shown in Fig. 2. However, we obtained very little information from the irregular shaped inclusion, which simulates a reef.

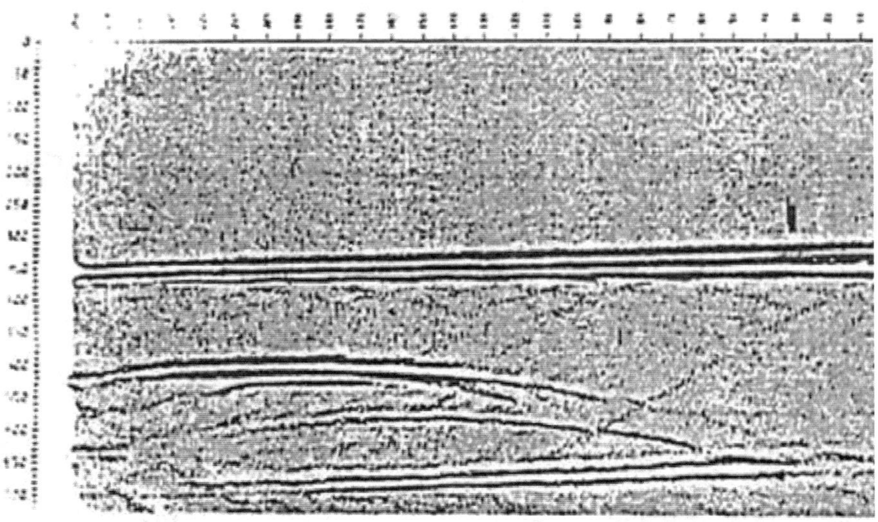

Fig.2 The synthetic seismogram of the displacement filed for a plane wave incidence.

Figure 3 and Figure 4 depict the snapshot view of the wave pattern of various physical quantities at 337.5 msec after the detonation of the compressional source.

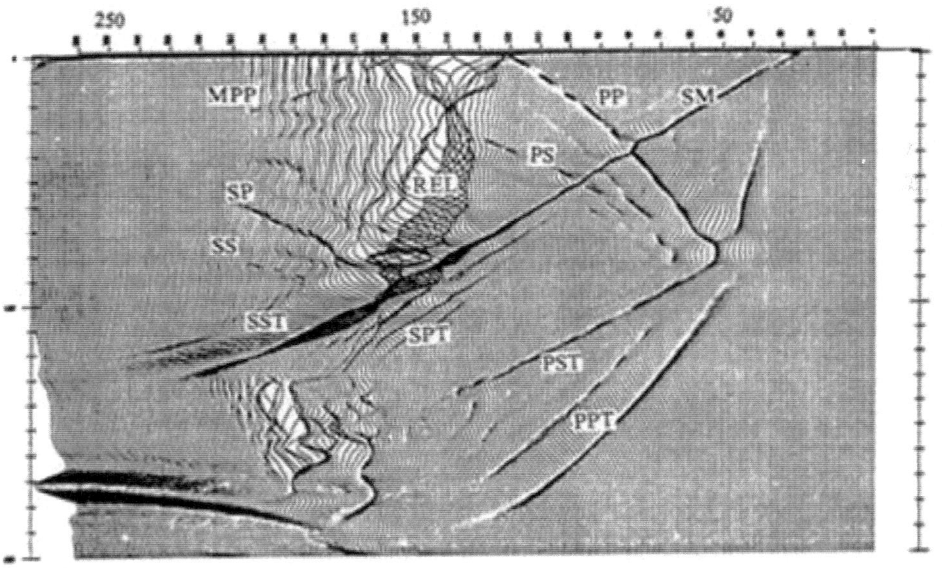

Fig.3 (a). The Snapshot View of the Wave Pattern for the Vertical Displacement at 337.5msec after the Detonation of the Compressional Source

Figure 3 (a) is the vertical displacement field and Fig. 3 (b) is the horizontal displacement field respectively. In Figs. 3 (a) and 3 (b), the reflected, transmitted and the converted waves from the wedge interface PP, PS, SS, SP, PPT, PST, SST, SPT can be clearly identified. The multi reflected compressional waves are designated as MPP. The Schmidt head wave SM and the Rayleigh wave REL are observed in the first layer only.

The characteristics of the wave responses caused by the inclusion, which simulates a reef, are also clearly depicted in Figs. 3 (a) and 3 (b).

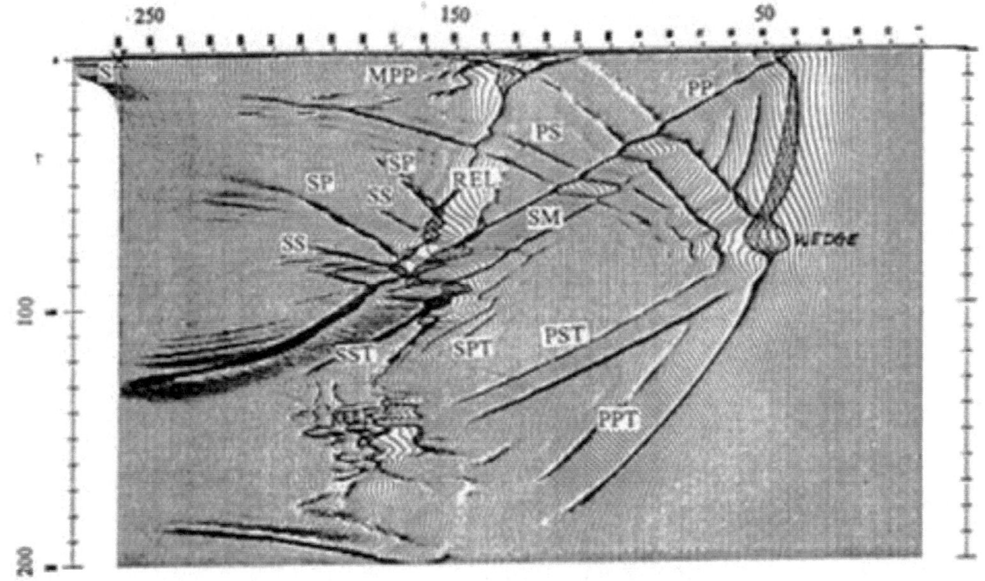

Fig.3(b). The Snapshot View of the Wave Pattern for the Horizontal Displacement at 337.5 msec after the Detonation of the Compressional Source

Figure 4 depicts the strain energy distribution for the wedged reef Model.

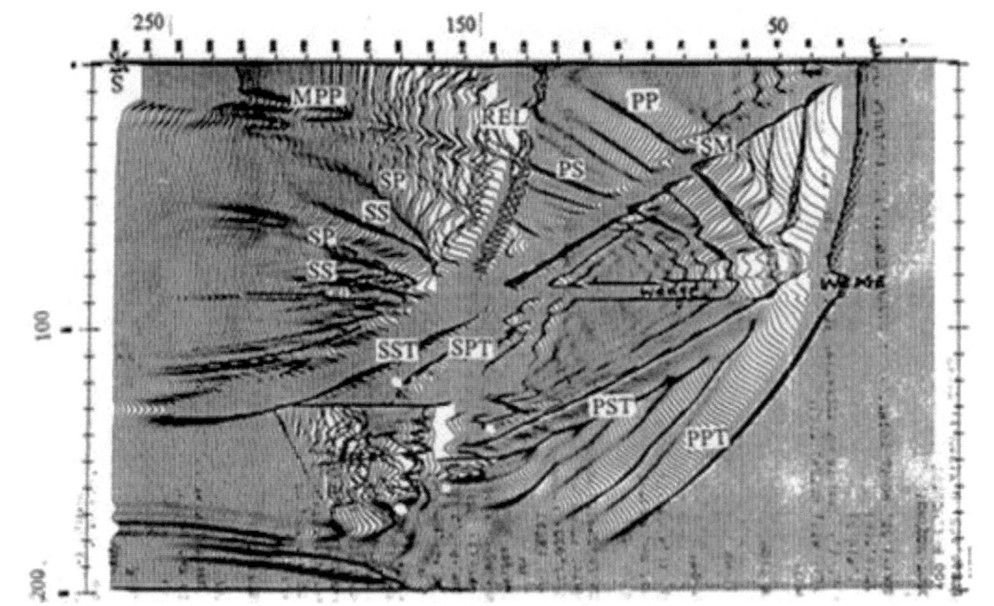

Fig. 4 The Snapshot View of the Wave Pattern for the Strain at 337.5msec after the Detonation of the Compressional source

Comparing the solutions of Figs. 3(a) , 3(b) and 4, we found a very important feature in the view of the strain energy. The magnitudes of the strain energy at the interface of two different media are greater at least 100 times than those in the regions of proximity of the interface. Therefore, the location of the top layer of the reef is sharply delineated as shown in Fig. 4. The display of strain energy possesses higher resolution than that of the displacement fields.

In Fig. 4, not only that the snapshot view of wave pattern of the strain energy can sharply delineate the interface of the irregular shaped reef, but also the interfaces of the thin wedge also delineate sharply, and most parts of the wedge's thickness are less than 1/4 of the wavelength of forcing function.

5. Discussion and Conclusion

(i) A two dimensional finite element model has been presented for the numerical simulation of viscoelastic wave propagation in isotropic media. The method is based on incorporation of the input parameters provided by well-logged measurements into the viscoelastic finite clement system.

(ii) From the two displacement components, several physical quantities such as dilatation, rotation, strain energy, can be deduced. Each of these physical quantities lends its support to the others.

(iii) The numerical results indicate that the snapshot view of wave pattern of the strain energy can sharply delineate the interface of the media as shown in Fig. 4.

(iv) In figure 4, the interfaces of the thin wedge also delineate sharply, Most parts of the wedge's thickness are less than 1/4 of the wavelength of the forcing function.

(v) With the using of an omni-directional (compressional) line source, better numerical results can be obtained.

We conclude that the finite element numerical modeling can he used to refine the interpretation of existing seismic profiles in some particular gas-oil-bearing area. The most powerful application of the finite element modeling technology is to simulate the problems with very complex geological structure, particularly for the cases with high contrast wave velocities between media.

Acknowledgments

The authors wish to thank Prof. John T. Kuo of the Columbia University and the Geophysical Research Institute (GRI) for their fully support and encouragement during the course of this research. The authors also thank Dr. Chung Gong, Mr. C.Y. Yan, Miss S.L. Fan, Misters B.K. Ke, M. Mao, F. L. Yang and Z.B. Meng for their valuable discussions and helpful assistance for the numerical calculation.

References

[1] Z. X. Fan, J.T. Kuo and Y.C. Teng, Statistical approach to the buried reef problem. Expanded Abstracts of the Technical Program. SEG Fifty third Annual International Meeting and Exposition. 1983, pp. 374-378.

[2] Z. X. Fan and Y. C. Teng, Numerical Modeling of Seismic Waves in the Isotropic and Viscoelastic Media. Acta Geophysoca Sinica, Vol. 31, No 2, 1988, pp. 198-210. (in Chinese)

[3] Y.C. Teng and J.T. Kuo, Up-dated version of the Aldridge 3D elastodynamic finite element

Code-AFEA3.B. PROJECT MIDAS ANNUAL. REPORT IV, Columbia University, New York, 1983, pp. 1-39.
[4] Y.C. Teng, and J.T. Kuo, Seismic source Simulation in finite element method, Special SEG Workshops V: Seismic Modeling Techniques, Atlanta, Georgia. 1984,
[5] Y.C. Teng, Three-dimensional finite element analysis of waves in an acoustic media with inclusion. Presented at the ll2th Meeting of the Acoustical Society of America, Anaheim, California, 1986.
[6] Y.C. Teng and J.T. Kuo. Finite element source simulation for elatodynamics. Presented at the Sixth International Seminar on Model Optimization in Exploration Geophysics,. Berlin. West Germany,. 1988.
[7] Y.C. Teng and J.T. Kuo, Finite element source simulation for elatodynamics, Model Optimization in Exploration Geophysics, Vol. 3,Vieveg Braunschveig-Viesbaden, 1988, pp. 277-298.
[8] Y.C. Teng, Three-dimensional finite element analysis of waves in acoustic media with inclusion: J. Acoust. Soc. Am., 86, 1989, pp. 414-422.
[9] Y.C. Teng, Three dimensional finite element source simulation in elastodynamics. Presented at the Ninth International Conference on Theoretical and Computational Acoustics, in Dresden Germany, September 7-11, 2009.
[10] Zienkiewicz, The Finite Element Method, 3rd ed. McGraw Hill, New York, 1977.

Theoretical Study on Axial Impedances of Fluid-Filled Orthotropic Pipes

Mingzhu Su [1], Yudong Sun[1], Fang An [1], Xiaying Hao [1]

1, National Key laboratory on Ship Vibration & Noise, Jiangsu Key Laboratory of Green Ship Technology, China Ship Scientific Research Center, Wuxi, Jiangsu, P. R. China

Email: sumz2016@163.com

Based on the elementary membrane shell theory and the stress-strain relation of the orthotropic material, considering the Poisson coupling, the axial governing equations of the fluid-filled orthotropic pipes are derived. And the analytical model of impedance matrix including acoustic, mechanical and coupling impedances, is developed. The numerical simulation model using finite element method for the pipe is established, its results are used for verification of the analytical approach.

Keywords: orthotropic pipe; Poisson coupling; axial impedance matrix

1. Introduction

The flexible pipe is an important component of the pipeline system, which can be used for displacement compensation and vibration/noise reduction. In the theoretical research of dynamic characteristics of isotropic flexible pipes, based on the 14×14 transfer matrix derived by Lesmez[1], Munjal and Thawani[2] studied the transmission losses of the hoses for longitudinal waves, sound waves and flexural waves, and parameters studies were made for different materials and geometries. Without considering the effect of Poisson coupling, Sun et al.[3] derived the analytical results of axial and transverse mechanical impedances and acoustic impedances, discussed the effects of materials and geometrical parameters on the impedances, and put forward some design suggestions for test specimens. Chen et al.[4] proposed a method of using complex wave speeds to describe the effects of viscoelastic wall of the flexible rubber pipe on inner fluid pressure ripple propagation.

With the development of science and technology, a large number of new composite materials with superior performance have been applied to pipeline systems. In order to clarify the vibration characteristics and vibration/noise reduction effects of such flexible pipes, Chen and Bert[5] analyzed the propagation of free harmonic waves in fluid-conveying, thin-walled, circular cylindrical shells of orthotropic or isotropic materials. Yu and Kojima[6] established the transfer matrix model of dynamic response in axial and circumferential directions for a type of thick wire-reinforced hydraulic rubber hose, and proposed a special test method to determine the mechanical property parameters of the hose wall. Pinnington[7] [8]established the coupled vibration equations of a orthotropic stiffened tube with a positive internal pressure, and studied the wave propagation characteristics of the tube wall and fluid. The research shows that, compared to single material tubes, the internal pressure has a stronger hardening effect on stiffened tubes, and the wave velocities were bigger. Drew et al.[9] obtained the frequency-dependent impedance matrix defining the relationships between pressure ripple and flow ripple at the hose ends by considering the viscoelasticity of the wall materials and fluid viscosity. Based on the anisotropic stress-strain relationship, Jeong and Inaba[10] analyzed the wave speeds and strains in axial and circumferential directions, and studied the influences of elastic anisotropic on fluid-structure interaction for water-filled carbon-fiber reinforced thin pipes.

Impedance is a physical quantity reflecting the dynamic characteristics of the component itself, which is defining as the ratio of force and response. In most cases, the dynamic characteristic parameters of composite pipes are obtained by actual measurement[11~14]. Very little work has been done on theoretical research. Sokolov[15] established the theoretical beam model of flexible hose by combining the orthotropic and viscoelastic properties of composite shell, gave the analytical formula of impedance matrix elements, and verified some elements.

In this paper, the main work is to establish the axial governing equations of the fluid-filled pipe based on the stress-strain relationship of orthotropic materials, derive the expressions for impedance matrix elements in analytical form, analyze the elements through examples, and show the effectiveness by finite element software ABAQUS.

2. Theoretical Model

2.1. FSI governing equations and their general solutions of fluid-filled flexible pipe

The stress equations of motion of the pipe wall are (Yu and Kojima[6])

$$hN_{\theta\theta} - rP = 0 \tag{2.1}$$

$$\frac{\partial N_{xx}}{\partial x} - \rho_p \frac{\partial^2 u_x}{\partial t^2} = 0 \tag{2.2}$$

Where N_{xx} and $N_{\theta\theta}$ are axial and circumferential stress components of the pipe wall, P is the pressure in the fluid, u_x is the displacement of the pipe wall, ρ_p is the density of the pipe wall, r and h are the nominal radius and the thickness of the pipe wall, and x is the axial coordinate, t is the time constant.

The stress-strain relationships in the axial and circumferential direction of the pipe wall composed of orthotropic materials are

$$N_{xx} = \frac{E_x}{1-\mu^2}\left(\frac{\partial u_x}{\partial x} + \mu_\theta \frac{w}{r}\right) \tag{2.3}$$

$$N_{\theta\theta} = \frac{E_\theta}{1-\mu^2}\left(\frac{w}{r} + \mu_x \frac{\partial u_x}{\partial x}\right) \tag{2.4}$$

Where E_x and E_θ are axial and circumferential Young's moduli, μ_x and μ_θ are axial and circumferential Poisson's ratios, $\mu^2 = \mu_x \mu_\theta$, w is the radial displacement of the pipe wall.

Substituting Eq. (2.4) into Eq. (2.1), combining Eq. (2.3), and eliminating $\frac{w}{r}$, the following equation is derived.

$$N_{xx} - \mu_x \frac{r}{h} P - E_x \frac{\partial u_x}{\partial x} = 0 \tag{2.5}$$

Multiplying the two sides of Eq. (2.5) by cross-sectional area of the pipe wall A_p ($A_p = 2\pi rh$), and taking its partial derivatives respect to t gives the first fluid-structure interaction equation as follows.

$$\frac{\partial F^x}{\partial t} - 2\mu_x A \frac{\partial P}{\partial t} - E_x A_p \frac{\partial^2 u_x}{\partial x \partial t} = 0 \tag{2.6}$$

Where F^x is the axial force in the pipe wall, and A is the nominal area of the pipe, $A = \pi r^2$.

Continuity equation in fluid:

$$\frac{1}{E_V} \frac{\partial P}{\partial t} + 2\frac{\partial}{\partial t}\left(\frac{w}{r}\right) + \frac{\partial^2 u_f}{\partial x \partial t} = 0 \tag{2.7}$$

Where E_V is the bulk modulus of the fluid, and u_f is the displacement of the fluid.

Combining Eq.(2.1), Eq.(2.4) and Eq.(2.7),eliminating $\frac{w}{r}$,the second fluid-structure interaction equation is obtained.

$$\frac{\partial P}{\partial t} - 2\mu_x E_V' \frac{\partial^2 u_x}{\partial x \partial t} + E_V' \frac{\partial^2 u_f}{\partial x \partial t} = 0 \tag{2.8}$$

Where E_V' is the modified bulk modulus, for thin-walled pipe:

$$E_V' = \frac{E_V}{1 + 2\left(1-\mu^2\right) rE_V \big/ E_\theta h} \tag{2.9}$$

As summarized, the axial coupling governing equations of fluid-filled orthotropic flexible pipe are

$$\frac{\partial P}{\partial x} + \rho_f \frac{\partial^2 u_f}{\partial t^2} = 0 \tag{2.10}$$

$$\frac{\partial P}{\partial t} - 2\mu_x E_V' \frac{\partial^2 u_x}{\partial x \partial t} + E_V' \frac{\partial^2 u_f}{\partial x \partial t} = 0 \tag{2.11}$$

$$\frac{\partial F^x}{\partial x} - \rho_p A_p \frac{\partial^2 u_x}{\partial t^2} = 0 \tag{2.12}$$

$$\frac{\partial F^x}{\partial t} - 2\mu_x A \frac{\partial P}{\partial t} - E_x A_p \frac{\partial^2 u_x}{\partial x \partial t} = 0 \tag{2.13}$$

Where ρ_f is the density of the fluid.

Solutions of the Eqs. (2.10) ~ (2.13) along the axial direction are supposed to be in the form of functions as

$$\begin{aligned} P &= \overline{P} e^{j\omega t} = \overline{\overline{P}} e^{\lambda x} e^{j\omega t} \qquad u_f = \overline{u}_f e^{j\omega t} = \overline{\overline{u}}_f e^{\lambda x} e^{j\omega t} \\ F^x &= \overline{f}_x e^{j\omega t} = \overline{\overline{f}}_x e^{\lambda x} e^{j\omega t} \qquad u_x = \overline{u}_x e^{j\omega t} = \overline{\overline{u}}_x e^{\lambda x} e^{j\omega t} \end{aligned} \tag{2.14}$$

Substitution of Eq. (2.14) into Eqs. (2.10) ~ (2.13) leads to a characteristic equation for λ.

$$\lambda^4 + \alpha\lambda^2 + \beta = 0 \tag{2.15}$$

Where

$$\alpha = \omega^2\left(\frac{\rho_f}{E_V^{'}} + \frac{\rho_p}{E} + 4\mu^2\frac{\rho_f}{E_\theta}\frac{A}{A_p}\right), \beta = \omega^4\frac{\rho_p}{E_x}\frac{\rho_f}{E_V^{'}}$$

And its root are found to be the following form, while considering the physical meaning of λ.

$$\lambda_{1,2}^2 = \frac{1}{2}\left(\alpha \mp \sqrt{\alpha^2 - 4\beta}\right), \lambda = \pm j\lambda_1, \pm j\lambda_2 \tag{2.16}$$

When $\mu = 0$, $\lambda_1^2 = \dfrac{\omega^2\rho_p}{E_x}$, $\lambda_2^2 = \dfrac{\omega^2\rho_f}{E_V^{'}}$, one-dimensional acoustic waves in the fluid and longitudinal waves in the pipe wall are independent of each other.

2.2. Derivation of axial impedance matrix

According to the definition of impedances of piping components, the relationship between state variables at two ends can be expressed by impedance matrix.

$$\begin{bmatrix} P(0) \\ P(L) \\ F^x(0) \\ F^x(L) \end{bmatrix} = \left[\begin{array}{cc:cc} Z_{11} & Z_{12} & Z_{13} & Z_{14} \\ Z_{21} & Z_{22} & Z_{23} & Z_{24} \\ \hdashline Z_{31} & Z_{32} & Z_{33} & Z_{34} \\ Z_{41} & Z_{42} & Z_{43} & Z_{44} \end{array}\right] \begin{bmatrix} A_f U_f(0) \\ A_f U_f(L) \\ U_x(0) \\ U_x(L) \end{bmatrix} \tag{2.17}$$

Where U_f and U_x are velocity of the fluid and the pipe wall, and A_f is the cross-sectional area of the fluid.

For fluid-filled pipes, the elements of impedance matrix satisfy the symmetry and reciprocity principles.

$$\begin{aligned} Z_{11} &= -Z_{22}, Z_{21} = -Z_{12} \\ Z_{33} &= -Z_{44}, Z_{43} = -Z_{34} \\ Z_{13} &= -Z_{24}, Z_{23} = -Z_{14} \\ Z_{31} &= -Z_{42}, Z_{41} = -Z_{32} \end{aligned} \tag{2.19}$$

According to the definition of impedance, it is easy to get the expressions of the element of the axial impedance matrix.

Acoustic impedances:

$$Z_{11} = \frac{P(0)}{A_f U_f(0)} = \frac{1}{\omega A_f}\frac{Z_1 N_2 \cot(\lambda_1 L) - Z_2 N_1 \cot(\lambda_2 L)}{M_1 N_2 - M_2 N_1} \tag{2.20}$$

$$Z_{21} = \frac{1}{\omega A_f}\frac{Z_1 N_2 / \sin(\lambda_1 L) - Z_2 N_1 / \sin(\lambda_2 L)}{M_1 N_2 - M_2 N_1} \tag{2.21}$$

Mechanical impedances:

$$Z_{33} = -\frac{1}{\omega}\frac{M_2 \cot(\lambda_1 L) - M_1 \cot(\lambda_2 L)}{M_1 N_2 - M_2 N_1} \tag{2.22}$$

$$Z_{43}=-\frac{1}{\omega}\frac{M_2/\sin(\lambda_1 L)-M_1/\sin(\lambda_2 L)}{M_1N_2-M_2N_1} \tag{2.23}$$

Acoustic-mechanical impedances:

$$Z_{13}=-\frac{1}{\omega}\frac{Z_1M_2\cot(\lambda_1 L)-Z_2M_1\cot(\lambda_2 L)}{M_1N_2-M_2N_1} \tag{2.24}$$

$$Z_{23}=-\frac{1}{\omega}\frac{Z_1M_2/\sin(\lambda_1 L)-Z_2M_1/\sin(\lambda_2 L)}{M_1N_2-M_2N_1} \tag{2.25}$$

Mechanical-acoustic impedances:

$$Z_{31}=\frac{1}{\omega A_f}\frac{N_2\cot(\lambda_1 L)-N_1\cot(\lambda_2 L)}{M_1N_2-M_2N_1} \tag{2.26}$$

$$Z_{41}=\frac{1}{\omega A_f}\frac{N_2/\sin(\lambda_1 L)-N_1/\sin(\lambda_2 L)}{M_1N_2-M_2N_1} \tag{2.27}$$

Where

$$N_1=-\frac{j\lambda_1}{\omega^2\rho_pA_p} \quad N_2=-\frac{j\lambda_2}{\omega^2\rho_pA_p}$$

$$Z_1=\frac{1}{2\mu_xA}\left(1-\frac{E_x}{\omega^2\rho_p}\lambda_1^2\right) \quad Z_2=\frac{1}{2\mu_xA}\left(1-\frac{E_x}{\omega^2\rho_p}\lambda_2^2\right)$$

$$M_1=\frac{1}{2\omega^2\mu_x\rho_fA}\left[j\lambda_1\left(1-\frac{E_x}{\omega^2\rho_p}\lambda_1^2\right)\right] \quad M_2=\frac{1}{2\omega^2\mu_x\rho_fA}\left[j\lambda_2\left(1-\frac{E_x}{\omega^2\rho_p}\lambda_2^2\right)\right]$$

3. Results and Discussion

A type of carbon-fiber composite pipe is used for calculation, the parameters are $\rho_p=1489\text{kg/m}^3$, $E_x=5.47\text{GPa}$, $E_\theta=15.52\text{GPa}$, $\mu_x=0.50$, $\mu_\theta=1.43$, $G_{x\theta}=28.1\text{GPa}$.

And the parameters of the fluid (water) are $\rho_f=998\text{kg/m}^3$, $E_V=2.18\text{GPa}$.

Geometric parameters are $L=1\text{m}$, $r=0.05\text{m}$, $h=10\text{mm}$.

In order to verify the above theoretical model, the finite element model of fluid-filled orthotropic pipe is established by ABAQUS software, and the harmonic response analysis is carried out. Fig. (2) illustrates the variation of axial impedance amplitudes with frequency for the fluid-filled orthotropic flexible pipe. It is shown that the curves of the analytical results and numerical results are in a good agreement in the frequency range of 0.1~1000Hz, where the former are obtained by the theoretical model and the latter are calculated by ABAQUS software with same parameters. It is obvious that the theoretical model is effective for determining the axial impedance matrix of the fluid-filled orthotropic flexible pipe.

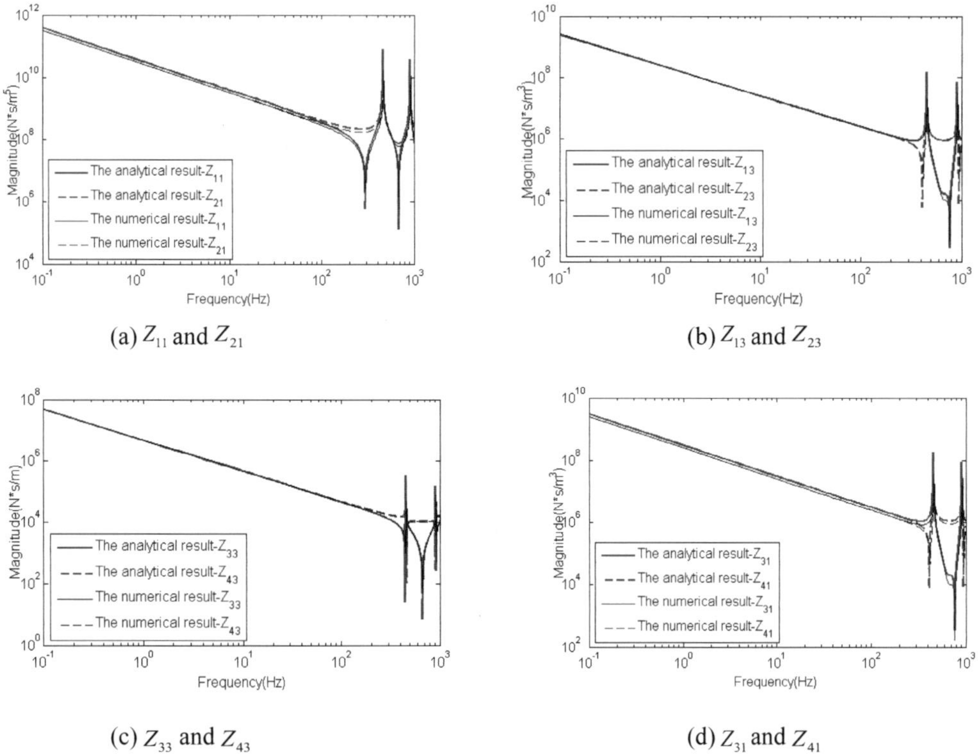

(a) Z_{11} and Z_{21} (b) Z_{13} and Z_{23}

(c) Z_{33} and Z_{43} (d) Z_{31} and Z_{41}

Fig. 2. Axial impedance matrix parameters

It can be also figured out that, at low frequencies, the input impedance curve coincides with the transfer impedance curve, as the frequency increases, the differences slowly emerges. The input impedances of acoustic impedances and mechanical impedances are first anti-resonant, then resonant, and there are no obvious anti-resonance peaks in transfer impedances. Under the influence of acoustic impedances, acoustic resonance frequencies appear in the amplitude-frequency curves of mechanical impedances. In contrast to the laws of acoustic impedances and mechanical impedances, acoustic-mechanical and mechanical-acoustic input impedance first resonant, followed by anti-resonant, meanwhile, the anti-resonance peaks appear before the resonance peaks in the curves of acoustic-mechanical and mechanical-acoustic transfer impedance.

4. Conclusions

Considering the orthotropic of the wall material and fluid-structure interaction (FSI), an analytical calculation model of the fluid-filled pipe is developed, and the analytical expressions of the axial impedance matrix parameters are obtained. The validity of the theoretical model has been investigated by comparing the calculated results with those obtained from the finite element method. It has been shown that the theoretical results can produce quite good results in the frequency range of 0.1~1000Hz.

Input impedances and transfer impedances overlap at low frequencies and differ at high frequencies. The difference between coupling impedances and acoustic impedances, mechanical impedances is that the input impedances first appears resonance and then appears anti-resonance, and the transfer impedances first anti-resonant and then resonant. Due to Poisson coupling, the mechanical impedances is affected by acoustic resonance.

Acknowledgments

The authors gratefully acknowledge the support of Jiangsu Natural Science Foundation, Youth Found (No. BK20160201) and Foundation for Key Laboratory of Ship Vibration and Noise (JCKY2019207CI02).

References

[1] Lesmez M W, Wiggert D C and Hatfield F J. "Modal analysis of vibrations in liquid-filled piping-systems." *J Fluid Eng* **112** (1990), 311-318.
[2] Munjal M W, Thawani P T. "Prediction of the vibro-acoustic transmission loss of planar hose-pipe system." *J Acoust Soc Am* **101**(5) (1997), 2524-2535.
[3] Sun Y D, Liu Z Z, Zhou Q Y, et al. "Research on Design of Test Specimen for Impedance Measurement of Elastic Pipe." *Shipbuilding of China* **45**(4) (2004), 42-47.
[4] Chen G, Zhu S J, He L. "Application of Complex Wavespeed to Flexible Rubber Pipe Dynamic Analysis." *Noise and Vibration Control* **23**(1) (2003), 41-43.
[5] Bert C W, Chen T L C. "Wave propagation in fluid-conveying piping constructed of composite material." *J Press Vess* **97**(3) (1975), 178-184.
[6] Yu J, Kojima E. "Wave propagation in fluids contained in finite-length anisotropic viscoelastic pipes." *J Acoust Soc Am* **104**(6) (1998), 3227-3235.
[7] Pinnington R J. "Axisymmetric wave transfer functions of flexible tubes." *J Sound Vib* **204**(2) (1997), 291-310.
[8] Pinington R J. "The axisymmetric wave transmission properties of pressurized flexible tubes." *J Sound Vib* **204**(2) (1997), 271-289.
[9] Drew J E, Longmore D K, Johnston D N. "Theoretical analysis of pressure and flow ripple in flexible hoses containing tuners." *Proc Instn Mech Engrs* **212**(6) (1998), 405-422.
[10] You J H, Inaba K. "Fluid -structure interaction in water-filled thin pipes of anisotropic composite materials." *J Fluid Struct* **36** (2013), 162-173.
[11] Longmore D K, Schlesinger A. "Transmission of vibration and pressure fluctuations through hydraulic hoses." *Proc Instn Mech Engrs pt* **205**(2) (1991), 97-104.
[12] Drew J E, Longmore D K, Johnston D N. "Measurement of the longitudinal transmission characteristics of fluid-filled hose." *Proc Instn Mech Engrs pt* **211**(13) (1997), 219-228.
[13] Johnston D N, Nigel T M. "Measured dynamic properties of flexible hoses." *J Vib Acoust* 210(2) (2010), 111-118.
[14] Popkov V I. "Defining dynamic properties (impedances) of the flexible inserts with fluid." *Acta Acust United Ac* **98**(6) (2012), 870-883.
[15] Sokolov A. "Impedance matrix of rubber-cord fluid-filled hose." I*nter-noise &Noise-con Congress & Conference*, 2014